THE
GOOD
HONEYMOON
GUIDE

LUCY HONE

includes
WHERE TO GET MARRIED ABROAD

Lucy Hone was born in London in 1968 and comes from a family of travellers. Lucy's first major trip on her own started with a six month stay in Southern Africa in 1986. In 1987 she moved to Scotland to study at Edinburgh University from where she graduated with an MA in History. Since then, both before and after her marriage, she has been all over the world in search of places offering romance, luxury or uniqueness. In the process she has tested beds, beaches, resorts and restaurants, with the aim of seeking out the best honeymoon destinations each country has to offer. She currently lives in London, working as a freelance writer specialising in travel and the media.

Acknowledgements

Many thanks to the following people who between them have contributed in no small way to the insight and detail of this guide: Philip Grierson, Kate Theobald, Katrin Holtkott, Erika Schule Grosso, Elizabeth Martin, Jane Roche, Toni Anne Leyland, Vanessa Janion, Edward Paine, everyone at ZFL and countless people at the various tourist boards, for allowing me to constantly pester them with queries; to Esther and Chris Henry, Andrew and Caroline Blatter, Tubes and Tan Thompson, Anthea and Biddy Fahey, Tre Petrie, Ian and Roo Cross, Miller Edwards, Doughlas Lochhead, Lizzie Howell, Tim Carter, Katie Stockton, Rodney and Vicky Theobald, Jess and Malcolm Wren, and Nige and Lizzie Walley for their much appreciated contributions; to Jane and Rick Field for the photo opposite p273, to Camilla Blood for her contacts and Scot McRae and Sally Blofield for the workspace.

Thank you also to the countless number of honeymooners I interviewed, for all their comments, tips and insight, and especially to those who made a special effort to take notes for me while they were away!

Thank you Gaby for coming to my rescue when I needed it most, and to Roo and my mother for their unfailing support, enthusiasm and interest.

I'm also very appreciative of the work Bryn Thomas and Anna Jacomb-Hood have put into transforming my text into this book.

But most of all I'd like to thank Andrew and Caroline for introducing me to Bryn and the idea of the *Good Honeymoon Guide*, and to Trevor for being big enough to let me go ahead with it.

A request

Every effort has been made by the author and the publisher to ensure that the information contained in this book is as up to date and accurate as possible. However, the quality and prices of resorts can change very quickly so we would welcome any constructive comments from readers.

Cover photo: Caribbean Island © Zefa Pictures

CONTENTS

PART 1: PLANNING YOUR HONEYMOON

PART 2: ISLANDS OF THE WORLD

PART 3: EUROPE

PART 3: EUROPE (cont)

PART 4: NORTH AMERICA

PART 5: CENTRAL AMERICA

PART 6: SOUTH AMERICA

PART 7: AFRICA

PART 8: SOUTH ASIA

PART 9: AUSTRALASIA

PART 1: PLANNING YOUR HONEYMOON

Your honeymoon is a holiday to look back on all your life. It is your chance, after all the hectic wedding preparations, to spend some time alone together: a time to enjoy one another and experience something together as a married couple. This holiday should be special, something to cherish in years to come and dream about on boring days at work.

Once you've got engaged

The first thing to do once you get engaged is to decide who is going to book the honeymoon. Although most couples choose to plan this important holiday together, there are those who still believe in the tradition that it's a man's job, especially in Europe. As one husband-to-be recently said to me: 'Melissa is sorting out everything else, I just want to have something that I can say is totally and utterly mine. She hasn't got a clue where we're going, but as soon as I saw it (in a brochure) I knew it was just perfect for the two of us and I am having such a great time planning it all in secret.' If you do decide to go it alone, note the Surprise Honeymoon section below.

The engagement is the hardest bit, once you've asked and she's said yes, the rest is easy. You can start having all those conversations that you wanted to have before but didn't dare. **Andrew Blatter**

Whatever you decide it's essential to get straight on with bookings as the best rooms, the best views and the best deals are the first to go. Look through the Contents List at the start of the book ticking off countries that appeal. Even if one of you loves the sound of Costa Rica or Morocco and the other hates it, tick it: you might be surprised at the kind of honeymoon you could have there. The golden rule of honeymoons is to go somewhere that neither of you has been to before as there's nothing more tedious than being given a blow-by-blow account of a holiday one of you enjoyed, or even didn't enjoy, with someone else.

Each chapter of the book is structured so that you can quickly tell whether or not the country is right for you, starting with the best time to visit. The Practical Information box tells you, amongst other things, approximately how long it takes to fly to that destination.

Flights are a big consideration when booking your honeymoon as you are going to be pretty exhausted after the wedding and may not necessarily feel like hours cooped up on an aeroplane. Don't think that romantic necessarily has to mean distant, it doesn't. Having said that, if you've absolutely set your heart on a country and a hotel that is thousands of miles away why not take the plunge? After all this is probably going to be the biggest holiday of your life and there is also a wonderful little trick called sleeping pills which can help the hours pass effortlessly (see Jet lag below).

What kind of honeymoon do you want?

Presumably you know each other well enough for it not to be a problem working out what your dream holiday comprises. But there are a few things to bear in mind: however much you long to flop on a white sandy beach and do absolutely nothing, it's a good idea to check that there are things to do when you decide it's time to venture off the lounger. The aim of this book is to inform you exactly what there is to do at or near each hotel: but check with the hotel or travel agent exactly what sports facilities are available at the time of year you are visiting and whether or not they will cost extra.

Take care to build plenty of time for rest and relaxation into your itinerary if you are planning an active honeymoon with touring, sightseeing and adventure activities. You will be amazed at how tired you are after the wedding, and even more so if you've got jet lag from a long flight. Consider having three days lying on the beach or in a mountain hideaway before you hit the trail; that way you'll both get much more out of the holiday. You don't have to dash around and see every single highlight of your chosen destination, even if you have decided on a really alternative place for your holiday. Tour operators, particularly the specialist ones, tend to push people into doing too much. You don't want to be exhausted, you're here to enjoy it: besides, you can always go back for more another year if you loved it that much and felt there was more to see.

Surprise honeymoons

Surprise honeymoons are great. They are romantic, dreamy and exciting – as long as you both feel that way. So do check that your other half is genuinely happy to go ahead with the plan before you take the ball into your own court. And check again a week or two before the wedding, and once more a day or two before the big day, that they are still happy to hang in there until the departure lounge. Bear in mind that half of the romance of your booking the honeymoon is that you've taken the trouble to think about what your partner would like, so there's nothing wrong in telling them a few days before you leave. This option often leads to a great deal of relief on both parts. Many people also find it difficult to get excited about a holiday they cannot visualise.

That aside, the key is to think about your partner and decide honestly what you think they would want. Don't book a trekking holiday in northern Thailand if all your fiancé(e) wants to do is lie on the beach. Perhaps best is to plan a two-centre honeymoon with something for you both: for example, a few days on the beach at either end and a few days in the middle for trekking, white-water rafting, canoeing, diving, looking around ancient temples or going on a safari. A good way to get an idea of where your partner would like to go, while still allowing you to keep it a surprise, is to get them to tick the countries they are interested in, on the Contents List. That way there's still plenty of scope but you know they'll approve of the basic destination.

Coping with tiredness

Most couples are extremely tired after their wedding. I can remember waking up the morning after and physically struggling to lift my head off the pillow, and I'm a morning person. It really does hit you: the emotion, the supreme effort that you've both put into the big day, and the excitement. All you'll want to do is flop, so bear this in mind when making your departure plans: try not to travel the very day of your wedding and consider whether you can both cope with a long-haul flight.

Costs

One thing you must get straight, right from the start, is how much you think you should allocate for the honeymoon. There's nothing romantic in talking about money and budgets, least of all for your honeymoon but there's also not a great deal of romance in starting married life broke. You simply won't enjoy a honeymoon if you end up scouring the cocktail menu trying to find something you can afford each time you're thirsty, or getting to some wildly exotic country and feeling you actually can't afford to go on the dug-out tour up the river to see the orang-utans' sanctuary. So talk about it and decide together what makes sense – which could of course involve the dreaded marital notion of **compromise**!

Make sure you think about all the expenses you are likely to incur, including extras like airport tax, service charges, tips, and shopping sprees. On your honeymoon, try not to go mad and spend way over your budget: I've talked to couples who are six months into their marriage and still paying crippling credit card bills – hardly the way to start married life.

However, it is worth noting that the room rates quoted in this book are rack rates only. These are the rates you would be charged if you walked into the hotel and asked for a room for one night only, and as such will very rarely apply to your honeymoon. A good travel agent or tour operator should be able to get a sizeable discount on this rate. For example, leading UK tour operators can expect to obtain discounts of 40-50% off the rack rate, depending on the time of the year and the length of your stay.

Order your foreign exchange and travellers' cheques at least a week before you leave and try to have some small change for taxis, tips on arrival etc. In many countries it's a good idea to have some US dollars in cash, as well as cash in the local currency. If you are not on a package tour it would be worth checking how you should pay your hotel bill: some hotels do not accept credit cards and they may even refuse to accept the local currency, or charge an extra premium for doing so. Throughout this book, prices are given as much as possible in both US$ and the local currency: where only a US$ rate is shown this is the principal currency used by tourists in that country.

Making a booking

Travel agents and tour operators around the world work in very different ways. You can book your chosen hotel **direct** by using the phone, fax or toll free number given for each hotel listing; through an **international booking agency** such as Small Luxury Hotels of the World, Relais & Châteaux and The Leading Hotels of the World; through **a travel agent**; or by using **a specialist tour operator** which has a range of hotels in a particular region with which its employees are well-acquainted, so you should get really expert advice.

I have tried to give the names of travel agents or tour operators through whom reservations can be made, for every hotel listed in this book. A large proportion of these tend to be UK-based tour operators as they often get the cheapest rates. Once you have decided which hotels you are interested in look at the companies listed below: they are grouped according to the country they specialise in. Do give a tour operator or a travel agent a call before you book direct, you might end up saving yourselves a lot of money, even if it costs you an international call. Using a travel agent or tour operator is also incredibly time saving, something you'll be grateful for as the wedding approaches; it's nice to know that your dream holiday is being taken care of.

WORLDWIDE OPERATORS
Abercrombie & Kent: UK (☎ 0171-730 9600, fax 0171-730 9376); USA (☎ 708-954-2944, fax 708-954-3324); Australia (☎ 39-699 9766, fax 39-699 9308); Hong Kong (☎ 2-865 7818, fax 2-866 0556)
Air France Holidays: UK (☎ 0181-742 3377)
American Express Vacations: USA (toll free ☎ 800-241-1700)
British Airways Holidays: UK (☎ 01293-723181, fax 01293-722624); USA (toll free ☎ 1-800-AIRWAYS); Australia (☎ 2-258 3300)
CV Travel: UK (☎ 0171-581 0851, fax 0171-584 5229)
Elegant Resorts: UK (☎ 01244-897888, fax 01244-897880)
GoGo Tours: USA (☎ 201-934-3500, toll free ☎ 800-526-0405)
Hayes & Jarvis: UK (☎ 0181-748 0088, fax 0181-741 0299)
Hideaways International: USA (toll free ☎ 1-800-843-4433)
Journeyworld International: USA (☎ 212-752-8308)
Kuoni: UK (☎ 01306-742222, fax 01306-744222)
Qantas Holidays: Australia (☎ 2-957 0538, fax 2-957 0781)
Silk Cut Travel: UK (☎ 01730-265211, fax 01730-268482)
Sunset Travel: UK (☎ 0171-498 9922, fax 0171-978 1337)
Thomas Cook Ltd: UK (☎ 01733-330111); Germany (☎ 0211-378087); Australia (☎ 2-229 6611); New Zealand (☎ 9-849 2071)
Travel Impressions: USA (toll free ☎ 800-284-0044)
Tropical Places: UK (☎ 01342-825123, fax 01342-822364)
Worldwide Journeys & Expeditions: UK (☎ 0171-381 8638, fax 0171-381 0836)

CARIBBEAN SPECIALISTS
Abercrombie & Kent: UK (☎ 0171-730 9600, fax 0171-730 9376); USA (☎ 708-954-2944, fax 708-954-3324); Australia (☎ 39-699 9766, fax 39-699 9308); Hong Kong (☎ 2-865 7818, fax 2-866 0556)
Alken Tours: USA (☎ 718-856-7711, fax 718-282-1152)
Fling Vacations: USA (☎ 215-266-6110, toll free ☎ 800-523-9624, fax 215-266-0280)
American Express Vacations: USA (toll free ☎ 800-241-1700)
British Virgin Islands Club: UK (☎ 01932-247617, fax 01932-229346)

CARIBBEAN SPECIALISTS (cont)

Caribbean Concepts: USA (☎ 516-496-9800, toll free ☎ 800-423-4433, fax 516-496-9880)
Caribbean Connection: UK (☎ 01244-341131, fax 01244-310255)
CaribTours: UK (☎ 0171-581 3517, fax 0171-225 2491)
Caribbean Vacation Planner: USA (toll free ☎ 1-800-356-9999, ext 304)
Caribbean World Resorts: USA (toll free ☎ 800-243-9420, ☎ 804-460-2343)
Elegant Resorts: UK (☎ 01244-897999, fax 01244-987990)
French Caribbean International: USA (☎ 805-967-9850)
GoGo Tours: USA (☎ 201-934-3500, toll free ☎ 800-526-0405)
Harlequin Travel: UK (☎ 01708-852780, fax 01708-854952)
Kuoni: UK (☎ 01306-742222, fax 01306-744222)
Ralph Locke Islands: USA (toll free ☎ 800-223-1108)
Sandals Resorts: USA (toll free ☎ 1-800-SANDALS or ☎ 305-284-1300, fax 305-667-8896); Canada (☎ 416-223-0028, fax 416-223-3306); UK (☎ 0171-581 9895, fax 0171-823 8758); Germany (☎ 089 592106, fax 089 550 1916)
Simply Caribbean: UK (☎ 01423-526887, fax 01423-526889)
Thomas Cook Ltd: UK (☎ 01733-330111); Germany (☎ 0211-378087); Australia (☎ 2-229 6611); New Zealand (☎ 9-849 2071)
Travel Impressions: USA (toll free ☎ 800-284-0044)
Unique Hotels: UK (☎ 01453-835801, fax 01453-835525)

INDIAN OCEAN RESORT SPECIALISTS

Abercrombie & Kent: UK (☎ 0171-730 9600, fax 0171-730 9376); USA (☎ 708-954-2944, fax 708-954-3324); Australia (☎ 39-699 9766, fax 39-699 9308); Hong Kong (☎ 2-865 7818, fax 2-866 0556)
Elegant Resorts: UK (☎ 01244-897999, fax 01244-987990)
Thomas Cook Ltd: UK (☎ 01733-330111); Germany (☎ 0211-378087); Australia (☎ 2-229 6611); New Zealand (☎ 9-849 2071)
Tropical Places: UK (☎ 01342-825123, fax 01342-822364)
Sunset Travel: UK (☎ 0171-498 9922, fax 0171-978 1337)

INDIA SPECIALISTS

Abercrombie & Kent: UK (☎ 0171-730 9600, fax 0171-730 9376); USA (☎ 708-954-2944, fax 708-954-3324); Australia (☎ 39-699 9766, fax 39-699 9308); Hong Kong (☎ 2-865 7818, fax 2-866 0556)
Cox & Kings: UK (☎ 0171-873 5000, fax 0171-630 6038); USA (☎ 212-935-3935, toll free ☎ 800-999-1758, fax 212-935 3863)
Hayes & Jarvis: UK (☎ 0181-748 0088, fax 0181-741 0299)

NORTH & SOUTH AMERICA SPECIALISTS

Blumar: Brazil (☎ 021-511 3636, fax 021-511 3739)
Canadian Connections: UK (☎ 01494-473173, fax 01494-473273)
Cathy Mathos Mexican Tours: UK (☎ 0171-284 2550, fax 0171-267 2004)
City Service: Argentina (☎ 1-312 8416/9, fax 1-313 9407)
Ecuadorian Tours: Ecuador (☎ 02-560488, fax 02-501067)
Journey Latin America: UK (☎ 0181-747 8315, fax 0181-742 1312)
Kuoni: UK (☎ 01306-742222, fax 01306-744222)
Last Frontiers: UK (☎ 01844-208405, fax 01844-201400, e-mail: travelinfo@lastfrontiers.co.uk)
Lima Tours: Peru (☎ 14-276624, fax 14-319878)
Mayaland Tours & Travel: Belize (☎ 2-30515/32810, fax 2-32242)
Passage to South America: UK (☎ 0171-602 9889, fax 0171-602 4251, e-mail: psauk@atlas.co.uk)
Thomas Cook Ltd: UK (☎ 01733-330111); Germany (☎ 0211-378087); Australia (☎ 2-229 6611); New Zealand (☎ 9-849 2071)
Ski Independence: UK (☎ 0131-557 8555, fax 0131-557 1676)
Sunny Land Tours: USA (toll free ☎ 1-800-783-7839)
Turismococha: Chile (☎ 2-230 1000, fax 2-203 5110)
Via Tur: Costa Rica (☎ 225 1411, fax 220 1080)
Worldwide Journeys and Expeditions: UK (☎ 0171-381 8638, fax 0171-381 0836)

ASIA SPECIALISTS

Abercrombie & Kent: UK (☎ 0171-730 9600, fax 0171-730 9376); USA (☎ 708-954-2944, fax 708-954-3324); Australia (☎ 39-699 9766, fax 39-699 9308); Hong Kong (☎ 2-865 7818, fax 2-866 0556)
Asian Affair Holiday: USA (toll free ☎ 1-800-742-5742)
Asia World: UK (☎ 01932-820050, fax 01932-820633)
British Airways Holidays: UK (☎ 01293-723181, fax 01293-722624); USA (toll free ☎ 1-800-AIRWAYS); Australia (☎ 2-258 3300)
Elegant Resorts: UK (☎ 01244-897888, fax 01244-987990)
Garuda Indonesia Holidays: UK (☎ 01753-687676)
Kuoni: UK (☎ 01306-742222, fax 01306-744222)

ASIA SPECIALISTS (cont)
Magic of the Orient: UK (☎ 01293-537700, fax 01293-537888, e-mail: 100635.2151@compuserve.com)
Thomas Cook Ltd: UK (☎ 01733-330111); Germany (☎ 0211-378087); Australia (☎ 2-229 6611); New Zealand (☎ 9-849 2071)
Symbiosis: UK (☎ 0171-924 5906)
Tropical Places: UK (☎ 01342-825123, fax 01342-822364)

AFRICA SPECIALISTS
Abercrombie & Kent: UK (☎ 0171-730 9600, fax 0171-730 9376); USA (☎ 708-954-2944, fax 708-954-3324); Australia (☎ 39-699 9766, fax 39-699 9308); Hong Kong (☎ 2-865 7818, fax 2-866 0556)
African Explorations: UK (☎ 01993-822443, fax 01993-822414)
Africa Tours: USA (☎ 212-563-3686, fax 212-563-4459)
Art of Travel: UK (☎ 0171-738 2038, fax 0171-738 1893)
Best of Morocco: UK (☎ 01380-828533, fax 01380-828630)
Carrier: UK (☎ 01625-582006, fax 01625-586818)
David Anderson Safaris: USA (c/o 905 Nemo Street, West Hollywood, CA 90069, USA)
Frontiers International: USA (☎ 1-412-935-1577, fax 1-412-935-5388)
Grenadier Safaris: UK (☎ 01206-549585, fax 01206-561337)
Nature Encounters: USA (☎ 213-852-1100, fax 213-852-1101)
Okavango Tour & Safaris: UK (☎ 0181-343 3283, fax 0181-343 3287)
Roxton Bailey Robinson: UK (☎ 01488-683222, fax 01488-682977)
The Legendary Adventure Company: (formerly known as Ker & Downey) USA (☎ 1-713-744-5244, fax 1-713-895-8753)
Theobald Barber: UK (☎ 0171-221 0555, fax 0171-221 0444)
Wilderness Travel: USA (☎ 510-548-0420, fax 510-548-0347)
World Archipelago: UK (☎ 0181-780 5838, fax 0181-780 9482, e-mail: 100711.3161@compuserve.com)
Worldwide Journeys and Expeditions: UK (☎ 0171-381 8638, fax 0171-381 0836)
Zanzique Ltd: Tanzania (Zanzibar) (☎/fax 54-31033)

AUSTRALIA AND NEW ZEALAND SPECIALISTS
Abercrombie & Kent: UK (☎ 0171-730 9600, fax 0171-730 9376); USA (☎ 708-954-2944, fax 708-954-3324); Australia (☎ 39-699 9766, fax 39-699 9308); Hong Kong (☎ 2-865 7818, fax 2-866 0556)
Air New Zealand: USA (toll free ☎ 800-262-1234)
Austravel: UK (☎ 0171-734 7755, fax 0171-494 1302); USA (☎ 212-972-6880, fax 212-983-8376)
New Zealand & Australia Reservations Office: USA (toll free ☎ 800-351-2323)
Qantas Vacations: USA (toll free ☎ 1-800-848-3579)
Silk Cut Travel: UK (☎ 01730-265211, fax 01730-268482)
Swain Australia Tours: USA (toll free ☎ 1-800-22-SWAIN)

EUROPE SPECIALISTS
Abercrombie & Kent: UK (☎ 0171-730 9600, fax 0171-730 9376); USA (☎ 708-954-2944, fax 708-954-3324); Australia (☎ 39-699 9766, fax 39-699 9308); Hong Kong (☎ 2-865 7818, fax 2-866 0556)
American Express Vacations: USA (toll free ☎ 800-241-1700)
Argo Holidays: UK (☎ 0171-331 7070, fax 0171-331 7065)
British Airways Holidays: UK (☎ 01293-723181, fax 01293-722624); USA (toll free ☎ 1-800-AIRWAYS); Australia (☎ 2-258 3300)
Crown International: USA (☎ 201-265-5151, toll free ☎ 800-628-8929, fax 201-712-1279)
CV Travel/CV Villas: UK (☎ 0171-581 0851, fax 0171-584 5229)
DER Tours: USA (☎ 310-479-4140, toll free ☎ 1-800-421-4243, fax 310-479-2239); Canada (☎ 416-695-1449, fax 416-695-1453)
Elegant Resorts: UK (☎ 01244-897888, fax 01244-987990)
Euro-Connection: USA (☎ 206-670-1140, toll free ☎ 1-800-645-EURO, fax 206-775-7561, e-mail: eceurope@wolfe.net)
Eurolynx: New Zealand (☎ 9-379 9716, fax 9-379 8874)
Greek Islands Club: UK (☎ 01932-220477, fax 01932-229346)
Ireland Vacations: USA (toll free ☎ 1-800-SHAMROCK)
InnTravel: UK (☎ 01653-628811, fax 01653-628741)
Invitation to Tuscany: UK (☎ 0171-603 7111, fax 0171-610 4175)
Magic of Spain/Italy/Portugal/Italian Escapades: UK (☎ 0181-748 4220, fax 0181-748 3731)
Meon Villas: UK (☎ 01730-268411, fax 01730-230399)
MLT Vacations: USA (☎ 612-474-2540, toll free ☎ 1-800-362-3520, fax 612-474-9730)
Qantas Holidays: Australia (☎ 2-957 0538, fax 2-957 0781)
Spanish Affair/Italian Affair/Portuguese Affair: UK (☎ 0171-385 8127, fax 0171-381 5423)
Simply Tuscany & Umbria: UK (☎ 0181-995 8277, fax 0181-995 5346)
The Best of Greece & Cyprus: UK (☎ 0171-255 2320, fax 0171-255 2321)
Thomas Cook Ltd: UK (☎ 01733-330111); Germany (☎ 0211-378087); Australia (☎ 2-229 6611); New Zealand (☎ 9-849 2071)

INTERNATIONAL HOTEL GROUPS

THE LEADING HOTELS OF THE WORLD
Australia: toll free ☎ 1-800-222033
Canada: toll free ☎ 1-800-223-6800
Germany: toll free ☎ 0130-852110
Hong Kong: toll free ☎ 800-2518
Japan: ☎ 03-5210 5131
New Zealand: toll free ☎ 0800-441016
United States: toll free ☎ 1-800-223-6800
UK: toll free ☎ 0800-181123

PRIMA HOTELS
Australia: toll free ☎ 1-800-676106
Canada: toll free ☎ 1-800-44 PRIMA
Germany: toll free ☎ 0130-854 278
Japan: toll free ☎ 0120-023723
New Zealand: toll free ☎ 0800-445366
United States: toll free ☎ 1-800-44-PRIMA
UK: toll free ☎ 0800-181535

REGENT INTERNATIONAL HOTELS
Australia: toll free ☎ 008-022800
Canada: toll free ☎ 800-545-4000
Germany: toll free ☎ 0130-852332
Hong Kong: ☎ 2-366 3361
Japan: toll free ☎ 0120-001500
New Zealand: toll free ☎ 0800-440800
United States: toll free ☎ 800-545-4000
UK: toll free ☎ 0800-282245

SUN INTERNATIONAL
UK: ☎ 01491-574546
Germany: ☎ 06171-57071
Japan: ☎ 03-3354 6151
United States: ☎ 203-622-1331

RELAIS & CHATEAUX
Australia: ☎ 1-800-815067
Germany: ☎ 0180-533 3431
Japan: ☎ 03-3567 4834
United States: ☎ 212-856-0115
UK: ☎ 0171-287 0987
Internet: http://www.integra.fr/relaischateaux

SMALL LUXURY HOTELS OF THE WORLD
Australia: toll free ☎ 008-251958
Canada: toll free ☎ 800-525-4800
Germany: toll free ☎ 0130-818912
Hong Kong: toll free ☎ 800-6378
New Zealand: toll free ☎ 0800-441098
UK: toll free ☎ 0800-964470
United States: toll free ☎ 800-525-4800
Internet address: http://www.slh.com

HYATT GROUP
Australia: ☎ 13-1234 (local call cost)
Canada: toll free ☎ 800-233-1234
Germany: ☎ 069-290114
Hong Kong: ☎ 2-956 1234
Japan: ☎ 092-483 1234
New Zealand: toll free ☎ 0800-441234
United States: toll free ☎ 800-233-1234
UK: ☎ 0345-581666 (local call cost)
Internet address: http://www.hyatt.com

ORIENT-EXPRESS HOTELS
Australia: toll free ☎ 1-800-818409
Germany: toll free ☎ 0130-818923
Hong Kong: ☎ 2-827 5566
Japan: ☎ 03-5561 0720
New Zealand: toll free ☎ 0800-442564
UK: ☎ 0181-568 8366
USA: toll free ☎ 0800-237-1236

FOUR SEASONS HOTELS
Australia: toll free ☎ 008-242907
Canada: toll free ☎ 800-268-6282
Germany: toll free ☎ 0130-852336
Hong Kong: ☎ 2-366 3361
Japan: toll free ☎ 0120-024754
New Zealand: toll free ☎ 0800-444141
United States: toll free ☎ 800-332-3442
UK: toll free ☎ 0800-526648

Plane tickets and seat reservations

If you are travelling independently ring several airlines or travel agents to get the best deal. Before you actually book a long-haul flight, you may want to look at the airline's seating plan and think about where you'd like to sit (some seats have extra leg-room). The travel agent may have a copy but if not ask the airline to send you their timetable. These timetables state the aircraft used on the flight and show seating configurations.

It's not always possible to book seats in advance (particularly if you are on a charter flight) but do make sure the airline knows you will be on your honeymoon. I've talked to honeymooners who were told at check-in that they weren't even sitting together: most airlines do all that they can to keep newly-weds together, even if they won't let you book seats in advance. You must specify any special dietary requirements in advance, however. Check in early, particularly if you're non-smokers and don't want to land up near the smoking section.

It's always worth getting someone responsible (perhaps the groom's mum) to confirm your outbound flight 24-48 hours before departure, just to be on the safe side.

Passports, visas and inoculations

Some countries require proof of citizenship, **visas** etc, so check with your travel agent or the tourist commission that you've got everything you **both** need as soon as you book, as it can take weeks or even months to get through the bureaucracy.

Take your marriage certificate with you if your plane tickets and your **passports** are in different names. Alternatively, arrange for your passport to be amended in advance. This is possible in Britain, but you can apply only three months before the date of your wedding and your passport will be valid only from the date you marry. Make sure you allow plenty of time for your new passport to be processed. Check out the procedure in your own country and again leave plenty of time for paperwork.

Consult your doctor about **inoculations**. Some countries require vaccination certificates and will not permit you to enter without one.

If necessary, make sure you take **anti-malaria pills** (prescribed by your doctor) both before and after your return from holiday and use **mosquito repellents** liberally at dawn and dusk. Drinking bottled water will help to avoid diarrhoea – not a wonderful honeymoon accompaniment.

Lastly, stock up on *all* necessary **prescriptions** (including contraceptives). Leave these in their original bottles and take a copy of the prescription, especially if you're going somewhere really exotic, so that you don't have them confiscated by Customs.

Packing

Have a really good think about what you want to take a good month before: this particularly applies to the bride of course, as not only are you likely to be more concerned about what you are wearing on your honeymoon, but the last few weeks will be so hectic you'll hardly give a moment's thought to life and your holiday after the big event. In fact, most of the hints below apply a great deal more to the bride than the groom.

Take a suitcase, even if you are a die-hard sailbag or rucksack type, because it protects clothes better, thus cutting down on the ironing.

Decant all big bottles of shampoo and toiletries into small containers or pick up trial sizes which are available in most pharmacies, so that these don't take up valuable space and weigh a lot. You could even get one of those gift-with-purchase cosmetic packs which have miniatures of everything from mascara to moisturisers. Before you pack your hair-dryer, call the hotel to check if they have one. Take plenty of sunscreen and insect repellent if required, both of which may be more expensive abroad. Put all bottles in a sealed plastic bag, even if they are brand-new, as some plane holds aren't pressurised and you don't want anything leaking on your clothes. Pack extra camera batteries and buy films before you leave to avoid having to pay costly resort prices.

Most guides tell you to 'think twice' about that extra T-shirt, dress or jacket: 'do you really need it?' they chastise, well I think you do. What the heck, this is your honeymoon, and even if you normally make a point of travelling light, make the most of the fact that for this one holiday you may want to wear something different every night, with shoes to match. Obviously this philosophy is not relevant if you're trekking through the jungle but you could leave the bulk of your clothes and your suitcase in a hotel while you go off trekking.

CAR RENTAL WORLDWIDE CENTRAL RESERVATION NUMBERS

AVIS: UK (☎ 01344-707070); USA (☎ 1-800-331-1084); Canada (☎ 1-800-TRY-AVIS, 1-800-879-2847); Caribbean Islands (☎ 1-800-228-0668); Germany (☎ 06171-681800); Australia (☎ 2-353 9000)
HERTZ: UK (☎ 0345-555888); USA (☎ 800-654-3001); Canada (☎ 800-263-0600); Germany (☎ 0130-2121); Australia (☎ 3-698 2555); New Zealand (☎ 0800-655955)
BUDGET: UK (☎ 01442-276000); USA (☎ 800-527-0700); Canada (800-268-8900); Australia (☎ 03-206 3222)

Jet lag

If you do opt for a long-haul flight, there are various ways of easing jet lag. Some countries have homeopathic pills designed to guard against jet lag. In New Zealand, for example, you can buy No Jet Lag pills, which are taken every four hours throughout the flight and have really helped me in the past. Aromatherapy oils are also a good idea. If you fancy something stronger, ask your doctor to prescribe you some sleeping pills: these will help you sleep for between six and eight hours and you don't even feel lousy when you wake up – just excited that you've got to the other end so quickly.

Getting married abroad

Every year, more and more couples decide to get married abroad. They are motivated by several considerations, the first and last of which is romance. It is also usually a great deal less expensive than having a big wedding at home, and lots of couples prefer to take their vows alone, or with a few close friends. As a result the number of places where you can be married abroad has also grown. Hotels all over the world are now geared up for weddings and can provide as many or as few extra trappings as you want. Whether you choose a secluded cove in Jamaica, a jungle lodge in Costa Rica, a hot-air balloon floating above the African plains of the Serengeti or a French château, there are certain legal requirements that you must fulfil in order to make your marriage a binding one. These vary considerably from country to country, so check *exactly* what you need when booking, and to avoid any confusion check everything with the embassy in your country before you depart.

Most countries request the following:
• your birth certificates
• valid 10-year passports and valid visas
• an affidavit confirming your marital status
• your previous spouse's death certificate if you are widowed
• a decree absolute if you are divorced
• a minimum residency requirement (anything from one to seven days)
• that you are both over 18 years old, or in some countries over 21 years old (in Bali men must be over 23 and women over 21)
• some countries require that you adhere to certain religious requirements

Feeling odd after the big day?

Having put so much effort into planning their wedding and their honeymoon many couples feel a little strange or end up rowing over nothing when they first get away: mainly it's the anticlimax of the big event being over and a feeling of guilt about not making the most of their 'holiday of a lifetime'. It does happen... so don't feel that you are odd or ill-matched if it happens to you, you're not alone. As Jessica Wren, a good friend of mine who married recently, said: 'When people talk about honeymoons, you always hear about holidays of a lifetime, but we both felt very weird for the first week, and this was made even worse by feeling guilty because it was supposed to all be so special. It was the first time we'd had that much time and space to be together for ages, plus we'd just done the massive thing of getting married. Looking back it was kind of inevitable that there'd be a getting-used-to-the-idea stage, and it did only last about four or five days. But it would have helped if someone had warned us, that way it would have taken some of the weirdness out of it.'

The Caribbean Islands
(BEST TIME: NOVEMBER TO JULY)

The name 'the Caribbean' can't help but conjure up romantic visions of dreamy days spent on secluded, white sandy beaches; watching the sunset with the sound of the ocean lapping near you; sailing from island to island, stopping to snorkel over coral reefs teeming with fish; and enjoying beach barbecues in the evenings with the rum punch flowing.

There are a lot of places in the world offering this kind of idyllic picture but there is one aspect of the above description that you won't find anywhere else in the world, and if you do, I guarantee it won't be quite the same or come anywhere close to having the magical ambience that it exudes in the Caribbean. That one unique aspect is of course, the rum punch.

It may sound ridiculous, but there is something particularly special about a rum punch served in the Caribbean. It has a lot to do with the people of course, the wonderful bar men and women grinning away at you as they conjure up their glorious concoctions nodding their head in time to the inevitable reggae music. It also has a lot to do with the rum: not its intoxicating strength, although that surely does play a part, but

---

THE CARIBBEAN ISLANDS

The ultimate tropical islands, some livelier than others, but generally offering great watersports and lovely sandy beaches

When to go: Peak season is between mid-December and mid-April, but the weather is usually just as good right through until the end of July and from November onwards

Average maximum temperatures °C

	JAN	FEB	MAR	APR	MAY	JUN	JUL	AUG	SEP	OCT	NOV	DEC
Barbados	29	29	30	30	31	31	30	31	31	30	30	29
BVI	25	25	25	26	26	27	28	28	28	27	26	25
Anguilla	26	26	26	26	27	28	28	27	28	28	27	25
St Kitts/Nevis	26	26	27	28	29	30	31	31	30	29	28	27
Antigua	26	27	27	27	27	27	28	28	28	27	27	26
St Lucia	28	29	30	31	32	33	32	31	31	30	29	28
Grenadines	29	29	31	31	31	31	33	33	33	31	30	29
Tobago	29	30	31	31	32	31	31	31	31	31	31	30
Jamaica	30	30	30	31	31	32	32	32	32	31	31	31

Capital: Each island has its own capital

Flight times: to Barbados from:
New York: 5 hours
LA: (via Miami) 9 hours
London: 8$^1/_2$ hours
Sydney (via LA and Miami): 20$^1/_2$ hours

Approximate exchange rates: Antigua and Barbuda, St Kitts and Nevis, St Lucia and St Vincent East Caribbean dollar (XC$) – £1 = XC$4.20, US$1 = XC$2.71, A$1 = XC$2.14; Barbados (BB$) – £1 = BB$3.13, US$1 = BB$2.02, A$1 = BB$1.59; Trinidad and Tobago (TT$) – £1 = TT$9.23, US$1 = TT$5.95, A$1 = TT$4.70; Jamaican dollar (JM$) – £1 = JM$52.87, US$1 = JM$34.09, A$1 = JM$26.94

Time difference: GMT minus four hours for most of the Caribbean

Voltage: 110/220v

Combine with: If you want a two-centre holiday combine two Caribbean islands, as they tend to differ quite markedly from each other

Country dialling code: ☎ Barbados 246; BVI 1-809; Anguilla 1-809; St Kitts and Nevis 869; Antigua 268; St Lucia 758; Grenadines 1-809; Tobago 1-809; Jamaica 1-809

SAILING IN THE CARIBBEAN

For some of the very best sailing in the world look towards either the **British Virgin Islands**, the world's largest yacht charter playground, or the **Grenadines**. Both areas provide interesting sailing around beautiful islands with only short day hops from anchorage to anchorage and lots of great bars and restaurants to discover each night. There is nothing quite like the freedom of a boat; if you don't like what you see when you arrive at a new island you can up anchor and find somewhere you do like. Sailing also enables you to see a great deal more of the islands and how much they vary from one another. The 15-20 knot Easterly trade winds are just perfect for easy and exhilarating cruising, although you can expect more squalls and gusts between June and November. Avoid August and September when there is a serious possibility of tropical storms and hurricanes.

There are essentially three ways to sail in the Caribbean. Charter a yacht through companies such as US-based **Sun Yacht Charters** (US ☎ 207-236-9611, US toll free ☎ 1-800-772-3500, fax 207-236-3972), in Maine, or **The Moorings**, which has a UK office (UK ☎ 01843-227140) and one in Florida (US ☎ 813-535-1446, toll free ☎ 800-437-7880, fax 813-530-9747): both of these companies have boats of varying sizes and cover the BVI and the Grenadines, either on a bareboat or crewed basis; charter a crewed yacht through professional agencies such as UK-based **Caribbean Connections** (UK ☎ 01244-341131) or **Camper & Nicholsons** who have offices in the UK (UK ☎ 0171-491 7181) and in the USA at Palm Beach (US ☎ 407-655-2121) and New York (US ☎ 212-938-0883): both companies have yachts with every kind of comfort you could imagine from air-conditioning to professional cooks and an itinerary made personally for you. The third option is to go for one of the 'sailaway holiday' packages offered by many Caribbean hotels involving time on shore in the hotel and a few days on a boat. Hotels that offer these kinds of deals include **Petit St Vincent (PSV)** and **Young Island** in the Grenadines and **Biras Creek** and **Peter Island** in the BVI (all are featured below). Rates vary a great deal from around US$1301/£840 for a week's bareboat charter of a 10m yacht in the BVI through the Moorings, to a week on *Disco Volante*, Camper & Nicholsons 'smallest' yacht measuring a cool 19m which will set you back a staggering US$11,500.

If you are sailing in the Grenadines try to pick up the yacht at **Marigot Bay** in **St Lucia** so that you can sail 'down' through the islands – it's much easier and is more fun than travelling northwards upwind.

Sample itinerary

Day One: Marigot Bay, St Lucia to the Pitons (lunch in Soufrière Bay at the Hummingbird Restaurant and pre-dinner drinks at Lord Glenconnor's Bang Between the Pitons)

Day Two: To Admiralty Bay on Bequia (last good food stop with excellent shops, fresh produce market and two delis, good choice of waterfront restaurants and Maranne's home-made ice-cream)

Day Three: Bequia to Mustique (rent a buggy and tour the island and dine at the infamous Basil's Bar)

Day Four: Mustique to Tobago Cays (spectacular setting, snorkelling and swimming, deserted sandy beaches)

Day Five: Tobago Cays to Petit St Vincent (need to pre-book dinner if you want to eat ashore)

Day Six: PSV to Carriacou (stop at Sandy Island for lunch, anchor overnight at Tyrell Bay)

Day Seven: Sail to Grenada (early start, lunch en route and arrive in time for Happy Hour at Secret Harbour Restaurant)

---

the very taste of Mount Gaye golden rum is in itself quite unique. The place is also special because of the West Indians themselves: there is something about their character, their music, their hot spicy food, the taste of coconut, and their laid-back attitude that will stay with you long after you've washed the sand and salt out of your hair.

The peak tourist season runs from the middle of December through until Easter. Although this is when the Caribbean really swings and when it attracts its most glamorous and style-conscious visitors, it is also much more expensive. If your wedding happens to fall after the middle of April, you'll find the prices drop significantly – sometimes by as much as 50% – while the weather stays pretty much the same until the middle of July, and to be honest I think it's much nicer when the beaches, bars and waters are quieter, making it feel that little bit more exclusive. I would avoid August and September as this is when the hurricanes and rains tend to hit, October is usually mixed but by November you're back into long sunny days and reasonable prices again.

Renting a Caribbean villa

Creative Leisure (US toll free ☎ 800-413-1000) has one-bedroom villas with ocean views starting from US$2600 for a 14-night stay, as well as villas that come with full-time staff but these are pricier. Also worth a call are US-based **At Home Abroad** (US ☎ 212-421-9165), the **Condo & Villa Authority** (US toll free ☎ 800-831-5512) and **Villas & Apartments Abroad** (US toll free ☎ 800-433-3020).

The **British Virgin Islands Club** (UK ☎ 01932-247617) operates a similar programme of villa rentals in the British Virgin Islands (BVI), with one or two properties just perfect for honeymoons and weddings. Ask in particular about **Sugar Mill Plantation House** on **Virgin Gorda**: it was designed by the same architect that Richard Branson used on his famous Necker Island just nearby. The house is set in its own private gardens above the sandy beaches of Spring Bay, a five minute walk away. The house is octagonal and has large open-plan living areas opening out on to a wide shaded balcony which encircles most of the property. It is beautifully decorated with rattan and cane furniture, ceramic floor tiles, high pyramid ceilings and huge wooden doors. There's one double bedroom with his and her bathrooms, each with a shower. One week's rental, including flights, transfers, taxes and maid service, in Sugar Mill Plantation House (from the middle of May to the middle of July) will cost around US$2634/£1700. If you want to be right on the beach ask about **Mango Bay Villas** in Mahoe Bay: a villa costs around US$2479/£1600 for a week.

UK-based **CaribInns** (UK ☎ 01453-835806 or toll free ☎ 0800-317185) is a select group of small hotels and villas which capture the spirit and charm of the Caribbean. The accommodation ranges from traditional guest houses to exclusive villas and the old-world charm of plantation inns. The group has properties on the following islands: Anguilla, Antigua and Barbuda, the British Virgin Islands, Dominica, Grenada, Montserrat, St Kitts and Nevis, St Lucia, and St Vincent and the Grenadines. For example **Plantation Beach Villas** (Trinidad & Tobago ☎ 639 9377, fax 639 0455), PO Box 435, Scarborough, Tobago, are a collection of private villas nestled high on a hillside looking down to the beach: they can be rented for US$255 a day, including taxes. For the ultimate in luxury go for the extraordinarily beautiful and quite unique **Cove Castles Villa Resort** (Anguilla ☎ 497 6801, fax 497 6051 or on US toll free ☎ 1-800-348-4716) on Anguilla. These incredible looking white villas are an intriguing cross between traditional Moorish architecture and something out of the 21st century. They are however expensive, costing either US$475 a night in the low season or US$2190 for a five-night Summer Dream Package which includes breakfast, champagne and fruit basket on arrival, transfers, lobster dinner for two and de luxe accommodation in a beach house.

BARBADOS

Barbados is a great place to go if it is your first visit to the Caribbean because it is big enough to give you lots of variety as well as a really good taste of Caribbean life. It stands on its own about 1610km out in the Atlantic, east of St Vincent and the Grenadines. Spanning 34km by 23km it has some of the most stunning beaches in the Caribbean as well as a selection of hotels to suit all pockets. The West coast, known as the millionaires' playground, is home to some of the finest and most expensive hotels in the Caribbean. While the island's British heritage was responsible at one time for earning it the nickname Little England, British influence over the island has waned considerably since it gained independence in 1966. American influences now dominate, as is typical of most Caribbean islands. Because Barbados is a relatively large island and one of the most developed in the Caribbean with lots to do and see it may be a good idea to combine a week on Barbados with a week somewhere quieter, such as the nearby Grenadines.

Sandy Lane

Sandy Lane is one of the longest established hotels in the whole of the Caribbean and has been the epicentre for Barbados's élite for decades now. It is the sort of hotel that somehow never ceases to remind its guests that they are staying somewhere very special. Like the Mount Nelson in Cape Town and the Cipriani in Venice, this grand old dame of a hotel is firmly etched in the hearts of the world's wealthier travellers. From the moment you are picked up at the airport in the customary white Rolls Royce you'll know you are participating in a very British and very stylish experience.

If you are looking for a small romantic hotel with secluded beaches forget Sandy Lane as it's too grand for that kind of honeymoon. Once you've found chilled champagne placed next to the orange juice on the breakfast table you know your expectations of hotels will never be the same again. Complimentary champagne at breakfast and entire bottles of Floris in the bathroom just about sums it up.

The bathrooms are sublime and the power showers so huge that you'll never want to leave them. The best suite is No 203, first used by Princess Alexandra in 1991, and the best rooms are Nos 210 and 310, because their corner aspect gives them unequalled views over the garden and on to the beach.

The beach is the very best in Barbados because of the absence of sea urchins and stone fish. And if you do decide to get active the range of facilities are quite overwhelming including an outstanding 18-hole golf course where green fees are complimentary, a hair and beauty salon and a fitness centre.

SANDY LANE
(☎ 432 1311, fax 432 2945), St James, Barbados, West Indies
Reservations: The Leading Hotels of the World toll free reservations numbers worldwide (see p12)
Getting there: Airport transfers are complimentary
Accommodation: 90 rooms, 30 suites
Amenities: Sailing facilities including yachting, hobie cat, sunfish sailing, windsurfing, snorkelling, scuba diving, deep-sea fishing, submarine tours, tennis, 18-hole golf course, fitness centre, two restaurants, bar, nightly entertainment
Dress code: Elegantly casual – no jeans, shorts, t-shirts, hats/caps after 7pm
Weddings: On request, couples must apply for a marriage licence, reception costs depend upon requirements
Minimum stay: None
Rates: Double room from US$302/£195 including dinner and breakfast; suite from US$774/£500 including breakfast.
Credit cards: Most major
Taxes and service charge: 5% Government tax is added to all room, food and beverage charges, 10% service charge

Cobblers Cove

Cobblers Cove has a wonderful English charm to it with all the amenities and sport facilities you would ever need. A member of the prestigious Relais & Châteaux grouping, Cobblers is located on the north-west coast of Barbados, near **Speightstown**, further up the beach from the other hotels on this famous stretch of coastline.

On arriving at the old stone fortress-style reception you are greeted with a big smile and the famous 'Cobblers Cooler' cocktail. Guests walk through the beautiful garden, a tropical paradise full of hibiscus flowers and tiny hummingbirds, to their suite. Complimentary bottles of wine, flowers and a big basket of exotic fruits are provided for honeymooners.

Having a surprise honeymoon and secretly thinking you are going to Canada is one thing, but finding out on the flight you are going to Barbados and then arriving at Cobblers Cove is another story – it was heaven! I couldn't have asked for a better honeymoon hideaway and I will definitely want to have my first anniversary back there!
Gabby Rance
Choosing a honeymoon place was going to be difficult as my wife to be is not only fussy, well-travelled and spoilt and likes to be in control, but Cobblers Cove seemed to be the place and it was!   **Hugh Rance**

Surrounding the old pink and white colonial building are 40 comfortable and spacious suites. Each suite has its own sitting-room with a balcony or French doors opening directly onto the garden and looking towards the sea. The bedrooms are tastefully decorated in colourful fabrics and have a fan and air-conditioning. The bathrooms are all marble with twin basins and plenty of towels – blue towels for the pool or beach are also provided. A great addition to each suite is a spacious kitchenette which enables you to add your own bits and pieces to the already full fridge and make tea or coffee when you want. Wicker-covered ice-buckets are filled up twice a day to keep those drinks cool.

Two sumptuous suites which have recently been redecorated are the Camelot and Colleton. They are both found on the top floor of the main building and have four-poster beds, private plunge pools and of course, a wicked view. These are the rooms to go for, for those who want to have the ultimate in luxury and privacy on their honeymoon!

The hotel has a wonderful terraced restaurant and bar right on the beach-front: both are open from morning until late at night. Complimentary afternoon tea is served by the pool every day – a selection of sandwiches, cakes, and of course scones and jam, but don't eat too much because you also get delicious hors d'oeuvres with your pre-dinner drinks. The menu is of an exceptionally high standard and is prepared by a team of French-trained chefs, who take advantage of the local fresh produce and fish, and yet successfully serve up the kind of dishes that would have you believe you were actually in France! The set five-course dinner menu is changed daily, or you can choose from an extensive à la carte menu and, if you still have room, fresh ground coffee is served with petit fours in one of the lounges. Some nights there is some light Caribbean music but this is always low key and unobtrusive. The manager, Hamish Watson, gives a weekly cocktail party: a great way to meet some of the other guests – after a few rum punches everyone seems only too happy to exchange stories.

This is the place for those who just want to relax on holiday, and also for those who want to relax and be active. Cobblers Cove has its own private beach, a pool, a floodlit tennis court and a good range of all-inclusive watersports facilities provided all day long. Golfers can take advantage of concessionary rates on the famous Royal Westmoreland golf course.

COBBLERS COVE

(☎ 422 2291, fax 422 1460), St Peter, Barbados, West Indies

Reservations: Relais & Châteaux worldwide reservation numbers (see p12)

Getting there: Taxi from the Airport costs BB$55

Accommodation: 40 suites including eight ocean-front suites and two de luxe suites, the Camelot and Colleton

Amenities: Dry cleaning, complimentary water-skiing, windsurfing, sunfish sailing, snorkelling; scuba diving and private yacht may be arranged for an additional charge; golf course 15 minutes drive away, car hire arranged

Dress code: Smart casual in the evening, but no jacket or tie required

Weddings: Can be arranged

Minimum stay: None

Rates: Double rooms from US$200 to US$850

Credit cards: Visa, Mastercard, American Express

Taxes and service charge: 5% Government tax is added to all room, food and beverage charges, 10% service charge

---

A FEW THINGS TO SEE AND DO IN BARBADOS

The best way to tour the island is to hire a **mini moke** (an open-sided jeep). Mokes can be rented for about US$50 a day from Dear's Garage in Bridgetown (☎ 429 9277). Make sure you take a good road map as sign posting on the island can be a bit haphazard. Start by visiting one of the old plantation houses, the **St Nicholas Abbey** (built in 1650), where sugar cane is still farmed, then go across to the district of **St Andrew** which takes you into the farming community and the old Bajan culture. Further south along the coast is **Codrington College**, a beautiful school perched on the cliffs, then head to **St John's Church**: from here one can go back down to **Bridgetown** and experience some

lively evening entertainment!

If you don't want to do much touring around **taxis** can be useful, but agree a price with the driver before you get in as there are no meters, and prices can vary considerably. **Tours** of the island can be organised through your hotel, but you could also try L E Williams Tour Company (☎ 427 1043) which has a reputation for organising good day trips to Scotland in the north of the island for around US$50 including lunch. If you want to learn to **scuba dive** or complete your PADI open-water certificate, Hightide Watersports (☎ 432 0931) offer competitive deals and very professional courses.

THE BRITISH VIRGIN ISLANDS (BVI)

Right up in the north of the Caribbean lie the Virgin Islands, both British and American. The BVI, as they are known, are much less developed than the US Virgin Islands where international hotel chains have developed sky-scraping resorts. So, if it's unspoilt islands you are seeking, go for the BVI.

Little Dix Bay

Little Dix Bay has to be one of the slickest, most stunning resort hotels in the Caribbean. To me it's one of those places with so many exciting things to do that when you first arrive you hardly know where to begin: do you pour yourself a large tumbler of the complimentary rum and coke; head straight for the beach and take a float out to sea; relax in a hammock; take part in the amazing array of activities on offer from the afternoon round robin tennisathon to diving, sailing, or simply sit at the beach bar watching the world go by?

This beautiful, spacious hotel was built by Laurance S. Rockefeller in the early 1950s, as a place where guests could relax comfortably amongst great natural beauty, without having to sacrifice the island's conservation in any way. The original architect was careful to use local materials such as stone, red cedar, purple heart, locust wood and mahogany. The hotel has recently been refurbished and is now looking its very best.

The focus of the hotel, apart from its huge crescent-shaped beach, is the main dining Pavilion which, supported by large purple heart beams reputed to weigh more than 1360kg, looks more like something in Thailand or Malaysia than a typical Caribbean resort. The views through the shaded arches of the Pavilion looking out over the brilliant turquoise sea in the Bay are quite incredible.

Little Dix is one of those hotels in which you could happily stay for a long, long time. The facilities are great, but best of all are the gardens (cultivated by British gardener, Ivon Brown); they make a wonderfully refreshing change from the beach, and for me really made the hotel.

The beach is awesome – it is certainly long enough to ensure that guests never feel cramped. In fact the whole hotel is very cleverly designed so that even when it is full the layout of the gardens and the length of the beach ensure that you'll have plenty of space to yourself. Every kind of watersport you could imagine is available on, or from, the beach, from sunfish and laser sailing, to kayaking and snorkelling, while a fleet of motor boats are on hand to take you water-skiing or scuba diving. The accommodation is spread out right along the beach with cream and dark wood two-storey cottages set about 50m back from the shore,

---

LITTLE DIX BAY
(☎ 49-55555, fax 49-55661), PO Box 70, Virgin Gorda, British Virgin Islands
Reservations: Through UK tour operator Simply Caribbean (UK ☎ 01423-526887)
Getting there: 20-minute transfer by private motor launch from the airport, check-in is on board accompanied by rum punches
Accommodation: 98 rooms: 12 garden view; 20 ocean view; seven de luxe; 38 premium; two suites
Amenities: Limited room service, hiking trails, early morning aerobics, Activity Centre for TV screenings of major sporting events, library, games room, seven tennis courts, complimentary watersports, dive centre, private yacht for overnight and day sails, sunset cruises on motor boats, private beaches for picnics à deux, three restaurants including a beach bar, once-weekly picnic at Spring Bay, car rental, health and beauty parlour
Dress code: Resort casual which means closed toe shoes and trousers for men in the evenings
Weddings: Little Dix is very popular for weddings, and usually does about three each weekend; receptions can either be in the hotel's main dining-room or at the beach house; the hotel will do its utmost to accommodate all your requests – brides can even pick their own bouquet straight from the beautiful grounds!
Minimum stay: None
Rates: Doubles from US$250 to US$650; suites from US$450 to US$1100
Credit cards: Most major
Taxes and service charge: 15% service charge on all food and beverages; plus a 5% service charge and a 7% sales tax on the room

amidst the mature gardens. The beautiful hexagonal premium rooms have lovely big balconies with views through the gardens straight out onto the beach and the sea stretching beyond.

The bedrooms are exquisitely decorated, but quite simple in style – there's no great swathes of material or chintzed bedclothes. Instead, most of the furniture is made of bamboo, rattan and pine, the walls are stone on two of the six sides with wood panelling and wide, shuttered windows on the other sides. The premium bedrooms have a walk-in closet and a good sized bathroom with shower and a turquoise tiled double basin, lots of wonderful toiletries (including the hotel's celebrated mango-coconut soap), new white cotton bathrobes, and white fluffy towels.

Each room has a fridge, hair-dryer, torch, an ironing board and iron, in-room safe and phone, as well as two comfortable rattan armchairs, a desk, and balcony furniture.

Biras Creek

Biras Creek amazed me. After staying in lots of hotels you tend to get immune to hotel furnishings. But then, once in a while, you stumble upon a special place, which not only makes you feel at home but you find yourself wishing your home was more like this. Biras is just such a place. It's not just the hotel's unique setting – it occupies a 56 hectare isthmus of land stretching out between the Atlantic Ocean with its crashing surf on one side and the calmly lapping waters of the Caribbean Sea on the other – but the feeling of space and the hundreds of little details that make it so special and ensure that it sticks in your mind forever.

Having arrived by motor launch you'll be whisked around the hotel for a quick tour on a mini moke, before being shown your room. There are 32 air-conditioned suites at Biras, 21 overlooking the ocean and nine with garden views, as well as two spacious and wonderfully romantic Grand Suites which have panoramic picture windows facing the sea and fabulous sunken baths.

But this is not a hotel where you have to have a premium suite to ensure a good room and view: the Ocean view suites are fabulous and just perfect for a honeymoon. They are all one-storey semi-detached cottages, but are laid out at an angle and are totally soundproofed so that you'd have no idea there were people staying next door. All the suites have three rooms: a sitting-room with wicker sofa, an armchair and a rattan desk, as well as a minibar, which comes complete with a complimentary bottle of Veuve Cliquot champagne and Perrier water; a bedroom which is naturally cooled by the wind coming off the Atlantic, although there is a fan; and an en suite bathroom with its alfresco shower.

BIRAS CREEK
(☎ 49-43555, fax 49-43557), PO Box 54, Virgin Gorda, British Virgin Islands

Reservations: Through UK tour operator Simply Caribbean (UK ☎ 01423-526887); from within the US and Canada through Ralph Locke Islands (US toll free ☎ 800-223-1108)

Getting there: The hotel will arrange your 25-minute transfer from Beef Island Airport, Tortola the capital of the BVI

Accommodation: 32 suites: 21 Ocean view suites; nine Garden view suites; two Grand suites

Amenities: Alfresco dining-room, library, terrace bar, fresh-water swimming pool with honesty bar, private beach at Deep Bay with beach bar and complimentary watersports, guest towels, two floodlit astro-turf tennis courts, full-time watersports instructor, enough bicycles for each guest, 14m luxury yacht, motor boats for water-skiing and smaller ones for private use

Dress code: Shirts with collars for men in the evening (polo shirt okay), smart shorts are allowed

Weddings: Biras does both wedding and honeymoon packages, the weddings can be held outdoors or on the resorts' luxury 14m yacht, but you must be on the island three working days prior to the ceremony

Minimum stay: None

Rates: Garden view suite from US$350; ocean view suite from US$425 which includes all meals and complimentary watersports, plus every seventh night free; a seven-night Sailaway plan including two nights on board the private yacht and five nights full board at Biras Creek costs from US$3230

Credit cards: Most major

Taxes and service charge: 7% government tax and 10% service charge

---

SAILING IN THE BVI

The hordes of deserted reefs, tiny green islands and remote sheltered bays that make up the BVI are interconnected with crystal clear seas making it the most popular yachting playground in the world. There are more charter boats in the BVI than there are in the rest of the Caribbean combined. Even if you choose to make your honeymoon a land-based one staying in one, or perhaps two, of the BVI's top class resorts, try to get out on the water for at least a day's sailing as the calm waters make this one of the safest and most enjoyable places to sail in the world. Most of the hotels have their own yachts so it's easy to organ-

ise a day trip, sunset cruise or even an overnight cruise.

Alternatively there are hundreds of boats for bareboat or skippered charters, which can either be organised privately through a yacht-broker in your own country or through one of the Caribbean charter companies, such as Sun Yacht Charters (US ☎ 207-236-9611, US toll free ☎ 1-800-772-3500, fax 207-236-3972), in Maine, see the box 'Sailing in the Caribbean'. As well as sailing, the BVI is also known for its scuba diving and fantastic snorkelling; it is not uncommon to see turtles and rays.

But it's the furnishings that really make the rooms at Biras so special, from the cheeky green wooden frog lolling on his back acting as a door stop to the large cool terracotta floor tiles, the colour-washed doors and shutters painted in aqua and lilac, and the fabrics which are designed and made locally. Everything has been done so tastefully and with such attention to detail that you'd never know you were in a hotel room.

The resort is spread out all over the isthmus: the cottages are lined up along the Atlantic ocean with its ripping surf and the outdoor swimming pool is set about halfway between the cottages. The beach on the Caribbean side and its bar are right on the edge of the isthmus along a sandy track (accessed either by your personal bicycle or on one of the golf carts). The resorts' small fleet of motor boats and yachts are anchored off the pier on the opposite side of the isthmus overlooking the **Sir Francis Drake Channel**. The main hotel buildings are arrayed on many different levels in what almost looks like a small castle, connected by a stone pathway spiralling up the hillside, with incredible views on all sides.

Since its recent multi-million dollar refit the hotel now has a redesigned restaurant, imported Italian tiles in the swimming pool, and new boats and watersports equipment. The hotel's facilities are just what you'd expect from a first-class resort: two floodlit tennis courts, a private beach with chaise longues scattered around under thatched huts for shade, a covered open-air pavilion and bar, as well as complimentary watersports such as windsurfing, sailing, snorkelling. There is also a fleet of small motor boats for guests to explore the **North Sound** under their own steam.

Lunch varies from barbecues served on the tranquil Caribbean beach about one kilometre away from the main body of the hotel to three-course meals in the dining-room; there is tea in the open-sided lounge looking out over the North Sound, while early morning coffee and pastries are served by the fresh-water pool, and full breakfasts and dinners are offered in the dining-room.

If you want the full-blown resort, with a big splashy hotel feel, then you may find Biras a little too quiet, but this is the place for you if you want to switch off and enjoy the odd drink or chat with other guests and staff. You may well find the general manager topping up your coffee at breakfast or the sales manager joining guests for a night-cap.

Peter Island Resort & Yacht Harbour

Peter Island Resort, owned by the multi-level marketing company Amway, is a 720 hectare private island located just south of Virgin Gorda. The hotel offers superb accommodation in an idyllic island setting.

Because the island is so big there is lots to keep you busy for a couple of weeks, as well as plenty of perfect beach spots on which to do nothing but gaze out over the varying shades of turquoise sea and the shadow of other islands in the distance.

Peter Island has five lovely sandy beaches ranging from the huge semi-circular **Deadman's Bay** which is the main beach and the base for all the watersport activities, to **Honeymoon Beach** where a lone thatched hut and two chairs occupy the small and intimate beach, or **White Bay Beach** which overlooks **Norman Island** and where the snorkelling is so fascinating you'll find the fish friendly enough to eat out of your hand. Guests are dropped at White Bay in the morning and left alone with a picnic: when they are ready to come home they contact the hotel via the two-way radio located on the beach.

There is a dive school on the island, as well as complimentary snorkelling equipment, sunfish sailing, hobie cats, sea kayaks and windsurfers, four tennis courts, a basketball court, a fitness room, and bicycles for guest use. There are also boats to charter and deep-sea fishing is available at local rates.

Deadman's Bay also has one of the best beach bars in the BVI, serving fabulous cocktails all day long, lunch between 12 and 3pm, and evening meals every night from December to May. After 1 May, the beachside restaurant is open only on Monday nights, which is a shame as it definitely has a much more convivial atmosphere than Tradewinds, the hotel's main dining-room. Wherever you eat look out for Jean, the restaurant supervisor, whose infectious personality has to be one of the best reasons to come here.

PETER ISLAND RESORT
(☎ 49-52000, fax 49-52500), PO Box 211, Road Town, Tortola, British Virgin Islands
Reservations: Through UK tour operator Simply Caribbean (UK ☎ 01423-526887); Peter Island Sales and Reservations (US toll free ☎ 800-346-4451), or Preferred Hotels and Resorts Worldwide US toll free (☎ 800-323-7500)
Getting there: 25 minutes by guest boat from Beef Island Airport
Accommodation: 50 rooms, plus three villas: 30 harbour-side rooms, 20 beach-front rooms
Amenities: Two restaurants, two bars, including beach bar; four tennis courts, fitness centre, swimming pool, extensive complimentary watersports, five beaches, Dive BVI centre, bicycles for guest use, heli-pad, gift shop, library lounge, masseur, laundry service, free ferry service to Tortola, picnic lunches, island tours and walking trails, deep-sea fishing and sailing trips organised locally
Dress code: Shirt with collar and smart trousers required for dinner in the Tradewinds restaurant; no swimming suits allowed for meals at Deadman's Beach Bar and Grill
Weddings: Wedding ceremonies are very popular at Peter Island and will be costed according to your requirements
Minimum stay: None
Rates: Garden view from US$195; ocean view from US$245; beach-front from US$325 (all rates depend on the season)
Credit cards: Most major
Taxes and service charge: 10% gratuity added daily for accommodation and 15% for all food and beverage charges, no further tipping is necessary

---

The hotel also has a swimming pool right next to the main Tradewinds restaurant, where shirts with collars, shoes and smart trousers are required of men in the evening. Reception, Dive BVI, the restaurant, pool and the 30 harbour rooms are on the harbour side of the island. On the other side of one of the island's many peaks are three of the beaches and the 20 beach-front rooms. The harbour rooms are housed in eight concrete two-storey houses with shiny white A-framed roofs. I would definitely go for the beach-front rooms as they are much more natural looking, though both are nice inside. Each room has an en suite bathroom with lots of white towels and full-sized bottles of toiletries, a fully-stocked minibar, a hair-dryer and iron and ironing board, a phone, radio and a good sized balcony or terrace with plastic loungers and table and chairs.

The interior decoration of the rooms is a bit of a confused mixture of styles from the pale pinks on the armchairs to the strong tones of the bedspreads, but the air-conditioning is great, the bed extremely comfortable, and the en suite bathroom facilities impressive. The views of Deadman's Bay from the beach-front rooms are also wonderful.

ANGUILLA

Regarded as one of the most romantic places in the Caribbean, Anguilla is a truly undisturbed haven for escapists. Only 26km long and 5km across at its widest point, you won't find any casinos here but you will find the best white sand beaches in the Caribbean – 30 of them in all. A must for visitors is a trip to one of Anguilla's offshore deserted islands where all you'll need is a picnic and a snorkel and mask.

Cap Juluca

If you are looking for the best beaches, full-on luxury and real exclusivity then look no further than Cap Juluca, where the hotel's white pavilions shimmer against a turquoise sea like something out of the Arabian Nights. Spread over 72 hectares, Cap Juluca boasts some of the Caribbean's most stunning beaches, with a garden stashed full of glorious palms, orchids and frangipani. But perhaps most telling of all is Cap Juluca's one to one ratio of staff to guests – we're talking serious pampering.

Cap Juluca, named after the Arawak rainbow god, was built in accordance with the Anguillan law that no building should be taller than a palm tree. The result is a stunning array of white-washed Moorish-style villas lining the perfect curve of **Maunday's Bay**, looking across to the mountains of the nearby chic French enclave, St Martin.

Rugs, stoneware, inlaid mirrors and leather articles from the Moroccan souks combine with cool white walls, Italian floor tiles and Balinese fabrics to create a feeling of effortless chic inside the suites.

The rooms are truly enormous: ranging from 67 sq metres to 198 sq metres. They all have private walled terraces for sunbathing with panoramic sea views, some even have their own private or shared pool. There are king-sized beds, air-conditioning, ceiling fans, in-room safes, fully stocked minibars with refrigerators and ice makers.

The 18 beach-front junior suites are the best rooms at Cap Juluca, largely due to their Italian marble bathrooms. In each of the large marble-and-glass bathrooms, one whole side – the one near the pillow-edged jacuzzi – is a sheet of clear glass looking on to your walled garden patio. What's more, the glass wall has a door in it, allowing you to step straight from the jacuzzi into the privacy of your own garden. Most bathrooms have a separate shower, bidet, dressing area and double basin, all have a hair-dryer, bath salts and Molton Brown of London toiletries.

Anguilla is also known for the quality of its food, and Cap Juluca offers guests four

---

CAP JULUCA
(☎ 497 6666, fax 497 6617), PO Box 240, Maunday's Bay, Anguilla, Leeward Islands, British West Indies
Reservations: Prima Reservations worldwide reservation numbers (see p9-10); or UK tour operators Abercrombie & Kent, Caribbean Connection, Elegant Resorts, Caribtours, Simply Caribbean (see p10); New York reservations US toll free (☎ 800-323-0139)
Getting there: Via scheduled air service from Antigua (35 minutes) from San Juan (50 minutes) or St Martin (5 minutes), guests are met at the airport on arrival
Accommodation: 12 two-storey 'hotel villas' housing 65 luxury and junior suites, seven suites and six pool villas with their own private or shared full size swimming pool
Amenities: Two restaurants: the Pool Terrace/Beach Pavilion and Pimm's; early morning coffee and pastries available in the main house library from 6.15 to 10am, otherwise breakfast is served on your terrace or at the Beach Pavilion, live music several nights a week, movies shown nightly, three omni-turf surface tennis courts (two are floodlit) plus professional coach, croquet lawn, junior Olympic-sized swimming pool, complimentary watersports including sunfish sailing, snorkel gear, kayaks, windsurfers, water-skiing; deep-sea fishing, scuba diving and day sails can be arranged at local rates; fitness centre, golf at local course, boutique and sundries shop, car rental, masseur
Dress code: No jacket or tie required
Weddings: Yes
Minimum stay: None
Rates: Doubles from US$255 to US$390 per couple per night in summer season; one bedroom suites from US$490, ask about packages
Credit cards: American Express, Visa, MasterCard
Taxes and service charge: 8% government tax and 10% service charge will be added to your bill

restaurants to choose from. The **Beach Pavilion** and the **Pool Terrace** are used during the day for tasty light lunches and cocktails, while most people look forward to a sumptuous dinner at **Pimm's** in the evening, where French, Chinese, Moroccan and Caribbean influences are all combined in dishes like Chinois fish with soy sauce, ginger and green onions. Those who are looking for something less formal head for the Pool Terrace and Beach Pavilion, or **Chattertons** for lighter dishes.

ST KITTS AND NEVIS

After a week of beach filled activity on some of the bigger islands, such as Antigua, time out on these smaller islands can provide the perfect contrast. St Kitts and Nevis are *the* islands to relax on. Spend long languorous days here in a totally unhurried environment that is filled with old colonial charm. The dense, tropical forests surrounding the summit of St Kitts' now dormant volcano contrast with the more cultivated, fertile valleys below. These islands seem lost in a dreamy past where the pace is slow and the best hotels are former plantations run as house parties where visitors mingle over cocktails and canapés in the evening.

Montpelier Plantation Inn

Montpelier, which nestles into the shoulder of Mount Nevis, is built on the ruins of a sugar plantation 195m above sea level. Today's hotel is famous as the wedding place of Lord Nelson and the young and well-off widow Frances (Fanny) Nisbet back in 1787 and is still just as romantic.

The Great House is reminiscent of a grand country manor run along the lines of an intimate house party, and while you certainly don't have to mix with the other guests it would be a shame not to as the convivial atmosphere is very much part of the hotel's endearing charm.

The 17 West Indian-style cottages each have their own trellised balcony with views out to sea and the bedrooms are wonderfully simple and clean, almost minimalist in tone.

Apart from having one of the prettiest pools in the Caribbean, guests can enjoy long lazy days down at the secluded private beach where sun loungers and thatched palm shaders are provided for guest use. You are dropped off at the beach each morning by the hotel's minibus which then picks you up again in time for afternoon tea. The watersports facilities are slightly limited – essentially this is a place for relaxation not activity, those who want full resort facilities can

> **MONTPELIER PLANTATION**
> (☎ 469 3462, fax 469 2932), PO Box 474, Nevis, West Indies
> **Reservations**: All leading Caribbean-specialist tour operators and travel agents worldwide (☎ see p9-10)
> **Getting there**: Flights to Antigua, Puerto Rico or St Martan and then LIAT or Windward Air to St Kitts or Nevis; taxi (19km) to the hotel approx US$20
> **Accommodation:** 16 rooms, one small cottage
> **Amenities**: Private beach, swimming pool, nearby golf course, tennis courts
> **Dress code**: Smart casual
> **Weddings**: The hotel does arrange weddings and has a set package from US$750, plus a photographer at additional cost from US$200
> **Minimum stay**: None
> **Rates**: Double room from US$178/£115 per night
> **Credit cards**: Most major
> **Taxes and service charge**: Included

head for the nearby **Four Seasons**. The kitchen will happily prepare you a sumptuous picnic, featuring the much-written about lobster butties, so that you can spend all day down at the beach, after which you'll really look forward to returning to the cooler hills in the evening.

Owned and run by old Etonian James Milnes Gaskell and his wife, Celia, Montpelier has the most wonderful laconic and relaxed atmosphere that confirms it as an established institution.

NISBET PLANTATION BEACH CLUB
(☎ 469 9325, fax 469 9864), St James Parish, Nevis, West Indies
Reservations: Leading tour operators and travel agents specialising in the Caribbean (see p9-10)
Getting there: Scheduled flights to Antigua, San Juan, St Kitts or St Martin and then take a short flight with LIAT or Windward air to Nevis, taxis available
Accommodation: 16 superior rooms, 10 de luxe suites, 12 premier units
Amenities: Dining-room, beach bar/restaurant, swimming pool and sun-deck, tennis, croquet, snorkelling, scuba diving, sport fishing, sailing, horse-riding, eco-rambles, mountain hiking and golf
Dress code: Daytime – casual, evening – smart casual, no jeans, t-shirts or shorts in main house after 6pm
Weddings: Special all-inclusive packages from US$1850
Minimum stay: None – four working days minimum for a wedding
Rates: Superior from US$255, de luxe from US$295, premier from US$325
Credit cards: MasterCard, Visa, American Express
Taxes and service charge: Government tax 7%, service 10%

Nisbet Plantation Beach Club

Also on Nevis is Nisbet Plantation, the family home of Fanny Nisbet, now a wonderful country house retreat offering accommodation in 38 bedrooms in airy cottages set around the grounds which are truly romantic – right down to the hibiscus petals scattered liberally over the bed for your arrival.

The hotel is the epitome of luxury and good taste: once there you can enjoy both the secluded one kilometre sandy beach with its beach bar and snorkelling and the old-world charm of the Great House where fabulous teas are served in the afternoon on the veranda.

Reports of the food at Nisbet are really good – it has been described as innovative, elegant and delicious. Dinner by candlelight on the veranda of the Great House is excellent.

There are mountain bikes for those who feel energetic and hammocks, or a drawing-room full of paperbacks and board games for those who don't.

A FEW THINGS TO SEE AND DO ON ST KITTS AND NEVIS

Nevis is just 15.54 sq km and is quite mountainous which makes it all the more dramatic. If you are feeling energetic it's possible to climb **Mount Nevis**, but the climb is pretty tough made more so by the dense rain forest: it's wise to take a guide. Try **Eco-Ramblers** (☎ 469 2091) and **Top to Bottom** (☎ 469 5371).

Horse-riding can be arranged through **Cane Gardens** (☎ 469 5464) or through the **Hermitage Inn** (☎ 469 3477), both of which will take you for an exhilarating gallop through the surf.

If beaches, not climbing or horse-riding, are your thing head for **Oualie Beach** on the north of the island, not far from Newcastle Airport: it has fantastic golden sands, a good beach bar and lovely views over to St Kitts. **Pinney's Beach** is the island's largest, stretching an amazing 6km which makes it a perfect place to stretch your legs, especially as there's a good selection of beach bars should you feel like the odd rum punch!

If you fancy a night out in true Caribbean style book a table at *Miss June's* (☎ 469 5330), where fantastic hot spicy food is served in a superb atmosphere.

A good way to see Nevis is to do one of **Mrs Swanson's** four hour tours – these can be booked at your hotel. But beware, by the time she's stopped for a gossip and mangoes en route it's likely to have taken considerably more than four hours. The houses in wonderfully named villages such as **Gingerland** and **Cotton Ground**, are brightly painted, while **Charlestown**, the capital, is a lovely port and especially worth visiting on a Saturday for the market. From here you can hop on a ferry and make the 40 minute journey to St Kitts for the day.

Basseterre, St Kitts' capital, is much busier than Charlestown, with its pavement cafés full of blaring music and its own shopping mall. Hop into a taxi and go to **South Friars Bay** where there is a lovely secluded beach, plus a vantage point from where you can see the choppy Atlantic on one side and the serene waters of the Caribbean Sea on the other. A good way to see the island is through an organised tour which includes **Brimstone Hill** and visits to the crater of **Mt Liamuiga**, talk to **Greg's Safaris** (☎ 465 4121). Bear in mind though that the walk to the crater is hard work and will take you all day.

ANTIGUA

For years Antigua has promoted itself as the island of 365 beaches, one for every day of the year. While this is somewhat of a romanticised cliché that has gradually lost its sparkle, the islands' beaches certainly haven't. Antigua also offers fantastic watersport facilities making it an ideal two-centre honeymoon combined with a week on Anguilla, St Kitts, Nevis or even the BVI. However if you want to submit yourselves utterly to the Caribbean way of life why not just stay in Antigua for a couple of weeks, giving yourself time to see some of its most beautiful beaches, maybe do a few days chartering and really start to unwind in true Caribbean style.

Curtain Bluff

Curtain Bluff has long been regarded as Antigua's best hotel, and is often included in the area's specialist tour operators' top three hotels in the Caribbean. Perched on a strip of land that juts out between two sandy beaches, one calm and tranquil the other windswept, Curtain Bluff is a resort hotel with a much more glamorous feel than quieter hotels included here such as the **Inn at English Harbour**.

Curtain Bluff is the ideal place for people who like impressive resorts where guests want for absolutely nothing and enjoy feeling safe in the knowledge that they are on a private estate. It is the perfect place for sport lovers who can take advantage of the complimentary sailing, water-skiing, windsurfing, snorkelling, ketch sailing and scuba diving if they are qualified. On top of this there is tennis, squash, a gym, and an 18-hole golf course nearby.

The hotel has everything you could possibly want including the most spectacular views of the sea from each of the 58 rooms and suites. The rooms themselves are decorated in pastel shades, with marble floors and en suite bathrooms which even have their own ceiling fans.

Curtain Bluff's restaurant has a solid reputation, thanks to its resident chef of 30 years, Reudi Portman, and the hotel's awesome wine cellar, which is said to have over 25,000 bottles. Dining is a formal affair with men required to wear a jacket and tie, so don't choose Curtain Bluff for your honeymoon if this kind of attitude is going to annoy you, especially as the hotel operates a full board policy.

> **CURTAIN BLUFF**
> (☎ 462 8400, fax 462 8409), PO Box 288, St John's, Antigua, West Indies
> **Closed**: Between mid-May and mid-October
> **Reservations:** US toll free (☎ 800-672-5833); or through tour operators specialising in the Caribbean (see p9-10)
> **Getting there:** 25 minutes by local taxi from the Airport
> **Accommodation:** 52 rooms and six suites
> **Amenities**: Complimentary sailing, water-skiing, windsurfing, snorkelling, ketch sailing and scuba diving (if qualified), four tennis courts, squash court, aerobics and gym; there is also an 18-hole golf course nearby
> **Dress code**: Jacket and tie are required after 7pm during the high season
> **Weddings:** Curtain Bluff is popular for weddings, particularly in the garden gazebo
> **Minimum stay**: None
> **Rates**: Doubles from US$595 per night in the peak season (mid-December to mid-April) and from US$495 from mid-October to mid-December and mid-April to mid-May
> **Credit cards**: Most major
> **Taxes and service charge:** 7% government tax, plus 10% service charge

The Inn at English Harbour

The Inn at English Harbour is a wonderfully relaxing hotel where guests stay in pale-green and white louvred one- and two-storey cottages along the beach, with green trellising dividing the semi-detached bungalows.

As soon as you enter the hotel's reception you'll know from the friendly service and wonderfully informal atmosphere that you are going to have a very private and relaxing stay. There is something about the Inn that makes it a very British hotel with an old world charm that puts you instantly at your ease.

The hotel is split between the public rooms which are high up on the hillside overlooking **English Harbour** (where there are also six bedrooms), and the beach-side cottages, set on one of the island's loveliest beaches. The hotel operates a shuttle service ferrying guests between the two levels.

The 28 rooms are all simply furnished but comfortable. Don't expect to find air-conditioning, a fully-stocked minibar, towelling robes or a marble bathroom but you will find a good-sized fridge, a decent hot and cold shower and an ample supply of towels, both for the beach and for the bathroom. In fact half the beauty about staying at the Inn is going across to the shops at **Nelson's Dockyard** on the hotel's dinghy and stocking up your fridge with your own favourite drinks.

Each of the rooms has the basic amenities such as hair-dryer, wall safe, fridge, ceiling fan, phone and ceiling fan, as well as mosquito nets draping down prettily in the superior rooms. The walls are white-washed wood, the floors tiled and the odd Caribbean painting brightens up the walls.

There are six beach-front superior rooms, three upstairs and three right on the edge of the beach. Although the downstairs rooms do have the advantage of allowing you to walk straight out on to the beach, the upstairs rooms are more private and definitely the ones to choose if lolling around in bed savouring the view is important to you.

There is plenty to do from the hotel which has its own speedboat for water-skiing (US$20 for 15 minutes), taking guests around the island or even packing them off to a deserted beach with a picnic and snorkelling kit for the day. There are also sunfish-sailing dinghies, windsurfers and snorkelling kits available for free on the hotel's private beach. Refreshments are served all day from breakfast through until 6pm at the beach bar.

But even more exciting are the hotel's own private classic ketch and smaller yacht, as well as a traditional Long Tail which Paul, the owner, brought all the way back from Thailand. A night on board *Flicka* would be the perfect getaway: the stunning 13m yacht was built 60 years ago and is a true classic. It has a large double bed in the forward cabin, so the skipper is more than happy to take guests off for a couple of days sailing.

After a day at the beach, the focus switches up the hill to where the main lobby, bar, restaurant and lounge are found. The bar is the perfect place for a drink in the evening: the varnished teak tables and chairs with green leather backs give the feeling of being in an elegant drinking club. Dinner is served outside on the terrace by candlelight, looking down over the harbour below.

THE INN AT ENGLISH HARBOUR
(☎ 460 1014, fax 460 1603), PO Box 187, English Harbour, Antigua, West Indies
Reservations: Simply Caribbean and most leading Caribbean specialists (see p9-10)
Getting there: 30 minutes by taxi from the airport costs US$21; the hotel can arrange a rental car to be waiting for you at the airport
Accommodation: 28 rooms including six hillside cottages; six superior beach-front rooms; and 16 standard beach-front rooms
Amenities: Complimentary sunfish sailing, windsurfing, row boat and snorkel gear; water-skiing, day sailing, scuba diving, deep-sea fishing and horse-riding can all be arranged at local rates; tennis and golf are both five minutes away; gift shop, 24-hour laundry service and a local masseur can be called in
Dress code: Smart casual in the evening but no jacket or tie required
Weddings: The hotel offers a US$450 wedding package which includes registration and legal fees, one-tier decorated wedding-cake, a bottle of champagne, plus decoration of the location
Minimum stay: None
Rates: Double rooms from US$186/£120 to US$527/£340 depending on room and season
Credit cards: Most major (not Diners Club)
Taxes and service charge: 18.5% service charge and government tax will be added onto your bill

Jumby Bay Island

Jumby Bay Island is a privately owned 120-hectare island just 3km off the east coast of Antigua. This stunning resort is the perfect place for honeymooners and is quite unusual in that it operates as a sophisticated, all-inclusive resort.

Jumby Bay is a place of utter peace: there are no cars on the island, just golf carts and the shuttle that collects guests for dinner, and the white bicycles with a good-sized pannier assigned to guests on arrival for ferrying themselves around.

Although the resort does boast some of the finest facilities of any Caribbean hotel it is above all a place where people come to do nothing and to get well and truly away from it all. To help you do so there are no phones or TVs in the bedrooms and the island is kept utterly private. Snoozing under a thatched umbrella or lying together in a hammock is how people spend their day at Jumby Bay Island, punctuated only by the occasional swim, snorkel, or a game of croquet on the immaculately manicured lawn.

The word 'immaculate' just about sums up this slick resort: the staff are unobtrusive but attentive, and the immense beach is perfect. For the energetic there's plenty to do – 7km of hiking trails (which are suitable for the resorts' bikes), a putting green, two all-weather tennis courts and a professional coach, and numerous water-based activities including water-skiing and sailing.

At the heart of Jumby Bay is the Estate House, an old English sugar plantation manor dating back to the 1700s, where

---

JUMBY BAY ISLAND
(☎ 462 6000, fax 462 6020), PO Box 243, St John's, Antigua, West Indies
Reservations: With leading tour operators and travel agents specialising in the Caribbean (see p9-10)
Getting there: Guests are met at the airport, five-minute drive and six-minute cruise to the island (rum punch served en route)
Accommodation: 38 de luxe rooms: including a 14-unit Mediterranean style villa and 24 junior suite style cottages
Amenities: Bicycles for each guest, hiking/cycling trails, three tennis courts with professional coach, large selection of watersports including sunfish sailing, water-skiing, floats, pedalos, windsurfing, snorkelling, and sailing on the island's yacht *Moonshine*, weekly sunset cruise, plus several swimming pools, both shared and private
Dress code: No jackets required
Weddings: The resort caters for both weddings and receptions
Minimum stay: None
Rates: Doubles from US$645; luxury villas from US$1195 per couple which includes all your meals, drinks and activities
Credit cards: Most major
Taxes and service charge: 7% government tax and 10% service charge will be added to your bill

---

guests gather for high tea on the veranda, candle-lit dinners in the downstairs dining-room or outside on the terrace if they prefer. Upstairs the hotel bar, better known as the Library, is well-stocked with reading material to keep you going through the day. Breakfast is either served at the beach pavilion or delivered to your room.

Guests can stay in Pond Bay House, the Spanish-style villa with a red, tiled roof and cream stone walls, which has 14 rooms, or in one of the 24 Mediterranean-style two-storey white cottages scattered along the beach and around the pools. All the suites are truly luxurious, decorated either in fresh white to contrast with the terracotta floor and dark wood louvred doors and ceiling, or in Caribbean tones of turquoise, coral, green and yellow. They either have king-sized or double beds, some are bamboo four-posters while others have iron bed frames. They all have a separate sitting-room with rattan armchairs, ceiling fan, hair-dryer, in-room safe, and wet bar (minibar). The wonderfully opulent bathrooms are something else with their open-air showers and pretty cream and turquoise tiling, Hermès toiletries and bathrobes with your names monogrammed on – which the resort sends to your home address when you leave.

If you view your honeymoon as the ultimate chance to see just how far you can both unwind and do nothing, this has to be one of the most beautiful islands on earth to do it. Day after day of lying on the beach, strolling through the gently lapping turquoise sea, and staring up at the starry sky night after night tends to do the trick.

A FEW THINGS TO SEE AND DO IN ANTIGUA

One of the best things about staying at the Inn at English Harbour is that you're right on hand for **Shirley Heights**, the old English garrison fort high up on the hill behind the hotel which commands the most incredible views of the bay and over to distant **Montserrat**.

I was talking to a couple recently who were so enamoured with their Sunday night trip to Shirley Heights that they insisted I should recommend that anyone going to Antigua organise their entire holiday itinerary around ensuring that they get at least one experience of this incredible event, if not two. The weekly 'jump up' at Shirley Heights has become so popular with locals, resident yachties and visitors alike that this sundowner party high on a hill looking down on English Harbour has now become a Caribbean institution. You can either walk up which takes about half an hour from the Dockyard or phone Ivor (☎ 460-1241 or on his mobile ☎ 464-0118) the local taxi man who will be happy to drive you up there and collect you later. Make sure you get up there for about 5pm so that you can order your rum punches and barbecued burgers before the 21-piece steel band kicks off and the crowd go wild. And they do! After the steel band finishes at around 7pm live reggae keeps the crowd entertained.

Because Antigua is one of the bigger West Indian islands it's great for couples who think they might get frustrated on tiny islands such as the Maldives. There's plenty to see and do in Antigua that would keep most people happy for a fortnight. The best thing to do is hire a jeep and see the island for yourselves, getting a real taste of what Caribbean life is like for the locals. The road system is good enough to find your way round but rough enough to make it quite an entertaining adventure as you pass stunning coastal views and tracks through the rain forest.

The interior is very arid, quite flat and not that beautiful but the beaches are just magical. **Half Moon Bay** is reputed to be Antigua's most beautiful beach, where the surf gets quite high up one end of the beach but remains flat and tranquil at the other. There's also a good bar set back off the beach itself. Closer to English Harbour is **Pigeon Beach** which is a great place to go if you are looking to get away from other tourists, as it's usually used by friendly locals and the crews from the yachts in the afternoons.

For a fantastic one-hour walk come out of the old Fort and walk up and over the ridge between the English Harbour and Falmouth Harbour across to Pigeon Beach: you just need to follow the white ribbons attached to the trees. You'll get stunning views of both harbours and the Caribbean Sea.

The Admiral's Inn (☎ 460 1027) and the *Copper and Lumber Store* (☎ 460 1058) are two historic hotels overlooking Nelson's Dockyard. They are both lovely places to enjoy a cocktail or even dinner, and are easy to get to if you're coming from English Harbour. Both hotels offer reasonably priced accommodation in a really beautiful setting and the food is apparently really good.

You don't have to have done much sailing to enjoy a few days chartering around Antigua, perhaps over to stunning **Green Island** or down to **Harmony Hall**. **Sun Yacht Charters** whose head office is in Maine in the USA (US ☎ 207-236-9611) operates both skippered and bareboat charters out of Antigua, for a minimum of four days, a 12m Centurion will cost you around US$2000 a week for a boat and skipper.

ST LUCIA

Imagine lush valleys covered in bananas, tropical rain forests, towering palms, lime trees, bushes covered in exotic flowers and two towering green volcanic peaks, and you're imagining St Lucia. This, the lushest and most exotic of all the Caribbean islands, is renowned for its friendly islanders and a climate that is so warm you'll want to skinny dip under the stars at midnight.

Sandals Halcyon Beach

Sandals run all-inclusive resorts all over the Caribbean designed as the perfect couples only holiday which means they make extremely good honeymoon destinations.

Of course Sandals won't appeal to everyone for the very fact that they are so popular with couples getting married abroad and with honeymooners – popular enough for them to claim they invented the so called Weddingmoon! However they certainly do have their benefits, and by paying up front at least you can start saving for your holiday well before and not have to continually dig into your pockets for that extra ten minutes' water-skiing or more rum punches. And better still, you won't spend the first six months of your married life paying off an extras bill.

Sandals Halcyon Beach is regarded as the most romantic and pristine of the company's nine Caribbean resorts. This lovely hotel is only ten minutes away from Vigie International Airport, and only ten minutes down the road from Sandals St Lucia, the facilities and restaurants of which are open to guests of Halcyon Beach.

The hotel has 170 rooms in all, comprising five different categories from de luxe to honeymoon beach-front. All rooms have air-conditioning, a mahogany four-poster, king-sized bed, ceiling fan, amenity kit, hair-dryer, phone, private bath and shower, clock radio and satellite TV. The grand de luxe and honeymoon beach-front rooms are fabulous with the most amazing beach and ocean views.

With so many watersports and land-based sports such as tennis, volley-ball and cards to play, there's no danger of getting bored at Sandals. There are three fresh-water swimming pools with swim-up bars, three whirlpools and three restaurants with food ranging from Italian to International or Caribbean in the **Pierhouse**, which is set out over the water's edge at the end of a 45m pier.

Anse Chastanet

Anse Chastanet offers the classic honeymoon experience. Whenever people ask me where they should go for a few days of total and utter relaxation at the start of their Caribbean honeymoon it's always top of my list.

This 200-hectare hideaway is wildly romantic, with bedrooms that seem to have been carved into the hillside they are so much part of the dense jungle surrounds. What makes this hotel so special is its premium rooms which have been designed so that there is nothing to impede the fantastic view over St Lucia's famous Pitons.

The higher up the hillside you go the better the rooms are, and needless to say, the better the views. While some guests have complained about the long hike up the many stone steps, when they were initially shown the room, they all seem to rapidly change their minds once they've seen the view. It really is quite staggering and most guests at Anse Chastanet seem to find themselves sitting for hours on end staring at the view.

The best rooms of all are No 7F and No14A, universally regarded as two of the Caribbean's most famously romantic bedrooms, where two whole sides are open to the view. Although unwanted wildlife might take advantage of the open walls you can both snuggle up under your mosquito net for protection. The alfresco bathrooms in suites Nos 7A to 7F are equally famous for their open-air experience: imagine rinsing away the beach sand and sea salt looking out upon the magnificent setting sun, as the sea turns gold and purple to match the sky.

The rooms are decorated with the bright madras checked material that is the traditional dress of the local St Lucian women. Combined with the wooden roofs, terra-

---

SANDALS HALCYON BEACH
(☎ 453 0222, fax 451 8435), Choc Bay, Castries, St Lucia, West Indies
Reservations: Through most tour operators and travel agents specialising in the Caribbean (see p9-10) and Sandals offices (also on p10)
Getting there: Just over one hour from Hewanorra International Airport and 10 minutes from Vigie International Airport, transfers are complimentary
Accommodation: 170 rooms in five categories: de luxe, premium, luxury, grand luxe, honeymoon beach-front
Amenities: Bayside International Restaurant, the Pierhouse Caribbean restaurant, Mario's Italian restaurant, three fresh-water swimming pools, three whirlpools, fitness centre, watersports, land sports, beauty salon with hair styling, facials, manicure, pedicure, massages, gift shop, money exchange bureau, piano bar and disco, car rental, golf
Dress code: No jackets required
Weddings: Sandals specialises in weddings, costs start at US$750, couples must allow a minimum of three working days in the Caribbean before getting married
Minimum stay: Three nights
Rates: For one week, per couple: double rooms from US$3400 in the high season, and from US$3230 low season; honeymoon beach-front rooms cost US$4330 in the high season and US$4110 low season
Credit cards: American Express, Visa, MasterCard
Taxes and service charge: Both included

ANSE CHASTANET

(☎ 459 7000, fax 459 7554), PO Box 7000, Soufrière, St Lucia, West Indies

Reservations: Most tour operators and travel agents specialising in the Caribbean (see p9-10)

Getting there: The hotel can arrange transfers from the airport, costing approx US$45 per car – it is best to try and share with another couple

Accommodation: 48 rooms: four Premium hillside rooms with open-sided views of the Pitons; 12 open de luxe hillside rooms with Piton or ocean views; 12 de luxe beach-front rooms; 16 Superior hillside rooms with wraparound balconies; four smaller hillside rooms

Amenities: Two restaurants, two bars, complimentary snorkelling, mini sailing and windsurfing, spa treatments and exercise equipment

Dress code: Elegant casual, men must wear trousers or long shorts at the Tree House restaurant

Weddings: Wedding and honeymoon packages available

Minimum stay: None

Rates: Double rooms from US$360 including breakfast and dinner from mid-December to mid-April; Premium suites from US$595

Credit cards: Most major

Taxes and service charge: 8% government tax and 10% service charge will be added to your bill

cotta floor tiles, and whole rows of wicker lamps, the overall effect is natural and stunning. Apart from the wicked views, the rooms all come with patios or balconies, fridge, tea and coffee-making facilities and hair-dryers.

Although there are some beach-side rooms at Anse Chastanet they only have garden views and are not nearly as romantic as the hillside extravaganzas. The beach, which is volcanic and therefore has blackish sand, is the scene for complimentary watersports such as snorkelling and sunfish sailing. Best of all are the scuba diving opportunities with the PADI dive school, which operates daily dives for the experienced and runs courses for beginners.

Windjammer Landing

The villas at Windjammer Landing were just made for couples seeking maximum privacy in first-class accommodation, with the added bonus of totally flexible dining. Windjammer overlooks **Labrelotte Bay** on the north coast of St Lucia and is a totally self-contained villa resort set in 22 lush green hectares.

The villas, scattered all over the hillside and inter-connected via stone pathways are Mediterranean in style, and are painted white with terracotta tiled roofs. The one-bedroom villas are huge – spanning almost 117 sq metres – and tastefully decorated with a pickled pine ceiling and floors, pastel scatter cushions on top of cream upholstery and wicker furniture, straw mats and sunny prints.

The one-bedroom villas have all the usual extras such as bathrobes, in-room safes, cassette players and cable TV. They also come with a separate lounge, which has open-air arches to maximise the sea views, a good-sized kitchen area, and a private sun ter-

WINDJAMMER LANDING

(☎ 452 0913, fax 452 9454), PO Box 1504, Labrelotte, Castries, St Lucia, West Indies

Reservations: Either direct or through tour operators specialising in the Caribbean (see p9-10)

Getting there: 90 minutes from Hewannora International Airport, 15 minutes from Vigie Airport

Accommodation: 42 superior and de luxe rooms, plus 91 one, two and three-bedroom villas

Amenities: Four swimming pools, four restaurants, mini-mart, complimentary watersports, complimentary shuttle bus, tennis courts (floodlit), fitness centre, aerobics, PADI school, golf and deep-sea fishing can be arranged, plus there is a 13m yacht for charter

Dress code: Informal

Weddings: The hotel does have wedding packages which cost around US$700 per couple for a villa upgrade and all the trimmings for the ceremony; however if you book 13 nights through Caribbean Connection you get their wedding package for free

Minimum stay: None

Rates: Doubles from US$230 per night in the peak season and from US$140 for the rest of the year; ask about their honeymoon packages

Credit cards: Most major

Taxes and service charge: 8% government tax and 10% service charge

race, while some even have their own private plunge pool. So while you have all the facilities of staying in a hotel, staying at Windjammer also feels like you're on a villa holiday, giving you a great feeling of independence.

For example, if you've had enough of dressing up for dinner and want to get away from everyone, you can either request a pizza from the hotel's extensive room service menu and snuggle up on the sofa for a video, or rustle up something special in your well-equipped kitchen and dine alone together in the privacy of your terrace looking out over the bay.

On the other hand, if you want to get involved there is lots to do at Windjammer, including four different restaurants, as many cocktail lounges, a good range of complimentary watersports such as water-skiing, windsurfing, and an introductory scuba diving lesson. There is also a nearby golf course, aerobic classes, two tennis courts, beach volley-ball and even sailing regattas for guests.

Other recommended hotels

Perched high up on a hillside, 300m above a lush valley with magnificent sea views below, is **Ladera Resort** (☎ 459 7323, fax 459 5156), PO Box 225, Soufrière, St Lucia. In my mind it is one of the most romantic hotels in the Caribbean. The bedrooms are open-sided so you can lie in the four-poster bed shrouded in mosquito netting and stare for hours on end at the totally uninterrupted view of the sea and the stars, and when it gets too hot you can take a dip in your own private plunge pool on your terrace. Days are spent relaxing on the superb wooden terrace by the horizon swimming pool, looking out over tropical rain forest to the awesome Pitons towering either side of the blue ocean beyond. An extremely tranquil hotel, which is well cared for, Ladera is the perfect place to flop for a few days in the mountains before moving on to a beach resort. A luxury pool villa costs US$550 in peak season from mid-December to the end of March and then goes down to US$350 between April and October. Ladera also offers seven-night honeymoon packages which cost US$4545 in peak season and US$2890 between April and October.

A FEW THINGS TO SEE AND DO IN ST LUCIA

Just 15 minutes outside **Rodney Bay** by car or a lovely rural walk to the north eastern tip of the island will take you to **Cas en Bas Estate**, where there is a superb windward beach on the Atlantic side. The beach is perfect for windsurfing as it is protected by a reef, you can hire boards from Cas en Bas beach bar. There is a real off-the-beaten track beach bar serving good food with lots of local flavour. The bar also organises 'Atlantic Fun Days' with windsurfing, mountain biking, horse-riding, walking, sea kayaking and a great Creole barbecue accompanied by pina coladas made with fresh coconut milk...heavenly.

The Bistro Restaurant at Rodney Bay Lagoon is a perfect spot for a romantic, waterfront dinner. The food is excellent, lots of fresh fish, fantastic cheesy garlic bread and there's also a good wine list.

Pigeon Island, bordering Rodney Bay, is a national park with well kept grounds, lots of interesting early naval history and superb views from the lookout points – there's even a small pagoda where you can get married.

Don't miss Friday night's regular carnival in the fishing town of **Gros Islet**: it was traditionally a small celebration for fisherman but has expanded into one big party for everyone.

From Ladera there are some wonderful walks down to *Bang Between the Pitons*, a great bar owned by the famous Englishman, Lord Glenconnor, who seems to be permanently in *Hello!* magazine. It's also worth visiting the **Tropical Botanical Gardens** in Soufrière and the mineral baths, which are unusually well kept for the Caribbean. If you go into **Castries**, St Lucia's capital, visit the wonderful colourful market on the harbour front particularly on a Saturday morning where, as well as lots of exotic fruit, vegetables, herbs and spices, you can find some good souvenirs such as T-shirts, baskets and sarongs.

If you are staying at Windjammer Landing make sure you do the boat trip to explore the golden coastline starting at **Marigot Bay**, one of the most secluded anchorages in the Caribbean where *Dr Doolittle* and *Superman 2* were filmed and where the charter crowd now put down their anchors. From there you'll sail on to Soufrière, the oldest town lying beneath **Petit Piton**, which was named after the nearby volcano. Here you can see the world's only 'drive in' volcano. Close by are the hot springs which feed the mineral baths on the Diamond Estate, where you can lie back in the warm water amongst waterfalls and botanical gardens.

ST VINCENT AND THE GRENADINES

Petit St Vincent

Petit St Vincent, or PSV as it is affectionately known, is the most ultimately romantic island of the Caribbean. If you've always fancied yourself as a castaway this is the place to do it, especially if you don't want to forgo the basic luxuries fundamental to any honeymoon.

Some 64km off St Vincent, PSV is luxurious but not opulently so; instead the 22 private cottages are rather low key letting this 45-hectare private island's beauty speak for itself. The low level cottages, built from local Bluebitch stone, are dotted all over the island, some on the hillsides, some set into the sides of cliffs, others set back from the beach.

All are rustic in style with a living room with two day beds, a bedroom with two queen-sized beds, dressing room, bathroom and a stone-encased deck with two canvas beach-back chairs, two chaise longues and a hammock. Toiletries, bathrobes, beach towels, insect repellent, hair-dryers, irons and an ironing board are also found in each room. Whichever cottage you choose, the views are spectacular and you're never far from a beach since the whole island is practically encircled by pure white sand.

This utter seclusion is what makes PSV so special, an aspect of the hotel exaggerated even further by the cunning use of red and yellow flags to tell the staff either that you don't want to be disturbed or that you require room service. Communication has to be by like this as there are no phones in the cottages at PSV – it's very much a no phone, no TV, no newspaper kind of place. Even when room service comes you don't actually have to be interrupted, as notes of requests are collected from your mailbox, which means it would be possible, if you wanted to, to spend your entire stay on PSV without seeing another person.

However that would deprive you of eating in the spectacularly located hilltop restaurant which looks down over the harbour where a lunch time buffet is served daily. If you do ever tire of whiling away the time in your hammock there are watersports such as snorkelling, hobie cats and sunfish sailing, as well as tennis.

> **PETIT ST VINCENT**
> (US ☎ 513-242-1333, fax 513-242-6951), PO Box 12506 Cincinnati, Ohio 45212, USA
> **Closed**: August to November
> **Reservations**: Either direct (see above) or through The Leading Hotels of the World toll free numbers (see p12)
> **Getting there**: Via 50-minute private charter plane from Barbados to Union Island (US$113 per person one way), hotel launch to PSV (a 25-minute journey)
> **Accommodation:** 22 luxurious cottages
> **Amenities**: Open-air dining pavilion, sailing trips to nearby islands, snorkelling, scuba diving, deep-sea fishing, hobie cats, windsurfers, sunfish sailing, tennis court, afternoon tea, room service
> **Dress code**: Casual, men are asked to wear trousers and shirts for dinner
> **Weddings**: Guests can be married in St Vincent, but you have to have been there for three days before you can fly to St Vincent for a licence; you have to pay for a minister to fly to PSV to perform the ceremony; wedding receptions cannot be catered for
> **Minimum stay**: None
> **Rates**: Full board: doubles from US$450 to US$740, ask about Summer Packages
> **Credit cards:** American Express
> **Taxes and service charge**: 7% tax and 10% service charge will be added to your bill

Other recommended hotels

Young Island (☎ 458 4826, fax 457 4567), St Vincent, West Indies, was one of the first 'whole island' resorts. Small, hilly and covered in lush vegetation and palm trees, there are only 30 wood-framed cottages with louvered windows, whitewashed walls decorated with colourful stencils, long cream calico curtains, and an open-air shower surrounded by bamboo walls and huge banana trees. The best is cottage No 10, one of the three luxury cottages: it has a sitting-room opening out onto your own patio, a plunge pool and a gazebo looking over to Mustique Island from where you can step straight down on to your own private beach. Meals are simple and cocktails are strong. Double rooms from US$275. From the US reservations can be made through Ralph Locke Islands (US toll free ☎ 800-223-1108) and through UK tour operators Elegant Resorts and Unique Hotels (see p10).

Plantation House (☎ 458 3425, fax 458 3612), PO Box 16, Bequia, is a charming hotel with a very relaxed atmosphere. The hotel is centred around the beautiful Main House and has 17 cabanas (thatched huts) and five suites in two cottages set amongst fragrant tropical gardens. Bedrooms are decorated in simple fresh-looking Caribbean style and are air-conditioned with good in-room facilities. If you're not into glitzy hotels and are looking for a quiet place to relax, Plantation House and Bequia itself as an island have immense charm. Doubles from around US$140 per night.

Both Plantation House and Young Island take advantage of their superb location in the Grenadines and offer sailaway packages to other islands and meals on board. The last time I heard one of the boats at Young Island needed a lick of paint, so check that this has been sorted out before you sail off into the sunset. Another word of warning: don't take an overnight sailaway if you are not familiar with sailing – seasickness could ruin the honeymoon! These two provisos aside, a sail to Mustique is worth it to see the island of the superstars and mingle with the rich. Stop for lunch at the famous **Basil's Bar** (you'll probably find the likes of Mick Jagger at the next door table) and for XC$40 you can have a personal taxi guide around the beautiful island and good look at the fantastic villas.

TRINIDAD AND TOBAGO

Located right at the southern end of the Caribbean chain of islands, just off the north eastern coast of Venezuela, Trinidad and Tobago, although politically related, couldn't be more unalike.

Trinidad is a large, lively island, where the capital **Port of Spain**, is much more commercialised and cosmopolitan than the capitals of most of its Caribbean neighbours. Tobago, on the other hand, is totally laid-back: the numerous deserted sandy beaches along its rugged coastline make it the perfect place to unwind after a wedding. It's an unsophisticated island which, unlike many of its neighbours, is relatively untouched by tourism. Instead, peace and harmony reign making it the best choice for couples in search of the 'real' Caribbean.

Blue Waters Inn

It's worth going to the north of Tobago, not just for the beaches, but to stay at the Blue Waters Inn. Located at Speyside this lovely moderately priced hotel has a really personal character.

This is one of the world's most classic hotels, not because it's big and flashy or even over the top in the luxury stakes, but somehow it has a magical feel that you'll always remember. It will appeal particularly to British couples who will appreciate the understated tone and the family-like atmosphere. When we stayed there one Christmas we ended up mixing our own cocktails from behind the bar and raiding the fridge late at night to make cranberry and turkey sandwiches. If that makes you think, 'well why didn't

---

BLUE WATERS INN
(☎ 660 4341, fax 660 5195), Batteaux Bay, Speyside, Tobago, West Indies
Reservations: US toll free (☎ 800-643-8938) or through UK tour operator Caribbean Connection (see p10)
Getting there: Transfers can be arranged, airport taxi costs US$38 one way
Accommodation: 38 rooms, including three bungalows with full kitchens, four self catering units, 31 standard rooms, all with ceiling fans, balconies/porches
Amenities: Scuba diving, kayaking, windsurfing, boat trips, tennis, deep-sea fishing, bird sanctuary tours, car rental, restaurant, bar, recreation/tv room
Dress code: Informal/casual
Weddings: Can be arranged, price depends upon requirements
Minimum stay: None
Rates: Standard double from US$80, self catering from US$105, bungalows from US$150
Credit cards: Most major
Taxes and service charge: Included

room service make them for you?' then the Blue Waters isn't for you.

The hotel is situated in one of the most beautiful bays in Tobago, well away from the island's main tourist area in the south. There is a superb beach and a PADI diving school which takes guests out to the numerous nearby dive sites to see incredible coral corridors, as well as manta rays at the right time of year.

A FEW THINGS TO SEE AND DO AROUND TOBAGO

Pigeon Point, the beach on all of Tobago's postcards where the water is bright turquoise, is a great place to watch the sun go down from the pier, armed with the ubiquitous rum punch, while nearby **Turtle Beach** is also worth a look.

Some of Tobago's most isolated and perfect beach coves can be found from the coastal road on the island's northern shore, so make sure you hire a car and find your very own private beach. A drive through the island's densely jungled interior is also a must, taking you through rickety shanty towns where the men sit all day on the side of the road waiting for nothing in particular.

If you want to experience a taste of local night life, then head down to **Buccoo Bay** for a bit of 'Sunday School' – the name given to the all-night party every Sunday. There will be very few tourists there, but it's a real piece of Tobagan life, with the air heavy with the smell of marijuana, jerk chicken on the barbecue and pop-corn. The music is loud, and mostly a mix of reggae and soca – a blend of reggae and calypso native to Trinidad and Tobago.

JAMAICA
Strawberry Hill

Strawberry Hill, nestled high up in Jamaica's **Blue Mountains**, is the perfect colonial retreat in the mountains. This wonderfully romantic hotel is the most idyllic place to unwind after a long flight and a hectic wedding, before moving on to a beach resort for a little more action once you are ready for it.

You know you are in for a treat as you approach Strawberry Hill – either by land cruiser or helicopter – climbing up through the Blue Mountains to one of the most magnificent natural settings on earth.

The dozen or so private cottages for guests are built entirely of Jamaican wood and furnished simply but elegantly with canopied four-poster beds and tiled baths. As part of Chris Blackwell's Island Outpost chain they are filled with the kind of tiny details which make his hotels so special, hand carved island antiques and the solid colonial comfort of the mahogany four-poster.

Each cottage has its own kitchen, parlour and best of all, private veranda so you can enjoy the breathtaking views across the mountains. Bird's Hill is the best choice for honeymooners as it comes with its very own garden and latticework gazebo that houses a private hot tub for two – the ideal place from

STRAWBERRY HILL
(☎ 944 8400, fax 944 8408), Irishtown, Jamaica
Reservations: UK Island Outpost toll free (UK ☎ 0800-614790); USA Island Outpost toll free (US ☎ 1-800-OUT-POST); or through UK tour operator Caribbean Connection (see p10)
Getting there: Complimentary shuttle from Kingston's Norman Manley Airport (about 50 minutes)
Accommodation: 12 villas: four studios, four one-bedroom, four with two/three bedrooms
Amenities: High tea and Sunday brunch, New-Jamaican cuisine served all day, room service, plunge pool and sauna; the Touring Society of Jamaica
Dress code: No jackets required
Weddings: Church weddings can be arranged at the local church at a cost of US$200, which includes a choir, minister and flowers; a wedding co-ordinator can also be arranged; you have to be on the island for three days before you can get married; receptions for up to 200 guests buffet-style costs around US$50 per head, or US$65 for a five-course sit-down dinner
Minimum stay: None
Rates: From June to October one bedroom suites cost US$175; from November to the end of May they cost US$250
Credit cards: Most major
Taxes and service charge: 22.5% government tax; 10% service charge

which to sip champagne at sunset and watch the lights go on in **Kingston Town**.

The **Touring Society of Jamaica**, based at Strawberry Hill, offers some great tours of the island including a visit to the **Old Tavern Blue Mountain** coffee estate, as well as mountain hikes after which you are rewarded with cocktails at the wonderful **Gap Café**, and guided walks through **Spanish Town**, Jamaica's original capital. But perhaps best of all is the Kingston Night-life tour which stops off at all the dance hot-spots for a real taste of the legendary Jamaican night-life.

Should you want to get married at Strawberry Hill, the staff are incredibly helpful and will arrange almost anything you want. They offer a summer wedding package costing US$300 per couple for which you get two nights at the hotel, a welcome cocktail on arrival, continental breakfast on Saturday morning and the most wonderful Sunday brunch overlooking the Blue Mountains.

Other recommended hotels

Jamaica Inn (☎ 974 2514, US toll free 1-800-837-4608, fax 974 2449), PO Box 1, Ocho Rios, St Ann, Jamaica, has long been one of the Caribbean's best loved hotels. This elegant hotel occupies a pretty private bay with a fabulous beach protected on either side by small headlands. If you're looking for refined colonial charm and a place to gracefully drift through the days, this is it. It's the sort of place where people really dress for dinner, some even wear black tie. Each of the 45 impeccable rooms has its own colonnaded balcony looking out to sea. Double rooms from US$250 include breakfast, dinner and tax, while the premier rooms on the beach are from US$310.

For a wonderfully well-priced alternative spend a few days seeing 'real' Jamaica at **Jake's Place** (☎ 965 0635, fax 965 0552), Treasure Beach, Calabash PO, Saint Elizabeth. Part of the Chris Blackwell (founder of Island Records) Island Outpost chain, this wonderful little hotel has bags of character and if you are into Jamaican culture has to be the perfect place to stay. The Blackwell signature colours are there, with bedrooms colour-washed in fantastic shades of cinnamon, cobalt and jade, and the kind of incredible attention to detail that makes his hotels so special but at the same time everything has been kept very simple with corrugated roofs over huts that look more like Jamaican rum shacks than hotel rooms. The most astonishing thing about Jake's is its price, with rooms costing only US$75 a night, and US$525 a week.

The Bahamas
(BEST TIME: DECEMBER TO JUNE)

THE BAHAMAS
Average maximum temperatures °C

JAN	FEB	MAR	APR	MAY	JUN	JUL	AUG	SEP	OCT	NOV	DEC
25	25	26	27	29	30	31	31	31	29	27	25

Approximate exchange rate: Bahamas dollars – £1 = BS$1.56, US$1 = BS$1, A$1 = BS$0.79
Country dialling code: ☎ 242

Compass Point

Compass Point is one of the world's most stunningly original hotels – if you like your primary colours that is. Compass Point is another of Chris Blackwell's inventions, part of the rapidly growing Island Outpost chain of enterprising, new, funky hotels that are proving so popular with younger people who are tired of the traditional hotel chintzes and characterless rooms. The success of the venture is illustrated by the fact that super models Cindy Crawford, Kate Moss and Naomi Campbell come here for their holidays. The colours were based on designs for the Bahamian carnival, Junkanoo, and even the sun loungers and parasols range from turquoise to teal, lavender to rust, cinnamon to sunflower yellow. The Junkanoo theme was also the inspiration for the owls, roosters, sunbursts and fish carvings on the cottages.

This wonderfully funky hotel consists of 13 rainbow-coloured octagonal huts and cottages, housing 18 rooms. The cottages are built on stilts, with wooden slat roofs, duck-boarded walls and louvred windows and are painted in many different, shockingly bright, colours. They all have their own private deck facing the ocean complete with rocking chairs and, while some have an open-air kitchenette and dining terrace on ground level, they all have an in-room fridge and coffee makers.

Eleven of the hand-crafted rooms face the sea, and each features tropical furnishings, batik fabrics, pretty wrought-iron lamps with bright coloured shades, hand-painted ceramics, and drift wood mirrors, along with mod cons such as CD players, satellite TV and VCR and king or queen-sized beds. Compass Point's best rooms are Rock Lobster, West Point and the Lookout.

Set on one hectare of the famous **Love Beach**, the hotel has its own ocean-side restaurant, a fresh-water pool, dive shop, tennis court, and an activities desk and boutique. The resort can arrange golf cart, bicycle or boat rentals and all sorts of tours and excursions. This is a totally different, quintessentially cool kind of honeymoon hangout.

COMPASS POINT

(☎ 327 4500, fax 327 3299), West Bay Street, Gambier, PO Box CB 13842, Nassau, Bahamas

Reservations: From the UK call Island Outpost (UK toll free ☎ 0800-614790); from the US call Island Outpost toll free (US ☎ 1-800-OUTPOST); or through UK tour operator Caribtours (see p10)

Getting there: 10 minutes from Nassau International Airport by taxi costing US$10

Accommodation: 18 rooms: 13 huts and cottages (one and two bedroom units, cottages are on stilts) and five studio cabanas

Amenities: Ocean-side restaurant, fresh-water pool, activities desk, dive shop, tennis court (floodlit), CD/Video library, boutique, fishing charters, watersports, boat rentals

Dress code: No jackets required

Weddings: A US$50 wedding licence can be applied for locally, while the hotel caters for wedding receptions for up to 50 people at US$45 per head, excluding wine and champagne

Minimum stay: None

Rates: Sea view cabanas from US$175 including breakfast; two-bedroom sea front cottage costs US$325

Credit cards: Most major

Taxes and service charge: 18% tax and service charge will be added to your bill

---

Pink Sands

The very best thing about this new hotel, as its name suggests, is the beach itself which honestly does have a pink hue to it. Condé Nast *Traveler* was so impressed that it pronounced Pink Sands 'quite possibly the finest beach in the world'.

Also part of rock promoter Chris Blackwell's Island Outpost chain, Pink Sands has long been a well-kept secret, but since its million dollar refit, it was relaunched last year with the kind of huge splash that this incredible hotel deserves. As yet, Pink Sands is relatively untouched by the honeymoon fraternity.

Situated on Harbour Island, just 5km by 2.5km, there are 26 rooms in separate cottages set among seven hectares of tropical gardens, overlooking the spectacular 5km beach. This is the Bahamas at its most charming; **Dunmore Town** even has a preservation order on it, it's such a fine example of Old Caribbean culture.

All meals are provided at the main Clubhouse, either inside or out, and lunch is also offered at the beach-side restaurant and bar. The restaurant, reception, library and pool table are all found in the main hotel building set around a small lily pond. The decor is true Island Outpost style, with imaginative use of colour, exquisitely elegant and the bedrooms are really comfortable. This is the perfect place to do nothing in, or if you feel the urge to get active you can jump on one of the windsurfers or hobie cats.

PINK SANDS
(☎ 333 2030, fax 333 2060), Harbour Island, Bahamas
Reservations: UK Island Outpost (UK toll free ☎ 0800-614790); USA Island Outpost toll free (☎ 1-800-OUTPOST); and specialist Caribbean tour operators (see p9-10)
Getting there: Miami to North Eleuthera or Nassau; Nassau to North Eleuthera by charter airline, North Eleuthera to Harbour Island by boat taxi costing US$10
Accommodation: 26 rooms: 23 one bedroom cottages and three two bedroom, all with air-conditioning and ceiling fans, walk in closets, CD players, minibar, private patio, room service
Amenities: Beach restaurant and Tiki bar, garden restaurant and bar; beach Palapa, a 5km stretch of pink sanded beach; fresh-water pool; three tennis courts, one of which is floodlit; exercise studio; Island Trading shop; Club House; PADI diving facilities; fishing charters; boat, golf cart and bike rentals; tours and excursions
Dress code: No jackets required
Weddings: A wedding licence costs US$50 and couples need to be resident for three days prior to their wedding; receptions can be arranged for up to 80 people at around US$60 to US$80 per head; from July to September Pink Sands runs Wedding Packages including a week's stay in the hotel on a half board basis
Minimum stay: None
Rates: Doubles from US$352 including breakfast and dinner
Credit cards: Most major
Taxes and service charge: 23% government tax and service charge

Hawaii
(BEST TIME: ALL YEAR ROUND)

Hawaii, the most isolated group of islands imaginable, is a string of eight islands located almost 3000 miles off the American coast. Because of its 'proximity' to California and Japan, most of Hawaii's visitors come from the sunshine state or elsewhere in north America and from Japan – fewer than 5% of visitors are from Europe – earning these naturally beautiful islands the reputation for being one big American (and now Japanese) holiday camp.

Over the years Hawaii has been a kingdom, a republic, a territory and it's now a state. These islands have wildly contrasting scenery from deserts and rain forests to snow and coral reefs: even the island's sandy beaches range from sugary white to red, green and even jet black.

HAWAII
America's most exotic state, Hawaii has a reputation for big glitzy resorts, but there are also some quiet hotels with long sandy beaches, as well as incredible rugged mountain interiors to explore
When to go: in general the islands have a warm balmy climate most of the year, but because temperatures vary from island to island check with your agent that you are going to the right place at the right time.
Average maximum temperatures °C

JAN	FEB	MAR	APR	MAY	JUN	JUL	AUG	SEP	OCT	NOV	DEC
24	24	25	26	27	27	28	28	28	28	27	26

Capital: Honolulu on Oahu
Flight times: to Oahu from:
   New York: 11 hours
   LA: $5^1/_2$ hours
   London $16^1/_2$ hours (via LA)
   Sydney: 10 hours
Approximate exchange rates: US dollar (US$) – £1 = US$1.55, A$1 = US$0.79
Time difference: GMT minus 11 hours
Voltage: 110v AC, 60Hz – two-pin plugs
Combine with: Los Angeles or San Francisco; or go island hopping within Hawaii
Country dialling code: ☎ 1-808

Despite the increasing commercialisation of the bigger islands, in particular **Oahu** and **Maui**, it is still possible to get away from it all and enjoy a dream honeymoon amongst truly stunning scenery and incredible beaches, and stay in some seriously impressive hotels. If you are looking for action opt for Maui, and if you are seeking seclusion head for quiet **Lanai**.

Getting to and around Hawaii

Both Aloha and Hawaiian Airlines offer frequent, daily jet services from island to island, with flights usually only taking a matter of 20 or 30 minutes.

On Oahu, Aloha's reservation number is (☎ 808-484-1111), while Hawaiian's is (☎ 808-838-1555). If you've always dreamed of having lunch on Lanai and Mai Tai cocktails on Maui, then the Hawaiian Island Pass from Hawaiian Airlines is the thing for you. Passes provide unlimited travel for all Hawaiian islands (even the smaller ones that have traditionally been much harder to get to), and come in five to 14-day packages, starting at around US$179 per person and going up to around US$279. From within the US, call Hawaiian Airlines on toll free number (US ☎ 800-367-5320).

Mahalo Air (☎ 808-833-5555) serves Oahu, Maui, Kauai, Molokai, Lanai, and Big Island with twin-engined prop planes.

Whichever island you are visiting renting a car will provide you with the most freedom and mobility. All the major car rental firms operate in Hawaii, and can be contacted through their respective toll free central reservation numbers (see p13).

MAUI
Four Seasons Resort Maui

The Four Seasons Maui is one of the world's most famous hotels. The very mention of it to anyone who has been there immediately seems to inspire a longing look. It's just that sort of place – once you've been there you'll dream about the ridiculous hedonism of the experience for years to come.

Where else are chilled face-cloths and Evian water sprays brought to you as you sunbathe, and a computer controlled fountain is programmed to react to the strength of the trade winds, so that the resort's precious guests don't ever get sprayed. This is one slick resort, where only the best is available,

---

FOUR SEASONS RESORT MAUI
(☎ 808-874-8000, fax 808-808-874-2222), 3900 Wailea Alanui, Wailea, Maui, HI 96753, Hawaii
Reservations: US toll free ☎ (1-800-332-3442); Canada toll free (☎ 1-800-268-6282); or through UK tour operator Elegant Resorts (UK ☎ 01244-897888)
Getting there: The hotel is 17 miles from Kahului Airport, airport transfers cost US$165 each way in the hotel's limousine
Accommodation: 380 guest rooms: 41 Four Seasons Executive Suites, 26 one-bedroom suites, four two-bedroom suites, the Ilima Suite, and the 5000 sq ft Maile Suite
Amenities: 24-hour room service, complimentary early arrival/late departure lounge, pool/beach attendants, Club Floor, beauty salon, use of Wailea Golf Club's three 18-hole championship courses, as well as nearby Makena and Silversword golf courses, use of Wailea Tennis Centre's 14 courts (three are floodlit), two floodlit tennis courts (on site), exclusive use of 60ft *Alii Nui* catamaran for snorkelling, whale watching and sunset cruises, 40ft by 80ft formal pool with fountain and whirlpool spas, free-form pool with waterfall and children's pool, snorkelling, scuba, sailing equipment and instruction available at the beach pavilion, putting green, volley-ball, badminton, croquet lawn, complimentary use of on-site health club, power-walking, aquacise and aerobics classes, bicycles, sport-fishing, helicopter rides, horse-riding, one-day tours by boat or plane to other islands, running paths, complimentary transfer service between hotel and Wailea Shopping Village and Golf and Tennis centres, Avis rental cars, several restaurants offering a wide range of dining options, shops
Dress code: Elegant casual
Weddings: Wedding ceremonies and receptions for up to 200 people can be held in an outdoor setting and up to 400 for an indoor wedding
Minimum stay: None
Rates: Doubles from US$295 to US$490; suites from US$515 to US$4700, ask about Romance for All Seasons (seven nights for US$4140 including lots of extras) and Romantic Interlude packages (three nights for US$1470 including some extras)
Credit cards: Most major
Taxes and service charge: 4.17% tax and 18% service charge

A FEW THINGS TO SEE AND DO ON MAUI

Maui boasts 42 miles of beaches, ranging from little **Red Sand Beach** to the black sands of **Waianapanapa State Park**. With the beaches comes great snorkelling, the best of which is to be found at **Honolua Bay** and the small islet of **Molokini**, a submerged crater. If you want to dive off Molokini you can sail out there on either the *Lavengro* or *Four Winds*. Call US toll free (☎ 800-736-5740).

But there's more to Maui than golden sandy beaches. Known as the Magic Isle, Maui is a lush, mountainous island made up of deep valleys, forested mountains, grasslands, open plains and the world's largest dormant volcano, **Haleakala**.

The island is effectively split into two contrasting halves, one with the mountainous **Iao Valley** and the sheer **Iao Needle** and the other dominated by the Haleakala Crater which rises a massive 10,023ft from sea level and over 16,000ft from the ocean floor.

You can drive from sea level to the summit in about an hour and a half, where you can look down on a lunar landscape 3000ft below and see **Science City**, an astronomical research centre where laser beams are bounced off the moon. Designated a National Park, Haleakala is one of only two places in the world where the rare silversword plant grows, and there is a good network of trails for hiking or riding. There's no better time to see Mt Haleakala than at sunrise; arrange to take a breakfast picnic with you and wear some warm clothes. You may not relish the prospect of getting out of bed at around 3am in order to reach the summit in time, but you'll realise it was worth it when you get there.

On the other side of the island, in the **West Maui Mountains**, the towns and roads cling to the shoreline. This area is nice for hiking but the best way to see the spectacular waterfalls and the high walls of the volcano's often cloud-cloaked interior is by helicopter. For a helicopter tour call **Papillion Hawaiian Helicopters** (☎ 808-367-7095). When you move to the dry, leeward side of the mountains you'll be rewarded with spectacular views over the islands of **Moloka'i**, **Lana'i**, **Kaho'olawe** and tiny crescent shaped Molokini, sitting like droplets in the still blue ocean beyond. On a good day you can see the snow-capped tips of **Mauna Kea** and **Mauna Loa** on Big Island.

The channel between Maui and its neighbouring islands, where the water is calm and shallow, is the winter home of the humpback whales: they arrive every October from the Bering Sea to give birth to their young. The best way to see the whale close up is to join one of the whale-watching cruises running from **Maalaea** and **Lahaina** harbours.

The old whaling port of **Lahaina** is a living museum to Hawaiian history. Initially settled by Polynesians, Maui was an autonomous kingdom until Kamehameha I united all the Hawaiian islands and made Lahaina his capital, in 1802.

Missionaries and whaling men arrived soon afterwards and Maui was torn apart by these opposing forces. During the peak whaling year of 1846, more than 50 vessels at a time were anchored in the Lahaina roadstead. Lahaina's tribute to whales is the **Whale Museum of the Pacific** (☎ 808-661-9918) at the Whalers Village Shopping Centre in **Kaanapali**. By 1860, the Civil War and the rise of the petroleum industry had brought the whaling era to an end.

Apart from the beautifully restored historic sites Lahaina with its richly coloured banyan wood architecture features many great restaurants and lots of interesting curio shops.

In rural Maui, or Upcountry as the islanders call it, sugar cane and pineapple fields give way to cattle ranches, fields of flowers and picturesque farms. With its distinctly Old West ambience, charming shops, restaurants, bars and art galleries, **Makawao** lies in the heart of Upcountry. This is cowboy country: every year on 4 July cowboys and cowgirls from throughout the state gather for a two day rodeo.

Hawaii may not be foremost in your mind as a wine growing region, but it is worth popping along to the **Tedeschi Winery** (☎ 808-878-6058) on the 20,000 acre **Ulupalakua Ranch**. A tour of the ranch and tastings of the winery's champagne and unique pineapple wine are available from 9am to 5pm daily.

No trip to Maui would be complete without a visit to **Hana**. You can jet down there in no more than 15 minutes from Kahului Airport in a prop plane, but arguably more exhilarating is the 55-mile drive. The road to Hana heads out of the north shore town of **Paia**, curving past **Hookipa Beach Park** (known as the Aspen of wind surfing!), and then takes you along more than 600 hairpin bends eastward into East Maui's spectacular rain forests. The drive takes you past the most spectacular scenery: waterfalls plunge to create natural swimming pools; emerald green patchworks jut out into the sea below; the roads hang perilously to the cliff edge. Hana itself is a place of sheer natural beauty: a huge round bay with black and red sand beaches, lush green pasture land and flowers in full bloom, and a totally unique atmosphere. Hana is definitely unmissable.

and the clientele is wealthy enough not to worry about keeping an eye on the tab.

Situated on the largest and most beautiful of Wailea's white sand beaches and set in 15 acres of gardens, the hotel is centred around an incredible array of swimming pools, fountains and jacuzzis, and set amongst swaying palms. There are so many wonderful places to nestle down for the day that it's almost hard to choose between the grassy lawns, the loungers on the various pool sides, and, of course, the beach. There's also no shortage of guest activities: in usual Four Seasons' style, everything is here from a health spa, tennis courts and croquet, to snorkelling, diving and sailing instruction and the use of not one but three golf courses.

Covering a massive 600 sq ft each, the Four Season's 380 guest rooms are the largest in the Hawaiian Islands, all have large lanais (terraces) ideal for private sunbathing and alfresco meals, while 85% have ocean views. The large marble bathrooms have separate showers and lovely bathtubs, and all come with soft terry bathrobes and toiletries. You won't want for anything and if you do, it will quickly be arranged.

ISLAND OF HAWAII

Mauna Lani Bay Hotel

Mauna Lani Bay Hotel on Hawaii Island (also called Big Island), is another vast resort hotel which is always popular with honeymooners. Mauna Lani epitomises the best kind of self-contained resort, where its guests needn't leave its walls until they are refreshed enough to go home again. Its commitment to guests, and the impeccable food and service are legendary among American resorts.

Once the private estate of Frances I'i Brown, the descendant of Hawaiian royalty, this secluded coastal retreat was a refuge for King Kamehameha himself. Situated along three and a half miles of Big Island's sunny and rugged **Kohala** coastline, the setting is just magical. On one side there are prehistoric fish ponds, on the other the snow-capped peak of **Mauna Kea**.

The hotel offers a good variety of accommodation from garden view rooms to ocean-front suites, bungalows and villas. All are decked out in teak and cane with air-conditioning, spacious lanais, remote TV/VCR, on-command movies, in-room safe, fridge, minibar, bathrobes and hair-dryer, while the really decadent will head straight for the hotel's five bungalows.

The ultimate in luxury, the bungalows are on the ocean front and are each named after a Hawaiian flower. Discreetly screened away from other guests, they comprise 2700 sq ft of living space, with an additional 1300 sq ft of lanai where there is a private pool and a jacuzzi. Each bungalow has two master

---

MAUNA LANI BAY HOTEL

(☎ 808-885-6622, fax 808-885-4556), 68-1400 Mauna Lani Drive, Kohala Coast, Island of Hawaii

Reservations: The Leading Hotels of the World toll free reservation numbers worldwide (see p12); toll free within the US (☎ 800-367-2323); and UK tour operator Elegant Resorts (UK ☎ 01244-897888)

Getting there: Arrangements can be made at time of reservation for the 30 minute journey from the airport (US$40)

Accommodation: 333 rooms, 12 suites and ocean villas, five bungalows

Amenities: Canoe House for casual, oceanfront dining with Pacific rim cuisine, Bay Terrace for breakfast and dinner, Ocean Grill for casual poolside dining, Atrium Bar, two championship golf courses, 10 court Tennis Garden, health spa, swimming pool, jacuzzi, sauna, jogging trails, watersports, travel desk, shops, beauty salon, clinic, complimentary morning coffee and newspapers, Hawaiian activities, games and crafts, tropical flower arranging, historic tours

Dress code: Resort attire, jackets not required for dinner

Weddings: Pinkie Crowe, the director of weddings and romance, is also a State Marriage License Agent and Notary Public and Wedding Consultant specialising in all wedding arrangements: packages begin at US$400 to US$1800, private dinners and receptions for two to 200 can be arranged, dinners from US$45

Minimum stay: None

Rates: Mountain view rooms from US$260; ocean view rooms from US$395; ocean front suites start at around US$795; bungalows from US$3350

Credit cards: Most major

Taxes and service charge: 10.17% tax

bedrooms and bathrooms to match, with whirlpool baths and steam rooms overlooking private gardens. We're talking serious luxury at a initial cost of around US$2 million per bungalow, with a cool US$175,000 spent on the interior decorations alone!

Guests in the bungalows get their own personal butler as well as a fully-equipped kitchen though a private chef is also available, so that you don't have to get your hands dirty. The list of goodies you can expect goes on and on: choice of cotton or satin linens, de luxe limo transfers, continental breakfast with fresh pastries and tropical fruits each day, full bar with cocktails, wines and sunset hors d'oeuvres. All of this with a million gallons of salt-water in lagoons full of tropical fish and the most staggering ocean views right on your door step – it doesn't come much better than that!

The **Mauna Lani Health Spa**, snorkelling equipment and a variety of other amusements are available free to all guests including historic tours and special 'Hawaiian activities'. Morning coffee and newspapers are also delivered to your room each day, along with breakfast if you wish – so that you can eat a long, lazy breakfast in the privacy of your lanai.

The Mauna Lani has always enjoyed a good reputation for its dining. The alfresco **Canoe House**, with its decked flooring and cane furniture, specialises in fresh local fish transformed into gourmet seafood dishes served on the ocean front by candlelight, while the serene and open-air **Bay Terrace** serves meals all day. For an elegant alternative try the wonderfully delicious French cuisine at **Le Soleil**, before heading to the bar for a little late night live music.

A FEW THINGS TO SEE AND DO ON ISLAND OF HAWAII

Of all the Hawaiian islands, **Big Island** (as Hawaii Island is commonly known) boasts the most variety in terms of climate, terrain and scenery. It is an intriguing combination of mile upon mile of black lava and green meadows, cool misty rain forests, and of course, long golden sandy beaches. Twice the size of all the other Hawaiian islands' combined, Big Island was formed 800,000 years ago by five volcanoes – Mauna Loa, Mauna Kea, Kilauea, Kohala and Hualalai. Today is spans over 4000 sq miles and is still growing; an estimated 500 acres of land have been added in the last dozen years.

The island is dominated by the peaks of two of these volcanoes, **Mauna Kea** and **Mauna Loa** which rise to nearly 14,000ft. Big Island's history is full of stories of Pele, the Fire Goddess whose home was in these mighty volcanoes. At the heart of the **Hawaii Volcanoes National Park** (☎ 808-967-7311), is Kilauea where you can feel the rumbling energy of this vast mountain through your feet as you hike the many trails. Kilauea is the world's most active volcano, but is safe enough to be seen by over one million visitors annually. Even if you're not regular walkers, do go for a wander through the lacy tree fern forests, blooming ohia trees, barren craters and yellow sulphur banks; the scenery is mesmerising. Just near the Park headquarters is the **Volcanic Art Centre** (☎ 808-967-7511) filled with the works of local artists, craftsmen and photographers, which is worth a look.

Take **Saddle Road**, going west out of **Hilo**: the road bisects the interior of the island and leads to an access road that meanders skyward to the 13,796ft peak of Mauna Kea, though this is often shrouded in snow during the winter months.

North of Hilo, the **Hamakua Coast Highway** takes you through lush green valleys and the sleepy town of **Honokaa** to **Waipio**, nicknamed the Valley of the Kings, because it was a favourite retreat with Hawaiian royalty. If you want to explore the stunning Waipio Valley you'll either have to go in on foot, on horseback or rent a four-wheel drive.

On the island's west coast you'll find the seaside resort of **Kailua-Kona** where, along with the numerous shops, hotels and condos, acre upon acre of coffee plantations are found. Visitors are welcome at many of the farms, and are encouraged to take a self-guided tour and sample Kona's famous brew.

For old Hawaiian culture visit **Puuhonua o Honaunau**, a stone-enclosed sanctuary used as a safe haven for defeated warriors of victims of war years ago. Just down the road from Honaunau, Puuhonua o Honaunau, now administered as a National Park (☎ 808-328-2326), is a good place to see kapa pounding, lau hala weaving and traditional dance, and hear local music.

LANA'I

Only recently opened up to visitors, Lana'i is still one of the lesser known, less developed, Hawaiian islands. For most of this century, Lana'i was known as 'the pineapple island', until the Dole Food Company which owns almost half the island, stopped commercial production of pineapple in favour of the more prosperous enterprise, tourism. As a result the island's two luxury hotels were built.

A FEW THINGS TO SEE AND DO ON LANA'I

The island doesn't offer much to do away from the recreations, such as fantastic diving and of course golf, offered by the resorts. Lana'i is a small island (approximately 13 miles by 18) and it is suited to the four-wheel drive vehicles which are available for hire from both hotels. There's not much to see in the interior, in fact the island's critics describe it as drab scrub-land, but it does have the advantage of being wonderfully empty, making it ideal if you like peaceful, private drives.

If you are keen to get out on foot, there are hiking and riding trails leading up through the forest to the ridge top: the **Munro Trail**, an eighteen-mile loop across the top of the island rewards your efforts with magnificent views of neighbouring islands.

A visit to **Kanepuu**, the region where the Garden of the Gods is located, is definitely worthwhile. Here you'll see colourful and strangely eroded rocks that take on an eerie aura at sunrise and sunset. The road is unpaved so it's wise to approach in a four-wheel drive vehicle. Pass through the **Kanepuu Nature Conservancy Preserve**, an area of native dry land forest plants on your way back.

The Manele Bay Hotel

The Manele Bay Hotel is a blaze of colour. From the moment you enter the hotel lobby where Aztec prints mix with Ming vases, Oriental rugs, and great towering Chinoiserie-inspired murals of emperors and nightingales on the walls, you know you are in for some kind of sensory colour extravaganza. It is an eclectic mix of oranges, yellows, blues and reds that is probably not for the faint hearted, but perfect if you like to think **big**!

This rather grand pavilion-style hotel is set in several different low-rise buildings with grey slate roofs, and is built around intimate courtyards filled with heavily manicured lush tropical gardens, waterfalls and tranquil pools, so you'd never know there are 250 guest rooms. The bedrooms are also rather lavish and are filled with accessories collected from throughout the world and custom designed furnishing. The guest bedrooms have vivid wall hangings and rich designer fabrics, as well as a full range of in-room facilities to match – even the bathrobes are a bright jazzy yellow.

The hotel is set among ornate, even sculptured gardens, on a red lava cliff overlooking the island's finest swimming beach. There are walking trails along the shoreline and a whole range of watersport activities should you feel the urge to get active: the hotel's leisure facilities are also impressive. There's a beautifully tiled fresh-water swimming pool with two jacuzzis and wonderful ocean views, a health and fitness spa, six ten-

THE MANELE BAY HOTEL
(☎ 808-565-7700, fax 808-565-2483), PO Box 310, Lana'i City, Hawaii, HI 96763
Reservations: Small Luxury Hotels of the World toll free numbers worldwide (see p12); toll free within the US (☎ 800-321-4666); or through UK tour operator Elegant Resorts (UK ☎ 01244-897888)
Getting there: 20 minutes from Lana'i Airport, free transfers arranged by the hotel
Accommodation: 224 rooms, 26 suites
Amenities: Three restaurants, library, lounge, music room, fitness centre, golf, tennis, biking, horse-riding, swimming pool, jacuzzi, lawn bowling, croquet
Dress code: Jacket/tie required for evening dining, ladies are expected to dress smartly
Weddings: Can be arranged, two specialised packages, from US$1000 plus tax
Minimum stay: None, apart from five nights' minimum over the Christmas and New Year periods
Rates: Doubles from US$315 to US$475; suites from US$600 to US$1500
Credit cards: Most major
Taxes and service charge: Not included

nis courts, horse-riding, helicopter rides, the hotel's own celebrated championship golf course designed by Jack Nicklaus, and a small harbour from where scuba diving excursions depart.

Lots of guests combine their stay on the coast at the Manele Bay with a few days at its sister hotel, **The Lodge** at **Koele**, a tranquil retreat in Lana'i's mountainous central highlands, just 15 minutes away by hotel shuttle. Designed to imitate an old Hawaiian plantation estate with heavy timbers and stone fireplaces in the public rooms and carved four-posters and quilted fabrics in the bedrooms, the Lodge is also very popular with golfers due to its championship golf course, designed by Greg Norman.

French Polynesia
(BEST TIME: MARCH TO NOVEMBER)

A few years ago my brother returned from months of sailing across the South Pacific declaring that he'd found the perfect place for his honeymoon – a stunning hotel in **Bora Bora** where the rooms were built on stilts hanging out over the turquoise waters. He showed me the photos and I was certainly convinced. He eventually chose Sark for his honeymoon and I went to Ireland, but we are both still firm believers that the thousands of islands in the South Pacific are indeed, paradise on earth.

French Polynesia comprises 130 islands divided into five archipelagos which constitute a French Overseas Territory. Of these the **Society Archipelago** is home to Tahiti, Moorea, Bora Bora and Huahine.

There is something quite magical about the Society Islands. They represent most people's blueprint for the perfect island, with an abundance of soft white sand, crystal clear waters in varying shades of brilliant blue, coral reefs and verdant interiors with majestic mountains. But they are quite different from other islands of the world, such as the Seychelles, the Maldives and the Caribbean Islands: the difference lying essentially in their space – 130 islands spread out over a water mass the size of western Europe – and their exotic inhabitants.

It was the people of French Polynesia who first captured the hearts of Robert Louis Stevenson, Somerset Maugham and Gaugin, all of whom managed to convey the native beauty and nobility in their work.

Bora Bora, with its immaculate powder-white sands and reef-protected lagoons has received worldwide acclaim for the quality of its hotels. During July and August Bora Bora really comes alive for the **Heiva Festival**, an all-dancing, all-singing, all-drumming party that attracts people from all over South Polynesia.

But there is much more to French Polynesia than just Bora Bora and many visitors like to do a little island hopping, either by boat or plane as there are lots of inter-island flights. One general word of warning: because of high import tariffs French

---

FRENCH POLYNESIA
130 islands clustered in five archipelagos spread across an expanse of water the size of Western Europe
When to go: Avoid December, January and February
Average maximum temperatures °C

JAN	FEB	MAR	APR	MAY	JUN
32	32	32	32	31	30
JUL	AUG	SEP	OCT	NOV	DEC
30	30	30	31	31	31

Capital: Papeete on Tahiti
Flight times: to Papeete from:
New York: 16 hours
LA: $8^1/_4$ hours
London: 20 hours
Sydney: $9^1/_2$ hours
Approximate exchange rates: Central Pacific Francs (CPF)
CPF 142 = £1, US$, Aus$
Time difference: GMT minus 10 hours
Voltage: 110 or 220v AC, 50 Hz
Combine with: Perhaps combine one or two South Pacific Islands, or stop off en route in Sydney, Auckland, Hong Kong, Singapore or Los Angeles
Country dialling code: ☎ 689

Polynesia is expensive and it is very difficult to have a really luxurious two-week honeymoon here for a great deal less than US$10,000, which is probably another reason why these islands have stayed so magical!

BORA BORA

Hotel Bora Bora

The 55 bungalows at Hotel Bora Bora boast the most exotic location of any hotel bedrooms anywhere in the world. Nestled on a palm-fringed promontory, with powder white beaches on either side spilling out into reef-protected lagoons, this incredible hotel is consistently rated among the world's finest. Owned by Amanresorts, a small chain of about a dozen incredible hotels, Hotel Bora Bora is just as amazing inside as the views are outside. When the Bora Bora Lagoon Resort first opened a few years ago it gave Bora Bora's primary hotel a real run for its money, but a recently completed refurbishment has made the Hotel Bora Bora even more exclusive than it used to be, restoring it to its former glory.

The overwater bungalows, the first to be built on Bora Bora, provide a spacious bedroom, bathroom and split-level sun terraces with steps leading directly into the lagoon. In the lovely white tiled and wood-panelled bathroom there is an elegant wood-trimmed Victorian tub, a separate shower, and a wooden-slat blind window looking onto the bedroom. The bedrooms are also wood-panelled, with large glass doors opening onto a balcony, so you can happily lie in bed gazing out at the lagoon beyond. The four-poster bed forms the focus of the bedroom, with its canopy of soft white muslin draped back at each corner, and soft glowing lamps either side of it.

The hotel's 17 'farés', or villas named after the Tahitian term for home, are set either on the beach or in the lush tropical gardens and like the overwater bungalows they feature thatched pandanus roofs. Each faré has a separate living room with bamboo and wooden furniture and plump cream cushions, a bedroom with en suite sitting-room, bathroom and large sundeck. Eight farés even have their own private swimming pool. Whichever room you choose they all come with bathrobes, complimentary toiletries, hair-dryer, minibar, in-room safe, stereo cassette player, overhead fans and coffee and tea-making facilities.

Dining at the Hotel Bora Bora is an event most guests look forward to all day: in the evening you can eat on the alfresco **Matira Terrace** staring out over the lagoon. During the day, lunch and refreshments are provided at the **Pofai Beach Bar** and once a week there is a beach barbecue.

The crystal clear waters of the lagoon form much of the focus for the day's activities with complimentary snorkelling and outrigger paddle canoes. The hotel also has

---

HOTEL BORA BORA
(☎ 60 44 60, fax 60 44 66), Point Raititi, Bora Bora, French Polynesia
Reservations: Prima Hotels worldwide toll free reservations numbers (see p12)
Getting there: Bora Bora Airport is 25 minutes away by complimentary boat transfer
Accommodation: 55 suites: five bungalows, 14 superior bungalows, four de luxe bungalows, nine overwater bungalows, six premium bungalows, six farés, eight pool farés, three premium farés
Amenities: Bar, restaurant, gift shop, tennis courts, watersports, scuba diving, deep-sea fishing, yacht charters onboard either catamaran, island tours in jeeps or on hired bikes, scooters or cars, jet skis, helicopter tours, island picnics, glass-bottom boat trips over the reef
Dress code: Smart casual
Weddings: Hotel Bora Bora offers couples a 'Marriage of Hearts', a non-binding, sentimental ceremony performed during a two-hour private sunset cruise aboard the hotel's 14m catamaran, followed by champagne and a romantic dinner with wine served at an intimate location in the hotel, for CPF65,000
Minimum stay: None
Rates: Bungalows from around US$400; overwater bungalows from around US$650; pool faré from around US$650
Credit cards: Most major
Taxes and service charge: All rates subject to 8% room tax

two yachts, a 15m and a 14m catamaran, available for sport fishing, day sails, dinners on board, or cruising through the Society Islands, as well as jeeps for safari excursions through the island's mountainous interior, and bicycles and motor scooters for hire.

Bora Bora Lagoon Resort

Bora Bora Lagoon Resort is so good that some people even argue that it has usurped the Hotel Bora Bora as the finest hotel in the South Pacific. When it first opened it was very definitely better than its older rival but since the Hotel Bora Bora's recent refurbishment the old favourite is now firmly back to its best.

Having said that the Bora Bora Lagoon Resort, set on its own tiny motu (a coral islet) one and a half kilometres out from the island of Bora Bora itself, is the more private hotel. Due to its positioning it is also blessed with truly incredible views looking back over the waters of the lagoon to the mysterious mountain peaks of **Otemanu** on Bora Bora.

Once you arrive at Bora Bora Airport you are met by hotel staff who take you on a private cruiser across the brilliant blue lagoon to the jetty on Motu Toopua. In that swift boat ride you are transported away from mainstream tourism into a private island paradise.

The 80 de luxe traditionally-styled overwater and beach bungalows are unashamedly modern inside. Although natural materials have been used there is nothing rustic about these bungalows with their oiled yucca wood floors featuring coconut shell inlay, timber venetian blinds covering the floor to ceiling louvred doors, and bright blue, yellow and orange cushions on the chairs, bedstead and chest at the foot of your king-sized bed. But it is the fantastic attention to detail that makes these rooms so wonderful, with incredibly imaginative touches such as the illuminated glass coffee table in the overwater bungalows which has sliding panels underneath so that you can sit at night watching the marine life rush about below you.

There are many lovely touches like this: from the huge stone-carved figures gracing the jetties and the complimentary sun block provided in each room, to the way your breakfast is brought out to your bungalow by a Tahitian couple in a traditional canoe. Everything about the resort is well-timed, cleverly thought out and perfectly executed. There's nothing like taking your time over breakfast on your overwater balcony, before heading off into the lagoon in a canoe of your own.

The fact that the Bora Bora Lagoon Resort has a fabulously large fresh-water swimming pool is a real plus point and is indicative of the quality of all the hotel's

---

BORA BORA LAGOON RESORT
(☎ 60 40 00, fax 60 40 01), Motu Toopua, BP 175, Vaitape, Bora Bora, French Polynesia
Reservations: Via the Los Angeles office (US ☎ 1-310-649-4570, fax 1-310-649-4566) or through The Leading Hotels of the World toll free reservation numbers (see p12)
Getting there: The resort provides complimentary transfers from Bora Bora Airport via private boat
Accommodation: 80 overwater and beach bungalows
Amenities: Café Fare, the Otemanu Restaurant, Hiro Lounge and Bistro, twice-weekly Tahitian feasts, limited room service, boutique, complimentary watersports, swimming pool, tennis courts, volley-ball, fitness centre, jacuzzi, games room, boat shuttle to Bora Bora, in-room videos, snorkelling, windsurfing and sailing; scuba diving, shark feeding and glass-bottom boating can also be arranged at local rates
Dress code: Casual during the day, summer dresses for women and trousers and short-sleeves shirts for the men are usually worn in the evening
Weddings: The hotel does not have a wedding licence, but does do 'romantic ceremonies' (not legally recognised) which include Tahitian dress for the couple, a waterfront ceremony with Polynesian music and dance, photos, sunset cruise on a pirogue and a candlelit dinner in the Otemanu restaurant
Minimum stay: None
Rates: Double rooms from around US$566/CPF52,000 to US$750/CPF69,000
Credit cards: Most major
Taxes and service charge: Tax 8%, service included

leisure facilities. At the front of the motu is a superb white sand beach from which guests can snorkel, scuba dive, paddle away in outrigger canoes, windsurf, or go for a morning's catamaran cruise. The lagoon is very much the focus of the whole resort; it is there that you will spend your days, when you dine you'll marvel at the views it provides and at night slide back that glass panel and enjoy your private slice of ocean.

A FEW THINGS TO SEE AND DO ON BORA BORA

Located 264km north-west of Tahiti, Bora Bora is the most spectacularly beautiful island, with emerald green hills and crystal clear lagoons. Bora Bora is about 32km in circumference, so it is easy to travel around the whole island in just a few hours.

Bora Bora Jeep Safaris (☎ 67 70 79) operate four-wheel drive round-island tours taking you through the interior and to all the remaining gun sites and radar stations left over from the Second World War.

If you want to go under your own steam, you can arrange car hire easily through your hotel or through any of the following: **Europcar Bora Bora** (☎ 67 70 03); **Maeva Rent-A-Car** (☎ 67 76 78); **Mautara Rent-A-Car** (☎ 67 73 16) and **Bora Bora Tours** (☎ 67 70 28) at the Hotel Bora Bora. Alternatively hop on a bike or scooter, both of which are available from most of the above car hire companies and from the big hotels for around US$50 for four hours.

If you'd prefer to see the island from the water, **Richard Postma** (☎ 67 77 79), a Californian who is now resident in French Polynesian, will take you out on his prototype 15m catamaran *Taravana*, based at the Hotel Bora Bora. Whether you choose to go on a sunset cruise or overnight charter with dinner on board, make sure you do get out on to the water and venture outside the barrier reef, as the views

of Bora Bora on the horizon are wonderful. Ask at either hotel.

There are two dive operators on the island: the **Bora Bora Dive Centre** (☎ 67 71 84), run by Mr and Mrs Michel and Anne Condesse, and the **Calypso Club** (☎ 67 77 85) which is run by Claude Sibani and is based at the Hotel Bora Bora. Both operations are International CMAS and have PADI certification facilities.

Wherever you stay in Bora Bora, don't miss out on one of the shark feeds, run by most hotels, where you are taken by a guide out to a part of the lagoon that is roped off. Your guide then enters the restricted area throwing meat out to a cluster of black-tip reef sharks, while you stay outside the area watching the feeding frenzy at a safe distance.

If you fancy getting out of your hotel for a drink or maybe a bite to eat, head to the notorious *Bloody Mary's*, near the Hotel Bora Bora, which has long been an island institution. A long-established celebrity hang-out, this sandy floored bar with its thatched roof and coconut tree stumps for chairs, serves grilled fresh fish and some mean cocktails, often accompanied by local music – an obvious inspiration for the famous Cheeseburger in Paradise as Jimmy Buffet's name is even etched on the huge slab of wood that acts as the bar's celebrity list.

MOOREA

Regarded as one of the world's most spectacular islands with its ragged cloud-topped peaks, deep valleys and emerald lagoons, Moorea is a really exotic place to explore.

Moorea Beachcomber Parkroyal

Moorea Beachcomber Parkroyal has been newly renovated and is now a fabulous hotel. Perched right on the lagoon edge with a spectacular mountain range rising up behind the hotel, the Moorea Beachcomber exploits its beautiful surroundings to the full. The only real problem with the Moorea Beachcomber Parkroyal is that, being so close to Tahiti, it tends to get very busy at weekends. It is also worth noting that although the beach is lovely, it is man made. However, for people who don't have thousands to fritter away, it gives you overwater accommodation for the price of a basic room at the Hotel Bora Bora, which is one very good reason why this hotel should be considered as a very romantic honeymoon destination.

The best rooms are the thatched roof bungalows set amongst the tropical gardens and looking out to the lagoon or those actually set out over the water. Whichever room you choose, it will be cool and comfortable with ample space provided by the separate

(Opposite) Top and middle: Hotel Bora Bora (see p46). **Bottom:** Beach in the Seychelles (see p71)

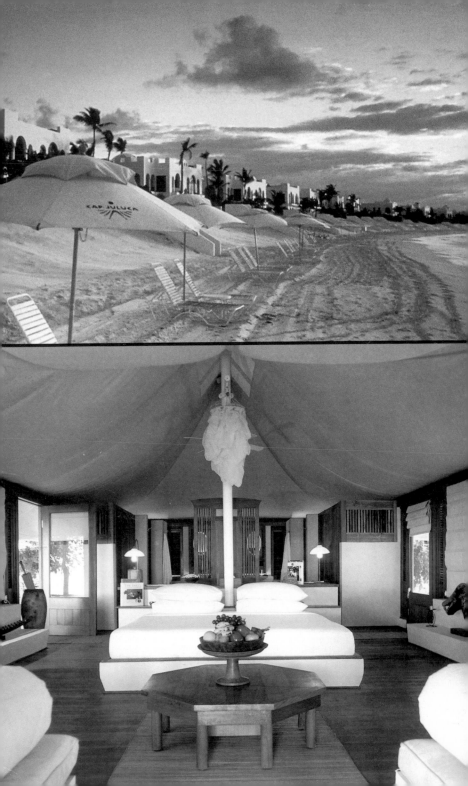

sitting area, en suite bathroom and good sized sundeck. Alternatively, there are standard rooms located in three-storey buildings but these have only small patios or balconies.

The hotel's sporting facilities are fabulous, whether you decide to launch your own outrigger or explore the lagoon on a glass-bottomed boat, play beach volley-ball, tennis or practice your water-skiing. The scuba diving in Moorea is also great.

There are two restaurants, the **Fare Hana** which offers day time snacks in a very relaxed atmosphere and the open-air **Fare Nui Restaurant**, where international dishes are enjoyed as the sun sets over the sea.

Other recommended hotels

Hotel Hana Iti (☎ 68 85 05, fax 68 85 04), BP 185 Fare, Huahine, French Polynesia, is a totally different kind of resort and should only be considered if you are both feeling quite adventurous and are avid nature enthusiasts. That being so, you'll find it hard to find such a fantastic hotel as this. Hana Iti is a 25-roomed hillside hideaway on Huahine, where many of the villas have no walls and where trees grow into the rooms. All the rooms are built in harmony with the environment using bamboo and native hardwoods. They cover around 90 sq metres and each has its own sleeping area with king-sized bed and mosquito net, a lounge with a refrigerator, and a bathroom which has an open shower and outdoor whirlpool spa. Because the villas are built into the hillsides, some on stilts and others actually built in the arms of giant trees, guests are collected by four-wheel drive vans when they are ready for dinner, which is served in the beach-side restaurant. You'll need some good insect repellent and a definite love of adventure, but the food is good and you'll be hard pushed to find bedrooms like these anywhere else in the world. That said, recent visitors to Hana Iti have come back saying that the hotel badly needs some smartening up and investment. This could have been attended to by the time you are planning your honeymoon but I would advise that you check with your tour operator or travel agent first. Doubles from around US$310 a night.

MOOREA BEACHCOMBER PARKROYAL
(☎ 55 19 19, fax 55 19 55), Papetoai, Moorea, French Polynesia
Reservations: USA and Canada toll free (☎ 800-835-7742) or any Forte, Utell, Delton Reservation Centre or through UK tour operators Air France Holidays (UK ☎ 0181-742 3377)
Getting there: There are daily flights from Papeete to Moorea (ten minutes), followed by a 25-minute taxi ride to the hotel (around CPF3000)
Accommodation: 150 rooms
Amenities: Two restaurants, tennis, beach volley-ball, scuba diving, outrigger canoes, glass-bottom boats
Dress code: Informal
Weddings: Can be arranged, there is no church but you can get married on the beach or in the hotel grounds; the hotel's traditional wedding ceremony where both wear Polynesian dress is also popular
Minimum stay: None
Rates: Doubles from US$305/CPF28,000; garden bungalows cost US$327/CPF30,000; beach bungalows from US$370/CPF34,000; over-water bungalows cost US$414/CPF38,000
Credit cards: Most major
Taxes and service charge: 8% government tax

COOK ISLANDS

Although officially part of Polynesia (not French Polynesia), the Cook Islands are included here because of their geographical affiliation: they are 1000km south-west of Tahiti and 3500km north-east of New Zealand, by which they are governed in 'free association'. Local currency is the NZ dollar, time difference GMT minus 10 hours.

The Manuia Beach Hotel (☎ 682-22461, fax 682-22464), PO Box 700, Rarotonga, Cook Islands, is a small secluded hotel set on the sparkling blue lagoon of **Raratonga**. Accommodation is in 20 Polynesian-style thatched bungalows which each has a queen-sized bed, fridge, phone, a well stocked minibar, tea and coffee-making facilities and hair-dryers, as well as a spacious veranda where dinner can be served.

(Opposite) Top: Cap Juluca, Anguilla (see p24). **Bottom:** Camping in style, Amanwana, Moyo Island, Indonesia (see p65).

Guests are greeted with champagne and baskets of fruit on arrival. The best thing about the Manuia Beach is its wonderful beach bar where guests gather to watch the sun go down over the lagoon. You can eat there or at the hotel's other restaurant, the **Bounty**, where international as well as local dishes are served, or you can arrange to have an intimate dinner in a quiet spot on the beach. The hotel's facilities are impressive with a swimming pool and spa, and there's an abundance of snorkelling, sailing and windsurfing. This is a really romantic island hideaway, where no children are allowed to spoil your peace. Doubles from around US$250/NZ$357 a night.

Fiji
(BEST TIME: MAY TO OCTOBER)

If your idea of paradise comprises deserted island hideaways fringed with powder white sand and brilliant turquoise waters, where coral reefs are home to hundreds of different varieties of vividly coloured tropical fish, and where you can sit alone on a private jetty to dine by candlelight, then dream no more, and book your honeymoon in Fiji.

Significantly less commercialised than the Caribbean, the independent republic of Fiji consists of a group of more than 300 islands spread out over 1,295,000 sq km of ocean in the heart of the South Pacific. Here the enthusiasm of the local people, a mix of Fijians, Indians, Europeans, Chinese and other islanders, also form part of the magic. Some visitors have found the islanders' welcome almost disarming it is so overwhelming, but everyone who has ever been to Fiji will tell you that it is the islanders who make these pearl islands so unique.

The Fijian islands are rightly renowned for their diving. Reputed to be one of the top four dive sites in the world, the clear warm water around the many lagoons offers ideal conditions in which to explore the ocean world. In addition to diving, there

---

FIJI

The perfect South Pacific hideaway for those looking for real escapism with little to do other than island hop, scuba dive and walk along empty white sand beaches

When to go: May to October

Average maximum temperatures °C

JAN	FEB	MAR	APR	MAY	JUN
31	31	31	30	28	28
JUL	AUG	SEP	OCT	NOV	DEC
27	27	27	28	29	30

Capital: Suva on Viti Levu

Flight times: to Viti Levu from:
New York: (via LA)
LA: 11 hours (direct)
London: 27 hours (via LA)
Sydney: 4 hours (direct)

Approximate exchange rates: Fiji dollar (FJ$) FJ$2.17 = £1, FJ$1.40 = US$1, FJ$1.11 = A$1

Time difference: GMT plus 12 hours

Voltage: 240v AC, 50 Hz

Combine with: Australia, Los Angeles, New Zealand

Country dialling code: ☎ 679

---

are lots of other beach and sea-related activities as well as exploring the jungle either on foot or on horse-back, but essentially the Fijian islands are a place to relax and truly unwind after the wedding and lose yourself to Fijian time. If you are looking for glamorous restaurants and evening entertainment, then you'd better look elsewhere, because being in Fiji is all about shedding your shoes, leaving your jacket and tie and jewellery at home, and walking barefoot along the beach to dinner on a moonlit shore.

I would suggest spending a week or a few days on Fiji's largest island, **Viti Levu**, and then venturing out to one of the countless offshore emerald dots. A little island hopping is a wonderful way to get a feel for the size and beauty of the South Pacific.

If you are looking for total luxury in a private setting and have a sizeable amount of cash to burn, fly out to the **Yasawa Islands**, a chain of six principal islands and a string of smaller ones stretching out north west from Viti Levu.

The Yasawa islands are home to some of the world's most luxurious and exclusive island hideaways. Arriving by sea plane, you'll be met by saronged Fijians carrying hibiscus with which to welcome you and saying 'bula, bula', the multi-purpose greeting that means health in Fijian.

You have to remove your shoes when you land because you step out of the plane into the turquoise shimmering water and you probably won't require them again until it's time to get back on the sea plane; the Yasawa islands are not known for their formalities. You can also put away your watch, so that you can thoroughly immerse yourself in Fiji time, the locals' own self-deprecating version of Spain's manana.

VITI LEVU
The Regent Fiji

The Regent Fiji is a slick Four Seasons resort only 15 minutes from Nadi airport making it the ideal place to just flop for a few days when you arrive in Fiji, before perhaps moving on to discover some of the other islands.

The kind of pampering you can expect at this Regent is indicated by the fact that the resort's staff outnumber guests by two to one. With 294 rooms, the Regent is not an intimate hotel rather a private South Seas village, but it does offer the unfailing luxury and facilities that this famous chain is renowned for worldwide.

Located on the 274-hectare **Denarau Island** in Nadi Bay, the hotel was designed to mirror the style of traditional Fijian villages, and is set among perfectly manicured tropical gardens fringed with brilliant white sandy beaches. Despite being such a slick Regent resort, the hotel is very conscious of maintaining its Fijian atmosphere and there's no doubt, from the moment you enter its high vaulted lobby that you will feel a sense of island heritage. Everywhere you look there are Fijian and Melanesian artefacts as well as traditional tapestries and the hotel is proud of its frequent folk evenings.

These Fijian motifs are carried through to the air-conditioned bedrooms which, spacious and wonderfully comfortable, have soothing garden or ocean views from their private verandas. Inside there are native Tapa wall-hangings, cool quarry tiles and rattan furnishings, as well as all kinds of modern amenities from light cotton robes to oversized bath towels and bathroom toiletries.

The hotel's facilities are just what you'd expect from a Regent resort. For the active

THE REGENT FIJI
(☎ 750000, fax 750259), Denarau Beach Resort, PO Box 9081, Nadi, Fiji
Reservations: UK toll free (☎ 0800-282245); US toll free (☎ 800-545-4000); Australia toll free (☎ 008-022 800); or through UK tour operators Elegant Resorts, British Airways Holidays and Kuoni (see p9)
Getting there: 15 minutes from Nadi International Airport by taxi or transfers can be arranged by the hotel
Accommodation: 285 rooms: 95 garden view, 100 de luxe garden view, 84 beachfront, six beach-front suites
Amenities: Five restaurants, Meke lounge and Garden Court Bar, swim-up bar, the Denarau Golf and Racquet Club with 18-hole golf course and 10 tennis courts, all watersports, lawn bowls, archery, volley-ball, massage rooms, on-call tennis professional, twice-daily maid service, gallery shops
Dress code: Smart casual
Weddings: Weddings can be arranged for couples who stay at the resort for a minimum of three consecutive nights, costs depend on what you want (licence costs FJ$14.30), the hotel's ballroom can accommodate up to 200 people
Minimum stay: None
Rates: Double rooms with a garden view start from US$189/FJ$265; one-bedroom suites with beach view start at US$493/FJ$693
Credit cards: Most major
Taxes and service charge: 10% tax, service is discretionary

there's an 18-hole golf course, four all-weather and six grass tennis courts, as well as a huge range of watersports, and a stunning swimming pool. Dining opportunities range from Asian and Fijian specialities, to the beach-front **Steak House** and the **Hamacho Japanese Teppanyaki** restaurant. There's so much variety on the menus of the four restaurants that the hotel claims you'll never have to eat the same meal twice, even if you stayed an entire month – if only!

A FEW THINGS TO SEE AND DO ON VITI LEVU

Aside from the obvious watersports and sun-worshipping, take a wander around the late **Raymond Burr's orchid garden**, where you can see over 2000 different varieties of this flamboyantly beautiful plant.

Up until the end of the 19th century, cannibalism was still practised in Fiji, and although the influence of visiting missionaries swept the practice away, the **human cooking-pit** is still there to be seen at **Tavuni Hill Fort**.

A water-born trip around the **Pacific Harbour Cultural Centre**, or the nearby **Sigatoka market**, confirms how little Fiji's culture has changed over the last few centuries. Browsing around both places is a wonderful way to pick up any presents or just a few reminders, such as coral jewellery and wooden carvings, of these mystical islands. More unusual artefacts, such as a hand-carved wife-beating club and forks for eating human brains

can also be found. There are lots of local treks to do around the hotel. Alternatively, they can arrange four-wheel drive tours through the hinterland, taking you through magical scenery and helping you to comprehend more of the heritage and culture of these mystical island people.

For the sheer romance of it, the hotel will helicopter you out to a remote waterfall, leaving you there with a sumptuous picnic before arranging a time to collect you later.

A two-hour ferry ride from **Denarau Marina** will take you to *Castaway Island* (☎ 661233, fax 665753), Private Bag, Nadi Airport: it's a great place to spend the day even if you're not planning to stay there. This breathtakingly beautiful small reef-ringed island has 66 traditional Fijian bures (thatched cottages, pronounced boo-rays), a huge range of watersports and great seafood lunches.

THE YASAWA ISLANDS

The Yasawa Islands are now home to a handful of extremely exclusive island resorts, aimed at couples who are seeking the perfect island hideaway and can afford to pay for it.

Yasawa Island Lodge

Arguably the best suited of the following four resorts for honeymooners is Yasawa Island Lodge, because unlike at the other hotels the clientele tends to be younger. It's also easy to arrange individual dining here.

Like the other Yasawa Island resorts, accommodation is in de luxe bures. There are only 14 one-bedroom bures, one two-bedroom bure, and one 'honeymoon hideaway' called **Lomalagi** with just one bedroom. The bures are all on the beach front and are really spacious, covering almost 90 sq metres on two levels, with a separate bedroom and living area, absolutely enormous timber sundecks and your own private mini-bure on the beach complete with a hammock.

Each bure has a traditional Fijian thatched roof and decor, a king-sized bed, air-conditioning, ceiling fans, minibar, private bathroom with bathrobes and lots of toiletries including sun tan lotion and coconut soap. There is also a fruit basket in your room which is replenished daily, tea and 'real' coffee-making facilities, and full room service. The meeting area for guests is the octagonal,

YASAWA ISLAND LODGE
(☎ 663364, fax 665044), Yasawa Island, PO Box 10128, Nadi Airport, Fiji
Reservations: Small Luxury Hotels of the World toll free reservation numbers worldwide (see p12); or through UK tour operators Elegant Resorts and Sunset Travel (see p10)
Getting there: 35-minute flight from Nadi International Airport in a light aircraft arranged by the hotel for US$117/FJ$165, plus 10% tax
Accommodation: 16 suites in luxury bures
Amenities: Restaurant, full room service, boutique, tennis court, four-wheel drive and walking tours, scuba diving, snorkelling, large horizon swimming pool; private beach picnics a speciality
Dress code: Smart casual for the evenings
Weddings: The lodge has a wedding licence and can host receptions for up to 32 guests
Minimum stay: None
Rates: Luxury bures from US$400 to US$750 inclusive of everything
Credit cards: Most major
Taxes and service charge: 10% tax will be added to your bill

open-sided **Bure Levu** where the bar, dining-room and relaxation area extend onto a split-level veranda overlooking the large horizon-style swimming pool. Dinner can either be taken in the restaurant overlooking the pool and ocean or on the beach by candlelight.

As well as the pool, guests can windsurf, snorkel, play tennis and croquet, scuba dive, sail catamarans and do some light game-fishing. The staff will also provide you with a champagne picnic and whisk you off to a secluded beach for the day, or guide you on local bush walks.

Vatulele

Vatulele was created by Australian television producer, Henry Crawford, and means 'ringing rock' in Fijian. Apparently it took him two years to choose the perfect island and another two to realise his dream of creating the ultimate hideaway for stressed out people.

The island itself is shaped like a foot; both the eastern and northern coasts are protected by a 11km long and 5km wide barrier reef just over one and a half kilometres from the shore. Most of the island is densely jungled, and apart from the resort the only habitations are the four villages with a total population of 900.

The very best thing about Vatulele is the peace, aided by the total lack of money, phones, newspapers, televisions, radios and children. (Children are only allowed on the island for two designated family weeks each year.) This is island living: no reception desk, no menus and no formal wine list. Vatulele is an informal and spontaneous place which is more like a private house than a resort. The management try hard to strike a balance between a private house party where guests eat together each night, and allowing couples the chance to dine on their own. Meals can be arranged à deux in the privacy of your own balcony but you would probably feel pressured eventually in to joining the other guests at dinner. If this doesn't appeal, choose somewhere else.

Located 32km south of Viti Levu there are 12 beautifully designed bures opening out

---

VATULELE ISLAND RESORT
(☎ 720300, fax 720062), PO Box 9936, Nadi, Fiji Islands
Reservations: Worldwide reservation office Australia (☎ 2-326 1055, fax 2-327 2764; US toll free (☎ 800-828-9146); the UK agent is Travel Portfolio (UK ☎ 01284-700444); Relais & Châteaux reservation numbers worldwide (see p12)
Getting there: Fly into Nadi and transfer to hotel via sea plane (about US$470 per couple return)
Accommodation: 12 luxurious bures
Amenities: Watersports, game fishing, PADI dive school, trekking, volley-ball, tennis, nature walks, extensive library, restaurant
Dress code: No dress code
Weddings: Fijian wedding ceremonies can be arranged for guests staying a minimum of six nights, and feature a Fijian choir, minister and feast
Minimum stay: Four nights, but five are recommended, average stay is eight nights
Rates: From around US$700 per couple per day all-inclusive
Credit cards: No credit cards but US$ cash and traveller's cheques accepted
Taxes and service charge: 10% Fijian government tax will be added to your bill, service charge is included

---

on to the beach and nestled in natural tropical foliage, providing absolute privacy from other guests. Each bure has a king-size bed on a raised platform with a separate dressing area, a spacious sitting-room and a large bathroom in a connecting wing. The furnishings are deliberately simple but extremely beautiful, with cane and canvas predominating, Italian white or terracotta floor tiles throughout, and cream stucco stone walls decorated with terracotta urns, heavy wooden bowls and primary coloured sofas and scatter cushions. The best thing about the rooms is that all areas open onto a spacious shaded terracotta terrace fronting the beach so, wherever you are, the views are amazing.

At Vatulele the emphasis is on food. Meals are taken on a terrace outside the large central pavilion, overlooking the lagoon, and by night tables are set out under the stars, lit by lanterns and candlelight. Much of the food is cooked outdoors in the large wood-fired pizza and tandoori ovens, the cuisine varying from Thai to Indian and Japanese: whatever you have you can be sure it will be superb enough to warrant the resort's Relais & Châteaux membership.

All the usual watersports are on offer; the diving on Vatulele is particularly spectacular and PADI courses are available. Apart from watersports and generally soaking up the sun, there are numerous alternative activities: tennis, hiking, volley-ball, nature walks and, best of all for this kind of relaxation, a well-stocked library.

Turtle Island Resort

Turtle Island Resort is another totally private island situated north west of Fiji's largest island Viti Levu and brought to international fame as the location for Brooke Shield's 1980 island epic, *Blue Lagoon*. It has since attracted serious praise from visitors and the industry and has been described as 'romantic, intimate, comfortable and friendly almost beyond belief, Turtle Island is a world entirely beyond time and obligations.' If you are looking for your very own island paradise, and can afford it, then this is it.

In 1972, Richard Evanson, an American businessman who was looking to escape the rat race of America's west coast, acquired Turtle Island to establish a private sanctuary. A few years, a hurricane and a major motion picture later, the tiny volcanic island is now the ultimate couples' hideaway with Richard still overseeing all the fun, like the host at a weekend house party.

One word of warning though: Turtle is very much run along the lines of a house party, if you don't fancy joining in, don't go. Although you'll get plenty of opportunities to be on your own during the day, the emphasis is very much on socialising with other guests at the cocktail parties and the mountain-top barbecues: some guests have found the socialising a bit intrusive. Dining alone in a private bay can be arranged but it is so popular that you're advised to request it when booking your holiday.

> **TURTLE ISLAND RESORT**
> (☎ 722780, fax 665220), Yasawa Islands, Fiji
> **Reservations:** US toll free (☎ 800-255-4347); Australia toll free (☎ 1-800-816 717); or with UK agents Travel Portfolio (UK ☎ 01284-700444)
> **Getting there:** Guests fly into Nadi and are met there and transferred to the island by sea plane (US$681 per couple)
> **Accommodation:** 14 bures
> **Amenities**: Horse-riding, jungle walks, scuba diving, snorkelling, sailing, windsurfing, canoeing, deep-sea fishing, 14 beaches, hammocks, private picnics on desert islands, mountain bikes, sunset cruise, mountain-top dinner, island tour
> **Dress code:** There isn't one
> **Weddings:** The hotel can arrange both western and Fijian ceremonies
> **Minimum stay:** Six nights
> **Rates**: From around US$975 per couple per day, all-inclusive
> **Credit cards**: Most major
> **Taxes and service charge:** 10% government tax, and guests can contribute to the staff's Christmas fund

The landscape of the 200-hectare island is extraordinarily varied, the smooth white sands and calm waters on the lagoon side contrast dramatically with the rugged black volcanic cliffs and rolling surf found on the windward side, while dense tropical forests give way to grassy highland interiors with breathtaking views.

Turtle's accommodation is restricted to couples who stay in one of the 14 thatched 'bures' which are dotted along the island's main beach, but which are discreetly designed so that they do not overlook each other. On arrival you'll find your names carved on a sign on your door, and frangipani and hibiscus blooms scattered all over the place.

Each bure is a spacious suite with two light, airy rooms, both looking out to sea. The bedroom has a queen-sized bed, there are rattan furnishings in the sitting-room, immaculately tiled bathrooms and a full stocked bar and refrigerator. The bures also come equipped with mosquito repellent, plenty of books, and even baseball caps and sarongs for use while you are there. The turtle motif is everywhere: green terrapin shaped soaps and little motifs on the bathrobes and towels. The vaulted ceilings are constructed in the traditional Fijian manner with hand-shaped and lashed native noko noko (wood) poles.

While you are there you can do as much or as little as you like: activities include horse-riding, jungle walks, scuba diving, snorkelling, sailing, windsurfing, canoeing and deep-sea fishing. On lazier days you can explore the island's 14 beaches, such as the aptly named, **Honeymoon Beach**, a secluded cove where you can lounge around in the double hammock. The hotel staff are always keen to take you out in the boat, dropping you off on a deserted beach with a sumptuous picnic of lobster and champagne, or whatever else you chose that morning.

FIJI'S OUTER ISLANDS
The Wakaya Club

The Wakaya Club is situated among 80 hectares of emerald forest, pearly beaches and turquoise coral-ringed sea, at the north-west end of Wakaya island. It's a slightly more formal resort than the other two: the staff will call you 'sir' or 'madam' and the average age of the clientele at the Wakaya Club is about 45 years old.

You'll be met at Nadi International Airport and whisked away to this wonderful private island by Wakaya Air – the island's own twin-engined 1992 Britten Norman Islander plane.

The island itself spans 880 hectares of soaring cliffs, a dense forest interior where wild horses, goats and boars roam free, ringed by shell-strewn beaches and aquamarine lagoons, protected by unspoilt coral reefs. Clichéd images I know, but this is very definitely the real thing.

Natural materials were used to create eight sumptuous, 'cathedral-ceilinged', 45 sq metre, guest accommodations, discreetly placed along the beach. Each bure has its own living room with hand-plaited woven bamboo walls, a fully-stocked bar and CD player, a four-poster king-size bamboo bed in the bedroom, and a separate bathroom with a stall shower, oversized bath tub, three sinks and a bidet. Crabtree and Evelyn toiletries, cotton bathrobes and hair-dryers make each bathroom a place to wallow in. There is a selection of books on your dressing table but more books, games and CDs are also available at reception.

The muffled beating of the 'Lali' drum summons guests to dinner in the **Palm Grove**

> **THE WAKAYA CLUB**
> (☎ 440128, fax 440406), Wakaya Island, Fiji
> **Reservations:** Australia toll free (☎ 14-800 126 205); US and Canada toll free (☎ 1-800-828-3454); UK toll free (☎ 0800-894465); New Zealand toll free (☎ 0800-440454); or through UK tour operators Elegant Resorts and Sunset Travel (see p10)
> **Getting there:** The hotel will arrange a light aircraft transfer from Nadi Airport (US$800 per couple)
> **Accommodation:** Eight elegant bures
> **Amenities:** Nine-hole golf course, tennis court, swimming pool, massage, deep-sea fishing, boules and croquet, resident masseur
> **Dress code:** No particular dress code; elegant casual
> **Weddings:** Fijian or Western wedding packages can be arranged: Fijian ceremonies cost around US$3000, Western from US$2500 which includes a church minister, use of church or other site, a choir, bouquet and floral decorations, wedding-cake, champagne cocktail reception and dinner, and the island band
> **Minimum stay:** Five nights
> **Rates:** From around US$1000 double occupancy per day all-inclusive but ask for promotional incentives
> **Credit cards:** Most major
> **Taxes and service charge:** 10% government tax, but service is included

dining pavilion, with its soaring 18m cathedral ceiling, while lunch can be taken overlooking the lagoon. The four resident chefs prepare all your meals using fresh seafood, locally grown organic vegetables and fruit, accompanied by wines imported from France and Australia. All meals and drinks are inclusive, so you don't have to worry what you choose, or how often you choose it! After dinner, guests can play pool, watch videos or just drink at the bar. Along with the usual watersport activities, from glass-bottomed boats to diving on the reef beyond the lagoon, there is a fresh-water grotto-like swimming pool, plus a nine-hole golf course, croquet and boules.

Other recommended hotels
Cousteau Fiji Islands Resort (☎ 850188, fax 850340), Vanua Levu, is a great alternative for enthusiastic divers. A joint venture between the famed Post Ranch Inn, one of the best hotels on the Californian coast and Jacques Cousteau's son, Jean-Michel, the resort is set in a seven-hectare coconut grove. Guests are accommodated in 20 traditional thatched-roof bures with 9m high ceilings and private decks. Diving is of course taken extremely seriously at the resort, which boasts one of the most powerful dive boats in the South Pacific. Jean-Michel Costeau and his guides will show you around the **Koro Sea** and protected **Savusavu Bay** and offer all forms of instruction and certification. Guests can even take part in Costeau's **Project Ocean Search**, a programme of investigative dives, nature walks, biology workshops, lectures and discussions, which provide the opportunity for you to expand your understanding of tropical ecosystems. For reservations it is easiest to call Prima Hotels worldwide reservations lines (see p12) or from the US toll free (☎ 800-246-3454). Prices start at around US$275 for a bure.

The Philippines
(BEST TIME: NOVEMBER TO MARCH)

The 7000 islands comprising the Philippine archipelago, surrounded by the Pacific, Sulu, the Mindanao, and the South China seas, are one of the most underrated destinations in Asia. These emerald green land masses with their lofty mountain ranges, seem to have been scattered randomly in a sea of a dozen different shades of brilliant turquoise. The Philippines are today a huge contrast of cultures and lifestyles, an exotic paradise where East meets West. From the peasants in the paddy fields to the cities with their seedy reputation, the whole country is a conundrum of Chinese, Spanish, American and Malay influences.

A honeymoon in the Philippines has all the perfect ingredients – tropical islands ringed by white sand and clear azure water, spectacular coral reefs teeming with exotic aquatic life, and the stunning mountainous interior where volcanoes sit beside ancient rice terraces. For couples who have previously visited Asia and think of Thailand or Malaysia as 'tired' this is the ideal, totally unspoilt island retreat.

THE PHILIPPINES
A great place to really get away from it all among perfect unspoilt islands.
When to go: November to March
Average maximum temperatures °C

JAN	FEB	MAR	APR	MAY	JUN	JUL	AUG	SEP	OCT	NOV	DEC
30	31	33	34	34	33	31	31	41	41	31	30

Capital: Manila
Flight times: to Manila from New York (via LA): 25½ hours
        LA: 17 hours
        London (via Bangkok): 17 hours
        Sydney: 8¾ hours
Approximate exchange rates: Pesos (P), £1 = P40.80, US$11 = P26.31, A$1 = P20.79
Time difference: GMT plus eight hours
Voltage: 220v AC, 60 Hz, although most hotels have both 220v and 110v, two flat-pin plugs
Combine with: Hong Kong, Singapore, Sydney, Bangkok
Country dialling code: ☎ 63

Amanpulo

Amanpulo has to be one of the most romantic hotels in the world. A newcomer to the famous chain of luxury hotels, Amanresorts, Amanpulo epitomises everything that is perfect, and of course vehemently expensive, about the group. If you've got the money and want to do nothing in a stunningly elegant hotel surrounded by some of the world's most beautiful, and remote, scenery then this is *the* place to do it.

Throughout this book, whenever it comes to writing about an Amanresort hotel I am faced with the same conclusion. None of these hotels is cheap but if you can possibly afford even one or two nights in one, then go ahead – you won't regret it and definitely won't forget it in a hurry.

Amanpulo, meaning 'peaceful island', is on the 88-hectare private island of Pamalican in the Cuyo group. Surrounded by pure white sandy beaches, turquoise water and a coral reef just 50m off shore, Amanpulo boasts some of the best snorkelling and dive sites the world has to offer.

You'll arrive via a one-hour private charter flight from Manila, and from then on the only transport on the island is on battery operated carts, which make exploring a marvellously lazy exercise.

Each casita (thatched hut), either down on the beach front or nestled up on the hillside, is modelled on a Filipino 'bahay kubo' house with polished timber floors. They are equipped with every luxury you could possibly want including CD player, phone, bathrobes and slippers, toiletries, minibar, satellite TV, hair-dryer and the most incredible sunken bath.

AMANPULO
(☎ 2-532 4040, fax 2-532 4044), Pamalican Island, Philippines
Reservations: Prima Hotels worldwide reservation offices (see p12)
Getting there: One hour flight from Manila by private charter costing US$275 per person
Accommodation: 29 air-conditioned beach-front pavilions; 11 treetop and hillside pavilions
Amenities: Air-conditioned panoramic restaurant, large swimming pool, beach club, lobby bar, 24-hour room service for private dining, snorkelling, scuba diving, sailing, rowing, fishing, tennis, library, boutique, picnic grove, massage
Dress code: Smart casual
Weddings: Non-binding ceremonies can be arranged at Amanpulo; the hotel is currently investigating the possibility of legal wedding ceremonies
Minimum stay: None
Rates: Treetop casitas from US$395; hillside and beach-front casitas from US$475
Credit cards: Most major
Taxes and service charge: 10% government tax and 10% service charge will be added to your bill

If you want complete seclusion Amanpulo really is the ultimate destination – you won't have to see anyone else, apart from the hordes of staff, from the day you arrive until the day you leave: even your meals can be taken in the privacy of your own outdoor terrace.

The hotel is of course well-equipped with a fabulous 30m swimming pool adjacent to the **Club House**, and a good range of complimentary watersports including hobie cats, laser sails, windsurfers and traditional Filipino 'banca' rowing boats. This kind of destination doesn't come cheap, but as the Nike advert says, 'just do it'.

Other recommended hotels

El Nido Pangalusian Palawan (☎ 2-894 5644, fax 2-810 3260), c/o Ten Knots Development Corporation, Ground Floor Exchange Corner Building, 107 Herrera Street, Legasbi Village, City of Makati, Philippines, is located on the island of Pangalusian in El Nido, north western Palawan. This extraordinarily beautiful hotel has 30 luxury cottages along the beach front, all air-conditioned, and just a few metres from the shore. Built using local materials and Filipino architectural styles, each has a writing desk, minibar, separate bath and toilet and private veranda. The hotel has its own games room, video room, library and boutique, as well as a wide range of watersports from windsurfing to scuba diving. Doubles from around US$130 per night.

A FEW THINGS TO SEE AND DO AROUND PAMALICAN ISLAND

Amanpulo offers guided **eco-walks** for its guests twice weekly in the afternoon, the guide points out local flora and fauna and explains the island's history as you go.

Surrounding Pamalican island, about 50m offshore, there are well preserved coral reefs and the most incredible array of tropical fish. With average water temperatures of 26°C and underwater visibility ranging between 15 and 30m, both snorkelling and diving are particularly good. Amanpulo's dive company, **Aquaventure**, offers courses for beginners and advanced divers. There can be few places as wonderful to start your diving as the stunning waters of Pamalican island because the sea water in front of the resort is calm and the drop-off very gentle. For those with more experience there is plenty of

exhilarating diving close by, and it is possible to rent one of the resort's boats and go off on your own to explore the many dive sites. Particularly impressive are **Fan Coral Wall** where turtles are quite common, **Windmill** where a resident 3m stingray has been sighted, and **South Point** where white-tip sharks, tuna, yahoo and mantra and eagle rays are common.

Back on top of the water, the island has a 5½km beach, two hills, and numerous paths to explore either on foot or on one of the hotel's mountain bikes available for guest use. Definitely worth a visit are the **giant clams**, some weigh up to 227kg, on the north-west side of the island. These are under the protection of the **Soriano Foundation**, which was formed to preserve them from the threat of extinction.

Pearl Farm Beach Resort

Pearl Farm Beach Resort enjoys the most spectacular location on the former site of the **Aguinaldo Pearl Farm**, framed by dense jungle and palm trees lining two small but perfect, white sandy beaches.

This beautiful resort was named after the white-lipped oysters that were farmed for their pearls on this spot over a decade ago. Nestling on the small island of Samal,

---

PEARL FARM BEACH RESORT
(☎ 2-832 0893, fax 2-832 0044), Samal Island, Kaputian, Davao City, Philippines
Reservations: Small Luxury Hotels of the World toll free reservations numbers (see p12)
Getting there: An 80-minute flight from Manila to Davao City, five minutes from airport to wharf and then 35 minutes to Pearl Farm by hotel boat (a one-way transfer organised by the hotel costs US$8.50)
Accommodation: 65 bedrooms: 17 Hilltop, 19 Samalhouse, two Junior suites, six Samal suites, 14 Mandaya Houses, seven Malipano Villas
Amenities: Maranao Restaurant, Parola Bar, swimming pool, tennis court, games room, room service, local tours and aquasports facilities
Dress code: None
Weddings: Pearl Farm does have a wedding licence and can host wedding receptions for between 100 and 150 people
Minimum stay: None
Rates: Doubles from US$150 to US$180; suites from US$185 to US$278
Credit cards: Most major
Taxes and service charge: Included

---

25 minutes offshore from the bustling metropolis of Davao, Pearl Farm is now a serene setting for this luxury hotel.

The resort has been beautifully designed with charming houses on stilts housing some of the 65 guest bedrooms, while others are set back with panoramic views of the secluded cove. The hotel has a lovely rustic feel, with rattan, bamboo and other local woods employed in its construction. All the bedrooms have air-conditioning, minibar, private toilet and bath, and a radio clock. The Samal suites also have hairdryers and other extras such as bathrobes and TV.

The best feature of Pearl Farm is the promenade that extends from the shore to the 'Parola', the multi-tiered lighthouse, where a ladder leads down from the open-air bar to a bathing platform below.

The resort provides all the facilities you'd expect of a hotel that is part of the international Small Luxury Hotels of the World group: the tropical and continental food at **Maranao Restaurant** is excellent, the water in the gleaming swimming pool seems to merge uninterrupted into the blues of the sea, and an impressive range of watersports keeps the more active guests busy during the day.

Other recommended hotels

Friday's (☎ 2-812 9139, fax 2-815 1415), c/o 5th Floor, Pacific Star Building, Machete Avenue, Corner Gill, Peat Avenue, Machete, Metro Manila, Philippines, is one of the original island-style resorts, located right in the middle of the island's finest dazzling white beach. An ideal setting and good quality accommodation and service makes this the best hotel in the Boracay area, and a dream situation for a honeymoon. The simply furnished but comfortable rooms are made out of rattan and bamboo, and all have showers, separate dressing areas, quality toiletries, phone, minibar and fresh towels. There is a great beach bar at Friday's, where grilled food is served at lunchtime, as well as the main restaurant. Other facilities include a fresh-water swimming pool, a games area and video room, a beauty salon with masseur, and lots of watersports including diving are available nearby. Doubles from around US$150 per night.

Bohol Beach Club (☎ 314020), Bolad, Panglao, Bohol, is one of the most reasonably priced top notch hotels in the Philippines. Although the accommodation in the 40 rooms is pretty basic, they are air-conditioned and the beach is OK. The resort also has a swimming pool, a spa and sauna, tennis court, poolside bar and restaurant. Bohol itself is quite unlike anywhere else in the Philippines with its famous Chocolate Hills, 1000 hummock-shaped limestone mounds rising spectacularly above the rain forest canopy. Standard twin rooms cost around US$75, while suites are around US$130. (Note that if you wish to call Bohol Beach Club direct you will have to go through the international operator.)

CALAMIAN CRUISES AND DIVING IN THE PHILIPPINES

Cruising in the Calamian Islands

At the northern tip of Palawan are a string of smaller, rarely visited islands. This group of satellite islands offers some of the most dramatic seascapes in Asia, prompting Jacques Cousteau to describe them as one of the most beautiful areas of the world. A four-day, three-night cruise aboard the 24m catamaran M/V *Lagoon Explorer*, stops in tranquil coves so you can swim ashore for a picnic or explore the coral world below. The ten air-conditioned cabins all have private toilet and shower facilities, with hot and cold water. The three-night cruise can be booked through most tour operators specialising in the Philippines and costs around US$1007/£650 per person, or directly with **Discovery Cruises** (☎ 2-815 3008, fax 2-819 0298), Cruise and Hotel Centre Inc, 2nd level, Ayala Wing, Shangri-La Hotel Manila, Ayala Avenue, Makati, Metro Manila, Philippines. The four day, three-night cruise departs every Monday and Thursday, while the seven-day, six-night cruise leaves every Monday.

Diving in the Philippines

The Philippines offers some awesome diving on its 40,000 sq km of coral reefs teeming with a wide variety of marine life.

Here in one of the most productive marine eco-systems in the world, the tropical waters are enriched by currents coming from Japan, the South China Sea, the Indian Ocean, and the Celebes Sea. As a result the country's waters are full of hundreds of different species of fish, shells as well as various marine invertebrates: there are no less than 800 species of corals.

There are dive sites of every description from perpendicular submarine cliffs covered with sponges, corals of varying shapes and sizes, gorgonians swarming with schools of pelagic fish, and dramatic drop offs that reveal the vibrant marine world below.

The Philippines' dive sites are grouped into four major areas, **Batangas, Mindoro,** Palawan, and the **Visayas.** If you are diving from Palawan, where Amanpulo and El Nido Pandalusian Palawan are located, you'll experience one of the last frontiers of the Philippines, where several endangered underwater species are found including manta rays, giant sea turtles, and the sea cow known locally as the dugong.

The diving from the Bohol Beach Club is equally superb and ideal for all types of divers because of its gentle slopes, magnificent walls and wide variety of marine creatures. At nearby **Cabilao Island** there are hammerhead sharks, tunas, dolphins and groupers.

Indonesia
(BEST TIME: APRIL TO MID-NOVEMBER)

Indonesia is an incredible archipelago of over 17,000 islands, of which only 6000 are inhabited, covering over 80,000 sq km of coastline making it, somewhat amazingly, the fourth largest country in the world. The name Indonesia comes from two Greek words, 'Indos' (Indian) and 'nesos' (islands), but the unique character of these islands is derived from the fact that they are neither Asian nor Australian, despite their location between the Indian and Pacific Oceans.

The waters of Indonesia offer some of the world's most dramatic and unspoilt diving. Islands are continually being revealed or removed by the fractious volcanoes marking the edge of a tectonic plate running through Indonesia, lyrically dubbed the 'Ring of Fire'. Along the arc lie numerous rugged islands where tropical flora and cultivated rice paddies stand by areas of dense untouched tropical jungle. This sprawling chain of islands offers a staggering amount of contrasting beauty from the snow-capped mountain peaks of **Irian Jaya**, and the spectacular Buddhist monument **Borobudur** on **Java**, to the volcanic craters of **Sumatra** and coral-fringed lagoons of **Bali**.

Over the last decade tourism has escalated so dramatically in Indonesia that the number of arrivals has increased by 350%. Most of the interest has focused on Bali and its beach resorts, with some parts now resembling an Australian suburb more than an idyllic hideaway: the beaches at **Kuta** and **Legian** in particular are now totally spoilt and full of backpacking Aussies and romantically named hangouts like **The Billabong Bar**. However Bali is big enough for you to avoid the busy bits and does still have some truly wonderful hotels, beaches and stunning countryside, so don't let people write it off as 'ruined'.

BALI

An exotic island of 20,000 temples, spectacular island scenery with unspoilt palm fringed beaches, stunning sunsets and creative, graceful people

When to go: During the dry season from April through to mid November, avoid Christmas and New Year when you can hardly move for tourists (most of them Australians)

Average maximum temperatures °C

JAN	FEB	MAR	APR	MAY	JUN
31	32	31	31	31	31
JUL	AUG	SEP	OCT	NOV	DEC
31	30	30	29	32	31

Capital: Jakarta (Java)

Flight times: to Denpasar (Bali) from:
New York: (via LA) 24 hours
LA: 18 hours
London: 22 hours
Sydney: 6$^1/_2$ hours

Approximate exchange rates: Indonesia Rupiah (R), £1 = R3400, US$1 = R2300, A$1 = R1600

Time difference: GMT plus 7 (west), 8 (central), 9 (east) hours

Voltage: Usually 220v

Combine with: Australia, Singapore, or combine more than one Indonesian island

Country dialling code: ☎ 62

BALI

The tiny volcanic island of Bali has lush green vegetation, coral seas and intriguing Hindu-Balinese culture. The best way to see Bali is to split your time between one of the many five-star beach resorts overlooking gleaming white beaches, and the hill-side village of **Ubud** in order to enjoy the cooler mountain air and soak up a little culture. Two weeks in Bali will enable you to experience all that the island has to offer and maybe see one or two of the other Indonesian islands as well.

Four Seasons Bali

The most famous hotel in Indonesia is the Four Seasons Bali, which, since it opened in June 1993, has come to epitomise the utmost in hedonistic luxury, setting benchmarks by which other hotels continue to judge their progress. Despite being located on the southern tip of Bali, the most developed part of the island, guests are so cocooned in luxury in the 14 hectares of tropical gardens that you'll forget the outside world exists anyway. The luxuriously appointed villas are built into the gently terraced hill in groups of 20, clustered around seven village squares, each with its own designated village chief and group of 'service' family members. There are very few places in the world as romantic as the Four Seasons Bali where, instead of rooms, guests are accommodated in Indonesian pavilions, each equipped with private plunge pool. Your own personal masseurs – one of the seven members of staff per guest – will pummel and swathe you to your heart's content in the privacy of your own villa.

The 139 one-bedroom villas are just perfect for couples and, with a minimum of 200 sq metres of outdoor and indoor living space, are really spacious. Three thatched-roof pavilions comprise an open-sided living and dining area, an air-conditioned sleeping pavilion with adjoining dressing area and closet, plus a luxurious bathing pavilion with a large soaking tub, double vanity, separate shower, toilet and another shower outdoors in the adjacent secluded garden. But it is each pavilion's 15 sq metre private plunge pool nestled amongst beautifully landscaped gardens with two separate sun decks that has become the trade mark extravagance of the Four Seasons Bali.

Being a Four Seasons resort your pavilion, and the resort itself, is equipped with every kind of luxury amenity imaginable from slippers, robes, toiletries, CDs, minibars and 100% white cotton sheets, to full spa and beauty services. There are also two floodlit 'supergrass' tennis courts, a 34m swimming pool which spills over into a seven-metre waterfall forming a free-form soaking pool below, and villa service around the clock so that you can enjoy all your meals in the privacy of your own dining area.

THE FOUR SEASONS
(☎ 361-701010, fax 361-701020), Jimbaran 80361, Bali, Indonesia
Reservations: Through the Four Seasons worldwide reservation numbers (see p12) and leading tour operators and travel agents worldwide (see p9)
Getting there: Chauffeured Mercedes Benz or BMW limousine service available for transfers from Ngurah Rai International Airport
Accommodation: 147 units: 139 one-bedroom villas; six two-bedroom villas; two Royal Villas
Amenities: Pool Terrace Café, Taman Wantilan Restaurant, the Terrace Bar and Lounge, PJs alfresco Mediterranean restaurant; full villa service; 34m swimming pool with free-form soaking pool; hot and cold spa pools; complimentary windsurfing, sailing, snorkelling and instruction; two floodlit 'supergrass' tennis courts, fitness studio, sauna; full selection of beauty services; comprehensive library; Ganesha art gallery; plus golf, scuba diving, white-water rafting, bicycling and trekking tours arranged nearby
Dress code: Elegant casual
Weddings: Ceremonies can be arranged on the beach or within the hotel's wonderful tropical gardens; the hotel's own Bali-based agent will help with the necessary paperwork; registration handling fees for a civil ceremony are currently US$165, with an additional US$50 for a religious ceremony; couples must be resident in Bali seven working days prior to their wedding and couples must be of the same religion in order for the wedding to be lawful
Minimum stay: None
Rates: One-bedroom pavilion from US$425; a five-night honeymoon package including private villa, transfers, champagne, flowers, full breakfast each morning, Bali by candlelight dinner in the villa, lunch at PJs and two Balinese massages costs around US$2500
Credit cards: Most major
Taxes and service charge: 21% tax and service charge will be added to your bill

Amankila

Amankila was voted hotel of the year in 1996 by the *Tatler* – 'the bottom line is that Amankila epitomises luxury'. As *Tatler* says any old five-star hotel should epitomise luxury, but Amankila does it better.   And one visit to any of the 10 Amanresorts will confirm that the word 'luxury' has indeed been redefined by the group. There's nothing flashy about Amankila, but wherever you look sophisticated elegance is combined with such simplicity of design that you'll immediately wish your own home was designed and decorated in the same vein. Built high on a hillside on the quieter eastern part of the island, commanding spectacular views of the **Lombok Straits** and the hotel's own palm studded beach, Amankila is far removed from the tourist hordes that flock to the island's south coast.

Designed in traditional Balinese fashion combining local thatched roofs and stone with timber frames, terrazzo floors and mirrored glass, this incredibly exclusive hotel attracts the likes of Mick Jagger and Jerry Hall, providing such celebrities with a polished haven of good style and taste.

Amankila has 35 free-standing guest pavilions elevated on the escarpment overlooking the sea. They are all decked out with the kind of luxury amenities you'd expect from an Amanresort – air-conditioning, bathrobes, complimentary toiletries, hairdryer, stereo cassette player, phone, minibar and in-room safe. Linked together by walkways to the main building, all the suites make the most of the hotel's elevated position affording breathtaking views. Each suite has an outdoor terrace designed for relaxing and dining, an air-conditioned bedroom with a carved four-poster bed, a dressing area with a day bed, and a fabulous bathroom with a luxurious sunken bath.

American architect, Ed Tuttle, designed the three-tiered swimming pool adjacent to Amankila's main building (which is also on three tiers) so that it overlooks the sea and appears to flow unchecked straight into the ocean. Down at the private beach, reached by a footpath, the **Beach Club** also has its own 45m swimming pool, an informal restaurant, as well as a superb range of complimentary watersports equipment. Aside from beach activities, Amankila also offers guests opportunities to discover the Bali that still remains untrodden by tourist groups, with individual tours organised to see the incredible water palaces, temples and nearby villages. Climb to the top of the nearby hills and you'll be rewarded with sweeping views of the fishing port, beaches and the temple complexes.

> **AMANKILA**
> (☎ 361-771267, fax 361-771266), PO Box 133, Klungkung 80701, Bali, Indonesia
> **Reservations:** Prima Hotels toll free reservations worldwide (see p12); and most leading tour operators and travel agents (see p9)
> **Getting there**: Complimentary transfer from Denpasar Airport included ($1^3/_4$ hours)
> **Accommodation:** 33 suites: 15 superior suites; nine de luxe suites; two de luxe ocean suites; six pool suites; the Amankila suite
> **Amenities:** Bar, two restaurants, Beach Club, two swimming pools, cruise boats, library, gift shop, watersports, trekking, 24-hour suite dining, massage, manicure, pedicure, library
> **Dress code**: Smart casual
> **Weddings**: Can be arranged
> **Minimum stay**: None
> **Rates**: Superior suites from US$430; pool suites from US$600
> **Credit cards**: Most major
> **Taxes and service charge**: All rates are subject to 100% government tax and 10% service charge

The Kupu Kupu Barong

The Kupu Kupu Barong is the perfect exotic mountain hideaway. Set high up among the rice terraces of Ubud, it is the most wonderfully relaxing and luxurious hotel and makes a superb place to spend the first few days of your honeymoon.

Guests stay in 19 beautiful Balinese-style bungalows which are spread out through the hotel's grounds so that you can't see any of the other bungalows from your balcony, just rolling green mountains with fantastic views over the **Ayung River**. One

Kupu Kupu Barong is very near to paradise: stunning views, we had the run of the place and we had our own bungalow in the jungle. We went white-water rafting down the Ayung river and saw the resort from a different angle which was fun. **Bruce Walker**

It was like being a very luxurious Tarzan and Jane only with air-conditioning and room service; waking up with the jungle all around us and from our bed we could see straight out to the other side of the hills. Whenever we went to the swimming pool we always seemed to be alone and with the petals floating on the water it was like an enchanted garden. **Vanessa Walker**

of the best things about staying at Kupu Kupu is the all-pervading privacy: the chances are that when you use the pool you'll be on your own and the only non-jungle noises you are likely to hear from your bungalow are the occasional cries of white-water rafters as they are hurled down river.

The bungalows are single-tiered with a sitting area which has a minibar and tea and coffee-making facilities and fabulous views through the huge window over the river. Beside the bed hangs a large mirror behind which is the bathroom. The bath, which is big enough for two, stands alone so that you can step in from both sides: there is also a separate shower. Batique-print robes are provided as well as a huge pile of properly fluffy white towels and another pile of striped swimming towels.

As well as the bungalows Kupu Kupu also has a luxurious suite, complete with its own private swimming pool, where Jerry Hall and Mick Jagger had their honeymoon.

The bungalows are connected to the rest of the hotel via a labyrinth of pathways along which the scent of the flowers and exotic plants and abundance of butterflies is quite overwhelming. The open-air restaurant is located in the hotel's main building and is

> **KUPU KUPU BARONG**
> (☎ 361-975478, fax 361-975079), PO Box 7, Ubud Bali, Indonesia
> **Reservations:** Utell Worldwide and most leading tour operators (see p9)
> **Getting there**: Transfer from Denpasar airport on request approx US$12 per person one way, one hour drive
> **Accommodation:** 19 bungalows most with separate sitting-rooms, spacious bedrooms, bathrooms. The Barong Suite has its own private pool
> **Amenities:** Free use of mountain-bikes, restaurant, room-service, pool-side restaurant, two swimming pools, massage; white-water rafting and golf can be arranged
> **Dress code**: Relaxed casual
> **Weddings:** Can be arranged, prices available upon request
> **Minimum stay:** None
> **Rates:** Doubles from US$335
> **Credit cards**: Most major
> **Taxes and service charge:** 21% tax and service

very relaxed indeed with more wonderful views. Kupu Kupu started life as a restaurant, famed for its views over the mountains, and the food is still good today. The best place to have lunch is by the bigger of the two swimming pools: the kind waitress does a very good job of keeping a low-profile while you're both swimming but still managing to respond quickly should you feel like a pool-side snack of satay or a salad.

There's lots to do from Kupu Kupu Barong, from mountain biking around the area to white-water rafting on the river Ayung, but essentially it is a hotel for some serious relaxation spending the days lounging around the swimming pools.

Other recommended hotels

Equally wonderful and luxurious are the three other hotels in Indonesia built, owned and run by the Amanresorts group. **Amandari** (☎ 361-975333, fax 361-975335), **Amanusa** (☎ 361-772333, fax 361-772335) and **Amanwana** (☎ 371-22233, fax 371-22288). Bali is a paradise for 'Aman-junkies', the growing number of people who having experienced one of these fantastic hotels want nothing more than to visit the others and for whom the group has now invented packages so that they can split their time between two or three different Amanresorts. If the description of Amankila appeals then make sure you ask your travel agent which of these four hotels most suits your particular needs because, although in terms of architecture and luxury all four are very similar, each also has its own qualities. For instance, Amandari is just outside Ubud, the inland centre of Balinese art, and set among rice paddies from where guests can enjoy walking in the **Monkey Forest**. In contrast, Amanusa is really focused around golf, while Amanwana has 20 luxury tents on **Moyo Island**, a large nature reserve off which some of the world's most incredible dive sites are found. Rates for all four Amanresort properties are pretty much the same, starting at around US$430 a night, although Amanwana is slightly more expensive with jungle tents costing US$500 and ocean-front tents US$575 – expensive, but absolutely worth it for the experience.

The Bali Hyatt (☎ 361-288271, fax 361-287693), PO Box 392, Sanur, is set in 14 hectares of beautifully landscaped tropical gardens. This 390-room resort hotel is furnished with traditional decor and has a huge range of facilities making it perfect for active couples after they've enjoyed a few days rest in Ubud. There are five restaurants, two bars, two outdoor swimming pools, lots of watersports and tennis courts. Doubles from US$145 to US$215; suites from US$400 to US$500; the Beach Villa with two bedrooms costs US$500-550 (all rates plus tax and service charge of 21%).

A FEW THINGS TO SEE AND DO AROUND BALI

Nusa Dua, the location of the Four Seasons and Amanusa, is an upmarket tourist enclave on Bali's south coast. The area is so self contained with its hotels, shops and golf courses, that you wouldn't experience much of the real character of this country if you didn't stray out of the area.

A visit to Ubud is a must, even if you don't actually stay there. Ubud is the island's cultural centre, located inland amidst the rice terraces, where the book shops, museums and craft centres make great browsing.

There is so much shopping potential in Bali that it's difficult to know where to start but try to get a look at some of the following: antiques and stone carving in **Batubulan**, silver in **Celuk**, wood carving in **Mas**, woven cotton fabrics in **Sideman**, as well as textiles in Ubud. Just ten minutes from Amankila is **Tenganan**, a unique village dating back from pre-Hindu times, where the locals make the most exquisite double ikat fabrics and intricate basketry to be found in Bali.

If you want to incorporate some soft adventure in your honeymoon, local tour operator, **Sobek** (☎ 361-287059) specialises in all sorts of white-water rafting, sea kayaking, mountain cycling, bird walks and jungle trekking tours. A three-hour jungle trek will cost around US$50, while four-hours' sea kayaking to idyllic **Turtle Island** costs around US$65.

For a gentler look at the coast, **Bali Hai Cruises** (☎ 361-720331) operates day and evening cruises aboard a sleek catamaran from US$38 for a sunset-dinner cruise.

Little explored east Bali is today often referred to as 'the old Bali'. Free from tourists and development, this stunning area remains very much within the Hindu lifestyle of ages past. The region offers some of the finest trekking available on the island, ranging from beautiful and sedate walks through the forests and rice paddies to more strenuous hikes through the lofty mountains. Amankila has its own drivers and guides with an intimate knowledge of the region to help you find the best sights, or alternatively, you can hire a car and explore under your own steam.

The volcanic mountain, **Gunung Agung**, can be approached from the foothills of this region, while further east lies the ruined water palaces of **Tirta Gangga** and **Ujung**, from where much architectural inspiration was drawn by Amankila's architect.

Klungkung, just 20 minutes west of the hotel, is the former capital of Bali and home to the superbly painted ceilings of the **Halls of Justice**, as well as the starting point for tours to the artists' village of **Kamasan**; the **Mother Temple**, **Besakih**; **Sidemen's** fine weaving and terraced rice paddies and **Kintamani's** panoramic views of the volcanic **Lake Bratan**.

OTHER INDONESIAN ISLANDS

If you are staying on Bali do try to see at least one of the other islands while you're in Indonesia, such as Sumatra, **Kalimantan**, Lombok, **Sulawesi**, Irian Jaya and Java. Each has differences in culture and landscape.

The natural jungles in south-east Sulawesi are predominantly National Parks, hence this area is described as being one of the world's last remaining untouched habitats. Garuda flies daily from Bali to **Ujung Pandang** departing at 8.35am and arriving at 9.55am for R158,800. Breathtaking scenery, archaeological sites and an abundance of culture are what allure travellers to Ujung Pandang. In particular it's worth visiting **Palenggo** village to witness the daily lifestyle of the Bugis people, the fishermen and their unique houses on stilts, the **Masaskar Fortress**, built in 1545, which has now been turned into a cultural museum, and **Paotere Harbour** where local ships are silhouetted against the sky during the breathtaking sunsets. If you want to stay the night try the **Makassar Golden Hotel** (☎ 411-314408, fax 411-320951), Jl Pasar Itan No

---

(**Opposite**) **Top:** Four Seasons, Bali (see p60). **Bottom:** Ladera Resort, St Lucia (p33).

52, Ujung Pandang, which offers comfortable accommodation from US$110 a night to US$150 for an Upper De luxe Cottage, plus 21% tax.

From Ujung Pandang take the ferry to **Bau Bau** which, located in the tranquil and picturesque **Takung Besi Islands**, is unlike any other place in the world. Visit **Kotana**, a small village in **Walio**, just 3km from Bau Bau, the incredible waterfall at **Tirta Pimba**, 5km from Bau Bau, and **Kawikawia Island**, a short boat ride from the harbour, which is a remote natural sanctuary with abundant bird and marine life. For accommodation try one of the small and intimate resorts, which, far away from mainstream tourism, are just ideal for honeymooners. Both the **Deborah**, Jl Kartini 15, Bau Bau and the **Liliana**, Jl Kartini 18, Bau Bau, are quaint bungalows where you don't have to book but can just turn up on the day.

Lombok is constantly compared to Bali as it was a decade ago because of its unspoilt landscapes and unhurried pace of life. While Bali is lush and equatorial, Lombok is much drier and more rugged with some of the most spectacular geological features you'll ever see. Lombok is accessible from Bali by Pelini ferries for R3400 departing several times daily, or by air with Garuda who fly to Mataram in Lombok almost hourly (R56,500).

As well as pristine beaches, there is plenty to explore from ancient temples, palaces and local villages, to the stunning **Sindenggile** waterfall and the magnificent sunrise at the **Puri Mayura Royal Gardens**. The best beach is **Kuta** where unbroken white sand stretches all the way to **Tanjuna**. **Sheraton Senggigi Beach Resort** (☎ 364-93333), Jl Raya Senggigi, overlooks the wonderful Senggigi Beach, and is the only really first-class hotel operating on the island, so if you don't want to compromise on creature comforts this has to be the place to stay. From Senggigi you can take the most incredible trip to **Gili Air**, **Gili Meno** and **Gili Trawangan**, three remote and unique islands which are only accessible by outrigger boats from **Bangsal Harbour**, which is an adventure in itself.

Moyo Island is a great place to go camping Amanstyle, where **Amanwana** (☎ 361-771267, fax 361-771266) houses guests in 20 seriously luxurious tents, either on the edge of the jungle or on the beach. Each tent has a teak floor, a library and a CD discman. Amanwana has been a wildlife sanctuary for 20 years now, so you are guaranteed absolute tranquillity and remoteness, accompanied by the unmistakable quality of service and furnishings that has come to be expected from Amanresorts. Double tents cost from US$500 per night (excluding meals) which, although extremely expensive, is arguably worth it for a night of unrivalled Aman hospitality.

Sri Lanka
(BEST TIME: AUGUST TO DECEMBER, FEBRUARY TO MAY)

Exploring the exotic scenery and rich culture and history of Sri Lanka makes an ideal combination with a lazy week in the Maldives, or as a contrast to an Indian honeymoon. Encompassing the relics of 25 centuries of different civilisations and their traditions, from the ancient Greeks and Romans to the latter-day invasions of the British, Dutch and Portuguese, Sri Lanka is fascinating. In just a week it is easy to see lots of wildlife, view 5th century frescoes on the top of the vast **Red Lion Rock**, explore

---

SRI LANKA
Approximate exchange rates: Sri Lankan rupee (Rs), US$1 = Rs56.54, £1 = Rs88.70
Time difference: GMT plus $5^1/_2$ hours
Country dialling code: ☎ 94

(Opposite): Cocoa Island beach, Maldives (see p67)

some of the many absorbing Buddhist ruins and temples, and relax in the cool wood and lake land retreat of **Kandy**. Images of Sri Lanka range from the timeless plodding of water buffalo in paddy fields to raging waterfalls, lofty mountain peaks and colonial hill-stations.

Since peace talks between the government and the Tamil Tigers (LTTE) broke down in April 1995 fighting has continued in the north and east of the country. Do not visit these areas. Although foreigners are unlikely to be directly targeted, it is wise to exercise caution in public places. The south and centre, including all the main tourist areas and the Cultural Triangle, remain largely unaffected.

The best way to see Sri Lanka is to hire a car and do a week's tour around the island taking in the following places:
• Kandy, the last stronghold of the Sinhalese kings, is a lakeland paradise where visitors can escape the heat and spend tranquil afternoons relaxing in this wonderful village, visit the **Temple of the Tooth** where Buddhists believe Buddha's tooth is housed, and explore the bustling bazaars
• Drive from Kandy up to **Nuwara Eliya** and see its tea plantations and hill stations
• Continue down the spine of the country through **The Gap** and on to the south-east coast and the **Yala National Park**, known for its leopards

The Maldives
(BEST TIME: JANUARY TO JULY, SEPTEMBER AND OCTOBER)

The Maldives really are the ultimate islands – small lush green forested dots ringed by perfect white sandy beaches and coral reefs in a turquoise sea to the south west of Sri Lanka. Some people love them and others wish they'd gone somewhere else, not because they were disappointed by the islands' beauty which is indisputable, but because they felt claustrophobic staying on islands so small that you can walk round most of them in less than half an hour.

The 1190 islands are scattered around 19 atolls spread over almost 800km of the Indian Ocean from north to south. Only 202 are inhabited, most of them home to Maldivian fishermen, but 56 have been transformed into tourist villages, each one occupying an entire island. These are found in the three central atolls: **Malé North**, **Malé South** and **Ari**.

THE MALDIVES
Idyllic tiny islands ringed by white sand and coral, just perfect for beach lovers, very quiet in the evenings
When to go: the temperature in the Maldives varies between 28 and 30°C throughout the year; towards the end of May and into June, and between November and December the monsoons bring intermittent showers, the best time to visit is meant to be November to Easter (that's the theory!)
Average maximum temperatures °C

JAN	FEB	MAR	APR	MAY	JUN	JUL	AUG	SEP	OCT	NOV	DEC
28	28	28	29	29	28	28	28	28	28	28	28

Capital: Malé
Flight times: to Malé from:
New York (via London) $18^3/_4$ hours
LA (via London) 25 hours
London: (via Dubai) 11 hours
Sydney: (via Singapore) $12^1/_2$ hours
Approximate exchange rates: Rufiya (R), £1 = R18.30, US$1 = R11.80, A$1 = R9.32
Time difference: GMT plus five hours
Voltage: 220/240v, AC 50 Hz – all sorts of plug sockets are found in the Maldives
Combine with: Sri Lanka, Singapore, India, Dubai
Country dialling code: ☎ 960

If you are totally self-sufficient and don't need people around you or space to escape from other guests, then the Maldives will suit you – in fact you'll love them; likewise, if you are both enthusiastic divers and are keen to spend your days in the immense underwater playground that surrounds the islands. But be warned that if you are active people who like to sightsee, look elsewhere because you'll feel like prisoners on your own island in the Maldives.

You should also be warned that the food is not that exciting. While the fish is of course really fresh and the barbecues delicious, everything has to be flown into the island so don't expect extensive gourmet menus to be laid on each night. And even if a hotel does have lots of wonderful things on the menu you'll have to get used to the waiters saying that they've 'just' run out of that.

Assuming you do both like the sound of these charming little coral islands the next stage is to pick the right island for you. There are all kinds of resorts on offer in the Maldives from perfectly tranquil hideaways with only a dozen or so bungalows to a group of islands linked together so you can have peace and privacy on one and bars and restaurants on another, and there are even islands which are run as much bigger resorts with tennis courts, night-clubs and a range of different restaurants. Whoever you book your holiday through make sure you state exactly what you expect from your island. Another good idea is to combine a week in the Maldives with some touring in Sri Lanka which is much bigger and more mountainous or, if you are coming from Europe, spend a few days acclimatising yourself back to reality in Dubai.

It is very difficult to say when is best to go to the Maldives. The weather pattern has changed so much over the years, it is hard to tell when you should and shouldn't go. The optimum time is supposed to be between December and April during the north-east monsoon period because the weather is hot and dry and showers are only occasional – theoretically. Having said that it always seems to rain at Christmas and New Year, February and Christmas are the busiest months, and weather charts show that June is wet but I've been there when it was wonderful. The best advice is to avoid August as the weather can be really mixed: otherwise take a chance and go – you may well get showers but they rush over the islands quickly because there are no mountains to trap the bad weather. Besides, you can always go to bed for the afternoon.

Cocoa Island

People dream of islands like Cocoa Island, in fact it is so perfect that Robert Louis Stevenson was prompted to describe it as one of the 'celestial islands in the Indian ocean'.

The water is so clear and the sand so white that at a distance, it is virtually impossible to distinguish where the beach ends and the sea starts. If you are looking for the desert island of your dreams, but don't want to compromise on food and accommodation, then you'll be interested to know that Cocoa Island is a member of the prestigious Relais & Châteaux group.

Looking down on Cocoa Island it looks just like an idyllic scene from Robinson Crusoe, with a handful of thatched roofs pointing out through the palm trees and dense green undergrowth, a perfect white beach and a patchwork of different colour blues all around. The eight beach bungalows are indeed ideal natural hideaways – they are

COCOA ISLAND
(☎ 44-3713, fax 44-1919), South Malé Atoll, The Maldives Republic
Reservations: Relais & Châteaux toll free numbers worldwide (see p12)
Getting there: Guests are collected from Malé by speedboat (45 minutes)
Accommodation: Eight bungalows
Amenities: Lagoon bar, restaurant, sailing, water-skiing, windsurfing, snorkelling, day trips to other islands, fishing
Dress code: Casual
Weddings: No
Minimum stay: None
Rates: Double bungalow from US$305
Credit cards: Visa, Eurocard, American Express
Taxes and service charge: Included

built from white coral and wood from the nearby coconut trees and are thatched with palms. Each one opens straight out on to the white sandy beach which surrounds this tiny island. There is no air-conditioning in the two-storey bungalows, but the natural breezes do seem to keep them cool, while each one has a shower and toilet attached.

The thing I like best about Cocoa Island is its bar which is built away from the beach on stilts and has 180° views of the lagoon. Here guests can linger over exotic cocktails and fruit punches before dinner.

Although the food at Cocoa Island is much better than most island resorts in the Maldives, people don't come here for the food. Instead it is the crystal clear water which provides the most perfect conditions for all kinds of watersports. Scuba diving is particularly good in the Maldives, and Cocoa Island now has its new **Soleni Dive Centre** which operates all standards of courses and takes guests to some spectacular reef dives. Alternatively if you just want to sit and do nothing the long sandbank stretching out away from the resort means you should be able to find a private spot.

Veligandu-Hura

Veligandu-Hura has one distinct advantage over the other Maldivian resorts in that it is one of three islands linked together via a causeway. So, although Veligandu-Hura is very tiny it is much the nicest of the three islands while the other islands give you the space and variety that the Maldives are so often criticised for lacking.

There are just 12 thatched bungalows situated along the edge of the beach. Each one is very private, has air-conditioning and is individually decorated in a simple fashion. Each bungalow also has a small patio with chairs and table from where you can look straight out to sea. You get your own towelling dressing gown and the fresh-water showers, although also very simple affairs, have both hot and cold water which is quite unusual in the Maldives. Most guests tend to get up pretty early, after retiring early too, but you can have breakfast brought to your room for an additional charge of US$2 per person.

The food isn't bad at Veligandu-Hura, another welcome change from many resorts in the Maldives. In addition to the main restaurant there is now a small Asian restaurant right by the breakwater wall. During the day this is a coffee shop but at 6pm it starts serving delicious Oriental cuisine. The bar on the island is small but quite sophisticated with a huge range of wonderful tasting cocktails.

The diving is particularly good around this island, although the lack of a house reef means there's no snorkelling on your doorstep: instead the hotel's boats take you out to the reef. Veligandu-Hura should fit the bill if you are looking for a simple but comfortable hotel in stunning island surroundings to crash out in for a week.

> **VELIGANDU-HURA**
> (☎ 44-3882, fax 44-0009), Palm Tree Island, PO Box 2014, Malé, The Maldives Republic
> **Reservations**: From the UK go through the Maldives local representative, Toni the Maldive Lady (☎ 0171-352 2246)
> **Getting there**: Transfers from the airport take approx 30 minutes by speedboat (US$175 per person return) or 90 minutes by local dhoni (US$65 per person return); speedboats don't travel after 6pm
> **Accommodation:** 12 thatched bungalows
> **Amenities**: Hotel safe, bar, main restaurant, Lotus restaurant/coffee-shop, table tennis, darts, badminton, volley-ball, diving, snorkelling, windsurfing, sailing, excursions to other islands, night fishing, deep-sea fishing
> **Dress code**: Casual wear and sportswear
> **Weddings**: No (if you book through Toni ask her about her villa in Sri Lanka where couples can get married; many then go on to honeymoon in the Maldives)
> **Minimum stay**: None, but at least three days recommended
> **Rates**: From US$150 per person
> **Credit cards**: American Express, MasterCard, Visa
> **Taxes and service charge**: US$6 bed tax per person per night, service charge 10%

What's lacking in material comforts is more than compensated for by some of the most stunning beach scenery in the world. **Katherine and Moray Wright**

Banyan Tree

The Banyan Tree resorts, of which there are only half a dozen worldwide, have in my mind got it pretty sussed. Here on Vabbinfaru, staying at the Banyan Tree means you can relax in the knowledge that you are on one of the most beautiful islands in the world, with accommodation to match.

Although the Maldives themselves are stunning islands, the resorts and hotels that have been built on them often don't live up to your expectations. At the Banyan Tree you can raise your expectations as high as you want and dream away of elegant four-poster beds, delicious meals, impeccable room service and even relaxing spa treatments and you won't be disappointed.

Dotted around the island are 48 villas, with conical thatched roofs and green louvered doors to allow you to make the most of the breezes coming in off the sea, and of course, the panoramic views. The accommodation is really classy for the Maldives, with a solid king-sized four-poster shrouded in cream muslin, stone-tiled floors, wrought-iron candles and ornaments, and ornate carved wooden furniture. Each villa has a spacious terrace from where you can watch the sun dip below the horizon, and a private garden where room service will set up an alfresco meal for you. Other amenities include ceiling fan, a phone, fully stocked minibar, hair-dryer, slippers and bathrobes, toiletries, coffee and tea-making facilities and an in-villa safe.

The hotel's spa is a fabulous way to unwind after a long flight. Treatment options vary from ancient Eastern healing and relaxation to European rejuvenation therapies, using organic essences from aromatic plants and indigenous essential oils.

BANYAN TREE MALDIVES

(☎ 44-3147, fax 44-3843), Vabbinfaru Island, North Malé Atoll, Republic of Maldives

Reservations: Small Luxury Hotels of the World toll free numbers (see p12)

Getting there: 25 minutes on the hotel's speed-boat from Malé International Airport

Accommodation: 48 private villas, most of which are sea facing, with an open terrace and private garden

Amenities: Spa facilities, badminton, volley-ball, table tennis, pétanque, indoor games, video room and library, watersports including snorkelling, scuba diving, fishing, deep-sea fishing, water-skiing, windsurfing, sailing, sea plane trips, canoeing and glass-bottom boat trips; Ilaafathi Restaurant serving international cuisine and local Maldivian food, Sangu Restaurant for barbecues, Naiboli Bar for cocktails and pastries with happy hour from 6.30 to 7.30pm; laundry, currency exchange

Dress code: Casual or beachwear

Weddings: The hotel does not cater for wedding ceremonies or receptions

Minimum stay: None

Rates: Suites from US$300 to US$450

Credit cards: Most major

Taxes and service charge: No taxes or service charge, but all guests must pay a US$6 bed tax per person per day

---

CHARTERING A YACHT IN THE MALDIVES

Perhaps the best way to see these incredible islands without having to worry about being marooned on just one of them is to charter a yacht and sail from one to another. A local Maldivian company called **Voyages** (fax 32-5336) runs dhoni charters which can be booked from the UK through **Andrew Brock Travel** (UK ☎ 01572-821330): a 15-day package on-board one of Voyages' 15m dhonis is from US$2540/£1640 per person which includes your flights, full board and a three-man crew.

Nika

The beautiful island of Nika in the Ari atoll is an idyllic honeymoon destination reputed to be one of the Maldives' most luxurious and private islands. There are only 25 thatched bungalows, all of which have just been redecorated and each comes with its own private beach. Nika is reached by either a two-hour boat trip or a 35-minute helicopter ride which is the most incredible way of seeing these stunning islands and arriving at your destination; when the pilot points and says 'that's Nika' it almost makes you quiver with anticipation. Do watch your flight times if you are going to Nika as

NIKA
(☎ 45-0516, fax 45-0577), PO Box 2076,
10 Fareedhee Magu, Malé, Republic of
the Maldives
Reservations: From the UK go through
the Maldives local representative, Toni
the Maldive Lady (UK ☎ 0171-352
2246)
Getting there: Nika's representative will
meet you at Malé International Airport
and assist your transfer to the island by
helicopter to Budafoludhu Island, five
minutes from Nika by boat
Accommodation: 25 guest bungalows
Amenities: Restaurant-bar, coffee
shop/bar, floodlit tennis court, bowling
alley, badminton, volley-ball,
snorkelling, windsurfing, canoes and
water-skiing, excursions to other islands,
barbecues and picnics on deserted
islands, fishing and big-game fishing,
scuba diving school
Dress code: Casual
Weddings: No, but they can arrange a
special Maldivian reception decorating
your bungalow with palm leaves and garlands and greeting you with champagne
and a wedding-cake
Minimum stay: None, but at least three
days recommended (14 days minimum
stay over the Christmas period)
Rates: From US$220 per person
Credit cards: MasterCard, American
Express, Visa
Taxes and service charge: US$6 bed tax
per person per night, 10% service charge

you'd have to stay on Malé for one night if
your international flight arrives at night –
which isn't an ideal way to start your honeymoon.

Each cottage is totally set apart from
its neighbour and is surrounded by a large
garden. They all have a good-sized bedroom,
a phone, a separate sitting-room with two
wicker chairs and a fully-stocked minibar.
There's also a lovely beach right on your
door step with a house reef for you to explore
with a snorkel. The recent renovations have
been careful not to spoil the magical character of Nika, so no extra guest rooms were
added and there is still no air-conditioning
but electric fans in the bedroom and sitting-
room just about do the trick. To make each of
the beaches even more private, 15 jetties
have been built perpendicular to the beach
dividing each bungalow's beach from the
next. Thanks to this new addition, all the
bungalows have a big wide beach.

Facilities include a floodlit tennis
court, scuba diving and an impressive range
of watersports. Under Italian ownership, the
hotel has a distinctly Italian feel to it, which
also means the food produced by the resident
Italian chef is better than most resorts in the
Maldives. You can expect pasta, raw fish
carpaccio, pizza, baked fish, fish curries and
steaks in the main dining-room, and there are
barbecues and Maldivian-style suppers twice a week. The best place for breakfast is
sitting outside your cottage making the most of the magical views of the ocean. A picnic lunch can easily be arranged on one of the nearby deserted islands: the staff will
drop you off in the morning and come back at sunset to pick you up.

Other recommended hotels
Soneva Fushi Resort (☎ 23-0304, fax 23-0374), Baa Atoll, a member of the Small
Luxury Hotels of the World is new to the Maldives. It is absolutely ideal for hedonistic escapists and occupies the largest of the Maldive islands given over to tourism. All
the 42 villas have garden bathrooms and stunning views of the lagoon. Doubles at this
incredible designer island will set you back US$310.

Nakatchafushi (☎ 44-3847, fax 44-2665), is an excellent middle of the range
island in the North Malé Atoll. Nakatcha, as it's called locally, has 51 pretty individual bungalows facing the beach with air-conditioning, phone, minibar, hot and cold
water and room service. With a choice of four restaurants, live bands, a disco, and a
fresh-water swimming pool, it will suit those who feel the other resorts are a little too
private, small and quiet. From US$150 per person per night plus US$6 bed tax per person per night.

Cheaper alternatives
If all of the above sound ridiculously expensive a really good way of getting a great
deal on a week or two in the Maldives is to call UK-based Kuoni (see p9) two months

before your wedding and ask them for their *Limited Edition* brochure; this has a wide variety of hotels and resorts at discounted prices. For example, two weeks in June at **Kurmati Village** is sometimes sold for as little as US$1700/£1100 per person which includes absolutely everything: your flights, transfers, watersports, all meals and all drinks.

Other islands to ask tour operators about are: **Makunudu Island**, a small two and a half hectare island under new management which has recently refurbished the 31 bungalows; **Angaga Island Resort**, a cheaper option with simple but comfortable rooms, currently British Airways Holidays' most popular Maldives resort; **Kanifinolhu**, a bigger medium-class hotel with more facilities than most Maldivian islands and which also operates an all-inclusive policy through Kuoni.

The Seychelles
(BEST TIME: MAY TO NOVEMBER)

The Seychelles, an archipelago of over 100 islands in the Indian Ocean, is all about beaches. If it's a romantic island setting you are after this place has all the right ingredients: palm trees, white sand beaches, brilliant aquamarine seas and totally unspoilt coral reefs – sheer escapism for true romantics.

Holidays here aren't cheap, but for those searching for an idyllic beach paradise a long way from anywhere, and who don't mind bumping in to other couples seeking the same, it is difficult to better the Seychelles.

Only a handful of these islands are visited by tourists. This part of the world may have been discovered a few centuries ago, but it was only when the international airport opened in 1971 that the Seychelles were put on the tourism map. Now over 100,000 visitors a year flock through the main island of Mahé.

Very few visitors remain on one island as it's so easy to take one of the many short boat or plane trips and go island hopping. Nature lovers will marvel at the different islands' diverse and unusual bird life, while snorkellers and scuba divers can swim with the 150 species of tropical fish occupying the surrounding waters.

The Seychelles are not known for their night-life, although there are bars dotted around Mahé – honeymooning here is all about being alone together on deserted

---

THE SEYCHELLES
Lazy days spent on perfect island beaches, staying in beach bungalows, great watersports, and ideal for island hopping
When to go: May to September when the south-east trade winds blow is relatively dry; from October to April the north-west trade winds bring humid weather; the main rainy season is in December and January
Average maximum temperature °C

JAN	FEB	MAR	APR	MAY	JUN	JUL	AUG	SEP	OCT	NOV	DEC
30	30	31	31	30	29	28	28	29	29	30	30

Capital: Mahé
Flight times: to Mahé from:
　　　New York: (via London) 24 hours
　　　LA: (via Singapore) 26 hours
　　　London: (via Nairobi or Europe)$11^1/_2$ hours
　　　Sydney: (via Singapore) 14 hours
Approximate exchange rates: Seychelles rupee (Rs) – £1 = Rs7.76, US$1 = Rs5, A$1 = Rs3.95
Time difference: GMT plus four hours
Voltage: 240v, AC 50 Hz – 3-point square pin plugs
Combine with: Mauritius, Réunion, Kenya, Europe
Country dialling code: ☎ 248

stretches of beach and eating delicious alfresco meals.

These islands make a wonderful combination with a week on Mauritius. One word of warning though: because the Seychelles' beauty is natural rather than man made, spend your first week in the Seychelles when lying on an empty beach will probably suit you both just fine; then go on to Mauritius, where the hotels' food, service, facilities and accommodation are undoubtedly superior.

MAHE

Le Meridien Fisherman's Cove

Fisherman's Cove has a very informal, club-like atmosphere which makes a few days here a very relaxing way to start your honeymoon. While it shouldn't be described as luxurious, Fisherman's Cove is without doubt the smartest hotel on Mahé.

Built in traditional Seychellois style, with its sweeping thatched roofs and rough hewn local granite, this low-level resort blends in well with the stunning shore line at the western end of **Beau Vallon** beach. The tropical gardens are beautiful and full of colour.

Each of the 19 standard rooms is housed in one or two storey buildings. They all have air-conditioning, phone, satellite television and video, radio, mini-fridge, private bath or shower, bathrobes and personal toiletries, and furnished balconies or terraces facing the ocean providing wonderful views. There are also 27 terraced cottages at Fisherman's Cove which open on to the gardens overlooking the sea. The decor is simple with white tiled floors, wooden walls, white cane furniture and colourful bed spreads and curtains to brighten up the room. Most of the rooms have sea views and a balcony or terrace but the best views of the water are undoubtedly from the cottages which are closer to the shore.

While the beach immediately in front of the resort is swallowed up at high tide, the adjacent beach, Beau Vallon, is only steps away. This beautiful beach is superb for swimming. Water-skiing, windsurfing, para sailing, deep-sea fishing and diving are all readily available at **Leisure 2000** across Beau Vallon bay at local rates, while the resort's own complimentary facilities include three tennis courts and a small fresh-water pool

---

FISHERMAN'S COVE
(☎ 247247, fax 247742), PO Box 35, Mahé, Seychelles
Reservations: Through Forte-Meridien Reservation International toll free numbers worldwide; or UK tour operators Elegant Resorts, Abercrombie & Kent, Sunset Travel (see p9)
Getting there: 30 minutes from Mahé airport, the hotel can arrange transfers
Accommodation: 48 guest rooms: 19 standard rooms, 27 cottages, two junior suites
Amenities: Two restaurants, one bar, entertainment four times a week, room service from 7am to 10pm, boutique, excursions desk, car rental, laundry service and hairdressing salon, three tennis courts (floodlit), billiards, table tennis, small fresh-water pool; water-skiing, windsurfing, deep-sea fishing and scuba diving at local rates
Dress code: Smart casual
Weddings: Minimum residency four days; US$635/£410 supplement per couple including all the trimmings
Minimum stay: None, apart from Christmas and New Year when five nights are required
Rates: Doubles from around US$431/Rs2150 bed and breakfast, US$512/Rs2550 half board
Credit cards: Most major
Taxes and service charge: Included

---

around which barbecued food is served at lunchtime from **La Carcassaille**, the poolside restaurant.

In the evenings guests can enjoy cocktails in the **Blue Marlin Bar** overlooking the Indian Ocean (men are asked to wear long trousers), and table d'hôte dinners in the **Petit Pot** restaurant. Red snapper and grouper are popular while meaty steaks of shark and barracuda come grilled with tangy 'rougaille' sauce or are delicately transformed into mouth-watering curries.

Other recommended hotels

Nestled on a rocky headland on the north west of Mahé is **Le Northolme Hotel** (☎ 261222, fax 261223), PO Box 333, Mahé, a charming small hotel in a perfect setting. Looking down over its own stunning beach with palm trees and exotic shrubs adorning the periphery, the atmosphere here is one of absolute tranquillity. Of the 19 seaview rooms, seven are classed as superior, with split-levels and a large balcony, the rest are standard. All 19 rooms have private bath/shower and toilet, air-conditioning, hair-dryer, radio and minibar, as well as a balcony/terrace. Doubles from US$239/Rs1190 bed and breakfast or US$311/Rs1550 half board, superior rooms cost around US$279/Rs1390 for bed and breakfast and US$351/Rs1750 half board.

Sunset Beach (☎ 261111, fax 261221), PO Box 372, Victoria, Mahé, perched on a bluff on the island's west coast, has an intimate feel and secluded atmosphere. The views over the hotel's perfect private beach and across the ocean to neighbouring **Silhouette Island** are absolutely stunning, especially, of course, at sunset. The hotel has only 16 de luxe rooms, six junior suites and one luxury villa, all of which have private bath and toilet, air-conditioning, mini-fridge, a patio and sea views. The hotel also has a fabulous fresh-water pool and sundeck overlooking the ocean, and although snorkelling equipment is available for use on the hotel's private beach, guests have to go to Beau Vallon beach for any other watersports. Doubles from US$257/Rs1280 bed and breakfast or US$329/Rs1640 half board, junior suites cost around US$335/Rs1670 bed and breakfast and US$407/Rs2030 half board.

A FEW THINGS TO SEE AND DO AROUND MAHE

Mahé is the largest of the islands in the Seychelles: it is home to its international airport and is also the most commercialised of all the islands. Like many other islands in the Seychelles, Mahé is surrounded by a **coral reef** which protects the coastline and makes the crystal clear waters calm and ideal for snorkelling, diving and swimming. Mahé has many beaches and coves of outstanding beauty: Beau Vallon is the largest and most sheltered beach and it offers an impressive variety of watersports, including the **Diables Des Mers Diving Centre**.

Mahé, with its two casinos, is the only island in the Seychelles to have any night-life: one is at the *Plantation Club* and another at the *Beau Vallon Hotel*.

There are six walking trails marked out on Mahé, most of which are graded either as easy or medium and take only an hour or two at the most. From **La Réserve** a trail passes through a mahogany plantation, allowing you to compare the difference between a planted forest and a relatively undisturbed natural forest, and through one of the best areas of palm forest remaining on Mahé. Many people find it as spectacular as the **Vallée de Mai on Praslin**, in spite of the lack of coco-de-mer. You'll see five types of palm unique to the Seychelles, together with numerous other native plants and animals.

Another fantastic walk takes you on the **Trois Frères** path through a section of the **Morne Seychellois National Park** to the summit of the mountain overlooking **Victoria**. The National Park was created in 1979 and embraces a large part of the uplands of central Mahé. Alternatively take the steady climb up through the Morne Seychellois National Park on to a huge expanse of granite rock (known locally as glacés) to **Copolia**, which at 500m above sea level has spectacular views of the east coast of Mahé.

PRASLIN

L'Archipel

L'Archipel on Praslin is without doubt one of the finest hotels in the Seychelles. Perched on the hillside, this charming little hotel has truly stunning views over the **Côte d'Or Bay**, and is the perfect place to escape for a few days.

Guests are accommodated in 22 hillside cottages built from local wood and granite, with Scandinavian-style interiors and green corrugated roofs. All the rooms measure 40 sq metres and have sea-facing verandas; they are either single or split-level with separate entrances to give you more privacy. Each comprises a double bed (some are four-posters) covered with pretty muslin mosquito netting hanging down from the

L'ARCHIPEL

(☎ 232040, fax 232072), Anse Gouvernement, Praslin, Seychelles

Reservations: Either direct or through Indian Ocean resort specialists (see p10)

Getting there: 20 minutes from Praslin airstrip, reached by a 15-minute flight from Mahé, the hotel can arrange for a taxi transfer for approximately US$45 return

Accommodation: 22 hillside cottages

Amenities: Cocktail bar, restaurant, beach bar serving light lunches; complimentary canoeing, snorkelling, and boat trips to nearby coves; scuba diving for qualified divers at local rates can be arranged

Dress code: Ties and jackets are not required but gentlemen are asked to wear trousers for dinner and women to dress up

Weddings: L'Archipel does occasionally do wedding receptions for small groups of up to 20

Minimum stay: None

Rates: Standard doubles US$425; junior suites US$556; suites US$718, all on a half board basis

Credit cards: Most major

Taxes and service charge: Included

polished wood ceilings. The rooms also have simple pieces of beautifully crafted furniture including a louvred wardrobe, cane chairs and table, and cool terracotta tiles on the floor.

They are also well-equipped with minibar, in-room safe, phone, satellite TV, music and an overhead fan. A large bathroom comes complete with lovely freebie toiletries, lots of towels, two basins and a separate toilet. Most important of all there is a full-width balcony offering superb views of the bay below, while being discreetly secluded from your neighbours.

The three luxury individual suites are quite magnificent: measuring around 100 sq metres they have a separate lounge and large wrap-around veranda where evening meals can be enjoyed, a walk-in wardrobe, bathroom with jacuzzi and shower, plus a second toilet and shower. Bathrobes and slippers are also provided in the suites, but not in the other rooms.

In the main building, higher above the small private beach, is the reception area, cocktail bar and a wooden open-fronted restaurant with wonderful views from the tables looking out over the ocean. All breakfasts and dinners are served in the restaurant, which offers some of the best food in the Seychelles, while light lunches, snacks and cold drinks are available from the **Beach Bar** during the day. L'Archipel has live music in the evenings twice a week.

Somewhat unusually for the Seychelles, L'Archipel has a good reputation for service; staff are continually being trained and retrained in Mauritius or in the south of France. Owner/manager Louis d'Offray and his wife, Cecile, have done much for the reputation of this hotel and are usually on hand to ensure guests are comfortable and their own high standards are met.

Snorkelling, windsurfing, hobie-cat sailing and canoeing from the hotel's white sandy beach are available free of charge, as are the boat trips to visit nearby coves, while deep-sea fishing and scuba diving can be arranged at local rates. L'Archipel prides itself on being able to offer its guests almost any kind of excursion whether it be a catamaran cruise to visit a few nearby islands, or beachcombing by helicopter.

Château de Feuilles

Château de Feuilles is the only Relais & Châteaux property in the Seychelles, and as such has an enviable reputation for both service and dining. This exclusive hotel has only 12 rooms and unusually for the Seychelles is not located on the beach. Its guests come instead for the gourmet food, the élitism and the distinctly French atmosphere. In fact, the Francophile influence at this hotel is so strong that guests even have to pay in French francs.

Located among two hectares of tropical parklands in the south of Praslin, the Château's hilltop location provides it with glorious views over the neighbouring islands and the dazzling surrounding ocean. Because the hotel is not actually on the beach, most guests hire a mini-moke (an open-sided jeep) which provides them with the freedom to choose their own beach each day: FF400 per day from the hotel's own rental office.

The hotel was built using natural materials with incredible thatched roofs in the reception, lounge and restaurant, lightened by the cream fabrics on the chairs and the sunlight flooding in on all sides. The whole effect is relaxed and rustic.

There is a wide range of accommodation, although the rooms are not particularly special; they are furnished in typical island decor with tiled floors, white walls, wooden-beamed ceilings and rattan furniture. Avoid the standard rooms and bungalows (unless you want single beds!) and go instead for one of the two apartments in the main building. Each has a large double bed, a separate living room, bathroom and either garden or sea views from their first floor location. Located in the tropical parklands are two mini-suites with double beds, and a terrace with a stunning sea view.

Dining at the Château de Feuilles will be one of the highlights of your stay. The restaurant, under the same management as Le Duc restaurants in Paris, serves absolutely delicious gourmet food, such as crabes et crevettes frits, poissons marinés creole and curries made from whatever is fresh that day.

Other recommended hotels

For those looking for a luxurious hotel with really fantastic food it is difficult to beat **La Réserve** (☎ 232211, fax 232166), Anse Petit Cour, Praslin. This beautiful old colonial hotel on the east of Praslin successfully combines old world charm with modern luxuries. It is an elegant destination where guests make an effort to dress up for dinner each night in anticipation of the five-course gastronomic feast that awaits them. Twice a week dinner is laid out on the jetty complete with white table cloths, silver and candles. Guests choose between bedrooms in colonial-style houses or the palm-thatched rondavels set in the grounds surrounded by lush vegetation. All the rooms are spacious and have similar facilities including king-sized four-poster beds, large bathrooms with shower and toilet, tea and coffee-making facilities, a minibar, and either terrace or a veranda with a sea view, but I have talked to honeymooners who felt that the bungalows were less private during the day when other guests were using the beach. Doubles from US$271/Rs1350 bed and breakfast, and US$331/Rs1650 half board.

Go for the rooms at La Réserve on Praslin which are much bigger and more private than the beach huts where people walk past you all day long. We spent a few days at La Reserve to start off with which was lovely but by the end we'd had enough of all that incredible French food. We then moved on to Denis which was just like something out of Treasure Island, much less commercialised, fewer people and a wonderfully relaxed atmosphere. **Martin and Joanna Pryke**

The **Village du Pecheur** (☎ 232224, fax 232273), PO Box 372, Glacis, Mahé, is a very basic but informal and comfortable hotel in a wonderfully secluded location in the centre of Praslin's largest and most beautiful beach, Côte d'Or. For a slightly more

---

CHÂTEAU DE FEUILLES
(☎ 233316), Baie Sainte-Anne, Ile de Praslin, Seychelles
Reservations: Relais & Châteaux worldwide reservation numbers (see p12); or through the hotel's 'No Problem' office in Paris (France ☎ 1-43 27 99 30, fax 1-43 20 46 73)
Getting there: The hotel can arrange transfers from Mahé Airport via plane and taxi at a cost of FF600 per person return
Accommodation: 12 guest rooms: three standard rooms, two apartments, four bungalows, two mini suites, plus The Suite
Amenities: Swimming pool, excursions, restaurant, bar, laundry, hair-dryer in rooms, but no TV or air-conditioning
Dress code: Relaxed attire, guests dress up for dinner
Weddings: The hotel does not cater for weddings
Minimum stay: Five nights
Rates: Double rooms from US$277 FF1400 bed and breakfast in the standard rooms; apartments from US$340/FF1720 bed and breakfast; bungalows from US$394/FF1990 bed and breakfast; suites from US$447/FF2260 to US$499 FF2520 bed and breakfast
Credit cards: Not accepted, payment must be to the French office, see Reservations, in FF (traveller's cheques, Eurocheques and French cheques), half board is a supplement of US$47/FF240 per person per day
Taxes and service charge: Included

authentic island experience book into one of the four beach bungalows and you'll actually be living on the beach. They are simply furnished, but do have a king-size bed, shower, toilet and bidet, phone, mini-fridge and air-conditioning, so not that spartan!

Life is very relaxed at the Village, so although men are meant to wear trousers after 7pm, shoes are redundant from the moment you arrive. Guests enjoy the laidback 'house party' atmosphere of the buffet dinners, beach-side lunches, and hours spent lying back on the big cushioned chairs in the cosy bar. Doubles from US$130/Rs650 bed and breakfast and US$172/Rs855 half board in a garden room, and US$160/Rs800 bed and breakfast or US$202/Rs1005 half board in a beach bungalow.

A FEW THINGS TO SEE AND DO ON PRASLIN

Praslin is the second largest island in the Seychelles and is quieter than Mahé. It is a good base from which to visit some of the other islands via inexpensive ferries. Approximately 40 km north east of Mahé, Praslin is reached by boat in two hours or in just 15 minutes by plane. There is enough to see and do on Praslin and its nearby islands to keep most couples entertained for a week, so it makes a good initial destination.

Once the haunt of Arab traders and treasure houses for pirates, Praslin is the perfect tropical island. Much of the interior is virtually virgin forest: the **Vallée de Mai** is an 18-hectare area of dense forested woodland off the road between **Grand Anse** and **Baie Sainte-Anne**. One of the Seychelles' most famous natural beauty spots, the Vallée, now a World Heritage site, is home to hordes of different plant life: the strangely shaped

coco-de-mer, an enormous indigenous coconut resembling the female pelvis, inspired General Gordon to dub the region the original Garden of Eden when he visited the island just over a century ago. Such is the rarity and notoriety of the coco-de-mer, the fruit from an extraordinary palm tree found only in the Vallée and neighbouring **Curieuse Island**, that it has since become regarded as an aphrodisiac.

Make a point of eating out at **Les Roches**, Le Pointe one night, as the food and beach-side setting are truly excellent.

Ferries run from Praslin to neighbouring **Cousin Island**, a bird sanctuary, on Tuesdays, Thursdays and Fridays. This tiny island, spanning less than one kilometre, is home to just six people and quantities of exotic flora and fauna, including tortoises, turtle doves and turtles.

LA DIGUE
La Digue Island Lodge

La Digue Island Lodge is the best known of the many lodges and guests houses stretching out along the west coast of La Digue. Here the lifestyle is simple, giving guests a real taste of Seychellois life. Accommodation at the Lodge comes in all shapes and sizes: most of the 24 simply constructed 'A' frame chalets are right on the beach,

---

LA DIGUE ISLAND LODGE
(☎ 234233, fax 234100), La Digue, Seychelles
Reservations: Either direct with the hotel or through UK tour operators Elegant Resorts, Silk Cut Travel and Sunset Travel (see p10)
Getting there: A short schooner journey from Praslin, once on the island you'll be met by an ox cart
Accommodation: Four first floor suites, five ground floor suites, 24 A-frame chalets and nine Rondavels, eight rooms in the Yellow House, plus 10 rooms in the annexe
Amenities: Restaurant, poolside snack bar with swim-up seating, hotel bar, entertainment, barbecues, billiards, games room, reading room, TVs in the reading room and lounge, two boutiques, foreign exchange, local trips by private yachts
Dress code: Casual elegance
Weddings: Ceremonies can either be carried out by local registrar or by a priest on the beach or at a location of your choice; most people opt for the registrar as it involves less paper work; receptions can involve whatever you like and the hotel is well-equipped with a band, video, photographer etc all on hand
Minimum stay: Three nights
Rates: Doubles from US$190/Rs945 for a non-air-conditioned annexe, up to US$299/Rs1490 for a beach-front chalet and US$336/Rs1675 for a suite, all prices are for half board
Credit cards: Most major
Taxes and service charge: Included

A FEW THINGS TO SEE AND DO ON LA DIGUE

Half an hour by boat from Praslin, La Digue is a place of tranquillity, where ox-carts and rusty old bikes are the only form of local transport, and times seems to stand still.

La Digue is famous for two things: its superb beaches and its bizarrely shaped granite rock formations, resembling vast Henry Moore sculptures. Most of the wide deserted beaches are just perfect for long walks, swimming and snorkelling, but particularly beautiful are the beaches on the west coast, between **Pointe Cap Barbi** and **Anse Pierrot**, while the most incredible rock formations are at **Pointe Source d'Argent** and **Pointe St Jacques**, three quarters of the way down the west coast.

The best way to see them is to find yourself a bicycle, grab a picnic and head off for a gentle pedal around the island, which, measuring only 3km by 5km, is very easy and enjoyable to cycle around. Look out for the rare Black

Paradise Flycatcher in the island's woodlands: although it was once judged to be near extinction recent estimates put the number at over 100 living on the island.

There is a lovely trail following the coastline road south from the jetty at **La Passe**, which it is possible to do either on foot or by bicycle. You'll pass several old houses built in the architectural style of the French colonial era and continue inland across a broad plateau, through agricultural land and fresh-water marshland. The path then takes you up a relatively gentle climb through woodland and orchards before descending through farmland and marsh and eventually coming to the white beach of **Grand Anse**. This is a lovely easy walk which will take a couple of hours on foot, or an hour by bike. Stop for a picnic at Grand Anse before returning the way you came.

---

and nine rondavels (thatched huts) are set among the palm trees and are ideal for couples. There are also eight rooms and nine suites in the pale Yellow House, a converted plantation house set on the other side of the road from the Lodge. If you need mod cons then go for the suites which have air-conditioning, minibars, tiled bathrooms with bath and a separate shower, as well as a balcony looking out to Praslin. The A-frame chalets and rondavels are quite adequate for couples and come with showers and air-conditioning. Whichever room you opt for, the lodge welcomes honeymooners with fruit and flowers in your room and also decorates your bed.

The large open-air restaurant overlooks La Réunion beach, which lies to the front of the hotel and is ideal for long lazy days in the sun. Creole cuisine is taken very seriously at La Digue Lodge: the restaurant is simple but superbly built with a cool sandy floor and a lofty thatched and beamed roof. The swim-up bar enables you to spend long afternoons indulging in fabulous cocktails while keeping cool in the water. Snacks are also served here.

The Lodge is family run and the staff are quite happy to organise trips to neighbouring islands, as well as fishing and scuba diving in association with **Marine Divers International**. Take a trip around La Digue, enjoy some fishing, snorkel off the beach, watch the birds at **Cousin**, **Aride** or **Fregate** islands, or venture further afield on one of the Lodge's yachts. The beauty of staying on La Digue is that there's plenty to do if you choose to, while you can just as easily lie on the beach and do nothing.

DENIS ISLAND

Denis Island Lodge

Denis Island is the place if you want to get right away from any signs of mainstream tourists. The island lies on the Seychelles Bank where several record-breaking Dogtooth tuna and Bonito have been caught. A wonderfully French ambience pervades this 140-hectare coral island hideaway making it the sort of place where you kick off your shoes on arrival and don't bother finding them again until it's time to leave.

Guests stay in 24 pretty thatched beach huts laid out along this beautiful island's most sheltered beach with wonderful views over the ocean. The bungalows are large and extremely comfortable, comprising a spacious en suite bathroom with a bath and shower, a separate toilet, a simply and traditionally furnished bedroom area and a little veranda at the front of the bungalow which is just perfect for escaping the sun. Although the beds aren't huge, they are comfortable and look very pretty shrouded in mosquito netting. Only one bungalow and the lodge's only suite are fitted with air-conditioning; phones and fridges are available on request.

The caring attention of the staff is what makes people enjoy their stay at Denis so much. When you come back to your room at night, mosquito coils have been put out for you, all the shutters will have been closed, and the floor is continually being swept. Denis's guests always remark upon how immaculately clean the rooms are kept: your sheets are changed every other day and both beach and bathroom towels are changed daily.

During the day guests either make the most of the incredible snorkelling or venture out to sea either for scuba diving, or deep-sea fishing which is reputed to be world class. There are also hobie cats, a tennis court and lots of inland walks through the jungle. A walk around the island is a lovely way to spend 45 minutes but do watch out for the tides, as you may end up swimming if you misjudge them.

Denis's food is just amazing. Unless you order breakfast in bed all meals are taken in the main lodge, a huge and very beautiful open-sided thatched building where the lounge, bar and a TV room are also located. The house speciality is their Creole curries: they are absolutely delicious and are accompanied by lots of salads, marinated tuna and other tasty raw fish dishes. Lunch is a buffet, while waiters serve French cuisine in the evening. The only thing to watch out for is the wine which is ridiculously expensive all over the Seychelles, a quite ordinary bottle will cost a good US$35!

Denis is a privately owned island which, the owners state very clearly, they do not wish to turn into a hotel. As their brochure says: 'Our sole ambition is to enable you to accomplish a dream' – they seem to be doing this pretty well!

DENIS ISLAND LODGE
(☎ 321143, fax 321010), PO Box 404, Victoria, Seychelles
Reservations: Direct or through Indian Ocean resort specialists (see p10)
Getting there: 30-minute flight from the International Airport on Mahé on Tuesday, Thursday, Friday and Sunday departing Mahé approx 12.30pm, costing around US$220
Accommodation: 24 thatched bungalows and one two-bedroom suite
Amenities: Breakfast room service, restaurant, lounge, bar and TV room, scuba diving, snorkelling, windsurfing, sailing, tennis, billiards, table tennis, visits to other islands, deep-sea fishing
Dress code: Casual attire, but men are asked to wear long trousers in the lodge after 7.30pm
Weddings: Denis does not specialise in weddings, but they can be arranged, however it is not possible to host a reception at the lodge
Minimum stay: Three nights
Rates: The bungalows cost between US$495 and US$550 per couple per day full board; the suite costs an additional US$100
Credit cards: Visa, MasterCard, American Express
Taxes and service charge: Included

Other recommended hotels

Bird Island Lodge (☎ 323322, fax 323335), Bird Island, Seychelles, comprises 25 bungalows on a tiny island where a million sooty terns mate between May and September, and other unique bird life can be seen year round. Also home to Esmerelda, the world's largest land tortoise, this private island offers peace and tranquillity to a maximum of 50 guests. Each bungalow has its own patio overlooking the gardens, with the sea just a few steps across the glorious pink sandy beach. This is real *Blue Lagoon* stuff, with a few well-chosen luxuries such as the king-sized four-poster bed, ceiling fans, a lounge area and a large shower room, in each of the simply designed, but cool, bungalows. The hotel has an informal bar and a small restaurant serving Creole seafood, after which most guests choose to retire early. There really isn't much to do on Bird, apart from wallow in the splendid isolation of it all, have an occasional rummage through the well-thumbed books in the library, or wade out into the turquoise waters snorkel in hand. If you stay for just one night a double room costs US$401/Rs2000 full board, including return airfares from Mahé, but the rate goes down considerably the longer you stay.

SAILING AND DIVING IN THE SEYCHELLES

Sailing and yacht charters

If you're into sailing a few days' island hopping has to be one of the best ways of seeing these stunning islands. Within the Seychelles, **VPM Yacht Charters** (☎/fax 241682), Inter Island Quay, Mahé, offers both yachts and catamarans for either bare-boat or skippered charters, and even day excursions. Alternatively, two UK-based companies offer flexible packages which allow you to plan your own route for as many, or few, days as you like.

UK-based **Sunsail** (UK ☎ 01705-210345) has a base at Port Victoria on Mahé, from where they take guests to La Digue in the north and to the unspoilt anchorages of Mahé's coastline in the south. From Victoria they will sail you east to the group of islands near **St Anne Marine National Park** where 150 different species of reef fish, crabs and sea urchins jostle in the crystal clear waters. Then sail south on a gentle cruise **to Anse Royale**, where silver sands stretch on endlessly, or further down still to **Takamaka Bay**, sheltering among the Takamaka trees and the unbelievable solitude and tranquillity. Prices per person for three days on a 10m yacht start at around US$1392/£899 including flights from the UK and transfers.

Elegant Resorts (UK ☎ 01244-897888) also arranges charters on three different yachts: *High Aspect*, a 21m yacht offering luxury accommodation in four double cabins with en suite facilities; *Mbjui Mayi*, a luxurious 16m catamaran; and *Panayotis*, a comfortable 14m catamaran. Guests usually join the yacht at Mahé and can embark on either a five- or seven-day cruise around some of the Seychelles most spectacular and remote islands.

Diving

The warm waters and shallow inshore reefs attract a myriad of iridescent fish making the Seychelles the perfect spot for scuba diving, even if you haven't tried it before.

There are a number of dive centres where you can be trained by professionally qualified instructors who are members of the Association of Professional Divers. Most dive centres offer one day introductory courses starting with a tutorial explaining safety precautions and the effects of diving and followed by a session in the swimming pool, familiarising you with the equipment and techniques. Then, if you feel ready, you can experience the marvels of the Seychelles' reefs.

The centres also offer more intensive four-day PADI certification courses encompassing tutorials, pool training sessions, and four open water dives.

For more experienced divers, holding a PADI or otherwise internationally-recognised certificate and log book, there are lots of exciting dive sites further offshore and on the outer islands. Manta rays, pelagic fish, ancient shipwrecks and even the wreck of the ill-fated naval tanker, *Ennerdale*, are there to be explored.

It is possible to dive in the Seychelles at any time of year, but the sea can be rough between June and September when the southeast trade winds blow, cutting visibility back to between 10 and 15m, while temperatures can fall as low as 24°C. From December to February the wind blows from the north-west making the Victoria side of Mahé sheltered. The very best months for diving are April/May and October/November when the seas are calm, visibility can reach over 30m on offshore sites and the water temperature is more likely to be around 29°C.

Most of the dives are from boats, on hard coral reefs (like the Barrier Reefs) and granite reefs encrusted with soft coral formations.

Dive centres

Marine Divers International (☎ 247141), PADI 5* Centre, Berjaya Beau Vallon Bay Hotel, Mahé
Diables Des Mers Diving Centre (☎ 247104), Beau Vallon Beach, Mahé
Praslin Beach Watersports Centre (☎ 232222), Praslin Beach Hotel, Praslin
Underwater Centre Seychelles (☎ 247357), PADI 5* Centre, Coral Strand Hotel, Mahé
Underwater Centre Desroches (☎ 224003), PADI 5* Centre, Desroches Island
Rainbow Divers (☎ 261222), Northolme Hotel, Mahé
Speedy Aquatics Dive Centre (☎ 378451), Berjaya Mahé Beach Hotel, Mahé
La Digue Lodge Dive Centre (☎ 234232), La Digue Island Lodge (Note: this is not a member of the Association of Professional Divers Seychelles and may not operate to their standards)

Mauritius
(BEST TIME: APRIL TO JUNE, SEPTEMBER TO NOVEMBER)

People go to Mauritius for the beaches and their palm trees, white sands and warm waters, but most of all they go for the unrivalled reputation of this island's upmarket hotels.

If you dream of a honeymoon filled with every conceivable luxury in an idyllic beach setting then this large tropical island 1932km off the coast of Kenya was made for you. It has to be the ultimate destination for people looking to drop their bags on the bedroom floor and head straight for the beach cocktail in hand, safe in the knowledge that they won't have to leave the resort's gates for anything until it is time to go home.

With a coral reef almost completely surrounding the island, the waters of the lagoons are warm and tranquil, making them ideal for year round watersports and allowing the island's devotees to refer to it as the 'world's largest swimming pool'. It certainly is the ultimate Indian ocean playground for beachcombers, swimmers, sightseers, fishermen, scuba divers, surfers and all escapists.

Unusually for idyllic islands Mauritius also enjoys an enviable reputation for fine cuisine, due largely to the ethnic variety of its people: dishes are touched with African, Indian, French and Creole influences.

The standard of service and the facilities of the hotels featured here are so impeccable that if you are going to combine a week in Mauritius with anywhere else in the world, such as a South African safari or a week in the Seychelles, you'd better leave Mauritius to last as no other hotel is likely to compare favourably afterwards. Mauritius's gourmet fare and its superior night life, also mean that it is better to come here for your second week once you've had a chance to relax and are ready for a bit of sophistication. And make no mistake, Mauritius is all about style and sophistication: the kind of hotels you will encounter are summed up by one of the brochures to the island that advises visitors to 'take their best beach and casual wear' – these are not resorts for scruffy Bermudas!

MAURITIUS

An exotic Indian Ocean island which has become one of the world's ultimate honeymoon destinations largely due to its stylish, sophisticated resorts with their reputation for first rate accommodation, service, facilities and best of all, food

When to go: The best weather is between April and June and September to November, although afternoon showers can occur at any time of year in Mauritius; avoid November and March because of cyclones

Average maximum temperatures °C

JAN	FEB	MAR	APR	MAY	JUN	JUL	AUG	SEP	OCT	NOV	DEC
28	27	27	26	25	23	23	23	24	25	27	28

Capital: Port Louis
Flight times: to Port Louis from:
New York: (via Paris) 19 hours
LA: (via NY and Paris) 27 hours
London: 12 hours
Sydney: (via Perth) 14 hours
Approximate exchange rates: Mauritian rupees (Rs) £1 = Rs32; US$1 = Rs20, A$1 = R16.33
Time difference: GMT plus four hours
Voltage: 240v AC, 50 Hz; UK-type three-pin plugs
Combine with: The Seychelles, South Africa, Réunion, Paris
Country dialling code: ☎ 230

Le Saint Géran Hotel

Laid out among fragrant tropical gardens the Saint Géran is Sun International's flagship property in Mauritius. This world famous hotel has long been popular with honeymooners seeking sophistication and elegance in a superb beach-front location. From the moment you enter the magnificent gateway and spectacular hall with its superb curving arcades leading to the interior gardens, you know you are going to be cocooned in luxury, pomp and grandeur.

The hotel's facilities are just wonderful: a nine-hole golf course with its 4500 palm trees, extensive watersports, floodlit tennis courts and even a casino. The cooking of chef Mesh is reputed to be the best on the island.

The bedrooms are not over large but they are decorated in pastel tones with pale, limed furniture and they have a light, breezy feel. The huge beds are comfortable and are covered in flowers when you come back from dinner at night. All over the room there are pieces collected from every corner of the world: a wooden carved Thai head board, a Chinese painting on the TV cabinet, and woven patent leather chairs that apparently come from the Philippines. The bathrooms are full of pink marble, with all the expected trimmings, and although very elegant are a little on the small side. The ground floor rooms are so close to the beach that you can be in the water within a minute of getting out of bed.

The beach is wonderful, a huge long curve arching right around the hotel grounds and into the lagoon. The hawkers can be annoying, but that aside the beach is fabulous and the watersports facilities excellent.

The hotel is also cleverly designed so that all motorised watersports take place in the lagoon, ensuring that they don't impinge upon the peace of those relaxing by the poolside. Aside from the complimentary watersports there are five floodlit tennis courts and a nine-hole golf course, and plenty of peaceful corners for those who want to retire with a book.

A honeymoon at the Saint Géran is all about enjoying an idyllic beach setting while being totally enveloped in your own private world of luxury. You name it and you've got it at this hotel: oysters in the middle of the night, a lagoon trip at dawn, a massage under one of the palm trees, nipping into the new pastry shop for freshly baked hot rolls in the morning, a chilled glass of champagne in the privacy of your balcony as the sun

---

LE SAINT GÉRAN
(☎ 415 1825, fax 415 1983), Belle Mare, Mauritius

Reservations: Sun International offices worldwide (see p12) and all leading tour operators and travel agents worldwide

Getting there: The hotel can arrange transfers from the airport (60 minutes)

Accommodation: 175 guest rooms: 163 de luxe rooms, eight junior suites, two de luxe suites and two Presidential suites

Amenities: La Terrasse Restaurant main dining-room, Paul & Virginie Alfresco Restaurant à la carte restaurant, Le Badamier Alfresco restaurant, Les Cascades gastronomique restaurant, Pool Bar, Casino Bar, Paul & Virginie Bar, beach trolley, golf bar, evening entertainment, casino, nine-hole golf course, five tennis courts (floodlit), volley-ball, bocciball, aerobics, sauna, massage and beauty salon, shuttle service to Le Touessrok and Ile aux Cerfs, car hire, excursions, shopping arcade, table tennis, bicycles, yoga class and aqua gym, large swimming pool, full range of complimentary watersports including unlimited water-skiing, mainsails, hobie cats, laser sails, paddle boats, canoes, glass-bottom boats, snorkelling, small-game fishing and windsurfing; scuba diving, fun board sailing, sailing cruises, big game fishing and para-sailing charged locally

Dress code: Although there is no formal dress code, Le Saint Géran is a smart hotel and guests usually dress up for dinner, especially in the à la carte restaurant

Weddings: The hotel operates a strict policy of only one wedding per day, you can get married three working days after your arrival (the legal formalities are carried out in Port Louis and the ceremony at your chosen location at the hotel), prices vary according to requirements, but virtually anything can be arranged; there are no set limits for reception numbers

Minimum stay: None

Rates: De luxe doubles cost around US$213/Rs4300, junior suites cost US$335/Rs6759

Credit cards: Most major

Taxes and service charge: Taxes are included, service is discretionary

sets. Some might find the service and sheer abundance of facilities a little over the top – they even present you with a rose when they bring you breakfast in bed – but others will delight in the knowledge that they are being pampered by 400 people in one of the world's most luxurious hotels.

Le Touessrok & Ile aux Cerfs

Sister hotel to the Saint Géran, Le Touessrok is the more romantic of the two. Built on a small promontory on the eastern side of the island, the Touessrok epitomises the kind of honeymoon hotels that we all at some stage in our life have dreamt about.

Everywhere you look impossibly deep blue skies meet towering palm trees, dark, thatched roofs and whitewashed facades. Marble pathways span the shimmering waters of a swimming pool that circles around the various parts of the hotel so that wherever you look you can see turquoise water. Clichéd yes, but absolutely perfect.

The architect's imaginative use of the location is what makes the Touessrok such an incredible resort to stay in. Many of the rooms occupy their own private islet, connected to the rest of the hotel via foot bridges over the vast twisting swimming pool so that it feels as if you're in some sort of mini Venice; others are fanned out along the private beaches of the main island. The standard of the rooms does vary considerably: standard rooms have been redecorated recently with small marble bathrooms and limed oak furniture; the decor in the larger premier rooms is more dated featuring lots of dark wood and a wooden bathroom, but they are very spacious and are generally cool and light due to the white walls, plus they have a large lounge area and a balcony accessed through patio doors. All the rooms have private balconies with a sea view, private bath and shower, colour TVs, air-conditioning and minibars. With twice daily maid service you are assured of a constant stream of fresh towels and toiletries with the Sun International sea shell logo.

Honeymooners are greeted with a bottle of sparking wine and a plate of fresh fruit on arrival and are also given a free upgrade to the French restaurant **Les Paillotes**, and a sunset boat ride. Half board guests eat in the main restaurant, **La Passerelle**, where typical meals are a mixture of buffet and à la carte service and a blend of different styles. The local Mauritian food is spicy and really excellent, however there is a disappointing lack of sea food though the fresh fish from

---

LE TOUESSROK & ILE AUX CERFS
(☎ 419 2451, fax 419 2025), Trou d'Eau Douce, Mauritius
Reservations: Sun International offices worldwide (see p12) and most leading tour operators and travel agents
Getting there: The hotel can arrange transfers from the airport (55 minutes)
Accommodation: 200 guest rooms: 80 de luxe rooms; 79 premier rooms; 37 junior suites; one Coral suite; one York suite; one Princess suite and one Royal suite
Amenities: Four tennis courts (floodlit), pétanque, volley-ball, football, 1600 sq m of pool surface and a smaller pool on Ile aux Lièvres, free watersports including hobie cats, laser sails, windsurfers, paddle boats, canoes, water-skiing, snorkelling, glass-bottom boat trips, three beaches with snack and bar service, nightly entertainment, Le Sega Bar, Les Paillotes Bar, La Passerelle main dining-room, Giannino Italian restaurant, Les Paillotes à la carte restaurant, 24-hour room service, shops, sauna, beauty and massage salon, free shuttle bus to Le Saint Géran; Ilot Mangénie private island; Ile aux Cerfs private island with two more restaurants, a bar and beach service; deep-sea fishing, scuba diving, sailing cruises, para-sailing, pirogue hire and golf are all charged locally
Dress code: Although there is no formal dress code Le Touessrok is a smart hotel and guests usually dress up for dinner, especially in Les Paillotes
Weddings: The hotel operates a strict policy of only one wedding per day, you can get married three working days after your arrival in Mauritius (the legal formalities are carried out in Port Louis and the ceremony at your chosen location at the hotel), prices vary according to requirements, virtually anything can be arranged; there are no set limits for reception numbers
Minimum stay: None
Rates: Double rooms cost around US$194/Rs3900, junior suites around US$248/Rs5000
Credit cards: Most major
Taxes and service charge: Taxes are included, service is discretionary

the lagoon was good. In the evening the meals can consist of as many as six or seven courses which can be a bit of a marathon. Overall the service is faultless and breakfast, when served in the room, was always prompt and delicious.

The Tousserok is a beach lover's paradise, with four superb beaches dotted around the hotel which never seemed to be very busy and were usually quieter than at the Saint Géran. The hotel has two private islands: **Ilot Mangénie** which has amazing, uncluttered beaches and the **Ile aux Cerfs**, which is open to the public and offers a good selection of watersports.

We stayed at both Le Saint Géran and Le Tousserok, but Le Tousserok was definitely the more romantic of the two. It's spread out over a large area so it's easy to find peace and tranquillity. If you are looking for a beautiful setting with a mixture of luxury and privacy then go to the Tousserok. Le Saint Géran was very elegant and sophisticated, but the clientele was older and we felt it would be more suitable for silver weddings than honeymoons!' **Carolyn and Roger Reynolds**

Le Pirogue

Although not as glamorous as its sister properties, Le Pirogue has just undergone a thorough refurbishment and looks superb. The fact that it has a more laid-back atmosphere will no doubt appeal to a great number of readers, particularly those who don't find relaxation in a collar and tie.

Stretching across 14 hectares of immaculately tended tropical gardens along four kilometres of dazzling white beach, the hotel is perfectly designed with thatched high arched 'pirogue' bungalows spread out throughout the gardens to avoid any crowding. La Pirogue is a popular hotel with families, so don't go if the mere sight of children will annoy you, but it does mean that it has a much more convivial atmosphere and is a lot less pretentious than its sister hotels.

Of the 180 rooms, 40 are Superior and two are Royal suites. All the rooms are lovely, light and airy, with air-conditioning, minibar, en suite bath and shower, in-house video, TV, radio and a terrace. The superior rooms and suites are much more spacious and are located in detached cottages right next to the beach.

Le Pirogue is Mauritius's third Sun International property and as such it has the same tremendous range of facilities as its sister hotels. There is absolutely everything you could possibly dream of doing: easy going glass-bottom boat trips and snorkelling; windsurfing, water-skiing, kayaking, laser sailing and para-sailing for the

---

LE PIROGUE
(☎ 453 8441, fax 453 8449), Wolmar, Flic en Flac, Mauritius
Reservations: Sun International offices worldwide (see p12) and all leading tour operators and travel agents
Getting there: The hotel can arrange transfers from the airport (50 minutes)
Accommodation: 248 guest rooms: 20 Standard Communicating, 180 Standard, 46 Superior, plus two Royal Suites
Amenities: Films, video, games, miniclub, ships, hair and beauty salon, laundry and dry cleaning, car hire, excursions, La Terrasse restaurant main dining-room, Paul & Virginie Restaurant, Pool side snack service and afternoon tea, La Terrazza pizza and pasta restaurant, Pool Bar, Casino Bar, Paul & Virginie Beach Bar, Beach Bar Trolley service, nightly entertainment, 24-hour room service, six tennis courts (floodlit), complimentary watersports including water-skiing, laser sailing, paddle boats, kayaks, glass-bottom boats, snorkelling, windsurfing; scuba diving, big-game fishing and para-sailing are charged locally
Dress code: Although there is no formal dress code most guests do dress up for dinner
Weddings: The hotel operates a strict policy of only one wedding per day, you can get married three working days after your arrival in Mauritius (the legal formalities are carried out in Port Louis and the ceremony at your chosen location at the hotel), prices vary according to requirements, but virtually anything can be arranged; there are no set limits for reception numbers
Minimum stay: None
Rates: Double rooms cost around US$124/Rs2500, Royal Suite costs US$397/Rs8000
Credit cards: Most major
Taxes and service charge: Taxes are included, service is discretionary

more active; land-based activities such as pétanque, aerobics and tennis; and La Pirogue's big two, scuba diving and big-game fishing for which this island is so famous. All are complimentary apart from para-sailing, diving and big-game fishing.

There are lots of dining options to choose from: breakfasts and barbecues at **La Terrasse**, fresh seafood at **Paul et Virginie**, Italian pizzas and pasta at **La Terrazza** for lunch, themed buffets, typical Mauritian fare and even Chinese dishes.

If you are looking for somewhere a little less formal, would like to feel you are actually in Mauritius and love doing things during the day but don't want to compromise on service or location, this is the Mauritian hotel for you.

Royal Palm

I have spoken to honeymooners who spent their first week at the Saint Géran and then moved on to the Royal Palm and definitely preferred the latter. The only Mauritian member of The Leading Hotels of the World chain, the Royal Palm is a truly first-class resort, continually laying claim to its reputation as the Indian Ocean's finest hotel. Obviously it depends on what you are looking for in a resort. Some British couples said they found the Royal Palm a bit too 'Royal', rather smart, plush and almost too grown up; others loved it.

Situated on a perfect beach in the north west of the island close to fashionable and more developed **Grand Baie**, the Royal Palm is a true 'resort' hotel. It is the sort of place where people come to be seen, armed with the hotel's own mobile phones designed to make ordering room service from the beach that bit easier, and where five out of the first seven sentences in the brochure end in an exclamation mark (!).

This stylish and sophisticated haven is a harmonious blend of stone, thatch and wood and is located right on the edge of a lagoon. The hotel's 82 rooms are set in manicured gardens, all are sea-facing with their own balcony, private bathroom with separate shower and toilet, sitting area with radio, TV and video channel, minibar, in-room safe, hairdryer, and individually controlled air-conditioning. The dark polished wood in the bedrooms provides a distinctly colonial atmosphere and all rooms have a private terrace where the tasteful wooden furniture makes it the perfect place to sit out for breakfast.

The Royal Palm's two à la carte restaurants, **La Goelette** and **Le Surcouf**, offer truly fantastic cuisine which has earned them their place among the island's best. The evening entertainment is quiet and discreet allowing you to enjoy your tranquil candlelit dinner in peace. In fact, this is a very quiet hotel in the evenings, but there are other restaurants and night-clubs not far away, or you could take a taxi to sister hotel **Trou aux Biches** only ten minutes away.

As part of the Beachcomber Hotels, guests of the Royal Palm are permitted to use facilities at the group's five other properties on the island which is a real advantage as it's lovely to drive round the island stopping for lunch at another fantastic hotel.

ROYAL PALM
(☎ 263 8353, fax 263 8455), Grand Baie, Mauritius
Reservations: Beachcomber Hotels and Tours (UK ☎ 01483-33008), The Leading Hotels of the World reservation numbers worldwide (see p12)
Getting there: The hotel can arrange transfers from the airport
Accommodation: 82 guest rooms in total: 66 de luxe rooms, four junior suites, three garden suites, eight senior suites and one Royal Suite
Amenities: Two à la carte restaurants, 24-hour room service, swimming pool, water-skiing, windsurfing, sailing, deepsea fishing, tennis, golf practice, hairdresser, sauna, massage, boutique, snooker; plus use of all other Beachcomber hotels' facilities in Mauritius
Dress code: Smart casual
Weddings: Beachcomber has a policy that only one wedding a day can take place in each of its six resorts, giving the event much less of a packaged production line feel, they can arrange anything you want
Minimum stay: None
Rates: Double rooms from around US$467/Rs9400, suites from around US$968/Rs19,500
Credit cards: Most major
Taxes and service charge: Not included

A FEW THINGS TO SEE AND DO ON MAURITIUS

Apart from lounging around under a palm tree and other beach-based activities there really isn't that much to do in Mauritius; it really is a resort based honeymoon. All the hotels featured here have an impressive range of sport and leisure facilities including tennis, watersports, sailing, cruises, scuba diving, deep-sea fishing and golf, which should keep you occupied for most of your stay and when you fancy a change hire a car for a day and drive around the island.

White Sand Tours (☎ 208 5424, fax 208 8524) offer a good selection of excursions, such as the day-long **Romance of the South** and **Romance of the North** tours. The southern tour includes **Trou-aux-Cerfs**, an extinct volcano crater, **Curepipe**, the sacred Hindu lake in the **Grand Bassin**, and the waterfalls and seven-coloured earths of **Chamarel**. The **Pamplemousse Gardens**, which have a large collection of indigenous and exotic plants, form part of White Sand Tours' northern tour, along with a boat trip to Grand Baie for lunch.

Another great boat tour is a day on *Isla Mauritia*, a lovely old schooner built in 1852, which now takes guests out for day sails stopping off for a picnic lunch; with music provided by the crew you might find this a bit tacky.

If you want to hire your own car, make sure you drive up to Chamarel as, apart from the beautiful scenery, there are some great restaurants up there. Try *Le Chamarel* (☎ 683 6421), a lovely airy French restaurant right up in the mountains with gorgeous views down to the sea, or *Le Domino* (☎ 683 6675) in **Le Monde** right up at the top of the mountain.

The best places to shop in Mauritius are at the market at **Port Louis**, the island's capital and main port, and at Curepipe, the main residential town; it has a good shopping area and is a fine place to escape the heat. Worthwhile buys include saris, silk shirts, basket work, pottery, wood-carvings and locally made jewellery – look out for the intricate models of 18th and 19th century sailing vessels which are crafted at Curepipe. If you do buy textiles it is worth getting something made up while you are there as local dressmakers can easily rustle something up in 24 hours.

For enthusiastic photographers looking to capture an insight into island life it's worth getting up early and driving to one of the many salt farms near the island's main beaches: the local workers come to collect salt once the sea water has evaporated.

Le Meridien Paradise Cove

Le Meridien Paradise Cove stands beside a secluded sandy cove at the north end of the island and is set in four hectares of landscaped gardens. It is a charming hotel which is owned by the Forte group and is Mauritius's only member of the prestigious Small Luxury Hotels of the World.

Le Meridien Paradise Cove is the smallest of all the properties featured in this chapter with only 64 air-conditioned rooms, so you'll never find too many people on the beach and will always be able to find a lounger around the lovely swimming pool. Its secluded location and the limited number of residents mean Le Meridien Paradise Cove is a perfect place to get away from it all in unspoilt and unpretentious surroundings. The hotel-keeping is impeccable, guests are always greeted by name and are treated pretty much as though they own the place.

Guests are accommodated in one and two-storey traditional Mauritian-style buildings clustered around the brilliant blue bay. All the buildings face the lagoon and have a terrace or a balcony and direct access to the beach. Each room has a TV with video channels, minibar, music system, en suite bathroom with hair-dryer and separate shower,

LE MERIDIEN PARADISE COVE
(☎ 262 7983, fax 262 7736), Anse Le Raie, Cap Malheureux, Mauritius
Reservations: Small Luxury Hotels of the World toll free reservation numbers worldwide (see p12), plus most leading tour operators and travel agents worldwide
Getting there: Taxis from the airport take about 25 minutes and cost approximately US$15
Accommodation: 64 rooms
Amenities: Outdoor swimming pool, tennis, heli-pad, free sports facilities including water-skiing, windsurfing, kayaking, snorkelling, hobie cats and glass-bottomed boat trips, while deep-sea fishing and scuba diving can be arranged at local prices, two restaurants, beach bar/restaurant, pool bar, cocktail bar
Dress code: Choice of informal or formal dining in the two restaurants
Weddings: No
Minimum stay: Two nights
Rates: Doubles from US$145
Credit cards: Most major
Taxes and service charge: Included

and a separate lounge area with two chairs and a low table. In tune with the decor around the hotel, the bedrooms are furnished with an appealing mixture of bright sunny colours and peaceful cream walls and solid, comfortable furnishings.

The hotel has three restaurants and two bars: the intimate thatched pavilions of **La Cocoteraie** on the shore line where delicious seafood is served in a casual environment, **Le Beach Bar** which provides light lunches and daytime snacks as well as being a bar, **La Belle Creole** restaurant which enjoys sweeping views over the lagoon and neighbouring islands. The cocktail bar and lounge is somewhat ridiculously named **Le Cosy Corner**! The watersports facilities are similarly extensive.

Only 8km away is fashionable Grand Baie, but you'll probably find days slip past very pleasantly at Le Meridien Paradise Cove without going anywhere else.

Réunion
(BEST TIME: APRIL TO NOVEMBER)

Réunion is not a place for a beach holiday but it is a truly spectacular island with wonderful opportunities for touring by four-wheel drive, and hiking. If you're both keen travellers and enjoy walking through breathtaking valley gorges and generally getting away from the tourist crowds, a four-day detour from either nearby Mauritius or the Seychelles provides the perfect contrast to a beach holiday. Because the hotel accommodation is so superior in Mauritius, it's best to do this tour first and then head to Mauritius for some pampering and a good flop on the beach.

Lying 193km west of Mauritius and only 40 minutes away by air, Réunion is very similar in size but totally different in terrain and it has less than half the population of Mauritius. The dramatic landscapes of Réunion are truly spectacular, with primeval rain forests, crashing surf on a rocky coastline, stunning valley gorges, cascading waterfalls and a semi-active volcano.

The best way to see Réunion is to hire a car and do a three or four-day tour around the island. The driving is easy, though inevitably some mountain roads need to be taken carefully. If you are booking from the UK a number of tour operators offer four-night self-drive tours of the island costing around £500 a head including flights from Mauritius: talk to Sunset Travel, Abercrombie & Kent and Silk Cut Travel (see p9). Work out a tour that takes in the following places:
• **Salazie** 'cirque' and the famous **Voile de la Mariée** waterfall
• **Piton de la Furnaise** volcano
• The lunar surface of **Plaines des Cafres** and **Vingt Septième**
• Drive up to **cirque de Cilaos** through the narrow and picturesque route along **Gorges du Bras de Cilaos** and stay at the charming **Le Vieux Cep** (☎ 262-317189, fax 262-317768), one of the most romantic hotels in Réunion; while you're there visit the thermal spa at **Cilaos**, up some 4000ft
• Relax in one of the lovely beach resorts on the west coast of **Boucon Canot**

Madagascar
(BEST TIME: APRIL TO OCTOBER)

If you are looking for something a little different Madagascar, known as the great red island because of the red hues of its undulating landscape, has to be one of the most exciting countries to visit. It is very definitely a place for travellers not tourists, for those who are interested in wildlife, mountainous scenery and the environment, rather than seeking out sandy beaches – not that Madagascar is lacking in beautiful beaches.

Most people get Madagascar confused with the Seychelles, the Maldives and Mauritius but, while it is close to Mauritius, it couldn't be less like these other islands. The most incredible thing about Madagascar is its size – it is the world's fourth largest island, more than twice the size of Britain with half of the population of London. You couldn't possibly feel claustrophobic here.

To make it even better Madagascar has, so far, remained largely untouched by tourism. There's plenty to explore in the stunning mountain landscapes, dense tropical vegetation, and breathtaking coastline. Many of the 200,000 species of flora and fauna are unique to the island, as are the 29 species of lemur with their long tails and feline features. Being relatively new to tourism, hotel development is in the early stages in Madagascar so don't go expecting fluffy white bathrobes or hair-dryers in every room.

Hire a car and do a three or four-day tour around the island taking in:
• **Fort Dauphin** and **Portuguese Islet** where the fort dates back to 1504
• **Berenty Reserve** via **Lac Anony**, spend the day in the forest reserve looking at the lemurs
• Spend Friday at the famous **Zoma market** in **Antananarivo** ('Tana') followed by lunch at **Le Carousel** and visit the botanical gardens, the **Queen's Palace** and the royal palace at **Ambohimanga**
• **Périnet Reserve** to discover the indri lemur, the largest of the species
• **Lake Mantasoa**
• Have a few days relaxing at the **Ile Sainte Marie** or on **Nosy Be** island off the north west coast

The Comores
(BEST TIME: MAY TO OCTOBER)

Situated in the Indian Ocean is the little known Comore archipelago, where lush green scenery is surrounded by deserted white sandy beaches and turquoise seas. The Comores are known as the Perfume Islands, renowned for almost five hundred years for their cinnamon, vanilla, clove and ylang-ylang essence, which form the base of the world's best perfumes.

Legend has it that King Solomon scoured these islands for the throne of the Queen of Sheba, which was supposedly hidden in the Karthala volcano, leading to the belief that ancient Israelites were the islands' earliest settlers. Not much has changed here, so if you are lovers of unspoilt white sandy beaches, exotic local cultures, and stunning

---

THE COMORES
Little known tropical islands offering some of the most spectacular diving in the world
When to go: May to October
Average maximum temperature °C

JAN	FEB	MAR	APR	MAY	JUN	JUL	AUG	SEP	OCT	NOV	DEC
30	30	30	30	29	28	27	27	27	29	31	31

Capital: Moroni, Grand Comore
Flight times: to Moroni from:
      New York: (via Johannesburg) 18 hours
      LA: (via NY and Johannesburg) 26 hours
      London: (via Paris) 18 hours
      Sydney (via Melbourne and Dubai) 16 hours
Approximate exchange rates: Comore Franc (KMF); £1 = KMF599.20; US$1 = KMF386.33; A$1 = KMF305.29
Time difference: GMT plus three hours
Voltage: 220v AC, 50 Hz, plugs with two square pins
Combine with: Mauritius, Réunion, South Africa, Madagascar, the Seychelles
Country dialling code: ☎ 269

scenery (including the world's tallest coconut groves and the largest volcanic crater), you'll love these barely discovered islands.

Over 2.5 million palm trees cloak the islands providing drink, food, construction materials, fuel, and copra, which is exported. Animal life is similar to nearby Madagascar, with the Indian mongoose effectively ensuring that there are no snakes.

The diving was unbelievable. Both Malcolm and I have done a lot of diving around the world, but we were hugely impressed with The Comores. Malcolm swam with dolphins which must have been great.
Malcolm and Jess Wren

One of the key attractions of The Comores is the scuba diving that the coral reefs provide. The diving here is virtually unbeatable, and somehow manages to suit all standards, from the novice who can shallow dive on the local house reefs, to the expert who will enjoy night dives and great wreck dives further afield. The tropical seas are teeming with fish of all species from wahoos, to marlin, bonito, groupers, rays, dolphins, turtles and sharks.

Four islands make up the Comore archipelago: **Grand Comore**, **Anjouan**, **Moheli** and **Mayotte**. All of them are situated in the Mozambique channel between northern Madagascar and the east African coast. As a result of their positioning, the islands are a mix-match of cultures; their people a combination of Arab, African and Malagasy, many of whom were brought over from Africa as slaves. Arabic and French are the principal languages, although hotels and most craft-sellers can speak English.

DIVING IN THE COMORES

Beginners usually start with underwater dives of around 12m to get them used to using the equipment confidently and safely. If you've never been diving before, you'd be hard pushed to find a better place to learn. The water is warm and crystal clear, the exotic fish are absolutely unbelievable and the whole experience of being part of a totally different, unexplored world is quite incredible. You don't need to worry about sharks, or any of the fish coming too close, as once you are down below with them, you become part of the whole ocean world and most species just swim straight past, ignoring you.

Just ten minutes north of the Galawa Hotel is **Tsada Beach**, from where you can dive at Coral Gardens, Treasure Cove and Castle Rock.

Qualified divers go to Msanga Drift, Oasis, Parrot Point, the Mosque, Black Coral Cove, Hahaya Wall near the airport and the Coelacanth and President's Palace at Moroni.

A **wreck dive** on the *Masiwa*, an old North Sea fishing boat, and night dives are also available.

One particularly magnificent dive is in the ocean 35km west of Moroni at **Banque Valheil**.

GRAND COMORE

The largest of the four coral islands, Grand Comore has lush green vegetation, dramatic volcanic peaks and endless palm-fringed beaches. The island is dominated by the Karthala volcano, the outline of which can be seen from 100km away. Standing over 2km high, it has the largest crater of any active volcano in the world.

Le Galawa Beach Hotel

Le Galawa Beach Hotel and Casino is *the* place to stay in The Comores. Nestling among giant coconut and baobab trees, the hotel has been carefully designed so as not to spoil its stunning location and is split into various sections, so although it is bigger than most of the hotels in this book, with 182 rooms, there is a feeling of space.

The hotel is named after the galawas, the local canoes with side-hanging outriggers, which are used by islanders for almost all of their fishing. Hewn from the trunk of a single tree they are surprisingly light and manoeuvrable.

Managed by the Sun International chain, which is renowned for its personalised service and comfort, Le Galawa Beach is on Grand Comore's northern coast at **Mitsamiouli**, along one of the island's most splendid beaches. It is very much a modern, resort hotel but because it is well appointed and informal, it doesn't feel overwhelming or impersonal.

The rooms are located in two long arms spreading out from the main body of the hotel, which means that each room faces the beach giving you a good view of the wonderful sunsets each night. All have bath, TV/video, tea and coffee-making facilities, air-conditioning, phone, radio and lounge area.

The main part of the hotel houses a large open-sided dining-room, which never feels crowded. Dinner alternates between table service and a buffet, both of which are excellent. The Comorans love dancing, and after dinner there is some type of 'themed entertainment', which later turns into a disco. Honeymooners I have spoken to said that all of this was very easily avoided!

The key to The Comores is their fantastic watersports. While you can quite happily laze around on the many beautiful beaches all day, the islands were made for couples who like to get out and about on, and especially under, the water.

As well as the swimming pool, which is just metres from the beach and has its own pool bar, there is complimentary tennis, plus fishing, sailing, para-sailing, volley-ball,

LE GALAWA BEACH HOTEL
(☎ 73-8118/9, fax 73-82 51), PO Box 1027, Moroni, Grande Comore
Reservations: Direct through Sun International's worldwide offices (see p12) and most leading travel agents worldwide (see p9-12)
Getting there: 40 minutes from the airport by taxi, or the hotel can arrange transfers
Accommodation: 182 double bedded rooms in two and three-storey buildings set in a crescent shape
Amenities: Casino, large swimming-pool, restaurant with theme evenings, boutique, pharmacy, free watersports include sailing, water-skiing, windsurfing, snorkelling, canoes, pedaloes, plus volley-ball, badminton, table tennis and floodlit tennis; diving and deep-sea fishing are available for a fee
Dress code: Informal
Weddings: A foreigner may obtain a legal marriage certificate in The Comores, although it is not possible to have a religious ceremony as there is no priest there; the hotel caters for receptions as small or grand as you like
Minimum stay: None
Rates: Doubles from around US$168/KMF850; suites from around US$336/KMF1700 on a half board basis
Credit cards: Most major
Taxes and service charge: Not included

canoeing, and best of all, scuba diving. You don't have to be a qualified diver in order to experience the many wonderful sights below the ocean's surface, as Le Galawa Beach has its own resort courses which enable you to do some spectacular dives.

A FEW THINGS TO SEE AND DO ON GRAND COMORE

It's worth taking a visit into Grand Comore's capital city, **Moroni**, with its old Arab Medina quarter, ancestral mosques, craft market and African customs. Take a walk through the narrow streets and winding alleys to the old waterfront, where you can watch the dhows move containers and cargo to and fro. Women would be advised to cover their shoulders and knees if you go into town, to respect local tradition, although the more stringent codes of Islamic dress have now largely fallen away in the Comores.

If you want to climb the **Karthala Volcano** and are sufficiently fit, find a guide at **M'Vouni**, but only go in the dry season between April and November. It takes about seven hours to get to the top, so you'll have to take a tent with you and stay up for the night. Alternatively

do a five-hour walking tour of the lower slopes past guava, banana and spice plantations. Both the full climb and the tour of the lower slopes can be arranged through **Tourism Services Comoros** (☎ 73-3044, fax 73-1533) once you're on the island or before you leave through the company's overseas operators in the UK (contact Dendy Barker on UK ☎ 0171-630 9490), in Australia (Leila Fiedler on Australia ☎ 2-368 1811, fax 2-358 5305), in Japan (Terry Inoue on Japan ☎ 03-3359 2390, fax 03-3359 2396), and the USA (Jean Walden on US ☎ 941-387-0027, fax 941-387-0028). Tourism Services Comoros offer a whole range of tours from shopping in Moroni and nature walks through the primary rain forest in the north of the island, to a full day tour of the island including a beach picnic and a visit to a ylang ylang distillery.

England
(BEST TIME: ALL YEAR ROUND)

In 1804, William Blake wrote of England's green and pleasant land in a poem, *Jerusalem*, which has since been adopted as an English anthem, every bit as much as *Land of Hope and Glory*, or even *God Save the Queen*.

Although almost two centuries have passed since Blake was writing, much of the English countryside remains unchanged. The England of historic stately homes set in rolling green pastures, cream teas in quaint tea shops and roast beef served in front of roaring log fires on a Sunday is still very much in existence. If you are both lovers of old-world living, history and culture, then you'll enjoy exploring the ancient cities of **Oxford** and **Cambridge**, **Bath**, **Cheltenham** and **York**, and the countless picturesque 16th and 17th century villages, scattered throughout this 'green and pleasant land'.

A honeymoon in England can be romantic whether it's winter, spring, summer or autumn, with different, quintessentially English things to do during each of the seasons. England in the spring is a place where new-born lambs cavort on the Yorkshire Dales and wild yellow daffodils line the road side.

The summer really is all about clotted cream teas served on immaculately mown lawns, with a game of croquet to follow; picnics washed down with jugs of cider in buttercup fields looking down on the Cornish coast; and the wonderful English summer sporting calendar including Ascot Races, rowing at Henley and, of course, tennis at Wimbledon.

The Lake District is the place to be in the autumn; once the crowds have gone you'll be left virtually alone with the rolling hills and stunning lakeland scenery as the trees turn a thousand different hues of red and gold.

If you can cope with the cold, then winter is arguably the best season of all to experience the English countryside: enjoy long frosty walks in the New Forest until you stumble across a 16th century pub for lunch and revel in the warm welcome inside as you settle down in front of a roaring log fire with a pint of beer and a steaming dish of steak and kidney pie. Bliss.

ENGLAND
Rolling countryside peppered with ancient castles and historic houses, beautiful cities such as York and numerous small villages to explore
When to go: All year round: summer is from June to September, winter from December to the end of March; rain is possible in any season
Average maximum temperatures °C (London)

JAN	FEB	MAR	APR	MAY	JUN	JUL	AUG	SEP	OCT	NOV	DEC
4	4	6	8	11	14	16	16	14	11	7	5

Capital: London
Flight times: to Heathrow from:
      New York: $7^1/_2$ hours
      LA: 11 hours
      Sydney: $21^1/_2$ hours
Approximate exchange rates: Pound sterling (£): US$1 = £0.64, A$1 = £0.51
Time difference: GMT (plus one hour from the last Sunday in March to the last Sunday in October)
Voltage: 240v AC, 50 Hz; three-pin plugs
Combine with: Ireland, the rest of Europe
Country dialling code: ☎ 44

Most of the hotels I have included here were originally country houses and were built two or three centuries ago: thus they have great character and a charm all of their own. But one word of warning, don't go to the country houses of Yorkshire, Devonshire, or the New Forest expecting to find vast bedrooms. Almost without exception the rooms in these hotels are quite small having been built so long ago and it is strictly forbidden by English law to alter the features of these 'listed' buildings. So try to look upon the size of the rooms not as a fault of the hotel, but instead as part of its charm.

LONDON

Claridge's

Claridge's is, in my mind, the most romantic of the capital's leading hotels. For almost one hundred years it has been used as a pied à terre by foreign royalty, diplomats and some of England's most distinguished families. Despite its size, the hotel still manages to make its guests feel as if they are part of a bygone age of elegance and refinement.

Claridge's has undergone some considerable refurbishment over the last year, with well-known designers such as John Stefanides and Tessa Kennedy brought in to give the suites a facelift. The results are stunning. Claridge's policy of repairing rather than replacing furniture means that the art deco furnishings in the rooms are authentic. From the moment you enter the glistening lobby with its black and white chequered flooring and ornate mirrors you will feel more like you've arrived in a museum than a hotel.

The magnificent Egyptian suite is just one of the hotel's fabulous newly decorated suites. Bigger than most flats in London it has an entrance hall, two entrance doors, a large sitting-room, an even bigger bedroom, a separate dressing-room, a separate toilet and a lovely bathroom. Adorned with clever paint techniques in deep greens and reds, with richly upholstered sofas to match and art deco lamps and other ornaments scattered throughout, the suite is truly amazing. Over half the suites also have real working fireplaces, which you'll find welcome if you are there in the winter.

All the rooms at Claridge's come with the sort of amenities that in many hotels are reserved for the best suites: air-conditioning, luxurious bathrooms with huge drench showers, bathrobes, slippers, heated towel rails, hair-dryers and full-sized bottles of Floris toiletries, satellite television, in-room safes, refrigerators with fully-stocked bars, two phone lines, modem and fax line, old-fashioned Roberts radio, as well as Claridge's famous push button room and maid service.

CLARIDGE'S
(☎ 0171-629 8860, fax 0171-499 2210), Brook Street, Mayfair, London W1A 2QJ, England
Reservations: From the US toll free (☎ 1-800-63-SAVOY); The Leading Hotels of the World toll free reservation numbers worldwide (see p12)
Getting there: 45 minutes from Heathrow Airport by taxi (around £25); by airport bus (around £8); and by underground (around £5); one hour from Gatwick Airport which has trains running into Victoria Station every 15 minutes; Bond Street is the nearest underground station
Accommodation: 198 rooms including 60 suites
Amenities: Dinner and dancing in the restaurant on Friday and Saturday nights, Smorgasbord buffets in the Causerie, drinks and coffee etc in the Foyer, the Reading Room serves morning coffee and afternoon tea; 24-hour room service, ladies and gentlemen's hair and beauty salons, overnight complimentary shoeshine, complimentary newspaper each morning, Japanese breakfast available from room service and in the Restaurant, laundry and dry cleaning service, twice-daily maid service, theatre desk, travel desk, florist; the hotel can arrange for residents who have a handicap to play golf at the world famous Wentworth Club free of charge
Dress code: Jacket and tie are required in the restaurants at lunch and dinner
Weddings: Claridge's has a wedding licence and will suggest locations for weddings and receptions
Minimum stay: None
Rates: Superior doubles from US$372 £240; junior suite US$604/£390
Credit cards: Most major
Taxes and service charge: 17.5% Value Added Tax (VAT) will be added, service is included

It is the thoughtful details that make Claridge's such a special hotel: there is always a lobby between your bedroom door and the corridor to cut out the noise. The beds are made especially by the Savoy Bedworks Company, they are covered in real Irish linen and will be remade whatever time of day you take a nap. In addition, liveried footmen come to your table in the foyer to take your drink orders, just as if you were staying in a private English country house in the 19th century.

The other main reason I rate Claridge's above its competitors is its position. Brook Street intersects Bond Street, where London's most famous designers, auctioneers and jewellery shops are found, not to mention scores of first-class restaurants. You are only minutes away from Oxford Street, Piccadilly, Regent Street and Soho.

Dorset Square Hotel

Dorset Square Hotel has to be one of the most special hotels in London. As you enter this pretty garden square, once the site of Thomas Lord's original cricket ground, and enter the lovely old fashioned entrance hall the tranquillity of the place envelopes you.

DORSET SQUARE HOTEL

(☎ 0171-723 7874, fax 0171-724 3328), 39/40 Dorset Square, London NW1, England

Reservations: Small Luxury Hotels of the World toll free reservation numbers worldwide (see p12)

Getting there: The hotel will arrange transfers from London's international airports; it is situated between Marylebone and Baker Street underground stations

Accommodation: 37 rooms: including one four-poster, eight coronet doubles, two junior suites with king-sized beds, 19 doubles, and seven singles, all en suite

Amenities: The Potting Shed restaurant and bar, 24-hour room service, drawing-room with honesty bars, key to Dorset Square gardens, all double rooms have air-conditioning, easy access to Regent's Park for jogging, walking, open-air theatre, and ten minutes from London's main shopping centres

Dress code: Informal

Weddings: No ceremonies, but lots of wedding receptions (about one a month because the hotel is so close to the famous Marylebone Registry Office)

Minimum stay: None

Rates: Doubles from US$178/£115; luxury doubles from US$209/£135; four-poster and junior suites are US$263/£170

Credit cards: Most major (except Diners Club)

Taxes and service charge: 17.5% VAT not included, 10% charged on food and beverage bills

---

The staff are all young, very unpretentious and friendly, and make a point of showing you the hotel's small and cosy lounge with its honesty bar on the way to your room. This lovely little hotel is a complete contrast to the big, flashy international hotels around London's Park Lane and makes a perfect place to come 'home' to after a hard day's sightseeing.

The bedrooms at Dorset Square are absolutely heavenly, the curtains have that reassuring thickness, the sofa is small but comfortable, the bed high up off the ground and covered in huge square pillows – all the bedroom trimmings and the large white fluffy towels in the bathroom are luxurious, but at the same time quietly understated. If you want a serene base in this fast-moving city, then make Dorset Square your home for a few days and you'll long to come back again and again.

If you can afford it ask for room No 202, or any of the coronet double bedrooms. Room No 202 is my favourite with its pretty terracotta and faded-green furnishings complementing the beautiful antique oak wardrobe, coffee table, wash-stand, bedside tables and the sturdy four-poster bed. It's a wonderful place to kick off your shoes and relax in old-style London and comfortable surroundings.

All bedrooms have two phones, TV, radio, hair-dryer, an assortment of books, air-conditioning, gas fireplace, and a sofa. The bathrooms are great with marble, mirrors, shiny china basins, chrome taps and low-voltage spotlights, reminding you that although you are staying in a restored Regency home the mod cons are thoroughly up to date.

We had breakfast in bed, served on an old wooden tray brimming over with croissants, toast and fruit and great fresh coffee (you can have the full-English breakfast if you want). Meals are also served in the **Potting Shed Restaurant and Bar** in the hotel's basement: despite being in the basement this has a surprisingly light and informal feel due to the garden-like decor and a large sky-light. The food at Dorset Square is definitely recommended, there's nothing pretentious about it because it, too, is designed to make you feel at home not intimidated. If you ask for a bowl of pasta they ask what kind of sauce you would like and will offer to make anything, and the dishes are very sensibly priced for central London – even if you don't eat dinner in the restaurant, do go down for a drink, as it is a lovely place to sit for a while.

The Portobello Hotel

Sitting near London's famous antique and bric-a-brac market on Portobello Road the Portobello Hotel has, over the last 25 years, built up quite a reputation for its sumptuous rooms and is ideally situated for exploring fashionable West London.

The Portobello Hotel is blessed with many features making it perfect for a few days' honeymoon in London, not least of all its enviably trendy W11 address, but most of all because it is unlike any other hotel I have ever visited. In contrast to the large international hotels on Park Lane where, however wonderful the hotel, you will still feel very much like a tourist: staying here will make you feel very much part of the London scene and will give you a rare insight into this village-like area.

All the hotel's 'special' rooms, as they call them, are decorated individually with lots of unique features. My favourites are room No 22, with its dusky pink decor, solid four-poster and light streaming through the lovely bay window; No 16 with its fabulous round bed and huge Victorian bathtub complete with brass taps and pipes only a few feet away from the bed and surrounded by mirrors; No 13 which has a huge four-poster with muslin drapes, steps leading up to it, painted cherubs looking down on you and a

> **THE PORTOBELLO HOTEL**
> (☎ 0171-727 2777, fax 0171-792 9641), 22 Stanley Gardens, London W11 2NG, England
> **Reservations**: Direct with the hotel
> **Getting there**: Transfers from Heathrow Airport can be arranged by the hotel, costing around £35
> **Accommodation:** 22 individually decorated rooms: 10 special rooms, five standard doubles, seven singles
> **Amenities**: Residents' bar and restaurant, lounge area, lift, discount at nearby and co-owned Julie's restaurant, one of West London's most popular restaurants
> **Dress code**: Informal
> **Weddings**: No
> **Minimum stay**: None
> **Rates**: Double rooms from US$209/£135 to US$325/£210
> **Credit cards**: Most major
> **Taxes and service charge**: Included

mahogany bath; and No 46 which is decorated in the deep ethnic tones of Morocco with kilim drapes and cushions on the sofa, dorma windows looking over the gardens, an old three-foot deep Victorian bath in the bedroom, and a mirrored head board on the bed.

These unique qualities aside, all the rooms are furnished with antiques, all the beds are covered in white striped sheets that are a mixture of Irish linen and Egyptian cotton, and with feather and goose down duvets, and they all have separate showers and toilets in addition to the ornate baths.

You cannot help but feel at home at the Portobello. If you want big bustling lobbies, full of uniformed bell boys and huge spacious suites then you can strike the Portobello off your list immediately. But if you are looking for a small, quirky, infinitely friendly hotel that is more like a home from home, where the staff don't have a uniform, and each of the individually decorated rooms seems to have been designed with romance in mind, then this is very definitely the hotel for you.

Our suite was compact but elegant with a four-poster bed and adequate seating, small tables etc. The en suite bathroom had a beautiful claw feet bath plus TV. It was all very quiet and private and overall a pleasant stay although we were disappointed to discover that an English breakfast was extra to the room rate!
Andy and Rose

THREE DAYS IN LONDON

There's lots more to London than the obvious sightseeing attractions of **Buckingham Palace**, the **Crown Jewels** and **Big Ben**. Get along to **Portobello Road** on a Saturday for its bustling antiques and bric-a-brac market, and stop off for breakfast in the *First Floor Restaurant* (☎ 0171-243 0072), where you can sit and watch the locals over a cappuccino, while the market gets into swing beneath you.

London is full of wonderful restaurants. Try *Mezzo* (☎ 0171-314 4000), Sir Terence Conran's new 700-seater on Wardour Street in the heart of **Soho**, the centre of London's café chic and also home to the theatres of the **West End** and **Chinatown**. Both Soho and Chinatown are great places to wander around soaking in the atmosphere, and safe enough even at night: however it's probably best to get a cab late at night. Good places to stop for snacks in Soho are the ever-popular *Soho Soho* (☎ 0171-494 3491) on Frith Street, and **dell'Ugo** (☎ 0171-734 8300) which is directly opposite: for romantic evening meals you can't beat the *French House Dining-Room* (☎ 0171-437 2477) on nearby Dean Street. More expensive and more upmarket but a fabulous place for celeb-spotting is *The Ivy* (☎ 0171-836 4751), West Street.

If you're into books you can walk from Soho into nearby **Charing Cross Road** which has just about every kind of specialist book shop you could imagine, one of which was the inspiration behind the legendary love story, *84 Charing Cross Road*.

A real find of a restaurant, and right off the tourist track, is *Julie's* (☎ 0171-229 8331) in Holland Park – a west London institution which must be one of the city's most romantic restaurants, despite the food not being as good as it should be. Dinner at Julie's doesn't come cheap: a three-course dinner with wine will probably set you back about £40 but it is the most beautiful location for a romantic supper. Around the same area, not far from Notting Hill underground station is one of London's quintessential drinking experiences, the *Windsor Castle* on Camden Hill Road – not the royal residence but named because it was once possible to see it from the pub! This wonderful old pub is perfect for long winter evenings in front of a log fire or, in the summer, outside under the oak trees in the pub's garden.

A great place to go any day but particularly on a Sunday is **Covent Garden**. Wander around the covered market in the Piazza, down Longacre, Floral Street and Neal Street (designer shopping streets) and stop for a drink or coffee at the *Opera Terrace*, or lunch at *Belgo's*, the new fangled Belgian beer-cellar on Neal Street, renowned for its bowls of 'moules' and chips. Or if you want a beer in one of London's oldest pubs head for *The Lamb and Flag* on Rose Street – it's a bit tricky to find but is a real English classic and is worth the hunt.

If you're after more designer shopping go to **Bond Street** (just off Oxford Street) or **Knightsbridge** where the legendary Harvey Nichols and Harrods are found, as well as several individual designer shops, such as Joseph, DKNY and Nicole Fahri. If you get hungry or thirsty while you are there take the lift up to *The Fifth Floor Restaurant* in Harvey Nichols – the perfect spot for a post-shopping livener.

At the other end of Sloane Street from Knightsbridge is **Sloane Square**, home to Peter Jones and the General Trading Company. **King's Road**, which was made famous in the 1960s and 1970s as the heart of London's punk fashion scene, leads off from Sloane Square: it still has some pretty interesting shops.

St James's and **Hyde Park** are lovely places for a walk in a park and you can't beat alfresco Shakespeare on a warm summer evening in **Regent's Park** or opera in **Holland Park**. For tickets ask the concierge at your hotel or just turn up as there are usually some left on the night.

Other recommended hotels

The Covent Garden Hotel (☎ 0171-806 1000, fax 0171-806 1100), 10 Monmouth Street, London WC2H 9HB, is owned by the same group as Dorset Square and has only recently opened. This is the perfect location for honeymooners – sandwiched between trendy Covent Garden on one side and Shaftesbury Avenue and Soho on the other, you couldn't be closer to the action. Like all hotels in this small family-run group, the Covent Garden Hotel's sumptuous interior decorations were overseen by its owner, Kit Kemp, who cleverly combines traditional furnishings with rather unorthodox colours. The lovely first-floor drawing-room is a complete panoply of fabrics and colours which works rather well and manages to create an informal, homely atmosphere far removed from that of most hotels, enhanced further by the unusual greenery arrangements found throughout the hotel. All the hotel's de luxe doubles come with king-sized beds, large TVs and videos, plus a CD player, the rest of the rooms have an old fashioned Roberts radio, three phones, air-conditioning, fully stocked minibar with half size bottles of spirits instead of miniatures and those little disposable cameras just perfect for holidays. Being so new, the marble bathrooms are breathtakingly shiny and full of sparkling chrome fixtures and really fluffy white towels. Luxury double rooms from US$271/£175, suites from US$403/£260.

Blakes (☎ 0171-370 6701, fax 0171-373 0442), 33 Roland Gardens, South Kensington, London SW7 3PF, has long been regarded as one of London's most romantic hotels. Created and owned by fashion designer Anouska Hempel, Blakes was one of the first examples of a designer-inspired boutique hotel. The incredibly stylish furnishings incorporating rich colours and voluptuous fabrics, as well as Hempel's signature bows, make it the ultimate quiet retreat for hedonists who appreciate life's little luxuries and don't like sharing them with hordes of other people. Room rates range from US$271/£175 to US$511/£330, and go up to US$930/£600 for the luxury suite. South Kensington is a great place to stay, just down the road from Harrods and within walking distance of Hyde Park.

Also watch out for the **Hempel** (☎ 0171-298 9000), Anouska's latest venture which has only recently opened. Situated on the other side of Hyde Park in Lancaster Gate, the Hempel is perfectly situated for exploring fashionable West London, minutes away from Notting Hill Gate and Portobello Road.

BERKSHIRE

Berkshire is typical of England's south-eastern counties: it is full of rolling green fields and is a prime commuter residence because of its close proximity to London. If you are flying in or out of London's Heathrow Airport it is the perfect place to stop for a night or two before journeying on.

Cliveden

There can be few places in England as beautiful as Cliveden with its 376 acres of graceful parklands overlooking the River Thames – and it's just 40 minutes west of London. The hotel seems to have it all: location, beautiful surroundings, a Michelin Star, and an extremely colourful history.

Designed by Charles Barry, who was also responsible for returning the Houses of Parliament in London to the Gothic style. It is a rare treat to stay in such a hotel and perfect for the first night of your honeymoon, or for your first couple of days in England since it is only 20 minutes from Heathrow Airport.

England's history has over the centuries been fashioned at Cliveden by some of the richest men and most powerful women: the love affair of the scheming Duke of Buckingham and Anna Maria, Countess of Shrewsbury resulted in a fatal dual on the house's side lawn; Queen Victoria, Winston Churchill and Franklin D Roosevelt were regular visitors; Nancy Astor, whose husband Waldorf was given Cliveden on their marriage, gathered the influential Cliveden set around her in the 1930s. She became the first woman to sit in Parliament; and subsequently the house formed the meeting point for one of the British government's most notorious scandals when John Profumo met Christine Keeler around the Pavilion swimming pool.

As you wander through the glorious gardens on a sunny day, or sip pre-dinner cocktails in the magnificent oak-panelled Great Hall surrounded by fine works of art, ancient stone masonry and suits of armour, you cannot but wonder what these walls have witnessed before you. One of the most magical things about staying at Cliveden is this all pervading sense of history.

The great house's interior is every bit as stunning as the ornate gardens in which it is set. There are 37 luxurious guest rooms in all, including ten suites. Everywhere you look in the rooms there are wonderfully personal touches all contributing to make your stay here that little bit more special and unbelievably comfortable. On the outside

CLIVEDEN
(☎ 01628-668561, fax 01628-661837), Taplow, Berkshire SL6 OJF, England
Reservations: The Leading Hotels of the World and Relais & Châteaux toll free reservation numbers worldwide (see p12); toll free within the UK (☎ 0800-454063); toll free within the US (☎ 800-747-6917)
Getting there: Cliveden can arrange transfers from Heathrow (20 minutes) and Gatwick Airports (90 minutes) in their chauffeur driven car, or from Burnham Station (five minutes) and 30 minutes from London Paddington, local taxis from the station cost around £6; the drive from London on the M4 or M40 takes about 40 minutes
Accommodation: 37 guest rooms: five full suites, five junior suites, five de luxe bedrooms with private dressing rooms and sitting-room areas, 12 superior doubles with sitting-room areas, five standard doubles with sitting-room areas, five small doubles
Amenities: Terrace Dining-Room, Waldo's Michelin Star Restaurant, four private dining-rooms, Pavilion restaurant, health spa, 376 acres of parkland, indoor and outdoor swimming pool, indoor and outdoor tennis courts, air-conditioned gym, billiards, snooker, boating on the Thames and horse-riding through the park, chauffeur
Dress code: Jackets are required in the dining-room at lunch-time (no jeans or trainers) and jackets and ties must be worn in the evening
Weddings: Cliveden does cater for the occasional wedding, with receptions in the magnificent private French dining-room
Minimum stay: Two nights at certain times of the year
Rates: Doubles from US$325/£210; junior suites from US$612/£395
Credit cards: Most major
Taxes and service charge: Included (a £4.80 fee per booking is added and contributed to the National Trust)

of each bedroom's large oak doors are brass plaques showing your name; the suites have music channelled into four different rooms, with individual volume controls in each one so that you can have your opera booming all around you as you stand under the drench shower without deafening your husband who's trying to read in the sitting-room; there are even individually designed bed mats for honeymooners that have the dates of your stay embroidered on both sides so that it says Saturday's date as you pass over it on your way into bed and Sunday's date as you get out of bed in the morning.

But without a doubt the best aspect of the rooms is their views. They have such a restful impact as you look down over the formal arrangement of box hedge encasing great bushes of swaying lavender, past the statue of Pluto at the end of the immense lawn and out to the shimmering River Thames. This view is what made my stay at Cliveden: we would return to the suite in the afternoon, place chairs in front of the two huge windows overlooking the lawn and sit and soak up the view that lay before us.

I could go on and on about Cliveden but, suffice it to say, the cuisine in both restaurants is world class, the service not snooty, just friendly and attentive, the house elegant and welcoming (if a little overwhelming when you first come up the drive), and the facilities of the health spa, an indoor and an outdoor swimming pool, horse-riding, tennis, dreamy sunset river trips down the Thames on an old Royal Navy launch, and the endless beauty of the gardens littered with elegant statues and fountains, all make it the most incredible place to stay.

NORTH YORKSHIRE

A few days in the Yorkshire Dales and you'll know you've seen the England epitomised by the Brontë sisters and Turner. North Yorkshire is a wonderful blend of wild fells, pastoral valleys and rambling villages. The countryside is so scenic that a large part of it has now been designated a National Park in order to conserve the landscape. North Yorkshire is home to many of British racing's most famous yards, so for horse lovers there can be few finer experiences than getting out on the Dales on horseback.

(Opposite): Cliveden, Berkshire

The Devonshire Arms Country House Hotel

The Devonshire Arms is a splendid country house hotel which has been in the Devonshire family since 1753. Still owned by the present Duke and Duchess of Devonshire this luxury hotel occupying 12 acres of the Bolton Abbey Estate, has been filled with fine furniture, paintings and antiques borrowed from the Devonshire family's stately home, Chatsworth in Derbyshire.

There is something very charming about staying at the Devonshire, it may have something to do with the green wellies and cloth caps lined up in the entrance hall, the magical views from the bedroom windows, or the smell of log fires that permeates the sitting-rooms, but I strongly suspect that it was the staff who made my stay there so enjoyable. I'm always reading about staff who anticipate your every need and have to say I think the phrase is utter twaddle, but I do love a place which provides unanticipated extras: when I asked for tea in the middle of the morning it came accompanied by freshly baked biscuits – which I hadn't asked for. The staff here will leave you alone if that's what you want but they are happy to chat about the local countryside and the hotel if you are looking for information.

The 41 rooms are not huge but they are extremely comfortable, with every trimming that you'd expect from a member of the Small Luxury Hotels of the World chain. Decorated with striped Laura Ashley-style

THE DEVONSHIRE ARMS
(☎ 01756-710441, fax 01756-710564), Skipton, North Yorkshire BD23 6AJ, England
Reservations: Small Luxury Hotels of the World toll free numbers worldwide (see p12)
Getting there: Taxis from York (35 minutes) or Leeds (25 minutes); heli-pad; 23 miles from M62 and M1 (four and a half hours' drive from London)
Accommodation: 41 rooms: eight four-posters, one twin and one family in the Old Wing; one lady executive suite, 17 twins and 12 doubles in the new Wharfdale Wing
Amenities: Health, beauty and fitness club with indoor heated swimming pool, spa bath, Turkish steam room, Scandinavian sauna, cold water plunge pool, high-powered sun bed, gym, beauty salon; all-weather outdoor tennis court, croquet lawn; one restaurant, cocktail bar and public bar; horse-riding, falconry, fly fishing, golf, clay-pigeon shooting can all be arranged nearby; 24-hour room service, laundry and pressing service and in-room safes
Dress code: Collar and tie in the dining-room; elsewhere smart casual
Weddings: The hotel does have a wedding licence and is very popular for both wedding ceremonies and receptions, couples can choose between a church service, registry office or a civil ceremony at the hotel (rates available on request)
Minimum stay: None
Rates: Doubles from US$217/£140 to US$349/£225 for the three suites mentioned
Credit cards: Most major
Taxes and service charge: Included

wall paper and floral furnishings, eight of the rooms have four-poster beds. I'd strongly recommend that you request a room in the Old Wing, particularly the Crace Room, the Park Top and Chatsworth, because they all have four-posters.

Each bedroom has a colour TV, phone, radio, hair-dryer, ironing board and iron, trouser press, tea and (fresh) coffee-making facilities and a selection of books and Christie's fine art catalogues, not to mention the most wonderful views of the Dales rising up all around you. The crisp white cotton sheets have 'The Devonshire' monogrammed in the corner, as do the white towelling robes in the bathroom. The bathrooms are well equipped – although the bath felt quite small when I was standing under the shower – and there are lots of white towels, Potter and Moore toiletries, and a vanity mirror.

Men are required to wear a jacket and tie in the hotel's award-winning **Burlington Restaurant**. Other facilities include a cocktail lounge for pre-dinner drinks or lunchtime snacks, the **Duke's Bar**, open to the public and run very much as a local Yorkshire pub, and a wonderfully luxurious beauty and fitness centre with indoor pool.

(**Opposite**) **Top:** Breakfast at the Hôtel de Crillon, Paris (see p121). **Bottom:** Château de la Treyne (p127)

A FEW THINGS TO SEE AND DO IN NORTH YORKSHIRE

From the Devonshire Arms, follow the trails to **Pickles Beck** or the **Cavendish Pavilion** along the banks of the River Wharfe, which will give you a good taster for the beauty of the surrounding countryside. Discover the nooks and crannies of the **Bolton Abbey Estate** which covers 75 miles of footpaths through spectacular riverside, woodland and open moorland scenery.

Wander around **Parcevall Hall Gardens**, which are open to the public daily from April to October and boast fabulous views of Simon's Seat and Wharfdale, or drive west over to **White Scar**, England's biggest cave.

If you happen to be in Yorkshire on a Sunday, hop on the **Embsay Steam Railway** for the two and a half mile trip from Skipton and back again or, for the more adventurous, join the **Leeds-Settle-Carlisle Railway**, which journeys through lowland valleys and into the mountainous **Pennines** – some of England's most spectacular scenery. Visit **Harrogate** with its wonderful healing baths, and numerous tea rooms,

the most famous of which is *Betty's*, or spend an afternoon in the historic town of **Richmond**, complete with its 11th century castle.

For a truly nostalgic trip, hire a car from **Craven Classic Car Hire** (☎ 01756-790202) for £50 a day and enjoy touring this stunning countryside in a twin-seater open-top 1959 TVR sports car, or breeze along in a 1955 split-screen Morris Minor.

A day's visit to **York**, with its medieval buildings and stout city walls is a must if you get to this part of the world. Make sure you take a look at the famous **York Minster** and the **Castle Museum**, plus you don't have to go far to get to places like **Castle Howard**, the fabulous stately home where Evelyn Waugh's *Brideshead Revisited* was filmed.

If you'd rather see all of this by air, a champagne balloon flight over the Harrogate countryside organised by **Aire Valley Balloons** (☎ 01423-340664) is a rare treat on a clear day.

Middlethorpe Hall

Middlethorpe Hall, an extremely elegant Queen Anne country house hotel, is a great place to stay if you want to visit one of Britain's most historic cities, York. Its position, right next to York's famous racecourse also means you could spend a wonderful day at one of the summer race meetings.

Set in immaculately kept gardens and parkland, and furnished throughout with antiques and objets d'art, the house was built in 1699. In 1980 Historic House Hotels 'rescued' it from an uncertain future and under their ownership it has been restored to its former glory. When I arrived at Middlethorpe the entire front façade was bathed in late afternoon sunlight, giving it a really magical and very English air. The front door opens on to a flagged stone entrance hall, off which are the gloriously appointed drawing-room, library and dining-room.

Of the eleven bedrooms in the main house, there are two beautiful four-poster rooms, with huge sash windows looking out over the grandest of cedar trees – one has

---

MIDDLETHORPE HALL
(☎ 01904-641241, fax 01904-620176), Bishopthorpe Road, York YO2 1QB, England
Reservations: Small Luxury Hotels of the World toll free numbers worldwide (see p12)
Getting there: Taxi from York station 1$^1/_2$ miles; transport from Manchester or Leeds airport can be arranged
Accommodation: In the main house: one main house suite, two four-posters, two de luxe doubles, three de luxe twins which can be zipped together; in the Classical Courtyard: two de luxe suites; a junior suite; six de luxe rooms; seven standard rooms; plus two cottage suites along the lane; and a garden suite
Amenities: Formal dining-room, Grill room in the summer months operates as an extended dining-room, croquet lawn, library, golf nearby, tennis, spa
Dress code: Jacket and tie in the dining-room, but less formal in the grill room
Weddings: The hotel does not have a licence to perform weddings, but receptions for up to 50 guests can be catered for, room hire £250 including flowers, menus and waitress service
Minimum stay: Two nights for the dinner, bed and breakfast package, but otherwise none
Rates: Doubles from US$194/£125; suites are US$308/£199; ask about the two-night dinner, bed and breakfast package which starts at around US$147/£95
Credit cards: Most major
Taxes and service charge: Included

a queen-size and the other (room No 2) a king-size bed. I'd definitely recommend one of these or the main house suite which has its own gas fire and where the trompe l'oeil window has a view of the racecourse. There are a further 15 bedrooms in the Classic Courtyard, a recently converted 18th century stable block adjacent to the hotel, plus another cottage with two self-contained suites, only one of which is a double.

In my mind the two four-poster rooms are perfect honeymoon material, with their wonderful window seats and view, an immensely comfortable and really solid four-poster bed, and the most invigorating drench shower in the bathroom. However the junior suites and de luxe doubles in the Courtyard are also very pretty and have spacious rooms, so don't rule them out if the four-posters aren't free.

As well as many fine antiques, rugs and paintings, all the rooms have a colour TV, radio, a bottle of mineral water, a collection of old books, a trouser press, and a well-lit vanity with hair-dryer. In the bathroom there are old-fashioned brass bathtaps, big white fluffy towels and a robe as well as an ample supply of toiletries from Crabtree and Evelyn.

THE LAKE DISTRICT

The north-western corner of the **Yorkshire Dales National Park** borders **Cumbria**: from there the hills, mountains and lakes of England's famous **Lake District** spill out before you. Avoid visiting the Lakes in July and August, because they are just so busy with tourists that driving becomes a nightmare and the wild beauty of this hilly region is hardly the same covered in families and campers. However, out of season you cannot beat the Lake District with its mass of peaks, shimmering lakes and traditional stone farmhouses.

Holbeck Ghyll

Holbeck Ghyll is run by resident proprietors, David and Patricia Nicholson, and it is their careful attention to detail and wonderfully warm service that makes this such a great place to stay. If you have plans to go to the Lake District a few days at Holbeck Ghyll is an absolute must.

Built by a Lancashire industrialist in the early part of the 19th century, the house was bought in 1888 by Lord Lonsdale, one of the richest men in the land. He used it as a country retreat and a hunting lodge. The house is full of original features such as the inglenook fireplace in the oak-panelled entrance hall. There are also many art nouveau features and stained-glass windows in the lovely lounges which look straight out over the lawns to the lake.

Surrounded by seven acres of fabulous woodlands and open fields and overlooking **Lake Windermere** and the **Langdale Falls**, this friendly little hotel has 11 bedrooms and three suites. Holbeck Ghyll looks much more like a private house than a hotel with its high stone walls covered in creeping ivy, stone-cased windows and steeple-like roof.

The rooms vary a great deal in size as this is an old house, but they are all individually decorated in country-house style with

---

HOLBECK GHYLL
(☎ 015394-32375, fax 015394-34743), Holbeck Lane, Windermere, Cumbria LA23 1LU, England
Reservations: Small Luxury Hotels of the World toll free reservation numbers worldwide (see p12)
Getting there: The hotel can arrange transfers from Windermere Station (five minutes, £4.50) or Manchester Airport (90 minutes, £40)
Accommodation: 11 rooms, three suites
Amenities: Two restaurants overlooking the lake, lounges overlooking lawns to lake, seven acres of grounds including woodland walks and jogging trails, tennis court, health spa with sauna, steam room, gym, beautician and masseur
Dress code: Smart casual
Weddings: The hotel has a wedding licence and can host receptions for up to 65 people, menus start at £17.95 per head
Minimum stay: None
Rates: Doubles from US$232/£150 to US$341/£220; suites from US$310/£200 to US$372/£240, including dinner, bed and English breakfast
Credit cards: Most major
Taxes and service charge: Tax is included, service is discretionary

either tartan or floral bedspreads, antique furniture and charming window seats with superb views. Each room has an en suite bathroom and is equipped with luxury toiletries, beautiful vases of fresh flowers and decanters of sherry.

Other recommended hotels
Linthwaite House Hotel (☎ 015394-88600, fax 015394-88601), Crook Road, Bowness-on-Windermere, Cumbria LA23 3JA, was voted the English Tourist Board's Hotel of the Year in 1994. It's set in 13 acres of private grounds, and also overlooks Lake Windermere. Because of the awards it has won and the coverage it has consequently received, prices have risen making it a good deal more expensive than many other properties in the area. But the difference is that much of the cheaper accommodation is in bed and breakfasts, while Linthwaite House is a lovely hotel with a full range of facilities such as phone, radio, TV and hair-dryer in your room, not to mention the luxurious interior decorations. Even if you don't stay there, do pop in for lunch which is served between 12.30 and 1.30pm each day. Doubles cost between US$186/£120 and US$279/£180 a night including breakfast.

    Pheasant Inn (☎ 017687-76234, fax 017687-76002), Bassanthwaite Lake, Cockermouth, Cumbria CA13 9YE, surrounded by its own gardens and woodland, has 20 rooms and three lounges filled with ancient oak beams, log fires and antiques. The wonderfully friendly and tranquil atmosphere here is very much in the manner of an old English pub or coaching inn, making it a really relaxing place to stop for a few days. Doubles from US$155/£100, all bedrooms are en suite.

    Pickett Howe (☎ 01900-85444, fax 01900-85209), Buttermere Valley, Cockermouth, Cumbria, CA13 9UY, is a delightful 17th century former farmhouse nestled in Buttermere Valley: it will particularly suit couples looking to get away from other tourists but who still want homely surroundings – being here is more like staying with friends on a farm than being in a hotel. Slate floors, oak beams and mullioned windows make this old farmhouse a wonderful experience. The three double bedrooms also have jacuzzis and Victorian iron bedsteads. Double rooms cost US$112/£72 for bed and breakfast, but they also do dinners.

THE COTSWOLDS
Here in the 'heart of England', amidst a patchwork of rolling green fields, are some of England's best known and best loved hotels. The Cotswolds has long been a favourite destination for tourists, and as such can be unbearably busy in the middle of summer, but if you don't mind the crowds then this is when these idyllic English villages, with their century-old houses, immaculate stone walls and beautifully kept gardens are at their best. Savour strawberries and cream on the lawn, or a glass of real lemonade after a game of tennis, and you'll immediately feel that you've been part of the English scene for ages.

Lords of the Manor Hotel
A grand 17th century country house turned hotel, the Lords of the Manor combines solid English comfort with food fine enough to merit a much coveted Michelin star, three AA red rosettes and the *Good Food Guide* prize for Country Restaurant of the Year in 1994. For 200 years it was the home of the Witts family and it was here that the Rev FEB Witts wrote his famous *Diary of a Cotswolds Parson*.

    Built from the pale honey-coloured stone so typical of the Cotswolds, the Lords of the Manor is part of the Small Luxury Hotels of the World chain and is set in nine acres of lovely formal gardens and parkland.

    Decorated in period furniture, with soft pastel fabrics and lovely water-colours on the walls, the hotel has a wonderfully understated elegance to it. All twenty-seven bedrooms have been named after various vicars' wives and are decorated in what has now become universally recognised as classic English country house chintz. They are all well-equipped with bathrobes, Molton Brown toiletries, hair-dryers, TVs, a sherry decanter, fresh fruit and radiant fresh flowers. 'Tracy', with its huge mahogany four-poster and vast bath easily big enough for two, was made for honeymooners.

The elegant and spacious dining-room overlooks the house's original walled garden and terrace, and features gourmet food and fine wines from the wine cellar beneath the manor.

The Lords of the Manor is the perfect base for touring the nearby Roman city of **Bath**, **Stratford-upon-Avon,** home to the Royal Shakespeare Company, and **Blenheim Palace**, and the staff are more than happy to help organise any trips you may want to go on.

The Lygon Arms

The Lygon Arms is situated right in the centre of Broadway, a mellow Cotswold village where stone houses surround a perfect village green. The hotel is a favourite with the Cheltenham Gold Cup racing brigade and has long been regarded as one of England's most celebrated country inns.

The inn, which has been here for almost 500 years, epitomises the fine English pub with a relaxed atmosphere produced by grandfather clocks, roaring log fires in winter and hearty food such as proper English steamed puddings. Now owned by the Savoy Group and turned into a world class hotel it is of course not quite like the old village pub it was for centuries but it is now famous for its first-class hospitality and fabulous modern-day luxuries.

Many historic figures and former Kings and Queens of England have slept in the 58 bedrooms and seven suites: Oliver Cromwell spent the night of the 2nd September

---

THE LORDS OF THE MANOR
(☎ 01451-820243, fax 01451-820696), Upper Slaughter, Cheltenham, Gloucestershire GL54 2JD, England
Reservations: Small Luxury Hotels of the World toll free reservation numbers worldwide (see p12)
Getting there: The hotel can arrange transfers from Moreton-in-the-Marsh station at a cost of £5 (20 minutes)
Accommodation: 27 rooms
Amenities: Fishing in the lake and river, croquet, local tours, eight acres of private gardens; golf, horse-riding and tennis are all available nearby
Dress code: Jacket and tie for dinner
Weddings: The hotel can arrange weddings and receptions for up to 60 people, menus start at £25 per head
Minimum stay: None
Rates: Double rooms from US$186/£120 to US$349/£225, but do ask about weekend and mid-week packages including dinner
Credit cards: Most major
Taxes and service charge: Taxes are included, service is discretionary

---

THE LYGON ARMS
(☎ 01386-852255, fax 01386-858611), Broadway, Worcestershire WR12 7DU, England
Reservations: The Leading Hotels of the World toll free reservation numbers worldwide (see p12); or from the US through the Savoy Group reservation numbers on (US toll free ☎ 800-63-SAVOY)
Getting there: The hotel can arrange transfers to and from Evesham or Moreton-in-the-Marsh Railway Stations (£15.50), or from London Heathrow Airport (£130) and from Birmingham Airport (£55)
Accommodation: 58 rooms (including five four-poster rooms) and five suites
Amenities: The Great Hall dining-room, Goblets wine bar, Patio restaurant, Country Club with pool, fitness room, sauna, solarium, steam room, beauty salon, table tennis, billiards room, tennis; plus horse-riding, clay pigeon shooting, golf, hiking, squash and ballooning all nearby, cocktail bar, private dining-rooms, 24-hour laundry, heli-pad, limo service
Dress code: Smart dress is requested
Weddings: Wedding ceremonies can be carried out in the Edinburgh Room (50 people) and the Torrington Room (80 people), receptions are usually held in the Great Hall (96 people) or the Russell Room (52 people)
Minimum stay: None
Rates: Doubles from US$228/£147 including breakfast; four-poster bedroom from US$302/£195; suites from US$345/£225 to US$473/£305
Credit cards: Most major
Taxes and service charge: Government tax 17.5%, service is discretionary

1651 in the suite that is now named after him, before the Battle of Worcester, the final and decisive battle of the Great Civil War. King Charles I stayed in the hotel the night after the same battle; he was in the first floor room that now bears his name. Both rooms have four-poster beds and many original features such as oak panelling, as well as a wide range of modern amenities including phone, remote control television with satellite channels, hair-dryer, in-room safe, trouser press and sumptuous bathrobes. All rooms have 24-hour room service, valet service and maid service.

The Great Hall, the hotel's splendid 17th century dining-room is resplendent with its original Minstrel's Gallery, stags' heads, heraldic friezes and barrel-vaulted ceiling. Dinner and lunch are served here, cooked by the Lygon Arms' award-winning chef, Roger Narbett. If you fancy something less formal, there is **Goblets Wine Bar** and the **Cocktail Bar** both of which serve light lunches. The patio is the perfect place for a late breakfast on a lovely summer's morning.

After all that eating it's reassuring to have impressive health, fitness and leisure facilities to hand (even if you don't use them!). The Lygon Arms Country Club was completed in 1991 at a cost of around £2 million. Guests have direct access to the club via the hotel, which means you don't even have to go outside to get to it. The central feature of the building is the swimming pool and spa bath, down on to which sunshine is filtered by an electronically operated skylight. There is a steam room, saunas, billiards, beauty treatment rooms and a fully-equipped gym in the club, as well as a fitness consultant on hand to help you at all times.

A FEW THINGS TO SEE AND DO IN THE COTSWOLDS

The Cotswolds have pre-historic as well as Roman remains with roads built as long ago as AD43-49. There are Roman remains throughout the area but the most famous are in **Bath**, a fine Georgian city in the Avon Valley.

Today the area performs a very important role in England's **social calendar**, hosting several world famous events including the Cheltenham Gold Cup in March, Badminton Horse Trials in April, polo matches throughout the summer at Cirencester Park, and Prescott motor-race hill climbs, a beautiful venue for a vintage meeting in August.

The Lygon Arms is set in a great area for walking and cycling: the track to the right of the church in the town of Broadway leads into open countryside and out eventually to the **Cotswold Way**, a 100-mile walk though some of England's most idyllic countryside running from Chipping Campden to Bath. Contact Broadway Tourist Office (☎ 01386-852937) for maps and things to see and do along the Cotswolds Way.

Places to visit nearby include: **Snowshill**, a mile away, where there is a large cottage garden; **Sezincote**, near Moreton-in-Marsh, a grander garden with glorious Cotswold views; **Hidcote Manor**, near Chipping Campden, which was created at the turn of the century by American, Lawrence Johnston, and which is now one of the UK's most famous gardens; and **Barnsley House Garden**, which was originally laid out in 1770 and is situated in Barnsley, a very attractive village with a Norman church.

You can visit **Stratford-upon-Avon,** where William Shakespeare lived and wrote in the 16th century. Wander around the houses where he lived, go punting down the beautiful river, stop for dinner in one of the many good restaurants before attending an evening performance by the resident **Royal Shakespeare Company.** If you fancy a pre-theatre dinner, try *No 6* (☎ 01789-269106) on Union St, which serves delicious food at reasonable prices in warm, bistro surroundings.

THE NEW FOREST

For centuries, the New Forest was a popular hunting ground for English Kings. This vast tract of countryside is now best known for the ponies who wander freely, and it is an idyllic place to enjoy long walks. 'Nova Foresta', as it was named by William the Conqueror, is still subject to the special laws that he created to protect the forest's red deer. Over 900 years later this nationally protected forest and heath land is a reminder of England's long established hunting heritage. Within easy reach of all of the hotels listed in this section are **Salisbury** and **Winchester Cathedrals, Stonehenge**, and

Beaulieu Abbey with its Cistercian cloisters and ruins. **Romsey**, where Lord Mountbatten's **Broadlands** estate, and the gardens at Exbury and Spinners are also close by, as is **Lymington**, which has a wonderful bustling market on Saturdays.

Local pubs and restaurants to look out for include: the **Chequers** pub down **Maiden Lane** on the outskirts of Lymington which is usually full of yachties, the **Bank House** which is a popular local haunt and is opposite the Post Office in Lymington High Street, and **Limpets** down the bottom of the High Street where the fish is particularly good. **The Trustee Servant** at **Minstead** where Arthur Conan Doyle is buried in the Norman churchyard is also worth a visit.

The Forest offers a wealth of leisure activities: horse-riding, golf, sailing, fishing and of course, mile after mile of walking through some of England's most glorious countryside.

Gordleton Mill Hotel

The Gordleton Mill Hotel, in Hordle, is a wonderful country retreat situated just outside Lymington, but within the New Forest National Park. The 17th century Mill is a privately owned hotel offering seven bedrooms in a spectacular riverside location on the banks of the Avon Water.

The bedrooms are all furnished with traditional English fabrics, using pretty pastel colours and Laura Ashley prints and borders. Each room has its own en suite facilities including whirlpool baths and showers, and colour television. Four bedrooms are exclusively reserved for non-smokers.

Gordleton Mill is particularly famous for the fine cuisine of its **Provence Restaurant**, which has earned it a coveted Egon Ronay star, the *Good Food Guide*'s 'Country Restaurant of the Year 1997', and a prestigious Michelin Star. The views from the dining-room and its adjoining terrace are quite wonderful. During the summer months, breakfast, lunch, and early evening aperitifs are served outside on the terrace.

Guests can relax in the informal library, collapsing into one of the many comfortable armchairs, or sit in the rattan chairs in the conservatory. The five and a half acres of private gardens boast their own mill pond, sluice gates, weir, rustic bridges, lily pond and formal gardens, while the surrounding woods and fields attract a great deal of local wildlife.

> **THE GORDLETON MILL HOTEL**
> (☎ 01590-682219, fax 01590-683073), Silver Street, Hordle, Nr Lymington, Hampshire, England
> **Reservations**: Contact directly, Egon Ronay guidebook
> **Getting there**: Five minutes by taxi from Lymington station, or fly to Bournemouth or Southampton airports (25-30 minute drive)
> **Accommodation**: Seven rooms, one standard double, five superior doubles and one suite
> **Amenities**: Fishing, restaurant, helicopter pad
> **Dress code**: Smart casual, but no jeans allowed at dinner
> **Weddings**: Able to host wedding receptions only (50-60 people)
> **Minimum stay**: None
> **Rates**: Weekend rates are more expensive, from US$174/£112 to US$211/£136, including full English breakfast
> **Credit cards**: Most major
> **Taxes and service charge**: Tax included, service at your discretion

Chewton Glen

Chewton Glen is the New Forest's biggest and most luxurious resort-style hotel. Set in 70 acres of immaculate parklands, gardens, lawns and woodlands, Chewton Glen dates back to the early 1700s, and was remodelled in the Palladian style in the early 1890s. Since 1966 this prestigious hotel has been owned and run by the same private owners.

Chewton Glen tries to create the atmosphere of a large private house, and although it is just too big to truly carry this off, it is a first-class resort with tastefully decorated rooms, exquisite antiques and fine art, mixed in with an abundance of fresh flowers and many other little extras.

CHEWTON GLEN
(☎ 01425-275341, fax 01425-273310),
New Milton, Hampshire BH25 6QS,
England
Reservations: The Leading Hotels of the
World toll free reservations numbers
worldwide (see p12)
Getting there: The hotel can arrange
transfers from Heathrow Airport (£145),
Gatwick Airport (£165), and
Southampton Airport (£65)
Accommodation: 45 rooms and 13
suites
Amenities: The Marryat Room
Restaurant, health club, beauty and spa
treatments, computerised gym, indoor
and outdoor pools, indoor and outdoor
tennis courts, golf course, croquet, billiards, hairdressing salon; fishing, horse-
riding, sailing and shooting nearby
Dress code: Informal during the day,
men are requested to wear jackets and
ties in the evening
Weddings: The hotel has a wedding
licence (ceremonies cost £350), receptions can be arranged for up to 120 and
cost £70 a head which includes a three-
course wedding breakfast, all wine,
champagne with the cake, floral decorations and room hire
Minimum stay: Usually none, but two
nights at certain times of the year
Rates: Doubles from US$287/£185;
suites from US$465/£300
Credit cards: Most major
Taxes and service charge: Tax inclusive,
service discretionary

The bedrooms want for nothing. As the brochure proudly states: 'There is scarcely an amenity you can imagine that has not been included in your bedroom and bath-room.' Antique knick-knacks sit alongside a decanter of sherry, home-made biscuits, chocolates and fruit, as well as more practi-cal items as in-room safe, trouser press, so many huge towels you won't know what to do with them and towelling robes. All the bedrooms are very romantic and pretty in true country house fashion, with Laura Ashley prints and chintzes, and private bal-conies or terraces looking out over the sur-rounding parklands.

The hotel's own health club provides a sanctuary where the body and mind can be refreshed and retuned. The centrepiece is a magnificent indoor swimming pool, sur-rounded by vast glass windows looking out onto the grounds, with an adjacent spa, steam room and saunas. Classically designed with trompe l'oeil frescoes, the pool uses the latest ozone treatment providing crystal clear water without condensation.

There's so much to do at Chewton Glen: indoor and outdoor tennis courts, gym, beauty treatments, croquet on the lawn, a nine-hole golf course, and the many walking and jogging trails to be explored close to the hotel. Riding, fishing, shooting and sailing can also be arranged at nearby locations.

The quality of the staff and facilities are the key attributes of Chewton Glen. The staff are as friendly as they are professional, and so attentive that they attempt to anticipate your every wish. Food at the Chewton Glen is taken seriously – a wonderful mix of local seasonal produce, such as game, fish and wild mushrooms, combined to create classic dishes.

DEVON AND CORNWALL
The ragged coastline of Devon and Cornwall is so pretty that it has always been a pop-ular holiday destination with the British. Explore the traditional fishing villages with their countless fish restaurants and visit the charming pubs where you can sample cider, particularly the local cider called scrumpy – a seemingly innocuous drink made from fermented apples with a powerful kick!

Danescombe Valley Hotel
A stay at Danescombe Valley Hotel is all about views and food. If these two criteria score pretty high on your list of priorities, then you won't go wrong here. This is a hotel for sheer relaxation where the tranquil atmosphere and beautiful countryside make it the ultimate escape.

Martin and Anna Smith run the hotel as their home, providing friendly hospitali-ty and service and making you feel most welcome. There are five bedrooms, all of which are individually decorated in a low-key manner with antiques collected over the years from various countries that Martin and Anna have visited. Each room has special touches such as Body Shop bath oil and shampoo, a pile of glossy magazines to flick through, San Peligrino water, paintings and books.

Rooms Nos 2 and 3 are en suite and have full length bay windows which open out onto the first floor balcony allowing guests to sit and observe the abundance of wildlife in the Tamar River, or watch the housemartins which have nested in the eaves. Room No 1 is also on the first floor and has a balcony on the side of the house, however its bathroom is across the landing. On the second floor, rooms Nos 4 and 5 make up for their lack of balcony by having huge luxurious bathrooms with wooden surround baths and plenty of room to lounge around in, making them much more like suites.

The hotel is situated on one of the most beautiful stretches of the **River Tamar**, known locally as the hidden valley: the views are so good that the hotel has been described as having the best views anywhere in the English countryside.

Danescombe Valley's pretty cottage garden is a perfect spot for tea, coffee or pre-dinner drinks and, like the rest of the house, is terribly informal. The dining-room is filled with vibrant oil paintings by a distinguished local artist, which sadly, aren't for sale. Martin hands out the set dinner menu when you arrive giving you time to build up a real hunger for the creations of his Italian wife, Anna. The four-course dinner is quite delicious with well-chosen local produce used wherever possible and a wide selection of local cheeses to choose from before dessert. Martin and Anna pride themselves on their wine list which is lovingly researched and compiled with in-depth descriptions of each wine and where they found it.

DANESCOMBE VALLEY HOTEL
(☎ 01822-832414, fax 01822-832446, e-mail http://www.danescombe.com/-lower/dvi), Calstock, Cornwall PL18 9RY
Closed: Between October and March
Reservations: Direct with the hotel
Getting there: The hotel will pick you up from Calstock station; there is also an airport at Plymouth from where you can take a taxi to the hotel
Accommodation: Five double bedrooms
Amenities: Restaurant, bar, garden, lounges with open fires (no TV!)
Dress code: Casual
Weddings: No
Minimum stay: Sometimes two nights over weekends
Rates: Double room with private bathroom, four course set dinner and coffee, extensive continental breakfast US$143/£92.50 per person per night
Credit cards: Most major
Taxes and service charge: All included

Staying at Danescombe Valley Hotel is an experience I shall never forget and would like to re-live as often as possible. The beauty of the setting is enhanced by the tasteful way Martin and Anna have created this magical hotel. If you are looking for somewhere totally off the beaten track with low key luxury and the utmost in good wine and delicious food this has to be the place, the only problem is that you have to leave at the end.
Ian and Roo Cross

A FEW THINGS TO DO IN DEVON AND CORNWALL

Devon and Cornwall are great for walking along coastal paths, or through woodland and open country with truly spectacular views.

From Calstock a local boatman takes passengers on trips along the river, downstream past the hotel to **Cotehele Quay** and up past **Morwell Rocks** which rise up sheer from the river bed to tower over you.

Just 15 minutes' walk from Danescombe Hotel is **Cotehele House**, one of the National Trust's estates. Set on the steep wooded slopes of the River Tamar, this medieval house has been in the Edgcumbe family for almost 600 years. Wander through the steep valley garden which contains some exotic plants, a domed dovecote,

and a 15th century chapel, before touring the ancient rooms of Cotehele. The Great Hall has a spectacular arch-braced roof and contains some amazing suits of armour and early dark oak furniture. A short walk through the estate woodland, alongside the Morden stream leads to the old corn mill which has been restored to working order, while the adjacent building now houses a cider press.

There are wonderful small fishing villages and quiet coastal coves to be discovered throughout Devon and Cornwall such as **Salcombe**, and **Burgh Island** where an amphibious tractor takes you from the beach out to the island for a pint of cider at the *Pilchard Inn*.

National Trust and Landmark Trust holiday cottages

One of the best ways of getting an idea of life in rural Britain is to rent one of the National Trust's, or the Landmark Trust's many wonderful properties. Both organisations were established to preserve Britain's countryside and the wealth of old buildings that were in danger of crumbling away. Two of the National Trust's properties on a beautiful stretch of the River Thames known as **Cliveden Reach** would make wonderful honeymoon hideaways. **New Cottage** and **Ferry Cottage** as they are called cost around US$775/£500 for a week in the summer months, and considerably less at other times of the year. Call the National Trust for further details (☎ 01225-791199). The Landmark Trust also has a whole host of quirky buildings for rent including coastal castles, a water tower, a gothic temple, the forebodingly named House of Correction (!), and even apartments in **Hampton Court Palace**. Prices start from around US$465/£300 for a week, depending on the kind of property and the time of year. Contact the Landmark Trust (☎ 01628-825925) for a copy of their Handbook. If you're in the US it may be easier to contact **Historic Inns of Britain** (US toll free ☎ 1-800-747-8035), which has a large portfolio of traditional and characterful pubs.

Scotland
(BEST TIME TO VISIT: ALL YEAR ROUND)

To me there is no more magical place than Scotland. There is nothing quite like standing on the west coast with the wind blowing around you, surrounded by wild terrain and some of the most spectacular scenery anywhere in the world.

If you're planning on going to Scotland you'd better be prepared to put concerns about the weather right out of your head, as there is absolutely no way you should go there if mixed weather will ruin your honeymoon. It's not that it rains any more than it does in England or Ireland, it's just that big weather is really what it's all about in Scotland – to pick this wonderful country for your honeymoon you've got to be the kind of incurable romantic that loves hilltop walks in the rain and huddling up together in front of a log fire with the wind whistling round the house. However I have had weeks on the west coast when we might as well have been in Greece it was so hot. In fact, the uncertainty of the weather adds to the mysticism of Scotland.

The hotels I've listed here epitomise for me everything that is great in Scotland. They are, by and large, not the sort of hotels that have 24-hour room service or TVs in the rooms (apart from Gleneagles of course!). Instead they have excellent home-cooked and often home-grown food, large comfortable beds, fantastically friendly and professional service, and are set in historic buildings surrounded by endless views of this beautiful country. They are, in short, the kind of hotels where you could easily wind up taking the proprietor's dogs with you on your walk, or sit up supping whisky

---

SCOTLAND
The attractive and lively cities of Edinburgh and Glasgow plus the staggering beauty of the west coast of Scotland and the wild grandeur of the Highlands
When to go: All year round in the south but snow makes travel difficult in the Highlands in winter; summer is from June to September, winter from December to the end of March
Capital: Edinburgh
Flight times: See England section
Approximate exchange rates: As for England: Pound sterling (£): US$1 = £0.64, A$1 = £0.51
Time difference: GMT (plus one hour from the last Sunday in March to the last Sunday in October)
Voltage: 240v AC, 50 Hz; three-pin plugs
Combine with: England, Wales, Ireland, the rest of Europe
Country dialling code: ☎ 44

TWO DAYS IN EDINBURGH

A week's touring around Scotland will give you a really good taster of this incredibly beautiful country. If you start in Edinburgh the best place to stay is the newly refurbished **Balmoral Hotel** (☎ 0131-556 2414, fax 0131-557 8740), 1 Princes Street, Edinburgh EH2 2EQ. This ornate gothic monolith, which was originally built as the North British Hotel in 1902, has fantastic views over the city and is centrally placed so that all the sights are within easy walking distance. Doubles from US$217/£140, suites from US$387/£250.

If you're coming from London then the train is a great way to arrive, as the journey up through the east side of England, particularly the last hundred miles along the coast, is really enjoyable: apart from which the views of Edinburgh as you come out of the station are breathtaking and fully warrant the city's appellation of 'the Athens of the North'.

The main tourist sights are: the 11th century castle which looms down over the city and where the original chapel, built around 1130 by King Malcolm's son, David, in memory of his mother, Margaret, still stands and is almost certainly the oldest building in the city; the **Royal Mile**, the cobbled street connecting the castle with Holyrood Palace; **Victoria Street** which winds downhill to the **Grassmarket** where you'll find all sorts of interesting shops selling lace, antiques and candles; the **National Gallery of Scotland**, just off Prince's Street, full of fantastic works by some of Europe's great masters; and **Calton Hill** and **Arthur's Seat** from where the views back over the city are fabulous.

The best way to experience this elegant city is to walk. A good place to begin is **New Town**, which is actually 200 years old and quite stunning with its huge Georgian buildings and cobbled streets. Start on **Dundas Street** and turn right when you get to the top of the hill on

George Street, before turning left down **Castle Street**: this brings you out directly opposite the castle. Pop into the National Gallery and then catch a bus up the **Mound** to save your legs and get off on the Royal Mile, where you can either go right to the castle, or left down to **Holyrood Palace** (the latter is too far to walk!). Victoria Street (see above) is also in the vicinity. When you're done with the Old Town go back over **North Bridge** so you can admire the fantastic views of the castle on one side, the sea and Salisbury Crags on the other.

The city really comes alive during the **Edinburgh Festival** (arts and drama) in August and at Hogmanay for Europe's biggest New Year's Eve party: if your honeymoon coincides with either of these periods you can't possibly miss a couple of nights in Edinburgh.

The city is also known for its many great restaurants, bars and cafés. There are so many it is hard to pick just a few but try some of the following: while you're on the Royal Mile stop for lunch at *Le Sept* down the steeply cobbled Old Fishmarket Close; for steaks there's no better place than the *Witchery*, a wonderfully atmospheric restaurant just below the castle at the very top of the Royal Mile; the *Queen's Street Oyster Bar* on the corner of Dundas Street and Queen's Street is a tiny little basement bar with good cheap meals and live music.

For seafood and fish head down to the gentrified parts of **Leith Docks** where *Skipper's*, *The Ship*, *The Shore*, *Vintners* and the ever-popular *Waterfront* all have great atmosphere and delicious fish; pop into the *Café Royal* on Rose Street for oysters, or to the **Abbertsford** close by for a pint of 'heavy' (bitter) in one of Edinburgh's oldest pubs, and last but not least, don't miss *Bar Kohl* on George IV Bridge which has over 50 different flavours of vodka and some wicked cocktail combinations.

with the owners and other guests into the early hours of the morning.

If you've not been to Scotland it may be an idea to pick two or three of these hotels and do a mini-tour starting in Edinburgh, so that you get a feel for the country and its vast open, unspoilt, spaces. Scotland is now one of the few parts of Europe where there is any real wilderness.

PERTHSHIRE

The Gleneagles Hotel

Set in the heart of Scotland on an 830-acre estate in Perthshire, Gleneagles is Scotland's most complete resort offering luxury accommodation and endless leisure facilities against a matchless scenic backdrop.

The hotel has 18 suites, one of which is the unbelievable Rob Roy Suite: interior designer Amanda Rosa was drafted in to create an 18th century Jacobean-style suite to mark the launch of the film *Rob Roy*. The two-bedroomed suite features a mixture of antique and reproduction solid oak Jacobean furniture including a barley twist four-

GLENEAGLES
(☎ 01764-662231, fax 01764-662022),
Auchterarder, Perthshire PH3 1NF,
Scotland,
Reservations: The Leading Hotels of the
World toll free reservation numbers
worldwide (see p12) or through Crown
International from the US (see p11)
Getting there: The hotel can arrange
chauffeur driven transfers from
Edinburgh or Glasgow Airports, £65 each
way
Accommodation: 234 bedrooms including 18 suites
Amenities: Four restaurants and The Bar,
lounge and Ballroom, private function
rooms, shopping mall and additional
fashion, sports and gift shops at all the
leisure locations, post office, three 18-
hole Championship golf courses, a nine-
hole course, Country Club and Spa, the
Gleneagles Mark Phillips Equestrian
Centre, the Gleneagles Jackie Stewart
Shooting School, the British School of
Falconry at Gleneagles, four all-weather
tennis courts, one grass court, two
salmon and sea trout angling beats on the
River Tay, lochs for brown trout, off-road
driving, lawn bowling, croquet, putting,
pitch-and-put, jogging trails
Dress code: There is no special dress
code at Gleneagles
Weddings: Civil and religious marriages
can be held either in the hotel or the
grounds, and receptions for up to 300
people can be catered for, menus start at
£41 a head; the hotel will cater for virtually anything you require from hair-
styling to a Highland piper
Minimum stay: None
Rates: Doubles from US$356/£230
including full Scottish breakfast; the Rob
Roy Suite costs US$1627/£1050 per
night including full Scottish breakfast;
ask about their honeymoon package
which for around US$697/£450 a night
gets you flowers in a suite, a champagne
breakfast in your room, a carriage drive
around the estate, and a chauffeur-driven
transfer to any airport in Scotland, as well
as a first anniversary dinner at the hotel's
Strathearn Restaurant
Credit cards: Most major
Taxes and service charge: Included

poster bed hung with Ralph Lauren shot rayon velvet drapes, a fur-effect bed throw and cushions by Pierre Frey of Paris. Specialist paint effects adorn the walls, while MacGregor tartan Knowle sofas, antique chests, books and rugs complete the picture. Costumes used by Liam Neeson and Jessica Lange in the filming of Rob Roy have also been incorporated into the decor. All this can be yours for just over £1050 a night.

All the suites have their own individ-ual colour schemes and are located at each corner of the hotel thus offering the best views over the surrounding countryside. Each suite comprises a bedroom, bathroom and lounge area with a dining table for those intimate room service breakfasts and dinners. There are Gleneagles branded toiletries in the bathrooms, a television, minibar, hair-dryer, and bathrobes. Two of the suites also have four-poster beds.

To most people Gleneagles means golf but the resort also boasts a wide range of leisure facilities. The list of pursuits with which to fill your days is staggering: there are of course the three 18-hole Championship golf courses (the King's, Queen's and Monarch's), as well as a pitch-and-put course and The Wee, a nine-hole course; but there is also a beautiful Country Club and Spa with a lagoon-shaped indoor swimming pool; the Gleneagles Mark Phillips Equestrian Centre – one of the best equipped centres in the world with fantastic riding to be had all around the estate; the Gleneagles Jackie Stewart Shooting School; the British School of Falconry at Gleneagles, two salmon and sea trout angling beats on the **River Tay** and lochs for brown trout, off-road driving; four all-weather tennis courts and a grass court, as well as lawn bowling and croquet.

A quick read through the above list will confirm for you that this is no ordinary hotel. Gleneagles is a totally self-contained luxury resort the like of which you won't very often come across in Britain, or even in the rest of Europe. You can choose between four restaurants and the bar, there are private function rooms which are per-fect for weddings, a complete shopping mall with branches of Harvey Nichols and Burberrys, and even a post office.

A ratio of more than one staff member per guest ensures you'll be utterly pam-pered, and this really is one of those hotels where no wish seems too much for the friendly, enthusiastic staff and management. Don't miss afternoon tea which comes with the most fabulous assortment of sandwiches, savouries, scones and cream cakes.

THE WEST COAST

The Altnaharrie Inn

The Altnaharrie is legendary but not for being a big luxury hotel. It is a small family-run residence with eight guest rooms, it is not accessible by road and it has no neighbours – it does however boast some of the finest food you are likely to eat in Scotland.

This old manor house with its dark slate roof is home to Fred Brown from Hamilton, Scotland and his Norwegian wife and chef Gunn Ericksen: her skills in the kitchen using local produce led to widespread acclaim for this friendly little inn. To call the Altnaharrie a hotel would be inaccurate, it would lead you to expect amenities such as air-conditioning, in-room safes and televisions. But you won't find any of these here; in their place are much more relevant things such as the torch by your bedside, which comes in handy when the generator is turned off at night.

The Altnaharrie lies on the southern shores of **Loch Broom** on the far north-west coast of Scotland, just opposite the fishing village of Ullapool. Don't make the mistake of thinking you can nip up there from either Edinburgh or Glasgow: Scotland is deceptively large with an awful lot of land between its lowland border with England and these far northern western shores.

The house was originally built a few hundred years ago as a stop-over point for drovers on their way to sell cattle in the south. To get to the house guests are asked to phone Gunn or Fred on arrival in Ullapool; they will then direct you to the ferry for your ten minute journey across Loch Broom. Be warned that the last ferry leaves at 6pm, but there are others at 2.45pm and 4.45pm (throughout the year) and make sure

---

THE ALTNAHARRIE INN
(☎ 01854-633230, fax 01854-633303), Ullapool, Wester Ross IV26 2SS, Scotland
Reservations: Must be made direct with the hotel
Getting there: On arrival at Ullapool guests are asked to call the Inn which will then direct you to the appropriate place to meet the ferry, last sailing 6pm
Accommodation: Eight bedrooms: five in the main house, three in separate cottages
Amenities: Restaurant, two lounges, bar
Dress code: Guests can wear whatever is comfortable, although people tend to look smarter for dinner
Weddings: Yes, but up to a maximum 16 guests
Minimum stay: Two nights over the weekend
Rates: Doubles from US$225/£145 to US$271/£175 per night per person dinner, bed and breakfast
Credit cards: Most major
Taxes and service charge: Tax included, service is discretionary

---

A DRIVING TOUR AROUND WESTER ROSS

Just three miles south of Ullapool are the lovely gardens of **Leckmelm** (open April to October), which are well worth a visit. There is a 10-acre arboretum and a walled garden which was laid out in the 1870s and which has been painstakingly restored over the last ten years.

Either on your way up to Ullapool or on the way back down again, take a detour off the A835 when you get to Braemore Junction and go back on yourself up the A832 towards Gairloch. Look out for a sign to **Corrieshalloch Gorge**, where water cascades into a 200ft box canyon creating a dramatic gorge and the **Falls of Measach**. Below the falls is a suspension bridge, a great place for photos. You can then continue back down the A835 through **Braemore Junction**. The scenery is breathtaking with the vertical cliffs of **Seana Bhraigh** on one side and the remote **Fannich Mountains** on the other.

At certain times of the year, usually on Wednesdays and Thursdays in June and July,

Dundonnel House Garden (☎ 01854-633206) is open to visitors. The house has the most incredible grassed walks and box-edged pathways in a pretty walled garden bounded by a river, but do call first to check if it's open.

If you've time, go on up the A832 to **Gruinard**, where **Stattic Point** and **Rumore Promontory** reach out with long arms to almost encircle the bay. A long strip of golden sand runs along the shore and you can look towards the horizon to the hills of **Sutherland**. The views are stunning. Then carry on along the A832 through **Aultbea**, a small crofting village on the shores of Loch Ewe, to **Inverewe Gardens** (open from 9.30am to 9pm all summer and to 5pm the rest of the year). The 19th century garden was created by Osgood Mackenzie and sub-tropical plants from all over the world flourish in magnificent surroundings. You can then either make your way back along the same road or complete the circuit along the edge of beautiful **Loch Maree**.

you take your wellies as getting on and off the boat can be a bit muddy.

The tranquillity at the Altnaharrie is so absolute that you can almost feel the silence weighing down on you as you cross the loch away from the town of Ullapool. If you can't cope with silence and nothingness give the Altnaharrie a wide berth, as days here are spent reading, walking in the surrounding heather-clad hills, fishing in a small boat out on the loch, sleeping and best of all, eating Gunn's fine food. You may well get to see golden eagles, seals and otters but you won't see many other people.

The atmosphere inside the Altnaharrie is relaxed and friendly and the two lounges with their open fires are just the place for those days when you decide that you can't actually be bothered to venture outdoors. Some of the rooms are in separate buildings away from the main house but don't worry if you get one of these as they are at least as comfortable as the rooms in the main house and have the added advantage of being even more private.

THE ISLE OF SKYE
Kinloch Lodge

Kinloch Lodge, Isle of Skye, is run by Lord and Lady MacDonald, and has been in the MacDonald family for over three hundred years. The hotel's gourmet food is now so celebrated that Claire MacDonald has written many books dedicated to Scottish food and drink.

Situated at the head of the loch (Kinloch means head of the loch) and at the foot of a hill at the southern end of Skye, this large white manor house with its slate-grey roof is more a house than a hotel. The MacDonalds are very careful to preserve this atmosphere, wishing to lure their guests on the promise of delicious food, fine wine, friendly company and truly comfortable surroundings rather than with the promise of extensive facilities and bedroom amenities. If you derive great pleasure from your food and drink, and enjoy being in relaxed and informal rural surroundings then you'd be hard pressed to beat this lovely lodge.

You start to get an impression of the lodge's remoteness as you travel down the mile long rough hewn track off the main (tiny single track!) road. The countryside of the Isle of Skye is rugged and wild and therein lies its beauty – walking in the nearby mountains and along the edges of the lochs is fabulous, and is the very best way of working up an appetite.

KINLOCH LODGE
(☎ 01471-833333, fax 01471-833277),
Sleat, Isle of Skye IV43 8QY, Scotland
Reservations: Direct with the hotel
Getting there: The hotel can arrange for a taxi to collect you from either Mallaig or Kyle of Lochalsh (£10 to £15)
Accommodation: 10 bedrooms
Amenities: Two lounges, bar, dining-room, limited room service, fantastic walking nearby, TV (for occasional use)
Dress code: Whatever is comfortable
Weddings: No
Minimum stay: None
Rates: Doubles from US$186/£120 to US$294/£190 bed and breakfast
Credit cards: Most major
Taxes and service charge: Included

Guests are encouraged to treat the place very much as their own and will find utter tranquillity and relaxation among the calming apricot walls of the drawing-room, while the strong green of the dining-room walls sets a richer tone for the sumptuous dinners produced in Claire's kitchen. The downstairs rooms are filled with elegant antiques, family portraits in gilt frames, photographs and piles of books, and from every window there are restful views. Upstairs are ten bedrooms, three of which are reasonably large but the rest fairly small although prettily and individually furnished.

If you must have a huge bedroom or need to be constantly entertained then this isn't the place for you, but if you're happy with a good book, a comfy sofa, good walks among fantastic scenery, and delicious meals to look forward to, it will suit you both down to the ground.

Renting a croft or a castle

Crofts and castles – from the tiny to the tremendous, both simple and splendid – and a whole range of wonderful holiday properties throughout Scotland can be booked by contacting **Crofts and Castles Ltd** (☎ 01835-870744, fax 01835-870711), Linthill Coach House, Melrose, TD6 9HU, Scotland. Talk to Nita Redfern who is more than happy to sort out almost anything you want. She'll find you a gorgeous and completely isolated croft for your honeymoon, or plan the perfect castle wedding with kilted piper and all. Shooting, fishing, stalking and catering can also be arranged.

Particularly suitable is the **Black House** on the shoreline at **Luib** on the Isle of Skye, it is one of the few original Black House crofts left that hasn't been turned into a museum. This almost unique humble abode has a heavy thatched roof, a pretty four-poster bed, exposed original stonework and a wood-burning stove for cooler evenings. If you're looking for something totally different you'll love the Black House: prices start at US$581/£375 for a week during the low season and up to US$697/£450 for a week in the high.

On a much grander scale you could consider **Stucan-T-Iobairt** a tranquil retreat right on the edge of **Loch Lomond** where a detached stone cottage has been convert-ed to offer a richly decorated hideaway. Inside, the house really is luxuriously fur-nished with flowing tartan drapes, old wooden beams, marble worktops in the kitchen and a glowing log fire. Surrounded by mature woodland there is a babbling burn and fantastic views over Loch Lomond to the mountains beyond. The cottage stands in the shadow of a thousand year old yew tree where Robert the Bruce is reputed to have assembled his troops. A week's rental at Stucan-T-Iobairt costs US$852/£550 through-out the year and goes up to US$1549/£1000 at Christmas and New Year.

Wales
(BEST TIME: ALL YEAR ROUND)

Wales is the perfect place to take life slowly and really unwind in beautiful mountain-ous scenery and there are few more magnificent places than **Snowdonia** in North Wales. Days can be spent driving along secluded lanes and narrow mountain roads, but you should leave the car in order to explore the many bridleways and footpaths which lead you to some of the wildest scenery in Europe. Wales is not a place for fair-weath-er travellers as the mountains in the north often bring rain and drizzle but if you are looking for views, privacy and peace then it's hard to beat.

Bodysgallen Hall

A member of the Small Luxury Hotels of the World grouping, Bodysgallen Hall is an absolutely beautiful hotel. Standing in 200 acres of its own parkland, you'd be hard pressed to find a more wonderful and relaxing place to spend a few days. It is set in some of Wales's most scenic countryside, just south of Llandudno, and looks down on **Conwy Castle** and towards the spectacular mountains of Snowdonia to the south.

From the moment you unbolt the huge front door of this grand old stone manor and enter the oak-panelled hall where an open fire burns in the hearth, you'll feel the tiredness of the journey subside.

The Hall has been carefully restored by the Historic House Hotels group, which own a handful of similar properties in Britain and are well known for their first-rate housekeeping, service and dining. The backing of this group has enabled the Hall to be refurbished exactly as it should be, using antique-style paints, original prints and fabrics, which sit well alongside the many antiques and fine paintings spread about the rooms.

BODYSGALLEN HALL

(☎ 01492-584466, fax 01492-582519), Llandudno, Gwynedd LL30 IRS, Wales

Reservations: Small Luxury Hotels of the World toll free reservation numbers worldwide (see p12)

Getting there: The hotel can arrange transfers from Llandudno Junction railway station but many guests arrive by car

Accommodation: 18 rooms in the main Hall and nine cottages

Amenities: The Bodysgallen Spa, historic gardens including a rare 17th century parterre of box hedges, two diningrooms, bar, library, tennis, croquet, sailing in Conwy Harbour, sea and river fishing, horse-riding and golf nearby

Dress code: Jacket and tie are requested for dinner

Weddings: The Hall's former stable block, the Wynn Rooms, has been converted and can be used for weddings

Minimum stay: None, apart from two nights for the Historic House Summer Breaks (see below)

Rates: Doubles from US$/£115, four-poster bedrooms from US$/£160, cottage suites from US$/£135; ask about their Historic House Summer Breaks which included two nights' accommodation, early morning tea, cooked breakfast, table d'hôte dinner, and free entry into the historic property of your choice

Credit cards: Most major

Taxes and service charge: Included

With only 19 bedrooms the Hall is an intimate place, making you feel that bit more special as a guest but for utter privacy choose one of the nine cottages situated in the grounds, all of which come with their own gardens and evocative names such as Dove Cottage or Gingerbread House. All the rooms are furnished with mod cons, including en suite bathroom, electric trouser press, TV, toiletries and bathrobes. Wherever you stay there's plenty of space to find a quiet corner of your own to snuggle up with a book, or enjoy afternoon tea in front of the fire in the beautiful first floor drawing-room.

Much of the Hall was built in the 17th century; the ancient look-out tower dates back to the 13th century. The views from the top of the tower are breathtaking and make the long climb up the winding stone staircase worthwhile. Despite being steeped in history Bodysgallen Hall also features just about every modern amenity that you would want on your honeymoon including a brand new sparkling health spa. Approached by a short walk through the garden, the spa occupies the original stone buildings of Bodysgallen Farm, but now houses a Club Room, a terrace, a good-sized indoor swimming pool, a whirlpool spa bath, as well as a steam room, sauna, three beauty salons and a gym.

Renting a cottage in Wales

Welsh Country Cottages (☎ 01328-864041) have some fabulous cottages ideally suited to honeymoons spread all over Wales. Choose from 500-year old, thick, white-washed wall cottages such as **Cwmmegan** which was originally a shepherd's cottage, or the cosy little **Retreat** in **Aberglaslyn** which is tucked away behind trees and shrubs with its own little garden. The cottages come well-equipped with mod cons such as microwave ovens and barbecues for the summer, and offer a unique insight into living in Wales.

Ireland
(BEST TIME: ALL YEAR ROUND)

Ireland is the perfect place for a honeymoon if you dream of walking round rugged coastlines hand in hand, riding across untouched sandy beaches and emerald green fields and lingering in local pubs for long lunches over pints of Guinness and a chat with the locals. It's also a place for fine dining on hearty, but gourmet, fare where everything from the lobster to the beef will be of local origin.

For some reason the Emerald Isles cannot fail to conjure up romantic images of a charmed existence now lost to most of the developed world, where the Irish charm and

(Opposite) Top: Château de la Chèvre d'Or, Côte d'Azur, France (see p134). **Bottom:** Villa San Michele, Fiesole, Italy (see p148), designed by Michelangelo.

THE REPUBLIC OF IRELAND
Country house hotels set in rugged scenery, delicious gourmet food washed down by pints of Guinness in a pub with fiddle-strumming locals
Capital: Dublin
When to go: May to October but you could go anytime as long as you don't mind the winter weather
Average maximum temperatures °C

JAN	FEB	MAR	APR	MAY	JUN	JUL	AUG	SEP	OCT	NOV	DEC
5	5	6	8	11	14	15	15	13	11	7	6

Flight times: to Dublin from:
New York: (via London) 8 hours
LA: 12 hours
London: 50 minutes
Sydney: 25 hours
Approximate exchange rates: Irish Punt (IR£) – £1 = IR£0.97, US$1 = IR£0.63, A$1 = IR£0.49
Time difference: GMT (plus one hour from the last Sunday in March to the last Saturday in October)
Voltage: 230v AC, 50 Hz, three-pin flat or two-pin round wall sockets
Combine with: Britain and Europe
Country dialling code: ☎ 353

wit still presides and holds a magnetic attraction for people from all corners of the world. Ireland is indeed a place of great history and romance, where the hospitality and local 'craque' – the Irish colloquialism for good times – will remain lodged in your heart forever.

We had our honeymoon in Ireland, touring about from place to place. We were drawn by the idea of staying in historic country house hotels, from which we could stride out to explore the surrounding countryside after a good hearty breakfast. We would return in time to take tea before a roaring peat fire, where we'd nestle for hours until it was time to change for our gourmet five-course dinner.

For us a honeymoon in Ireland was all about eating and drinking – and what wonderful food we had! Perhaps our judgement was swayed by being on our honeymoon but I always swear I've never experienced better food than at **Ballymaloe** or **Ballylickey**. All the hotels I have listed offer such high standards in cuisine, accommodation and service that they'd be quite at home among the very best hotels in the world, but they have somehow managed to remain some of Europe's best kept secrets.

You might like to make Ireland just a three-day stopover in a longer European tour, in which case just pick one or two hotels close to each other. But the best way to see Ireland is by car, staying in three or four hotels dotted around the country. Driving is easy in Ireland although the lack of major roads tends to mean journeys take a little longer, so give yourself a few days in each hotel to truly savour the slow pace of life and wonderfully warm hospitality.

COUNTY CORK

Cork, down in the south west is the Republic's largest county. The town itself is the sailing capital of Ireland and in the summer months it's a really bustling place – its many great pubs are full of tanned sailors.

Ballymaloe House

If you fly into Cork, then Ballymaloe House is a good place to start your honeymoon as it's only an hour's drive north-east from Cork airport: it is easy to hire a car at the airport. A lovely Georgian manor turned hotel, Ballymaloe House has long been famous for its exceptionally fine food. Owner and chef, Myrtle Allen, who has won awards from critics and been praised by food lovers throughout the world, has overseen a resurgence in the popularity of traditional Irish dishes and now runs a cookery

(Opposite) Top: Dromoland Castle, County Clare, Ireland (see p120). **Bottom:** Château de Bagnols, Beaujolais, France (see p126).

BALLYMALOE HOUSE

(☎ 021-652531, fax 021-652021), Shanagarry, Co Cork, Republic of Ireland
Getting there: 40 minutes drive from Cork Airport
Accommodation: 13 rooms in the main house; 10 in the old coachyard; eight larger rooms opening out over the lawns; plus one room in the Gatehouse
Amenities: Heated outdoor pool, tennis court, craft shop on site; horse-riding, fishing, and championship golf all nearby
Dress code: Smart casual
Weddings: No
Minimum stay: None
Rates: Double rooms from US$89/IR£55 to US$105/IR£65 between May and the end of September; ask about special offers because they often do a three-day dinner, bed and breakfast package
Credit cards: Access, Visa
Taxes and service charge: Taxes are included, service charge is optional

school close to the hotel. The kitchens at Ballymaloe produce food from a bygone era, when summertime was all about freshly squeezed lemonade, and when people had time for full breakfasts. Still a working farm, everything is prepared for you on site that day – from the white triangles of toast baked that morning to the hand-churned butter, with fish having only arrived in the kitchen minutes before it arrives at your table. This small luxurious hotel has an incomparable homely feel with flowers fresh from the garden in the 32 bedrooms, wonderfully pressed white cotton sheets on king-sized beds, huge towels in the en suite bathrooms, and no television, radio or even locks on the door to bring you back to the present day. Thirteen of the bedrooms are located in the main house while five new larger rooms open on to the lawn and a stream on the north side of the building. Further bedrooms are housed in the old coach yard – if you get offered these because the main house is full don't turn them down as they are lovely spacious rooms and the food in the restaurant is just the same!

Days at Ballymaloe are spent walking, riding or touring the countryside by car. This part of Cork has rolling fertile farmland and a mixture of sandy beaches, deserted headlands and rocky inlets along the coastline. The family's 160-hectare farm also has its own outdoor swimming pool, tennis court, a small golf course and excellent craft shop. Sea and river fishing as well as a championship golf course are available close by. Whatever you do, try to get back to the hotel for tea by the fireside: you can easily while away the time before getting ready for the main event of the day – dinner.

Ballylickey Manor House

BALLYLICKEY MANOR HOUSE

(☎ 027-50071, fax 027-50124), Ballylickey, Bantry Bay, Co Cork, Ireland
Closed: From November to end of March
Reservations: Relais & Châteaux reservation numbers worldwide (see p12)
Getting there: The hotel is 82km from Cork Airport and 300km from Dublin
Accommodation: Five cottages and five suites
Amenities: Two restaurants, drawing-room, room service from 8am to 10pm; swimming pool, croquet; salmon and trout fishing, treks, golf and horse-riding nearby
Dress code: Smart in restaurants
Weddings: Ceremonies and receptions are not catered for
Minimum stay: None
Rates: Doubles from US$72/IR£45 in the cottages and up to US$145/IR£90 in the main house
Credit cards: Visa, Eurocard, American Express
Taxes and service charge: 10% on rooms and food and beverages

Ballylickey Manor House is a wonderful hotel overlooking **Bantry Bay**, in the very south of Co Cork. Built 300 years ago, the Manor House was originally used by Lord Kenmare as a shooting lodge. The hotel enjoys the most wonderful setting between the rugged inlets of Bantry Bay and the heather-covered mountains behind.

Over the last 50 years the current owners of this lovely white house have extended it so that guests can now choose between the elegant and spacious suites in the main house or the more rustic bedrooms and suites in the garden cottages. All the rooms have recently been refurbished and are beautifully decorated in pale yellows and mild apricots with floral prints and large white bedspreads.

The immaculately kept gardens are the perfect place for a mid-afternoon potter, a game of croquet on the lawn with some of the other guests, or just a sumptuous tea while looking out to sea. Everywhere you look there are different coloured roses, purple and white hydrangeas, and rhododendrons that are more like trees and hedges than bushes.

As well as being close to the sea which provides great fishing and walking, the hotel has its own outdoor swimming pool and can easily arrange golf at either one of the two courses within 5km of the hotel. There is also a really good riding school just up the road, with fine eventing horses which can be taken out on two or three-hour treks if you are experienced.

Inside, the house is filled with antiques and fine art. There is a small drawing-room, with a log fire, 17th century furniture and subtly-lit oil paintings, and an intimate dining-room which most guests are tempted to eat in due to the exceptional standard of the cuisine. I had the most fantastic lobster soufflé at Ballylickey I've ever tasted anywhere.

A FEW THINGS TO SEE AND DO AROUND CORK

Nearby **Kinsale** is considered to be Ireland's gourmet capital and is a really super place to visit for a taster of old Ireland. Among its 12 restaurants, *The Loft* (☎ 021-772803) and *The Vintage* (☎ 021-772502) are particularly good and if you're there at the end of September or early October you'll catch the city's annual Gourmet Festival. You can get details of the festival from Peter Barry (☎ 021-774 026). If you just fancy a couple of pints of Murphy's, head for *1601* on Pearse Street which is always popular, or *The Spaniard* out at Scilly which is much more cosy and a really lovely pub.

On the road to **Clonakilty** pop into the **Timoleague Castle Gardens** if you're at all into horticulture and take a detour via quaint **Courtmacsherry**. Clonakilty is a great town which was founded in the 17th century by the first Earl of Cork is now very Irish and very Catholic.

Another rare treat is *Heir Island Restaurant* (☎ 028-38102) situated on Heir Island in **Roaringwater Bay**. You have to catch a boat across to the small restaurant: the boat from Cunnamore drops you off as the sun sets and returns just before midnight to take you home again. In between you'll have had one of the best set meals of your life and the whole evening will seem like some kind of magical dream. Do book early as the restaurant gets

booked up well in advance: it only seats 16 people and it will only take you if it has a party of eight booked in, but persevere as it's worth it.

A drive down the **Mizzen Head Peninsula** is worthwhile for the beautiful scenery around **Mount Gabrielle**, the views of **Fastnet Rock** which is the turning point for the sailing race of that name that marks the end of Cowes Week each year, and the lovely sailing village of **School**, at the foot of Mount Gabrielle. Drive on to **Crook Haven** and stop for a pint at *O'Sullivans* bar. The views all around here are amazing.

Make sure you also make a detour to kiss the Blarney Stone in **Blarney Castle** (open from 9am to 7pm or sundown Monday to Saturday and Sunday 9.30am to 5.30pm or sundown), although it's painfully touristy it just has to be done: the theory goes that if you kiss the stone you'll never be at a loss for words. Other touristy places worth visiting are beautiful **Bantry House** (open daily from 9am to 6pm, and to 8pm in the summer) and the town of Bantry itself, the **Jameson Heritage Centre** in **Midleton** where whiskey has been distilled since the early 19th century, and catch the ferry across to Cape Clear and the **Skerkin Islands** for their lovely sandy beaches and two great pubs, the *Jolly Rodger* and *Garrison House*, both of which serve food.

COUNTY KERRY
Park Hotel Kenmare

Park Hotel Kenmare is without doubt one of Ireland's most popular hotels. Built on the estate of the Marquis of Lansdowne, a descendant of the Cromwellian landlord Sir William Petty who designed the local town, the building was later turned into a resting place for travellers on the Great Southern and Western Railway. It stands amidst four hectares of parkland with spectacular views over Kenmare Bay and is perfectly positioned for the Ring of Kerry.

The hotel's public rooms, full of exquisite antiques, grand interior furnishings and roaring fires, welcome you with the kind of atmosphere aimed to make you feel you

THE PARK HOTEL KENMARE
(☎ 064-41200, fax 064-41402), Kenmare, Co Kerry, Republic of Ireland
Reservations: Small Luxury Hotels of the World toll free reservations numbers worldwide (see p12)
Getting there: $1^1/_2$ hours from Cork Airport; one hour from Kerry Airport; the hotel can arrange transfers for about IR£45 each way
Accommodation: 41 rooms, nine suites
Amenities: 18-hole golf course, tennis court, fitness centre, croquet; horse-riding and fishing nearby, restaurant with Michelin star, 24-hour room service
Dress code: Neat dress after 6pm
Weddings: The hotel can have wedding ceremonies for up to 65 people, and hosts receptions for up to 120 people, prices start at IR£33 a head for dinner
Minimum stay: None
Rates: Double rooms from IR£142/US$228 to IR£214/US$344, suites from IR£252/US$405 to IR£320/US$515; ask about their 'Enchanted Breaks'
Credit cards: Most major
Taxes and service charge: Included

have just stepped back in time to a Victorian country home. Somehow owner Francis Brennan's hotel seems to epitomise all that should be expected of a truly great hotel.

Although there are only 50 bedrooms, don't expect a small, quaint hotel as the Park Hotel Kenmare is an imposing grey stone building which resembles a rather austere château. The bedrooms and suites are all spacious with rich, dark wooden furniture enhanced by pretty pale fabrics, and en suite marble bathrooms. All the standard rooms have lovely views over the surrounding mountains, while spectacular sea views can be enjoyed from all the superior rooms and suites. They are all equipped with bathrobes, Floris toiletries, TV and hair-dryer.

A member of Relais & Châteaux and Small Luxury Hotels of the World, the hotel restaurant serves a mix of classic and progressive Irish cuisine, and has received numerous international awards, including one Michelin star. Because of the culinary expertise and extensive wine list most guests dine at the hotel. The lounge, bar, alfresco drinks terrace and dining-room boast stunning views over the gardens and the estuary.

During the day there are a whole host of activities on offer including the hotel's own fitness suite, an 18-hole golf course and a tennis court. Fishing, horse-riding and some watersports can easily be arranged nearby.

A FEW THINGS TO SEE AND DO AROUND CO KERRY

The stunning **Ring of Kerry** is one of the most scenic parts of Ireland. The 177km stretch from Kenmare to Killorglin and back via the MacGillycuddy Reeks, that comprises the Ring of Kerry, has to be seen. It is easy to do the circuit, by car, in a day or two but don't try to do it in the middle of summer unless you are known for your patience with caravans and tour buses on single track roads. If you are there in the height of the season the best option is to go clockwise: the opposite direction to most of the other tourists who will be doing it the 'right' way.

I'm not a fan of Kenmare, the so-called 'jewel of the Ring of Kerry' with its pastel-painted shops and houses, or indeed Sneem, mainly because they are both so popular with tourists, but there is lots to do in the surrounding area.

Call the local tourist board (☎/fax 064-41688) for details on **cycling** routes and where to hire bicycles, **pony trekking** over the mountains and along the beaches, **salmon and trout fishing** and even deep-sea fishing, and of course for information on how to play at the two championship courses in **Killarney** and **Waterville**.

Kerry is also brilliant **walking country** with routes and paths to suit all kinds of fitness and

abilities. To the north lie the MacGillycuddy Reeks, Ireland's highest peak **Carrantuohill** (over 1000m) as well as several other munros (peaks that are smaller than mountains) and 40 peaks over 600m. To the south of Kenmare are the gentle **Cahas** which are usually covered with a rich layer of blanket bog (peat) and which stretch from Gougane Barra to the Atlantic Ocean. Or you can walk the **Kerry Way**, Ireland's longest footpath with a marked trail which starts and finishes in Killarney – just don't expect to be the only ones doing so in the summer time!

Other great driving routes in the area are the 21km scenic route over the twisting **Moll's Gap** road to Killarney and the 130km tour of the **Dingle Peninsula**, which is a great deal less touristy and just as beautiful.

For a classic Irish night out try *Nick's* (☎ 066-61219), Lower Bridge Street, Killorglin, where good hearty food such as a rack of lamb will no doubt be washed down by several pints and a sing-song around the piano, and for a delicious night out in Kenmare you can't beat *Packie's* (☎ 064-41508), Henry Street, where Maura Foley serves simple but delicious dishes in lively bistro surroundings.

COUNTY GALWAY

A few days on Ireland's west coast and you'll soon really understand why the place has always been known as the Emerald Isle. The west coast of Ireland is, in my mind, its most beautiful, and Connemara boasts some of the most splendid scenery on earth.

Cashel House

Cashel House is a small, mid-19th century country home standing at the head of Cashel Bay in 20 hectares of award-winning gardens. Owned and run by Dermot and Kay McEvilly who offer guests a warm Irish welcome, this lovely white Georgian manor house is the perfect environment in which to unwind and take in the many pleasures of the surrounding Connemara countryside.

The house is full of inviting public rooms where leather and floral-patterned sofas give guests lots of opportunity for private relaxation, in front of well-laid peat fires. Ornately framed oil paintings adorn the walls, which are painted in warm cinnamon and deep red tones. Throughout the house, there are lots of oak antiques and wonderful fresh flower arrangements from the garden.

The bedrooms are also very comfortable and all individual, with TVs, en suite bathrooms and vivid floral prints. Avoid the standard rooms as they are all very small but the garden suites are extremely spacious with their separate living and sleeping areas.

The service, accommodation and food at Cashel House are good enough to have earned it membership of the prestigious Relais & Châteaux group. Largely due, no doubt, to the hotel's excellent location on **Cashel Bay** which ensures that the lobster, scallops, salmon and mussels are all really fresh. In the summer meals are served outside in the garden or in the pretty conservatory where guests dine by candlelight on lobster, oysters au gratin, Connemara lamb and fine Irish cheeses.

Days at Cashel House are spent either out on the hotel's own fine horses, walking in the nearby Connemara hills or along the many deserted beaches taking in the scenery along the nearby and aptly named Sky Road, or enjoying the 25-minute sail out to the nearby **Aran Islands**. Tennis, golf, and salmon and sea fishing are also close to hand and can be easily arranged for you by the hotel. Rowing boats are available for residents and are ideal for exploring the coastline – make a day of it by taking a picnic. There are also a number of paths through the woods and up the summit of nearby **Cashel Hill**.

> **CASHEL HOUSE HOTEL**
> (☎ 095-31001, fax 095-31077), Cashel, Co Galway, Republic of Ireland
> **Closed**: Mid to end January
> **Reservations**: Relais & Châteaux reservation numbers worldwide (see p12)
> **Getting there**: 67km from Galway Airport; $2^1/_2$ hours from Shannon Airport and 280km from Dublin via the N59
> **Accommodation**: 32 rooms including 13 garden suites
> **Amenities**: On-site equestrian centre offering guided treks, lessons, jumping; tennis; golf at nearby Ballyconneely, salmon and sea fishing also nearby; conservatory restaurant
> **Dress code**: Most guests do wear a jacket and tie in the evening, but there is no official requirement to do so
> **Weddings**: Not catered for
> **Minimum stay**: None
> **Rates**: Doubles from US$158/IR£98 per night; garden suites from US$222/IR£138 per night
> **Credit cards**: Most major
> **Taxes and service charge**: Taxes are included, but there is a 12.5% service charge on the room and food bills

Other recommended hotels

Rosleague Manor (☎ 095-41101, fax 095-41168), Letterfrack, Connemara, Co Galway, is a lovely manor house that sits looking down on **Ballynakill Harbour**. It is not as luxurious as some of the hotels in this chapter but it will really suit you if you are looking for something a little more understated. It is comfortable but the bedrooms are ever so slightly austere with their dark wood furnishings, though the ones at the front of the house have the most dreamy views over **Diamond Hill**, **Speckled Hill** and

Letter Hill. We loved Rosleague Manor for its tranquil, laid-back atmosphere. The food is delicious and the gardens were inundated with that ubiquitous Irish rhododendron. Doubles from around US$193/IR£120 including breakfast.

A FEW THINGS TO SEE AND DO IN CO GALWAY

Connemara is all about long, leisurely strolls, island hopping from one emerald dot in the shimmering blue sea to another, and of course oysters, for which the area is famous.

Make sure your stay here incorporates a visit to the **Aran Islands**, **Dunguaire** and **Portumna** castles and as many of the **idyllic beaches** – Ballyconneely, Gurteen and Dog's are particularly beautiful – as you can.

There is a regular boat service from Galway to the Aran Islands: the journey takes around an hour and a half, or alternatively go from Rossaveal, which only takes 30 minutes. A round trip fare from Galway costs IR£15 to IR£18 and IR£12 to IR£15 from Rossaveal, for further details call (☎ 091-568903).

There are lots of wonderful restaurants in the area. Even if you don't stay there, do go along to *Rosleague Manor* (☎ 095-41101, fax 095-41168), Letterfrack, Connemara for afternoon tea or dinner. The food is delicious and the beautiful wooden dining-room very elegant.

Clifden, the capital of Connemara, is a curious place, a strange mix of tourist seaside resort and working fishing village, but it is very nice and is blessed with two great restaurants.

We went for a light snack one evening, having eaten delicious meals for days on end, but I got so over-excited about the menu at *O'Grady's Seafood Restaurant* (☎ 095-21450) that I ended up ordering the dressed lobster. O'Grady's is a bit like that, something about the menu (not the surroundings!) and the smells from the kitchen tells you to expect some seriously good seafood and you end up ordering accordingly. Just outside Clifden is the area's other most famous restaurant, *High Moors Restaurant* (☎ 095-21342), Dooneen, Clifden. Located in the somewhat unlikely setting of a room in the owners', Eileen and Hugh, bungalow, High Moors which is only open for dinner has a great atmosphere and even better food, especially the Connemara lamb.

If you feel you need to work off the seafood, it is possible to hire bicycles from **Mannions** (☎ 095-21160), or just head on foot for the hills in the **Connemara National Park**, just outside Letterfrack. The park's visitor's centre (☎ 095-41054) usually has small local exhibitions and maps for all grades of walks. If you do make it to the top of one of the famous **Twelve Bens** the sea views are incredible.

COUNTY KILDARE

Home to the famous Kildare Club, this Irish county is noted for its outdoor pastimes such as horse-racing, fishing and hunting. Spend a day at the Curragh, the famous race course where the Irish Derby and St Leger are run.

The Kildare Hotel and Country Club

The Kildare Hotel and Country Club is definitely Ireland's most complete and slick resort hotel. Set among 132 hectares of lush green woodland, the 19th century manor house was bought by Dr Michael Smurfit in 1988. It took him three years to transform the former private home into his dream hotel but the result is a truly first-class resort, with incomparable facilities.

The accolades have rolled in: Andrew Harper's Country House Hotel of the Year in 1994, a blue ribbon award from the RAC, the only Irish Gold Property Member of Relais & Châteaux.

However, the Kildare won't suit everyone: strike it off your list if you are looking for small country hotels that epitomise Irish character and hospitality because Kildare is quite simply too professional to be

THE KILDARE HOTEL
(☎ 01-627333, fax 01-627312), Straffan, Co Kildare, Republic of Ireland
Reservations: Relais & Châteaux (see p12); or Elegant Resorts (see p11)
Getting there: 40 minutes from Dublin
Accommodation: 45 bedrooms and two courtyard suites
Amenities: 18-hole par 72 championship golf course, tennis courts, squash court, swimming pool, saunas, beauty salon, gym; horse-riding, clay pigeon shooting, salmon and trout fishing all nearby.
Weddings: Can be arranged
Minimum stay: None
Rates: Doubles and suites from IR£260/US$419
Credit cards: Most major
Taxes and service charge: Included

regarded as homely. But look no further if you like your luxuries and feel safer knowing that the full health spa package is at your well-manicured finger tips. There isn't another hotel in Ireland that can compete with the Kildare's leisure facilities.

As well as an absolutely stunning indoor swimming pool with French windows opening out on to the gardens, there are saunas, professional beauty treatments, an exercise room and gym, indoor and outdoor tennis courts, and a squash court. But the real pièce de resistance at the Kildare is its 18-hole golf course, designed by Arnold Palmer and home to the Irish PGA Championships, featuring 11 lakes and covering 88 hectares of unspoilt woodland.

The rooms are pretty smashing too, each with their own satellite TV, video, and minibar. The 19th century manor house, bedecked with its fine art collection and bespoke carpets is still the focal point of this outstanding property. The **Cocktail Bar** makes a wonderful setting for early evening drinks, and the **Byerley Turk** restaurant serves up gourmet meals.

COUNTY KILKENNY

County Kilkenny, like Co Kildare, is one of those traditional Irish hunting, shooting and fishing counties where the beautiful surrounding countryside provides the perfect playground. Try to visit the 12th century Cistercian Abbey at **Jerpoint**, just south of **Thomastown**. Shopping in Kilkenny itself is also really good – a great place to buy presents to take back home and especially for your own home.

Mount Juliet Estate

Mount Juliet Estate is one of the most famous country house hotels in Ireland. There is so much for guests to do in the 640 hectares of woodland and gardens that there probably won't be much time to see anything of the rest of the county.

This beautiful grey building with its ivy-clad stone walls stands majestic, but welcoming. Most guests opt for one of the lovely rooms in the Georgian manor house itself where antique furnishings, lifted by pastel fabrics, take you back to the house's former age of glory. Many have sweeping views over the surrounding countryside. Around the stable, and not far from the main building, Hunters Yard offers less formal rooms with old timber beams, stone walls and wooden ceilings, producing a rustic, sporting atmosphere. Hunters Yard also has its own **Loft Restaurant**, which offers more casual dining than the main house's elegantly appointed pale blue **Lady Helen Dining Room**.

Mount Juliet offers its guests a broad range of facilities: two restaurants, three bars, an impressive leisure centre with a swimming pool, gym, steam room, tennis, croquet, an 18-hole Jack Nicklaus golf course, its own equestrian centre with riding trails, and a stretch of river for fishing.

You'll want for nothing at Mount Juliet: the fresh fruit and flowers in your room are changed daily, there is a fine wine list and distinguished Irish cuisine and the impeccable service pervades every aspect of your stay.

MOUNT JULIET ESTATE
(☎ 056-24455, fax 056-24766), Thomastown, Co Kildare, Republic of Ireland
Reservations: Small Luxury Hotels of the World toll free reservation numbers worldwide (see p12)
Getting there: Two hours from Dublin airport; the hotel can arrange transfers at a cost of IR£140 one way
Accommodation: 32 bedrooms: 11 in Mount Juliet House, 13 rooms in Hunters Yard, eight two-bedroom Rose Garden Cottages
Amenities: 18-hole par Championship golf course, three-hole golf academy, driving range, David Ledbetter Golf Academy, tennis, indoor swimming pool, sauna, steam room, leisure centre and beauty therapist, gym, horse-riding, croquet, fishing, clay pigeon shooting, archery, two restaurants, three bars and room service
Weddings: No
Minimum stay: None
Rates: Doubles from IR£140/US$225 to IR£230/US$370, suites from IR£325 US$523 to IR£395/US$636
Credit cards: Most major
Taxes and service: Included

Other recommended hotels in Ireland

Dromoland Castle (☎ 061-368144, fax 061-363355), Newmarket-On-Fergus, Co Clare has always been one of the most famous castles in Ireland. Standing proud among almost 160 hectares of private estate, Dromoland must be incorporated into your stay if you've always dreamt of sleeping within castle walls. Some honeymoon-ers might be put off by the size and opulence of the castle – with 73 rooms, state rooms and suites the castle is not exactly intimate. Dromoland is all about impressive chandeliers, suits of armour, crystal glassware and taking tea in the kind of drawing-room where the Queen Mother wouldn't look out of place – if you are after a bit of grandeur then this baronial seat is hard to beat. Dining is taken seriously at Dromoland: the restaurant has been awarded a Michelin and an Egon Ronay Star. There are plenty of distractions to help burn off the calories during the day, from golf at the castle's own 18-hole championship course to tennis, trout fishing, riding and shooting. Doubles from USS$180/IR£112 to US$312/IR£194, suites from US$193/IR£120.

France
(BEST TIME: ALL YEAR ROUND)

France and romance have always been synonymous. Much is due to the language itself which, like Italian, sounds so innately sensuous. But I also suspect that this long established reputation has been passed on in the minds of individuals who believe that there are very few things more romantic than sharing a three-course lunch washed down with a good bottle of wine. And nobody lunches better than the French.

Think for a minute about your images of France and you'll soon realise that they all revolve around food and drink: cycling up to the village in the morning to pick up freshly baked croissants, and coming home to sit on the terrace, dunking them in great bowls of steaming coffee; wizened old men huddled around small tables in a café, the air thick with the blue smoky haze from their Gitanne, their gnarled hands raising small shots of Pernod to their lips; sitting outside bustling Parisian cafés enjoying a mid-morning espresso; the historic châteaux and rivers of the Dordogne where the set gastronomic menu will guide you through six or seven hearty courses; or just long sunny evenings sipping kir or Provençal rosé. Whatever your favourite thoughts of France are, they are bound to include food and drink.

The strength of this association has ensured that France has long been a popular honeymoon destination but its attraction also lies in the large number of romantic châteaux spread throughout the countryside and the many amazingly unaltered medieval villages.

There are literally thousands of suitable destinations and combinations for a French honeymoon: skiing in the **Alps**, the glitzy, glamorous beaches of **St Tropez** or the elegant chic of **Cap-Ferrat**, the châteaux of the **Dordogne**, the vineyards of the **Loire** and, of course, **Paris**, long regarded as the world's most romantic city – so romantic that they have somehow succeeded in convincing us that even a rainy day in Paris is the stuff that dreams are made of.

My idea of the perfect French honeymoon would be to find an open-top sports car, pick out three hotels and enjoy leisurely driving along the lanes of the French countryside. If you stay off the autoroutes and stick to these local lanes you will see how little rural France has changed over the last century. You'll find the most memorable views doing it this way while also discovering wonderful village cafés to stop for lunch: you'll sit alongside builders and bankers as the nation halts at 12 noon to enjoy a three-course lunch and carafe of house red.

FRANCE
A honeymoon for gastronomes with hundreds of châteaux to stay in and beautiful countryside to explore
When to go: All year round: summer is from June to September, winter from December to the end of March
Average maximum temperatures °C

	JAN	FEB	MAR	APR	MAY	JUN	JUL	AUG	SEP	OCT	NOV	DEC
Paris	8	8	10	15	16	22	24	24	20	16	12	8
Lyons	8	7	11	15	17	24	26	26	22	16	11	8
Nice	12	12	14	18	20	25	27	27	24	21	16	14

Capital: Paris
Flight times: to Charles de Gaulle from:
     New York: 8 hours
     LA: 15 hours
     London 1 hour 10 minutes
     Sydney: 25 hours
Approximate exchange rates: French Franc (FF) – £1 = FF7.98; US$1 = FF5.15; A$1 = FF4.07
Time difference: GMT plus one hour (GMT plus two hours from the last Sunday in March to the last Sunday in October)
Voltage: 220v AC, 50 Hz- plugs with two round pins
Combine with: Britain, Ireland and the rest of mainland Europe
Country dialling code: ☎ 33

PARIS

It may sound a little clichéd but there are very few things more romantic in life than walking along the banks of the **River Seine** hand in hand, stopping for a mid-morning espresso at a pavement café, or dining at the **Jules Verne** restaurant in the **Eiffel Tower** looking down over Paris as the city lights up beneath you. Paris is dreamy, and there is something unmistakably chic about going there on your honeymoon. Paris also has a good range of hotels to suit every budget, from the grand hotels around the **Champs Elysées** to smaller more intimate hideaways in the **Marais** quarter. Now that Eurostar is fully operational it also makes it easier and much more enjoyable to get between London and Paris. It is however, very definitely worth avoiding Paris at Easter when there are too many children, and in August when the city is so inundated with tourists and many of the restaurants close.

Hôtel de Crillon

The celebrated Hôtel de Crillon continues to be the city's most impressive hotel. Standing as one of the two majestic façades of the celebrated Place de la Concorde, which was commissioned in 1758 by Louis XV, the Crillon continues to be very much *the* place to stay in Paris – providing you can afford the very best.

If you want to lose yourselves in the Paris of old, the Crillon is very definitely for you. The hotel's public rooms are so grand, with many fine antiques that wandering around this incredible 18th century palace is rather like viewing galleries at the **Louvre**. The hotel is only a few steps away from the exclusive boutiques of the Champs-Elysées and **Faubourg Saint Honoré**.

The 163 rooms are flamboyantly furnished but at the same time they are incredibly refined and softened with the help of French designer Sonia Rykiel's exquisite taste. All the rooms are soundproofed and air-conditioned. If you really want to lose yourself in the France of Louis XV go for rooms No 101, No 105 or No 158, where the original 18th century panelling has been completely refurbished and restored.

The former ballroom, now the palatial **Restaurant Les Ambassadeurs**, has one of the most amazing views you'll ever see and Christian Constant, one of France's

THREE DAYS IN PARIS

When you've seen the **Eiffel Tower**, **Notre Dame**, **Montmartre** and **Place Vendôme** and taken a trip on the Seine, it's time to explore some of the lesser known parts of the city.

Head up to **Villiers** in the 17th arrondissement and stroll round **Parc Monceau**, with its beautiful gold studded gates, ornamental rocks and statues and perfectly-clipped lawns. You'll pass nannies walking their charges in one of the city's most elegant neighbourhoods. Nearby **rue Levis** is an altogether different scene, where the all-day market is open seven days a week and you're more likely to bump into locals hurrying home with their baguettes than into other tourists. The stalls and shops, piled high with fresh fruit and vegetables, fish, meat, cheese and bread, are a wonderful sight.

If you're still around the 17th by dinner time, try *Le Bistro du Dix-Septième*, on Avenue de Villiers, for a classic French meal; the set menu is really good value including an aperitif, three courses and coffee.

One area you shouldn't miss is the **Marais**, over in the 4th arrondissement: it is full of interesting arty shops and boutiques at much more affordable prices than the rue Faubourg St Honoré. Walk along **rue Temple** and you're sure to find at least one little café suitable for morning coffee. The lovely **Musée Picasso** is tucked away at 5 rue de Thorigny, but provides a splendid setting for some 200 of Picasso's paintings as well as sculptures, ceramics and drawings, and is well worth a visit. Less well-known but just as impressive in architectural style is the Musée Cognac-Jay at 8 rue Elzevir. The Marais is studded with little bars, cafés and restaurants but two of the most authentic have to be *Le Coude Fou*, at 12, rue du Bourg-Tibourg, and *Au Gamin de Paris*, at 51, rue Vieille-du-Temple. The former's walls are painted with colourful frescoes and the place has a wine bar feel about it, coupled with a friendliness not always found in Parisian restaurants. The food and wine are reliably delicious which explains its popularity with the locals. The Gamin is always busy, in no small way due to the fantastic steaks they serve.

Don't miss the **Musée Auguste Rodin**, at 77 rue de Varenne in the 7th arrondissement for not only is the inside of the lovely 18th century **Hôtel Biron** home to his works, but you can also wander round the picturesque gardens and stand face to face with some of his finest sculptures.

If you fancy a French film there's no better place than **La Pagode**, 57 bis rue de Babylone also in the 7th; unquestionably the most unusual and also the loveliest cinema in Paris.

Rue Vignon is a good place for lunch, especially if you're shopping in Fauchon, near Place de la Madeleine. Rue Vignon is just around the corner and home to the most incredible cheese shop, *La Ferme Saint-Hubert* with its 180 different varieties of cheese. Either grab a snack lunch at *Tarte Julie*, where a mouth-watering variety of freshly-baked tarts is available, or at **Le Vin Vignon** a little further up the road where scrummy sandwich platters and snack lunches are served at reasonable prices.

The series of little arcades, where the 2nd arrondissement meets the 9th, is one of those often undiscovered gems of Paris. Start in **Passage des Panoramas**, at 11 boulevard Montmartre, and then head into **Passage Jouffroy**, at 10-12 boulevard Montmartre and 6 rue de la Grange-Batelière. You'll see the **Hôtel Chopin**, with its charming little dolls' house entrance, at the end of the first arcade, and plenty of antiquarian book shops and artisan gift shops. Then find **Passage Verdeau**, at 6 rue de la Grange-Batelière and 31 bis rue du Faubourg-Montmartre. This is the most elaborate of the arcades and it is full of shops with old books, postcards and posters. The Galerie Vivienne, at 4 rue des Petits-Champs, has obviously been renovated in recent years and now has a luxurious feel about it; *Le Grand Colbert* serves the ultimate hot chocolate (melted chocolate served separately with a jug of fresh cream) surrounded by huge brass lanterns and immense green palms reaching up to the high ceilings. *Le Brin de Zinc... et Madame*, at 5 rue Montorgueil will really get your taste-buds going with a huge variety of dishes served in pleasant, unassuming surroundings.

A ramble through the wonderful shops under the arches at **Place des Vosges** is a must: this lovely tree-lined square has to be one of the most romantic places in Paris. It was originally built to house the King's state apartments on one side and the Queen's on the other. There are now lots of intriguing shops to wander in and some lovely cafés and restaurants too. Alternatively take a book and sit in the park in the middle of the square and watch the Parisians as they come and go.

A final must for a delicious meal in a typically Parisian bistro is *Chez Paul*, at 13 rue de Charonne in the 11th arrondissement – superb food, French clientele and a bustling atmosphere, but make sure you book.

greatest chefs, creates French cuisine good enough to warrant two coveted Michelin stars. Alternatively try regional French dishes in the less formal **l'Obélisque**, the piano bar for early evening aperitifs, or sip afternoon tea in the **Jardin d'Hiver**, accompanied by harps. In the summer both drinks, tea and evening meals are served in the Crillon's regal courtyard.

The Crillon is the most fabulous first night hotel, especially as it offers a Romancing The Crillon package comprising a de luxe double room, a stunning bouquet of flowers, a Baccarat crystal heart and a garment bag with the hotel's crest embroidered on which would be perfect for storing your wedding dress, plus a champagne breakfast served in your room the next morning.

Other recommended hotels

Hôtel de Vigny (☎ 01-40 75 04 39, fax 01-40 75 05 81), 9-11 rue Balzac, 75008 Paris, is currently very much in vogue with the travelling cognoscenti. If you've got the money and really fancy pushing the boat out, this discreet, modern boutique hotel is hard to beat. It has the kind of unobtrusive service and peaceful atmosphere that makes it feel as if you are staying in a private residence.

The Hôtel de Vigny is located on the Rue Balzac, right in the heart of Paris and two minutes' walk from the Champs Elysées. The hotel's 37 rooms and suites are all individually decorated and have air-conditioning, minibars, marble bathrooms with hair-dryers, and TVs. Doubles from US$376/FF1900 to US$435/FF2200, suites from US$514 FF2600.

Relais Christine (☎ 01-43 26 71 80, fax 01-43 26 89 38), 3 rue Christine, 75006 Paris, is a pretty, converted 16th century monastery in the heart of the Latin Quarter. With its lovely garden and courtyard the Relais Christine is a peaceful haven in the middle of Paris. All the 35 rooms are air-conditioned and most look out over the courtyard or into the garden. Double rooms from US$360/FF1820, or book through UK tour operator Abercrombie & Kent (UK ☎ 0171-730 9600) which offers four-night packages including flights from around £625 per person.

Hôtel Le Tourville (☎ 01 47 05 62 62, fax 01-47 05 43 90), 16 av de Tourville, 75007 Paris, sits between the dome of the Invalides and the gardens of the Rodin Museum. The 30 bedrooms are fully equipped with air-conditioning and satellite TV making the Tourville a comfortable place to stay. Rooms start at around US$156 FF790; suites are available from US$295/FF490.

HÔTEL DE CRILLON
(☎ 01-44 71 15 00, fax 01-44 71 15 02), 10 Place de la Concorde, Paris 75008, France

Reservations: The Leading Hotels of the World toll free numbers worldwide (see p12) Relais & Châteaux (see p12); or UK toll free (☎ 0800-181591) and France toll free (☎ 05 05 00 11)

Getting there: Approximately 30 minutes from Charles de Gaulle Airport, 30 minutes from Orly Airport and 10 minutes from Gare du Nord; collection from either airport can be arranged for FF900 one way and from Gare du Nord for FF700

Accommodation: 120 rooms, 43 master suites, some of which overlook the Place de la Concorde; room Nos 101, 105 and 158 have had the original 18th century panelling completely restored

Amenities: Les Ambassadeurs, the principal two Michelin star restaurant, l'Obélisque restaurant serving traditional French cuisine, Le Bar, Salon de Thé for afternoon tea, seven 18th century salons for receptions, 24-hour room service, boutique, parking

Dress code: Jacket and tie are required for dining

Weddings: Although ceremonies cannot be performed at the Crillon, receptions for up to 450 guests are catered for – a cocktail reception would cost approximately FF350 per person, a sit-down dinner FF750

Minimum stay: None

Rates: Doubles from US$633/FF3200; suites from US$970/FF4900

Credit cards: Most major

Taxes and service charge: Included

THE LOIRE VALLEY
The Domaine des Hauts de Loire

The Domaine des Hauts de Loire is one of the best run and best known of all the French châteaux: it may not be cheap but it is fabulous. There can be no more luxurious base for touring the wineries of the Loire Valley than this.

Built as a hunting lodge in 1860 by publisher Panckouche, the Domaine des Hauts de Loire is the very model of a classic French château. Facing a beautiful lake, its white shuttered windows poke through rambling ivy below a grey slate roof.

This very grand château is full of Louis XIV furniture and ormolu decorated antiques, Oriental rugs, polished parquet flooring and rich organdie curtains, so you may find the grand salon a little over the top but the pretty dining-room has the most wonderful, serene atmosphere. As it's a member of Relais & Châteaux you can expect the food to be delicious, accompanied of course by the very best local vintages. A spiral staircase leads up to the hotel's bedrooms and suites decorated in traditional French style with fine antique armoires, thick cream carpet and heavy cream curtains with apricot piping matching the warmth of the apricot walls. The bathrooms are just as stunning with either oak panels or pretty honey-coloured marble and the odd oak beam running through the middle. There are several rooms in the adjacent timbered wing which are also tastefully furnished and decorated.

There's lots to do at the Domaine apart from visiting this region's numerous other châteaux and their wineries. The hotel has its own tennis court and outdoor swimming pool; you can borrow bicycles and explore the forest paths running throughout the hotel's 70-hectare private park, fish on their river or even look down on the glorious countryside from a hot-air balloon.

DOMAINE DES HAUTS DE LOIRE
(☎ 02-54 20 72 57, fax 02-54 20 77 32),
Route de Herbault, 41150 Onzain, Loire-et-Cher, France
Reservations: Relais & Châteaux worldwide reservation numbers (see p12)
Getting there: Most guests tour the Loire by car: from Tours follow the River Loire (N152) towards Blois, in Chaumont-sur-Loire go to Onzain, then follow signs to Mesland and Herbault for 3km to the hotel (200km from Paris Orly Airport)
Accommodation: 25 rooms, 10 suites
Amenities: Swimming pool, tennis court, restaurant, walks around the park, fishing; nearby golf, horse-riding, hot-air ballooning, hunting
Dress code: Jacket and tie in the restaurant
Weddings: No
Minimum stay: None
Rates: Doubles from US$129/FF650 to US$277/FF1400; suites from US$317 FF1600 to US$435/FF2200
Credit cards: Visa, Eurocard, American Express, Diners Club
Taxes and service charge: Included

A FEW THINGS TO SEE AND DO IN THE LOIRE VALLEY

A stay in the Loire usually revolves around seeing the region's many wonderful **châteaux**. There are in excess of a thousand fabulous castles strung out along the Loire River valley of which around a hundred are open to the public. If you possibly can, try to avoid July and August when the European school holidays mean the roads, not just the châteaux themselves, become unbearably crowded – hardly a honeymoon scenario!

From the Domaine des Hauts de Loire the most worthy are **Chenonceaux**, which spans the River Cher and one of the most beautiful of all the châteaux; **Amboise**, which was visited by Leonardo da Vinci and was at one time home to Francis II and his wife Mary, Queen of Scots;

and the fabulous **Cheverny** where many of the original 17th century decorations and furnishings can still be seen.

From Chenonceaux you can take to the skies in a **hot-air balloon**, which is the most superbly relaxing way to view the stunning countryside, call (☎ 02-47 23 57 64).

Aside from the famous **Valois** château, the Loire Valley is also famous for its wines, in particular for the great estates of Vouvray (☎ 02-47 52 75 03) and Chinon (☎ 02-47 93 20 75), both of which can be visited and offer wine tastings.

The charming old town of **Beaugency** is also definitely worth a visit with its majestic arched bridge spanning the river and intriguing narrow medieval streets.

BURGUNDY
Château de Gilly

Château de Gilly at Vougeot is a simply amazing château set deep in the heart of the famous Burgundy vineyards, half way between Dijon and Beaune.

The palatial, moated abbey was built in the 14th century by Cistercian monks and has since been transformed into a 48-bedroom hotel with the most wonderful atmosphere. The owners were careful to retain the abbey's ancient charm and authenticity, and with such success that this really is one of those properties in France that people now rave about.

The lounges are grand enough to make the Château feel more like a former palace than an abbey while all the bedrooms are individually decorated and are very comfortable. There is a honeymoon suite set apart from the main building, located in the grounds of the park close to the river, with its own 'salon', a balcony and a king-size bed.

The Château operates a variety of honeymoon packages offering guests either a de luxe room or the honeymoon suite, a welcome aperitif, a gourmet dinner served in **Le Clos Prieur**, tours of the local vineyards and ancient castles by horse-drawn carriage, and lunch at Bernard Loiseau's celebrated restaurant, **La Côte d'Or**, nearby. The prices vary depending on which package you go for: although they are all pretty expensive they do make a really good way of seeing the surrounding countryside.

French cuisine at its best and local vintage Burgundies are served in the impressive 14th century vaulted dining-room which was formerly the palace's cellar. Fresh produce from the Château's own grounds are used to prepare such delights as filet de boeuf de Charolias à la lie de vin, while breakfast

---

CHÂTEAU DE GILLY
(☎ 03-80 62 89 98, fax 03-80 62 82 34), Gilly-les Citeaux, 21640 Vougeot, Côte d'Or, France
Closed: From end January to early March
Reservations: Relais & Châteaux worldwide reservation numbers (see p12)
Getting there: Gilly les Cîteaux is 5km off the Nuits Saint Georges exit from A31
Accommodation: 39 rooms and eight suites
Amenities: Tennis court, table tennis, bowling green, bicycles; room service until midnight; a local beautician and hairdresser can visit the hotel if requested
Dress code: Informal but elegant dress
Weddings: Buffet receptions can be arranged for up to 150 people, and sit-down dinners for up to 230 guests; the hotel is not licensed to perform wedding ceremonies
Minimum stay: None
Rates: Double rooms from US$131 FF660; suites from US$315/FF1590
Credit cards: Visa, Eurocard, American Express, Diners Club
Taxes and service charge: Included

A FEW THINGS TO SEE AND DO IN COTE D'OR

The Côte d'Or, originally named after an abbreviation of Côte d'Orient, or 'eastern slope', is home to some of France's finest vineyards. The Côte d'Or is divided into the **Côte de Beaune** to the south, where legendary names such as Volnay, Meursault and Pommard are found, and the smaller **Côte de Nuits**, named after Nuits St Georges in the north from where Burgundy's most famous and long lasting reds derive.

Make a start at **Beaune**, the former home of the Dukes of Burgundy and the area's capital. Beaune has obviously prospered from the wine trade: there are many lovely houses rich in architecture, delightful cobbled streets and squares. The more famous local vineyards have their own shops in Beaune where you can happily while away the hours in tastings, but the best way to really get to grips with the vineyards is by doing one of the tours. **Safari Tours** (☎ 03-80 24 79 12) organise a variety of tours which depart daily (between May and October) from the **Hôtel Dieu**. At other times of the year tours must be booked in advance. Alternatively do a tour under your own steam by joining the Route des Grands Crus in **Gevrey Chambertin**: the route takes you right through the most important wine growing villages.

A bit further afield, but definitely worth the drive is one of France's best restaurants, *La Côte d'Or* (☎ 03-80 90 53 53, fax 03-80 64 08 92), where the celebrated chef Bernard Loiseau holds court.. Book well in advance.

is served in the **Pierre de Nivelle** room, with its lovely adjoining loggia.

The hotel has its own tennis court, table tennis, a bowling green and bicycles for guests' use, not to mention the 'Jardins à la Française' which are lovely for a pre-dinner stroll. It is also very well placed for discovering the surrounding Burgundy countryside and its celebrated vineyards, either by hot-air balloon or horse-drawn carriage, or even bicycle. Make sure you visit the **Clos de Vougeot**, the **Abbaye de Cîteaux**, and the **Hospices de Beaune** and **Dijon**, the former capital of the Burgundy Dukes.

BEAUJOLAIS
Château de Bagnols

Château de Bagnols is without doubt one of the most gracious, luxurious and spectacularly romantic places to stay in the whole of Europe, let alone France.

Located right in the heart of Beaujolais country this enchanted castle encircled by lavender, stands alone in terms of service and beauty. The region is constantly likened to Italy's Tuscany because of the rolling hills with their historic hilltop villages, châteaux and ancient churches. There are wonderful authentic markets to visit where you can pick up local cheeses and woven basketwear, while the abundance of vineyards makes this one of the best areas of France to tour around.

Owned by English publisher, Paul Hamlyn and his wife, and managed by Amanresorts, a small chain of exquisite properties and exceptional standards of hotelkeeping, the Château de Bagnols is a Grade 1 Listed Building which has been artistically renovated. It has been decorated so perfectly that you could easily convince yourself you've travelled back centuries into the lands of medieval knights.

Described by *Tatler* magazine as the grandest small hotel in the world – 'so luxurious as to be almost sensual' – the Château is, of course, expensive. But even if you can only stay there one night, do so, because you'll quite simply never find another hotel like it, anywhere. Four hundred craftsmen and FF319 million were required to turn this 700-year old castle with its golden stone walls into a 20th century luxury hideaway. Everywhere you look there are fine antiques, most of them priceless, collected by Mme Hamlyn from all over Europe: there is the Renaissance fireplace in the Grand Salon, the Napoleonic bath in the Suite aux Bouquets,

CHÂTEAU DE BAGNOLS
(☎ 04-74 71 40 00, fax 04-74 71 40 49), 69620 Bagnols, France
Closed: October to mid-April
Reservations: Prima Reservations worldwide toll free numbers (see p12); or through tour operators, Elegant Resorts, Abercrombie and Kent, CV Travel (see p11)
Getting there: 45 minutes from Lyon Satolas Airport; the hotel can arrange transfers at an approximate cost of FF500 one way
Accommodation: 20 double rooms: two Château Chambre, six Château Grande Chambre, one Grande Chambre Chapelle, one Suite Cheminée, one Suite Aux Bouquets, one Suite Madame de Sévigné, two Residence Chambre, five Residence Grande Chambre, one Residence Suite
Amenities: Restaurant, bar, library, tennis, pétanque, croquet, boutique, badminton, mountain bikes; the hotel can also arrange vineyard tours, walking tours, ballooning, horse-riding, horse carriage rides
Dress code: Smart casual
Weddings: Ceremonies and receptions can be arranged at the Château
Minimum stay: None
Rates: Double room from US$519 £335; suite from US$805/£520
Credit cards: Most major
Taxes and service charge: Included

17th century sofas, and many original wall paintings. All this combined with latter-day comforts such as heated floors, complimentary toiletries, bathrobes, hair-dryers, TVs and pristine Swiss linen, makes for a pretty hedonistic experience.

There are 20 double rooms; all are en suite. Each has been individually decorated with exceptional attention to detail: the soft velvets extravagantly inlaid with gold ribbons and the draped silks will surely take your breath away as you enter your room.

A FEW THINGS TO SEE AND DO AROUND BEAUJOLAIS

The ravishing countryside around the Château de Bagnols is the perfect place for a leisurely stroll. A really good **walk** leaves Bagnols eastward towards Frontenas and past the 'pigeonnier', which was once a local status symbol as only the Lord of the Manor was allowed to keep pigeons. Otherwise take the walk westwards towards Légny, which is also really scenic.

There are lots of wonderful villages to be explored by car, in particular Frontenas and Theizé, Le Bois d'Oingt, St Vérand and Ternand, Chessy, Bully and Le Breuil.

Wine enthusiasts will also enjoy following the **wine trail** around the many 'caves' in the Beaujolais region which are open to visitors. Start at Beaujeu, where the huge, multi-roomed cellar has an effigy of Anne de Beaujeu, daughter of Charles XI and once ruler of the area. If you are planning to visit the caves during the week, when things tend to be quieter, it's probably a good idea to ask the Château to make appointments for you.

If you fancy an evening out, you can choose between **21 gourmet restaurants** all within a 40-minute drive of the Château, of which 14 have Michelin stars. Don't miss *Alain Chapel* (☎ 04-78 91 82 02), in Mionnay, *Georges Blanc* (☎ 04-74 50 90 90) in Vonnas, or the *Léon de Lyon* (☎ 04-78 28 11 33) in the centre of Lyon, the gastronomic capital of France.

Few of the local châteaux are open to the public but **Lyon** has an abundance of historic buildings, two dozen museums celebrating the city's 2000-year old history and a maze of fascinating back streets in the old town to explore.

In the summer, guests can eat outside on the south-facing terrace under the lime trees, looking out over the surrounding fields. The Château's restaurant has recently been awarded a much sought after Michelin star and is now also offering guests a Sunday 'bruncheon' of typical Machon fare in the **Salle de Cuvage**.

On summer evenings, the Château holds baroque music concerts in the Cuvage, followed by drinks in the garden and then returning to the Cuvage for a full gourmet banquet. There can be few more romantic ways to spend an evening than listening to Beethoven in the magnificent surroundings of the Château Bagnols, so do make sure you ask before you book your stay which nights the concerts will be held.

A lavish swimming pool is proposed in the Roman ruins, but for now guests will have to make do with tennis, pétanque, croquet, badminton and mountain bikes.

However, one of the most enjoyable things to do from the hotel is a horse carriage ride taking you through the country lanes and stopping off for a sumptuous picnic prepared at your request by the hotel. Although not cheap at US$50 the picnic is just heavenly. Similarly wonderful are hot-air balloon trips organised by the hotel, taking off either first thing in the morning or for a couple of hours in the early evening before dinner.

SOUTH WESTERN FRANCE
Château de la Treyne
Château de la Treyne is a wonderfully isolated château set deep in the heart of the Lot Valley and spectacularly situated on the banks of the river Dordogne.

This lovely hotel really is a classically romantic Dordogne château, set on a lofty clifftop with golden stone walls, turrets and mullioned windows. The earliest of the surviving structures date from the first half of the 14th century when the Vicomte de Turenne

---

CHÂTEAU DE LA TREYNE
(☎ 05-65 27 60 60, fax 05-65 27 60 70), Lacave 46200, Lot, France
Closed: Mid November to end March
Reservations: Relais & Châteaux reservation numbers worldwide (see p12)
Getting there: 180km from Toulouse-Blagnac Airport, 200km from Bordeaux; RN20 south of Souillac, D43 towards Lacave (6km)
Accommodation: 12 rooms and two suites
Amenities: Billiards, piano playing, tennis, heated swimming pool, kayaking, fishing on the Dordogne river, hunting in season; horse-riding and golf nearby
Dress code: Casual elegance
Weddings: Wedding ceremonies in the Château's chapel which seats 60 people, otherwise an outdoor wedding in a marquee with a reception can be organised for a maximum of 150 people
Minimum stay: Guests are asked to stay two nights in low season
Rates: Double rooms from US$152 FF770; suites from US$317/FF1600
Credit cards: Most major
Taxes and service charge: Included

authorised the local lords of the manor to erect a fort at a place called Treyne. After being burnt down during the Wars of Religion, the Château was rebuilt by the de Cluzels family under Louis XIII.

Inside, the Château has been restored tastefully with traditional furnishings and a particularly beautiful painted ceiling in the Louis XIII formal drawing-room. You'll enjoy excellent hearty dinners in true Dordogne fashion, either outside on the terrace overlooking the river or inside, on colder nights, with silver candlesticks in front of a roaring fire.

The 12 bedrooms and two suites are decorated just as you'd imagine a castle should be: walls covered in deep red damasks, polished floors with intricate rugs, solid four-poster beds with hand-carved posts, and lovely large sash windows with views over the river. Honeymooners are welcomed with flowers in their room, a slice of cake and a glass of champagne.

Among the 120 hectares of gardens and woodland there is a classic formal French garden as well as several ancient trees including two magnificent cedars of Lebanon, and a Romanesque chapel which is used for piano recitals in the summer and for weddings. There is a swimming pool, a tennis court and plenty of opportunity for touring the beautiful surrounding countryside by kayak, horseback or on foot. The Château de la Treyne would make a great base for a few days' relaxation and for touring the Dordogne.

Hostellerie la Source Bleue

Hostellerie la Source Bleue is a beautifully converted mill on the south bank of the river Lot and is surrounded by the Cahors vineyards. Owned for generations by the Bouyou family, the Hostellerie dates back to the 15th century and was built from those wonderful big caramel-coloured stone blocks that one associates with medieval castles. Surrounding the hotel is the most enchanting garden with lots of unusual aspects, such as the giant bamboo around the spring of lagoon-blue water that gives this lovely little hotel its name.

Seventeen comfortable, rustic bedrooms, many of which have exposed beams, are spread between the two main buildings. They are all en suite with either a bath or shower and most have TV and phone. The rooms vary a great deal in size, the biggest and definitely the best is No 10. Located in the mill it is prettily decorated with floral curtains and bedcovers, and has exposed wooden beams, an old oak wardrobe, a large bathroom and great views over the gardens.

The separately-run restaurant, **La Source Enchantée**, is rustic and spacious and serves good quality regional cooking, accompanied by friendly service. The hotel also has a fine swimming pool which is lovely to come back to after an afternoon walk.

> **HOSTELLERIE LA SOURCE BLEUE**
> (☎ 05-65 36 52 01, fax 05-65 24 65 69), Moulin de Leygues, 46700 Touzac, Puy L'Eveque, France
> **Closed**: January to end March
> **Reservations**: Direct or through UK tour operator, Inntravel (UK ☎ 01653-628811)
> **Getting there**: Most guests hire a car from Toulouse airport (160km)
> **Accommodation:** 17 double rooms
> **Amenities**: Gardens, outdoor swimming pool, sauna, fitness room, bar, restaurant, private parking
> **Dress code**: Informal
> **Weddings**: The hotel can host weddings and receptions
> **Minimum stay**: None, but three nights if you book through Inntravel
> **Rates**: Double rooms from US$59/FF300, No 10 costs US$93/FF470 (20% discount in winter); Inntravel's seven night fly-drive holiday including Air France scheduled flights to Toulouse, seven nights' Avis car hire and seven nights' half board costs from £616 per person
> **Credit cards:** Most major
> **Taxes and service charge**: Included

Other recommended hotels

Le Moulin de L'Abbaye (☎ 05-53 05 80 22, fax 05-53 05 75 27), 1 route de Bourdeilles 24310, Brantôme-en-Perigord, Dordogne, is one of the most romantic hotels in

A FEW THINGS TO DO IN THE SOUTH WEST

The south west of France, deep in the gulf of Gascony, is all about truffles, dwarf oaks, vineyards and orchards. This is my favourite area of France: the countryside is undulating and sometimes surprisingly cliffy, the scenic villages are overshadowed by small charming castles, and every moment of the day evolves around gastronomy.

Brantôme, in the north of the Dordogne, is a lovely village on the banks of the river Dronne. Walk across the unusual elbow bridge to the abbey or just linger in the village's characterful cafés.

Most visitors to this area visit the **Lascaux Caves** lured by their incredible 15,000-year old paintings: but the very fact that they are so popular, attracting 2000 visitors a day in the height of the summer, combined with the fact that you are no longer allowed to see the originals but are taken round a 1960s copy, cunningly named Lascaux II, is reason enough to avoid them altogether.

Much further down the Dordogne valley is **Beynac**, a small hamlet nestled beneath a cliff upon which sits a 12th century fortress. The castle is open between March and October and is well worth a visit, mainly for the views. Equally picturesque are **La Roque Gageac** which clings to the cliff edge and, just upstream, Domme which is a wonderful medieval walled village.

A good day-trip from Château de la Treyne is to **Rocamadour** where the castle, chapel, houses and streets are all built right on the edge of the steep cliff-face.

France. This is the place for you if you like small, personal hotels set deep in the heart of the countryside and where you can eat delicious food. Any stay in the Dordogne must include **Brantôme**, the 'Venice of Perigord' where a Benedictine abbey is tucked into the cliffs, and **Le Moulin** which is situated right on the edge of the beautiful river **Dronne**. Guests stay in one of the hotel's three residences: the ivy-covered 15th century mill, the miller's home set against a cliff, or the home of Pierre de Bourdeilles, the abbot of Brantôme. There are only 12 bedrooms and three suites so make sure you book early. Doubles from US$109/FF550 to US$168/FF850; suites from US$178 FF900 to US$237/FF1200.

SOUTH EASTERN FRANCE

There is such a mixture of landscapes in south-eastern France that it is easy to spend time at glamorous coastal resorts and also in the numerous unspoilt medieval hillside towns. **Nice** is the focal point of the south east, and probably your arrival point: the famously chic seaside resorts of **Cannes**, **St Tropez** and **Monte Carlo** are within an hour and a half's drive. At the coastal resorts there is no getting away from the feeling that you are right in the very midst of the fashionable élite.

Auberge de la Vignette Haute

Set deep in the heart of Provence, the Auberge de la Vignette Haute is the perfect little hotel for escaping the summer crowds and experiencing this wonderful region of France at its very best.

Nestled halfway between **Grasse**, the capital of perfumes, and glamorous Cannes, this charming 17th century inn seems a world away from the bustling coast. It has been lovingly restored by its owners and offers 12 guest rooms, each of which is individually decorated. There are wonderful views of the

AUBERGE DE LA VIGNETTE HAUTE
(☎ 04-93 42 20 01, fax 04-93 42 31 16), 370 Route du Village, 06810 Auribeau sur Siagne, Cannes, Provence, France
Closed: Mid November to end March
Reservations: Small Luxury Hotels of the World toll free numbers (see p12)
Getting there: The hotel is situated on the D509 just off the D109 between Cannes and Grasse through Mandelieu; it is 40km or 45 minutes from Nice Airport
Accommodation: 12 guest rooms
Amenities: Outdoor swimming pool, terrace, garden, river fishing, hiking, restaurant and bar, room service; tennis, golf, and fishing nearby
Dress code: Informal
Weddings: Weddings for up to 150 people at a cost of US$100/FF520 per person including food, champagne and music
Minimum stay: None
Rates: Doubles from US$250/FF1300
Credit cards: Most major
Taxes and service charge: Included

undulating countryside from the rooms' tiny balconies. All the rooms are well equipped with colour TV, minibar, in-room safe, air-conditioning, a jacuzzi-bath, toiletries, hair-dryer, make-up mirror, trouser press, bathrobes and slippers.

The terrace is the perfect place to sit either during the day under one of the large umbrellas or, at night, to look down over the swimming pool.

All around the inn, the rolling hills of **Auribeau sur Siagne** are covered with fields of lavender and huge wild sunflowers, punctuated only by the odd stone house. If you've never been to Provence you'll be amazed at the vivacity and vastness of this rolling carpet of purple, green and yellow.

Eating in the restaurant is very romantic: the flames from the oil lamps flicker on the rough stone walls, you sit at solid oak tables, pour your wine from pewter jugs and drink from goblets. The local cuisine is hearty Provençal in style and absolutely delicious.

Hôtel Le Calalou

The lovely Hôtel Le Calalou nestles below the picturesque hilltop village of Moissac, amongst some of Provence's most breathtaking scenery. The impressive Provençal manor house has been built in the typical long low style with a wonderfully cool interior which is simply but elegantly decorated.

The hotel's 35 bedrooms are comfortable and beautifully appointed. There are two mini suites which have a small sitting area, while all rooms are en suite with TV, phone, minibar and hair-dryers. If you can, try to get room No 18; it is decorated in white and blue and has a small sitting area and a magnificent view of the surrounding countryside.

There is a bar, a restaurant which draws much inspiration from the local region and specialises in dishes from the Antilles, and a reading and video room. There are spacious gardens of cork-oak and ancient olive trees and a shady terrace which is a perfect place to sip the local rosé and dine.

From the lovely swimming pool you can stare out to the south across field after field of purple lavender swaying in the breeze. This is Provence at its best, a land of lavender, cork-oaks and chirping cicadas. The hotel is close to **Moustiers-Ste-Marie**, a village famed for its beautiful ceramics and the start of the dramatic **Gorges du Verdon**. The sheer scale of the gorge is breathtaking, at points the cliffs are 900m high with dizzying views down to the turbulent river below.

> **HÔTEL LE CALALOU**
> (☎ 04-94 70 17 91, fax 04-94 70 50 11), 83630 Moissac-Bellevue, Provence, France
> **Reservations:** Direct or through UK tour operator Inntravel (UK ☎ 01653-628741)
> **Getting there:** Most guests hire a car from Marseille Airport (46km)
> **Accommodation:** 35 bedrooms, including two suites
> **Amenities:** Restaurant, bar, reading and video room, tennis court, heated outdoor swimming pool, private parking
> **Dress code:** Informal
> **Weddings:** The hotel can cater for receptions for up to 160 people
> **Minimum stay:** Three nights
> **Rates:** Inntravel's seven day fly-drive package including scheduled Air France flights to Marseilles, seven days' Avis car hire and seven nights' half board costs £724/US$1122 per person
> **Credit cards:** Most major
> **Taxes and service charge:** Included

Other recommended hotels

Hostellerie de Crillon Le Brave (☎ 04-90 65 61 61, fax 04-90 65 62 86), Place de l'Eglise, 84410 Crillon le Brave, Vaucluse is the most fantastic hotel situated above the charming medieval village of Crillon le Brave, not far from **Avignon**. Most of the 24 bedrooms and suites enjoy superb views over the vineyards and olive groves, while Souleiado fabric and strong tones of ochre complement the original stone and woodwork perfectly. Dining on the hotel's terrace, perched on the edge of the hillside is really romantic or, in cooler weather, you can eat inside in the impressive vaulted dining-room. Surrounded by famous vineyards, and with lovely countryside for walking and rustic hilltop towns, this is a fabulous base for touring Provence. Doubles start at around US$158/FF800, or you can book a four-night package with flights through UK tour operator Abercrombie & Kent for £516 (UK ☎ 0171-730 9600). However it is closed from January to early March.

A FEW THINGS TO SEE AND DO AROUND THE GORGES DU VERDON

The Verdon is home to endless stretches of purple lavender fields, bubbling green waters in awe-inspiring gorges, **Provençal markets** where a rich variety of local produce can be found alongside traditional craftwork. Look out in particular for pretty jars of olive oil containing herbes de Provence, lavender soaps, huge tins of olives, and prettily decorated steep-sided bowls from which the French drink coffee. **Canoeing** and **kayaking** are very popular in the Gorges du Verdon and can be organised through **Club Nautique d'Esparron** (☎ 04-92 77 15 25), **canyoning** is arranged by **SERAC** (☎ 04-31 08 96 08, fax 04-92 64 00 74), while the best people for **rafting** are simply called **RAFT** (☎ 04-92 83 72 75, fax 04-92 83 75 81).

Dégustation tours of the Provence area are a must for anyone remotely interested in food and drink: try Vignobles Maison des Vins (☎ 04-94 47 47 70, fax 04-94 73 36 13) in Les Arcs.

THE COAST
Grand Hôtel du Cap-Ferrat

Grand Hôtel du Cap-Ferrat is a living legend and has long been known as one of the world's most luxurious hotels, so it is difficult to imagine quite how fantastic it is now after its recent US$40 million refit!

This grand old dame of a hotel is blessed by a wonderfully private location right on the tip of the exclusive Cap-Ferrat peninsula. The views are quite unbeatable but even the grand white façade of the hotel itself contributes to the grace, elegance and unmistakable chic of this part of the world. Huge palms tower over the stately marble archways, while the water from the pool glides seamlessly over its invisible edge.

The facilities are all first rate: from the hotel's own beach club, the Club Dauphin, to the funicular which takes you effortlessly down to the Mediterranean past five hectares of semi-tropical hotel gardens. The exquisite cuisine of Jean-Claude Guillon, who after 25 years in residence has become as much a part of this French institution as the rocky coastline itself, has earned him a Michelin star. The restaurant itself, called **Le Cap,** is the epitome of opulence with its original marble floors, murals on the walls and mosaic dolphins. It is divided into two sections, a terrace lined with umbrellas pines and a classic hall overlooking splendid gardens. During the day you can tuck into great alfresco snacks beside the pool.

The 59 bedrooms and suites are furnished in pastel shades with huge French windows, while they all boast air-conditioning, TV, minibar, and views of either the sea or the pine woods behind the hotel. The marble bathrooms have everything you would

GRAND HÔTEL DU CAP FERRAT
(☎ 04-93 76 50 50, fax 04-93 76 04 52), Boulevard du Général de Gaulle, 06230 Saint-Jean-Cap-Ferrat, Alpes-Maritime, France
Reservations: Relais & Châteaux worldwide toll free reservation numbers (see p12); or through tour operators Elegant Resorts and Abercrombie & Kent (see p11)
Getting there: 20 minutes from Nice Airport, the hotel can arrange transfers which cost around FF450
Accommodation: 59 rooms, including junior, senior and the massive Presidential suite which occupies the entire fourth floor
Amenities: Olympic sized swimming pool, pool-side restaurant, Le Cap restaurant, funicular railway running between hotel and beach, tennis; plus golf, watersports, climbing, casinos and museums nearby
Dress code: Informal during the day, but jacket and tie are required in the restaurant in the evening
Weddings: Can be arranged
Minimum stay: 2 nights over a weekend
Rates: Double rooms from US$257/FF1300; suites from US$564/FF2850, breakfast included
Credit cards: Visa, Eurocard, American Express, Diners Club
Taxes and service charge: Included

expect, such as bathrobes, toiletries, wonderful power showers and a separate toilet.

The best thing about staying at the Grand Hôtel is that you can have it all: either relax with a kir royal at the **Piano Bar** before enjoying a sophisticated night in with an alfresco dinner or don your glad rags and hit the roulette tables at nearby Monte Carlo.

One word of warning, if you are intending to stay during July or August make sure you book really early as the hotel is always fully-booked during the peak season.

La Réserve

Following a vast renovation plan La Réserve, a 19th century Florentine-style palace overlooking the Mediterranean, can once again be counted amongst the very greatest hotels in the world. It is reputed to be so good that most top hoteliers would give it their vote as the world's most professionally run hotel – not a bad recommendation.

Just 20 minutes from Nice, La Réserve has been operating as a hotel since 1894. The hotel's Mediterranean character along with its famous apricot hew was preserved during the refit, but the bedrooms have been totally renovated making them bigger. Better views over the bay have been created by enlarging the bay windows.

Throughout the interior, pastel shades predominate blending with soft coloured fabrics and Bottichino marble. Many of the bedrooms are shades of cream, with fine antique furniture and elegant light fittings. La Réserve is an intimate hotel with 37 rooms, each of which is air-conditioned and each has a minibar, satellite TV, radio, phone, in-room safe, hair-dryer, toiletries and bathrobes.

The Michelin-rated restaurant offers truly gastronomic dishes, while there is also a lovely alfresco dining terrace. Service at La Réserve is impeccable, due largely to the expertise of Gilbert Irondelle, who has previously run both Le Crillon in Paris and the Mandarin Oriental in Hong Kong.

La Réserve is an extremely refined hotel, with an exceptionally elegant, not to mention famous, clientele. The hotel has its own heated salt-water pool, with wonderfully comfy pink and white striped loungers and parasols lining its edge and an adjacent restaurant, as well as boat trips and watersports, and use of the beach at the nearby Royal Riviera hotel. Monte Carlo and Cannes are just 20 minutes away.

> **LA RESERVE**
> (☎ 04-93 01 00 01, fax 04-93 01 28 99),
> 5 Bd General Leclerc, Beaulieu-Sur-Mer,
> 06310 France
> **Reservations:** Small Luxury Hotels of the World toll free reservations numbers worldwide (see p12); or through UK tour operator Elegant Resorts (see p11)
> **Getting there:** 30 minutes from Nice International Airport; hotel transfers are available on request and cost FF400 one way
> **Accommodation:** 21 rooms and 16 suites
> **Amenities:** Gastronomic restaurant, bar, sea and garden view lounge, heated outdoor sea-water swimming pool, restaurant by the pool, private port providing access to the hotel by boat and watersports, local tours and activities organised on request
> **Dress code:** Ties and jackets are required at the gastronomic restaurant
> **Weddings:** La Réserve caters for wedding receptions for up to 120 people, costing upwards of FF500 per person
> **Minimum stay:** None
> **Rates:** Doubles from US$406/FF2100; suites from US$610/FF3150
> **Credit cards:** Most major
> **Taxes and service charge:** FF6 per person per day city tax

Le Saint Paul

Le Saint Paul is definitely one of the most romantic small hotels in France. Located in the heart of this superb medieval village, the hotel is a great place to spend three or four days savouring the exclusivity of remaining in Saint Paul long after the crowds have departed each night.

Because it is so lovely with its winding cobbled streets, medieval ramparts, profusion of tiny dwellings housing exclusive shops and bustling restaurants, Saint-Paul-de-Vence is the second most visited village in all France, so don't come here expecting to find an undiscovered hideaway. If you like your hotels small, intimate and old, and are also passionate about wining and dining then you'd be hard pressed to beat this lovable 16th century bourgeois house.

The hotel's 15 rooms and three suites, are all individually furnished with warm Provençal-style fabrics producing a light and elegant atmosphere in contrast to the rustic stone walls of the lounge/bar area. The rooms are air-conditioned and have a TV, minibar and en suite bathroom, but they are small and you shouldn't expect the facilities of a big hotel. While some rooms overlook the village the best views are out over the valley. If you really want to splash out, there is a wonderful honeymoon suite and another suite with a beautiful flower-filled terrace.

> **LE SAINT PAUL**
> (☎ 04-93 32 65 25, fax 04-93 32 52 94), 86 rue Grande, 06570 Saint-Paul-de-Vence, Alpes-Maritimes, France
> **Closed**: Early January to mid February
> **Reservations**: Relais & Châteaux worldwide reservation numbers (see p12); or through Elegant Resorts (see p11)
> **Getting there**: 20 mins to Nice Airport
> **Accommodation**: 15 rooms and 3 suites
> **Amenities**: Lounge/bar, restaurant and terrace
> **Dress code**: Elegant casual
> **Weddings**: No
> **Minimum stay**: None
> **Rates**: Double rooms from US$139 FF700 to US$277/FF1400; suites from US$247/FF1250 to US$416/FF2100
> **Credit cards**: Most major
> **Taxes and service charge**: Included

The first-class cuisine and service found here can be credited to Olivier Borloo, the former managing director of Relais & Châteaux. Since taking over Le Saint Paul, Borloo has had it completely refurbished so that its Provençal-style rooms are now immaculate. While all is elegant and pristine inside, the outer walls of this ancient hotel are ancient sandstone so eating outside under the stars on the dining terrace leaves you in no doubt that you are in the very heart of rustic Provence. Book your place in this restaurant when you book your room as it is small and very popular.

Hôtel de la Cité

Hôtel de la Cité is a truly excellent hotel in the most unbelievable setting. Located in a delightfully sheltered position behind the ramparts of the incredible medieval city of Carcassone, this former episcopal palace has been transformed into a luxury hotel.

Inside the hotel is just as exciting as outside. There are magnificent tapestries, original wood panelling, a superb library which is the oldest part of the hotel and the most wonderful place to sit and read the paper or a good book over afternoon tea. The best bedrooms overlook the ramparts from where the views are breathtaking.

The restaurant **La Barbacane**, with its mock Gothic windows and miniature golden fleurs-de-lys shield and lion motifs on the deep green walls, has won two Michelin stars securing its ranking among the world's most famous restaurants. For a more casual alternative there is **Les Coulisses du Théâtre**, a bistro situated in the square next to the hotel.

Set in beautiful gardens, the hotel overlooks the town and the surrounding **Languedoc** countryside with its vineyards and Cathar castles. I can think of few places more unusual to be on your honeymoon – this really is a fairytale place where, crossing that heavily fortified drawbridge, you step back into a completely different world.

> **HÔTEL DE LA CITÉ**
> (☎ 04-68 25 03 34, fax 04-68 71 50 15), Place de l'Eglise, 1100 Carcassonne, France
> **Reservations**: Small Luxury Hotels of the World toll free reservations numbers worldwide (see p12)
> **Getting there**: The hotel does not arrange transfers from Toulouse the nearest airport (90km away), but you can take a train to Carcassonne from where the hotel's van will pick you up
> **Accommodation**: 23 rooms, three suites
> **Amenities**: Outdoor swimming pool, golf nearby
> **Dress code**: Casual, even in la Barbacane
> **Weddings**: The hotel cannot perform wedding ceremonies but does host receptions for up to 250 people, menus start at FF400 per person
> **Minimum stay**: None
> **Rates**: Doubles from US$202/FF1020 to US$274/FF1250; suites from US$317 FF1600 to US$366/FF1850
> **Credit cards**: Most major
> **Taxes and service charge**: Included

Other recommended hotels

There is a continual debate between the travelling cognoscenti as to the relative merits of the two world renowned cliff-edge hotels in tiny **Eze Village**. The village is just incredible, with its narrow cobbled streets, medieval château, steep panorama of the Mediterranean and hundreds of tiny houses with terracotta-tiled roofs occupying every inch of space. It can only be reached on foot and is therefore not for the faint-hearted – donkeys are even used to carry guests' luggage up to the hotels. Both hotels are indisputably romantic, both have breathtaking views looking down on Cap Ferrat and both have small, well-decorated bedrooms in medieval châteaux.

The Château Eze (☎ 04-93 41 12 24, fax 04-93 41 16 64), 06360 Eze Village, Côte d'Azur, France (Closed: November to April), perched right on the cliff-edge is a former residence of a Swedish Prince. With only ten bedrooms the problem with the Château Eza is managing to get a room in the first place. Everything about the hotel is stunning: the views, the half-timbered bedrooms some of which have four-posters and many of which have terraces or balconies, and the Michelin-star Provençal restaurant. Double rooms from US$396/FF2000; suites from US$495/FF2500.

The Château de la Chèvre d'Or (☎ 04-92 10 66 66 , fax 04-93 41 06 72), Moyenne corniche, rue du Barri, 06360 Eze Village, Côte d'Azur, France (closed: end November to early March) has some truly wonderful rooms and the views from the dining-room, the bar or the terrace pool are simply dazzling. The addition of two swimming pools is one factor in the Chèvre d'Or's favour, and the lovely suites perched right on the cliff-edge in detached cottages make the perfect room with a view. Double rooms from US$257/FF1300; suites from US$514/FF2600, but do ask about their honeymoon package which offers two nights' accommodation in one of their best rooms, breakfast each morning, dinner at the Chèvre d'Or on one night and one lunch at the Grill du Château, for around US$866/FF4375 during the week off season and US$1070/FF5407 during the week in peak season.

THE ALPS

Le Melezin

Le Melezin, overlooking the French Alps in Courchevel, has to be the ultimate honeymoon destination for winter sports enthusiasts. Resting at the foot of the Bellecote run in one of Europe's premier ski resorts, it is difficult to imagine a more superior ski chalet. Owned by Amanresorts, the super luxurious chain, Le Melezin is terribly expensive but worth it. The hotel enjoys a prime location in the heart of Courchevel so that you can ski in and out of the front door. However, it is not the hotel's location that is so amazing, but the incredibly sophisticated and elegant decorations and the awesome standards of hotel-keeping that have become recognised as hallmarks of Amanresorts.

The 34 bedrooms are beautifully appointed with typically Aman understated but wonderfully designed, furniture, as well as low voltage spot lighting and every possible amenity including bathrobes, satellite TV, hair-dryers, in-room safe, complimentary toiletries, phone and slippers. Where else in the Alps are your boots warmed for you before

---

LE MELEZIN
(☎ 04-79 08 01 33, fax 04-79 08 08 96), rue de Bellecote, 73120 Courchevel 1850, France
Reservations: Prima Hotels (see p12)
Getting there: For FF2000 the hotel can arrange transfers from Geneva (162km) or Lyon (225km); alternatively get the train up to Moutiers and a taxi from there
Accommodation: 34 guest rooms: six chambre junior, eight chambre vallée, 15 chambre ski piste, three chambre Melezin, two suites
Amenities: Restaurant, bar, room service
Dress code: Smart casual
Weddings: No
Minimum stay: None
Rates: Junior chambre from US$396 FF2000, chambre ski piste from US$594 FF3000, chambre Melezin from US$693 FF3500, suites from US$1187/FF6000, all inclusive of breakfast
Credit cards: Most major
Taxes and service charge: Included

you leave each morning, where else can you lie back in your huge foam filled bath looking straight out across the surrounding snow-capped peaks, and where else is afternoon tea provided outside on tables hewn out of local logs? Like all Amanresorts this place is just magical.

Spain
(BEST TIME: ALL YEAR ROUND)

While travel snobs may wince to hear that you are heading off to Tuscany or the Dordogne on your honeymoon (despite being heavenly both areas are 'just too clichéd') it is currently quite acceptable to have fallen in love with Spain. Not the southern coast of course, that was effectively ruined over a decade ago, but the interior where places like **Catalonia**, **Andalucia** and **Salamanca** are reassuringly undiscovered and you can find your own pace of life in traditional rural communities.

A week or two touring in Andalucia or Catalonia is a great way to see this amazing country. Pick one hotel to stay in for a week and maybe another one or two for just a few days each: this will enable you to relax, see the lovely countryside and explore its countless historic Moorish towns and cities, the vast mountains, parched plains, verdant forests, mass of olive groves and the many remote hilltop villages.

SPAIN

A dignified land with a rich heritage of castles, culture and gastronomy where rural life still continues as it has for centuries

When to go: All year round, but March to June and September and October are the best months for warm sunshine and fewer crowds

Average maximum temperatures °C

	JAN	FEB	MAR	APR	MAY	JUN	JUL	AUG	SEP	OCT	NOV	DEC
Madrid	10	11	15	18	20	26	29	28	24	18	13	10
Costa del Sol	17	17	19	20	22	26	27	28	27	22	19	17
Majorca	14	15	17	19	21	25	27	27	26	22	18	16

Capital: Madrid

Flight times: to Madrid from:
New York: 7^1/$_2$ hours
LA: 13 hours
London: 2 hours
Sydney: 29 hours

Approximate exchange rates: Pesetas (P) – £1 = P198, US$1 = P127.66, A$1 = P100.88

Time difference: GMT plus one hour (two hours from the last Sunday in March to the last Sunday in October)

Voltage: 220v AC, with two-pin plugs

Combine with: Anywhere else in Europe

Country dialling code: ☎ 34 (omit the first digit 9 on the numbers below when calling from outside Spain)

CATALONIA

Many people underestimate Catalonia: close to **Barcelona**, it is the country's undisputed gastronomic capital. People are forever telling me that they couldn't believe the quality of the cuisine: I hear many 'I've never eaten so well in my life' kind of comments. For shopaholics, duty-free Andorra is close by, and all around you are charming medieval villages and staggering Pyrenean scenery.

Hotel El Castell

If fine food and wine are likely to play a pretty important part in your honeymoon I can strongly recommend a stay at the Hotel El Castell. Standing on a hill beneath the ruins of an old castle, just outside the atmospheric medieval village of La Seu d'Urgell,

HOTEL EL CASTELL

(☎ 973-350704, fax 973-351574), Route N-260, km 229, Apto. 53, E-25700, La Seu d'Urgell, Spain

Reservations: Relais & Châteaux toll free reservation numbers worldwide (see p12); or with UK tour operator Magic of Spain (UK ☎ 0181-748 4220)

Getting there: 200km from Barcelona, most guests drive to the hotel, although they can arrange a taxi to collect you from Barcelona

Accommodation: 34 rooms, four suites

Amenities: Restaurant, bar, lounge, terrace, swimming pool (towels provided)

Dress code: Jackets and ties are not required, but gentlemen are asked to wear long trousers for dinner

Weddings: Small wedding parties can be arranged, but only up to 60 people

Minimum stay: None

Rates: Doubles from US$123/P15,500; suites from US$203/P25,000

Credit cards: Visa, Eurocard, American Express, Diners Club

Taxes and service charge: 7% tax will be added to your bill, service is included

the hotel is surrounded by the lovely mountain scenery of the high Pyrenees.

Built in local rustic style no more than two storeys high, it has a really relaxed atmosphere, with sufficient luxury and impeccable service to remind you that you're staying somewhere very special. What makes the El Castell particularly special is undoubtedly its owner managers, Jaume and Katia Tapies: nothing is too much for them. Jaume was formerly at England's Chewton Glen and he now heads the Spanish arm of Relais & Châteaux. The hotel's cuisine, recognised by a Michelin star, is matched by its wine. The cellars are reputed to be the second largest in Spain with nearly 15,000 bottles accumulated from all over the world.

The 38 comfortable bedrooms are all elegantly furnished with en suite bathroom, toiletries, TV and minibar. Some rooms have incredible sunset views from their balconies and terraces. There's lots to see and do in the surrounding mountainous countryside, be it a balloon flight over the **Cadi-Moixero National Park** or one of the hotel's terrific jeep tours into the local forests. These are a must as you not only see much more of the countryside than you ever could on foot, but the jeeps are met by the most incredible picnic lunch all laid out for you on the forest floor: waiters in black tie stand ready to pass you a glass of champagne and quails' eggs. Heaven.

The perfect Catalonian honeymoon would be to combine four or five days in El Castell with the much simpler, but equally gastronomic, **Ca'n Boix**, (☎ 973-470266) just 45 minutes away in the lower Pyrenees. The lovely Ca'n Boix has 50 bedrooms, but do make sure you request a superior suite as it's not much more expensive and it is certainly worth the extra cost.

A FEW THINGS TO SEE AND DO IN CATALONIA

Catalonia is an autonomous region with a totally distinct culture, language and history. It is one of Spain's most prosperous areas and is as rich in its cultural heritage thanks to Dalí and Picasso, as it is in its gastronomy. The region is particularly noted for the way its kitchens combine meat and seafood in one dish, known locally as Mar y Montana, producing meals such as 'pollo con langosta' (chicken with langoustines).

There is much to experience in Catalonia, quite apart from **Barcelona**. The rugged coastline of the **Costa Brava** is full of undiscovered retreats and the national parks, and peaks and valleys of the Pyrenees are magnificent in their beauty.

Whether or not you are staying at El Castell the hotel can arrange a whole host of visits and activities, such as balloon flights over the

Cadi-Moixero National Park or cultural tours and duty-free shopping in **Old Andorra**. One thing you mustn't miss are the jeep tours through the surrounding forests over big terrain which culminate in a sumptuous picnic with champagne served by waiters in black tie.

From the Mas de Torrent there are many wonderful **small villages** to explore, including nearby Pals and Peratallada, as well as Monells, Ullastret, Vulpellac and Fonteta all of which are within a 14km drive of the hotel and have many historical monuments and churches of interest. La Bisbal is also worth a visit to wander round the numerous ceramic shops which have gained this city international recognition.

The **Dalí Museum** in **Figueres**, the second most visited museum in Spain, is a definite must for art lovers and is only 40km from Torrent.

Mas de Torrent

The Mas de Torrent is a simply gorgeous hotel in the countryside just outside the hamlet of Torrent. If you are looking for total relaxation in absolutely beautiful, tranquil surroundings, this has to be a contender.

The main part of the hotel, including the gourmet restaurant and lounges, is housed in a converted 18th century farmhouse reminiscent of Provence's golden stone buildings, while some of the bedrooms are scattered amongst the hotel's lovely gardens, close to the swimming pool.

The bedrooms, most of which are named after flowers, are very comfortable and spacious. They have rustic furniture and good amenities including bath/toilet, air-conditioning, minibar, in-room safe, satellite TV and fresh fruit on arrival. Most of the bedrooms in the main building have a balcony, while the individual bungalows all have their own private gardens rich with the smell of lavender, agapanthus and green cypress trees. My favourites are Iris with its lilac colour-washed walls, the Garden bedroom which is more modern with fresh cream and blue striped fabrics and rattan furniture, and Geranium for its carved wooden bed.

The gourmet restaurant was decorated by contemporary Spanish artists as a tribute to Picasso and offers fine Catalan cuisine incorporating lots of seafood. A typical dish might be a fresh pasta salad over a carpaccio of prawns, or monkfish medallions on a bed of mushrooms.

Located just 10km from the beaches of the **Costa Brava** the Mas de Torrent makes a great base for touring the most picturesque parts of this coastline, such as **Palafrugell** and **Begur**. With comfortable rooms and delicious food to return home to each evening you can join the long list of people who rave about this hotel.

ANDALUCIA

Finca Buen Vino

About 100km from **Seville** and near **Aracena**, the Finca Buen Vino, which is owned by Sam and Jeannie Chesterton, is a perfect private hotel. With only six rooms, guests are guaranteed a feeling of warm hospitality in very special, homely surroundings.

The Finca (a farm) is located amidst 60 hectares of woodland, which makes it a wonderful place for walking and horse-riding. It's a romantic hotel and is ideal for those who like peace and quiet and prefer not to be surrounded by lots of other guests. Upstairs

---

MAS DE TORRENT
(☎ 972-303292, fax 972-303293), E-17123 Torrent, Spain
Reservations: Relais & Châteaux reservation numbers worldwide (see p12); or through UK tour operator Magic of Spain (UK ☎ 0181-748 4220)
Getting there: The hotel can arrange a taxi from Barcelona (P18,000)
Accommodation: Six suites and four double rooms in the main building and 20 suites in bungalows in the garden
Amenities: Restaurant, lounge, bar, outdoor swimming pool, terraces, tennis court, mountain bikes, tour desk, 24-hour room service, library
Dress code: Smart casual, jacket and tie are not required
Weddings: Available on request, there are a variety of different menu prices
Minimum stay: None
Rates: Doubles from US$214/P27,000; suites from US$254/P32,000
Credit cards: Most major
Taxes and service charge: 7% tax added to your bill, service not included

---

FINCA BUEN VINO
(☎ 959-124043, fax 959-124034), Los Marines, 21203 Huelva, Spain
Reservations: Either direct or through CV Travel (UK ☎ 0171-581 0851)
Getting there: The Chestertons recommend a charter flight to Seville from where they can organise a taxi for about £65/P13,000; or fly to Faro and hire a car (a $2\frac{3}{4}$ hour drive)
Accommodation: Six rooms
Amenities: Pool, fabulous natural surroundings for horse-riding and walking
Dress code: Informal
Weddings: None
Minimum stay: Minimum stay is three days at the main house and one week in the poolhouse cottage (rental from Friday to Friday, but you can stay an extra night in the main house)
Rates: Doubles from US$201/P25,650
Credit cards: EuroCheques and cash (Spanish pesetas) only
Taxes and service charge: 7% tax and staff gratuities

there are two charming bedrooms each with its own bathroom – one has a double bed, the other a twin – while the downstairs bedrooms have adjoining bathrooms. All the cooking is done by Jeannie, who is Cordon-Bleu trained and who enjoys using ingredients from the surrounding area, giving her creations a distinctly Mediterranean flavour.

The villa has been tastefully decorated using English and Spanish country furniture and fabrics producing a wonderfully welcoming and lived-in feel. The view from the large sitting-room overlooks the surrounding hilly countryside. Further up the hill from the house is a lovely pool and a poolhouse cottage which is great for honeymooners, though the noise and the presence of other guests may be distracting. Drinks are taken by the pool or in the conservatory – you just help yourself, fill in the bar-book and are billed at the end of your stay.

If you are looking for peace and quiet in a rural setting and are not into large pampering hotels then Finca Buen Vino is the place. The tranquillity is absolute.

Casa de Carmona

Staying at Casa de Carmona is just like being a guest in a private house, and a very beautiful one at that.

This 16th century conversion of the former Lasso de la Vega Palace retains many beautifully preserved original features and is furnished throughout with lovely antiques and stunning fabrics. The 30 individually decorated bedrooms are all provided with central heating and air-conditioning, bathrobes, toiletries, minibar, TV, videos and a stereo in the de luxe suites. Although it is lovely to have such luxuries, it is the exceptional decor and architecture of the rooms that make people so enthusiastic about the Casa de Carmona. The rooms couldn't be more romantic with their draped fabrics hanging over four-poster beds, and strong imaginative use of colour on the arched walls.

The most wonderfully relaxed atmosphere really does make you feel as if you are in a private home, a sentiment enhanced by welcoming touches such as the free bar in the library: guests help themselves to drinks. The hotel's restaurant is open from 1.30 to 4.30pm for lunch and from 8.30 to 11.30pm for dinner, which gives you plenty of time to explore in the mornings, eat a long, lazy, late lunch, followed by an even longer and lazier siesta and then dine at a typically late Spanish hour.

Carmona is ideally situated for exploring the famous cities of **Jerez**, **Granada** and Seville, and lesser known towns like **Cordoba**. Carmona itself is a beautifully preserved hilltop town, with some of the buildings dating back to Roman times. The Roman walls and necropolis are well worth visiting and hotel staff are more than happy to arrange local excursions as well as horse-riding, tennis, and tickets for local events such as a flamenco show.

CASA DE CARMONA
(☎ 95-414 3300, fax 95-414 3752), Plaza de Lasso 1, 41410 Carmona, Seville, Spain
Reservations: Either direct or through UK tour operator Magic of Spain (UK ☎ 0181-748 4220)
Getting there: The hotel can offer transfers from the nearest train station and airport for P4000
Accommodation: 30 guest rooms: 12 standard rooms and 18 de luxe suites
Amenities: Outdoor swimming pool, sauna, small gym, free parking area, 24-hour room service, restaurant, free bar; golf, horse-riding, tennis, flamenco shows can be arranged
Dress code: No jacket or tie required
Weddings: The hotel can host weddings and receptions, prices depend on your requirements
Minimum stay: None
Rates: Standard doubles from US$175 P22,000, de luxe suites from US$206 P26,000
Credit cards: Visa, American Express, Diners Club
Taxes and service charge: 7% tax, service is included

Hotel La Bobadilla

If you are driving up from Malaga it's quite likely you will be utterly convinced you are in the depths of nowhere, and you will be about to reach for the map, when up looms the Hotel La Bobadilla, one of the most amazing purpose-built hotels imaginable. King Juan Carlos of Spain and Tom Cruise are among the countless celebrities who have been drawn to this remote spot by tales of its privacy and tranquillity.

Built a couple of decades ago by a German engineer, the hotel was designed to echo the fabulous Moorish architecture that originally made this region famous. While the Alhambra Palace in Seville and the Mezquita in nearby Cordoba may have been built many centuries ago, this new addition is just as sensual and ridiculously extravagant in its grandeur.

Set in the middle of a vast area of olive and vine groves in the rolling Andalucian countryside, La Bobadilla is more like a Moorish village than a hotel – it even has its own church. The sprawling white buildings with their rustic tiled roofs, pillars and arches are interconnected via a labyrinth of stone walkways, flower covered overhangs, pretty courtyards and soaring marble colonnades.

Inside, the rambling hotel is equally impressive, tucked away off pebbled plazas are some of the most incredible hotel suites ever built. Each of the 60 rooms is architecturally different and individually decorated. They have lots of ethnic furnishings, kilim rugs and cushions, and beds so high that steps are provided as well as a sumptuous bathroom with a huge sunken jacuzzi bath. They are also well-equipped with air-conditioning, minibar, colour satellite TV, hair-dryer, in-room safe, and bathrobes and there is 24-hour room service.

Apart from being a heavenly place in which to do next to nothing, La Bobadilla makes a perfect base from which to explore Andalucia. You can either jump in the car and head off to nearby Seville and Granada, or hop on a horse, bike or just don your walking shoes and explore the estate. Most of the facilities are complimentary; there are two swimming pools, a beauty parlour with masseur, a fitness club and lots of unusual sports on hand, such as clay pigeon shooting and archery.

> **HOTEL LA BOBADILLA**
> (☎ 958-321861, fax 958-321810), Finca La Bobadilla, 18300-Loja, PO Box 52, E 18300 Loja, Granada, Spain
> **Reservations:** The Leading Hotels of the World toll free reservation numbers worldwide (see p12) or through UK tour operator Magic of Spain (UK ☎ 0181-748 4220)
> **Getting there:** Most guests hire a car from Malaga and drive the 70km to Loja; transfers from airport cost P9000, plus 7% tax
> **Accommodation:** 60 rooms: nine suites, 21 junior suites, 28 double rooms, two single rooms
> **Amenities:** The award winning La Finca specialises in international haute cuisine, El Cortijo serves traditional Spanish fare, poolside barbecues in summer, two terraces, reading lounge, 24-hr room service, a 2000 sq m outdoor heated pool, heated indoor pool and jacuzzi, four saunas, two Turkish steam baths, two Finnish saunas, hiking tracks, horse-riding, archery, small game hunting, clay pigeon shooting, cycling, pétanque, fitness club facilities, boutique, beauty parlour, massage, organ concerts, two tennis courts; plus watersports on the coast at Iznajar (20km from the hotel) and golf on the Costa del Sol (60km from the hotel)
> **Dress code:** Jackets and ties are recommended at dinner time, but not required
> **Weddings:** Ceremonies and receptions are available, the cost depends on what you want; use of the chapel is free; gala dinner for two people including wedding-cake and cava P11,000
> **Minimum stay:** None
> **Rates:** Doubles from US$255/P32,550 to US$290/P37,000 including breakfast; suites from US$438/P55,900 to US$498 P63,600
> **Credit cards:** Most major
> **Taxes and service charge:** 7% tax added to your bill, service charge is included

Molino de Santo

Molino de Santo is a family-run converted watermill situated just 15 minutes outside Ronda. Set in lovely gardens beside a mountain stream and waterfall, it is the perfect place to relax for a week or even longer, as there's plenty to do around historic Ronda

MOLINO DE SANTO

(☎/fax 95-216 7151), Bda Estación s/n, 29370 Benaoján, Málaga, Spain
Reservations: Either direct or through UK tour operator Magic of Spain (UK ☎ 0181-748 4220)
Getting there: Most guests hire cars and drive from Malaga Airport, a journey that costs around £50/P10,000 by taxi, but it is possible to get a train to Benaoján from where the hotel is only a five minute walk, they will collect your luggage
Accommodation: 12 double rooms, 7 with double beds and 5 with twin
Amenities: Swimming pool heated with solar panels, gardens, residents' lounge with games, car park, mountain bikes for hire, well-stocked library, information service on excursions and maps for walks, air-conditioned bar and dining-room, terraces by the river
Dress code: None
Weddings: The hotel cannot do ceremonies, but can do receptions for up to 50 people from around P3500 per person
Minimum stay: None
Rates: Doubles from US$54/P6800 to US$71/P8900
Credit cards: Most major
Taxes and service charge: Included

and the hotel is one of those great places in which to laze around and do nothing.

The Molino has 12 white-washed bungalow style cottages set amongst its lovely tree-filled gardens, 10 of which have terraces. All the rooms are en suite, mostly with showers but some do have baths. They are simply but very comfortably furnished in local style with white walls, terracotta tiles and pine furniture. Each has a phone, tea and coffee-making facilities, heating and electric fans. Hair-dryers are available at reception.

In the summer, meals are served outdoors on the terrace and traditional English tea and cakes are served every afternoon. The homely cooking is superb, it has made the hotel famous within the region, and the service both from its English owners and Spanish staff is friendly and helpful.

The hotel is in a splendid location just below the village of Benaojan and there is lots to see in the area. Hop on the quirky local train down to **Ronda** or talk to the English owners about walks in the area and places to visit by car. You can also hire mountain bikes which are great fun for a day.

Posada Real

On a hot summer's day in Ronda, with the temperatures soaring around the high 30°C mark, walking into the Posada Real is like entering another world: the cool floors and tranquil atmosphere are enough to return you to sanity. This converted nobleman's

POSADA REAL

(☎ 95-287 7176, fax 95-287 8370), Calle Real 42, 29400 Ronda, Spain
Reservations: Either direct or through InnTravel (UK ☎ 01653-628811)
Getting there: Most guests either fly to Gibraltar Airport and hire a car for the 97km journey to the Posada, but the hotel will arrange collection from nearby Ronda Station at no extra charge
Accommodation: 12 guest rooms: 10 double/twin rooms and two communicating rooms in the tower
Amenities: Restaurant, café/bar, small outdoor swimming pool, sauna, garden
Dress code: Informal
Weddings: The hotel can cater for receptions for up to 23 people
Minimum stay: Two nights
Rates: Seven days' fly-drive including flights, car hire and half board accommodation costs from around US$945 P120,000 per person
Credit cards: Most major
Taxes and service charge: Included in the above package

house in one of the oldest streets of Ronda is exquisite. Five centuries of history are contained within its walls which, in their time, have acted as palace, boarding house, town hall and tenement. The current owners are architects whose skills are evident in the attention to detail that has made it a wonderfully harmonious and beautifully decorated place to stay.

There is a small garden and patio where sunshine, trickling water and quiet conversation immediately make you feel as if you've escaped from the hustle and bustle of the surrounding town. The restaurant, bar and all the downstairs rooms are furnished in local style, with heavy dark-stained furniture, cooling terracotta tiled floors and intricate tiling and wood carving.

Original medieval doors are used for the bedrooms, all of which are individually decorated and furnished with antiques. There are ten double or twin rooms with en suite bathrooms, TV and air-conditioning. No 10 has a romantic four-poster bed, exposed beams, and a small balcony and is decorated in red and a yellow-gold colour.

From Ronda you are also ideally placed to explore the **Grazalema National Park** where there are many fine walks and excursions. Ronda too is famous for its leather industry making it the perfect place to pick up presents, and when you've tired of shopping settle yourself down in one of the many tapas bars for a long, lazy lunch.

Other recommended hotels

There are lots of other wonderfully personal fincas and country houses throughout Andalucia, many of which make perfect rural locations for honeymoons. Talk to UK specialist tour operator **CV Travel** (UK ☎ 0171-581 0851) about Cortijo Torre de la Reina, Las Casas De La Juderia, Cortijo El Puerto del Negro and La Almoraima, and **Elegant Resorts** (UK ☎ 01244-897 777) or the **Magic of Spain** (UK ☎ 0181-748 4220) about Hacienda de San Rafael in Seville.

A FEW THINGS TO SEE AND DO IN ANDALUCIA

The **Alhambra** in Granada, the **Mezquita** of Cordoba, and the **Alcazar** in Seville, are among the most awesome, sensual and romantic monuments to be found anywhere in Europe. These legacies of the Moorish Kings of Granada have to be seen to be believed: walk around the old Santa Cruz quarter of Seville and the maze-like narrow streets surrounding the Mezquita, and the amazing water world of the 14th century Alhambra.

To see the undulating Andalucian countryside from another perspective arrange a hot-air balloon flight with Graham Elson (☎ 95-287 7249), whose trips over **Grazalema National Park** are a wonderfully serene way of experiencing the dramatic Andalucian countryside. Graham offers two options: you can either go first thing in the morning from the National Park at Ronda for a 90-minute flight with a champagne breakfast on landing, or go in the evening along the coast near Marbella for one hour. Both trips can be booked directly through Graham or if

you are coming from Britain talk to the Magic of Spain (UK ☎ 0181-748 4999).

Most of the above hotels either have their own horses or an arrangement with the local riding school. **Riding** in Andalucia is wonderful and in most places you will be given a horse and left to explore the surrounding countryside on your own, so it's probably more suited to those with some experience.

Ronda is a charming town, reached by a bridge across a steep gorge. Home to the oldest bullring in Spain, the village is packed with Spanish heritage and history. Avoid it in July and August when it gets crowded and much too hot, but during the rest of the year it is a lovely place to walk around.

Further south takes you to the coast which, to be honest, has been largely ruined by mass-tourism, but it can be good fun to head down to the coastal town of **Puerto Banus** for a night of gin and tonics at *Sinatra's* on the marina-front and watch the holiday-makers go by.

MAJORCA

If Majorca immediately conjures up images of British lager louts eating egg and chips and packed night-clubs in built-up holiday villages, then think again. **Magaluf** aside, which is definitely worth avoiding if you want to get away from the crowds, Majorca is one of the most beautiful, tranquil and unspoilt islands in the Mediterranean. If you are looking for two weeks of absolute peace and quiet after your wedding you'd be hard pressed to beat it. Unless you are looking for some hectic night life, the best time to go is from March to June, and between September and November, when you should get lots of sunny days, and the temperatures and the crowds won't be unbearable.

La Residencia

There can be no finer way of experiencing the very best of Majorca than a stay at Richard Branson's La Residencia. This beautiful hotel, created from two 16th century Majorcan manor houses, is so exquisite that it is justly regarded as one of the finest hotels in the Mediterranean. La Residencia owes much to its glorious location being

LA RESIDENCIA
(☎ 971-639011, fax 971-639370), Deia, Majorca, Spain
Reservations: Either direct or through leading tour operators specialising in Spain (see p11)
Getting there: From Palma follow signs to Valldemossa, then Soller and take the Deia exit (a hire car is essential)
Accommodation: 50 rooms: 13 junior suites, two superior suites with private pool
Amenities: Restaurant, breakfast room and terrace, cocktail bar, poolside bar with grill, tennis court, two swimming pools, fitness room, Turkish bath, beauty centre, private access to sea, car hire, room service, fax, boat availability, gym, beauty centre
Dress code: There is no strict dress code but diners usually dress well for El Olivio
Weddings: The hotel is not licensed to perform wedding ceremonies but does cater for receptions for up to 60 people
Minimum stay: None
Rates: Double rooms from US$137 P17,250 to US$326/P41,000; suites from US$369/P46,500 to US$810/P102,000 including breakfast
Credit cards: Visa, MasterCard, Diners Club
Taxes and service charge: 7% tax will be added to your bill, service is included

set in the middle of one of the island's most idyllic rural villages, Deia. The village has, for years, attracted artists seeking tranquillity and natural beauty. Entering the village is rather like stepping back in time, where the rustic stone buildings with their red-tiled roofs and green shutters and doors blend in superbly with the citrus groves and cyprus trees which cover the rocky hillsides.

During the two years spent converting La Residencia, particular attention was paid to preserving the building's existing features – only traditional materials were used in the renovation. The painstaking attention to detail was worth it as the finished result is stunning. While the hotel is immaculate throughout, you really do still get a feeling of the heritage of the building and this is enhanced by the beautiful antiques in each room. The rooms are a classic Mediterranean combination of pale cream and white walls with dark wooden furnishings and beamed ceilings, while large terracotta tiles and cool white linen complete the effect. The two suites with private pools and fantastic views over the mountains and sea are particularly wonderful.

Days at La Residencia are extremely tranquil: although there is a floodlit tennis court most guests choose to lie on one of the loungers by the 32m pool, or find a quiet spot in the beautifully terraced gardens amongst the fruit trees.

In the evenings, chef Joseph Sauerschell, who has been at the hotel for ten years, prepares the kind of exquisite dishes that have won him international acclaim and a Michelin star three years running. Somehow the decor of the restaurant seems to epitomise everything that is special about La Residencia. Dining there is wonderful: there are scores of candles on huge wrought-iron stands, the dusky red walls blend in with the huge slabs of terracotta on the floor and wicker chairs and terracotta urns make the perfect contrast to the formal crisp white linen and crystal glassware on the tables.

Renting a villa in Spain

The best way to experience Spanish life is to rent a villa. There are hordes of tour operators offering non-descript villas in Europe, but for something really special talk to **CV Villas** (UK ☎ 0171-581 0851), **Meon Villas** (UK ☎ 01730-268411), **Spanish Affair** (UK ☎ 0171-385 8127) and **Magic of Spain** (UK ☎ 0181-748 4220). Many of these villas are high up in the mountains in the middle of nowhere so you can busy yourself with little more than staring out across the olive groves, or just lying in the pool, with a glass of wine close at hand. If you want to relax on your own, free from the tyranny of hotel meal regimes and other guests, this is the way to do it.

Ask CV Villas about **Casa Larga** in **Gaucin**, Andalucia. Located on a broad street leading up to the church, this large senorial house has been stylishly restored and would make the perfect honeymoon hideaway. You can either stay in the Bodega House, set in the garden grounds and formerly used for wine making, or the Upper House. Both are ideal. The two houses share the most beautiful deep, fresh-water swimming pool set within the walled garden and surrounded by terracotta tiles and lush green foliage. There are also lots of lovely private corners and terraces where you can sit with a book or just a glass of wine marvelling at the view. Seven nights at either house in peak season will cost you about US$860/£555 per person including flights and US$650/£420 in low season. If Casa Larga is booked up go for **La Casita De Pedro** near **Los Marines** (also in Andalucia and available through CV Villas): it's an idyllic cottage hidden away in a wooden valley with a small stream and a pond in the garden.

A FEW THINGS TO SEE AND DO IN MAJORCA

PALMA
As you'll fly in and out of Palma, Majorca's capital, it's a good idea to spend a couple of days either at the beginning or at the end of your honeymoon exploring this beautiful city, except in July or August when it's best avoided because of the holiday crowds.

The best place to stay in Palma is *Hotel Son Vida* (☎ 971-790000, fax 971-790017), one of Europe's most famous hotels built in a medieval castle high up on a hill amongst 560 hectares of sub-tropical parkland with incredible views over the bay of Palma. With over 150 rooms Son Vida is not a small hotel, but it has fantastic facilities and is a welcome retreat from the bustle of Palma at the end of the day. Double rooms from US$183/P23,300 to US$334 P42,000.

Palma's magnificent Gothic **cathedral** dominates the city and is definitely worth a visit. Below the cathedral, the intricate labyrinth of narrow winding streets stretching outwards from the city's main square, **Plaza Major**, is a great place to explore. You'll find all sorts of wonderful ceramics painted in bright Mediterranean colours and beautiful coloured glassware at much more reasonable prices than you'd get at home.

Stop for lunch at *Parlament Restaurant* (☎ 971-726026), which is essentially a local hangout so it's a good place to escape the tourists. We stumbled across this restaurant quite by chance and were inspired to go in by the hordes of Majorcans flocking up the steps one Friday lunch-time. And what a find it was. Order the paella (everyone does despite being local!) and wash it down with a bottle of Rioja.

Spend at least a day in Palma, hopping from bar to bar for tapas and into pavement cafés for coffee and the delicious local pastries, called emsaimadas. Try *Bon Lloc* (☎ 971-718617), on San Felio 7 for lunch: dishes have a vegetarian and healthy bias and you'll be with the locals. Booking is essential. But best of all, make sure you leave time for cocktails at *Abaco*. Hidden away behind imposing wooden doors just off La Llonga, Abaco has to be one of the world's most romantic bars. Inside, the stone floor of the immense courtyard is crowded with great piles of oranges and lemons, small green box shrubs protrude from every corner, and the most ornate flower arrangements and Mediterranean statues, fountains and wrought-iron work, all make you feel that you've somehow stepped back into the land of the gods: stirring classical music completes the picture. Drinks are of course expensive here, but no more so than in most major cities, and infinitely more wonderful for the decadence of the surroundings.

After drinks, dine at *Caballito del Mar* (☎ 971-721 074) one of the best restaurants in Palma, on one side of La Llonga the palm-fringed square next to the Cathedral and overlooking the port.

AROUND THE ISLAND
The north of the island and the west coast are the best places to head for if you are looking for unspoilt areas. Good places to visit include **Inca** where you can pick up good quality leather jackets, shoes and handbags for bargain prices. Sunday morning in **Pollensa** is market day, an event which throws this normally sleepy town into chaos with mounds of olives and giant piles of tomatoes and lettuces strewn across the streets.

If you want to pack a picnic and get out and discover your own sites, the **west coast** is a great place to do it. There are lots of craggy paths leading down to deserted sandy beaches, and others that will take you through pungent pine woods and remote villages where old men in berets really do sit outside cafés all day long. Walk up **Puig da Maria**, 'puig' meaning peak, to the monastery at the top, from where you can look back over the 365 cypress-lined steps that lead up to Pollensa's **El Calvari** and the 700-year old statue of the Virgin.

Visit **Porto Petro** where the quay is lined with palm trees, and white Majorcan fishing boats are tied up along the water's edge.

If you like your walks to have a hearty reward at the end of them, drive to **Alaro** and ask anyone there to point you in the direction of the ancient **Castillo d'Alaro**. The drive takes you halfway up the mountain on a very steep rubble path (just made for hire cars!). Park your car and continue on foot. The views from the castle are breathtaking and there is a wonderful rustic restaurant where you can tuck into roast lamb before driving back down again.

Italy
(BEST TIME: APRIL TO OCTOBER)

Italy has to be the ultimate destination for any romantic holiday. Nowhere else in the world does the past combine with beautiful scenery in such a stylish and evocative way.

This amazing country stretches thousand of kilometres from the snow-capped Alps to balmy southern climes. Wherever you go, the grandeur of the architecture will transport you back to the many different ages of antiquity as images of the Etruscans, the mighty Roman empire and Renaissance artists capture your imagination.

While you will no doubt be drawn by the reminders of Italy's incomparable past, today's Italy is just as romantic: imagine tucking into bowls of perfectly cooked fresh pasta, sipping local wine in the cool shade of cypress trees, and looking out over the endless olive groves.

Whether you dream of the cocooned luxury of the Venice Simplon Orient-Express, exploring the waterways of **Venice**, the languid elegance of the Italian lakes, the Renaissance palaces and museums of **Florence**, the rolling countryside and terraces of **Tuscany** and **Umbria**, or an exotic hideaway retreat perched 90m up on **Positano**'s cliff edge, it is difficult to go wrong with a honeymoon in Italy.

There is so much to see and do that a book entirely devoted to Italy as a honeymoon destination could still barely do justice to the country and its multitude of treasures. I have therefore picked out the most romantic of the country's hotels, and arranged them in three sections – cities, rural and coast – on the assumption that you'll want to incorporate a bit of each into your stay.

ITALY

A stunning coastline, 3000 years of classical history, delicious food and even better wine enjoyed overlooking the rolling fields filled with olive groves and vines – there is nowhere as magical as Italy

When to go: April to the end of October (avoiding August because it is so busy and hot)

Average maximum temperatures °C

	JAN	FEB	MAR	APR	MAY	JUN	JUL	AUG	SEP	OCT	NOV	DEC
Florence	6	6	10	13	17	21	24	23	20	15	12	7
Positano	9	9	12	14	17	21	23	24	21	17	13	10
Rome	8	8	12	14	18	22	24	24	21	17	13	9
Venice	5	5	9	13	17	20	22	22	20	15	11	6

Capital: Rome

Flight times: to Rome from:
New York: $9^3/_4$ hours
LA: $15^1/_2$ hours
London: $2^1/_2$ hours
Sydney: $24^3/_4$ hours

Approximate exchange rates: Lira (L), £1 = L2370, US$1 = L1528.05, A$1 = 1207/52

Time difference: GMT plus 1 hour (2 hours from the last Sunday in March to the last Sunday in Oct)

Voltage: 220v, mostly three round pins

Combine with: Anywhere else in Europe

Country dialling code: ☎ 39

VENICE
Hotel Cipriani

The most celebrated hotel in Venice is the Hotel Cipriani. Guests can enjoy the best views of Venice from a magical hideaway: as one travel writer recently wrote: 'The Cipriani is irresistibly there, like Everest.' Of course, this kind of élitism and luxury doesn't come cheap and, as they say, if you need to be looking at the bill you shouldn't be staying there. It's not just expensive, it's exorbitant, but if you have got the money and enjoy rubbing shoulders with the world's élite, this is *the* place to stay in Venice.

In Venice yet not in Venice because the hotel was built on its own island, Giudecca, you can see the Campanile of **San Giorgio Maggiore**, the rooftops of **Dorsoduro** and the **Zattere**, the floating pink square of the **Doge's Palace**, and the domes of the Basilica of **St Mark's** from the hotel.

Dining outside on the terrace among fragrant flowers and looking out over this view is one of the most truly romantic experiences imaginable. Now an Orient-Express hotel the Cipriani really does incorporate the very best in luxurious accommodation, attentive service and fine cuisine, in an all-pervading atmosphere of tranquillity and seclusion.

Completed in 1958 by restaurateur extraordinaire, Guiseppe Cipriani, the hotel is set around its own formal gardens and Olympic-sized swimming pool. Each room is different and elegant in its simplicity: the rooms to the south look onto the lagoon; to the east and north, the San Giorgio Maggiore Church.

It is partly the fabulous pool which accounts for the cost of staying at the Cipriani as it's the only hotel in Venice to have a swimming pool (and is for residents only), so insist on at least having a poolside room if you're going to splurge out all that money – and get it in writing so that they can't shove you in a back room at the last minute when some celebrity turns up.

Alternatively, you can stay in the **Palazzo Vendramin**, adjacent to and part of the Cipriani. Regulars in Venice argue it has better views and more elegant accommodation than the main body of the Cipriani, although it is even more expensive. Linked to the Hotel Cipriani by an ancient courtyard and flowered loggia, only part of this 15th century Palazzo is open to guests. Seven de luxe apartments with full butler service and easy access to all the adjacent hotel's facilities make the Palazzo one of the city's most exclusive destinations. Both hotels are incredibly expensive, but you are paying for the very best and the most prestigious Venice has to offer.

Hotel Danieli

Hotel Danieli is a great alternative to the Cipriani if you haven't got a small fortune to fritter away and don't want to sacrifice the sense of history. Besides, the only real difference between the Danieli and the Cipriani is the latter's swimming pool: so if you can suffer without a pool for a few days and if you book through one of the UK tour operators shown below you can stay for half the price in equally elegant surroundings – in fact some would argue that the Danieli has a greater feeling of history than its rival.

Set in a 15th century Doge's palace, the Danieli was first converted into a hotel in the early part of the 19th century and, although the atmosphere is still very much part of a bygone era, it has all the modern amenities that you'd expect from a hotel that is

---

HOTEL CIPRIANI
(☎ 041-520 7744, fax 041-520 7745), Giudecca, 10, 30133 Venice, Italy
Closed: November to March
Reservations: Orient-Express Hotels, or The Leading Hotels of the World toll free reservations numbers worldwide (see p12)
Getting there: The hotel's private launch crosses the lagoon from Piazza San Marco in just four minutes; 30 minutes from Marco Polo Airport, 15 minutes from the station
Accommodation: 66 rooms and 28 suites
Amenities: 24-hour room service, hairdresser, boutique, swimming pool, sauna, massage, hydro-system, tennis court, private yachting marina, 24-hour motorboat service to St Mark's Square, de luxe motorboat available for outings in the lagoon; golf can be arranged at the Lido, 40 minutes away by boat
Dress code: Elegant casual
Weddings: Weddings and receptions can be arranged, prices on request
Minimum stay: None
Rates: Doubles from US$428/L654,000; suites from US$610/L932,000; ask about honeymoon, spring and autumn packages which give a much better deal
Credit cards: Most major
Taxes and service charge: Included

HOTEL DANIELI
(☎ 041-522 6480, fax 041-520 0208),
Riva degli Schiavoni, 4196 – 30122
Venice, Italy
Reservations: Either direct or through
UK tour operators Italian Escapades,
Abercrombie & Kent and Elegant
Resorts (see p11)
Getting there: Transfers from the airport
vary from L80,000 to L130,000, depend-
ing on the number of pieces of luggage
Accommodation: 231 rooms, 178 are
doubles, 44 single, three junior suites,
and six suites
Amenities: Piano bar and in the summer
a terrace bar
Dress code: Generally casual, but the
hotel does prefer jackets for dinner
Weddings: Are available and costs vary
depending on what is requested
Minimum stay: None
Rates: Double room with lagoon view
US$454/L690,000, junior suite US$691
L1,050,000 and suites US$1381
L2,100,000
Credit cards: Most major
Taxes and service charge: 10% tax
added to all above rates

one of ITT Sheraton's chain of luxury
hotels.

Inside there are many grand and elegant rooms including the most impressive
galleried entrance hall with its glass chan-
delier and marble arches. All the guest
rooms have been recently refurbished and
although they vary a great deal in style and
character they are all very luxurious featuring air-conditioning, hair-dryers,
bathrobes, toiletries, slippers, minibar, TV
and phone.

The Danieli enjoys one of the most
superb positions in Venice, situated on the
edge of the lagoon only a few steps away
from St Mark's and the entrance to the
Grand Canal. The views from the rooftop
restaurant are quite magical, especially in
the early morning light.

Other recommended hotels
At around half the price of the Cipriani, the
Hotel Flora (☎ 041-520 5844, fax 041-
522 8217), Calle larga 22 Marzo, 2283/a,
30124, Venice, is a charming small hotel
situated down a little alley-way, just off St Mark's Square. There are no canal views,
but three sides of the hotel frame a pretty walled garden with wrought-iron furniture,
rampant greenery and the soothing sound of a fountain, making it the ideal place to
escape the city heat. The 44 rooms vary considerably but all have traditional antique
furnishings: it's very popular so book early. Doubles from US$184/L280,000.

Pensione Accademia Hotel (☎ 041-521 0188), Dorsoduro 1058, 3123 Venice, is
just off the Canal. This wonderul rambling 17th century villa also has the advantage
of being in one of the prettiest and least touristy parts of Venice, on a small piece of
land almost completely surrounded by canals. Unusually for Venice it has two gardens,
one of which overlooks the **San Trovaso** canal: some of the rooms have views over
the garden and canal. There are all sorts of styles and sizes of rooms: some are in the
wisteria-covered palazzo and others in a neighbouring building; some are in a better
state of repair than others as the owners are gradually restoring the hotel. With doubles
at around a very reasonable US$75/L114,500 you need to book as early as possible.

THE VENICE-SIMPLON ORIENT EXPRESS

Undoubtedly the most romantic way to enter Italy
is on the legendary Orient-Express from London
to Venice. Since 1883, this train service has
embodied luxury and refinement. The cream and
umber British Pullman leaves London's **Victoria
station** at 11am on Thursdays and Sundays
between mid-March and mid-November. The
journey starts with a champagne lunch on the way
to the coastal town of Folkestone in Kent, before
the short crossing to France by **SeaCat** (high-
speed catamaran). By 5pm you'll be ensconced
aboard the magnificent blue and gold train, swept
up in a world of absolute luxury and fine dining,
on your way to Venice. By about 9pm the train
draws briefly into Paris and then continues its
journey while you enjoy dinner in one of the
train's three restaurant cars. As you start your
ascent up into the spectacular Alps and Dolomites
the next morning full-breakfast is served. Lunch
is served as you descend towards Verona, followed by tea and pastries just before you draw
into **Santa Lucia Station** on Venice's Grand
Canal. The one-way trip from London to Venice
costs US$1542/£995 for a double cabin. For
reservations contact Orient-Express's international reservation numbers (see p12).

THREE DAYS IN VENICE

For the first time visitor there is so much to see in this staggeringly beautiful city that it's difficult to know where to start. The 'must see' tourist sights are **Palazzo Ducale** (Doge's Palace), **St Mark's Square** and **Basilica, Bridge of Sighs** and **Rialto Bridge**. The best way to explore is on foot – with the occasional *vaporetti* or water bus – so that you can really take in all there is to see. Go into the various churches as you stumble upon them to see works of great masters such as **Tintoretto**, **Titian**, **Bellini** and **Canaletto**. Wherever you go in Venice the churches are full of Byzantine mosaics, St Mark's Basilica being perhaps the most beautiful and exotic of all Europe's cathedrals. Take a good map; you'll no doubt get lost along the way but that is all part of the fun and often leads to real finds.

One of the most incredible sights in Venice is **The Rialto**, Venice's biggest market where barges are stacked high with produce. A good place to eat in this area is the **Osteria Antica d'Olo**, it's a really unpretentious restaurant which serves authentic Venetian food. The fish is good, especially when washed down with a glass of Prosecco, dry sparkling wine from the Venetian region.

Another good day out is to visit the islands in the lagoon – **Murano**, **Burano** and **Torcello** – famous respectively for their Venetian glass-blowing, lace-making and the 7th century cathedral.

There are of course numerous fantastic restaurants in Venice. Here are just a few worthy of note: **Harry's Bar** (☎ 041-528 5777), Calle Valaresso, is legendary and no trip to Venice would be complete without a visit to this famous restaurant; right next door is the **Grand Canal Restaurant** (☎ 041-520 0211), Hotel Monaco e Grand Canal, Calle Vallaresso, which is one of the stalwarts of Venice. The Hotel Cipriani's supremely elegant **Ristorante dell'Hotel Cipriani** (☎ 041-520 7744), Guidecca, is undoubtedly one of the best and most romantic restaurants in Venice; at the other extreme entirely is **Da Bruno** (☎ 041-520 6978), 2754/A Dorsoduro, where you can get fried fish; the best pizza place is **Aé Oché**, near the Frari church on Santa Croce; it's very popular with the locals and is always busy; **Da Gianni** (☎ 041-528 6497), Castello 6418, is also a good local restaurant in an interesting locality.

If you've got some energy left after dinner and want to see where the Venetians go after dark, head for **Paradiso Perduto**, near Fondamenta della Miscricordia, a late night drinking hole with live jazz and blues in the north of the city quite near the station. Alternatively try **Ca'droma**, Fondamenta dei Carmini, near Campo Magherita, which is the coolest place to hang out and play chess, backgammon, cards or a whole range of quirky Italian board games, as you sip your wine. Ca'droma is very well known among young Venetians and has a great atmosphere.

This whole area is totally off the tourist route but it's really worth seeing: choose one of the many cafés in the square and just sit and watch the world go by – **Café Rosso** serves a Venetian aperitif called Aperol and is adjacent to one of the best patisseries in town.

FLORENCE

Torre di Bellosguardo

The Torre di Bellosguardo is a fabulous 13th century villa perched on a hill overlooking Florence. It was built by a nobleman friend of Dante's once he felt confident that he'd found the perfect location for his home. The view, very definitely one of the finest vantage points over the city, is just fantastic – you can just about see the façade of every church in Florence.

Don't come here expecting to find all sorts of modern facilities in your room: there's no minibar, few rooms have air-conditioning largely because few need it, and if you want a hair-dryer you have to borrow one from reception. But this is part of the authentic old world charm of this lovely romantic villa: it bears no resemblance to a

TORRE DI BELLOSGUARDO
(☎ 055-229 8145, fax 055-229008), via Roti Michelozzi 2, 50124, Florence, Italy
Reservations: Direct
Getting there: Taxis from the station cost between L12,000 and L17,000
Accommodation: 16 guest rooms: eight doubles, six suites, two single rooms
Amenities: Small bar open 24 hours, outdoor swimming pool
Dress code: Casual
Weddings: The hotel is able to organise wedding ceremonies from October to April when it is less busy
Minimum stay: None
Rates: Double rooms from US$255 L390,000; suites from US$320/L489,000
Credit cards: Most major
Taxes and service charge: Included

modern resort hotel with its many restaurants, tennis courts and tour desks, but the small house bar is open 24 hours a day and the views and immense character of the place make up for anything the hotel lacks.

People return time and again to the Torre di Bellosguardo having fallen in love with the serene atmosphere of its homely rooms, and the immaculate gardens with their unsurpassed views. In summer, guests eat lunch around the outdoor swimming pool, but when it comes to dinner you have to go down the hill to Florence as there is no restaurant in the hotel. But, before you go, get yourself a long, cool drink from the bar and settle down on the terrace to watch the setting sun turn the whole city a magical pinky hue beneath you.

Villa San Michele

Villa San Michele, perched high on the wooded hillside in Fiesole with the most magnificent views over Florence, is perhaps even more exclusive and luxurious than its sister Orient-Express Hotel, the Cipriani in Venice. Where else in the world can you sit in such complete seclusion looking down across a whole bustling city.

The façade of this 15th century Franciscan monastery was built by Michelangelo, thus its beauty should probably not come as a surprise. With its traditional terracotta tiled roof, ancient masonry, classical loggia, original frescoes and graceful pillars it is one of those few places in the world that is quite overwhelmingly graceful and elegant.

Guests dine either in the elegant **Cenacolo Restaurant** overlooking the gardens, where the bar boasts the most magnificent fresco of *The Last Supper* and many other original oil paintings, or less formally in the **Loggia**. Dining outside on the Loggia's terrace, which stretches the full length of the building, on a balmy summer's evening has to be one of the most romantic experiences imaginable; as you look down through the cypress trees at the lights coming on over Florence you can observe the most incredible transformation from daylight through dusk to the light-studded cityscape before you.

The Orient-Express Hotel group has furnished the villa with a perfectly minimalist Italian sense of design, as a result the modern furnishings sit effortlessly beside the classical features of the building. While the hotel's public areas are full of antiques, oriental rugs and glistening candelabra arranged in a very traditional fashion, some of the bedrooms and suites have more modern overtones. The only problem with the hotel is that unless you go for one of the superior rooms or the suites the bedrooms are actually incredibly poky, which for this kind of money isn't great especially as the very high windows mean there are no views from your bedroom at all.

The suites, however, are of course fantastic. The Limonia has an unmistakably contemporary theme to its decor – a sort of Mulberry meets Conran image – combining honey-coloured walls, large terracotta floor tiles and cream-covered sofas, with the

---

VILLA SAN MICHELE
(☎ 055-59451, fax 055-598734), Via di Doccia, 50014 Florence, Italy
Reservations: Orient-Express Hotels' toll free reservation numbers worldwide (see p12); The Leading Hotels of the World reservations numbers worldwide (see p12); or through UK tour operators, Elegant Resorts, Italian Escapades and Abercrombie & Kent (see p11)
Getting there: The hotel operates a shuttle bus to and from Florence
Accommodation: 26 rooms, seven junior suites and three suites
Amenities: Swimming pool, Italian terraced garden, horse-riding, golf and tennis nearby, courtesy shuttle bus to/from Florence, chauffeur service,
Dress code: Jacket and tie are requested in the Cenacolo Restaurant
Weddings: The hotel is very small and more suitable for honeymoons than wedding ceremonies and receptions
Minimum stay: None
Rates: Per person half board is from US$325/L497,000 to US$411/L628,000; suites from US$573/L875,500; ask about honeymoon spring and autumn programmes which give a much better deal
Credit cards: Most major
Taxes and service charge: Included

dark tones of fine antique chests and wrought-iron furnishings. All the rooms are equipped with air-conditioning, minibars, phone and spacious bathrooms, while the junior suites have four-poster beds and many have jacuzzis.

The Villa San Michele is stunning and so grand, but it was really expensive, especially the food with a tomato and mozzarella salad at lunch costing around £15. But you are paying for the absolute exclusivity of the house, the huge amount of space and privacy and the surroundings, not the bedrooms. We felt really it was more of a long weekend place, as it's too expensive to relax in unless you have an awful lot of money.
Nick and Vanessa McDonald Buchanan

The hotel's swimming pool and adjacent bar also enjoy stunning views over Florence and have the wonderful feel of a private garden, making it a lovely place to relax if you feel like escaping the bustle of the city for the day. Or you can wander through the immaculate landscaped gardens past cypresses and olive trees to two small chapels, a reminder of this incredible villa's impressive heritage. Despite the hotel's seclusion it is only minutes from Florence and is within easy reach of **Bologna** and **Pisa**, making it an ideal base for touring this glorious area, providing you can afford its staggering room prices!

Other recommended hotels

The Brunelleschi (☎ 055-562068, fax 055-219653), Piazza Santa Elisabetta, 50122 Florence, is also very special. Built around an unusual 6th century Byzantine tower and the medieval church of **San Michele** in **Palchetto** right behind the Duomo, the 96-roomed Brunelleschi with its distinctive façade is a superior hotel with antique walls and ceilings but no shortage of modern comforts. Doubles from US$296/L450,000 including breakfast and taxes during the low season.

The Rivoli (☎ 055-282853, fax 055-294041), Via Della Scala, 50123, Florence, is one of the best value hotels in the city. There is nothing flash or grand about staying at the Rivoli, but this pretty little hotel with its jacuzzi in the middle of the central courtyard is wonderfully comfortable and stylish for the money. Doubles from US$164/L250,000 including breakfast, tax and service charge during the low season.

THREE DAYS IN FLORENCE

Home of the court of Lorenzo the Magnificent, power-house of art and thought in the Renaissance period and today famous for its fashion and antiques, this city has to be part of any honeymoon in Italy.

Florence, built predominantly on the patronage of the church and the Medicis, is a complete work of art unto itself. The wealth of artistic achievement within its ancient walls is, at times, totally overwhelming. The basic sights are: the **Uffizi**, though try to leave it until late in the afternoon when it is quieter; the Michelangelos at the **Accademia**, Donatello at the **Museo dell'Opera del Duomo**, Titian, Raphael and Veronese at the **Palazzo Pitti**, Renaissance sculpture at the **Bargello** and Fra Angelico at the **Museo di San Marco**; the Brunelleschi cathedral domes and church interiors of **San Lorenzo** and **Santo Spirito**; and finally a climb to the top of the **Duomo** is well worth it for the views. Do your touring on foot as most of the sights are within a very small area.

If you're not staying at the Villa San Michele, it is worth driving out to **Fiesole**, the aristocratic hilltop suburb where Florentines go to escape the heat and enjoy the summer plays and concerts at the well-preserved amphitheatre.

When you've had enough of sightseeing it's time to relax in some of Florence's wonderful restaurants and bars. *Canietta Antinori* (☎ 055-292234), Palazzo Antinori, serving Antinori wines by the glass is a great place for a drink or light snack and very stylish surroundings. *Aqua al Duo*, behind the National Museum, serves some of the best pasta in town. It is cheap, cheerful and always bustling. Even cheaper is *Il Cantinone del Gallo Nero* (☎ 055-218898), Via S. Spirito, which serves authentic and hearty Tuscan food. For something much smarter try *Enoteca Pinchiorri* (☎ 055-242777), Via Ghibellina, one of Florence's most famous restaurants which although very expensive is perfect if you feel like spoiling yourself.

For a totally authentic Tuscan experience spend a few hours looking round **Sant' Ambrogio** market and then pop into *Cibrèo* (☎ 055-234 1100), Via dei Macci, for lunch. Unless you want to get totally embroiled in a long, long, lunch stick to the simple trattoria, where you might have to share tables with the locals but the food is unbelievable. You'll need to be able to understand a bit of Italian as there's no menu and the complex names of the dishes are not easy to catch when the waiter reels them off to you.

ROME

So much is said about Florence and Venice that I was totally unprepared for the out-standing beauty and magnificence of Rome. Unlike other European capital cities where new-fangled creations stand alongside historic monuments, you can walk for ages in the centre of Rome and never see a modern building. And there is something in the chaotic nature of the Romans – the way young and old charge round the city on scooters without helmets – that gives the whole place a wonderfully spirited atmos-phere that I've never come across anywhere else.

Hotel Eden

Hotel Eden is quite special for a grand old hotel and is very much *the* place to go in Rome at the moment. This classic apricot-coloured hotel, a stone's throw from the **Piazza di Spagna**, **Via Veneto** and **Villa Borghese**, was totally refurbished and restructured back in 1994 at a cost of L30 billion and is now clearly reaping the ben-efits.

The Eden is currently so popular with the locals that you'll find the fifth floor restaurant completely booked most nights. This renaissance in the hotel's popularity is predominantly due to the success of chef Enrico Derflinger (former chef to the Prince and Princess of Wales). Since he came to the **Terrazza dell'Eden** he has become the darling of Rome's food lovers and, in 1995, earned the restaurant a much coveted Michelin star. The **Terrazza Bar** is a wonderful spot to enjoy early evening cocktails in the roof-top garden, overlooking the squares, domes and ancient monuments of Rome, against the magnificent backdrop of gently rolling hills. And after dinner it's well worth slipping into the cosy **Piano Bar** for a nightcap, where jazz musicians Luca Jacovella and Andrea Bianchi provide the perfect backdrop to the end of an evening.

For a big, city centre hotel, the Eden has a remarkably friendly atmosphere with unusually helpful staff; it somehow manages to feel like a palace but without being formal. Over the 100 years since it first opened, the Eden has had some pretty famous guests: Ingrid Bergman, Ernest Hemingway, Liam Neeson, Tom Cruise and Nicole Kidman, and Emma Thompson and Kenneth Branagh.

The Eden's public lounges are full of fine antiques, oil paintings, open fireplaces and other fine furnishings which combine to produce a lovely old world atmosphere. The 112 rooms, decorated in peaceful creams and taupe, come equipped with all modern facili-ties including air-conditioning, bathrobes, slippers, two phones, satellite television, VCR, CD player, hair-dryer and in-room safe. The two-tone marble bathrooms are lux-urious with sparkling chrome furnishings and an abundance of white towels, healthy look-ing plants and Etro toiletries.

HOTEL EDEN
(☎ 06-478121, fax 6-4821584), Via Ludovisi 49, 00187 Rome, Italy

Reservations: The Leading Hotels of the World toll free reservation numbers worldwide (see p12); or through UK tour operator Italian Escapades (UK ☎ 0181-748 4220)

Getting there: The Eden can arrange transfers from Leonardo da Vinci' Airport (32km) for around L110,000, or from Termini Railway station (2km), but taxis from both are much cheaper (L70,000 from the airport)

Accommodation: 112 rooms: one Royal Suite, one Presidential Suite, nine one-bedroom suites, 38 de luxe doubles, 54 superior doubles, nine singles

Amenities: La Terrazza dell'Eden, Piano Bar, La Terrazza, car park nearby, laun-dry, dry cleaning, gym, 24-hour room service, three guest lifts, theatre and opera reservations, car rental with or without chauffeur; golf, horse-riding, swimming and tennis can all be arranged nearby

Dress code: Jacket required for lunch and dinner in the restaurant

Weddings: The Eden can cater for wed-ding receptions for up to 110 in its largest banqueting room or up to 60 people in the panoramic Sala Bellavista, menus start from L170,000 including beverages, tax and service charge

Minimum stay: None

Rates: Double superior rooms from US$425/L649,000 to US$495/L756,000; suites from US$935/L1,429,000

Credit cards: Most major

Taxes and service charge: Included

THE DOLOMITES
Berghotel Zirmerhof

This delightful mountain hotel is a real find. Set in a superb mountainside location above the **Val di Fiemme**, the Zirmerhof, originally a working farm, dates from around 1600 and has been run by the Perwanger family for over a century.

Peacefully situated just outside the tiny hamlet of **Radein**, the hotel has magnificent views of the valley below and the surrounding mountains, including the **Weisshorn** and **Schwarzhorn**.

It is currently run by Sepp Perwanger and his family: they offer warm and genuine hospitality giving the Zirmerhof a really special feel. Traditional, regional cuisine is served in the restaurant using recipes created by Sepp's grandmother, Hanna, whose imaginative and delicious creations have been published locally. The superb restaurant has a fresco, painted by Ignaz Stolz, covering two of the walls and splendid views out over the countryside.

The hotel has the feel of a traditional farmhouse; it has old hand-crafted wooden furniture, timbered ceilings and wonderful creaky wooden floorboards. Rooms No 6, No 14 and the suite, No 11, are the best because they are the largest and most recently renovated and they have a balcony or loggia with panoramic views over the valley. The bathrooms are marble but only four of the hotel's 31 rooms have baths, the rest have en suite showers.

> **BERGHOTEL ZIRMERHOF**
> (☎ 0471-887215, fax 0471-887225), Radein, I-39040, Italy
> **Reservations**: Either direct or through UK tour operator Inntravel (UK ☎ 01653-628811)
> **Getting there**: The hotel is 241km from Verona Airport, most guests hire a car but the hotel can arrange transfers from Ora railway station
> **Accommodation**: 31 rooms and one suite, all en suite
> **Amenities**: Restaurant, bar, library, lounge, terrace area with outside seating, private parking
> **Dress code**: Informal
> **Weddings**: The hotel can host receptions for up to 80 people
> **Minimum stay**: Three nights
> **Rates**: Doubles from US$64/L98,000 to US$112/L170,000 for No 11 half board; Inntravel's seven-night package including flights to Verona, seven days' Avis car hire and seven nights' half board in a superior room costs around US$1038 £670 per person
> **Credit cards**: Credit cards are not accepted, bills must be settled by Eurocheque or cash
> **Taxes and service charge**: Included

Few places can rival this delightful little hotel if you are looking for somewhere cosy in a stunning mountain setting and where you can be guaranteed delicious meals. There's lots to do in the area, apart from walking: you can go swimming, mountain biking or horse-riding and play tennis.

THE LAKES
Villa D'Este

Villa D'Este has a huge crowd of devotees who will tell you that it is the best hotel in the whole of Italy. Those who go there come back raving about it, which is all very well providing you can afford it: even if you think you can, do watch out for the extras bill which has a nasty habit of getting way out of control.

There is a long, romantic tradition behind the Villa D'Este. The first photos of Edward VIII with Mrs Simpson, following his abdication were taken at the villa and the couple returned many times as the Duke and Duchess of Windsor. Rita Hayworth stayed there with Orson Wells, and other guests include Ava Gardner and Frank Sinatra.

Located on the far side of Lake Como in Cernobbio, this fabulous 16th century villa used to belong to Cardinal Tolomeo Gallio, before being transformed into a grand hotel in 1873. As its management are fond of telling you, the Villa d'Este is 'more than

VILLA D'ESTE
(☎ 031-511471, fax 031-512027), Via Regina 40, Lake Como, 22012 Cernobbio, Italy
Closed: December to February
Reservations: The Leading Hotels of the World toll free reservations numbers worldwide (see p12); or through UK tour operators, Elegant Resorts, Abercrombie & Kent, Italian Escapades (see p11)
Getting there: The hotel can arrange transfers from Milan Airport on request, L270,000 from Linate Airport and L255,000 from Malpensa Airport
Accommodation: 108 rooms, 48 suites
Amenities: Two restaurants, four hectare private park, night club, disco, piano bar, beach bar, Sports Club with three swimming pools, eight tennis courts, squash court, gym, putting green, windsurfing, canoeing, water-skiing, hang gliding, excursions on the lake, sauna and Turkish bath, massage rooms, boutiques and beauty salon; seven 18-hole golf courses nearby
Dress code: Jacket and tie are required for dining in the Veranda Restaurant
Weddings: Weddings and receptions for a maximum of 200 people, menus start at L200,000 including cocktails, wines, coffee and spumante
Minimum stay: None
Rates: Doubles start at around US$411/L625,000
Credit cards: Most major
Taxes and service charge: Included

just a hotel, it is an idea born in the minds of a group of people dedicated to anticipating every wish of their guest' – an encouraging start. The legendary service will indeed make a big difference to your stay, but what really makes this villa so incredible is its awesome lakeside position in four hectares of spectacular gardens. Some parts of the gardens are so beautiful they inspire the same kind of veneration as the gardens of the English stately home, Cliveden. The formal design, perfect box hedges and elegant statuary make you want to stay there for ever.

The villa is extravagantly furnished: ceremonial staircases sweep down to marble floors, gleaming chandeliers hang from lofty ceilings supported by mighty pillars, and dainty French ormolu-decorated chairs are arranged throughout the public rooms – this isn't really the place to snuggle down with a good book or put your feet up! The bedrooms are equally ornate being decorated with rich colours and great swags of heavy fabrics and furnished with fine antiques. They're also not short of modern amenities: most of the rooms have a jacuzzi, and they all come with TV, in-room safe, minibar, toiletries, bathrobes, slippers and lots more goodies.

If you like your hotels to be self-contained resorts with every kind of facility and hundreds of formal staff at hand, you'll love the Villa d'Este. Somewhat unusually for Europe, it is the kind of big resort hotel that has everything: there are two restaurants serving Italian haute cuisine, a disco, piano bar, beach bar, indoor and outdoor swimming pools, eight tennis courts, a squash court, a gym, sauna and Turkish baths, seven golf courses nearby and a whole range of watersports – you could stay here for two weeks not leaving the grounds and want for nothing.

Obviously this is not the place to come for a quiet intimate stay, but if you love the glamour of big hotels and can drag out the odd Hermès scarf and Prada beach bag, then this is about as chic and slick as it gets.

Other recommended hotels

Hidden on a rocky outcrop, just off the main body of **Lake Garda** is the ancient domain of **San Vigilio**. Here at the end of a tree-lined pathway and narrow cobbled street, the **Locanda San Vigilio** (☎ 045-725 6688, fax 045-725 6551), 37016 San Vigilio, Lake Garda, is the perfect romantic hideaway. It is set in lush gardens of cypress and olive trees, and lemon and orange groves. With just three suites and four bedrooms, a small restaurant with tables right on the edge of the lake and a private harbour and beach, the Locanda has been receiving guests for five centuries. Although the Locanda is expensive, it's a good deal more reasonable than staying at any of the really flash hotels further along the lake. This hotel will really suit you if you are looking for a tranquil place to be alone together and like to avoid the kind of hotels where you feel you have to speak in hushed tones. Double rooms cost around US$197/L300,000.

THE VENETO

The Veneto, just a short drive from Venice, is home to some of Italy's most beautiful countryside and the former residences of the Venetian nobility. The following hotels are all within a couple of hours' drive of Venice.

Villa Cipriani

The Villa Cipriani is one of those honeymoon classics. If you are planning a surprise honeymoon and you take her to the Villa Cipriani she'll love you forever. I would! Just an hour from Venice, at the foot of the Dolomites, the villa is found in the small, walled hill town of Asolo, a haven since the 15th century for artists, musicians and writers from Titian to Robert Browning. One of Italy's most famous hotels, the Villa Cipriani which no longer has anything to do with the celebrated Venetian hotel of the same name, truly is a place favoured by the gods.

Today's hotel offers the unique and unchanging charms of a patrician 15th century residence with honey-coloured stone and dark green shutters; it is ever so slightly dilapidated with rough patches and cracks showing in the exterior walls but, to the kind of people suited to this hotel, the slightly shabby feel only augments its charm. It seems to assert an almost mystical attraction on its guests, causing many to pledge undying love for the villa and vow to return again.

The 26 rooms and five suites are all en suite and air-conditioned, and enjoy fabulous views over the surrounding countryside and the English-style garden, while cool corridors of polished stone lead to the excellent restaurant where you'll discover Italian cuisine that brings out the finest provincial and Mediterranean flavours.

Although there is no pool at the hotel, guests can use one nearby, and tennis and golf can also be arranged. But somehow these activities don't quite fit in with life in Asolo, where a gentle stroll around the gardens, or a leisurely rootle around the shops is much more appropriate.

> **VILLA CIPRIANI**
> (☎ 0423-952166, fax 0423-952095), Via Canova 298, 1-31011, Asolo, Treviso, Italy
> **Reservations:** Relais & Châteaux (see p12) and ITT Sheraton toll free reservation numbers worldwide
> **Getting there:** From Venice take the A27 towards Treviso north, and then the SS248 towards Bassano del Grappa or take a taxi from Treviso Airport (20km)
> **Accommodation:** 26 rooms and five suites
> **Amenities:** Lounge, bar, restaurant divided into two rooms Veranda and Contarini, room service from 6am to midnight, English garden; golf, tennis, swimming all nearby
> **Dress code:** Casual, but formal for dinner
> **Weddings:** The hotel does cater for wedding ceremonies and receptions
> **Minimum stay:** None
> **Rates:** Doubles from US$210/L320,000; suites from US$304/L462,000; US$33 L50,000 supplement for valley view rooms and US$92/L140,000 for half board
> **Credit cards:** Visa, Eurocard, American Express, Diners Club
> **Taxes and service charge:** Included

La Foresteria Serego Alighieri

La Foresteria Serego Alighieri, an absolutely stunning private villa, is without doubt one of the most heavenly places to stay in Northern Italy. Set in the heart of the beautiful Valpolicella wine region, La Foresteria forms part of a vast wine and olive oil producing estate which has been run by the same family for six centuries and twenty generations, and all of them are direct descendants of the poet Dante Alighieri.

The present Count Alighieri, who lives on the estate with his family, has carefully transformed the stables and farm buildings into eight immaculately furnished apartments in super-chic Milano style. Each apartment combines parquet floors, rustic beams and brass rods supporting muslin drapes, with pristine grey kitchens.

Best of all the rooms is No 8, La Colombara, the dove tower, which covers two floors and can only be reached through a trapdoor staircase. Just made for honeymooners, the bedroom is tucked away up in the eaves where light streams in through

LA FORESTERIA SEREGO ALIGHIERI
(☎ 045-770 3622, fax 045-770 3523), Via Stazione 2, 37020 Gargagnago di Valpolicella, Italy
Reservations: Direct or through UK tour operators, Magic of Italy and Abercrombie & Kent (see p11)
Getting there: La Foresteria is 18km north west of Verona and 20km east of Lake Garda
Accommodation: Eight apartments with kitchens
Amenities: Kitchens and dining areas, vineyard and cellar tours, small estate shop, light continental breakfasts served
Dress code: There isn't one
Weddings: No
Minimum stay: None
Rates: Double apartments from US$125 L190,000 per night in the low season going up to US$171/L260,000 during the high season; weekly rates are cheaper, costing US$79/L120,000 per night (low) and US$112/L170,000 (high); La Colombara costs US$132/L200,000 (low) and US$178/L270,000 (high)
Credit cards: Most major
Taxes and service charge: Included

the original dove holes. The bed virtually runs from one wall to the other, and there are the most fabulous views of the countryside.

You can buy balsamic vinegar, olive oil and jams from the estate shop, tour the vineyards and even help with the harvest in October. Don't be put off by the thought of self-catering as there are lots of superb restaurants in other country house hotels nearby and breakfasts can be provided. **Verona**, with its famous opera, is only 16km away. The opera season at the **Arena Di Verona** runs from the beginning of July until September.

Other recommended hotels

Relais El Toula (☎ 0422-440751, fax 0422-440754), Via Postumia 63, 1-31050, Ponzano Veneto, another Relais & Châteaux hotel in this gorgeous area, is a spacious 18th century residence with a noble exterior located at the end of a lane walled with tall vines. The hotel's eight rooms and two suites overlook either the fountains or its swimming pool and there is lots to do nearby, including surfing and skiing, as well as **Padua** and Venice to discover. The hotel's cuisine is particularly good and accompanied by the finest wines of Piedmont, Tuscany and Venice. They will prepare honeymoon packages to suit your individual requirements. Double rooms are from US$210/L320,000.

The **Hotel Villa del Quar** (☎ 045-680 0681, fax 045-680 0604), Via Quar 12, 37020 Pedemonte, at the gates of Verona in the beautiful Valpolicella valley, has recently become a member of Relais & Châteaux, a tribute to its fine cuisine and accommodation. A stone wall circles the hotel enclosing vineyards, fields, a clover-shaped swimming pool and velvety green lawns. Much of the family-run villa is built in a U-shape around a spacious courtyard with gardens dating back to 1539. The 18 bedrooms and four suites are en suite, and have air-conditioning, satellite TV and in-room safes and feature wood beams, waxed parquet floors and antique French and Italian neo-classic furniture. The hotel has its own private family chapel and wonderful restaurant, and will happily arrange wine tasting in local Venetian villas, hunting or fishing. Doubles from US$164/L250,000.

Also within an hour's drive of Venice is another Relais & Châteaux hotel, the splendid 16th century mansion, the **Hotel Duchessa Isabella** (☎ 0532-202121, fax 0532-202638), Via Palestro 68/70, 44100 Ferrare. This typically Italian hotel is ornately furnished with an abundance of crystal chandeliers, brilliant white columns, marble floors, coffered ceilings, original 16th century doors, Ferrara school frescoes and glistening gold antiques in every corner. The 21 guest rooms and six suites are extravagantly decorated in true romantic style. In the grand Duchessa Isabella suite flowing lace curtains hang beside striped damask silks, brilliant pink bows are tied to huge gold candelabras and a frilly canopy hangs down over the bed. Junior suites Nos 10, 11 and 12 all have terraces, overlooking the hotel's private park, which are just perfect for alfresco breakfasts or lunches. All honeymooners are greeted with a bottle of champagne and guests are free to use the hotel's horse-drawn landau for sightseeing tours. Doubles from US$217/L330,000, the suites start at around US$362/L550,000.

WINE ROUTES OF THE VENETO

One third of Italy's classified wines (recognised under the DOC and DOCG labels) come from **Veneto**, **Trentino-Alto Adige** and **Friuli-Venezia Giulia**, and the countryside that produces them is absolutely stunning. Whether you are on your way up to the Lakes, staying close to Verona itself or even based in the heart of Valpolicella country at La Foresteria Serego Aligieri, it would be a crime to miss out on seeing some of this glorious wine country. Long sunny days spent meandering along picturesque rural lanes and popping into the odd estate for a tasting is sheer bliss.

From the Lakes the nearest wines of note are produced in **Bardolino**, close to Lake Garda, where there is a clearly marked wine route, *strada del vino*, to follow. Even if you don't follow the prescribed route make sure you take in **Lazise**, **Cisano**, **Calmasino** and **Affi**.

You'll find some of the most splendid vintages in the Classico hills of **Valpolicella**. Close to the Alighieri estate is the famous **Masi Winery**, but you can continue exploring in both directions. To the west is **San Giorgio**, with its beautiful 18th century church and the *Trattoria dalla Rosa Alda* (☎ 045-770 1018), a popular place with the local growers and a splendid location for lunch on the outdoor terrace, and to the east lies the high wine country of towns such as **Fumane** and **Marano**, linked by classically rugged Valpolicella terrain. Further east still will take you into the **Negrar Valley** until you reach Negrar, where Giuseppe Quintarelli's wines are legendary, and the tiny hamlet of **Mazzano**.

TUSCANY AND UMBRIA

Once you've had your fill of Florence, hire a car and drive south through magical Tuscany and adjacent Umbria, where the rolling hills are filled with green cypresses and an ocean of olive and vine groves. Follow the **Chianti Route** through hundreds of vineyards perched on steep hillsides. Don't miss **San Gimigniano**, Italy's best preserved medieval town, with its 15 towers dominating the landscape. Between Florence and Siena, in the rolling Tuscan countryside lie some of Italy's most classic hotels.

La Suvera

Staying at La Suvera, a gorgeous 12th century villa about 30 minutes west of Siena, is rather like living in your own private medieval castle. Set right in the very heart of Tuscany, La Suvera is surrounded by olive groves and green fields, making it a perfectly secluded and tranquil retreat.

Created around a medieval castle, La Suvera later became the papal villa of Pope Julius II and is now the home of the Ricci family who live in one part of the castle. The entrance to the villa is dominated by a large square with several different buildings along one side including a tiny, beautiful ancient church. Guests are accommodated either in junior suites in the papal villa itself, which are magnificent, or in two sets of former stables, **La Scuderia** which has 15 bedrooms many of which have four-posters, and the **Oliviera** where there are three and four-bedroom suites.

Each room is decorated in a highly individual theme, for instance one has a butterfly collection, and they are all full of antiques and artefacts picked up from all over the

LA SUVERA
(☎ 0577-960300, fax 0577-960220), 53100 Pievescola di Casole d'Elsa, Val d'Elsa, Italy
Reservations: Direct or through UK tour operator Italian Escapades (UK ☎ 0181-748 2661)
Getting there: Most guests hire a car, approx $2^1/_2$ hours' drive from Pisa Airport, and $1^1/_2$ hours from Florence Airport; the hotel does not arrange transfers
Accommodation: 24 rooms
Amenities: Room service, swimming pool, tennis court, restaurant, several lounges, library, music room, bar; horse-riding is available nearby
Dress code: Jackets for men and dresses for women are requested at dinner
Weddings: The hotel is happy to host ceremonies and receptions, its lovely little church can take up to 60 people
Minimum stay: Two nights
Rates: Double rooms from US$243 L370,000 to US$329/L500,000; suites from US$309/L470,000 to US$460 L700,000
Credit cards: Most major
Taxes and service charge: Included

world by the Ricci family's ancestors. There are several lounges, a library and a music room and all are adorned with fine oil paintings and magnificent antiques, making it more like staying in some sort of medieval artefacts' exhibition than being in a hotel.

The Oliviera, across the road, also houses the hotel's restaurant where produce from the farm is incorporated into delicious and typically Tuscan cuisine is accompanied by estate wines. The gardens are equally amazing: the beautiful swimming pool is surrounded by ancient statues and rambling ivy, swans glide across the lake, and more statues peep out from the topiary.

Tenuta di Ricavo

In the heart of the fabulous Chianti countryside this lovely little residence is a real slice of heaven. If you are searching for a remote and tranquil base to explore Tuscany among very private surroundings then look no further, as Tenuta di Ricavo is truly out of this world. The hamlet of **Ricavo**, whose medieval origins date back to the year 994, was transformed into a comfortable country residence back in the 1950s using traditional Tuscan architectural techniques to maintain the historic ambience.

Eight of the 23 rooms are located in the main house, while the other 15 are in the former hamlet's cottages, so staying here is hardly like being in a hotel but much more like renting a cottage in a small private village. Very few of the rooms have televisions, as this is a quiet hotel and the views are much better than any television programme. The rooms are rustically furnished with solid antique furniture, wrought-iron beds and lovely Persian or Tuscan carpets. Lots of them have exposed original wooden beams and 14th century tiles and are all equipped with hair-dryers and fridges.

When you make your booking ask for room No 5, which is particularly beautiful and really spacious. It boasts a wooden renaissance double bed, marble floor, antique paintings and furniture and even prayer stools. It also has a marble bathroom.

Charming gardens surround the cottages and the main building so you can easily find a private place to sit with a good book, or take a walk further afield on one of the many marked trails through the estate's 178 hectares of idyllic countryside. These often take you along old dirt roads, so bring some good walking shoes. Meals are taken outside in the summer months, and often well into October if the weather lasts, in Ricavo's main square. Local Tuscan cuisine created by chef Alessandro Lobrano is accompanied by the delicious wines of Chianti.

TENUTA DI RICAVO

(☎ 0577-740221, fax 0577-741014), 1-53011 Castellina in Chianti, Italy

Closed: December to May

Reservations: Through UK agencies Representation Plus (UK ☎ 0181-392 1589) or DER Travel Services (☎ 0171-408 0111); US agents Euro-Connection toll free number (US ☎ 1-800-645-EURO)

Getting there: It is essential for guests to hire a car as there is no public transport to and from the hotel, the nearest airport is Florence (taxi costs L180,000), the nearest station is Siena or Florence (NOT Castellina Stazione!)

Accommodation: 23 guest rooms: nine suites and 14 rooms

Amenities: Walking trails, two outdoor swimming pools, boccia (an Italian ball game), table tennis, tandem bikes, gym, library, chess, cards, TV room with satellite, à la carte restaurant La Pecora Nera, bar, limited room service

Dress code: The hotel requests that guests be well dressed even if casually so when dining in the restaurant, but ties are not required

Weddings: The hotel cannot cater for wedding parties

Minimum stay: Five to seven nights in high or mid season, although they will accept you for just one night if you call at the last minute and they have a vacancy

Rates: Double rooms from US$145/L220,000

Credit cards: Visa, Eurocard, Master Card

Taxes and service charge: Included

We had eight days here and drove out each morning for an adventure. Siena, Florence, San Gimigniano are all within easy driving distance so that we were usually home by 4pm in time for a swim and relaxing in the sun. The only thing to break the perfect silence at this lovely small hotel are the pigeons cooing, the swallows nesting and the cuckoo calling, it really is quite dreamy. **Biddy and Morgan Fahey**

UMBRIA
Hotel Le Tre Vaselle

The Hotel Le Tre Vaselle, set in the centre of the old fortress town of Torgiano, is a charming rustic hotel. Being owned by the Lungarotti family, producers of Umbria's finest wines, the Tre Vaselle is also becoming increasingly well-known for its fabulous cuisine.

This is the place for you if you are looking for an unpretentious and friendly village inn from where you can explore the Umbrian countryside, safe in the knowledge that you've got a charming room and a delicious meal to return to each night. Dishes are pure and wholesome in time-honoured Umbrian fashion, based on ingredients supplied by the hotel's own farms and good enough to warrant a recent visit from British television chef, Keith Floyd.

This lovely old 16th century home is a traditional Umbrian residence with thick stone walls the colour of sand, wooden beams, terracotta roof and floor tiles and impressive stone fireplaces. The interior decoration is also traditional featuring handwoven fabrics from central Italy, oil paintings, embroidery, antique etchings of viticultural scenes, and the three 17th century monastic jugs displayed in the lobby from which the hotel derives its name. The hotel actually consists of two buildings, connected via an underground arcade, one of which has just recently undergone a thorough refurbishment programme which has also seen the addition of a swimming pool.

All the hotel's 61 rooms are decorated with antique furnishings, have separate bath and shower and are air-conditioned. They also feature a good range of modern amenities including phones in the bedroom and the bathroom, satellite TV and radio, radio alarm, hair-dryer and in-room safe.

Just a short walk from Le Tre Vaselle is **La Bondanzina**, a small dusky pink house with dark green shutters, which has the most incredible interior. Huge swathes of yellow, white and cream fabrics are draped around the beds, one a lovely wrought-iron four-poster, while on the walls are painted the most brilliant frescoes depicting gazebos, more drapery and tranquil pastoral landscapes. The whole effect is rather clever making the house a very serene place and just perfect for a honeymoon.

> **HOTEL LE TRE VASELLE**
> (☎ 075-988 0447, fax 075-988 0214), Via Giuseppe Garibaldi 48, 06089 Torgiano, Perugia, Italy
> **Reservations**: Can be made either directly or through UK tour operator Italian Escapades (UK ☎ 0181-748 2661)
> **Getting there**: The hotel can arrange complimentary transfers from Perugia Station, transfers from Rome Airport (approx 200km) cost L350,000
> **Accommodation:** 48 double rooms and 13 junior suites
> **Amenities**: Outdoor swimming pool, indoor swimming pool with whirlpool, sauna, gym, small outdoor amphitheatre, private parking, shuttle bus to Perugia and Assisi, Le Melagrane restaurant, Il Fauno bar
> **Dress code**: Elegant casual
> **Weddings**: The hotel caters for wedding receptions for up to 200 people and there is a lovely little church attached to the hotel where you can get married, costs start from L95,000 per person including Lungarotti wines
> **Minimum stay**: Two nights
> **Rates**: Double rooms from US$191 L290,000 including breakfast; executive doubles with jacuzzis from US$230 L350,00 including breakfast
> **Credit cards**: Most major
> **Taxes and service charge**: Included

Hotel le Silve di Armenzano

You could very easily pass through Assisi without ever knowing about this wonderful little hotel perched high up above the town on the peaceful hillside, mainly because its devotees (most of whom are Italians) don't want to spoil the tranquil atmosphere by publicising it. But once you have found your way up the 13km of steep winding road to Armenzano, you'll find the most perfect seclusion where you can unwind.

Such is the peace of Le Silve that a glorious silence seems to descend upon you as you arrive, no doubt enhanced and fed by the awe-inspiring views across the valley

LE SILVE DI ARMENZANO
(☎ 075-801 9000, fax 075-801 9005)
06081 Localita Armenzano, Assisi, Italy
Closed: November to March
Reservations: Either direct or through
UK tour operators Magic of Italy (UK ☎
0181-748 7575) and Abercrombie &
Kent (UK ☎ 0171-730 9600); from the
US through American rep Euro-
Connection (US toll free ☎ 800-645-
3876)
Getting there: Rome Airport is two
hours away, Assisi is 30 minutes by car or
a taxi costs around L40,000, most guests
hire a car
Accommodation: 21 rooms
Amenities: Outdoor swimming pool, ten-
nis court, mini golf, restaurant, bar, pool-
side bar, fantastic walking around the
estate
Dress code: Casual
Weddings: No
Minimum stay: Three nights during
August and September
Rates: Bed and breakfast from
US$89/L135,000 per person per day, half
board from US$115/L175,000 per person
per day
Credit cards: Most major
Taxes and service charge: Included

and the timeless beauty of the hotel's ancient stone buildings some of which date back almost a thousand years.

The hotel has 21 rooms: all of them are individually decorated in a rustic fashion and incorporate vital honeymoon modernities such as minibars, hair-dryers, bathrobes and wonderful toiletries.

Most guests spend their days either exploring the hotel's 200-hectare estate on horseback, lazing around the outdoor pool, or visiting Assisi or Spello, two of Umbria's most splendid hilltop villages. Meals are taken on the terrace of the separate restaurant building, where the ambience is extremely laid back and there are lots of local dishes to set your mouth watering.

Renting a villa

Renato's Tower is one of the most unusual little country hideaways. This 1000-year old tower has one room on each of its four floors, starting with a kitchen/dining-room on the first floor, then leading up to a second floor sitting area, a double bedroom with a shower room on the third, another sitting-room on the fourth, and last, but not least, a delight-fully bizarre battlement rooftop terrace complete with reclining chairs, sun umbrella and a small swimming pool. You don't have to worry about hours of clearing up as a maid comes for two hours a day three days per week, and you can eat out in nearby **Calzolaro** on the other nights! This delightfully quirky tower can be booked through UK agents, CV Travel (UK ☎ 0171-581 0851), for around US$1193/£770 (high sea-son mid-July to third week in August) and US$906/£585 (low season) for seven nights' villa rental only. Make sure you book Renato's Tower as soon as you can as it is very popular. If it is booked up ask about **Colombaia** and **La Torreta**, which are both also on the Tuscan/Umbrian border and similarly lovely. Seven nights in La Torreta costs around US$1123/£725 (high) and US$728/£470 (low). Prices for Colombaia are similar.

THE COAST

Il Pellicano

Porto Ercole has long been the holiday destination of well-to-do Italian families, many of whom have their summer villas here making it a very swish kind of place. But the best thing about Porto Ercole is the lovely Il Pellicano.

Much is made at Il Pellicano of the extraordinary love and bond that existed between Patsy Daszel and Michael Graham, the Anglo-American couple who built it, but quite why the fact they were so in love should make it such a romantic place slightly mystifies me. It is however indisputably romantic, mainly because of

We went to too many hotels in two and a half weeks, but it was at Il Pellicano that we unwound the most. When we arrived we had a late lunch for a few hours and by the end of it we felt we'd been there for weeks. It's the most wonderful, friendly hotel and completely unsnobby – you don't have to tip them to be nice to you. The interiors are very tasteful, in fresh English style, but it's the location that really makes it. **Nick and Vanessa McDonald Buchanan**

A FEW THINGS TO DO AND SEE IN TUSCANY AND UMBRIA

Tuscany has long been synonymous with romance, while Umbria is less well known and is very much like Tuscany was 30 years ago. Despite rumours that Chianti is about to be renamed Chiantishire (making it another British county!) the countryside is still just as beautiful now as it has always been. All that has changed is the ownership and while it is true that more of the hillside villas are holiday homes than permanent residences, the magic of the place still exists. And if you do feel strongly about going somewhere authentic, not packed with fellow tourists, visit Umbria.

A stay in Tuscany and Umbria is all about long relaxing days spent either lying by the pool gazing at the smooth rolling hills rising and falling like waves; wandering the medieval streets of hilltop towns such as **Assisi**, **Orvieto**, **San Gimigniano**, and splendid **Siena**; or exploring the vineyards of **Chianti**, **Monetepulciano** and **Montalcino**. If you want to drive the wine route through Italy's most famous vineyards symbolised by the black rooster symbol of Chianti Classico, follow the *strada del vino* between Florence and Siena, and give yourselves time for plenty of enjoyable diversions en route.

One of the most romantic ways to see this beautiful countryside is in a hot-air balloon. Talk to Konstantin Turnau who runs the **Chianti Balloon Club** (☎ 0577-363232) and who will take you up in the skies at first light on a journey over the Chianti hills where you'll watch the early morning mist rise up off Siena, culminating in a hearty full-breakfast an hour later. Thoroughly recommended.

But whatever you do the days will no doubt revolve around eating, just as it has always been for the region's locals. The following restaurants should give you a taste of the area. On the main road between Florence and Siena, the SS22 (not the autostrada), about a kilometre north of Castelini en Chianti, is the fabulous bar/restaurant *Pietrafitta* (☎ 0577-741123), set on a hilltop with panoramic views over the surrounding vineyards. Pietrafitta is run by a British man who is conveniently fluent in Italian, German and French. Guests dine outside on the large terrace beneath parasols and the yellow tablecloths reflect the glorious sunsets (try to get there before 8pm to witness this stunning sight). The delicious food is produced by an Australian chef so, although the dishes are essentially Italian, they do have a cosmopolitan slant. There are always at least two fresh fish dishes on the menu, which is unusual in rural Chianti, as well as fresh pasta and the best carpaccio to be had in Italy. Typical dishes are rabbit with tomatoes and olives, fresh porcini mushrooms which melt in the mouth and scrumptious desserts. At about £50/L119,000 for two with lots of wine, the Pietrafitta is well worth a visit.

In Greve in Chianti, the *Cantinetta di Rignana* (☎ 055-852601), Via Rignana, serves some of the finest steaks you are ever likely to eat, in a farmhouse restaurant.

Radda in Chianti has several lovely restaurants, in particular try: the *Podere Terreno* (☎ 0577-738312), Via Terreno alla Via della Volpaia, which is another farmhouse restaurant and is a must, providing you can book a table; for a cheaper meal, try the *Ristorante Le Vigne* (☎ 0577-738640), Podere Le Vigne, which is a charming old farmhouse restaurant surrounded by vineyards and representing exceptionally good value; *Vignale* (☎ 0755-738094), run by a Swiss-Italian team, has a Michelin star and is renowned for its delicious figs wrapped in pancetta – expensive, but a real treat.

If you find yourselves in San Gimigniano around lunchtime pop into the *Ristorante Dorandò* (☎ 0577-941862), Vicolo dell'Oro just off the Piazza Duomo, where medieval dishes are rustled up in cool 14th century surroundings. Lots of the items on the amazingly descriptive menu are strange combinations but there is also pasta if you're not feeling adventurous.

its location – it is built into a recess of the rocky peninsula, snugly enclosed by pines and cypresses hanging out over the dark, blue sea of this beautiful stretch of coastline. Romantic, too, are the perfectly decorated bedrooms which manage to be smart as well as elegant with their bold reds and ochres juxtaposed against cool white walls and dark wooden beams. There are also individual touches such as the huge basket of Molton Brown toiletries and knuckle jointed towel rails in the bathroom.

But it is the staff that really makes Il Pellicano so special. Everyone is helpful, courteous and takes time to get things right. Unlike most hotels, for instance, where your breakfast is plonked down on a tray, at Il Pellicano they make the effort to lay the whole ensemble out on the balcony for you, complete with starched tablecloth, English jams, croissants, pain au chocolat, brioche, rye bread and even French toast, just to ensure they've catered for every taste. Apart from choosing a superb location, the lov-

IL PELLICANO
(☎ 0564-833801, fax 0564-833418), Cala dei Santi, 1-58018 Porto Ercole, Grosseto, Italy
Closed: Early November to end March
Reservations: Relais & Châteaux worldwide reservation numbers (see p12); or through UK tour operators Abercrombie & Kent and Italian Escapades (see p11)
Getting there: The hotel can arrange transfers from Orbetello (14km), otherwise guests get a taxi or rent a car from Rome (150km), Florence (193km) and Siena (125km); from Rome, take the A12 towards Civitavecchia, exit at Orbetello towards Porto Ercole
Accommodation: 26 rooms, eight junior suites and six de luxe suites
Amenities: Piano bar, candlelight barbecues, dinner and dancing every Friday during July and August, sightseeing to Roman and Etruscan ruins, salt-water heated swimming pool, rocky beach, all-weather tennis court, water-skiing, beauty centre; horse-riding nearby and golf an hour's drive away
Dress code: Informal
Weddings: Wedding receptions for up to 120 people are catered for, but the hotel is not licensed to perform wedding ceremonies
Minimum stay: None
Rates: Double rooms from US$156/L 237,000 half board per person; suites from US$273/L415,000 half board per person
Credit cards: Visa, Eurocard, American Express, Diners Club
Taxes and service charge: 10% tax, service included

ing couple also did well to create such a classically Italian villa, so that despite being merely decades, as opposed to centuries, old the rambling rust-coloured villa with its heavy cloak of ivy and terracotta roof tiles looks as if it has been around forever.

The management claims that this is not a glamorous hotel and indeed it does have a very discreet atmosphere, rather like a private club, but for these very reasons Il Pellicano has for years attracted all sorts of celebrities from Charlie Chaplin to Leonard Bernstein, so it's hardly a rustic retreat.

Dining at Il Pellicano is a rare treat, especially by candlelight out under the trees, with food delicious enough to merit Relais & Châteaux membership for the past 15 years and regular favourites such as riz aux langoustines al dente and the fabulous spaghetti Il Pellicano. It is pretty expensive but well worth it, though the barbecues seem overpriced at around L95,000 a head.

During the day, guests make the most of the hotel's lovely cliff-edge swimming pool which is surrounded by deck chairs and tasteful cream parasols. The views from the pool over the sea to the neighbouring islands of **Giglio** and **Giannutri** are truly dreamy, especially in the early morning light and again as the sun sets. Alternatively you can go down the steps to the water's edge and the rocky beach where several comfortable loungers are lined up on small individual terraces. From here you can dive straight out into the deep waters of the sea.

La Posta Vecchia

La Posta Vecchia is without doubt one of Italy's most exclusive hotels. Built right on the edge of the Mediterranean this grand palace was the former residence of John Paul Getty and, as such, boasts incomparable architecture and facilities.

When the brochure describes La Posta Vecchia as a place that 'speaks of harmony and beauty – luxury, peace and pleasure' it doesn't exaggerate. The villa is so elegant with such a timeless air of refined beauty and splendour that you really will be able to imagine yourselves as house guests of the big JP himself.

Because of the sheer size of the place and the fact that it has only 10 rooms and eight suites there seems to be endless space wherever you look. Originally a Roman post house and built as early as 1600, La Posta Vecchia is filled with priceless artefacts: Roman antiquities, exposed Roman mosaics, Venetian lamps, elegant marble busts, hand-woven French tapestries and the original fine art adorning the walls. A series of salons occupies the ground floor, each one appointed with objets d'art gathered from all over the world.

Despite the existence of the beautiful terrace, just a few easy steps away from the sea, John Paul was encouraged by one of his mistresses to build an indoor swimming pool hewn out of solid granite. The pool is surrounded by huge arched windows through which the sunlight pours on to the shimmering pool below.

Each of the suites is decorated differently and is furnished with wonderful antiques from the 16th and 17th centuries, but modern comforts such as satellite TV, hair-dryers and phones are not forgotten. La Posta Vecchia has developed a tradition whereby honeymooners who present a slice of their wedding-cake to the hotel are offered the house's best suite on arrival, either the Medici with its pink marble tub, or the Getty, if they are available.

Fine Italian cuisine, worthy of its Relais & Châteaux membership, is served formally in the dining-room each evening on beautiful marble tables set with sparkling crystal and silverware. During the day, guests spend their time around the pool, down at the villa's private beach or exploring the adjacent parklands. Horse-riding, tennis and golf can also be easily arranged, while **Cerveteri**, **Tarquinia** and Rome itself, are not far away.

PORTOFINO
Hotel Splendido

The Splendido is another one of those hotels that has etched its way into people's minds

---

LA POSTA VECCHIA
(☎ 06-9949501, fax 06-9949507), Palo Laziale, 1-00055 Ladispoli, Rome, Italy
Closed: Mid January to mid March
Reservations: Relais & Châteaux worldwide reservation numbers (see p12) or through leading travel agents and tour operators to Italy (see p11)
Getting there: 30 minutes from Rome Airport, 45 minutes from Rome city centre; from Rome take the SS1 towards Ladispoli, then follow signs to Paol Laziale
Accommodation: Nine double rooms and eight suites
Amenities: Restaurant, and large ocean-terrace for dining in the summer, 24-hour room service, limousine service, car rental, horse-riding, golf courses 20 and 40 minutes away, excursions, indoor swimming pool, private beach, park, archaeological Roman museum, heli-pad, beautician and masseur on call
Dress code: Jacket and tie are required in the evenings
Weddings: Wedding receptions for up to 80 people are catered for in-house, but up to 250 can be accommodated if outside catering is used; La Posta Vecchia is not licensed to perform wedding ceremonies
Minimum stay: None
Rates: Double rooms from US$387 L591,000
Credit cards: Most major
Taxes and service charge: Included

---

so firmly that it has become an institution in its own right. Get any serious traveller to name the ten most luxurious hotels in the world, and the Splendido would be there.

The greatest thing about the Splendido is its marvellous location providing some of the most stunning views in the whole Mediterranean. You'll never tire of the picture postcard view of the pretty pink and yellow houses crowding the edge of the harbour,

---

HOTEL SPLENDIDO
(☎ 0185-269551, fax 0185-269614), Viale Baratta, 13, 16034 Portofino, Italy
Reservations: Through Orient-Express Hotels and The Leading Hotels of the World toll free reservation numbers worldwide (see p12); or through UK tour operators Elegant Resorts, Abercrombie & Kent, Italian Escapades (see p11)
Getting there: The Splendido can arrange transfers from Genoa and Milan Airports and the local railway stations, but most guests arrive by car
Accommodation: 63 guest rooms: 42 bedrooms, 13 junior suites and eight suites
Amenities: Outdoor swimming pool, all-weather tennis courts, water-skiing, private speedboat charter with chauffeur, sauna, solarium, two restaurants; golf nearby
Dress code: Elegant casual (European chic)
Weddings: Can be arranged
Minimum stay: None
Rates: Bed and breakfast from US$201/L307,000 per person, half board from US$325/L497,000; suites from US$372/L568,000 to US$527/L805,000, but ask about spring and autumn breaks which give a much better deal
Credit cards: Most major
Taxes and service charge: Included

or studying the comings and goings on the yachts bobbing around in the waters below.

But there is also more to this hotel than impressive vistas: much of the hotel's character is derived from the clientele itself where elegant guests sit in their finely coutured Italian blazers and Gucci loafers, beside Versace sunglasses and Hermès scarves. You could never be in any doubt that a stay at the Splendido puts you in the epicentre of the sophisticated social life of this chicest of resorts. You probably won't realise quite what an art there is to lying on a sun-lounger until you've seen the elegant Italian women gently lower themselves in practised fashion – the whole place is just one long pose, nobody speaks to anyone and at times the place is so hushed that it's almost like being in a church!

The hotel is a former monastery, which is somewhat hard to relate to the amazing luxury and opulence that the same building houses now. The trompes l'oeil in the bedroom are exquisite, the jacuzzis an enjoyable extra, the salt-water pool terraced into the hillside is wonderful. Lunches washed down by chilled white wine on the Terrazza with the lattice of vines above and views of the port below are infinitely romantic.

Wander down the hill into the village for a drink, play tennis on the all-weather courts or else charter the hotel's private speedboat for chauffeur-driven trips to nearby villages and water-skiing.

Hotel San Pietro

Perched high up above picturesque Positano, the jewel of the Amalfian coast, clinging to 100m of craggy rock face, it is certainly difficult to imagine a more spectacular location for a hotel. The panoramic views are incredible and the San Pietro is one of those hotels that could have been designed for honeymooners. With its terraces and balconies projecting over the sea, shaped according to the contours of the cliff edge, exterior staircases and sloping gardens full of massed bougainvillaea, you'd be hard pressed to find anywhere more romantic.

Each of the 58 bedrooms has its own balcony, every one offering breathtaking views across the **Tyrrhenian Sea**. Neapolitan ceramics, in yellow, blue, green and white hues, adorn the benches on the immense terrace, the floors of the rooms and the pink marble bathrooms. Everywhere you look there are views, facilitated by the clever use of glass panels.

Guests can either enjoy the hotel's small pool, or take the lift from the reception hall down an 88m shaft excavated into the cliff-edge to the beach where there are watersports, a tennis court and a sundeck and bar nestled between the rocks and the sea.

Dinner is taken by candlelight outside on one of the hotel's terraces looking out over the bay. The cuisine pays tribute to the aromas and flavours of the south, with such favourites as langoustines sautés and risotto aux langoustines, and is good enough to have earned the hotel Relais & Châteaux status long ago. It is difficult to fault this gracious hotel with its antique ambience, the only problem you are likely to encounter is managing to get a room in the first place.

THE HOTEL SAN PIETRO
(☎ 089-875455, fax 089-811449), Via Larito 2, 1-84017 Positano, Italy
Reservations: Relais & Châteaux worldwide reservation numbers (see p12); or through UK tour operators Elegant Resorts, Abercrombie & Kent and Italian Escapades (see p11)
Getting there: From the north take the A2 Napoli, A3 towards Salerno, exit Castellanmare di Stabia; 17km south of Sorrento, 55km south of Naples
Accommodation: 55 rooms and five suites
Amenities: Tennis court, swimming pool, restaurant, bar, terraces, private beach with sundeck and bar, water-skiing, jacuzzi, fishing
Dress code: Gentlemen are requested to wear long trousers in the restaurant, and although jackets and tie are not needed people usually dress up for dinner
Weddings: No
Minimum stay: None, but most guests stay for four or five days
Rates: Doubles from US$342/L520,000; suites from US$493/L750,000
Credit cards: Visa, Eurocard, American Express, Diners Club
Taxes and service charge: Included

Other recommended hotels

People keeping telling me that their favourite hotel on the coast is **La Sirenuse** (☎ 89-875066, fax 89-811798), Via Colombo 30, 84017 Positano, described to me by one recently returned honeymooner as 'spectacular, it might be my favourite hotel ever'. La Sirenuse has long been regarded as one of Italy's loveliest hotels and, apart from its dramatic cliff-top location overlooking the beach, La Sirenuse is celebrated for its perfect taste, quiet elegance and intimate European charm. There are 58 bedrooms and four suites: superior and de luxe bedrooms and junior suites have balconies overlooking the sea, and there are an abundance of charming details such as the Nina Ricci toiletries and jacuzzis in the bathroom. The hotel even has its own culinary school. Doubles from US$316/L480,000 including breakfast and taxes.

Hotel Santa Caterina

Hotel Santa Caterina on the Amalfi coast is one of the world's top honeymoon hotels. Sitting majestically on a clifftop surrounded by lemon groves and terraces, this charming villa boasts uninterrupted views out to sea and along the superb coastline.

The lounge and bar are linked by huge floor-to-ceiling windows which look onto a spectacular terrace where bougainvillaea grows on a pergola-style frame, making it the perfect spot from which to soak up the view. The gardens lead down to the sea and, just above sea level, to the hotel's beautiful pool and sun terrace. The pool can be reached by a lift or a flight of stairs. The only problem with the pool is that it loses the sun by about 3.30pm prompting guests to make an early start with their sunbathing and producing competition for the best spots. Otherwise you can't fault this hotel.

Built during the early 1900s, it became a favourite venue for artistic, political and cultural figures of the time. The original interiors are beautiful, and all the bedrooms are tastefully decorated in understated style.

The Santa Caterina has always been popular as a romantic destination due to its lovely gardens, immaculate service and incredible location, but the recent addition of its two garden cottages make it one of the most sought after destinations in Europe.

What makes the two cottages, La Follia Amalfitana and Casa dell'Arancio, so special is their superb layout maximising the Santa Caterina's prime asset, the views. You can lie back in the huge white sunken jacuzzi, with only a plate glass window separating you from the cliff edge and the views beyond. The two semi-detached suites are totally isolated and are reached via a pathway through the lemon grove. Each one has a lounge with TV and minibar, a mini jacuzzi in the bathroom, and a private terrace situated right above the sea.

> **HOTEL SANTA CATERINA**
> (☎ 089-871012, fax 089-871351), SS Amalfitana 9, 84011 Amalfi, Italy
> **Reservations:** Prima Hotels toll free reservations numbers worldwide (see p12)
> **Getting there:** The hotel can arrange transfers in its air-conditioned Mercedes from either Naples Airport (L170,000) or Rome Airport (L650,000)
> **Accommodation:** 58 rooms, 12 suites
> **Amenities:** Panoramic restaurant, open-air restaurant above swimming pool, piano bar, swimming pool, private beach, lift from hotel to pool and beach
> **Dress code:** Casual
> **Weddings:** Wedding receptions for between 50 and 300 people can be catered for
> **Minimum stay:** None
> **Rates:** Doubles from US$237/L360,000 to US$329/L500,00 bed and breakfast; suites from US$414/L630,000; the cottages cost US$625/L950,000 bed and breakfast
> **Credit cards:** American Express, Eurocard, MasterCard, Visa
> **Taxes and service charge:** Included

The Santa Caterina is a really lovely, very private hotel with an old world elegance about it. The food was wonderful, the swimming off the rocky beach was nice and our bedroom was quite large and very comfortable and it had a private balcony overlooking the sea. Surrounded by interwoven lemon groves built into the cliffs it was so tranquil, and we enjoyed walking into Amalfi each afternoon to explore the town.

Diana and Peter Pásint Magyar

Greece
(BEST TIME: MAY/JUNE AND SEPTEMBER)

Greece is known for its incredible coastline of heavily indented shores and sandy beaches. Inland, however, are the vast mountains, such as the Pindus range which forms the country's backbone and Mt Olympus, which were immortalised in Greek mythology, as well as hundreds of villages where the pace of life has been little altered by modern society.

Greece, consisting of mainland Greece and the islands of the Aegean and Ionian seas, forms Europe's southernmost tip. The Aegean Sea, with its crystal clear waters, dolphins, and wonderful fresh fish is host to some of the most idyllic islands in the Mediterranean area. One of the Aegean Islands is **Chios**: it lies just off the coast of Turkey and claims to be the birthplace of Homer. Chios has remained beyond the reach of mass tourism but it is a fantastic island to explore because each village has a different façade and it has scores of unspoilt beaches.

Crete is the largest island in Greece and forms the border between the Aegean and the Libyan seas and between Europe and Africa. This mountainous island comprises rocky coasts, vast sandy beaches, pebbled shores and over 3000 large and small caves, with impressive stalactite and stalagmite formations. Dotted throughout the countryside are dry-stone farm buildings, villages perched on high plateaux, monasteries, isolated castles and chapels. Home to Europe's very first civilisation, the Minoan (2800-1150 BC), today's Crete is the product of a succession of invading nations, each having left its influence over the years. Apart from its beaches, Crete is a fabulous place to hang out in the hundreds of cafés sipping a sweet or medium coffee, or a glass of raki while playing backgammon.

GREECE

Sparkling seas, soaring mountains, magic skies, and that perfect little taverna on the waterfront – so good that even the gods chose it as their heaven on earth

When to go: May/June and September (July and August are too hot and busy)

Average maximum temperature °C (Athens)

JAN	FEB	MAR	APR	MAY	JUN	JUL	AUG	SEP	OCT	NOV	DEC
12	12	14	17	20	24	26	26	23	20	17	14

Capital: Athens

Flight times: to Athens from:
New York: $10^1/_4$ hours
LA: $18^1/_2$ hours
London: $3^3/_4$ hours
Sydney: 22 hours

Approximate exchange rates: Drachmas (D) – £1=D374, US$1 = D241.13, A$1 = D190.55

Time difference: GMT plus two hours (plus three hours from the last Sunday in March to the last Sunday in September)

Voltage: 220v AC, 50 Hz, round two-pin plugs

Combine with: Turkey

Country dialling code: ☎ 30

CRETE
Kalimera Kriti Hotel and Village Resort

Kalimera Kriti Hotel and Village Resort is one of Greece's top luxury resorts. If you want to be thoroughly pampered and are looking for the sort of honeymoon where all you do is switch from the bedroom to the beach to the restaurant and back to the beach, this is *the* place in the Greek islands. Positioned on the northern coast of Crete, facing Sissi bay and the endless blue of the Aegean sea, the hotel enjoys a fantastic location and being spread over 210 sq km it never feels crowded. It took ten years to build the Kalimera and the result is a hotel built for the 21st century with every conceivable facility on hand and a very mixed European clientele. There are two full-sized outdoor and one indoor swimming pools, two private golden sand beaches, a cafeteria, a snack bar, a Greek Kafenion (bar/café), a gourmet and seafood restaurant and a shopping centre. In short, this is not a hotel, but a cleverly designed Cretan village.

There are, in fact, three separate villages as well as the main building, and all incorporate neo-classical elements in their traditional Cretan-styled one and two-storey bungalows. The decor is a good combination of traditional materials with solid wooden furniture, cool marble floors and marble bathrooms. All the rooms are well proportioned with impressive facilities including proper king-sized beds, air-conditioning, phones, radio, satellite TV, minibar and in-room safe.

With so many different dining options to choose from you won't get bored with the same old Greek dishes every night and, unusually for this part of the world, the staff have been trained to let guests linger over their meals if they want. Try the Kafenion which serves Cretan raki, Greek coffee and sweets and which is located just beside a large natural cave which has recently been excavated: the perfect spot for the classical concerts which are held weekly during the summer.

What makes the Kalimera such an incredible hotel is the attention to detail: the tables and chairs in the taverna are aligned each day according to the direction of the wind and the position of the sun, at breakfast there are even small packets of Nutella and chocolate dipped croissants for the Europeans, while at night rose petals and sugared almonds are scattered on the bed. Pretty impressive really.

KALIMERA KRITI HOTEL AND VILLAGE RESORT

(☎ 0841-71603, fax 0841-71598), 72400 Sissi, Lassithi, Crete, Greece

Reservations: Prima Hotels worldwide toll free reservation numbers (see p12), or through UK tour operator Argo Holidays (UK ☎ 0171-331 7070)

Getting there: Fly to Heraklion Airport from where the 45km journey to the hotel in local taxis costs approximately D12,500

Accommodation: 416 bedrooms, including 141 hotel and bungalow suites and 40 waterfront and VIP bungalows

Amenities: Six tennis courts, mini golf, two squash courts, volley-ball, table tennis, large selection of watersports, indoor heated swimming pool, two outdoor heated swimming pools, large natural cave, the Dionyssos taverna, snack pool bar, cafeteria, Kafenion, shopping centre, three restaurants and terraces, fish and barbecue evenings

Dress code: No code but Euro-chic and lots of Armani jeans

Weddings: The hotel doesn't have a wedding licence, but Argo Holidays can organise your wedding at a nearby chapel

Minimum stay: None

Rates: Standard room with garden view from around US$200/D48,000 half board; waterfront bungalows from US$242/D58,000 half board; sea view one bedroom suites from US$260 D63,000 half board

Credit cards: Most major

Taxes and service charge: Included

Other recommended hotels

Elounda Beach Hotel (☎ 0841-41412/4, fax 0841-41373/75), 721 00 Aghios Nikolaos, Crete, is widely acknowledged as an outstanding hotel. If you want the full-blown luxury resort hotel and have money to burn go for one of Elounda Beach's waterfront bungalow suites. Built in traditional Cretan-style with white plastered and stone walls, the bungalows have fantastic balconies with steps down to private platforms and the shimmering blue water below. Both the sea-view bungalows and the waterfront bungalows have luxury marble bathrooms with jacuzzi tubs, TV in the bathroom and CD players. Inside, the rooms are white-washed with traditional furnishings, rattan sofas, and refreshing blue and white striped cotton fabrics on the beds.

As a member of The Leading Hotels of the World, its facilities are superb, but in my mind the best feature of the hotel is the **Veghera Bar**, located at the end of a jetty with 360° sea views. Sea-view bungalows cost from US$116/D27,500, while the waterfront bungalows are around US$137/D32,500.

Hotel Elounda Mare (☎ 0841-41102/03, fax 0841-41307), PO Box 31, GR-72100 Aghios Nikolaos, Crete, is also in the village of Elounda, but has the additional advantage of having 46 rooms with their own private, or shared, swimming pool. From an aerial view this Relais & Châteaux hotel looks just incredible – a sprawling confusion of pristine white bungalows nestled along the contours of the Aegean, with scores of turquoise swimming pools separated from the similarly coloured sea by a lush band of fertile gardens. The 49 rooms in the main body of the hotel start at US$139/D33,000, while the 46 bungalows are from US$190/D45,000.

Hotel Doma (☎ 0821-51772, fax 0821-41578), 24, Venizelou, Chania, Crete, is the sort of hotel that you either love or hate. It is a rather quirky, but very romantic old neo-classical mansion with large Grecian pillars and intricate wrought-iron work, built on the shore in Chania. The Doma is particularly popular with writers and artists. There are three air-conditioned suites, two of which cost US$139/D33,000 per night, while the third one costing US$190/D45,000 occupies the top floor and has a terrace where meals can be taken.

A FEW THING TO SEE AND DO AROUND CRETE

The best way to get a feel for Crete is to hire a car. Don't miss the **Samarias Gorge**, at the western end of the island. It is the largest and most imposing gorge in Europe and it is only possible to go through it in the summer months. The route is not difficult but it will take around four to five hours and you'll need good footwear. Its width ranges from just three metres at its 'doors' to 150m in places, while the steep, vertical walls towering up to 500m high, are absolutely staggering. It makes a lovely walk with wild vegetation, a huge variety of grasses and the constant smell of wild herbs.

In the middle of the gorge is **Samarias village**, where the church of Osia Maria has some beautiful wall paintings. At the other end of the gorge stop off at **Aghia Roumeli**, an isolated fishing village built on top of ancient Tarras, where you can revive yourselves with a dip in the crystal clear waters.

Further back down the coast lies **Hora Sfakion**, a beautiful, historic community with old houses and churches, from where it is possible to take a boat out to the island of **Gavdos**, or to the picturesque seaside communities of **Loutro** and **Aghia Roumeli**.

SANTORINI

The Tsitouras Collection

THE TSITOURAS COLLECTION
(☎ 0286-23747, fax 0286-23918), Fira, Firostefani, 847 00 Thira, Santorini, Greece
Reservations: Head office in Athens (☎ 01-362 2326, fax 01-362 2326)
Getting there: Ferries from Piraeus (Athens) to Santorini (Kos has daily connecting ferries to Piraeus); TC will collect you from the airport or port for no extra charge
Accommodation: Five guest houses
Amenities: Hair-dryer, minibar, CD player, bathrobes
Dress code: Smart casual
Weddings: Yes
Minimum stay: Three nights
Rates: From US$420/D101,000 to US$500/D120,000
Credit cards: Most major
Taxes and service charge: Included

The Tsitouras Collection (TC as it is modestly referred to!), in exclusively upmarket Santorini, must be one of the most romantic places to stay in the Mediterranean. Perched on the top of a 300m cliff, this traditional style villa has the most spectacular views.

The brochure, which itself is worthy of coffee table status, describes the Tsitouras Collection as 'a work of sculptural art in that it is ravishingly beautiful from every possible angle, its spaces, its volumes, its ornamentation, its colours are all flawless'. The ridiculous thing is, that this is not just a load of over exuberant narrative, but the place does actually do the brochure justice! It seems inaccurate to call the TC a hotel, because it is more like a work of art and a gallery than a private villa, let alone a hotel.

The TC comprises five suites all of which are designed, decorated and furnished in accordance with their names. The **House of the Sea** has fabulously framed English, Italian and German sea charts from the 16th to the 19th centuries adorning its walls, while a ceramic dish by Pablo Picasso sits in a glass case on top of an antique chest; the **House of the Winds** has high, vaulted ceilings in an airy light blue and a silver Venetian oil lamp adorned with cherubim hangs down from the ceiling; the **House of Portraits** has beautifully framed portraits gracing its walls, a 19th century wooden baptismal font makes a novel coffee table, while the bedroom ceiling is covered in a fresco with cherubs at each corner; the **House of Porcelain** derives its name from the valuable white and blue 19th century Minton and Royal Copenhagen porcelain plates that it contains; and the **House of Nureyev** is the most romantic of them all, perched above the others and named after the collection of sketches depicting the late Rudolf Nureyev. This last house is the only one with its own veranda overlooking the caldera.

Elegant, decadent, serenely beautiful, the TC is all about aesthetics. It is the most stunning collection of rooms imaginable and if you can possibly afford to spend a few days there you'll never forget them.

CHIOS

Chios was under Genoese control from the mid-13th century until it fell to the Ottoman Turks in 1566, only finally escaping Turkish rule and united to Greece in 1912. It has successfully managed to escape the trappings of mass tourism, with the exception of the small seaside village of Karfas. In fact it is only really known in travel circles for one reason, the staggeringly beautiful and exclusive, Villa Argentikon.

Villa Argentikon

It has amazed me how many people have heard of the Villa Argentikon. Not many have actually been there of course but it is just one of those magical places that seems to find its way into the pages of glossy magazines and which people hear about by word of mouth. This magnificent classical villa was built in the 16th century as part of the Genoese settlement. It has been in the Argenti family for centuries and has recently undergone considerable refurbishment restoring it to its former glory. With only five suites and one de luxe room, the exclusivity of the villa speaks for itself. The Villa Argentikon is a place of quiet, discreet and simple elegance.

Set in the corners of the villa's brilliant, one hectare garden, the private suites offer total privacy, well appointed interiors and stunning views. There are no bars, no swimming pools and no televisions at the Villa Argentikon – happily it's not that kind of place. The villa's few guests are staying effectively, not in a hotel, but in a private house which the owner, the Marquis Lorenzo Argenti, is very happy for you to treat as your own.

All the rooms are light and airy and beautifully decorated, with large marble

---

VILLA ARGENTIKON
(☎ 0271-31599, fax 0271-31465), Chios Island 82100, Greece
Reservations: Either direct or through Greek Islands Club, Best of Greece and Cyprus or Abercrombie & Kent (see p11)
Getting there: The villa will arrange the 15-minute transfer from Chios Airport (there are 5 flights from Athens daily)
Accommodation: 5 suites, 1 de luxe room
Amenities: The alfresco dining-room, drinks and light snacks will be brought to you in the secluded gardens, Francesco d'Afflitto, the Marquis' personal assistant will take care of anything you need from a private tour of the island to contact with the outside world (No TV!)
Dress code: Men are required to wear trousers at dinner, but not jacket and tie
Weddings: No
Minimum stay: No minimum stay but the hotel recommends three days
Rates: Doubles from US$232/D56,000 to US$310/D75,000 depending on season
Credit cards: None, payment must be by Eurocheque or in cash
Taxes and service charge: No taxes, but there is a 10% service charge on dinner

bathrooms, relaxing sitting-rooms, polished wooden floors and brass beds. Only the villa, **Christopher Columbo**, and the de luxe room, **Meridiana**, are equipped with air-conditioning, but with large doors on to your private patio and open windows in the elegant bedrooms you'll hardly need it. Besides, all that whirring and droning would detract from the very reason people come to the Villa Argentikon – the utter and absolute tranquillity.

All meals are served in the peace of the sunny courtyard, where white-gloved staff bring you sumptuous dishes, accompanied by Italian, Greek and Turkish wines. Guests are welcome to either eat on their own at a table for two, or to join with other guests at a larger table. There is absolutely no pressure to do either. At night a pianist gently plays as you dine under the stars by candlelight.

The garden is perfect for a lazy afternoon walk: stroll through the rose garden, the ancient lime avenue, or the many arbours and bowers. And when you're feeling more adventurous there is the rest of this lovely island with its 62 rustic villages, pine forests and 11th century monasteries to explore.

A FEW THINGS TO SEE AND DO ON CHIOS

Chios, a 1554 sq km island has 62 villages which have retained their medieval character, so there's plenty to explore. The south part of the island is famous for producing mastic, otherwise known as 'the chew in chewing gum' which comes from trees unique to Chios. The villages in this area are known as *mastichohoria*, quite literally mastic villages.

Heading south from Chios town the first village you come to is **Armolia**, known for its pottery and magnificent 14th century Genoese castle. Then there is **Pyrgi** which, with its central square of tiered balconies, narrow and often roofed alleyways, and intricate *xysta* blue and grey geometric stonemasonry, has changed very little since medieval times. Not far from Pyrgi traces of a 6th century BC temple of Apollo remain in the archaeological site of **Phanes**, while just 10km south of Pyrgi you can lose yourself for an afternoon in the confu-

sion of cobbled backstreets and stone-walled tunnels in 9th century **Mesta**, before stopping off in the square where the shaded *taverna* serves a host of delicious traditional dishes.

On the west coast **Volissos**, one of the island's most beautiful villages, is spread over the lower slopes of a hill where the remains of a Byzantine castle still hold court.

Drive north through the valleys clothed in pine forests, corn fields and olive groves, taking in the island's most striking Byzantine monument, the 11th century monastery of **Nea Moni** with its frescoes and mosaics of the life of Christ, en route. In the same area it is worth visiting the virtually abandoned medieval villages of **Anovatos** and **Dietcha**, before driving on to the very north of the island where the mountainous landscape gives way to valleys full of pine, chestnut and oleander and some idyllic unspoilt beaches.

Renting a villa in Greece

The luxurious **Terrace House**, in Nissaki, Corfu, is a true honeymoon hideaway and one of the most elegant and stylish places to stay in Corfu, particularly for a couple who want to be alone. The white-washed interior with its sumptuous royal blue cushioned-sofas and lovely framed prints perfectly complement the simple outdoor living on the spacious terrace overlooking a seemingly endless ocean. The Terrace House is just one of a range of villas represented by UK tour operator, **CV Villas** (UK ☎ 0171-581 0851) – ask them in particular about the **Cottage**, the **Bijou Studio**, **Villas Eleni** and **Margarita**, and **Trelawny**. As a rough guide a week's holiday in the Terrace House would cost around US$852/£550 (peak season) and US$674/£435 (low season) per person including flights, transfers and maid service, while a week at the Bijou would cost about US$666/£430 (peak) and US$511/£330 (low).

The **Greek Island Club** (UK ☎ 01932-220477) has the most wonderful one-bedroom house built in a dramatic clifftop location with views of the west coast of Skopelos. Two weeks at **Anilio House**, including hire car in the peak season costs around US$2169/£1,400. Other recommended villas on the Greek Island Club's books are **Liakada House** and **Papaki House** in Panormas, a village in south **Skopelos**.

PART 4: NORTH AMERICA

Canada
(BEST TIME: ALL YEAR ROUND)

There can be few parts of Canada as breathtaking as the province of Alberta, where the soaring mountains, blue-green lakes and glaciers are majestic both in summer and in winter. So despite the undeniable lure of Quebec City and Montreal I've concentrated on the Rockies, the epitome of Canada, the country of the great outdoors.

CANADA

Skiing and hiking in the Rockies and scenic journeys by luxury train

When to go: All year round

Average maximum temperatures °C

	JAN	FEB	MAR	APR	MAY	JUN	JUL	AUG	SEP	OCT	NOV	DEC
Toronto	-2	0	2	12	19	24	26	24	20	12	5	1
Calgary	-3	-2	2	10	10	18	23	21	17	12	4	0

Capital: Ottawa

Flight times: to Vancouver from:
New York: 8 hours
LA: 3 hours 10 minutes
London: 10 hours
Sydney: 18³/₄ hours

Approximate exchange rates: Canadian dollar (C$) – £1 = C$2.13, US$1 = C$1.37, A$1 = C$1.08

Time difference:
Toronto: GMT minus 5 hours
Vancouver: GMT minus 7 hours

Voltage: 110v AC, 60 Hz , two-pin plugs

Combine with: USA, Central America, the Caribbean as a stopover, Australia, New Zealand, South Pacific,

Country dialling code: ☎ 1

THE CANADIAN ROCKIES

The Canadian Rockies really reveal their awesome beauty from the slopes, as you look down on thousands of acres of tree-covered wilderness. Between them, Jasper, Banff and Lake Louise cover Canada's second largest ski area. But the Rockies are just as impressive in the summer when you can canoe on the lakes, white-water raft down the rivers or just enjoy the stunning mountain scenery on leisurely walks.

Lake Louise is the archetypal winter wonderland: you can take a horse-drawn sleigh ride on a moonlit night with only the dark shadows of the vast craggy mountains all around you, or be pulled on a sled by pure bred huskies through the trees and snow-covered creeks.

Jasper National Park is Canada's largest and oldest Rocky Mountain park and it boasts some of the most magical lake and mountain wilderness you are likely to encounter anywhere in the world. The park spans 4200 sq miles of rushing rivers, sparking lakes, virgin forest and majestic snow-clad mountains. The best thing about Jasper is its relative quietness, especially compared to Banff which is much more touristy.

It is surrounded by emerald lakes, the most incredible of which is **Maligne Lake**, the second largest glacier-fed lake in the world. There is a spectacular walk from the very top of **Maligne Canyon** right down to the canyon floor. If you are looking for a thrill, Maligne River is the scene for white-water rafting – you can book at Jasper Park Lodge.

Jasper, Banff and Lake Louise are within easy driving time of each other, so you can easily leave Jasper after lunch and arrive in Lake Louise before dinner.

Jasper Park Lodge

Jasper Park Lodge owns 1000 acres of the incredible National Park, making it a superb destination for any couple who love big scenery, whatever the time of year. The skiing (between December and April) is, of course, superb but in summer this mighty region is perhaps even more breathtaking and certainly provides a great setting for horse-riding, canoeing, mountain biking or just staring at the scenery.

Without doubt the most prestigious hotel in Jasper, the lodge is located a small way out of town overlooking **Lac Beauvert**. Originally built as an 80-room bungalow by the Canadian National Railway, the lodge now comprises 442 guest rooms all in authentic log cabins or cedar chalets spread along the lake shore. Many of the rooms and all the suites have sitting-rooms with fire-places and minibars, while some have private jacuzzis. Room service is by bicycle!

The best thing about the Jasper Park Lodge is that it is in fact a lodge. This may sound silly but I hate hotels that call themselves lodges and end up being more of a brick building. Not here, whether you are in one of the public lounges or your bedroom you'll never forget that you are in a mountain lodge: moose heads stare down at you from the walls, glass chandeliers are replaced by light fittings made from antlers, real log fires roar in stone hearths, and deep cushioned sofas are covered in plaids in warm country colours.

The hotel's facilities are awesome.

> **JASPER PARK LODGE**
> (☎ 403-852-3301, fax 403-852-5107), PO Box 40, Jasper, Alberta, Canada
> **Reservations:** US toll free (US ☎ 800-441-1414) or through UK tour operator Canadian Connections (UK ☎ 01494-473173)
> **Getting there:** 225 miles west of Edmonton and 275 miles north-west of Calgary
> **Accommodation:** 442 guest rooms including 55 suites
> **Amenities**: Four restaurants, two lounges, café, night-club, 18-hole championship golf course, horse-riding, tennis, mountain biking, hiking, fishing, boating, white-water rafting, swimming, cross-country skiing, canyon ice crawling, sleigh rides, ice-skating, heli-skiing, snowmobile tours
> **Dress code:** Casual/smart
> **Weddings:** Ceremonies and receptions are catered for
> **Minimum stay:** None
> **Rates:** Doubles from US$83/C$114, suites from US$176/C$241 during peak ski season (from December to February); doubles from US$62/C$85, suites from US$82/C$112 during the summer season (May to August)
> **Credit cards**: Most major
> **Taxes and service charge:** 5% room tax and 7% Government Service Tax (GST)

You can choose between skiing, hiking and fishing, there's an 18-hole championship golf course, four restaurants, two lounges featuring regional Canadian cuisine, a café, a night-club, and of course a health club.

Château Lake Louise

Château Lake Louise enjoys an incredible picture postcard setting. In the shadow of Mt Victoria this stunning cream-coloured château stands alone on the shores of Lake Louise with nothing but mountains and pine trees around it and the vast lake in front.

From Bavarian curling on the frozen lake to dog-sled and horse-drawn sleigh rides, Lake Louise in winter is truly romantic. This wonderful Canadian Pacific hotel really has got it sussed, they build bonfires and make hot chocolate on a cold winter evening, serve fondues in the **Walliser Stube** wine bar, and provide pack lunches whether you are going for a summer-time walk around the lake or on a challenging cross-country ski along the Moraine Lake Road.

Don't expect a small intimate chalet as the Château Lake Louise is pretty vast with 513 guest rooms but with scenery and space like this you're hardly going to feel claustrophobic. All rooms come equipped with a colour TV and in-house movies, phone, minibars, bathroom with bath and bidet, individual climate control and are decorated in alpine style.

Like all Canadian Pacific hotels the leisure facilities are superb. There are four restaurants, a wine bar, a night-club, an Alpine lounge (open in summer only) with views over **Victoria Glacier**, and the hotel's own deli where you can buy freshly-baked muffins and sandwiches to order. The recreation centre features an indoor pool, whirlpool, steam room and gym, as well as massage. In summer you can choose from canoeing, hiking, mountain biking, horseriding, white-water rafting, tennis and fishing, while the opportunities for winter sports are endless. The three ski mountains around **Banff** and Lake Louise jointly form Canada's second largest ski area and the runs suit everyone from beginners to intermediate with an average of 30ft of snow guaranteed.

CHÂTEAU LAKE LOUISE

(☎ 403-552-3511, fax 403-522-3834), Alberta, TOL 1EO, Canada

Reservations: US toll free (☎ 800-441-1414); or through UK tour operator Canadian Connections (UK ☎ 01494-473173)

Getting there: Two hours drive from Calgary International Airport, daily bus transfers

Accommodation: 513 guest rooms, including 66 suites

Amenities: Restaurant, three dining-rooms, wine bar, saloon night-club, lodge bar, deli, indoor pool, whirlpool, steam room, sunbed, massage, canoeing, hiking, skiing, tobogganing

Dress code: Casual/smart

Weddings: The hotel can cater for receptions up to a maximum of 450 people

Minimum stay: None

Rates: Doubles from US$83/C$114, suites from US$176/C$241 during peak ski season (from December to February); doubles from US$62/C$85, suites from US$82/C$112 during the summer season (May to August)

Credit cards: Most major

Taxes and service charge: 5% room tax and 7% GST

THE ROCKY MOUNTAINEER

The Rocky Mountaineer is a luxury train that makes two-day excursions through the Canadian Rockies.

The 'most spectacular train trip in the world', as the company quite rightly calls it, takes you through vast landscapes where you could see mighty bears swiping at salmon in the river one minute, an eagle soaring overhead the next and numerous elk, deer, moose and osprey.

Only seven years old, this fabulous blue and white train has to be the most romantic way to see this untamed landscape – up close but cocooned in luxury – with every last detail of the train and the journey carefully planned so as to maximise viewing potential and comfort.

You can choose from several different routes, between Vancouver and Jasper, or between Vancouver and Banff and onto Calgary.

If you can afford it do opt for the super-luxurious newly-launched **Gold Leaf Service**, a C$400 supplement. Not only does this give you better seats travelling on an upper deck in a brand new dome car with all-glass sides, but there is a fabulous observation platform below which is great for taking pictures and videos, and a proper art deco-style restaurant car complete with silver cutlery, white linen and china where you can enjoy gourmet meals.

Whichever route you take, the train stops overnight in **Kamloops**, where you get off and stay at the *Towne Lodge* which, although pretty basic, does serve good hearty food.

The next morning the train departs at 7.30am and goes either on to Jasper (perfect for the Jasper Park Lodge) or on to Banff, where there is another fantastic Canadian Pacific hotel, *Banff Springs*.

The Rocky Mountaineer can be booked from the US and Canada (US and Canada toll free ☎ 800-665-7245), or through tour operator Thomas Cook Ltd (see p10).

Melissa Graham's *Trans-Canada Rail Guide* is a useful guidebook that gives full details about what to see along the way on this fascinating rail journey.

USA
(BEST TIME: ALL YEAR ROUND)

The USA has so much to offer from the sunny Californian coast, and the awesome scenery of the **Grand Canyon**, to the **Arizona** desert and the snowy slopes of **Colorado**, as well as the glittering cities of **New York**, **San Francisco** and **New Orleans**, and the famous art deco hotels of fashionable **Miami Beach** and the islands of the **Florida Keys**.

The options are endless, so I've picked some of the United States' most famously romantic hotels and some destinations to give you a taster of the country's enormous honeymoon potential.

USA

Everything from cruising the Californian coast to skiing in Colorado and some of the most exciting cities in the world

When to go: All year round

Average maximum temperatures °C

	JAN	FEB	MAR	APR	MAY	JUN	JUL	AUG	SEP	OCT	NOV	DEC
Los Angeles	18	18	18	19	20	21	23	24	24	22	20	18
San Francisco	12	15	16	17	19	20	21	21	22	20	17	14
Phoenix	17	19	23	27	32	36	38	36	34	29	22	18
Denver	6	8	10	15	20	26	29	29	25	19	11	8
New York	5	5	9	15	20	24	27	26	23	18	12	6
Tampa	21	22	23	26	29	30	30	30	30	27	24	22

Capital: Washington DC

Flight times: to LA from:
New York: $5^1/_2$ hours
London: 11 hours
Sydney: 11 hours
to New York from:
London: $7^1/_2$ hours
Sydney: $20^1/_2$ hours

Approximate exchange rates: US dollar (US$) – £1 = US$1.55, A$1 = 0.79

Time difference: West coast: GMT minus 8 hours
East coast: GMT minus 5 hours

Voltage: 110v AC, 60 Hz , two-pin plugs

Combine with: Canada, Mexico and Central America, the Caribbean, Australia, New Zealand, South Pacific as a stopover

Country dialling code: ☎ 1

LOS ANGELES

Until I went there I have to admit that I wasn't too convinced about California as a honeymoon destination but one look at the sun-drenched coastline, lined with its characteristic petticoat palms, and I was won over.

The really classic thing to do is to fly into either **LA** or **San Francisco**, hire a car – perhaps some kind of racy red convertible or a sleek Cadillac – and drive the 400-mile coastline, along the famous Highway One, between these two fantastic cities. It is truly stunning and the hotels en route couldn't be more romantic.

Los Angeles, the city of beautiful people and, when they are passed their prime, facelifts, is a fun place to start or finish your honeymoon. Wander down **Sunset Boulevard**, shop on Rodeo Drive, or take a tour around the affluent streets of **Hollywood** and Beverly Hills. For a hassle-free honeymoon I'd avoid down town LA, and stick to the beaches, such as **Venice** and **Malibu** for your entertainment instead. LA is also ideally placed for visiting **Disneyland** or **Universal Studios**.

The Regent Beverly Wilshire

The Regent Beverly Wilshire, which over-looks Tiffany & Co, Saks and Valentino, on Beverly Hills' **Rodeo Drive**, cannot fail to give you a romantic start to your holiday, with its trademark strawberries and cream presented to your room on arrival. But as the hotel used in the filming of *Pretty Woman*, the Regent has now gone down in the annals of history as one of those places that epito-mises romance: as you stroll through the lobby you cannot forget the images of Julia Roberts strutting along in her thigh-length boots and Richard Gere's long rain mac.

Although the Regent has 295 rooms in all, it certainly doesn't have the feel of a big hotel. While some of the decor is a tiny bit shabby, with pastel colours in the bedrooms that seem to have faded a bit, the Regent has something magical about it, some kind of feeling that you truly have arrived – which makes your walk just that little bit more swanky as you stride out on to Rodeo Drive.

All the rooms have air-conditioning, colour televisions in the bedroom and anoth-er in the bathroom, in-room safe, two phones, and wonderfully comfortable beds. The bathrooms are marble and divided from the bedroom by a spacious walk-in closet. There is an abundance of white fluffy towels, large bottles of toiletries, a separate shower, white bathrobes and, best of all, a perfectly positioned TV so you can lie back among the foaming bubbles and watch classic movies.

The hotel's facilities include an outdoor swimming pool, and a spa with sauna and workout rooms, as well as a wide variety of places to eat and drink.

The Hotel Bel-Air

The Hotel Bel-Air has long been recognised as one of the world's most incredible hotels. As travel journalists are fond of saying: 'it's not so much a hotel, as a way of life'. The only problem is it can be difficult getting a room if you are a mere nobody!

Located in the prestigious Bel-Air dis-trict, just a mile down the road from **Beverly Hills**, the Hotel Bel-Air has 91 rooms, including 39 suites. These are all built in one and two storey red-tiled Mediterranean villas set amongst 11 acres of beautifully main-tained gardens, giving the hotel a tranquil atmosphere in this frenetic city.

The best suite is No 160, named the Grace Kelly suite, with a sitting-room and

---

THE REGENT BEVERLY WILSHIRE
(☎ 310-275-5200, fax 310-274-2851), 9500 Wilshire Boulevard, Beverly Hills, CA 90212-2405, USA
Reservations: The Leading Hotels of the World toll free reservation numbers worldwide (see p12)
Getting there: 30 minutes by taxi from LA's international airport; the hotel can arrange transfers at an approximate cost of US$86 one way
Accommodation: 275 rooms, including 69 suites
Amenities: 24-hour personal room atten-dant, three phone lines in each room, voice-messaging for guests, in-room safes
Dress code: Elegant casual, jackets are required in the dining-room, but a tie is not necessary
Weddings: The hotel does cater for wed-ding receptions
Minimum stay: None
Rates: Doubles from US$275 to US$400; suites from US$450 to US$4000
Credit cards: Most major
Taxes and service charge: 15.2% tax

HOTEL BEL-AIR
(☎ 310-472-1211, fax 310-476-5890), 701 Stone Canyon Road, Bel-Air, CA 90077 USA
Reservations: The Leading Hotels of the World's toll free reservations numbers worldwide (see p12)
Getting there: 13 miles from LA's inter-national airport
Accommodation: 52 rooms, 39 suites
Amenities: 24-hour fitness centre; beau-ty salon; 24-hour room service; video library; on-site limo and car rental; multi-lingual concierge; outdoor heated oval swimming pool; tennis, golf and other sporting facilities available nearby
Dress code: Jacket in dining-room after 6pm
Weddings: Can arrange weddings and receptions, contact Miss Maddelena
Minimum stay: None
Rates: Doubles from around US$306/£198; suites from US$536/£346
Credit cards: Most major
Taxes and service charge: 14% tax, ser-vice is included

bedroom opening on to its own private terrace, while the best room is No 240, which also has a private terrace and its own tangerine tree. But all the rooms have air-conditioning with individual controls, cable TV and VCR, plus all the toiletries and bathroom goodies you could possibly imagine, right down to bathroom scales and nail files.

CALIFORNIAN COASTAL ROUTE

Four Seasons Biltmore

Nestled on **Butterfly Beach** at the foot of the **Santa Ynez Mountains** the Four Seasons Biltmore with its splendid Moorish architecture, turreted rooms and individual cottages spread throughout blossoming gardens is, not surprisingly, popular as a wedding location.

> **FOUR SEASONS BILTMORE (SANTA BARBARA)**
> (☎ 805-969-2261, fax 805-969-4682), 1260 Channel Drive, Santa Barbara, CA 93108, USA
> **Reservations:** Four Seasons reservation numbers worldwide (see p12) or US toll free (☎ 800-332-3442); UK (☎ 0171-936 5019); Japan (☎ 03-3288-9511); Australia toll free (☎ 008-242907)
> **Getting there:** 20 minutes from Santa Barbara Municipal Airport
> **Accommodation:** 234 rooms and suites, including 34 cottages
> **Amenities:** Bar, three restaurants featuring California Mediterranean cuisine and ocean views; two health clubs, massage rooms, three floodlit tennis courts, croquet and shuffleboard, putting green, the American game horse-shoes, bicycles, two swimming pools; nearby golf, horse-riding, sailing, hiking, wineries and quaint shops
> **Dress code:** Smart casual
> **Weddings:** The Biltmore is a very popular venue for wedding ceremonies and receptions, from small private gatherings in the gardens to a reception for 500 people in Le Pacific Ballroom
> **Minimum stay:** None
> **Rates:** Superior doubles from US$325; suites from US$475
> **Credit cards:** Most major
> **Taxes and service charge:** 10% tax, service charge discretionary

The Four Seasons Biltmore has the feel of a really lavish, grand hotel with 234 rooms spread out over 20 acres of tropical landscaped grounds. It is obviously a resort for those looking for the ultimate in everything – from the 164ft beach-side swimming pool, to the health centre, the two large dining-rooms, the croquet lawns and tennis courts. Like its sister Regent properties throughout the world, the Biltmore is run impeccably offering guests every kind of facility and luxury imaginable in very slick surroundings.

The bedrooms are certainly full of all mod cons, with twice-daily maid service, terry-cloth bathrobes, marble bathrooms, complimentary newspapers delivered each morning, a fully-stocked private bar, TV and VCR, radio, in-room safes and hair-dryers. Some rooms also have fireplaces which are wonderful on spring evenings when there's a chill in the air.

The views out to sea, looking across to the **Channel Islands,** are what really make the Biltmore, with its beautiful, long sandy beach: you can even walk the whole way round the bay into town. One of the most magical experiences is to sit out on the front terrace at dawn watching groups of whales as they swim across the bay.

The Biltmore offers great Romance Packages during the week, with two nights' accommodation, a bottle of champagne on arrival, and a candle-lit dinner in **La Marina** restaurant where you can gaze out across the Pacific Ocean, for US$590 each.

San Ysidro Ranch

For a more intimate hotel with a more personal feel go for the San Ysidro Ranch, up in the foothills of **Montecito**, the other side of Highway 101. With 43 rooms and suites housed in 21 separate cottages, the San Ysidro is the perfect place to get away from it all. The emphasis is on simple, exquisite furnishings in elegant colours, with oak floors, exposed beams and French windows – nothing is over-chintzed here making it the definite choice if you don't like your furnishings too over the top. Don't think I mean by this that it's not luxurious – it's romantic enough to have been chosen by Jackie and John F Kennedy as their honeymoon destination, while Lawrence Olivier married Vivien Leigh on the lawn.

Each cottage has its own private deck, many with spa pools, and inside there are real log fireplaces which are lit on winter evenings. They have all the usual amenities such as VCR, king-size beds, goose down comforters and newspapers delivered to your room each morning. The layout of the cottages has been cleverly designed so that you feel totally secluded once you've walked up your own private pathway. It's rather like having your own summer home in the countryside, so much so that one cottage has recently been bought from the hotel as a private residence.

The nearby hills are great for walking, whether it's just a short amble you are looking for or a more challenging day-long hike with a picnic provided by the hotel. The hotel can arrange a whole host of activities in the area from hang-gliding to Channel Island Cruises, Polo, winery tours and ocean or lake fishing. There's also a 49ft heated swimming pool, tennis courts, exercise facilities, and a full array of body and beauty treatments are available in the privacy of your own cottage.

THE SAN YSIDRO RANCH
☎ (805-969-5046, fax 805-565-1995), 900 San Ysidro Lane, Montecito, California 93108, USA
Reservations: Relais & Châteaux offices worldwide (see p12)
Getting there: 85 miles north of Los Angeles, 20 minutes from Santa Barbara Municipal Airport
Accommodation: 42 bedrooms/suites in 21 cottages
Amenities: Stonehouse Restaurant featuring American regional cooking, outdoor poolside dining and 24-hour room service, the Plow & Angel Pub built in 1893, 49ft heated swimming pool, health club facility with cardiovascular equipment and free weights, two tennis courts, tennis professional, hiking trails, golf nearby
Dress code: Elegant casual
Weddings: Popular for weddings and receptions
Minimum stay: None
Rates: Double rooms from US$240; de luxe cottage from US$575
Credit cards: Most major
Taxes and service charge: 8% tax will be added to your bill, service is included

I loved the San Ysidro. To me it was the perfect combination of comfort, luxury and privacy in very informal, relaxed surroundings. As a Relais & Châteaux hotel, the ranch will provide you with the type of service you won't forget in a hurry. The staff, dressed casually in denim shirts, floral ties and chinos, always seem to be walking smartly off towards a cottage armed with champagne in an ice bucket, a plate of strawberries and a friendly smile. Stylish and efficient but casual, which just about sums up the hotel itself.

The Post Ranch Inn

The Post Ranch Inn has long been recognised as one of the world's most incredible hotels. This is where the likes of Jackie Collins and the Hollywood jetset come to get away from it all.

The Post Ranch is particularly famous for its architecture, which is a combination of post-modern and environmentally friendly steel, concrete and red wood huts. The architects were so careful to protect the surrounding environment that only one tree was moved during building. The result is the most awesome hotel protruding from and nestled into the cliff edge, with the particularly stunning **Sierra Mar** restaurant where huge sheets of glass, held together by steel tubing, stand between you and the Pacific.

Some of the 30 lavish rooms are virtually submerged in the earth and surrounded by wild flowers, others are amid the trees looking out over the giant redwood forest towards the mountains.

But the most famous rooms of all are the ten coast houses which hang right out from the cliff edge some 1200ft above the Pacific, so that all you can see through the large glass windows is the seemingly endless ocean.

POST RANCH INN
(☎ 408-667-2200, fax 408-667-2824),
Highway 1, Big Sur, Monterey County,
CA 93920, USA
Reservations: Relais & Châteaux and
Small Luxury Hotels of the World toll
free reservations numbers worldwide
(see p12)
Getting there: 35 miles from Monterey
County Airport; the hotel does not
arrange transfers as guests really need
their own car to drive around the area
Accommodation: 29 rooms and 1 suite
Amenities: Outdoor swimming pool,
exercise room, health and beauty facili-
ties, nearby beaches and horse-riding,
Sierra Mar restaurant with bar, limited
room service, gift shop
Dress code: None
Weddings: The hotel can host weddings
and receptions for up to 50 people, cost-
ing upwards of US$65 per person for
food only, plus tax, service and drinks
Minimum stay: None
Rates: Double rooms from US$285 to
US$545; the suites cost US$660, both
prices include breakfast
Credit cards: American Express, Visa,
MasterCard
Taxes and service charge: Not included

Each room comes complete with the kind of
luxuries that are standard in this quality of
hotel, such as king-sized beds, stereo systems, minibar and hair-dryers. But what
makes this hotel quite so incredible is all the
not-so-standard extras: each room has its
own massage table – inspired by Barbara
Streisand – its own spa baths, a selection of
walking sticks, a roaring open fire for when
you come in from your walks, and a private
deck so that you can gaze out over the magical Big Sur wilderness day and night. There
are even star-gazing lectures to help you
make the most of the area's incredible night
skies.

Highlands Inn

Highlands Inn, just as the brochure says, is 'a
visual masterpiece'. The awesome surroundings can certainly take much of the credit for
making this hotel so incredible, but credit
must also go to the architects and interior
designers who have made this such a magical place, especially since its recent renovation. Located on the **Monterey Peninsula**,
only four miles south of pretty Carmel and
just up the road from Big Sur, the hotel occu-
pies a remote stretch of cliff-side pine forest overlooking **Point Lobos** with fabulous
views of the big, blue Pacific stretching out beneath you. Wherever you are in the hotel
the views seem to dominate.

Outside, the hotel is built along the contours of the hillside with weather-boarded
cottages clustered in small groups and
arranged to provide the best views from the
rooms. The lovely suites all feature spa
baths, separate living areas, wood burning
stoves, decks with fantastic views, plus their
own fully stocked kitchens. The bedrooms
are modern in style and have good amenities
such as bathrobes and great aromatherapy
toiletries in the bathrooms, king-sized beds,
TV and VCR, minibar, iron and board, hair-
dryers and binoculars to maximise the views.

Below the cottages is the hotel's lovely kidney-shaped swimming pool, surrounded by comfortable loungers and café-like
tables and chairs.

While the outside decor is essentially
rustic, inside the Highlands Inn is a masterpiece of design made up of glass walls, sky
lights, precisely angled beams and beautifully lacquered wooden floors and pillars, the
whole effect set off by cleverly placed low
voltage spotlights.

HIGHLANDS INN
(☎ 408-624 3801, fax 408-626 1574), PO
Box 1700, Carmel, CA 93921, USA
Reservations: Small Luxury Hotels of
the World toll free reservations numbers
worldwide (see p12)
Getting there: The hotel is 10 miles from
Monterey Peninsula Airport and 90 miles
from San Francisco Airport, transfers are
complimentary upon availability
Accommodation: 42 rooms and 100
suites
Amenities: Restaurants, lounge,
concierge, fine dining, complimentary
trail bikes, swimming pools, plus tennis,
golf, horse-riding and fishing nearby
Dress code: None
Weddings: Ceremonies and receptions
for up to 150 are catered for
Minimum stay: Guests staying at the
weekend must stay for two nights
Rates: Doubles from US$245 to
US$290; suites from US$325 to US$495
Credit cards: Most major
Taxes and service charge: Not included

A FEW THINGS TO SEE AND DO ON THE CALIFORNIAN COASTAL ROUTE

Just an hour and a half's drive up the coast from LA is **Santa Barbara**, a relatively small city renowned for its year-long sunshine, sheltered coastal location and stunning backdrop of the Santa Ynez mountains. The architecture of the town and the surrounding area as well as street names such as Castillo Drive, give the place a Spanish feel. Santa Barbara is a heady mixture of celebrity estates, sun-drenched golden beaches, rugged mountains and terraced vineyards. The actual town is very beautiful and a really lovely place to wander around and browse through the shops. There are shops devoted to olive oils and nuts, antiques, children's clothes, shoes and lots of home interior and houseware stores. Stop for coffee and a Danish at the *Santa Barbara Coffee Roasting Company*, just off State St, or for the most wonderful pizzas and a bottle of cold Budweiser at the *California Pizza Kitchen*.

Moving up the coast, it's a good idea to take **Highway 154** from just outside Santa Barbara. This is the mountain road and will take you high up into the spectacular Santa Ynez mountains, past **Lake Cachuma** which is great for boating, fishing or even just picnics, and on to the towns of Solvang and Santa Ynez.

Solvang itself is certainly worth a look, for its remarkable Danish architecture. The whole town was only built around 40 years ago, and resembles something out of a Hans Christian Andersen fairy tale: there is a museum commemorating the writer and many of the streets have Danish names.

The advantage in staying in Solvang is that it is a great base from which to see the dozen or so surrounding **wineries**, for which this region is famous. All the local vineyards are open daily for tastings and tours, but perhaps the best and most original way of touring the area is by bicycle. Ask at the visitor centre in Solvang about cycling winery tours – you can always get a taxi home and pick up your bikes the next day should you get carried away sipping chilled glasses of Sauvignon Blanc overlooking the vineyards.

Another possibility is taking to the skies in a glider. For around US$135 you can take the 35-minute Mile High flight from Santa Ynez Airport and see this truly spectacular landscape from above, not to mention looking out for red-tailed hawks and the occasional golden eagle, and even taking a hand at the controls. For further details contact **Windhaven Glider Rides** (☎ 805-688-2517).

The stretch of road along Highway One between **Hearst Castle** and **Monterey** is breathtaking, mainly for its views but quite often due to the 1,000ft cliff drops and numerous narrow bridges – it's an experience! Make sure you stop off at **Big Sur** where the Santa Lucia mountains meet the Pacific Ocean – the views from the rugged clifftop are fantastic. North of Big Sur, perched on a rocky cliff 100ft above the pounding surf, is a lovely place for lunch – *Rocky Point Restaurant* (☎ 408-624-2933). If you stop off in Big Sur for a few days make sure you visit the *Ventana Inn* (US toll free ☎ 800-628-6500) and sample its famous gourmet food.

Go to **Carmel** to shop but only stay if you have an abundance of cash as it is wildly expensive and if you don't mind the mass of tourists in the summer. Sunday lunch at *Blums* in downtown Carmel is legendary.

The **Monterey Peninsula** is a good place to base yourselves for a few days as there's loads to do both inland and of course, out on the water. If you want to get out on the water why not try sea-kayaking with **Cannery Row's Adventures by the Sea** (ABTS). Apart from kayaking trips to see the sea otters, ABTS has mountain bikes and roller blades for hire as well as guided bike tours to Big Sur, Carmel and 17-Mile Drive. A great roller-blading trail runs from the easterly end of Monterey to **Lovers' Point** in Pacific Grove out to Seaside. There are hordes of fantastic **restaurants** in Monterey, far too many to list, but you might try *Montrio* (☎ 408-648-8880), 414 Calle Principal, where chef Brian Whitmer prepares dishes with American, French and Italian influences well enough to have been voted Restaurant of the Year 1995 by *Esquire* magazine, or *Tarpy's Roadhouse* (☎ 408-647-1444), a charming vine-covered stone house on Highway 68, which has a sunny courtyard that would not be out of place in Provence. Each of the rooms has its own kind of ambience and chef Michael Kimmel prepares good hearty country dishes using rabbit, duck and fresh fish.

The Highlands Inn has long been popular for weddings – this is where Madonna married Sean Penn – the hotel's large decked terrace looking out over the ocean makes the perfect place to take your vows. The hotel's cliff-hanging restaurant, **The Pacific's Edge**, with its dramatic ocean views, is the scene of the annual Masters of Food and Wine event, and during the day the **California Market** offers guests casual alfresco café-style dining.

Other recommended hotels

Simpson House Inn (☎ 805-963-7067, fax 805-564-4811), 121 East Arrellaga St, Santa Barbara, is a beautiful Victorian inn right in the middle of Santa Barbara, offering remarkably priced bed and breakfast in 14 beautifully decorated bedrooms, suites and garden cottages. The rooms in the main house are the most reasonable but if you can afford it go for one of the weather-boarded cottages or suites in the converted barn. Each has its own stone fireplace and an in-room jacuzzi, concealed TV and VCR and small fridge. With many original features including stained-glass windows, high beamed ceilings, a wood-burning fireplace and solid-oak floors, the Inn is the perfect place to relax in tranquil and unpretentious surroundings. You can take your breakfast tray full of freshly squeezed fruit juices, home-made granola and yoghurt, and apple French toasts out in to the lovely gardens or sit on your own patio admiring the foliage, plants and beautiful topiary. Bed and breakfast from US$130 in the main house to US$270 for the cottages.

If you want to stay in **Solvang** a somewhat quirky choice of hotel is the **Chimney Sweep Inn** (☎ 805-688-2111, fax 805-688-8824), 1554 Copenhagen Drive, Solvang, with its 'enchanted cottages' in the **Narnia Gardens**, built in memory of C S Lewis's tales. The hotel itself, like the village, is perhaps a little over-ornate for some tastes, but the cottages are perfect. Traditional furniture, such as antique chain-pull toilets, private decks with their own spa baths, a small basic kitchen, and huge beds covered in crisp white linen make this a perfect getaway from hotel life. Bed and breakfast in one of the cottages costs between US$145 and US$225, but ask about their weekday three night packages. You may not be convinced when you come up the driveway and three days may be a little too long in a two week holiday, but take a look at a cottage and I'm sure you'll have found your bed for the night.

The **Crystal Rose Inn** (☎ 805-481-1854, fax 805-481-9541), 789 Valley Road, Arroyo Grande, a bright pink Victorian bed and breakfast about an hour or so up the coast from Solvang, is a good place to stop. Out of the nine rooms we went for the honeymoon bedroom: it has a supremely comfortable bed which is covered from top to toe in white cotton and lace and an abundance of pillows; and it also has a pretty white iron bedhead. The en suite bathroom has an old Victorian bath, as well as separate shower and plenty of white towels and toiletries. The Inn, built in 1890, serves wonderful breakfasts, great afternoon teas as well and complimentary pre-dinner sherry and snacks: these can be served in the immaculately kept garden in the summer. The Crystal Rose Inn is extremely popular for weddings and receptions. Doubles from US$85 to US$175.

SAN FRANCISCO

The Sherman House

The Sherman House is generally recognised as the greatest little townhouse in the world. Originally built, in 1876, for Leander Sherman, the famous music patron, this fabulously elegant white stucco four-storey mansion is situated in the prestigious **Pacific Heights** area of San Francisco, minutes away from chic **Union St** and **Nob Hill**. The success with which the present owner, Manou Mobedshahi, transformed the house into a hotel in the late 1970s, is illustrated by the hotel's membership of both the Relais & Châteaux, and the Small Luxury Hotels of the World groups. Mobedshahi was responsible for hiring interior designer William Gaylord to restore the house to its former glory. Hardwood floors were polished, new moulds were made to recreate the original cornicing and another staircase was added, in addition to the dramatic double staircase.

The decor of the hotel is now a hedonistic combination of Victorian detail and French extravagance. Heavy draperies now serve as bed canopies and frame cushioned window seats that look out over the **Golden Gate Bridge** and **Alcatraz**. Wood-burning fireplaces in most of the suites and rooms make the hotel a snug refuge on chilly evenings, and decadent details such as sound systems hidden by upholstered walls, beds piled high with Scandinavian down comforters, sprays of orchids, and writing paper embossed with your name make the hotel that little bit extra special. The lovely garden with its gazebo, Victorian greenhouse and cobbled pathways, is the perfect place to retreat to at the end of a hard day's sightseeing.

Of the hotel's six suites and eight guest rooms the Sherman Suite (No 401) and the Biedermeier Suite (No 302) are without doubt the best. The panoramic views of the Golden Gate Bridge and Alcatraz from the private brick-floored terrace of the Sherman suite are so incredible that most people forget to leave the hotel and have been known to spend their entire stay on the terrace. If you do manage to drag yourself inside it will probably be to the wonderful Roman-style bathtub or to sit in front of the open fire in the fine English-style sitting-room.

THE SHERMAN HOUSE
(☎ 415-563 3600, fax 415-563 1882), 2160 Green St, San Francisco, CA 94123, USA
Reservations: Relais & Châteaux and Small Luxury Hotels of the World toll free reservation numbers (see p12)
Getting there: The hotel can arrange to collect you from the airport, this can be in a 1962 white Vanden Plas limo if you like
Accommodation: Eight rooms and six one-bedroom suites
Amenities: Restaurant, 24-hour room service, private formal garden with a gazebo and a Victorian greenhouse, the Gallery sitting-room and the music room; golf, horse-riding, fishing and sailing nearby
Dress code: Casual attire for breakfast and lunch in the dining-room, jackets (but not ties) are required in the evening
Weddings: The hotel does cater for small wedding parties: guests must be resident in the hotel; ceremonies can either be in the garden or on the roof-top terrace
Minimum stay: Two nights on major holiday weekends
Rates: Doubles from US$275 to US$400; suites from US$600
Credit cards: Most major
Taxes and service charge: Not included

The Biedermeier suite and the Biedermeier room are all brocade bed hangings, thickly upholstered walls and the kind of bronze Doré chandeliers typical of this period. Both rooms have romantic window seats with bay views, although the view is much better from the suite.

The hotel's dining-room is reserved exclusively for hotel guests and is always very popular. Chef Timothy Au prepares great California-French cuisine for a prix-fixe and an à la carte menu: dishes such as pepper smoked duck breast salad with satsuma tangerine vinaigrette, or roasted rack of lamb with vanilla-whipped sweet potatoes cranberry sauce and chestnut purée are sure to tempt you.

Hotel Triton

Hotel Triton, right across the road from one of the huge gates in **Chinatown**, gives its guests a real flavour of this fantastic city at very good value for money – where else would you get Nintendo and environmentally friendly bedrooms!

The Triton is a hotel devoted to style. As soon as you enter the lobby it is obvious that this is not your average hotel. It has plush red sofas and towering Egyptian-style gold columns, beautifully designed lamps and tables, and murals painted on the walls.

You won't confuse a Triton bedroom for any standard hotel room – there's no wishy-washy patterned carpet or dreadfully unassuming standard-issue prints on the walls here. Instead each of the 140 guest rooms is decorated with real flair and minute attention to detail: there are hand-painted wall finishes, art deco sun mirrors, beds covered in combination white, black and striped linen, mock-Zebra skin sofas and armchairs and beautifully designed pieces of modern furniture.

Each room also comes with a fully-stocked honesty bar, remote control TVs with cable and on-demand movies, Nintendo, voice-mail, hair-dryers, irons and boards. There are terry cloth bathrobes, CD players, VCRs and two phone-lines in the suites

HOTEL TRITON

(☎ 415-394 0500, fax 415-394-0555) 342 Grant Avenue, San Francisco, CA 94108, USA

Reservations: Either direct or US toll free (☎ 800-433-6611)

Getting there: The Triton does not provide transfers although it can arrange limo service, guests can get the shuttle from the airport (every 15 minutes, around US$10)

Accommodation: 140 guest rooms: seven suites (4 designer suites, two junior suites and one Triton suite) and 24 eco-rooms

Amenities: Aioli and Café de la Presse Restaurants, 24-hour valet parking, room service, complimentary evening wine hour and morning coffee service, work-out facilities

Dress code: Casual (no jacket or tie required)

Weddings: No

Minimum stay: None

Rates: Salon doubles US$105 to US$125, Queen US$125 to US$145, King Premier US$145 to US$175, suites from US$195 to US$285

Credit cards: Most major

Taxes and service charge: Room tax 14%, service is discretionary

and King Premier rooms, while every room receives complimentary morning coffee service. Try one of the four designer suites where top notch design gurus like Joe Boxer and Suzan Briganti have been allowed to run riot, or for the eco-conscious there are 24 environmentally sensitive eco-rooms.

Other recommended hotels

Auberge du Soleil (☎ 707-963-1211, fax 707-963-8764), 180 Rutherford Hill Road, PO Drawer B, Rutherford, is located outside San Francisco in **Nappa Valley** wine country. The Auberge's 31 rooms and 19 suites have a really Mediterranean feel and the cuisine is superb enough to warrant its membership of the Relais & Châteaux group. Set among olive trees and grapevines the rustic colours and tranquil ambience make this a delightful haven to spend a few days of unadulterated luxury. There is a two-night minimum stay at weekends but it would be almost sinful to spend only one night in the Auberge! Guests very rarely stray out of the hotel at night, attracted by the delicious cuisine of Claude Rouas' restaurant, but during the day there's lots to do aside from lying by the pool – cycling, horse-riding, or even browsing for antiques nearby. Doubles from US$295, suites from US$550.

THREE DAYS IN SAN FRANCISCO

San Francisco is one of the most user-friendly cities in the world as it is relatively compact and has a very easy transport system, which is just as well as it's too hilly to cover on foot. The best areas to explore are **Haight Ashbury**, where flower power flourished so radically in the 1960s, and the restaurant and club-filled **SOMA** (South of Market), **Chinatown**, **North Beach** and **Hayes Valley**, the bohemian centre of today's San Francisco.

The food in San Francisco is particularly good: if you go to *Kate's Kitchen* (471 Haight/Filmore) for breakfast on the weekend, *Suppenküche* (601 Laguna/Hayes) for lunch and on to *Stars* (150 Redwood Alley/Van Ness) for dinner – you can live safe in the knowledge that you've been to all the right places. Hayes Valley is great for shopping if you want to see goods by young designers and artisans, but stay between blocks 300 and 500 for safety and don't turn up until after lunch when the shops open. **North Beach**, San Francisco's Italian district, is good for breakfast. It's also worth visiting the church where Marilyn Munroe married the baseball player Joe DaMaggio.

Take one of the ferry boats from Fisherman's Wharf to **Sausalito**, a pretty fishing village and an expensive suburb on other side of the bay, passing Alcatraz on the way. Stop for lunch at one of the many little restaurants and bars. Afterwards hire bikes and cycle up to the **Marin Headlands**. If you've got a car, it's worth crossing the Golden Gate Bridge, stopping off in Sausalito and then driving up to the Marin Headlands. There's nothing quite like standing with a panoramic view of the city before you as the fog rolls in off the ocean like a cotton wool quilt, leaving the bridge suspended above it.

San Francisco is big on acid jazz, so if you want to hear the best get along to the **Elbo Room**, or supermodel Christy Turlington's **Eleven** and the **Up and Down Club**. Visit the new **San Francisco Museum of Modern Art**, and take a stroll around **Yerba Buena Gardens**, which are a great place to people watch. For views, you can't beat the top of **Telegraph Hill**: it is easily recognisable because of its landmark, the **Coit Tower**.

ARIZONA
The Boulders

The Boulders is one of those hotels that was made for honeymoons. It combines the natural splendour of the Arizona desert with the utmost luxury, in a way that you'll dream about long after your honeymoon.

Set among some of the many 12 million year old granite bolder formations and towering cacti that are littered all over the **Sonoran Desert**, the Boulders has been so sympathetically constructed that from the other side of the pond you can hardly make out the hotel building: even the corners on the granite-coloured walls were carefully rounded off.

Consistently ranked as one of the best resorts in America, the Boulders is a place for hedonists but it still has a homely, relaxed atmosphere. The spacious adobe-like one-bedroom casitas (thatched huts) where guests stay are located along paths flanked with butterfly bushes and lush trees. Each of the 160 casitas features air-conditioning, wood-beam ceilings with fans, wood burning fires placed opposite king-sized beds – ideal for when the temperature drops in the evening – wet bars, a large dressing area and lovely tiled bathroom with bathrobes, slippers, hair-dryers and complimentary toiletries. They also all have either private patios or decks with the most incredible views.

The hotel is the perfect place to unwind after a wedding, not just because of the immense space around you but also because of the hotel's new **Sonoran Spa**. The facilities here seem endless: from the Boulders' Club with its six tennis courts, to a hi-tech Fitness Centre as well as the Spa.

Most of the restaurants are in the main lodge: the alfresco, but quite intimate, **Palo Verde**; the indoor **Latilla**, from where you can see water cascading over the boulders; and the **Discovery Lounge**, which has live music most nights. **Boulders** restaurant serves lunches and dinner on the terrace overlooking the hotel's wonderful golf course.

The best way to experience the area's stunning scenery is on a guided tour along the ancient trails to the ruins of former villages, long ago deserted. The views of **Phoenix** and **Scottsdale** beyond are fabulous. If you feel like getting out of the hotel check out the country and western bars at nearby **Cave Creek**.

THE BOULDERS

(☎ 602-488-9009, fax 602-488-4118), 34631 N Tom Darlington Drive, PO Box 2090, Carefree, Arizona 85377, USA

Reservations: Small Luxury Hotels of the World toll free reservation numbers worldwide (see p12); US toll free (☎ 800-553-1717)

Getting there: The hotel can arrange transfers from both Scottsdale Airpark (13 minutes) and Phoenix Sky Harbor (33 minutes); US$27 per person one way and US$35; the hotel has its own heli-pad

Accommodation: 194 luxury casitas: 157 rooms, 34 pueblo villas (villas clustered together in a village) and three suites

Amenities: Five restaurants, room service, lounge, two Championship 18-hole golf courses, outdoor swimming pool, tennis, spa, sauna, jacuzzi, health and beauty, hiking, trekking, horse-riding and hot-air ballooning nearby

Dress code: Jackets are required in the main restaurant, and no shorts or jeans are allowed in any of the restaurants in the evening

Weddings: Can be arranged for up to 550 people

Minimum stay: None

Rates: Doubles from US$230 to US$580; suites US$325 to US$1000 including continental breakfast

Credit cards: Most major

Taxes and service charge: 10.25% Government tax on accommodation; 6.7% on food and beverages; US$15 night service charge, excluding food and beverage waiters

Other recommended hotels

The Phoenician (☎ 602-941-8200, fax 602-947-4311), 6000 East Camelback Road, Scottsdale, and the **Scottsdale Princess** (☎ 602-585-4848, fax 602-585-0086), 7575 E Princess Drive, Scottsdale, constantly vie for the title of Scottsdale's best resort. In fact both hotels are large, extravagantly luxurious self-contained resorts surrounded by dramatic scenery and there is very little to choose between the two. A stay at either represents a foray into the world of hedonistic luxury where accommodation, service and cuisine is pretty much faultless, resulting in both hotels' membership of The Leading Hotels of the World chain. Double rooms in both hotels start at around US$180 for a night.

If you want to stay in the Grand Canyon, the best hotel is the **El Tovar Hotel** (☎ 602-638 2631, fax 602-638 9247), Grand Canyon National Park, PO Box 699: it is perched 50ft from the South Rim. Although it can be painfully crowded during the day, it is a blissful feeling to be left alone with the views in this friendly hunting lodge-style hotel once the crowds do eventually go. The hotel has 78 rooms and it is extremely popular so do book early and do insist on having one of the north-facing suites because they have staggering views over the Canyon. Double rooms from around US$100.

A FEW THINGS TO SEE AND DO IN ARIZONA

The main attraction of **Scottsdale** is its resorts, and once installed in one of these fabulous self-contained hotels you probably won't want to venture out until it's time to leave. Scottsdale is home to block after block of art galleries and arts and crafts shops, many of the latter featuring the handiwork of Indian craftsmen. Nearby **Old Town Scottsdale** is also worth a look for its blacksmith shop that has been there since 1880, the mission church and the old red schoolhouse.

Heading south on Scottsdale Road to McDowell, west to Galvin Parkway, and then south again will take you into the rugged desert of **Papago Park** and the **Desert Botanical Gardens**, where one of the world's most complete collections of cacti and other desert plants is found.

North-east of Scottsdale lies **Fountain Hills**, which at 560ft is the tallest fountain in the world. It is run on recycled water and only flows for 15 minutes every hour. Desert jeep tours are very popular around **Cave Creek** and can easily be organised, ask the concierge at your hotel.

But, of course, the main reason most people come to Arizona is to visit the spectacular vistas and majestic rock formations of 'canyon country'. A mile deep, 277 miles long and two billion years old, the **Grand Canyon** has to be seen to be believed. The myriad of colours and striking features are enhanced by the beautiful waterfalls and pools and the mighty Colorado River. *Grand Canyon National Park* has accommodation ranging from lodges to camp grounds. *Phantom Ranch*, on the Canyon

floor, can only be reached by hikers or via the famous mule ride, while air tours over the Canyon take off from Tusayan, along the South Rim. All types of accommodation and the mule rides can be booked by calling the National Park office (☎ 602-638-2401). The Park Service recommends booking accommodation and tours 11 months in advance.

To the south is Sedona and **Oak Creek Canyon**, one of the most beautiful places on earth. The great rock monoliths of Oak Creek Canyon – Bell Rock, Courthouse Butte and Capitol Butte – are the awesome bi-product of millions of years of erosion. As the weather changes and the hours in the day pass so too do their colours and shapes. State Route 89A, heading south from **Flagstaff**, descending into Oak Creek Canyon and winding on over **Mingus Mountain** to **Prescott**, is one of America's top scenic highways. If you want to get off the road and explore the canyon on foot or on horseback (**Apache Stables** ☎ 602-638-2424), go to nearby **Sycamore Canyon**, a wildly beautiful remote wilderness where there are no roads to spoilt the tranquillity. Or if the more leisurely pace of a train journey appeals, hop aboard the **Verde River Canyon Railroad** (reservations ☎ 602-639-0010) which begins at Clarkdale taking you into the Verde River Canyon on a five-hour round trip through the red cliffs aboard a diesel powered train. Quite magical.

In order to avoid long queues and over-booked hotels the best time to visit the Canyon is March/April and September/October, either side of the main tourist season.

COLORADO

Names like **Vail**, **Aspen** and **Steamboat Springs** cannot fail to conjure up romantic images of crisp sunny days spent out in the snow followed by long cosy evenings – just the two of you snuggled up in front of a roaring log fire with the snow falling silently outside. Going to a ski resort can make a wonderfully romantic honeymoon, but only if you are both around the same standard as you don't really want to spend your days apart or with one of you always miserably trying to catch up.

And remember, you don't have to ski like lunatics for 10 hours a day, nor do you have to be expert skiers to enjoy this kind of winter wonderland. This is your honeymoon so don't feel guilty about getting up late, skiing to a mountain restaurant and tucking into the wine and chips at lunch time!

Vail is the ideal resort for a two-centre holiday and can easily be teamed up with **Jackson Hole** (for a completely different style of holiday), nearby **Aspen**, or even **Whistler** in Canada. The ski season runs from December to the middle of April.

The Little Nell

The Little Nell is one of the world's best mountain resort hotels. Ringed by 14,000ft peaks, alpine meadows and snow-fed streams, the Little Nell is a snug base at the foot of the Aspen Mountains.

The hotel's management set out to blend the finest attributes of an intimate country inn with the personalised service and amenities of a grand hotel, and they do it rather well.

It is a very special little hotel, a far cry from normal ski resort accommodation. Guests are surrounded by fine antiques and the kind of old-world, understated furnishings that you dream of having in your own home.

No two rooms are alike and all feature the quintessential assets of any mountain holiday – a fireplace and a view. Soothing tones of cream, ochre and chocolate brown make the bedroom a cosy place to return to for a pre-dinner snooze in front of the fire. Down-filled sofas and lounge chairs are just the thing for tired limbs, and if you don't have the energy to leave the room there's 24-hour room service and a remote control TV with VCR.

The king-sized beds have down comforters and there is a Belgian wool carpet to add to that feeling of cocooned luxury. The en suite marble bathrooms are well-equipped and fitted with deep baths and more fluffy white towels and toiletries than anyone could possibly need.

The living rooms are filled with leather armchairs, comfortable sofas, and fine paintings hanging on dark rust and deep ochre-coloured walls. You can warm up with a steaming bowl of soup and watch skiers swooshing down The Little Nell slope from the restaurant and courtyard café.

> **THE LITTLE NELL**
> (☎ 970-920 4600, fax 970-920 4670), 675 East Durant St, Aspen, Colorado 81611, USA
> **Reservations:** Relais & Châteaux toll free numbers worldwide (see p12); from the UK book through Ski Independence (UK ☎ 0171-713 5337)
> **Getting there:** 186 miles from Denver, take the I-70 towards Glenwood Springs, then Highway 82 to Aspen; 4 miles from Aspen-Sardy Field Airport from where the hotel can arrange complimentary transfers
> **Accommodation:** 78 rooms and 14 suites
> **Amenities:** The Bar, the Grand Salon, the Restaurant and Courtyard Café, several adjoining private dining-rooms, swimming pool, ski concierge, jacuzzi, spa and thalassotherapy, dry cleaning and laundry, 24-hour room service, plus hiking, fishing, tennis and golf in the summer
> **Dress code:** Casual
> **Weddings:** Can be arranged in the private dining-rooms, such as the oak-panelled library
> **Minimum stay:** Three nights over a weekend in summer and four nights over a weekend in winter
> **Rates:** Doubles from US$255 in summer to US$425 in winter; suites from around US$325 in summer and US$700 in winter
> **Credit cards:** Visa, American Express, Diners Club
> **Taxes and service charge:** Tax 8.2%, service is discretionary

Located right in the heart of the town, The Little Nell is only steps away from the many shops, restaurants and galleries that have made Aspen famous, but is also ideally situated beside the Silver Queen gondola (the resort's main ski lift). Of course, this kind of location and elegant living doesn't come cheap, but this is Aspen and if you can afford it The Little Nell is just about the best place to stay.

The Bavaria Haus Sonnenalp Resort

The Bavaria Haus Sonnenalp Resort is right in the centre of Vail and strives to be the most European hotel in America. Known for its world-class skiing, Vail boasts the largest single ski mountain in the whole world, stretching seven miles across with 4000 skiable acres serviced by 25 lifts – pretty impressive stuff.

The best thing about Sonnenalp is that it has reinvented all that is romantic about skiing in the Alps and transported it to America. Deservedly one of Vail's most prestigious hotels, the resort is made up of three different 'hauses', **Bavaria Haus**, **Swiss Haus** and **Austria Haus**. In my opinion, Bavaria Haus, the largest and most luxurious of the three, is the most suitable for honeymooners. With 88 suites, two restaurants, a piano bar, library and a vast area given over to every kind of spa treatments, it's hard to beat as a mountain retreat.

You are bound to fall in love with Bavaria Haus as soon as you see it: the attractive white building with its red and white striped shutters, little wooden balconies protruding from French windows, its stone arches at ground level. Inside the hotel is designed like any chalet in Europe with hand-crafted woodwork and traditional stonework.

Everything is done in European style from the comforter on your king-sized bed to the freshly-baked croissants and coffee in the morning, and the traditional Austrian-style uniforms of the staff. The bedrooms are the best place to unwind when you come in from the slopes, and they are all furnished with a gas fireplace, a TV and VCR and a fully-stocked minibar. The marble floors in the bathrooms are heated, there are double basins, a large soaking bath with separate shower, robes, iron and ironing board and hair-dryers. The best suites are the **Bald Mountain Suite** overlooking the Gore Creek, the **Blue Spruce Suite** and the **Lodgepole Suite**.

The resort helps you plan your day by providing the latest snow and trail conditions with your breakfast, but Vail also has a lot to offer if you fancy a day away from the slopes. The hotel arranges the most incredible hot-air balloon rides taking you peacefully over the majestic mountains or go for a moonlit sleigh ride or even dog-sledding.

> **THE BAVARIA HAUS SONNENALP RESORT**
> (☎ 970-476 5656, fax 970-476 1639), 20 Vail Road, Vail, Colorado 81657, USA
> **Reservations:** US toll free (☎ 1-800-654-8312); from the UK book through Ski Independence (UK ☎ 0171-713 5337)
> **Getting there:** 100 miles away from Denver International Airport, take the 1-70 to exit 176 in Vail; Eagle County Airport is 35 miles away
> **Accommodation:** 88 suites
> **Amenities:** Ludwig's Restaurant serves breakfast and dinner, Bully Ranch Restaurant serves south-western and western cuisine at lunch and dinner, King's Club has fireside piano music nightly, the Spa-Steam rooms offer sauna, indoor and outdoor jacuzzis, light spa menu and an extensive range of spa treatments, indoor/outdoor heated pool, juice bar, full bar
> **Dress code:** Casual, apart from jacket and tie in Ludwig's
> **Weddings:** The hotel does cater for weddings and receptions
> **Minimum stay:** None
> **Rates:** Doubles including full breakfast from US$253 to US$283; suites including full breakfast from US$358 to US$1200 during the winter season
> **Credit cards:** Most major
> **Taxes and service charge:** 8% tax added to bill, service is discretionary

Other recommended hotels

The Peaks (☎ 970-728 6800, fax 970-728 6175), 136 Country Club Drive, PO Box 2702, Telluride, is one of North America's best kept secrets. This lovely hotel, a member of Small Luxury Hotels of the World, is perfectly placed to take advantage of the powder snow this region is renowned for, and also pretty good for those who don't ski, with a vast 42,000 sq ft given over to the most incredible spa, offering an impressive 44 different programmes. Surrounded by some of the most awesome scenery, but off the beaten path on the far slopes of the Colorado Rockies, the hotel is as good in summer as it is in winter. The 181 lavish rooms, suites and penthouses have sweeping views of Mt. Wilson and the 14,000ft **San Juan Mountains**. Rates start at around US$130 in the summer and US$290 in the winter: ask about the Peaks Alpine Honeymoon package which includes five nights' accommodation, champagne and gift on arrival, breakfast in bed each day, in-room 'couple's massage' for around US$1972 in peak season and as low as US$897 between mid-May and mid-June.

The Gant (☎ 970-925-5000, fax 970-925-6891), 610 West End St, Aspen, has a wide selection of privately owned condos for anything from US$150 a day in low season to US$395 a day in peak holiday season. Each condo in the Swiss-style wooden chalet is individually owned and has a private patio or balcony, wood-burning fireplaces and fully equipped kitchens. Be warned there are only about eight or nine one-bedroom condos so you'll have to book early. Morning newspapers are delivered to your door and there is a once-daily maid service (even your washing up will be done for you). All guests have use of the Gant's two heated outdoor swimming pools, three outdoor hot tubs and dry saunas. One of the best aspects of staying at the Gant is the services of the 'Gantman' who, equipped with a van and complete knowledge of the area, will meet you at the airport, collect you after dinner or a concert, deliver your firewood and generally make sure every aspect of your stay is comfortable and convenient.

The Lodge at Cordillera (☎ 970-926 2200, fax 970-926 2486), PO Box 1110, Edwards, Vail Valley is a wonderfully elegant château-like retreat hugging a curve high up on the mountainside with an unimpeded view of the rugged **New York Mountain Range**. If you are looking for a snowy mountain honeymoon without crowds of people to spoil the tranquillity this is the place for you. With just 28 rooms, the Lodge is unlike any of the other properties in this section: it is a peaceful mountain haven far away from it all. The hotel's inside was designed to echo a Spanish hacienda with flagstone floors and hand-trowelled plaster walls, enhancing the lodge's European feel. The rooms too are filled with old world furnishings like the wrought-iron desks and carved armoires, but there is nothing old world about the hotel's stunning spa facilities. Swimming in the beautifully lit indoor pool at night, with the outlines of the mountains silhouetted beyond the arched windows is just magical. De luxe rooms with two queen-sized beds cost from US$355, de luxe loft suites from around US$385.

VERMONT
Twin Farms

Twin Farms must be one of the most luxurious country retreats ever constructed. So exclusive is Twin Farms that it even has its own ski slopes, and so romantic are its Japanese soaking tubs known as *furos*, set in the vast surrounding forest, that you can't help but dream about the place long after you've left.

The main house where the four suites are found has been decorated with a total disregard for expense. But if you really want to

---

TWIN FARMS
(☎ 802 234 9999, fax 802-234 9990), Barnard, Vermont 05031, USA
Reservations: Either direct with the hotel on the above numbers or through US toll free (☎ 1-800-TWIN-FARMS)
Getting there: Twin Farms can arrange transfers from West Lebanon Airport in New Hampshire (40 minutes)
Accommodation: 14 guest rooms: four suites in the main house and 10 cottages
Amenities: 24-hour room service, pub, lounges, health and beauty club and fitness centre, Japanese tubs; seasonal activities include lake swimming, croquet, skiing, biking, tennis, fishing, canoeing, ice-skating and golf nearby
Dress code: Casual
Weddings: Both ceremonies and receptions are catered for; prices on request
Minimum stay: Two nights at weekends, three on public holidays
Rates: Suites in the main house from US$700, cottages from US$1050, the Studio from US$1500 (rates include all meals, drinks and sporting facilities)
Credit cards: Most major
Taxes and service charge: 8% tax and 15% service charge

go the whole hog, book into one of the ten cottages – however expensive, you won't regret it. Choose from the most exclusive **Treehouse**, and the **Studio**, or one of the new themed cottages. Each cottage is unique and set apart from the others in Twin Farm's 300 acres of grounds. The spectacular interior designs were the work of Jed Johnson, one of America's most celebrated interior designers who died tragically, in July 1996, in the TWA disaster. Twin Farms remains a show case for Johnson's work.

The bedrooms are absolutely perfect for a winter honeymoon: you sleep in a magnificent four-poster bed, and can snuggle up together in front of a roaring log fire in the privacy of your own cottage. The cottages and suites are all undeniably romantic and were specifically designed to accommodate one couple each.

Widely regarded as the most exclusive hotel in America and understandably popular for celebrity weddings since privacy is guaranteed, Twin Farms could also be the most expensive place to stay. But then, as its manager is quick to remind you, a night at Twin Farms is actually particularly good value considering the monumental costs of running such an establishment. Luckily the extortionate price of the rooms includes everything: your skiing, canoeing, massages, breakfast, lunch, dinner, room, endless wine and anything else you'd care to order.

Other recommended hotels
The Point (☎ 518-891 5674, fax 518-891 1152), HCR1, Box 65, Saranac Lake, New York 12983, is a Relais & Châteaux hotel and has recently been named one of the top ten resorts in the US. Located on the Canadian border between **Montreal** and **New York** and situated in the **Adirondack** wilderness The Point has the most amazing setting: right on the edge of the peninsula overlooking the lake and all its splendid surrounding wilderness. The A-lined log cabins sit amongst the tall pine trees, and when you walk inside it's difficult not to warm to the homely atmosphere created by the wood-panelled rooms filled with hunting trophies, oriental carpets and antique furniture.

The Point is superb in all seasons: summer days are filled with sailing, fishing or taking a speedboat ride around the lake; autumn is the time for horse-riding, canoeing or hiking or even a gentle stroll around the lake edge, while **Saranac** golf course is a few minutes away; and in winter months you can snuggle up in front of the log fire or brave the outdoors with some cross-country skis, snowshoes or even try out the ice skating. Everything is inclusive at the Point: breakfast, lunch and dinner and unlimited wine. The food, cooked by one of the world's most renowned chefs, is really quite extraordinary. Rates start from US$825 to US$1175 for two people but don't include NY State taxes (7%) or service charges (15%).

NEW YORK
The Mark
The Mark is now regarded as one of the best hotels in New York. This Upper East Side hangout even attracts local New Yorkers, so you can be sure you'll feel you're in the right place. It is also perfectly situated for shopping on Upper Madison Avenue, where some of New York's most exclusive art and antique galleries are located, as well as numerous fashion boutiques and great restaurants.

The bedrooms are equipped with king-sized beds, overstuffed chairs, and prints reflecting the hotel's style which lies somewhere between new-classic and English-Italian. Throughout the hotel, dark green and red velvets sit beside heavy custom designed curtains and bedspreads, while Biedermeier furniture stands on marble floors.

Most guest rooms have wonderful black pantries equipped with refrigerator, sink and stove. All rooms have two phone lines and in-room fax capability, while the very largest suites have everything you could ever dream of including a foyer, library, stereo system with CD players, wet bars and the most incredible large landscaped terraces with views over **Central Park**.

There is marble everywhere in the bathrooms, lovely large soak tubs, hair-dryers and scales (not that you should be looking at them on your honeymoon!).

The best way to stay at the Mark is on their US$450 Honeymoon Package which gives you a night in a junior or executive suite, half a bottle of champagne, cocktails for two, a dozen red roses, and continental breakfast in your room. Considering a junior suite usually costs US$500 and an executive US$625 this is a relatively good deal.

The cosy **Mark's Bar** has a club-like atmosphere which is perfect for pre-dinner cocktails or post-theatre snacks: more substantial meals, a great Sunday Brunch, and afternoon tea are all served in **Mark's Restaurant**.

The Royalton

The Royalton is a must for design-gurus. Without doubt one of the funkiest hotels in New York, the Royalton is also home to one of the city's greatest bars. From the outside the hotel is unassuming with two big stone

---

THE MARK
(☎ 212-744-4300, fax 212-744-2749), Madison Avenue at East 77th St, New York, NY 10021, USA
Reservations: Small Luxury Hotels and The Leading Hotels of the World toll free reservation numbers worldwide (see p12); US toll free (☎ 800-THE-MARK)
Getting there: 45 minutes from JFK International Airport, 25 minutes from La Guardia Airport, transfers are available
Accommodation: 120 guest rooms; 60 suites. There are various categories of luxury rooms and suites: superior and de luxe rooms, junior suites, one-bedroom suites, two-bedroom suites, the Tower and the Presidential suites
Amenities: Clefs d'Or concierge; 24-hour room service; limousines; Marks Bar; Sunday brunch; afternoon tea; cocktails and after-theatre drinks and desserts; banquet facilities; shuttle to the theatre district on Friday and Saturday nights and to Wall St during the week
Dress code: Jacket and tie required for dining
Weddings: Ceremonies and receptions catered for up to 180 people, the cost of which varies depending on your requests
Minimum stay: None
Rates: Doubles from US$325; suites from US$500
Credit cards: Most major
Taxes and service charge: Not included

---

columns and a very plain wooden door to distinguish it. However, open the door and you enter a purple haze of exquisite design full of beautiful New Yorkers sipping cocktails.

The hotel lobby and bar area are very subtly lit, with seats covered in rich tones of reds and purples and a lot of calico-covered chairs; the concierge and porters are dressed in black jackets with Nero collars, a Parisian barman operates a cosy Vodka bar, and fresh flowers have been replaced by Japanese fighting fish swimming around in bowls. However, the most legendary aspect of this wonderful bar is the gents' toilet where, instead of using conventional urinals, men urinate against a fountain of water cascading down from the ceiling to the floor. Somehow this says it all about the Royalton, the hotel created by former Studio 54 disco kings, Ian Schrager and the late Steve Rubell.

If you are at all interested in design you'll love this hotel. It was the first of Schrager's projects to employ design guru Philippe Starck, and the result proved so successful that the partnership is still producing new hotels today. The hotel rooms lead off from long, weaving corridors, which are so dark that when you first come out of the brightly-lit lifts it's difficult to see anything at all. The bedrooms are painted a dark matt grey and furnished minimally with just a comfortable low-level mattress bed covered in white linen sheets and big square pillows. Without doubt the most impressive thing about staying at the Royalton is the

The Royalton is very trendy, and a little bit mysterious because of the way it sits so discreetly on W44th St. The rooms were luxurious without being opulent and were very cool. It wasn't just a place to stay, it felt like we were at the centre of trendy New York life.

Lizzie and Nigel Walley

THREE DAYS IN NEW YORK

The best way to see **Manhattan** is to get off the island and up into the air. Several companies operate **helicopter rides** from heliports around 12th Avenue and 34th St, whisking you over the Hudson River and hovering by the Statue of Liberty within a matter of minutes. The views are stunning, not just of Lady Liberty but also of the skyline dominated by the twin towers of the World Trade Centre. Make sure your helicopter tour takes you over the Downtown area, and that it flies along 5th Avenue passing the Empire State Building and the Rockefeller Centre on your way to Central Park. Within the space of 15 minutes you'll have seen most of New York's landmarks.

Times Square is close to the heliport. While you're there book tickets for a **Broadway show**: the best place to go is the discount ticket outlet in the middle of the square.

No visit to New York would be complete without a wander down **5th Avenue**: in winter you can ice skate at Rockefeller Plaza and in summer just sit in the café which replaces the ice rink; Saks, the famous spires of St Patrick's Cathedral and the pink marble Trump Tower are all worth a look.

One of the best places for breakfast is the *Barking Dog Luncheonette* on Third Avenue at 94th St. It's small and you might have to queue, especially at weekends, but it's worth it.

Central Park in many ways epitomises New York – immense and diverse – it is the very heart of the city. Approximately 850 acres, it contains a zoo, the Woolman Ice Rink, an open-air theatre, an observatory, numerous lakes and walkways and a six-mile loop around which New Yorkers jog, roller blade and cycle. Serene and peaceful in winter when the lakes are frozen over and snow lies everywhere but providing an escape from the heat in summer when you can lie and watch kids dancing and roller-skating. A great place to watch some of the best in New York is outside the *Tavern on the Green*: groups congregate here and try to out-do each other.

Close to the Park, and still on the 5th is the **Metropolitan Art Museum**, housing impressive collections of 18th, 19th and 20th century art, an armoury and musical instrument section, many wonderful statues and vast sections recreating the palaces of pre-Revolutionary France. Also definitely worth a look is the **Guggenheim**, close to the Met, which houses an incredible modern collection in a wonderfully groovy building.

Once you've done all your culture bashing it's time to relax in **SoHo**, so-called because of its location south of Houston St. A hip and trendy area to hang out and be seen in, SoHo is home to many of New York's contemporary artists. The main drag, **West Broadway**, and the surrounding area are full of galleries, chic coffee bars and restaurants. Particularly good are *Felix's*, on the corner of Prince St, and *Bar 89*, at 89 Spring St. Lots of small designers have shops in the area selling individually designed jewellery, clothing and art. The best way to experience SoHo is to just wander around for a few hours: the hordes of converted warehouses with their external fire escapes will make you feel you've seen the real New York.

However, you haven't really seen it until you've seen it at night. Take the **Staten Island Ferry** – a bargain at 50 cents round trip – from the tip of **Battery Park** to **Staten Island**. The ferry passes the **Statue of Liberty** and provides fantastic views of the financial district.

Once back on Manhattan Island, provided you've a head for heights, you could eat at *Windows of the World* at the top of the World Trade Centre: the food is good, the wine list huge and the views are absolutely breathtaking.

Little Italy is another great place to wander around, especially in the evening when it is usually bustling largely due to the number of popular restaurants there. Walking down Mulberry St you are greeted by the strong aromas of espresso and parmesan, and incredible displays of cakes and pastries. Everywhere you look in Little Italy there are stretch limos – a hint that this formerly notorious area's past is not so distant!

And then there's **Harlem**. You'd be wise to take a cab there, but there's nowhere like *Sylvia's Restaurant*, 328 Lenox Avenue (in between 126th St and 127th St) for soul food and cool jazz music on a Sunday morning. Right in the heart of Harlem, Sylvia's is the original soul food restaurant, frequented by the likes of Jesse Jackson and Woody Allen.

A great place for cocktails is the *Rainbow Room*, up in the **Rockefeller Center**. Looking straight out onto the Empire State Building, the art deco surroundings are fabulous and the cocktails pretty lethal too. Don't let the Rainbow Room's dress code – no jeans or trainers, jackets and ties for men, skirts for ladies – put you off, as it is definitely worth dressing up for. Brunch on Sundays is a good option, otherwise there is dinner and dancing, a big band and cabaret bar.

Round off your evening by nipping across to the **Empire State Building** and ascending to the viewing platform so that you can spy on the people who are eating where you've just been.

bathrooms – all slate, chrome, copper and stainless steel – with the best showers in **Manhattan** taking up half of the entire bathroom space and encased by a floor to ceiling glass wall with a door cut into it.

The standard rooms are very small so if you need your space go for a superior. Make sure you ask for a room overlooking the street, as they are definitely the best, with great views of the Big Apple, and if you really want to push the boat out go for the immense Studio Suite.

Other recommended hotels

The Inn at Irving Place (☎ 212-533-4600, fax 212-533-4611), 56 Irving Place, New York, is a wonderfully romantic hotel with art deco furnishings, right in the heart of New York's historic Gramercy Park, off Park Avenue. A typical townhouse hotel, the Inn has 12 guest rooms with separate sitting-rooms, brass beds, lovely antiques and all mod cons including a fridge which the hotel will fill with anything you want. Doubles from US$250 including continental breakfast either in bed or in the guest parlour, and newspapers.

The Paramount, (☎ 212-764-5500, fax 212-354-5237), 235 West 46 St, New York, a sister hotel to the Royalton, embodies Schrager's notion of 'cheap chic' and with rooms costing from US$190/£100 a night it is a great place to take a peak at the real New York. The focal point of the Paramount is the **Whiskey Bar**, a super trendy ground floor bar, which has turned into a huge literary and media hangout, so you can lunch surrounded by editors of glossy magazines. Conveniently located close to Broadway, the fashion district and just south of the Rockefeller Center, Radio City Music Hall and Carnegie Hall. Double rooms from US$190 to US$245, suites from US$395, plus 13.25% sales and local tax.

THE ROYALTON
(☎ 212-869 4400, fax 212-869 8965), 44 West 44th St, New York, NY 10036, USA
Reservations: Either direct with the hotel on the above number or toll free within the US toll free (☎ 1-800-635-9013)
Getting there: The hotel can arrange all sorts of transfers to/from the airports, a limo will cost around US$140, plus 20% for tax and tips
Accommodation: 168 rooms and 20 suites
Amenities: A fitness room, plus an arrangement allowing guests to use the Go Vertical club
Dress code: Dressy casual
Weddings: Wedding parties can be arranged in the penthouse but prices are subject to negotiation
Minimum stay: None
Rates: Doubles from US$295 (reduced to US$210 at the weekend); suites from US$425 (reduced to US$325 at the weekend)
Credit cards: Most major
Taxes and service charge: 13.25% sales and local tax plus US$2 per room

---

FLORIDA

The last few years have seen a wave of hotel gentrification and new hotels springing up around Miami, making the area the perfect destination for honeymooners in search of chic design-conscious hotels. The art deco hotels in particular, many owned by Chris Blackwell, promoter of Bob Marley and U2 and owner of the Island Outpost chain, have regained their former popularity and funk status. Past guests at The Marlin and Casa Grande have included Madonna, Paloma Picasso, Lenny Kravitz and Jamie Lee Curtis, so you would be in good company.

The Delano

The Delano on Miami Beach symbolises elegant but simple chic. Owned by Ian Schrager and designed by Philippe Starck, it was conceived as the next generation urban resort – the hub of social activity and at the same time a sophisticated, serene retreat. Everything is whiter than white at the Delano, from the remote control for the TV and the stereo in your bedroom to the abundance of white orchids. It was designed to be soothing and tranquil and the large blocks of white colour were used as a direct response to the era of 'over design'.

THE DELANO
(☎ 305-672-2000, fax 305-532-0099),
1685 Collins Avenue, Miami Beach,
Florida 33139, USA
Reservations: Either direct or US toll
free (☎ 800-555-5001)
Getting there: The hotel can arrange
limo transfers
Accommodation: 238 guest rooms,
lofts, suites, apartments and duplex pool-
side bungalows
Amenities: Water Salon, private beach
area for Delano guests, watersports, pool-
side private cabanas, state of the art 24-
hour gym, rooftop women's bathhouse
and solarium with health bar, gift and
magazine shop, US$1 movie theatre,
entertainment centre, 24-hour room service, portable phones and computers
available, video on demand
Dress code: Informal (white!)
Weddings: Can be arranged in the ballroom
Minimum stay: Two nights over weekend
Rates: Doubles from US$225 to US$300
in the winter; suites cost US$550; pool-
side bungalows cost US$600
Credit cards: Most major
Taxes and service charge: 11.5% tax,
service is discretionary

Located on Collins Avenue, directly on the beach, the core of this 16-storey hotel is its lobby area spanning both in and outside, where rigid functional spaces such as reception desks and waiting chairs have been replaced by a more fluid series of areas given over to an **Eat-in Kitchen**, the fully upholstered **Rose Bar** with roving service, and various other indoor and outdoor eating and drinking areas in which to mill about.

The Delano also boasts the most incredible collection of art and furniture from all over the world, including pieces by Man Ray, Salvador Dali and Antonio Gaudi. Instead of a swimming pool, Starck designed a Water Salon, modelled on ancient Roman baths and comprising several different areas of floating, meditating, sleeping, underwater classical music, waterfalls and furniture not around but in the pool.

There is nothing conventional about the Delano, even in the orchard and garden there is a huge chess board designed by Starck, as well as a bed, while the on-site movie theatre costs only US$1 a film. Throughout the hotel the emphasis is on natural materials. The 228 bedrooms, which all come with the full range of amenities, feature poured-in-place art gallery floors, furniture and lamps designed specifically for the hotel by Starck, and many examples of his design cheek, such as angels hovering over the bed and ceiling to floor mirrors.

The Marlin

Three years ago Blackwell spent US$4.5 million on the Marlin making it one of America's funkiest and most radiant hotels. This incredible little hotel combines art deco with Jamaican funk in a way that only Blackwell could make work.

This is where the fashion and music world flock for their holidays, the latter inspired by the world renowned recording studio on site, the former drawn by the buzz of **South Beach** and the hotel's modelling agency. As a result the Marlin is *the* place for people-watching. The desire for a glimpse of the stars means the hotel bar gets painfully crowded at night, but to the right clientele this can only be considered an advantage, not a drawback!

An American publication, *Metropolitan Home*, described the Marlin as 'a combination of aquatic glamour and island junk', which about sums up the way the rooms are decorated. Each of the 12 guest suites is designed as its own tropical world and filled with original Jamaican, Haitian and Cuban art.

Echoes of the seashore are found throughout the hotel, from the jellyfish bar stools to the scallop-shaped bar. The whole hotel is an absolute riot of colour from deep indigo to acid yellow. The roof terrace with its Jamaican-style bar is a great place to hang out, with its brightly coloured scatter cushions, cane furniture, silk drapings and sunflowers in tin buckets. Alternatively there is the **Shabeen Cookshack** and bar, where the food is spicy and the Shabeen Punch a euphoric mix of a ridiculous number of different rums, topped up with fruit juices.

All the rooms are well kitted-out, with their own kitchenette and coffee-maker, CD radio cassette player, TV and VCR, minibar, iron, hair-dryer and in-room safe. As you'd expect there are batik robes in the place of impersonal white hotel bathrobes, and a great video and CD library to raid for your own use. One of the best rooms is the African room, with its varying shades of violet and original Jamaican and Haitian artwork.

Other hotels in Miami Beach

While the Marlin and the Delano are not actually on the beach, **The Leslie** (☎ 305-534-2135, fax 305-531-5543) and **The Cavalier** (☎ 305-534-2135, fax 305-531-5543), two cheaper Chris Blackwell properties are right on legendary **Ocean Drive**, the street opposite the beach where it all happens. While the Cavalier is a true art deco hotel, having been built in 1936, the Leslie is all wildly exaggerated tropical-funk, with yellow walls, pink satin counterpanes combined with vermilion cushions – not for the faint-hearted, but a perfect personification of Florida and life on the beach. Both are fun hotels to be in, and all their rooms are brilliantly executed; with rates from US$105 a night they also offer extremely good value.

THE MARLIN

(☎ 305-673 8770, fax 305-673 9609), 1200 Collins Ave, Miami Beach, Florida 33139, USA

Reservations: UK Island Outpost toll free (☎ 0800-614790); USA Island Outpost toll free (☎ 1-800-Outpost); UK tour operator Earth Travel (UK ☎ 0171-734 3426)

Getting there: 15 minutes from Miami International Airport, taxi costs US$20

Accommodation: 12 suites

Amenities: Shabeen Cookshack and bar, roof-top deck with Jamaican-style bar, video and CD libraries, international newspapers, Ian Innocent guest services and tour desk; video and CD library; laundry and dry cleaning

Dress code: Casual

Weddings: The Marlin allows guests to make their own arrangements for a licensed minister or Justice of the Peace to conduct the ceremony, and caters for buffet-style receptions for up to 40 people on the rooftop or in the Marlin bar; rooftop rental fee costs US$550 plus food and beverages

Minimum stay: None

Rates: Studio suites cost US$200; a one-bedroom de luxe suite costs US$265

Credit cards: Most major

Taxes and service charge: 11.5% tax is added to your bill, service charge is optional

---

A FEW THINGS TO SEE AND DO AROUND SOUTH BEACH

The white sandy beaches of Miami have long attracted tourists to South Beach, but what is much newer and just as exciting is the art deco renewal that has hit the area over the last decade. There are more **art deco buildings** concentrated in South Beach than anywhere else in the world.

Things have certainly changed in South Beach: back in 1980 the average age of its punters was a somewhat shy and retiring 66, by 1995 it had dropped about three decades.

The rows of small hotels built here in the 1930s have undergone some serious face-lifts and the result is the creation of one of America's hippest, most happening places. The strip that is known as South Beach, the bottom third of Miami Beach, is fringed on one side with deep blue ocean and on the other with a veritable rainbow of art deco condos and hotels, scores of brilliant shining convertibles and a few thousand palm trees. Home to Versace, and clubs owned by the likes of Sean

Penn, Prince and Mick Hucknell the place is just one long party and has to be seen to be believed.

All you have to do is rent a convertible, lace up your roller blades or simply stroll the streets, and join in. Check out *News Café* on Ocean Drive, the new *Van Dyke Café* on Lincoln Road, and if you fancy something smart and quite delicious try *Pacific Time* also on Lincoln Road, and then late at night slip into *Bash* (partly owned by Sean Penn) for a bit of celebrity dancing, and *The Strand* which really kicks on Friday nights.

The shops are also quite incredible. You can pick up anything from zany wigs to funky clothes and tasteful house and garden goodies. There are late night book stores such as the famous **Books & Books** on Lincoln Road, along which you'll also find gays and galleries, roller-bladers and African drummers, and even the Miami City Ballet.

The other big honeymoon thing to do in Florida is to hire a car in Miami and head down to the Florida Keys, the 31 islands arranged in an arc around the southernmost tip of Florida. The 110-mile drive down the **Overseas Highway** from **Key Largo**, just 40 miles south west of Miami, to Key West, will take you past some spectacular scenery and great hotels.

The Gardens Hotel

The Gardens Hotel, located in the heart of the historic district of **Key West**, was formerly the largest private estate in Old Town and today's hotel contains almost a quarter of an Old Town city block within its walls.

The hotel captures all the colonial charm and elegance of a Caribbean homestead, with its white pillars and balconies peeking through lush green gardens overflowing with huge palm fronds. The property underwent a complete renovation in 1993 to create a 17-bedroom hideaway within the island's best known tropical botanical gardens, providing a place of calm and tranquillity in marked contrast to the bustling wining, dining and shopping centre just a few blocks away.

Guest accommodation is in the original buildings – the main house, the carriage house and the cottage – as well as two new buildings which were designed to be consistent with the existing architecture. The hotel's rooms are decorated with European-style floral chintz and stripes, with subtle lighting to set off the many American antiques and impressionist paintings of the island and its gardens by New Zealand's Peter Williams. All the rooms have hardwood oak floors, king-size beds with antique headboards, pristine white marble bathrooms with jacuzzi baths, white cotton robes, Nina Ricci toiletries, TV, phone, make-up mirrors and a fully stocked minibar with imported beers.

> **THE GARDENS HOTEL**
> (305-294-2661, fax 305-292-1007), 526 Angela St, Key West, Florida 33040, USA
> **Reservations:** Small Luxury Hotels of the World toll free reservation numbers worldwide (see p12)
> **Getting there:** In the centre of the Old Town at the corner of Simonton St and Angela St, four miles from Key West International Airport; 160 miles from Miami International Airport
> **Accommodation:** 15 rooms and two suites
> **Amenities:** Swimming pool, jacuzzi, poolside bar; golf, health and beauty, fishing, diving, flying and canoeing all nearby
> **Dress code:** None
> **Weddings:** The hotel does not cater for wedding receptions
> **Minimum stay:** Two nights at weekends
> **Rates:** Doubles from US$200 to US$435; suites from US$475 to US$625, including breakfast
> **Credit cards:** American Express, Visa, MasterCard
> **Taxes and service charge:** Not included

The best rooms are the two 'historic' bedrooms on the second floor of the main house, **Eyebrow Cottage** tucked away in a corner of the estate which has the most incredible cathedral ceiling and a huge jacuzzi bath and shower, and the **Master Suite** which has a separate sitting-room overlooking the courtyard, pool and garden from its cloistered terrace and a sauna and steam shower as well as the jacuzzi.

Key West is unlike any other part of America, having evolved a culture of its own. Once a haven for contrabandistas, this tiny island only two miles by four now plays host to poets, pirates, artists and tourists alike. This unlikely combination makes Key West a bizarrely sophisticated small town, one of the wealthiest cities in America and a great place to visit with a good selection of bars, restaurants and shops.

Little Palm Island

This fabulous little island is the perfect southern seas' island hideaway, but on Florida's doorstep. The rustic looking but very luxurious thatched cottages lined up along the island's edge really make it seem as if you've stepped on to some South

Pacific island, rather than being 28 miles from Key West.

Originally a favourite retreat of US Presidents, Truman and Roosevelt, Warner Bros selected the island for the filming of *PT 109*, a film about JF Kennedy's WW II experiences in the South Pacific. The island has now been transformed into a luxury hotel that attracts the likes of Robert Wagner and Ivana Trump, and is impressive enough to warrant membership of the exclusive Relais & Châteaux group.

The hotel was certainly created with escapism in mind: in place of TVs, radios, phones and computers, there are hammocks, outdoor showers, sauna and massage rooms, in-room whirlpools and a poolside tropical bar. There are only 30 suites on this tiny three-mile long island so you can be assured of privacy, and the peace won't be disturbed by screaming kids as none are allowed on the island.

The 14 thatched-roof villas, each housing two suites, are scattered discreetly among flaming bougainvillaea, oleander, hibiscus and palm, and all have ocean views. They are equipped with private sundeck, ceiling fans and air-conditioning (though the louvred windows and doors mean you'll hardly need them), wicker and rattan furnishings, coffee-maker and minibar, as well as the famous outdoor showers and whirlpool baths.

Unusually for the Keys, the island is blessed with a lovely white sandy beach which is just great for sunbathing, kayaking and windsurfing, both of which are complimentary. The hotel also has a lovely fresh-water swimming pool and lots of other activities to keep you occupied during the day; scuba diving to **Looe Key National Marine Sanctuary**, sunset sails, Key West excursions, nature tours and fishing charters.

Little Palm is not the place to come if you want to avoid other honeymooners or feel you might get claustrophobic on such a small island eating dinner with the same guests each night – most of whom are Americans. But if you only ever want to wander as far as your hammock, or to the bar for a drink or the library for a book, and like your luxuries such as a whirl-pool bath to return to each evening, then this is the perfect island paradise.

LITTLE PALM ISLAND
(☎ 305-872-2524, fax 305-872-4843), 28500 Overseas Highway, Little Torch Key, Florida 33042, USA
Reservations: Relais & Châteaux and Small Luxury Hotels of the World toll free reservations numbers worldwide (see p12)
Getting there: The hotel can arrange a limousine for the two and a half hour drive through Florida Keys from Miami Airport, or will collect you from Key West or Marathon Airports and transfer you to the island by private boat
Accommodation: 30 suites
Amenities: Fresh-water swimming pool, sauna, exercise room, kayaks, canoes, windsurfers and instruction, hobie day sailers, snorkel gear, fishing gear, beach loungers and towels, beach floats, fishing charters, nature tours, Key West excursions, cellular phones, seaplane tours, sailing trips, motorised sunkats, pontoon boats, snorkelling and scuba diving trips, sunset sail, therapeutic body massage, room service, two restaurants
Dress code: Collared shirts with sleeves are to be worn by men in the dining-room
Weddings: The hotel has a selection of wedding packages such as the Crystal Water Cruise which costs US$1296 for a ceremony aboard Chimera, the hotel's beautiful 40ft sailing yacht, with photographer, flowers, private champagne and cake reception, or Tropical Breezes costing US$450 for a ceremony on the island with champagne and cake
Minimum stay: Two nights at weekends, three nights on public holidays, seven nights over Christmas and New Year's Eve
Rates: Doubles from US$465 in the winter, US$290 in the summer; ask about their five night honeymoon package which costs around US$3500 depending on the time of year and includes accommodation, full board, two snorkelling trips to Looe Key National Marine Sanctuary, one full body massage each, sunset sail aboard Chimera, and complimentary watersports
Credit cards: Most major
Taxes and service charge: 7% tax and 15% service charge will be added to your bill, unless otherwise stated by your honey-moon package

Mexico
(BEST TIME: NOVEMBER TO APRIL)

Mexico's tourist industry is the best developed of all the countries in Latin America, which doesn't mean that Mexico itself is developed although some parts of it undoubtedly are: rather that it has the widest choice of the kind of hotels that you want for a honeymoon.

The best thing about Mexico is that it is easy to combine a wonderfully relaxing beach holiday – lots of great watersports – with a few days experiencing some of this country's amazing 3000 years of history. Mexico is the ideal destination if you fancy something a little adventurous but don't want to rough it.

There are some truly fantastic beaches in Mexico. Some like **Cancún** and **Acapulco** have become very touristy: rows of sky-scraping international hotels now line the water's edge, while others can be found in small villages where local fishermen still cast their nets each morning. But with over 9600km of coastline covering four distinct bodies of water, you should be able to find something to suit your taste and budget.

With Mexico's regular and efficient system of internal flights it is easy to visit two, or even three, different places in a two-week holiday. I've organised this chapter in two sections to help you plan a honeymoon that combines the best beach hotels with a few days' sightseeing: the first section deals with the Pacific and Caribbean coasts, while the second suggests different places to visit for cultural insight or archaeological interest. Having said that, the proliferation of wonderfully romantic, first-class hotels makes Mexico the best country in Latin America if you just want to stay in one place for your entire holiday.

MEXICO
A great combination of palm-fringed beaches and ancient Mayan culture
Capital: Mexico City
When to go: The temperate dry season is November to April (avoid Christmas and Easter because the Mexicans crowd the beaches and everything is booked up)
Average maximum temperatures °C (Mexico City)

JAN	FEB	MAR	APR	MAY	JUN	JUL	AUG	SEP	OCT	NOV	DEC
19	21	24	25	26	24	23	23	23	21	20	19

Flight times: to Mexico City from:
New York: 5 hours
LA: $5^1/_2$ hours
London: 10 hours
Sydney: 19 hours
Approximate exchange rate: Peso (P) – £1 = P11.73, US$1 = P7.56, A$1 = P5.98
Time difference: GMT minus six hours
Voltage: 110v AC, 60 Hz, US-style two-pin (flat) plugs
Combine with: Belize, Guatemala, Costa Rica, Los Angeles
Country dialling code: ☎ 52

ACAPULCO
Stretching out along the Pacific coast Acapulco was the birthplace of the Mexican tourist industry. Today the town that was responsible for giving the world cliff-diving, tequila slammers and swim-up bars, is one large, glittering, glamorous resort with a slightly has-been feel to it. It is an extremely popular destination for America cruise ships so, if it's small, intimate, romantic hideaway beaches you are looking for, avoid

Acapulco. There's no doubt that Acapulco Bay, the U-shaped, mountain-framed, natural harbour is one of the most stunning in the world but you have to be a fan of really big resorts, and all that comes with them, to decide upon Acapulco.

Las Brisas

Las Brisas continues to be the one good reason to choose Acapulco as your honeymoon destination. Famed for years as one of the world's most romantic hotels, the pink and white *casitas* (thatched huts) of Las Brisas span the hillside, each with either private or shared swimming pool.

The 300 casitas and suites of Las Brisas offer guests a relaxed kind of elegance amidst 44 hectares of beautiful gardens filled with bougainvillaea, fuchsias, and the hotel's trade mark, hibiscus blooms, plus endless stunning views of the vast Acapulco Bay. It's definitely worth asking for one of the higher casitas where the views are better.

Each room has glass sliding doors opening on to stone terraces and contains all the extras that you'd expect of a luxury hotel, including air-conditioning, ceiling fans, in-room safe, phone, minibar, wet bar, lots of toiletries beside the marble bath, a separate vanity unit, hair-dryer and bathrobes. However, the rooms themselves are rather simply decorated.

The multi-levelled suites have their bedrooms on the upper level, which also has a terrace and a jacuzzi, while the lower level features a separate dining area, sitting-room, patio and pool, so it feels as if you've got your own private house.

Each morning your breakfast will be delivered through a small cupboard built into the bedroom wall which can be opened from either side, so room service can leave your orders in it allowing you to enjoy a relaxing breakfast alone without any form of interruption.

There are three restaurants to choose from: one serving international cuisine, another offering local dishes, and a restaurant and bar at **La Concha**, the hotel's own private beach club. Guests can either eat outside on the terrace looking out over the bay, or get room service delivered through the magic box.

One of the best features of Las Brisas is La Concha, the hotel's fabulous leisure club a short drive away. Guests are driven to the club in one of the hotel's signature pink and white jeeps. An attendant meets each jeep and helps guests select pool-side sun loungers and lays their towels out for them – and then keeps them supplied with a constant stream of refreshments from the bar. The club has a good range of facilities including water-skiing, sailing, deep-sea fishing and scuba diving. There's also tennis at the hotel, golf nearby, a shopping arcade and delicatessen and the jeeps are always available for touring the scenic grounds, transporting you to your casita, or for getting into town for some night-life.

LAS BRISAS
(☎ 748-41580, fax 748-46071), PO Box 281, 39868 Acapulco, Guerrero, Mexico
Reservations: The Leading Hotels of the World worldwide toll free reservation numbers (see p12)
Getting there: 20 minutes from Acapulco International Airport; guests staying in suites are met at the airport
Accommodation: 300 casitas and suites: 96 casitas have semi-private pools, 104 have private pools, 38 royal beach casitas, 22 junior suites or villas, five one-bedroom suites, three two-bedroom suites
Amenities: Five floodlit tennis courts, private swimming club with fresh-water pool, two saltwater lagoons, shopping arcade and delicatessen, jeeps and petrol station and of course the 250 swimming pools!
Dress code: Casually elegant; jackets optional for men
Weddings: Can be arranged in the Chapel of Peace on the top of the hill
Minimum stay: None
Rates: Doubles from US$165 to US$345
Credit cards: Most major
Taxes and service charge: 15% Government Tax, service charge US$16 daily per person

IXTAPA AND ZIHUATANEJO

Ixtapa is another large coastal resort teeming with modern hotels, much like Acapulco and Cancún. But just down the coast from Ixtapa is Zihuatanejo, a small fishing village with some of Mexico's most intimate and romantic hotels scattered around the edge of its beautiful bay. If you want to get away from the big international hotel chains and are searching for the charm of a classic Mexican pueblo, this is the place to come.

Hotel Villa del Sol

The Hotel Villa del Sol has long been regarded among the cognoscenti as one of Latin America's best retreats. As a member of both Relais & Châteaux and Small Luxury Hotels of the World, guests can be assured of finding luxurious accommodation, delicious food and stylish surroundings in this wonderfully romantic beach-front hideaway. No children are allowed in the hotel during the high season so you are guaranteed complete and utter peace.

> **HOTEL VILLA DEL SOL**
> (☎ 755-42239, fax 755-42758), PO Box 84, Playa la Ropa, 40880 Zihuatanejo, Guerrero, Mexico
> **Reservations:** Relais & Château and Small Luxury Hotels of the World toll free reservation numbers worldwide (see p12)
> **Getting there:** 15 minutes from Ixtapa-Zihuatanejo Airport International Airport
> **Accommodation:** 22 mini suites; eight de luxe suites; six master suites
> **Amenities:** Beauty parlour, laundry and valet service, two fresh-water pools, golf, fishing and horse-riding nearby, two tennis courts, private beach with hobie cats, water-skiing, snorkelling
> **Dress code:** Casual
> **Weddings:** Ceremonies and receptions can be arranged for up to 150 people
> **Minimum stay:** None
> **Rates:** Mini standard suites from US$143 to US$198; suites from US$330 to US$506
> **Credit cards:** Most major
> **Taxes and service charge:** 15% tax and 10% service

Set on one of Mexico's loveliest beaches, the **Playa la Ropa**, among palm trees, lush gardens and cascading fountains, the Villa del Sol has 36 de luxe split-level thatched bungalow suites, all appointed with traditional furnishings and colourful native artworks. Each bungalow has a king-sized canopied bed, ceiling fan, air-conditioning, minibar, TV, a spacious bathroom and a separate sitting area: some even have whirlpools.

The bungalows also have their own private terrace, so guests can either relax there in the hammock or wander down to the beach where all the usual watersports are on offer. Other facilities include a beauty parlour, a beach-bar, two floodlit tennis courts, a golf course and two swimming pools.

The alfresco restaurant serves both Mexican and international dishes and on Fridays offers a buffet to a background of live Mexican folk music. The cuisine at the Villa del Sol is particularly good and has won several awards.

La Casa Que Canta

Also overlooking Zihuatanejo, with staggering views of the bay, is the La Casa Que Canta, described by many travellers to Mexico as the country's prettiest hotel. The 'house that sings' has been so beautifully built among terraces set on the edge of a steep cliff, and its terracotta architecture has been blended so well into its surroundings that you'd never know the hotel was built this decade. Everywhere there are terracotta pots sprouting lush green foliage, huge palm fronds rising up from the balcony below, and thatched roofs sitting atop rust-coloured adobe suites.

I've only heard good things of La Casa. It is a truly wonderful hotel, adorned throughout with traditional Mexican artefacts and furnishings. The hotel has a very personal but relaxing feeling: as the brochure says 'we invite you to share our lifestyle at our home and yours', which just about sums up the atmosphere of this luxurious, but unpretentious hotel.

The individual decor of the 18 suites has been inspired by Mexican folk art, using wonderfully cool shades of palest blue and cream, with red-tiled cool floors, brightly coloured fabrics draped effectively over the wooden king-size bed frames and hand-painted furniture everywhere. All the suites have magnificent views of the dazzling bay from the bedroom balcony and the living room terrace, as well as air-conditioning, fans, minibars, in-room safes, marble bathrooms with double sinks, bidets, walk-in showers, and enormous towels.

The architecture of La Casa enhances your privacy: you can walk through your suite's wooden louvred doors on to your patio, which is partially thatched for seclusion. It would be easy to spend all day there on the two comfy loungers, eating from the brightly painted wrought-iron garden furniture, or just lounging in your hammocks enjoying the view.

Meal times at La Casa are very informal with delicious salads and grilled snacks offered at both poolsides during the day, while candlelit dinners on the terrace overlooking the bay in the evening are extremely romantic.

> **LA CASA QUE CANTA**
> (☎ 755-47030, fax 755-47040), Camino Escenico La playa la Ropa, Zihuatanejo, Guerrero 40880, Mexico
> **Reservations:** Small Luxury Hotels of the World toll free reservations numbers worldwide (see p12)
> **Getting there:** 20 minutes from Ixtapa-Zihuatanejo International Airport, 45-minute flight from Mexico City; the hotel will provide transfers by arrangement
> **Accommodation:** 23 rooms
> **Amenities:** Fitness centre, boutique, fresh and salt-water swimming pools, salt-water jacuzzi, boutique and restaurant; plus golf, fishing, horse-riding, all watersports, scuba diving and tennis nearby
> **Dress code:** Casual
> **Weddings:** Can be arranged for up to 34 people
> **Rates:** Suites from US$200 to US$285; pool suites from US$290 to US$480
> **Credit cards:** Most major
> **Taxes and service charge:** 15% government tax, plus 10% service charge recommended

One of the best aspects of La Casa is its salt-water jacuzzi and its two stunning swimming pools. One of the pools is a fresh-water horizon pool – the water seems to flow endlessly straight out into the Pacific way down below – while the salt-water pool is set amongst boulders and towering palm trees at the bottom of the cliff. As well as the pools, the hotel has its own private beach club on **La Ropa**, a five-minute walk away, with bed chairs and refreshments.

Other recommended hotels

I have chosen two very different alternative destinations on the Pacific coast, one truly exclusive with a price tag to match and the other offering basic, inexpensive accommodation in a superb beach setting.

Las Alamandas (☎ 328-55500, fax 328-55027) is one of the world's most exclusive and ultimate resorts, set halfway between **Puerto Vallarta** and **Manzanillo**. Owned, designed and decorated by Isabel Goldsmith, Las Alamandas has long been popular with celebrity guests. Most people fly directly into the resort's private airstrip on private charter flights from either Puerto Vallarta or Manzanillo airports, costing around US$200 per couple each way. A maximum of 22 guests are accommodated in four villas of varying size. Each room is large with high vaulted ceilings and is beautifully decorated in bright Mexican fabrics and warm colour-washed walls with stunning hand-carved wooden furniture. They all have a Mexican tiled bathroom, equipped with bathrobes and toiletries, a private terrace, a full-sized living-room and a dining-room, so that you can eat alone if you want. Bed and breakfast rates start at US$302/£195 per person per night, including tax and service, with a US$201/£130 supplement for full board. While the hotel is exceptionally pricey, you get what you pay for – a really exclusive hotel where you are made to feel like guests instead of customers. For reservations call Robert Reid Associates – US (☎ 1-800-223-6510); Canada (☎ 1-800-424 5500); Europe (France ☎ 01-40 49 02 34); or book through UK representatives Cathy Mathos Mexican Tours (UK ☎ 0171-267 2004).

The Sotavento y Catalina Beach Resorts (☎ 755-42032, fax 755-42975), PO Box 2, Playa La Ropa, Zihuatanejo, Guerrero 40880, Mexico, also enjoy a prime location on the beautiful Playa la Ropa. This is a great alternative if you are looking for something less pricey but in a similar location to La Casa Que Canta and Hotel Villa del Sol. The Sotavento and the Catalina beach resorts, run by the same management team, are located side by side, perched on the cliff edge overlooking this most beautiful bay and beach. The resorts offer a wide variety of accommodation from casitas with standard sized terraces, guest rooms, larger terrace suites, and de luxe bungalows. Although the rooms are simply furnished, all the terrace suites come with hammocks, chaise longues and a sitting corner with wonderful views. The guest rooms have a smaller terrace and ocean view, while the bungalows have both inner roofed terraces and outer open terraces for sunbathing. There are three bars with ocean views and two restaurants, one of which is right on the beach, where guests can also participate in sailing, windsurfing, snorkelling and diving. Golf, tennis, horse-riding and deep-sea fishing are all available nearby. You won't find the same sort of privacy as you'd expect at the more expensive hotels, but the beach is wonderful and the views just the same. Doubles from US$45, cottages from US$70 and the honeymoon suite costs US$70, all rates are subject to 15% tax.

CANCUN AND THE YUCATAN PENINSULA
If you like big, buzzing resorts, you'll love Cancún where international high-rise hotels, discos, and sports facilities abound.

Casa Turquesa
Casa Turquesa is unique among the hotels on Cancún beach in that it is very small and personal making it much more classically romantic than any of its neighbours. Needless to say, it is also much more expensive but exclusivity doesn't come cheap and the Casa Turquesa is very definitely the most exclusive hotel in the area.

This magnificent white Mexican-style mansion is the personification of the boutique hotel and its 31 luxury suites boast fabulous views of the Caribbean. Casa

> **CASA TURQUESA**
> (☎ 98-852924, fax 98-852922), Blvd Kukulcan Km 13.5, Zona Hotelera, Cancún 77500, Mexico
> **Reservations:** Small Luxury Hotels of the World toll free reservation numbers worldwide (see p12)
> **Getting there**: The hotel will arrange transfers from Cancún Airport (5km), there is a charge of US$20 per person if staying less than three days
> **Accommodation:** 31 suites
> **Amenities**: Outdoor swimming pool, fitness centre, jacuzzi, health and beauty centre, breakfast and lunch café, swim-up bar, dining-room; plus golf, fishing and a wide selection of watersports nearby
> **Dress code**: Elegant casual
> **Weddings**: The hotel does not cater for weddings or receptions
> **Minimum stay**: None
> **Rates**: Suites from US$302.50 to US$385; executive suites cost US$550
> **Credit cards**: Most major
> **Taxes and service charge**: Included

Turquesa is a very modern hotel in terms of the quality of its service and its first-class amenities, which include an outdoor swimming pool, tennis, fitness centre and a health and beauty parlour.

The rooms are all spacious junior suites with marble flooring, light wood and wrought-iron furniture, pastel shades and matching floral bedspreads. The air-conditioned rooms also have minibars, phones, TV, CD players and videos, and best of all a large private balcony with its own jacuzzi overlooking the ocean – perfectly designed so you can lie there, cocktail in hand, staring out over the vast expanse of deep blue sea with your favourite CD playing. The marble floored bathrooms have double sinks, bath, a separate shower and lovely rose-scented toiletries.

The pool area is reached by a wide staircase which forms the focal point of the hotel's facade. The area is shaded by blue and white striped awnings which provide a cool spot where you can recline on a lounger and gaze out at the ocean. As well as the gloriously refreshing swim-up bar, the hotel has a breakfast and lunch café, while dinner is served in the dining-room.

Other recommended hotels

You need not spend a fortune on accommodation in Cancún. The best deals are to be found through British tour operators, like Kuoni and BA Holidays (see p10), who offer fantastic packages to Cancún in really top class hotels, many of them on an all-inclusive basis. For example, Kuoni offers a week at the **Diamond Resort** (☎ 98-850638) for around £850 per person in May including flights, transfers, accommodation, all meals and drinks, and lots of free watersports. Diamond Resort is located on **Playa del Carmen** about 64km south of Cancún and is therefore a much quieter destination. This is a great hotel if you want to get away from it all amongst laid-back, peaceful and friendly surroundings. The hotel is set in six hectares of landscaped gardens, there's a wonderful pool with a swim-up bar at the centre of the complex and plenty to do during the day from tennis to volley-ball, free bikes to tour around on, aerobics classes, and lots of free watersports, including sunfish sailing, snorkelling, windsurfing and paddle boats. There's also a long sandy beach.

A FEW THINGS TO SEE AND DO IN THE YUCATAN PENINSULA

Just off Cancún, **Isla Mujeres**, is a great place to visit with a really rustic atmosphere. The island is a bird-watchers' paradise but it is also great for diving and snorkelling and, because it is so small, it is easy to cycle from one end to the other. The beaches at the north end of the island are the best while the coast at the south end is rocky. Isla Mujeres is easily accessible for a day trip: a ferry goes 16 times a day from Puerto Juarez, north of Cancún.

Cozumel is Mexico's largest island and it has the same friendly, laid-back attitude as any Caribbean island as well as excellent beaches and diving. Only 56km away from Cancún, Cozumel is perfect for those who are seeking to get away from it all, in hotels that are unpretentious and which have lots of Mexican charm. Cozumel is reached by a 50-minute flight from **Merida**, a ferry from Playa del Carmen, or a 20-minute flight from Cancún with Aerocaribe.

If you want to dive, the best dives are at Palancar, Santa Rosa and Colombia. There are plenty of certified **dive schools** on the island to choose from.

It is easy to fly from Cancún or Cozumel inland to **Chichen Itza**. Originally a Mayan city, Chichen Itza became the capital of the Toltec Empire in the 12th century, before the Mayans reclaimed it a century later. To see these incredible ruins from the air is an awesome experience. Equally worthwhile is a visit to the Mayan site of **Tulum**, where the white city walls are set against a backdrop of cliffs and coastline. Approximately 125km south of Cancún, the ruins were dedicated to the worship of the setting sun and have to be seen to be believed. If you take your swimming gear you can scramble down the rocks to the sea and dive on the reef.

Playa del Carmen, a very Mexican port which is especially colourful on Sundays, is also worth visiting for its relatively peaceful beach and slow pace. The best white sandy beaches are north of the town but the sandflies can be annoying.

OAXACA

Founded in 1529 this historic and quite magical city is the place to come if you want to discover the real charm of this amazing country. Oaxaca has to be one of the most romantic colonial cities in Mexico; it is very easy to fall in love with it because of its exquisite baroque architecture and charming cobbled winding streets. The city sits on an arid plateau, high up in the **Sierra Madre del Sur** mountains, giving it a wonderfully fresh spring-like climate all year round. Try to be there on a Saturday as the Indian market is one of the best in Mexico for hand-embroidered clothing and jewellery. Even a short stay in Oaxaca will give you ample opportunity to visit some of the area's extraordinary archaeological sites, created by the Zapotec and Mixtec

Indians long before the Spanish conquest. The three best sites, **Monte Albán**, **Mitla** and **Yagul**, all lie within 40 km of the city. With a direct flight from Acapulco to Oaxaca it is very easy to combine these two destinations.

Camino Real

Camino Real, built within the hallowed walls of the 16th century convent of Santa Catalina, is the best place to stay in Oaxaca. The hotel boasts 400-year old frescoes overlooking flagstone walkways, set amidst cooling fountains and scenic gardens. The frescoes and the treasured canvases line the passageways, giving the hotel a very old world air.

> **CAMINO REAL OAXACA**
> (☎ 951-60611, fax 951-60732), Calle 5 de Mayo 300, 68000 Oaxaca
> **Reservations**: Either direct with the Mexico City office (☎ 5-227 7200), from the US and Canada (☎ 800-722-6466) or from the UK (☎ 0-800-897571)
> **Getting there**: Taxis from Oaxaca International Airport cost 50 pesos (15 minutes)
> **Accommodation**: 91 rooms and suites
> **Amenities**: Swimming pool, restaurant, two bars, phones, laundry, room service, tour desk
> **Dress code**: Casual
> **Weddings**: Wedding ceremonies and receptions can be arranged either in the hotel grounds or in the private chapel
> **Minimum stay**: None
> **Rates**: Doubles from US$150 to US$210
> **Credit cards**: Most major
> **Taxes and service charge**: 15% tax, service included

The hotel has 91 rooms and suites which are all decorated in authentic Mexican style, using brightly coloured rugs and Mexican artefacts. Whitewashed walls set off dark wooden furniture, terracotta tiled floors and wooden beamed ceilings. Facilities in the bedroom include TV and a phone, and many of the rooms come with two double beds.

Guests can choose between eating outside beneath the convent's majestic arches or in the dining-room, and drinking in either the **Bugambilias** bar or enjoying cocktails at **Las Novicias**.

At weekends the chapel hosts traditional folk art displays called Guelaguetza, an ancient Oaxacan ritual stemming from the tribe's belief in giving without expecting anything in return. The festivals involve handicrafts, dances in colourful costumes, and a lavish buffet.

There's plenty to do from and at the Camino Real: I'd recommend a three or four-day stay so that you can see some of this country's culture. This, combined with a week or so on a beach resort, would be a great honeymoon

CENTRAL MEXICO

If you want to see some of Mexico's colonial heritage, then a visit to the beautiful central highland region of **Bajio**, is a great way to experience the impact of the country's 300 years under European rule. Wonderfully unspoilt colonial cities, such as **Querataro**, **San Miguel de Allende** and **Morelia**, are within a day's drive of Mexico City. These cities have plenty of old world charm, fine-art and handicrafts shops, museums, and hundreds of colonial buildings, many of which have hardly changed for centuries.

La Casa de la Marquesa

La Casa de la Marquesa, in Queretaro 217km north of Mexico City, is one of the most beautiful and romantic hotels you'll ever see. As part of the Small Luxury Hotels of the World chain, this recently restored architectural jewel makes a wonderfully luxurious base from which to explore the picturesque nearby towns of San Miguel de Allende and Morelia.

The palace is located in the heart of the historic downtown and is one of the oldest and most impressive mansions in the city of Queratero. A baroque building dating back to 1756, the ornate, pale yellow sandstone exterior, and the lavish, but totally in keeping, interior decorations have to be seen to be believed. The carved stonework, intricate design and Moorish details, the living room and the chapel, are overwhelmingly beautiful.

The hotel has 25 air-conditioned suites, all of which have original decor, either double or king-size beds, cable TV and phones, as well as homely touches such as fresh flowers.

The menu in La Casa de la Marquesa's dining-room reflects traditional flavours and aromas, while the **Don Porfirio** bar is a great place to relax.

This hotel is the perfect contrast to a beach hotel, giving you another, much more authentic, insight into Mexico.

Las Mananitas

Las Mananitas, 70km south of Mexico City, is one of Mexico's most elegant small inns, and has long been a popular destination for honeymooners. This pretty pink hotel is set in the beautiful mountain city of Cuernavaca, a place which the Aztecs called 'the city of eternal spring'. The hotel was built in colonial fashion with terracotta tiled roofs and is covered with foliage. It is filled with sculptures and authentic paintings by the country's greatest artists and is surrounded by exotic gardens.

Inside, the hotel is decorated using traditional Mexican techniques and artefacts. The long, arched white corridors connect the 20 suites, all of which have Spanish colonial furnishings, huge king-sized beds, rustic pillars and beams, and brightly upholstered sofas in separate sitting-rooms.

All the rooms have a patio or terrace overlooking the hotel's lush gardens and a private pool area, but ask in particular for rooms No 19, No 21 or No 23: they are perfect for honeymooners.

The hotel's excellent reputation stems not from the accommodation, good though it is, but from the wonderful cuisine which has earned it a loyal international clientele as well as many awards.

Currently a member of Relais & Châteaux and recently named as one of the world's most famous restaurants by Franklin Mint, guests can dine alfresco on one of the covered terraces or in one of the dining areas overlooking the gardens. Sitting out on the rattan chairs in the shade of the trees or on the hotel's sweeping veranda enjoying a pre-dinner drink is a wonderful experience.

LA CASA DE LA MARQUESA
(☎ 42-120092, fax 42-120098), Madero No 41, Centro Querataro, QRO 76000
Reservations: Small Luxury Hotels of the World toll free reservations numbers worldwide (see p12)
Getting there: Five minutes by taxi from Querataro
Accommodation: 25 suites
Amenities: Restaurant, bar, 24-hour room service; golf, horse-riding and a swimming pool are all available nearby
Dress code: Elegant casual
Weddings: The hotel can host weddings and receptions for up to 120 people
Minimum stay: None
Rates: Suites from US$126.50 to US$345 including continental breakfast
Credit cards: Most major
Taxes and service charge: Not included

LAS MANANITAS
(☎ 73-141466, fax 73-183672), Ricardo Linares 107, Apdo 1202, 62000 Cuernavaca, Mexico
Reservations: Relais & Châteaux reservations numbers worldwide (see p12)
Getting there: Mariano Matamoros Airport is 12km away
Accommodation: 20 suites and two twin-bedded rooms
Amenities: Swimming pool, tennis courts, restaurant, room service; plus golf nearby
Dress code: Casual
Weddings: Las Mananitas caters for wedding ceremonies for a maximum of 500 people and receptions for up to 1000 people
Minimum stay: Guests are required to stay Friday and Saturday at weekends
Rates: Suites from US$156 to US$270
Credit cards: American Express
Taxes and service charge: 5% service charge on rooms

THE COPPER CANYON

A great four-night, five-day tour into the heart of northern Mexico is the spectacular train ride from **Los Mochis** into the Copper Canyon at **Chihauhua**. The Copper Canyon is without doubt one of the most stunning sights in the world. Deeper and four times larger than the Grand Canyon, the 644 km railway line links the wild beauty of the **Tamahumara Range** with the Pacific coast.

Fly from Mexico City to Los Mochis and stay the night at the **Hotel Santa Anita** (☎ 681-57046, fax 681-20046), ready for the train's early departure the next day. The five-hour train journey takes you through a diversity of scenery from tropical forests, peach and apple orchards, and semi-arid plains to snow-covered mountain peaks and upland lakes. The best hotels to stay in are at **Divisidero**: they also have the best views of the canyon. Stay at the **Hotel Divisidero Barrancas** (☎ 14-103330, fax 14-156575) for at least two nights as there is lots of see and do in the area, all of which can be arranged by tour companies based in the town. Although this pretty pink hotel is not luxurious, it is simply and comfortably furnished and has one of the most wonderfully romantic locations set right on the edge of the canyon. Each of the 32 rooms in the two-storey building has a private terrace with staggering views.

Two trains run daily in each direction so, if you stop another night in Los Mochis on your way out, the whole trip will take you five days. **Balderrama Hotels and Tours** (☎ (681-57465, fax (681-20046), based in Los Mochis, are the best people for the Copper Canyon tour if you want to book direct. Alternatively you can book a four-night package through **Cox & Kings** (for US and UK offices see p10) which includes accommodation (four nights), the train both ways and flights from and to Mexico City for £485 per person.

DRC Rail Tours (US ☎ 713-659-7602 or toll free ☎ 800-659-7602), an American company, operates luxury tours into the Copper Canyon using restored vintage carriages known as the South Orient-Express. Trips range from three to nine days and start at around US$1000 per person.

PART 5: CENTRAL AMERICA

Belize
(BEST TIME: OCTOBER TO MAY)

Although not exactly what you'd call a classic honeymoon destination, the tropical rain forests, coral reefs, mountains, stunning offshore islands and Mayan culture of Belize cannot fail to fascinate visitors.

Belize is best suited to people looking for somewhere far off the tourist track, who are keen to visit the jungle and who don't mind sleeping in simple accommodation. But most of all you should be avid scuba divers because the best thing about Belize is the spectacular diving, particularly on the world's second largest barrier reef. If you're not enthusiastic divers then I would recommend you do your culture bashing and jungle treks elsewhere, as nearby Mexico has stacks of both, as well as some much classier hotels, with better food, for you to relax in.

The **Cayes** (pronounced 'keys'), the string of small islands along the reef where all the diving takes place, does have some good hotels with beach-front casitas, but don't expect the kind of luxury accommodation or service that you'd find in the nearby West Indies. Between the months of June and September the sand-flies can be so dreadful that they'd ruin your honeymoon – you have been warned!

The best places to stay are on **Ambergris Caye**, the biggest of the Cayes and home to hundreds of dive schools offering *the* most spectacular diving to be found anywhere in Belize. Don't go to Ambergris Caye expecting to find the true Belize as much of the island is owned and operated by North Americans. Regular ferry services operate to the island from **Belize City**: services depart from the pier in front of **Bellvue Hotel**, Monday to Friday 4pm, Saturday 1pm, no service Sunday, costs US$10. There are also frequent, daily flights from Belize City, plus direct flights from **Corozal** in the north of Belize if you're coming from Mexico.

For accommodation, try **Victoria House** (☎ 2-62067, fax 2-62429), PO Box 22, San Pedro, Ambergris Caye, which has the best reputation for consistent standards of all the island's hotels. This very elegant and comfortable beach-side hotel was where Harrison Ford chose to stay when he filmed *Mosquito Coast*. The beach cabanas are air-conditioned and look onto the hotel's private beach where there is a good selection of watersports. As one of the island's best hotels it tends to get booked up way in advance, so make your reservations early. Beach bungalows from US$145 without air-conditioning, or US$165 with air-conditioning, plus 17% tax. Victoria House can also be booked through the US office in New Orleans (US ☎ 504-865-0717).

Alternatively, **Ramon's Village Resort** (☎ 2-62071, fax 2-62214), San Pedro, Ambergris Caye, has a collection of beach cabanas which look very rustic from the outside, but are much more luxurious inside, with fans or air-conditioning, depending

BELIZE
Average maximum temperatures °C

JAN	FEB	MAR	APR	MAY	JUN	JUL	AUG	SEP	OCT	NOV	DEC
27	28	29	30	31	31	31	31	31	30	28	27

Approximate exchange rates: Belize dollar (BZ$) – US$1 = BZ$2.01
Time difference: GMT minus six hours
Voltage: 110v/220v AC, 60 Hz
Country dialling code: ☎ 501

how much you pay. There is a private beach, as well as a pool, bar and restaurant. Doubles from US$125 for a garden view to US$150 for beach-front cabanas, but if you book one of their three-day packages the rates are reduced to US$105 and US$125 respectively, plus 7% tax.

The best surviving examples of ancient Mayan culture are at **Altun Ha** and **Xunantunich**, deep in the jungle: exotic wildlife, like the native black howler monkey, is also common here. Most of the accommodation in the jungle is in very simple bed and breakfasts on locally-owned farms, but there are two more luxurious jungle lodges.

Chan Chich Lodge (☎ 2-75634, fax 2-76935, US toll free ☎ 1-800-343-8009), c/o 2 South Park Street, Belize City, is reached by a 30-minute charter flight from Belize City to **Gallon Jug**. This extraordinary hotel is set amidst the ruins of an ancient Mayan city in the **Rio Bravo Conservation Area**, located within 50,000 hectares of untouched rain forest. The owners had to get the government's permission to be allowed to build within the plaza of these classic protected ruins. This is paradise for nature lovers: you can see monkeys, all manner of exotic birds and other wildlife from your balcony; some guests have even been lucky enough to see a jaguar. The lodge has 12 thatched cottages made from local wood and tastefully decorated, each with its own en suite shower, two queen-sized beds, private porch and two hammocks. The hotel will organise wonderful archaeological tours as well as fabulous rides in the surrounding reserve, canoeing and river swimming. Doubles from US$110 plus 7% tax during the low season and US$130 during the high season.

The best place to stay in the forest reserve, near San Ignacio, is **Blancaneaux Lodge**, (☎ 92-3878, fax 92-3919, US toll free ☎ 1-800-PINE-RIDGE), Mountain Pine Ridge Road, Central Farm, PO Box B, Cayo District – Francis Ford Coppola's former mountain retreat. Although the lodge is very isolated and a pain to get to, the views over the river and waterfalls are stunning, the food is good and the accommodation pretty luxurious for Belize. Double cabanas from US$115 including breakfast in the low season and US$160 including breakfast in the high season, all rates plus 15% tax.

Guatemala
(BEST TIME: NOVEMBER TO APRIL)

Guatemala is the most typically Indian of the central American countries, and makes a truly fascinating side-trip from either Mexico, Belize or Costa Rica. With one of the largest indigenous populations in central America, Guatemala comprises over 100 different ethnic groups. What it lacks in beaches, Guatemala makes up for with its culture, history and spectacular scenery. Visit the **Western Highlands**, the centre of Indigena culture where each mountain village has its own traditional brightly coloured dress and you can shop in the bustling markets. The highlands, with their lakes and active volcanoes, are still home to the Mayan tribes whose ancestors settled there thousands of years ago.

GUATEMALA
Average maximum temperatures °C

JAN	FEB	MAR	APR	MAY	JUN	JUL	AUG	SEP	OCT	NOV	DEC
23	25	27	28	29	27	26	26	26	24	23	22

Approximate exchange rates: Queztal (Q) – US$1 = Q6.08
Time difference: GMT minus six hours
Voltage: 110v/220v AC, 60 Hz
Country dialling code: ☎ 502

Antigua, founded in 1543, is one of the most spectacular towns in Guatemala. It is the former cultural capital and is now considered a national historical site due to its splendid colonial mansions, palaces and churches. Set at the foot of a valley, with mountains and volcanoes towering over it on all sides, Antigua is still a wonderfully romantic and very relaxing place to walk. Stroll down the quiet cobbled streets and peer through the many large wooden doors which open to reveal inviting garden courtyards and strikingly elegant colonial architecture. Look out in particular for the main plaza and the cathedral, as well as Popenoe House, Capuchinas Convent and La Merced Monastery. The best place to stay is the **Hotel Casa Santo Domingo** (☎ 09-320140, fax 09-320102), 3 Calle Oriente No 28, Antigua, located in one of the city's oldest convents and set amidst formal gardens, with historic crumbling arches and fountains. Doubles from US$87.50 plus 20% tax.

Lake Atitlán, one of the world's most beautiful lakes, is only a couple of hours' drive north of Antigua up the pan-American highway. It is surrounded by three volcanoes, breathtaking mountain scenery and many Indian villages. The view across the lake is magical and there can be few places in the world more romantic at sunset. There are lots of interesting Indian villages in the area to be explored, such as **Santiago**, and it is possible to climb the 3000m **San Pedro** volcano in a few hours, with a local guide. **Hotel Atitlán** (☎/fax 962-1416), Panajachel, Guatemala, is the best of the lake-side hotels. It offers luxurious accommodation and extremely good facilities so you'll definitely want to stay there for a few days. The hotel, a three-storey flower-covered building, is set right on the edge of the lake a kilometre away from the main tourist village **Panajachel**. Colonial in ambience, the hotel's rooms are furnished in native style, with wooden-framed beds, wooden hand-carved tables and chairs, polished floors, and brightly coloured rugs, bed spreads and wall hangings. The gardens are a wonderful place in which to relax, but the hotel has its own private beach with all sorts of watersports such as boats, canoes and windsurfers, as well as a pretty swimming pool, fishing and tennis if you want to be active. It also has a shop, bar and restaurant. Doubles from US$88, suites from US$180, including tax.

Chichicastenango, or Chichi, as it is known, has a totally distinct character, due largely to its Mayan inhabitants and their traditional culture. Set on a steep hill, Chichi, with its quaint cobbled streets, is particularly famous for its wonderful market every Sunday and Thursday: it's a really great place to buy all sorts of local crafts from weavings to rugs and embroidered clothes. Everyone who goes to Guatemala goes to Chichi, so it's usually packed with tourists especially on market days, however it is still a must. The best place to stay in Chichi is the **Hotel Santo Tomás** (☎ 056-1061, fax 056-1306), 7 Av, 6-32, Chichicastenango. It has recently been converted from a colonial mansion and the rooms are set around a courtyard with an ornate fountain in the centre. The 43 rooms have good, though simple, facilities including an open fireplace and a private bath. Most of the rooms have a balcony with extensive views of the surrounding countryside. The hotel also has a good restaurant and bar, sauna and jacuzzi and swimming pool. Doubles from US$78 including tax.

Close to **Flores**, right in the heart of the Guatemalan jungle in the north of the country, is the lost city of **Tikal**. Tikal lay totally undiscovered for over a thousand years until 1848: it is the largest Mayan site to be discovered and its ruins and scenery are really impressive. From Flores, you can easily arrange jungle tours with a private local guide: you can go on the rivers or on horse-back. The best way to get to Tikal is to fly to Flores from Guatemala City, and from Tikal it is easy to cross the border into Belize. A honeymoon combining a week or so touring in Guatemala, taking in Antigua, Lake Atitlan, Chichi, and Tikal, and then going on to Belize for a few days' diving from Ambergris Caye would be wonderful, but would only suit very ambitious and adventurous travellers. Alternatively you could fly from Flores to Cancún for some sun on the beach. The **Camino Real** (☎ 2-334633, fax 2-374313, UK ☎ 0800-282565,

US and Canada ☎ 1-800-228-3000), Lote 77, San José, Péten, Guatemala, is the best place to stay while visiting the ruins, although it is about an hour's drive away: being situated halfway between the ruins and Flores. Because the hotels at the ruins aren't so good, it's well worth the effort. This new hotel was built using traditional fabrics and methods, so the thatched bungalows blend sympathetically with their jungle surroundings. Set on the shores of **Lake Petén Itzá**, the hotel has 120 comfortable rooms with marvellous views across the lake. Each has air-conditioning, phone, cable television, minibar, and private bathroom. Double rooms cost from US$110 plus 20% tax.

Costa Rica
(BEST TIME: DECEMBER TO APRIL)

After Mexico, Costa Rica is the Central American country most suited to honeymoons. You'd both have to have a thirst for adventure, but there are some truly idyllic beach resorts and plenty of opportunity to see some of the wonders of the jungle and its abundant wildlife.

A honeymoon in Costa Rica is all about beautiful scenery and eco-tourism. There's no real Indian culture, no markets and no impressive colonial buildings to speak of but the landscape is so dramatic that you'll be truly swept away. The natural beauty of Costa Rica is world renowned; you'll see it all here, cloud forest, rain forest, iguanas, sloths, extraordinary birds and hundreds of brilliant and rare butterflies.

Rich it indeed is, but not in the way it was originally anticipated. The country got its name from Columbus, who, when he landed in 1502, believed the area was full of gold and named it Costa Rica, meaning rich coast. Now a haven of peace and tranquillity in the middle of Central America, sandwiched between volatile Nicaragua to the north and equally chaotic Panama to the south, Costa Rica has somehow managed to escape the political and social unrest of its neighbours.

Although it is very possible to combine Costa Rica with other Central American countries, such as Mexico, there is so much to see and do here and travelling around is so easy, that I'd recommend spending two weeks in just this one country alone.

Costa Rica was a fabulous place. Don't go expecting the beaches to be the kind that you find in resorts – all manicured and perfect with lots of comfy bed chairs – because they are all natural, windswept and misty from the jungle, which we loved. Make sure you hire a car as half the excitement was driving around on our own.
Victoria and Piers Hankinson

COSTA RICA
Perfect for adventurous couples who are keen on wildlife, the jungle and idyllic beach resorts and who also like being far away from other honeymooners
When to go: December to April
Average maximum temperatures °C

JAN	FEB	MAR	APR	MAY	JUN	JUL	AUG	SEP	OCT	NOV	DEC
24	24	26	27	27	27	26	26	27	26	25	24

Capital: San José
Flight times: to Juan San José from:
New York: (via Miami) 6 hours
LA (via Miami): $7^3/_4$ hours
London: (via Miami) $9^1/_2$ hours
Sydney: (via LA) 20 hours
Approximate exchange rates: Colón (C) – £1 = C330.41, US$1 = C213.03, A$1 = C168.34
Time difference: GMT minus six hours
Voltage: 110v AC
Combine with: It's best to concentrate on Costa Rica alone
Country dialling code: ☎ 506

SAN JOSE

There's very little point in staying in San José, as the city is a bit of a dump but only 15 minutes away is one of Costa Rica's most perfect romantic hideaways, Finca Rosa Blanca.

Finca Rosa Blanca

Finca Rosa Blanca is a real treat. Without doubt one of the most individual hotels in Central America it makes a wonderful place to unwind and relax at the start or end of your holiday.

The Finca is as extraordinary from the outside as it is within. Looking up at the turreted white building from below it looks a pretty strange shape – an intriguing combination of traditional Hispanic ranch house with two levels and white walls and something not unlike a lighthouse tower in the middle. This is a pretty odd description but it's hard to put this unique building into words, and if I've made it sound ugly I've done it a vast injustice because it's not at all.

Because of its unusual architectural design the Finca is the most incredible building inside with irregularly-shaped glass windows letting light in on every side. In the middle of the house you come into a central foyer with a circular seat and lots of lush green foliage and various interesting artefacts displayed about you. This is used as the hotel lounge and there is an honesty bar for guests.

Each of the eight guest rooms in this small, family owned inn is furnished differently or, as the owners like to put it, 'each has its own name and personality'. The **Rosa Blanca Suite**, in particular, is out of this world with a huge sunken bath painted turquoise, surrounded by stone flagging and ornate murals of jungle scenes on the walls and light streaming in from an adjacent window looking out on to the gardens. There's even a separate shower painted in bright tones of aqua, turquoise and royal blue. It's not only the sunken bath that has helped this room to work its way into the pages of glossy magazines all over the world: up an amazing spiral staircase is the bedroom where lace covers the bed and windows open out onto balconies on all sides. The entire room is incredible.

Meals are expensive but good: they are taken with the finca's other guests around a large central wooden table which seats about 20 people. Guests spend their days either by the lovely oval swimming pool which appears to flow seamlessly into the coffee plantation below, or out on day tours to the **Braulio Carillo National Park Cloud Forest**, **Barva**, **Poás** and **Irazú** volcanoes, coffee plantations and butterfly farms. If you are thinking about Costa Rica do make a point of fitting in a couple of days at the Finca Rosa Blanca either at the beginning or the end of your trip as it's a wonderfully friendly little hotel and the bedrooms are quite an experience.

> **FINCA ROSA BLANCA**
> (☎ 269 9392, fax 269 9555), Apdo 41-3009, Santa Barbara de Heredia, Costa Rica
> **Reservations**: Through UK tour operator Worldwide Journeys and Expeditions (UK ☎ 0171-381 8638)
> **Getting there**: The hotel can arrange transfers
> **Accommodation**: Eight rooms, standard to suite
> **Amenities**: Swimming pool with cascades, library, horses, three hectare fruit orchard
> **Dress code**: Casual
> **Weddings**: Can be arranged, with a maximum of 50 guests
> **Minimum stay**: None
> **Rates**: Doubles from US$135
> **Credit cards:** American Express, Visa, MasterCard
> **Taxes and service charge**: 18.45% on lodging and breakfast

> *At **Finca Rosa Blanca** our only complaint was with the food which we felt was a bit of a rip off, although it was good – sort of middle of the road French with local bits and pieces like the gallo pinto, a traditional dish of black beans, rice and onion, which we had for breakfast. Otherwise it was a very quiet, very relaxed and a very friendly hotel and was quite unusually decorated.* **Moyra and Alastair Murdoch**

Lapa Rios

Lapa Rios is the best jungle lodge in Costa Rica, and it offers first-rate accommodation, service and dining, among primary and advanced secondary forest 90m above sea level. Wherever you stand at Lapa Rios the views of the **Golfo Dulce Forest Reserve** are absolutely magnificent. The 400 hectare property was the brainchild of John and Karen Lewis from Minnesota; they decided to build the luxury lodge to help finance rain forest conservation.

The first-class facilities have been built in total harmony with their natural habitat, incorporating local woods, bamboo and thatch roofing over zinc and white concrete to create typical palenque-style cottages. The Lewises have kept the buildings as open as possible, so although the cottages have bamboo roll-down shades, the 'walls' are actually just screens, and the aspect has been designed carefully so that the cottages are completely private. You do get insects in your room but that's the price you pay for this kind of jungle experience and there are mosquito nets for protection.

In the main lodge there are bamboo settees with pillows in vivid jungle prints, and bamboo and smoked glass tables in the dining-room, where the food is quite good. The focal point of the dining-room is the somewhat adventurous addition of a spiral wooden staircase which winds up three storeys and out on to a roof-top walkway affording a breathtaking 360° view above the forest canopy and out to the ocean beyond. After dinner everyone goes straight to their rooms, so don't come here expecting any kind of evening entertainment or late night drinking. The 14 thatched cottages at Lapa Rios are really comfortable and airy, with two double beds in each, covered in lovely white and green striped cotton sheets and prettily draped mosquito nets. Particularly nice touches are the screened windows in the en suite shower room giving the illusion of bathing outdoors with the most incredible views of the gulf, and the second shower outside in your private garden where there really is nothing between you and the view! The bedrooms have ample towels, white blankets in case it gets chilly at night, electric ceiling fans, kerosene lamps for power cuts, and heavy tropical vanity units, closets, bamboo easy chairs and a writing desk. Each bungalow has an ocean view, private deck and patio garden.

Lapa Rios, part of the Golfo Dolce Forest Reserve, has many private, uncrowded trails for guests to explore. You can go with guides who are trained to point out the remarkable wildlife – make sure you do the walk to the large waterfalls. The hotel also offers horse-riding, kayaking, game fishing and a huge sandy beach to stroll along, but do watch out as their activities can be a bit pricey.

> **LAPA RIOS**
> (☎ 735-5130, fax 735-5179), Box 100, Pto Jimenez, Costa Rica
> **Reservations**: Either direct or through UK tour operators Worldwide Journeys and Expeditions (☎ UK 0171-381 8638) and Cox & Kings (see p10)
> **Getting there**: Via charter flight or the domestic airline, Travel Air, to Puerto Jimenez, from where Lapa Rios is a 40-minute journey in the owners' four-wheel drive
> **Accommodation:** 14 thatched bungalows
> **Amenities**: Restaurant and bar; uncrowded jungle trails accompanied by naturalist guides; riding; kayaking; game fishing; surfing; boat tours of Golfo Dulce; swimming pool and poolside bar service
> **Dress code**: Informal
> **Weddings**: Weddings and receptions can be held here but they require a minimum of 20 and a maximum of 78 guests
> **Minimum stay**: Two nights
> **Rates**: Bungalows cost US$159, plus US$52.50 full board
> **Credit cards**: American Express, Visa and MasterCard
> **Taxes and service charge**: 18.45% room tax

PACIFIC COAST

At one point the Pacific and the Atlantic coasts are only 113km apart, but they couldn't be more different. The Pacific coast consists of long deserted beaches, while the

(Opposite): Hotel Salto Chico enjoys the most spectacular location amongst the Patagonian wilderness of Torres del Paine, Argentina (see p222). Facilities include an outdoor jacuzzi.

Atlantic side is wind-lashed with roaring surf, so head south if it's beaches you are after. The province of **Guanacaste** boasts some of the most exotic and idyllic beaches in Central America. Although this coastline is more heavily developed there are still some long stretches of unspoilt sandy beaches with a few really great hotels which are perfect for recharging your batteries before you do some serious touring.

Hotel Villa Caletas

Hotel Villa Caletas is located up in the hills, 457m above sea level with magnificent views over the **Gulf of Nicoya**. One of the most romantic hotels in Costa Rica, the Villa Caletas is an unusual combination of coastal, mountain and tropical resort. As you lie beside the wonderful swimming pool which appears to be spilling out over the horizon you can detect the sea breezes mingling with the mountain air.

Set in six hectares of land near **Jacó** high above the Pacific Ocean the hotel is just 68km from Santamaria International Airport in Costa Rica's capital, San José. The 360° panoramic views look out on the **Nicoya Peninsula**, gulf islands, the crescent beaches of Jacó, **Herradura** and **Punta Leona** as well as the mountains.

The hotel's design was influenced by French colonial architecture and the Victorian homes still found in San José. The eight guest rooms and 20 villas are painted in bright colours such as yellows, oranges and green, and all come with a private terrace or balcony. The double rooms have either queen-sized or twin beds, ceiling fans and a private bathroom with hot and cold water, while the villas also have a good sized living-room and all have queen-sized beds.

The airy restaurant and bar where international cuisine is served also have incredible views. The hotel staff are more than happy to arrange transportation to any of the nearby beaches for you, as well as trips to volcanoes, Tortuga Island or activities such as horse-riding and sailing.

HOTEL VILLA CALETAS
(c/o ☎ 257 3653, fax 222 2059), PO Box 12358-1000, San Jose, Costa Rica
Reservations: Through tour operator Cox & Kings (see p10)
Getting there: The hotel can arrange transfers from San José Airport costing US$90 one way per couple
Accommodation: Eight double rooms, 17 villas, two junior suites and one master suite
Amenities: 74 sq m swimming pool, bar-terrace, two restaurants, cellular phones, security deposit boxes, laundry, towels for the swimming pool, tour desk, transfers to Caletas beach, plus horse-riding, scooter and bicycle hire, seadoos, water-skiing, boating, fishing, island hopping, scuba diving and snorkelling all arranged nearby
Dress code: Casual
Weddings: Can be arranged
Minimum stay: None
Rates: Double rooms from US$115; villas from US$136; suites from US$163
Credit cards: Visa, MasterCard, American Express
Taxes and service charge: 3.3% ICT (tourism) tax and 10% sales tax not included

Other recommended hotels

Hotel Capitan Suizo (☎/fax 680-0853) Playa Tamarindo, is regarded as one of the best of Costa Rica's beach hotels. This very friendly informal hotel enjoys a prime beach location in the Province of Guanacaste which is a great area with lots to do. The hotel has eight bungalows and 22 rooms, all of which have been carefully decorated by its Swiss owners. Every room has an ocean view, a terrace or a balcony, and a white tiled en suite bathroom. This isn't a really luxurious beach resort, so don't come here expecting Four Seasons pampering or facilities, but if you are looking for a small hotel with a relaxed atmosphere and simple but comfortable accommodation this will suit you well. The large free-form swimming pool is a great place to spend quiet days engrossed in good books, punctuated by walks along the beach and a cold beer with lunch at the poolside restaurant and bar. Although there are some other wonderful

(Opposite) Top: Château Lake Louise, Canada (see p170). **Bottom:** The Post Ranch Inn, USA (see p175)

hotels in Costa Rica, perched up on the headland looking down over the sea with amazing views, if you want to be actually on the beach this is the best option. The hotel will also arrange to collect you from Tamarindo Airport. Doubles from US$88 without air-conditioning, US$99 with air-conditioning and US$113 for the bungalows (which don't have air-conditioning). All rates include taxes.

In contrast, if you do like your hotels to have a bigger, more resort feel about them opt for **El Parador Hotel and Beach Club** (☎ 777 1411, fax 777 1437), Punta Quepos, which is located amid a 161-hectare densely forested peninsula just 4km from the entrance to **Manuel Antonio National Park**. This region boasts some of the most spectacular wildlife imaginable: you might see three-toe sloths, whiteface spider and howler monkeys, sea turtles, squirrel monkeys and many other of the 109 species of mammals living in the area. The beaches are bordered by evergreen forest and on the north side of the peninsula is a cove about 305m deep. The hotel itself is Spanish colonial in style featuring oak beams, Spanish roof tiles, white stucco and many Spanish artefacts inside. All the rooms have private terraces, king-sized beds, TV and air-conditioning. Doubles from US$105.18, suites from US$176.16.

A FEW THINGS TO SEE AND DO IN COSTA RICA

The **Tortuguero National Park** in the north of Costa Rica, on its Caribbean coast, is particularly spectacular and worth visiting for its animal life. Flat bottom boats will skim you along the twisting labyrinth of canals and creeks, where the dense jungle hangs down over the water's edge and your guide will slow down to point out small alligators, birds, monkeys and huge butterflies in the trees.

Tortuguero is famous for its enormous turtles, and is the place to see them dragging themselves laboriously up the beach to dig pits in which to lay their eggs, before covering them up and returning to the sea again, exhausted.

There are lots of basic jungle lodges offering accommodation in Tortuguero, try the *Rio Parismina Lodge* (☎ 222 6633) which is simple, but comfortable. The Lodge offers two-day/one-night packages which include a tour of the Tortuguero Park, a walking tour near the lodge and all meals and transfers for US$169 per person including tax.

Another wonderfully romantic place to visit in Costa Rica is **Arenal**, home to both **Lake Arenal** and **Volcano Arenal**. The live volcano last erupted in 1968 but it still rumbles and billows smoke today: though the proliferation of bubbling geysers and mud pools in the vicinity means it is unlikely to blast ever again. At night, the views of the volcano are mesmerising, as small bursts of fiery red lava erupt, pushing incandescent material down the sides of the volcano. A visit to the nearby hot mineral springs at **Tabacon** is highly recommended, allowing you to lie back in the pool's warm waters at night and watch the spitting volcano.

From the *Tilajari Hotel* (☎ 469 9091, fax 469 9095), PO Box 81-4400, Ciudad Quesada, you'll see all sorts of wildlife, and can easily take day trips to the volcano 35 minutes away.

Guests often see crocodiles, giant iguanas and a broad diversity of birdlife from the hotel, and because there's so much to do in the area it's probably worth staying for a few nights. Only 113km from the capital, Tilajari is found in the lush landscape of the **San Carlos** valley. The hotel is set in 12 hectares of magnificent gardens in Costa Rica's most famous eco-system. The 56 rooms and four family suites are well furnished and have air-conditioning. Tilajari has two swimming pools, three floodlit tennis courts, two racquetball courts, a games room with billiards and table tennis, a sauna, gift shop, bar and restaurant. The hotel also organises fishing on Lake Arenal for rainbow bass, and guests can easily visit nearby waterfalls and soak in the hot mineral springs at Tabacon. Doubles from US$71.07, suites from US$88.83 including taxes.

En route for the Pacific coast from Arenal, you'll pass through **Monteverde**, one of the world's most famous cloud forests, with its own micro-climate. A biological reserve since a US conservationist saved it from logging in the 1970s, Monteverde is now Costa Rica's top tourist spot. Despite the abundance of gringos, it is still definitely worth seeing for the jungle experience, the views and the wildlife. Trails lead through dense forest where trees covered in orchids fight for space against a multitude of tropical plants. Sloths hang from branches and monkeys leap from tree to tree high above your head.

Stay at the *Belmar Lodge* (☎ 645 5201, fax 645 5135) Monteverde, Puntarenas, which is a beautiful wooden chalet nestled in the mountains adjacent to the Monteverde Cloud Forest Reserve. All the 34 rooms have private bath with hot and cold water and a balcony with fantastic views. Double rooms cost US$60 plus tax.

PART 6: SOUTH AMERICA

Venezuela
(BEST TIME: ALL YEAR ROUND)

Venezuela, quite simply, has everything: a beautiful and unspoilt Caribbean coastline; the power of the **Angel Falls**; the timeless majesty of the snow-capped **Andes**; the wide open spaces of the **Llanos**; and vast areas of dense Amazonian rain forest.

Although undeniably spectacular, a honeymoon in Venezuela won't suit everyone, but it will lure those who have had enough of lying on beaches and want to start married life by experiencing something new and exciting together.

My only real tip if you do choose Venezuela is not to do too much. Spend a good four days on the coast either at the start or end of your holiday so that you can unwind, go to **Canaima** to see the Falls and choose just one other destination, especially if you've only got two weeks – there's nothing worse than trying to fit too much in and just getting more and more tired, especially as you are likely to start off pretty exhausted in the first place. If you love it that much you can always go back another time.

With this in mind I have picked **Villa Mangrovia** on the coast as it is absolutely heavenly, **Hacienda Guataparo** which is a lovely farm just outside **Valencia**, not far from **Caracas**, and given you information on what to expect from Canaima and **Merida**. In Canaima the only accommodation is at **Hoturvensa Camp** which, luckily, is fine. The best way to find somewhere good to stay in Merida is to ask your travel agent or the Venezuelan Tourist Board at the time of booking, particularly as the quality of accommodation changes so rapidly. If you want to stay on a working Venezuelan ranch, **Hato Pinero**, high in the Llanos, is fabulous.

VENEZUELA

A excellent starting point to explore the grandeur and beauty of South America as it has just about everything: jungle, stunning coast, Andean mountains and the world's highest waterfall

When to go: The climate is fairly constant throughout the year, although it varies with altitude; to see the Falls at their best you have to go between July and September

Average maximum temperatures °C (Caracas)

JAN	FEB	MAR	APR	MAY	JUN	JUL	AUG	SEP	OCT	NOV	DEC
26	26	28	28	28	27	26	27	27	25	27	26

Capital: Caracas

Flight times: to Caracas from:
New York: (via Miami) 5 hours
LA: 9 hours
London: 12 hours
Sydney: (via LA and Miami) 22 hours

Approximate exchange rates: Bolivar (B) – £1 = B738, US$1 = B475.82, A$1 – B376.01

Time difference: GMT minus four hours

Voltage: 110v, 60 cycles AC is used all over the country, US-type flat two-pin plugs

Combine with: Miami, Trinidad/Tobago, but there's so much to see in Venezuela that you'll probably want to concentrate your time there

Country dialling code: ☎ 58

THE CARIBBEAN COAST
Villa Mangrovia

The Villa Mangrovia is the perfect place to get away from it all. The villa is located in the **Morrocoy National Park** high up above the mangrove trees. The park is a

VILLA MANGROVIA
Parque Nacional Morrocoy, Estado Falcon, Venezuela
Reservations: As contact with the villa is only by local radio you have to book through UK tour operator Last Frontiers (UK ☎ 01844-208405, fax 01844-201400, e-mail: travelinfo@lastfrontiers.co.uk)
Getting there: Four hours from Caracas by car, about US$150 by private transfer
Accommodation: Three double rooms: two with twin beds, one with a double bed
Amenities: All meals provided on the villa's veranda, trips to neighbouring islands and beaches, and to the river Yaracuy, scuba diving can be arranged
Dress code: Informal
Weddings: No
Minimum stay: None
Rates: US$95 per person per night including full board, drinks and all trips; or US$491 per person for a four-day/three-night package through Last Frontiers including transfers
Credit cards: Most major
Taxes and service charge: Included

collection of sand-fringed islands and mangrove swamps about four hours' drive west of Caracas.

The villa is the home of Irina Jackson who, because she takes only six guests in at any one time, will make you feel more like house guests than hotel visitors. This is a really magical place to spend a few days: the white sand, palm trees and turquoise water provide the ideal environment for utter relaxation. If you want to spend some time on the coast during your trip to Venezuela this is the place to do it, not at **Margarita** which is full of high rise hotels.

The best cabin to request is the one set on its own in the villa's garden: it is the only one out of the three with a double bed. The two double rooms in the villa have twin beds.

Don't expect luxurious accommodation or even air-conditioning or hot water. Villa Mangrovia doesn't have any of these things and in my mind is better for it: the rooms are simple but comfortably furnished, you won't need hot water, the ceiling fans are quite adequate and the excellent food and really personal service are far more important than a minibar, gold taps and marble bathrooms. Villa Mangrovia is unique in Venezuela and is the perfect place to start or finish your honeymoon.

All six guests have their breakfast on the veranda of Irina's elegant white-washed house. Then each couple is taken by the boatman to one of the beautiful nearby islands with their Caribbean-style beaches. Guests are provided with a delicious picnic, a hammock and snorkelling equipment. This is the key to Villa Mangrovia, and what makes it such a special place to stay. While **Margarita Island** attracts people looking for big resort hotels, Villa Mangrovia is the perfect alternative for couples who long to be alone on their own private Caribbean retreat.

Everything is included in the price at Villa Mangrovia, from the beers with your lunch-time picnic to all your meals and drinks at the Villa, and the island trips. Irina can also arrange, at extra cost, excursions to local sites of interest such as the river **Yaracuy** and local farms for bird-watching, or scuba diving at the **Tucacas NAUI-approved Centre** where the dives on the coral reef are marvellous.

Hacienda Guataparo

This lovely old colonial house with its traditional terracotta tiled roof and white walls, is just outside Valencia. Situated in its own valley the Hacienda is a tranquil place to base yourself for a few days.

All around the house are mature gardens with lovely places to sit and read a book or take a gentle afternoon stroll. There is also an amazing outdoor spring-water swimming pool with a grassy bank on one side and terracotta tiles on the other. Meals are served around a large outside table when the weather is warm enough and are often cooked on a barbecue.

You can either spend your days doing very little and relaxing into the rhythm of this serene place, or take advantage of the unlimited horse-riding available and explore

TWO WEEKS IN VENEZUELA

The best way to see Venezuela is to spend a night in **Caracas** on arrival: if you want to go into town stay at *Hotel Avila* (☎ 2-515128, fax 2-523021), Áv Washington, San Bernadino, Caracas 1011. Doubles from US$80 per night. Alternatively stay out at the coast by the airport in *Hotel Meliá Caribe* (☎ 31-945555, fax 31-941509) Caraballeda, Caracas, which has comfortable rooms and saves you the hassle of going into Caracas. Doubles from US$95 including tax.

Caracas is the kind of hot, smelly, bustling city that epitomises South America and although it has an intriguing mix of Latin and American influences with some amazing cathedrals, plazas, museums and botanical gardens, it is not worth spending much time there if you only have a couple of weeks.

Most people then fly straight into the jungle at **Canaima**, close to the **Angel Falls**, the world's highest waterfall dropping a staggering 979m. The only accommodation is at *Hoturvensa Camp* in individual grass-thatched cabins built on white sand overlooking the lagoon. The falls must be seen during the wet season, so only go between July and September. The hotel's location is outstanding, overlooking the lagoon as the Carrao river plunges over a series of falls right in front of you. The only access to Canaima is by air with Avensa, one of Venezuela's national airlines. The airline also owns the hotel so prices tend to be pretty high. If you are booking from the UK, specialist Venezuelan tour operator Last Frontiers (UK ☎ 01844-208405) offers three-day, two-night packages including all meals, internal flights, a fly past of the Angel Falls in an ageing Douglas DC3 and short trips around the lagoon for around US$545 per person. If you book the trip direct with Avensa it will cost you about US$724 for two nights per couple: this is without flights the cost of which are rising all the time but are currently about US$200 each.

Canaima is also a great place to explore the rain forest with local guides who will take you on short walks through the dense jungle to rivers full of natural swimming holes. Alternatively do one of the day-long canoe trips. The local tours can be arranged when you get there through tour companies operating out of Canaima.

Sierra Nevada de Mérida, 1600m up in the snow-clad Andes, is one of Venezuela's most popular destinations. The best way to explore the region is to either hire a car or fly in from Caracas. Due to the altitude, Mérida is a welcome cool retreat from the heat of the jungle or the coast and is a fabulous place if you enjoy walking. The mountain scenery is just fantastic: look out for the frailejon, an indigenous flower, as you walk through the dense pine forests to dark lagoons. One of the key attractions of Mérida is the famous **Teleférico**, the world's highest and longest cable car which spans 12km and climbs 4765m taking you rapidly from banana trees to snow-capped mountain peaks.

You can **fish** in the deep blue lakes or discover the more remote and interesting villages high up in the mountains, accessible only by mule. If you fancy **trekking**, talk to Rowena Hill or Andreas Fajardo at Torcaza Trails (☎/fax 74-445694) who are based in Mérida and can organise all kinds of tours. One trip takes you across a spectacular river gorge up to the high páramo with its hardy shrubs and brightly coloured flowers, and down a long ride through the cloud forest to the plains near Barinas. The best places to stay in Mérida are the local guest houses offering bed and breakfast for around US$40. However, the standards change rapidly so it's best to check which one is currently in favour with a local tour operator once you arrive in Venezuela. On the winding road down to the east stay at *Hotel Los Friales* Santo Domingo, Estado Mérida, a converted 17th century monastery which for US$58 per room is a mere snip for one of the most beautiful locations in the Andes. The hotel's service can be a little patchy, so don't go expecting Four Seasons' treatment, but it is a wonderful place to stay. There is no telephone or fax but bookings can be made through UK-based Last Frontiers (UK ☎ 01844-208405).

Enter **Los Llanos** and you will find a completely different landscape. Instead of mountains there are mesas (flat-topped hills) and an abundance of wildlife. This open, flat savannah land is a perfect haven for ornithologists with over 340 different bird species and frequent sightings of such exotic birdlife as big white and grey herons, pink spoonbill ibis and fire red scarlet ibis, as well as a great number of wild horses, cattle and deer.

The best known and best loved of the Venezuelan ranches is *Hato Pinero* (☎ 2-916965, fax 2-916776), El Baúl, Estado Cojedes, a fabulous estate in the 'high' Llanos. Rates start at US$240 per room plus 16.5% tax which includes all meals, an open bar, twice-daily guided excursions and land transfers from Caracas. Last Frontiers in the UK (UK ☎ 01844-208405) also does four-day/three-night packages to Hato Pinero costing US$693 in the low season and US$845 in the high season, including transfers from Caracas (five hours).

HACIENDA GUATAPARO
☎ 41-235314, fax 41-239919), Centro Comercial Guaparo, Valencia, Estado Carabobo, Venezuela
Reservations: Either direct or through UK tour operator Last Frontiers (UK ☎ 01844-208405, fax 01844-201400, email: travelinfo@lastfrontiers.co.uk)
Getting there: The Hacienda is 15 minutes from Valencia which is two hours from Caracas by private road transfer
Accommodation: Three double rooms
Amenities: Horse-riding, mountain bikes
Dress code: Casual
Weddings: No
Minimum stay: None
Rates: US$100 per person per night including full board, drinks and all activities; or US$490 per person for a three night package through Last Frontiers
Credit cards: Most major
Taxes and service charge: Included

the gorgeous surrounding countryside either on your own, if you are experienced enough, or with a guide. There are also mountain bikes.

This lovely private house has only three guest rooms so it's quite likely that you'll have the run of the place to yourselves: you are very much encouraged to treat the house as your own. The rooms are traditionally furnished with cane furniture, paintings by local artists and wonderful features such as cow-hide rugs on the floor. It's worth noting that there is only one bathroom to be shared between the three rooms but as the house is rarely full it doesn't present too many problems and is definitely a worthwhile sacrifice for being a guest in such a peaceful place.

Ecuador
(BEST TIME: ALL YEAR ROUND)

A visit to Ecuador isn't complete without a cruise round the **Galapagos Islands**, famous for their incredible wildlife, or a stay in some of Ecuador's beautiful haciendas (privately-owned homes) which have now opened their doors to visitors. A very easy itinerary for a fabulous two-week honeymoon would be to spend one week on a boat in the Galapagos and another week relaxing in Ecuador's famously beautiful Andean countryside visiting the various local markets and walking in the Andes.

ECUADOR
Average maximum temperatures °C (Galapagos Islands)

JAN	FEB	MAR	APR	MAY	JUN	JUL	AUG	SEP	OCT	NOV	DEC
31	32	32	32	30	29	27	26	26	27	28	29

Approximate exchange rates: Sucre (S) – £1 = S5118, US$1 = S3299.81, A$1 = S2607.63
Time difference: GMT minus five hours
Voltage: 110v/220v AC
Country dialling code: ☎ 593

THE GALAPAGOS ISLANDS
Although discovered by the Spanish Bishop of Panama in 1535 while on an exploratory mission for the King of Spain, the Galapagos Islands were only really brought to the world's attention three centuries later when, in 1859, Charles Darwin published his famous tome, *Origin of Species* following a five-week exploration of these fascinating islands on HMS *Beagle*. Today, the Galapagos islands are still worth discovering and remain very much a living laboratory of evolution where birds and animals live without fear of man. Anyone remotely interested in animals, ecology or natural history will be impressed by these graceful islands where blue and red-footed boobies, flight-

less cormorants, playful sealions, land and sea iguanas, and giant tortoises roam freely.

The best way to experience the 13 major islands and the dozens of smaller islets is by boat. The boats travel at night in order to maximise the area covered. December to April is the best time of year to go because the water is pleasantly warm and the sea is at its calmest. The only problem with this is that you miss the celebrated albatrosses, who usually arrive in the islands in April and can be seen at their best, during courtship, in June.

Quasar Náutica, UK (☎ 01962-779317, fax 01962-779458) and US (☎ 305-599 9008, fax 305-592 7060), have a fleet of six boats (yachts and motor cruisers) ranging from 17m to 38m in length. Two of their boats, *Mistral* and *Lammer Law*, have diving equipment. Seven nights in a cabin with en suite facilities on the *Lammer Law*, a 28m motorsailer trimaran, will set you back US$2200 in high season (November to May) per person and US$2000 in low season, including all meals. On top of this you have to add your flights from Quito which currently cost US$378 (high season), the National Park entry fee of US$80 payable in cash on arrival, tips for the staff on your boat which can be as high as US$100 and Municipal Ports Tax when you land in Baltra (US$12) or at San Cristóbal (US$30). These islands don't come cheap but they really are a holiday of a lifetime.

Alternatively there are a number of UK-based tour operators who offer packages to the Galapagos. **Worldwide Journeys and Expeditions** does an 11-day trip on *Beagle III*, a lovely boat with really good sheltered outside seating (which is absolutely crucial) but without en suite facilities, for US$3408/£2200 per person including all flights, stopovers in Quito, transfers, accommodation and meals on *Beagle III*. Tour operators **Abercrombie & Kent**, **Cox & Kings** and **Last Frontiers** also operate in the Galapagos (see p10).

Although some companies offer three or four-day cruises I've never met anyone who regretted going for the whole week. It is also possible to go on a two-week cruise, allowing you to cruise between **Isabela** and **Fernandina** which are grander and much more beautiful than the comparatively austere islands you visit in the first week: the only problem is that you may not want to spend two weeks of your honeymoon cooped up on a boat with strangers!

STAYING IN HACIENDAS

Some of these haciendas continue to operate as farms or mills while others have abandoned their original raison d'être in order to focus on tourism. You can either book the haciendas direct or through **Metropolitan Touring** in Quito (Ecuador ☎ 02-464780, fax 02-464702). If you choose the latter I suggest you fax them your dates of arrival and needs and ask them for a brochure and some sample prices. They can also suggest combinations of properties to enable you to experience different types of haciendas in different areas of Ecuador.

One of the loveliest of these country retreats is **Hacienda Cusin** (☎ 06-918 013, fax 06-918 003), San Pablo del Lago, Imbabura, Ecuador. It was originally built in the 1600s but was carefully renovated in 1990 to retain the old charm. Guests are accommodated in either the main building, the garden rooms or the Monasterio where an additional 14 guest rooms have recently been built in the same style as the house. The Monasterio is a five-minute walk from the house through the gardens. All the rooms have private bathrooms (some with baths), lovely garden or mountain views, and are furnished with antiques and local art and artefacts. In addition, many have open fireplaces. They are not big on in-room facilities, but this is part of the feel of staying in a hacienda. There is loads to do including 15 spectacular valley walks, hill and mountain climbs for which you can take a guide (or a picnic!), 14 horses for guest use, eight mountain bikes, a four-wheel drive vehicle for local touring and several hundred books. Guests are required to stay a minimum of two nights and double rooms start at

US$80 for the room, or US$160 for all-inclusive. The Hacienda Cusin can be booked from the UK through either Cox & Kings (UK ☎ 0171-873 5000, fax 0171-630 6038) or Worldwide Journeys and Expeditions (UK ☎ 0171-381 8638, fax 0171-381 0836) or Last Frontiers (UK ☎ 01844-208405, fax 01844-201400), and from the US through Andean Treks (US ☎ 1-617-924-1974, fax 1-617-924 2158 or toll free 800-683 8148) or through Cox & Kings (US ☎ 212-935-3935, fax 212-935 3863, toll free ☎ 0800-999-1758).

Peru
(BEST TIME: JUNE TO SEPTEMBER)

Along with the Pyramids and the Taj Mahal, Machu Picchu is one of those magical places that many people long to visit once in their life. Somehow the very name Machu Picchu, and indeed Peru itself, is synonymous with mystery and romance.

CUSCO AND MACHU PICCHU

This lost Inca citadel was discovered only in 1911 by the American explorer, Hiram Bingham, and is undoubtedly the best known and most incredible archaeological site on the continent. Very little is actually known about the origins of Machu Picchu, but from the buildings' scale and ornamentation it is clear that it held some very significant ceremonial value.

Although **Hotel Ruinas de Machu Picchu** (Peru ☎ 014-287815 or 014-428696) may not be the most luxurious in the world there are few more dramatic locations from where to experience sunrise and sunset. What's more you can now start and end your stay at **Hotel Monasterio del Cuzco** (Peru ☎ 014- 408043), a converted 17th century monastery built on the remains of a pre-Columbian royal palace. It has only just reopened after an extensive overhaul and is now one of the most splendid colonial hotels in South America. A five-day tour starting and ending with a night in **Cusco** and incorporating the return train journey to the ruins, as well as one night in Las Ruinas will set you back around US$600 per person with a quality tour company (see p10 for details of specialist South American tour operators).

It is of course possible to see Machu Picchu under your own steam: trekking the **Inca trail** to the ruins takes three full days and offers awesome views of snow-capped mountains and the cloud forest en route but it is wise to travel in a group as robbings are quite common.

Brazil
(BEST TIME: ALL YEAR ROUND)

It is the wide variety contained within one country that draws people to Brazil: in just a couple of weeks you can move from city to jungle to waterfalls to beach, and explore historic civilisations and colonial ruins. Many of these sites are in a marked contrast to the latter-day extravagance of **Brazilia**, the nation's capital city that was purpose built only thirty years ago. Names such as **Rio**, **Salvador**, **Ipanema** and the **Amazon** cannot fail to evoke powerful images of this awesome country that occupies a vast chunk of the entire South American continent.

This chapter does not try to guide you around this huge country but instead suggests some hotels that you might try to work into your itinerary as each, in its own way, expresses Brazil's multifarious character.

Designed like an aeroplane, Brazilia was the first capital in the world purpose-built in an attempt to open up the country's interior. For architecture and design enthusiasts the city is totally mind-blowing with its incredible modern architecture rising out of the Central Plateau like some kind of sci-fi film.

In total contrast is Salvador, one of the great cities of South America, where lavish churches boast breathtaking baroque gold interiors and numerous impressive colonial buildings stand as reminders of former settlements. Salvador is the capital of **Bahia**, an area which is a melting pot of Africans, Latin Americans and Europeans and which has a totally distinct culture with unique food, lots of rhythmic music with heavy drum beats and even a little black magic.

Most visitors to Brazil try to visit the mighty **Iguazú Waterfalls** on the border with Argentina and Paraguay (see p221 for details); **Pantanal**, the flood plains on the border with Bolivia and Paraguay – a wilderness region full of cowboy characters and colourful wildlife; and spend a few days at an Amazon lodge.

If you have time **Angra**, a little coastal town on the **Costa Verde** about three hours' drive west of Rio, has lovely beaches, lots of islands and secluded bays to discover. **Paraty**, a small fishing village close by is particularly pretty and well worth a visit. And then there's Rio, with its fantastic beaches and Carnival. Rio is always an unbelievable and exhilarating place to be, even if it's not Carnival season. Don't be put off by Brazil's 'dangerous' reputation, both Rio and Salvador have put in a big effort to clean up their act and now have a really good tourist police. However it's always wise to leave your valuables in the hotel safe and not to walk along empty beaches or blatantly carry a camera.

BRAZIL

An incredible concoction of vibrant cities, beautiful beaches, elegant colonial cities and the Amazonian jungle

When to go: All year round

Average maximum temperatures °C

	JAN	FEB	MAR	APR	MAY	JUN	JUL	AUG	SEP	OCT	NOV	DEC
Rio	29	29	29	27	25	24	24	24	24	25	26	28
Salvador	29	29	29	29	28	27	26	26	27	28	28	29
Manaus	30	30	30	30	31	31	32	33	33	33	32	31

Capital: Brazilia

Flight times: to Rio de Janeiro from:
New York: 10 hours
LA: 14 hours
London: 11 hours
Sydney: 20 hours

Approximate exchange rates: Cruzeiro (C) – £1 = C1.59, US$1 = C1.02, A$1 = C0.81

Time difference: GMT minus three hours (Rio de Janeiro)

Voltage: 110v and 220v, most hotels have adapters

Combine with: Concentrate on Brazil, there is so much to see

Country dialling code: ☎ 55

RIO DE JANEIRO
The Copacabana Palace

The Copacabana Palace is Brazil's most famous hotel, which also means that it is one of the country's most expensive. But at least you get the kind of luxury that will make you smile deep inside your pampered soul time and time again.

The rooms have recently been renovated and are equipped with the furnishings and facilities that you'd expect from a hotel owned by the elegant and lavish Orient-Express Group. Just about everything you could possibly need, as well as a comforting amount of things you probably won't, is there – frigobar, in-room safe, satellite TV

COPACABANA PALACE
(☎ 021-255 7070, fax 021-235 7330), Av Atlantica 1702, CEP 22021-001 Rio de Janeiro, Brazil
Reservations: Through Orient-Express Hotels' worldwide reservation numbers (see p12)
Getting there: The hotel can arrange transfers from the airport about 35km away, or you can get a taxi costing around US$45
Accommodation: 226 rooms
Amenities: Outdoor swimming pool, florist, bookstore, hairdresser, car rental, laundry service, 24-hour room service
Dress code: Elegant casual, people do dress up for dinner
Weddings: Can be arranged
Minimum stay: None
Rates: Doubles from US$210; suites from US$360; ask about their four-night honeymoon package which includes a suite, breakfast in bed, dinner including wine, flowers and champagne, two bathrobes as a gift, and limo transfers for US$1440
Credit cards: Most major
Taxes and service charge: 15% service tax will be added to your bill

and air-conditioning are just a few of the goodies.

The Copacabana Palace was one of the first buildings in Rio over two storeys high and today it is one of the few original buildings still standing on the beach front. Of course it is really quite ritzy and particularly grand, but I can think of nowhere finer to start or end your honeymoon in Brazil.

Apart from its legendary status, the hotel has a number of features which put it head and shoulders above its neighbours, including a much bigger swimming pool than the tiny roof-top efforts that are so common here.

Food in the restaurant is very good and you can enjoy light lunches overlooking the beach and retreat to the English tea room in the late afternoon.

My only word of warning is that you make sure you get a proper sea view when you're booking as you don't want to end up looking out at the next door hotel: the extra price of the beach-front rooms is definitely worth it.

A FEW THINGS TO SEE AND DO IN RIO

Known familiarly as the Cidade Maravilhosa, or the marvellous city, Rio will always be known as the **Carnival City**, and even if your visit doesn't coincide with the extravagant festivities that occur between the Friday and Tuesday preceding Lent (usually in February), you can't help falling for the infectious atmosphere.

The safest way to get to **Sugar Loaf Mountain** is by taxi to the bottom of the cable car, so that you can take your camera and not be worried about thieves. Do, however, be wary if you get vertigo as the second cable car really does dangle a long way up. There are bars, knick-knack shops and snack restaurants at the top as well as fantastic views. The best time to go is in the early evening: the queues shouldn't be too long and you can see the sunset. To see the **Corcovado**, the 40m high statue of Christ, get a taxi to the funicular railway station or

right to the top. The Corcovado is surrounded by rain forest and, being really high, the views overlooking the city, the coast and its islands are just amazing, whether it's day or night.

Maracana Stadium, the biggest football stadium in the world, may not automatically find its way on to your list of honeymoon activities but the atmosphere at a football match on a Sunday afternoon is unbeatable and totally mad: it will give you a better insight into life in Brazil than any mainstream tourist attraction.

Copacabana and **Ipanema** (the next beach round) are still the best beaches. They are both quite mind blowing with thousands of people everywhere, and huge volley-ball tournaments, concerts and festivals going on all year round. It's just a really groovy place to wander around. All along the beach there are bars and restaurants serving massive barbecue grills – not exactly a haven for vegetarians.

OURO PRETO

Ouro Preto, founded in 1711 and the former capital of the state of **Minas Gerais**, with its unspoilt churches, colonial architecture and winding cobbled streets is a superb place to wander around. Ouro Preto developed as a mining town and the wealth of gold and other minerals in the area funded the wonderful array of buildings which are still immaculately preserved. Built on rocky ground 1000m above sea level, the city was declared a national monument in 1933. Gleaming mansions, fountains, churches and gardens all combine to give the town a delightful 18th century feel. Of particular interest in many of the churches and museums are the baroque carvings, in wood and soapstone, by the sculptor Aleijadinho: many of them were created with tools strapped to his feet after his hands were crippled by illness.

Places worth visiting outside the town include **Mariana** and **Congonhas do Campo**, two colonial towns with beautiful churches, as well as the deserted gold mines.

Pousada Mondego

The Pousada Mondego is an imposing colonial mansion which was built in the 18th century. Located right in the heart of Ouro Preto, the mansion is almost baroque in style. The 22 rooms and two suites have colonial-style decorations, a heavy wooden wardrobe and table, and good facilities including TV, minibar and a stereo music system. There are three different categories of room, **Mirante Standard**, which are really quite small, **Mirante Superior** which are bigger and the **Sacada** which have balconies overlooking the street front. All the rooms are en suite and five have balconies, so make sure you request a balcony at the time of booking. The Pousada has recently been renovated and is now looking quite superb.

POUSADA MONDEGO
(☎ 031-551 2040, fax 031-551 3094), Largo de Coimbra 38, Ouro Preto, Brazil
Reservations: Through local ground operator, Blumar/Brazil Nuts (Brazil ☎ 021-511 3636, fax 021-511 3739), or through tour operator Cox & Kings (see p10 for UK and US numbers)
Getting there: The closest airport is at Belo Horizonte, 150km away, private transfers with English speaking guides are available for around US$113 per person each way so it's better to hire a car
Accommodation: 22 rooms and two suites
Amenities: Bar, restaurant
Dress code: Casual
Weddings: The hotel performs wedding ceremonies and has receptions for up to 50 people, rates depend on exactly what you want and the time of year, available on request
Minimum stay: None
Rates: Doubles from US$129 to US$163; suites from US$182 to US$220
Credit cards: Most major
Taxes and service charge: 10% service tax will be added to your bill

---

ILHEUS

Hotel Transamerica

Hotel Transamerica is reputed to be the best resort on Brazil's north-eastern coast. Located on Comandatuba island, guests are brought across on a quick boat journey.

The island itself is absolutely stunning, wherever you look there are coconut trees, coconut trees, and more coconut trees, and of course a fabulous beach from which you can watch the sun slowly slip past the horizon. The Transamerica is the sort of place that immediately has its guests calculating how soon they could return again and, for some I've spoken to, how easily they could secure a job there and stay forever.

The hotel is beautifully decorated in light colours with ocean themes (shells and fish) running through a number of the rooms. Every guest room is equipped with individually controlled air-conditioning, phone, minibar, in-room safe, satellite TV and complimentary in-house movies, plus a private terrace or balcony. Transport, in small cars, is provided to and from the hotel's wooden main building for guests staying in one of the bungalows.

One of the best features of the Transamerica is its astonishing sculpted fresh-water swimming pools, canals and waterways covering a massive 1200 sq metres of space. The hotel has five pools in all, one competition size, one for leisure featuring an artificial waterfall, a third for exercising, one for underwater massage and one with a swim-up bar.

Watersports certainly play a big part in relaxing here; there's jet-skiing, water-skiing, windsurfing and sailing all on hand, with instruction too. Or you could sail off for

HOTEL TRANSAMERICA
(☎ 073-613 1122, fax 073-613 1114), Canavieiras Road, Km 79, City of Una, Comandatuba Island, Brazil
Reservations: Through local ground operator, Blumar/Brazil Nuts(Brazil ☎ 021-511 3636, fax 021-511 3739), or through tour operator Cox & Kings UK (☎ 0171-873 5001) or US (☎ 212-935-3935, toll free ☎ 0800-999-1758)
Getting there: The hotel will meet you at Ilhéus Airport about 100km away
Accommodation: 326 rooms and 14 suites in the main building and 108 rooms and three suites in bungalows
Amenities: 24-hour room service, daily laundry service, resident doctor, watersports including jet-skis, water-skiing, and sailing (with instruction), sailing trips on the hotel's private schooner, 1200 sq metres of freshwater swimming pools, deep-sea fishing, eight floodlit tennis courts, fitness centre with massage, sauna and gym, games room, Hibiscus Restaurant for international dining, Brisa Restaurant for grills and Brazilian regional specialities, Do Canal Restaurant for seafood and Bahia specialities, Cravo & Canela for informal meals throughout the day, Capitania Bar for live piano music and entertainment, Carambola Bar, Deck poolside Bar
Dress code: Casual
Weddings: Can be arranged
Minimum stay: None
Rates: Doubles from US$342
Credit cards: Most major
Taxes and service charge: 10% service tax will be added to your bill

a day in the hotel's private schooner around scenic Comandatuba Island, or try some deep-sea fishing in one of the hotel's private fleet of motor boats. Whatever you fancy doing, the hotel is well-equipped with eight floodlit tennis courts, a fitness centre with sauna, massage and exercise machines and other gym equipment – not on your honeymoon surely!

Other recommended hotels

Hotel do Frade (☎/fax 0243-692244), Praia do Frade BR 101 Km123, Angra dos Reis, RJ, Brazil, is more charming than posh, but its close proximity to **Paraty** makes it well placed for day trips. The hotel's accommodation is good with 118 rooms, three suites and 20 chalets all facing the sea and furnished with brightly coloured curtains and blankets, a TV, frigobar, air-conditioning and phone. There are three restaurants, a buffet, a grill and an à la carte serving good food, and six different bars – as well as room service. The hotel also has a golf course, although its upkeep is a bit patchy. Doubles from US$200; suites from US$360, plus 12% service tax.

The **Pousada Porto Paraty** (☎ 0243-712323, fax 0243-712111), Rua do Comércio s/n, Paraty, is a much smaller hotel with only 48 rooms and a really simple and charming atmosphere. Bedrooms are furnished in colonial style and equipped with TV, phone, air-conditioning, in-room safe deposit boxes, minibars and have room service. Situated in Paraty's historical square, the Pousada is a pretty, tropical home with an airy veranda overlooking beautiful gardens. Doubles from US$60 to US$85 and suites from US$110, plus 15% service tax.

Argentina and Chile
(BEST TIME: NOVEMBER TO MARCH)

Argentina and Chile are quite unlike any other part of the South American continent: they are a great deal more European and have a smaller population of indigenous Indians. They're also a lot safer and are easier to travel around. Because these two countries sit side by side along the length of the southern half of this astonishing continent, most travellers visit both in one trip. Once you are in the **Lake District** (in the lower half of both countries) or even further south still in the mountainous wilderness of **Patagonia** it's very difficult not to find yourself wandering across the border between the two.

The hotels I have chosen here are pretty much the best that Argentina and Chile have to offer. They are by no means cheap, but they are really first class and each one is individual. Although you are unlikely to go to all four of them these are special places to relax in after or before your adventures in Patagonia or on a cattle drive, a soothing reminder that you are on your honeymoon and not on an expedition.

BUENOS AIRES

If you fly into Buenos Aires, the most gloriously luxurious and the most elegant hotel is the **Alvear Palace Hotel** (☎ (54) 01-804 4031, fax 01-804 9246), Av Alvear 1891, 1129 Buenos Aires. It is also rumoured to be the most expensive hotel in the whole of South America. The Alvear really deserves to be called a palace. Set in the heart of **La Recoleta** with the city's best shops and restaurants only a stone's throw away, the Alvear would make the most incredible hotel for the first night of your honeymoon. There are just over 200 rooms with all mod cons and an excellent health club with indoor swimming pool, tailor-made for soothing jet lag. Doubles start at US$270, suites from US$290, but watch out for the 21% tax, and do ask about the honeymoon packages which feature a night in a junior suite with champagne, flowers, canapés and chocolates, as well as continental breakfast in bed, use of the health club and a delayed 5pm checkout, all for US$270.

A visit to a cemetery is probably not something most honeymooners would contemplate but the cemetery in La Recoleta is quite something. Not only is it the place where Eva Peron is buried but it is also full of wonderful statues and marble tombstones. Some tombs are built above ground but many are below including that of Eva Peron, for fear that her remains might be stolen.

IGUAZU FALLS

Whether or not you've seen the film *The Mission* a visit to the Iguazú waterfalls on the border with Brazil and Uruguay is a must. Make sure you have a day to spend on each side so that you can properly admire the stunning rainbows produced by the waterfall. Stay at **Hotel Internacional** (c/o Buenos Aires ☎ (54) 01-311 4259, fax 1-311 20488) in the national park here. The hotel has a swimming pool, a casino and good restaurants. Double rooms overlooking the Falls are from US$155/£100 including buffet breakfast and service but a 21% tax is added to this rate. Rooms with a garden view are cheaper. Reservations through the above number or through Utell International in the UK (☎ 0990-300200).

THE LAKE DISTRICT

No trip to Argentina or Chile would be complete without a visit to the Lake District. When I first toured the region I thought it the most beautiful place I'd ever seen and vowed to go back and live there someday. White-water rivers flood into scores of vast blue lakes surrounded by dense pine forest, above which snow-capped volcanoes tower into the sky. You can be as active or inactive as you want, simply enjoying a gentle stroll around the lakes or hiring a bike from one of the many rental places, trekking up volcano sides, windsurfing on the lakes, white-water rafting on the rivers and even snow-skiing on the sides of the volcanoes. The region's towns have that wonderful feel of anticipation and exhilaration akin to a ski-resort. There are also lots of good bars to retire to at the end of the day where you can talk about your adventures over addictive pisco sours – the Chilean national drink similar to a margarita only better!

On the Argentinian side, people flock to **Bariloche** in the winter (June to September) to ski and also in the summer to spend the Christmas holidays in their summer houses. Not far from Bariloche is **Lago Nahuel Huapi**, a glacial relic over 100km long which is surrounded by beautiful alpine scenery and great blankets of flowers in summer-time. There are two particularly good hotels in Bariloche. The first is a Relais & Châteaux member, the **Hosteria Las Balsas** (☎ (54) 0944-94468, fax 0944-94308), Villa la Angostura, 8407 Neuquen, a luxurious rambling manor house on the edge of

Nahuel Huapi. This pretty blue house is a place where you can relax or from where you can go walking or riding during the day, before returning to gastronomic meals in the evening. Doubles from US$220. The second is the **Llaa Llao Hotel** (☎ (54) 0944-48530, fax 0944-48222) which, with 164 rooms, is much bigger and is a very popular local haunt. Doubles from US$115 in the low season to US$135 in the high, while superior suites costs US$370 in the low season and US$450 in the high, all rates are subject to 21% tax.

Whichever hotel you opt for, take the **Cerro Campanario** chair lift which affords panoramic views of the lake, and the chair lifts and cable car up **Cerro Catedral**, a ski centre 20km west of Bariloche, which also has incredible views and several good walking trails.

Only go between November and April or the weather will be too cold: many of the hotels are closed between June and September.

PATAGONIA

Deeper into Argentinian Patagonia the ultimate destination for riding and big country enthusiasts is **Estancia Huechahue** (☎ (54) 0944-91303, fax 0972-27111), 8371 Junin de los Andes, Provincia del Neuguen. This incredible estancia (ranch) has opened its doors to just a handful of paying guests. It is a good base from which to ride out each day into the foothills of the Andes or into areas only accessible on horseback on a few days trail-riding into the land of the gauchos. An experience like this doesn't come cheap and you'd be looking at around US$150 per person each day, but imagine a few days' riding out alone, just the two of you with your guide, into one of the least populated areas of the world, and camping under the Southern hemisphere stars at night.

If you don't ride (although you don't have to be experienced riders to go to Heuchahue) there is another way of experiencing the incredible landscapes of Patagonia by crossing the border and heading down to **Torres del Paine National Park**, north of Puerto Natales in Chile.

Here, in the middle of what is universally recognised as South America's finest national park, is the extraordinary **Hotel Salto Chico, Explora** (☎ (56) 02-699 2922, fax 02-699 0137), Parque Nacional Torres del Paine s/n, Patagonia. If you are readers of the travel pages of glossy magazines then you may have seen pictures of this incredible hotel. It is set amongst Patagonia's wildest granite peaks, emerald lakes, raging waterfalls, sprawling glaciers and dense forests. At first glance it looks like some modern Antarctic research station but on closer inspection is one of the world's most design-conscious hotels. For anyone interested in architecture and modern design, and enthusiastic enough to explore this unbelievable land, the Salto Chico has to be seen. The hotel's brilliantly polished interior, made from local wood, is quite magnificent. There are roaring fires, huge deep baths with windows looking out over the mountains, a stunning swimming pool totally surrounded by polished pine, bed linen brought from Barcelona, chinaware from England and tapestries from New York. There's even an outside jacuzzi where you can lie back and drink champagne with the snow falling all around you.

Each day the Explora team take you off on any one of 16 'explorations' offered, by boat, on foot, on horseback, mountain bikes, or in four-wheel drive vehicles. Now that you're convinced, here's the painful part: three nights and four days per person will set you back from US$1040 to US$1773 for a suite, which includes all meals and house wine, transfers to/from Punta Arenas Airport, and all Explora excursions which, of course, are the highlight of the trip.

Morocco
(BEST TIME: OCTOBER TO MAY)

If you are coming from Europe, Morocco makes a particularly good honeymoon destination as it is a truly exotic country with a fascinating panoply of cultural styles and landscapes, and best of all you don't have to endure a long-haul journey to get there.

Most travel agents' brochures tend to paint a very different picture of Morocco to the one described here, instead of concentrating on the overcrowded beaches of **Agadir** there's a much more enchanting side to Morocco, a land rich in history, colour and mystery where not much has changed since the coming of Islam.

Morocco's contrasting landscapes, the bustling Imperial cities of **Fez** and **Marrakech**, the fertile agricultural lands of the north, the vast craggy wilderness of the **Atlas mountains** with their Berber kasbahs and the endless dry emptiness of the **Sahara**, mean that this is a honeymoon with a difference.

From the moment you land you'll be in no doubt at all that you have entered another world: a world where the smells, wails and colours of a way of life virtually untouched by the modern world will continue to surprise and even shock you at every turn. But the great thing about going to Morocco is that you don't have to compromise on hotels: two of the world's most extravagantly luxurious hotels, **La Mamounia** and **La Gazelle d'Or** are found in Morocco as well as plenty of other hotels with character and old world charm.

My only word of warning is that you avoid the inland sights, including Marrakech and the Atlas mountain ranges, during the summer months (June, July and August), as the heat and volume of tourists rise to quite unbearable levels – not at all romantic. These months aside Morocco is pretty much a year round destination.

MOROCCO
Step back in time to an intriguing world of mosques, minarets and palaces, the bustling and colourful labyrinth of souks and the timeless majesty of the Atlas Mountains
When to go: October to May are the best months to visit Morocco but southern Morocco is really a year-round destination
Average maximum temperatures °C

	JAN	FEB	MAR	APR	MAY	JUN	JUL	AUG	SEP	OCT	NOV	DEC
Marrakech	20	21	22	25	27	28	31	34	29	26	23	20
Taroudant	21	22	25	26	28	30	34	34	33	30	24	21

Capital: Rabat
Flight times: to Casablanca from:
New York: $6^{1}/_{2}$ hours
LA: 13 hours
London: 3 hours
Sydney: 23 hours
Approximate exchange rates: Dirham (D) – £1 = D13.58, US$1 = D8.76, A$1 = D6.92
Time difference: GMT
Voltage: 110v/220v AC, 50 Hz is also common, two-pin round plugs
Combine with: It's best to devote your time purely to this one fascinating country
Country dialling code: ☎ 212

MARRAKECH

A visit to Marrakech, the city of madness, magic and miracles, gives one an awesome insight into a life that most of us assume is all but forgotten. It is one of the world's enchanted cities where time seems to have stood still, and through the open doors of its souks and temples today's visitor can catch a glimpse of another world.

La Mamounia Hotel

La Mamounia Hotel is legendary. A member of The Leading Hotels of the World it is unbelievably ornate and ostentatious. From the moment you are greeted by the Berber dressed porter, all in white with a sword hanging at his side, you'll know you've arrived somewhere quite out of the ordinary.

Having first opened its doors in 1925, La Mamounia was totally remodelled in 1986 to produce interior decor that is a staggering combination of art deco with Moorish influences. Set in seven hectares of fruit and flower-filled gardens within the massive ochre ramparts of Marrakech, the hotel has some kind of magical essence, imbuing its guests with that strangely thrilling feeling that only comes from staying in a really special hotel.

The 171 guest rooms and 57 suites are all decorated to a theme with co-ordinating fabrics, architecture, furnishings and colours. Most of the 110 garden and pool view rooms have their own nine metre balcony equipped with table and chairs making it the perfect spot for breakfast. There are a further 45 rooms on the Koutoubia mosque side of the hotel and 16 overlooking the courtyard. Whichever room you opt for, it will have one of those snappy little control panels by which you can control the TV, radio, central heating and air-conditioning and even call room service or house porters without so much as having to move a muscle.

The suites at La Mamounia are of course outrageous. They're huge, they're lavish and they're really rather expensive. In the Churchill Suite everything is British in style and it is more like a museum to the great man than a hotel room with Chesterfield furniture, a Regency desk and wood panelling as well as numerous original documents and photos. The suite was named after Sir Winston Churchill, one of La Mamounia's numerous visiting dignitaries. Churchill developed a lasting affection for the place returning year after year to paint from his balcony. His legacy remains in the now famous Churchill

---

LA MAMOUNIA HOTEL

(☎ 04-448981, fax 04-444660), Avenue Bab Jdid, Marrakech, Morocco

Reservations: The Leading Hotels of the World toll free reservation numbers worldwide (see p12) and most travel agents and tour operators specialising in Morocco (see p11)

Getting there: The hotel operates a courtesy shuttle bus to and from Marrakech Menara Airport 4km away; two and a half hours by road from Casablanca and three hours from the seaside resort of Agadir

Accommodation: 171 rooms: 110 garden or pool view rooms; 45 rooms on the Koutoubia mosque side of the hotel; 16 overlooking the courtyard

Amenities: The Marrakech L'Imperiale restaurant, L'Orangerie, L'Italien, Les Trois Palmiers, Le Churchill Piano Bar, Le Bar du Soleil, Le Bar des Trois Palmiers, Le Bar du Squash, Le Bar du Club La Mamounia, Le Grand Casino, range of boutiques, swimming pool, jacuzzi, hair and beauty salon, massage, sauna and hammam (Turkish bath), tennis, squash, gym, boules games area, table tennis, 18 hole golf course near the hotel, snow-skiing within 72km

Dress code: Jacket and tie required for dining

Weddings: Wedding ceremonies and receptions are catered for, depending on time of year and availability

Minimum stay: None

Rates: Double rooms from US$220/D1900 to US$487/D4200, but the hotel does offer three-night honeymoon packages which include full Moroccan or American breakfast each day, a bottle of champagne, flower and fruit in your room and a horse-drawn carriage ride starting from US$1419/D12,240 for a room overlooking the gardens in high season

Credit cards: Most major

Taxes and service charge: D30 city tax per person per night, service charge is included

---

(Opposite) **Top:** The luxurious Blue Train, South Africa (see p260). **Bottom:** La Mamounia, Morocco

Piano Bar, a superb place for a nightcap. Similarly the Orient-Express suite is furnished with original pieces from the celebrated train.

The food in the six restaurants is universally impressive and is served in elegant surroundings.

La Mamounia won't suit you if you're looking for a quiet hotel to be alone together: you could hide away here but it would somehow be a waste – it's one of those places to see and be seen. La Mamounia is the ultimate hotel for the first night of your honeymoon or, if you can afford it, the first few nights, providing you with the kind of glitz, glamour and hedonistic spring board that will become your bench-mark for hotels for years to come.

Other recommended hotels

La Roseraie Hotel (☎ 04-439128, fax 04-432094), c/o BP 769, Gueliz, Marrakech, is a haven of tranquillity high in the Atlas mountains standing at 914m. Just an hour's drive from Marrakech, the hotel is set in 20 hectares of flower-filled gardens in the heart of Berber countryside. La Roseraie has 21 rooms and suites all of which contain wood-burning stoves, en suite bathrooms and a patio leading into the gardens. This is the place to come if you fancy a few days of real adventure such as horse-riding through the incredible mountain villages and even staying in remote Berber houses en route. It's also a great place for walkers and those who like wildlife, wild flowers, or even just lying by a pool. Regular rooms cost around US$71/D612 per person for half board, while junior suites are US$94/D812, rates include tax.

For a more realistically priced hotel in Marrakech go for the **Hotel Tichka** (☎ 04-448710 fax 04-448691), Casablanca Street, Semlalia, a quiet four-star property where the poolside rooms are particularly recommended. This lovely hotel has been recommended by lots of people who didn't feel they could relax amid the ostentation of La Mamounia. Located five minutes by taxi or 15 minutes by horse-drawn carriage from Marrakech's central square, the Tichka benefits from being removed from the frantic city life and acts as a peaceful retreat at the end of the day. The 146-bedroom hotel has been beautifully decorated using superb Moroccan fabrics, intricate tiling and each room has a small balcony. There is also a lovely pool surrounded by carefully maintained gardens – all in all, a very relaxing hotel with a friendly atmosphere. Double rooms from US$122/D1050 excluding breakfast, which costs D80 per person.

A FEW THINGS TO SEE AND DO IN MARRAKECH

The only way to discover Marrakech is to grasp each other firmly by the hand and launch yourselves upon the mad frenetic world of the city's **souks**. Amidst all the confusion, calls and colour you'll find hand-made Moroccan carpets, rugs, leather goods and silverware all of which are good buys, especially if you enter into the haggling spirit. If you don't fancy getting lost you can always arrange to be shown round by an official English-speaking government guide (just ask your hotel concierge). The guide will also be able to steer you towards the best quality shops and help if the French-Moroccan haggling gets too much for you.

The best way to see the **Djemaa el Fna**, the city's main square, during the day is to head for the Hotel de France's roof terrace: you can gaze down on the bustling market while enjoying a relaxing meal of couscous, washed down with the ubiquitous cup of sweet mint tea. At

dusk the square really starts to come alive with its cacophony of snake charmers, preachers, tumblers, singers, sorcerers and herbalists all vying for your attention. Try a few spicy nibbles from the stalls surrounding the square or splash out and eat at *Stylia*, where diners sit on low sofas set around candlelit tables strewn with rose petals, and you'll soon discover why the famous chef Robert Carrier has made this fine city his second home.

Other points of interest are **Koutoubia Minaret**, the **Ben Youssef Mosque**, **Medina** (the old city), and the **Saadian Tombs**, or just wander around the city's lush gardens, the **Jardins de Majorelle**.

Among the best day trips from Marrakech is a trip to see the spectacular waterfalls, the **Cascades d'Ouzoud**, or the drive into the Atlas Mountains to the top of the **Tichka Pass** at a breathtaking elevation of 2255m.

(Opposite) Top: Sundowners on safari. **Bottom:** Bird House, Tongabezi Lodge, Zambia (see p251).

TAROUDANT

A three-hour drive from Marrakech brings you to Taroudant, a majestic ochre-walled city famous for its rambling souks, ruddy clay houses and stark Atlas mountain backdrop. After a few frenetic days in Marrakech you'll welcome the change of pace in Taroudant. From Taroudant you can make easy day excursions into the Ante-Atlas (the western end of the Atlas range) by car, or even head off on horseback or mountain bikes for a couple of days exploring the countryside and its Berber villages.

La Gazelle d'Or

La Gazelle d'Or is a place where people come to celebrate, usually an anniversary, a wedding or some other landmark in their lives. It's just that kind of place: special beyond your dreams where self-indulgence is de rigueur. The hotel's guest book is unbelievable: it's crammed full with celebrity names.

Set amongst ten hectares of mature gardens, the hotel is cocooned by orange groves with the majestic Atlas Mountains providing a time-honoured backdrop. The hotel originally started life as a retreat for a French aristocrat but fell into neglect until it was reincarnated as a hotel. Days at La Gazelle d'Or are all about hours spent relaxing by the palm-fringed pool with a good book, punctuated only by gourmet meals or perhaps a visit to the steam baths and some aromatherapy, or a stroll around the nearby souks.

The hotel's decorations give it an incredibly opulent feel with polished marble floors, tented ceilings, the Berber-motif lounges and white robed staff, but the atmosphere is more of a country club. The hotel provides a rare combination of Moorish architecture and metropolitan chic, where guests are encouraged to feel that they are part of a house party rather than staying in a hotel.

Huge buffet lunches are served by the pool with views over the snow-capped mountains while gastronomic, seven-course dinners comprising international and Moroccan cuisine are served in the tented Moorish-style dining room and are the high point of each day.

> **LA GAZELLE D'OR**
> (☎ 08-852039, fax 08-852737), BP 260, Taroudant, Morocco
> **Closed**: Mid-July to early August
> **Reservations**: Direct with the hotel or through leading tour operators and travel agents specialising in Morocco (see p11)
> **Getting there**: The hotel's cars and drivers are available for transfers to/from Agadir Airport (about one hour), costing D500 each way
> **Accommodation**: 30 double rooms, including one suite and one junior suite
> **Amenities**: Large outdoor swimming pool (heated in winter), two clay tennis courts, golf practice, croquet, horse-riding, steam bath, massage/aromatherapy and beauty treatments, guided excursions and walking/trekking in the surrounding countryside and up in the Atlas Mountains, room service from early morning to late evening
> **Dress code**: Jacket and tie preferred for dinner
> **Weddings**: No
> **Minimum stay**: None
> **Rates**: Double rooms from US$417 D3600, junior suite US$520/D4485, suite US$847/D7310 full board
> **Credit cards**: Most major
> **Taxes and service charge**: Included

Accommodation is in 30 creeper-covered non air-conditioned bungalows curving away from each side of the hotel's central pavilion. All the rooms are beautifully appointed with exquisite furnishings, mosaics, ornate decor, hand-woven rugs, log fireplaces and private terraces for long drawn out breakfasts.

Within the hotel, there are tennis courts and horses available for desert rides, although most guests get their recreation by taking advantage of the hotel's close proximity to the walled town of Taroudant: a five-minutes walk away. Give yourself at least three days here and up to a week if you can afford to and are feeling especially self-indulgent.

Other recommended hotels

Palais Salam (☎ 08-852312, fax 08-852654), Milie Palais Salam, Taroudant, within the walls of Taroudant, is a really good cheaper alternative to the renowned but expensive La Gazelle d'Or. The four-star Palais Salam was once the palace of a Pasha (a local governor) and is now a tranquil unpretentious hotel offering 100 rooms decorated in Moorish style.

There are also two swimming pools each with an adjacent bar as well as a restaurant serving Moroccan and international food. Doubles from US$75/D645 including breakfast or US$113/D975 for half board; suites from US$98/D845 without breakfast, plus D12 tax per person.

ESSAOUIRA

If you want to escape the hagglers and find a quiet spot off the beaten tourist track, Essaouira is the place. Originally planned by a French hostage in 1760, this delightful walled town is a closely guarded Moroccan secret. Located on a sandy bay with shallow, clean water, the mood at Essaouira is more akin to that of a Greek island than that of Agadir, a comforting 160km down the coast. Get grilled sardines and can of Coke from down by the harbour and just relax in the sun.

Villa Maroc

If you want to get away from the star-studded pampering havens described above and are looking for somewhere more individual, Villa Maroc in Essaouira is a great place right off the tourist route. At Villa Maroc you'll see the real Morocco without having to feel you've got to dress for dinner each night.

Located within the historic ramparts of Essaouira, Villa Maroc was formed by the joining together of two extraordinarily beautiful 18th century houses built in Spanish-Moroccan style. With only seven double rooms, six suites and two apartments staying at the Villa is more like being a guest in a private house than a hotel resident.

White-washed walls and cobalt blue railings and other trimmings adorn the villa's exterior while the inside is an interior designer's dream. Rooms are gathered around a central courtyard, three or four to each floor. The white-washed walls are hung with Moroccan tapestries, old traditional costumes displayed on poles and paintings by local artists.

The bedrooms feature carved beds and wooden floors while the bathrooms are individually designed and just fantastic, some have mosaic-tiled baths and others have shower cubicles made from coloured glass. The hotel rooms don't come with TV,

> **VILLA MAROC**
> (☎ 04-473147, fax 04-472806), 10, Rue Abdellah Ben Yassin, Essaouira 44 000 Morocco
> **Reservations**: Direct with the hotel or through leading tour operators and travel agents specialising in Morocco (see p11)
> **Getting there**: The hotel can arrange a taxi to collect guests from Marrakech Airport (D500), Agadir Airport (D600), or Casablanca Airport (D1000)
> **Accommodation**: Seven double rooms, six suites and two apartments
> **Amenities**: Private residents' bar, private dining-rooms for all guests
> **Dress code**: Jackets and ties are not required
> **Weddings**: Wedding ceremonies for up to 50 people can be held at the hotel
> **Minimum stay**: None
> **Rates**: Doubles from US$64/D555, mini suite from US$82/D705 (bed and breakfast)
> **Credit cards**: Most major
> **Taxes and service charge**: D6 per person per night accommodation tax, service is not included

in-room safe or minibar, because the villa's ethos is to stick to Moroccan style and keep the structure of the rooms as simple as possible. If you feel you need to use a safe ask in the office.

One of the highlights of staying at Villa Maroc is the evening meal, which is prepared only on request. Dinners are served in different lounges dotted around the hotel courtyard, so that each couple or party of guests gets their own private dining space. There is also a private bar for use by hotel guests only.

The villa has the intimate feel of a private house, rooms are filled with antiques and Moroccan wall hangings, candlelit dinners are served in private rooms off the central courtyard and there is cobalt blue woodwork everywhere. A wonderful end to a Moroccan honeymoon and we resolved to return.
Vanessa and Bruce Jones

There is no swimming pool, no night club and no tennis court at the villa – as the management are keen to remind you, this is meant to be a place of relaxation and charm, not some kind of holiday resort. Besides you'll find plenty of entertainment just wandering around the souks and bazaars of Essaouira where, unlike Marrakech and Fez, you won't get hassled, or you could nip down to the beach which is only minutes away.

Other recommended hotels
Le Mirage (☎ 09-333491, fax 09-333492), Grottes d'Hercule, BP 2198, Tangiers, a new hotel is a real contender for the most beautiful hotel in Morocco. Located just south of Tangiers, Le Mirage looks down on the most incredibly long, deserted beach at least 275m wide and stretching out as far as the eye can see. Although physically not that far from Tangiers, metaphorically you couldn't be further away from the hassle and crowds up the coast. The hotel is built with dazzling white walls, stucco columns and steps leading down to the beach. The 22 bungalows (all of which are suites) are quite unlike most that you find in Morocco – you'd be forgiven for thinking that interior designers Colefax and Fowler stepped in and took over. There is a lovely swimming pool and a good restaurant overlooking the Atlantic serving international food. Le Mirage really is the perfect honeymoon hideaway on an amazingly beautiful beach. Rates start at US$93/D800 per person per night. Reservations can either be made direct or through UK tour operator, the Best of Morocco (UK ☎ 01380-828533).

Egypt
(BEST TIME: ALL YEAR ROUND)

The land of the Pharaohs cannot help but conjure up exotic images of former civilisations and, with 5000 years of noble heritage, Egypt is certainly an exotic honeymoon destination for those looking for something out of the ordinary. No trip to Egypt would be complete without a visit to one of the famous Seven Wonders of the World, the **Great Pyramids** at **Giza**, towering out of the desert sands – although **Cairo** itself is an extremely aggravating place to visit, so it's best to limit your time there to a couple of days. It pays to be patient if you are planning to visit Egypt for your honeymoon: everything takes about three times as long as you'd normally anticipate so think seriously about doing an organised trip which will instantly cut down on the hassle-factor.

EGYPT
Average maximum temperatures °C

JAN	FEB	MAR	APR	MAY	JUN	JUL	AUG	SEP	OCT	NOV	DEC
19	21	24	28	33	35	35	35	32	30	26	21

Approximate exchange rates: Egyptian pound (E£) – US$1 = E£3.40
Time difference: GMT plus two hours (plus three hours from May to September)
Voltage: 220v AC, 50 Hz
Country dialling code: ☎ 20

There are hotels to suit all budgets in Egypt from five-star luxury to basic bed and breakfasts. If you want to set aside a few days to relax in colonial splendour it's hard to beat the legendary **Old Cataract Hotel** (☎ 97-316001/8, fax 97-316011), Abtal El Tahrir Street, in **Aswan**. Doubles start from US$75 per night.

NILE CRUISES

From Aswan you are ideally placed for one of the world's most romantic journeys, a luxury cruise down the Nile, northwards to **Luxor** and the **Valley of the Kings**. If you prefer to start your holiday in Cairo this trip can just as easily be done from Luxor going upriver to Aswan. The best way to see the many ancient temples and observe life is on the river.

If you can afford it, it's well worth spending a little extra on your cruise, thereby guaranteeing you better (and safer) food and a nicer cabin. From the UK and the US, cruises can be booked through Abercrombie & Kent or Cox & Kings (see p11 for tel). Both companies offer truly luxurious cruises in full Edwardian splendour aboard ships equipped with swimming pool, sundecks, and en suite cabins, some of which even have their own private balconies. You'll be welcomed on board with afternoon tea, and have just enough time to relax and get your bearings before dressing for the cocktail reception which is, of course, followed by dinner – all guaranteed to get you in to the swing for this kind of sophisticated, elegant travel. A ten-day tour of Egypt, including four nights on the beautifully decorated *Oberoi Philae*, built in the style of an old paddle-wheeler but only completed in 1995, and short stays in Cairo and Aswan costs around US$1700/£1100 with Cox & Kings.

Kenya
(BEST TIME: JULY TO END OF MARCH)

Kenya has become one of the most popular tourist destinations on the African continent, largely because it offers an impressive and easily accessible range of safaris and beaches at prices that are often a good deal cheaper than many of its neighbours. Situated on the east coast of Africa, close to the equator, there can be no doubt that

---

KENYA

The famous Masai Mara with its incredible game viewing and the warm Indian Ocean coastal waters with their golden sandy beaches and great diving opportunities

When to go: The coast rarely dips below 20°C so Kenya is a year-round destination, but avoid April to June when the rains come

Average maximum temperatures °C

	JAN	FEB	MAR	APR	MAY	JUN	JUL	AUG	SEP	OCT	NOV	DEC
Nairobi	25	26	26	24	23	22	21	22	24	25	23	23
Mombasa	32	32	33	31	29	29	28	28	29	30	31	32

Capital: Nairobi

Flight times: to Nairobi from:
  New York: 16$\frac{1}{2}$ hours
  LA: 21$\frac{1}{2}$ hours
  London: 7$\frac{1}{2}$ hours
  Sydney: (via Johannesburg) 20 hours

Approximate exchange rates: Shilling (S) – £1 = S87.30, US$1 = S56.29, A$1 = S44/48

Time difference: GMT plus three hours

Voltage: 220v/240v AC, 50 Hz, although some hotels are equipped with 110v wall sockets for American plugs

Combine with: The Seychelles, Tanzania, Uganda (for gorillas) and Zanzibar

Country dialling code: ☎ 254

Kenya makes a perfect honeymoon destination. Kenya is difficult to beat if you've never been to Africa before and like the idea of going on safari but don't want to spend too much time in the bush. Home to the legendary game reserves of the **Masai Mara** and **Tsavo**, Kenya offers plenty of opportunities to see the big five – lion, leopard, elephant, rhinoceros and buffalo – in some of Africa's greatest game parks while staying in safe, comfortable lodges.

The Kenyan coast also offers a good selection of watersports, particularly scuba diving on the immense coral barrier reef that fringes the coast, great snorkelling not far from the shore and world renowned big-game fishing.

Safaris

When booking your safari make sure you let the tour operator know exactly what kind of safari experience you want. If you have been to Africa before you may be looking for a much wilder safari experience, perhaps sleeping out at night and tracking on foot with your own personal guide, well away from the buzz of other Land Rovers. But if you haven't been before, a first-timer safari where you'll be driven around one of the bigger parks in closed Land Rovers will probably suit you better and will still give you a really good feel for this vast country and its inhabitants. Many British tour operators, such as Tropical Places (UK ☎ 01342-825123) and British Airways (UK ☎ 01293-723191) offer one to three-day safaris in minibuses straight from your hotel in Mombasa. If you want to visit the more exclusive and less commercialised parts of Kenya, head for **Ol Donyo Wuas** or the private lodges on the **Rift Valley** lakes, but understand that these are specialist safaris, with prices to match so they are probably best suited to those who have been out in the bush before.

SAMBURU

Wilderness Trails at Lewa Downs

One of Kenya's longest established and most popular hosted homestays, Lewa Downs is the perfect base for walking and riding out in the African bush amongst really beautiful scenery.

Your hosts, the Craig family, have owned the ranch since 1924 when the grandparents of today's owners, William and Emma Craig, arrived from England and began raising cattle. Now, William and Emma welcome just a few privileged guests to their private 24,000-hectare game ranch on the northern slopes of **Mt Kenya**, an hour's drive north-east of **Nanyuki**.

Guests stay in one of three stone and thatch cottages which all have two double rooms, unfortunately with twin beds. Each cottage has a central rondavel-style living-room with an open fireplace and easy chairs, plus a large veranda with lovely comfortable

---

WILDERNESS TRAILS AT LEWA DOWNS
(c/o ☎ 2-571661, fax 2-571665), PO Box 56923, Nairobi, Kenya
Closed: April, May and November
Reservations: Most leading specialist African tour operators and travel agents or direct through Bush Homes of East Africa (see above number for Lewa Downs)
Getting there: Guests can either take a charter flight to Lewa Downs airstrip, a schedule flight to Nanyuki and then transfer by road to Lewa Downs or drive from Nairobi which takes about four hours
Accommodation: Six twin rooms en suite in the three cottages
Amenities: Small swimming pool, dining-room, safaris on foot, in four-wheel drive, on horseback or by camel, day and night drives
Dress code: Informal
Weddings: No
Minimum stay: Three or four nights are recommended
Rates: US$220 per person per night full board including all game drives, horse-riding, bush walks and camel treks, excluding drinks and Lewa Wildlife Conservancy fee of US$25 per person per night
Credit cards: Are not accepted, payment of extras must be by cheque (British) or cash (US$); most people book their stay through one of the above companies who will accept credit cards
Taxes and service charge: Included, but tips welcomed

seats which are just ideal for napping. Days at Lewa Downs are spent either in four-wheel drive vehicles on game drives or out in the bush on foot, tracking game with an experienced and incredibly knowledgeable guide. Lion, leopard, cheetah, black and white rhino and two types of zebra reside on the ranch, as well as countless other game such as giraffe, warthog, impala, gazelle and buffalo.

Horses, and even camels, are available for rides through the local countryside. The ranch's horses are very well trained and will enable even the most novice rider to get much closer to the game than on foot – sometimes it's almost possible to touch a giraffe. In the evening, guests can cool off with a refreshing dip in the lovely pool and enjoy tea on the lawn for a restful hour or so before dinner.

Other recommended camps

Borana Camp (☎ 2-567251, fax 2-564945), c/o Tandala Ltd, PO Box 24397, Nairobi, is perfect honeymoon material. This luxury camp has six individual cottages built from local materials, and decorated using attractive fabrics sourced locally and in South Africa. The cottages are huge compared to most bush camps and are exquisitely decorated with local wood incorporated into their design. Guests can go horse-riding, walking, on game drives in open-top vehicles, or on a helicopter ride over the bush. There is also a rhino sanctuary nearby. Borana has been carefully conceived and executed with impressive results – this has to be the most luxurious, non chichi, bush accommodation in Kenya. Rates are US$280 full board per person per night and Borana can also be booked through Theobald Barber Travel in the UK (UK ☎ 0171-221 0555, fax 0171-221 0444).

Absolutely wonderful, wonderful time, loved every minute. We've had the most amazing three weeks and have now decided we want to be posted out here. Borana was fantastic and so unlike a hotel, we were very, very sad to be leaving.
Kathryn and James Redfern

Private lodges and bush homes

One of the best ways to start a holiday in Kenya is to avoid Nairobi all together: instead fly straight out to **Lake Navaisha**, only one and a half hours by plane from the capital. The Lake is a beautiful and tranquil place to start your holiday: you can spend long lazy days watching the pink flamingos and spotting the myriad of birdlife around, take a boat out on the fresh-water lake, or explore the surrounding bush on horseback. **Loldia House**, on the shores of Lake Naivasha, is a pretty red-brick private house set amongst well tended lawns and acacia and fig trees. The family-run farm offers luxury accommodation to 16 privileged guests, either in the main house or in cottages within the grounds: all the rooms have private facilities and magnificent views across the lake over to **Mount Longonot**.

While dinner is served in the dining-room, day-time meals are taken under the shade of Loldia's beautiful giant fig tree. The lodge's staff will take you to visit Lakes **Nakuru**, **Elementait** and **Bogoria**, the hot-springs at **Hell's Gate**, as well as boat trips on Lake Naivasha to see the amazing birdlife. Just opposite **Hippo Point** is **Elsamere**, the former home of Joy Adamson and her lions, made so famous by the book and film *Born Free*. Loldia can be booked through the Governor's Camps (☎ 2-331871/2, fax 2-726427), PO Box 48217, Kenya, doubles from US$390 including all meals and laundry.

Alternatively, **Bush Homes of East Africa** (☎ 2-571661, fax 2-571665), PO Box 56923, Nairobi, Kenya, have a number of properties worth looking at, including **Rekero** and **Mundui**. The private home of the Earl and Duchess of Enniskillen, Mundui is a great place if you don't want to see anyone else for days on end. The estate covers 480 hectares of private acacia woodland and grass plains offering fantastic walking and private game viewing. The two houses, the Enniskillen's own and the

Hunting Lodge where guests stay, are set in landscaped gardens which run down to the lake shore. There are two bedrooms in the two-storey Hunting Lodge, a master bedroom with fireplace, one smaller bedroom and two bathrooms. Downstairs there is a large sitting-room with another fireplace.

Guests have exclusive use of the cottage, the estate and the lovely swimming pool set in a courtyard. Mundui is a one and three quarter hour flight from Nairobi by charter aircraft. Prices available on request.

THE MASAI MARA

To the south west the Masai Mara, which adjoins Tanzania's Serengheti, is practically the only place where you can see game in the kind of abundance that was common a century ago.

A 50-minute flight from Nairobi will take you to the open rolling savannah grassland that is home to the proud Masai tribes, who continue to live alongside their cattle and the hordes of big game roaming the plains. You are likely to see zebra, wildebeest, lion, leopard, cheetah, elephant, antelope and giraffe. Take a hot-air balloon trip at sunrise: soaring high above the African plains is a magical experience and certainly worth getting out of bed for – especially as you are rewarded with an alfresco champagne breakfast once you touch down.

Little Governor's Camp

Extremely upmarket, exclusive, and unspoilt, each of the Governor's Camps offers four-wheel drive safaris and lots of bush walking, picnicking and sundowners in wonderful vantage points. Set among immaculately kept grounds and lit at night by paraffin lamps, these are the most romantic safari camps.

LITTLE GOVERNOR'S CAMP
(☎ 2-331871/2, fax 2-726427), PO Box 48217, Nairobi, Kenya
Reservations: Leading tour operators and travel agents specialising in Africa worldwide (see p11); JE Marketing London (UK ☎ 0181-742 7780, fax 0181-742 7655)
Getting there: Air Kenya flight to Governor's Camp approx US$160 per person return
Accommodation: 17 tents – bathrooms with hot/cold showers and bidets.
Amenities: Game viewing; variety of bird-life, walking safaris daily; hot-air ballooning daily for one hour, after landing a traditional champagne and full English breakfast served
Dress code: Casual
Weddings: Can be arranged, prices on request
Minimum stay: None
Rates: US$390 for two people sharing – includes all meals and laundry, but not park fees or beverages
Credit cards: Most major
Taxes and service charge: Included

Little Governor's Camp is the smallest of the three main Governor's Camps. Approached by boat, crossing over the Mara River, the small site has 17 de luxe, en suite tents arranged close to a popular watering hole. It is a great place to catch sight of large herds of migrating wildebeest between July and October.

Each day there are three game drives in four-wheel drive Land Rovers, half-day morning walks with bush breakfast outside the Reserve, and incredible hot-air ballooning trips to choose from. The camp staff will also arrange a picnic for you and take you off to the **Oloololo** escarpment where the last scene of *Out of Africa* was filmed. Breakfast and lunch are served outside under the shade of the trees, while dinner is in the dining tent after drinks at the bar. There is also a swimming pool.

It's also worth asking about **Paradise Camp** which is more expensive but even smaller than Little Governor's and truly fabulous.

AMBOSELI NATIONAL PARK

This park is situated south of Nairobi near the majestic snow-capped **Mt Kilimanjaro**: you are likely to see elephant, giraffe, buffalo, wildebeest and zebra.

Ol Donyo Wuas

Ol Donyo Wuas, meaning spotted hills in Masai, is an exclusive hideaway among the open plains and rolling **Chyulu hills**, looking over to the snow-capped peaks of Mt Kilimanjaro. Here is Africa as it used to be a century ago: abundant game and the Masai herdsmen continue to live side by side in an unspoilt corner of Kenya.

This private home-stay, owned by Richard Bonham one of Africa's most famous guides, accommodates guests in six individual thatched cottages. The open front of the cottages and the main building give stunning views over the surrounding Masai land to Mt Kilimanjaro which looms large and impressive in the distance. Each cottage has an en suite bathroom, electric lighting, an open fireplace and a veranda. The beds are covered in mosquito netting and there is a cupboard with hanging space, as well as bedside lights and locally made decorations. The whole experience is fabulous – very exclusive and of course, very expensive.

Bonham set his heart on building his home in this spot after scouring the land in his light aircraft. Once he started building the ranch, in 1986, he also assumed honorary game manager status for ten thousand hectares of Masai land.

Game viewing usually starts soon after dawn. Having been woken with a cup of tea, guests head out either on horseback or on foot, or in one of the camp's specifically converted open-top Land Rovers. Among common sightings are antelope, zebra, eland, cheetah, lion, giraffe and wildebeest. The camp staff then catch up with you around 9am armed with breakfast which they lay out under the shade of an acacia tree. Viewing continues until lunch-time which is usually back at camp. After a good lunch of cold meats, salad and cheese most guests take the opportunity for a siesta in the heat of the day. At around 4pm there is tea to refresh you before returning to the bush for a few more hours tracking the game. Bonham and his crew are always careful to find you a wonderful spot in which to enjoy the magical sunsets with a chilled sundowner, before heading back to camp for a well-earned wash up and dinner as darkness and the noises of the jungle close in around you.

OL DONYO WUAS

(☎ 2-884475, fax 2-882728), PO Box 24133, Nairobi, Kenya

Reservations: Either direct or through UK reps Roxton Bailey Robinson (UK ☎ (01488-683222, fax 01488-682977) and Theobald Barber (UK ☎ 0171-221 0555, fax 0171-221 0444); or through leading safari specialists (see p11)

Getting there: Access is by charter aircraft, usually from Nairobi (50 minutes) to a private airstrip near the lodge, from where guests are transferred to the lodge; charter aircraft cost US$350 and take three people

Accommodation: Six large secluded thatched cottages

Amenities: Main dining-room, game viewing by four-wheel drive, on foot and on horses, and fly camping

Dress code: Informal

Weddings: Have been arranged

Minimum stay: Although there is no minimum stay, two to six days are recommended

Rates: From US$280 per person per night, including transfers, meals and game viewing, not including drinks and fly camping (US$330 per person per night)

Credit cards: The camp itself will not accept credit cards so any extras must be paid for in cash (preferably US$); most people book their stay through one of the above companies who will accept credit cards

Taxes and service charge: Included, although tips are welcome

TSAVO NATIONAL PARK

Exceptional birdlife and elephant viewing, the distant views of Mt Kilimanjaro, and the vast sense of space are what makes Kenya's largest wildlife stronghold, Tsavo, so incredible.

Galdessa

Galdessa, part of a huge rhino release project, is one of Kenya's best kept secrets. This is *the* place to go if you want to get totally away from it all and experience the wild, pure Africa where nature remains untouched by time.

> **GALDESSA**
> (☎ 2-890480, fax 2-891307), PO Box 15095, Nairobi, Kenya
> **Reservations:** Through Galdessa's head office (Switzerland ☎ 22-311 0002, fax 22-311 0021); or through UK tour operator World Archipelago (UK ☎ 0181-780 5838)
> **Getting there:** Guests can be flown in from Malindi or Mombasa for around US$200 per person
> **Accommodation:** Seven twin-bedded luxury tented rooms, one double-bedded honeymoon tented room
> **Amenities:** Game drives in four-wheel drive vehicles, walking and camel safaris, fishing trips (all included in the price)
> **Dress code:** Casual
> **Weddings:** Can be organised, costs depend on what you want
> **Minimum stay:** None
> **Rates:** From US$220 per person for standard full board accommodation, VIP rates from US$350 which includes all drinks and additional services
> **Credit cards:** The camp itself will not accept credit cards so any extras must be paid for in cash (preferably US$); most people book their stay through the head office or through World Archipelago who will accept credit cards
> **Taxes and service charge:** Included, but tips and park entrance fees of US$31 a day are not included

Right in the heart of the Tsavo, overlooking the Galana river, Galdessa Camp comprises eight canvas tents providing spacious luxury accommodation in the finest safari tradition.

Eighteen people are at your service in the camp and nothing in your tent is left to chance so there's no reason to feel unsure about your safety or the camp's cleanliness: your laundry is washed and ironed each day, the bread is baked each morning and food is cooked on a wood fire.

The canvas tents are covered in coconut leaf thatching, they each have their own mosquito netting, an en suite bathroom with showers connected to tarpaulin water drums and lovely fresh white cotton sheets on your bed. So, after an evening of alfresco dining, you can retire to the safety of your tent and listen to the noises of the bush just beyond the canvas walls, safe in the knowledge that they will stay that way.

The guides at Galdessa, under the direction of co-owner Anthony Russell, are all highly experienced. Whether you travel on foot, on horseback, by camel, jeep, or in a hot-air balloon, they are sure to provide you with moments of sheer magic, as you encounter game in a way that few even dream of.

OTHER SAFARI LODGES AND CAMPS

Tortilis Camp (☎ 154-2551, fax 154-22553) is nestled in an unspoilt corner of the park, far away from the busy lodges, close to the Tanzanian boarder and in an ideal position for exploring **Amboseli**. This relatively new camp was awarded British Airways' Tourism for Tomorrow Award in 1995. Tortilis offers its 30 guests four-wheel drive safaris and lots of bush walking, picnicking, and a lovely sitting/dining area on a small hill looking down on the camp and over to fabulous views of Mt Kilimanjaro. It is reached by a 45-minute flight from Nairobi. Rates from around US$180 per person per night, but you'll have to pay extra for things like bush dinners.

Lake Victoria is the perfect stop off after a few days in the Mara, especially if you're keen on fishing and ornithology. Stay on the unspoiled island of **Mfangano** on the southern tip of the lake at **Mfangano Island Camp** (☎ 2-331871/331872, fax 2-726427) where there are only six double-roomed clay and thatched cottages. You'll get a real feel for the local culture and you can also fish for Nile perch and go bird-watching. Mfangano is owned by the same people who own the Governor's camps. Rates from US$220 per person per night full board.

THE COAST

Kenya's coastline stretches for more than 322km and it offers seemingly endless pristine white sandy beaches, fringed by palm or casuarina trees, and lapped by turquoise waters where diving, deep-sea fishing and snorkelling are all fantastic. To the north are the unspoilt beach hideaways of **Lamu** and **Manda** islands, perfect for true escapists, an exotic combination of African and Arabian cultures.

Hemingways

Hemingways is recognised as one of the best beach hotels on the Indian Ocean. Twenty nine kilometres south of **Malindi**, perched on quiet **Watamu Beach**, Hemingways has the most wonderful relaxed atmosphere. In front of you lie the waters of the Indian Ocean while behind are the mighty green hills of Africa.

Relaxed it may be, but the service and cuisine at Hemingways are pretty well faultless and all the bedrooms have air-conditioning and other essential extras, as well as plenty of inessential but very welcome ones too, like the strawberries and roses that are left in your room on arrival.

The 'makuti' (traditional thatched) roofs of Hemingways contain the reception, the main bar and restaurant. The large round sit-up bar, with its relics of old fishing battles and lovely wicker chairs, opens out on to the ocean terrace. Guests can choose between eating here alfresco or, if a wind picks up, in the sunken main restaurant with its high-vaulted thatched roof. The terrace is the best place to watch the outstanding sunsets.

Of the resort's 72 rooms only the 26 standard ones are in the hotel's original block, while the superior and de luxe rooms are all in the new wing – superior rooms occupy the second and third floors and de luxe are on the ground floor. All rooms have en suite bathroom, mosquito nets, phone, in-room safes, slippers and kimono, and a terrace or patio, while the de luxe have a luxury bathroom with both a shower and a bath. But do note that there are no double beds in the de luxe rooms, so it's best to go for the superior rooms that overlook the ocean and swimming pool.

Hemingways is renowned for its leisure facilities, in particular deep-sea fishing and scuba diving. When you've tired of lazing about on the beach there's water-skiing, windsurfing, snorkelling and dhow excursions, as well as two fabulous swimming pools: one fresh and one with salt water. You can swim in the safe, warm waters inside

---

HEMINGWAYS
(☎ 122-32624, fax 122-32256), PO Box 267, Watamu, Kenya
Reservations: Most leading African-specialist tour operators and travel agents worldwide (see p11); or through the UK office (UK ☎ 01295-272747)
Getting there: The hotel can arrange free transfers from Malindi Airport, and from Mombasa Airport costing US$100
Accommodation: 72 guest rooms: 26 standard rooms, 28 superior rooms and 18 de luxe rooms
Amenities: Main restaurant, pool bar, hotel bar and Terrace restaurant, fully-equipped gym, windsurfing, snorkelling, diving, deep-sea fishing, glass-bottom boats; squash and tennis are available nearby
Dress code: Jackets and ties are not required but men are requested to wear long trousers or smart tailored shorts for dinner
Weddings: No
Minimum stay: None
Rates: Double rooms from US$150, superior room from US$200, suites from US$232
Credit cards: Visa, MasterCard, Access
Taxes and service charge: Taxes included, service is discretionary

the reef, snorkel out to the coral gardens, or take a small boat to watch the local dolphins frolic beside the boat and even slip in beside them.

Hemingways' success lies in its ability to combine informality with punctuality. While you'll never feel pressured by pompous staff, they'll also never fail to deliver on a promise. The seafood is wonderful, the accommodation comfortable and the beach just perfect – although be careful to avoid the end of April through to October when the changing winds tend to cover the beach with seaweed.

Indian Ocean Lodge

Indian Ocean Lodge is one of the most beautifully appointed lodges on the whole of the Kenyan coast. A grand old Arab-style building, full of antiques, the lodge has the most incredible views of the Indian ocean. This is exclusivity at its best – relaxed not snobby and very, very private.

Located south of Malindi town, the Indian Ocean Lodge sits out on a coral peninsula with two private beaches flanking either side of it. On windier days you can feel the spray if you sit on the ground floor veranda looking through the baobab trees out to the brilliant blue waters beyond.

With only six double rooms accommodating guests in the upstairs of this lovely old white house, it's a very special place. Old Lamu in style, the en suite rooms are incredibly romantic with wooden four-poster beds shrouded in mosquito netting, beamed roofs and ceiling fans adding to the cool ocean breezes coming through the shuttered windows.

Downstairs is the sitting-room full of antiques, the dining-room and a spacious veranda running the length of the front of the house. All around the house are immaculately cared for gardens shrouded in white, pink and purple bougainvillaea.

Apart from lazing by the pool or snorkelling from the beach there's lots to do from the lodge. Peter and Jo Nicholas, the owners, will arrange anything: a trip in to Malindi for a bit of shopping or a visit to the **Gede Ruins,** or even a guided bird walk through the **Arabuko Sakoke Forest** – and everything is included in the price.

> **INDIAN OCEAN LODGE**
> (☎ 123 20394), PO Box 171, Malindi, Kenya
> **Reservations**: Either direct or through UK tour operator World Archipelago (UK ☎ 0181-780 5838)
> **Getting there**: The lodge can arrange transfers from Malindi Airport, if you travel with World Archipelago they are included in the price
> **Accommodation**: Six double rooms with en suite facilities
> **Amenities**: Ceiling fans, swimming pool, snorkelling, excursions
> **Dress code**: Relaxed
> **Weddings**: Weddings and receptions can be organised, prices depend on exactly what you want
> **Minimum stay**: Two nights
> **Rates:** US$250 per person which includes all meals, activities and drinks other than champagne
> **Credit cards**: Not accepted at the hotel itself so extras must be paid for in cash (preferably US$); your hotel bill will probably be paid through your travel agent/tour operator
> **Taxes and service charge**: Included

Peponi Inn

The Peponi Inn, Lamu is one of the world's most perfect honeymoon paradises. From the moment you arrive at the airport and are transferred to Peponi by dhow you'll know that you're in for a rare treat.

John Hemingway's quotes in the Peponi brochure sum up this unique hotel. He says: 'There are too many luxury hotels around the world and they offer the same: a chocolate on the pillow, canned romance and a cuisine called haute because it's spelled in French. Peponi stands apart from them all...yes, you come here to be pampered, but at Peponi, luxury is the engine not the destination.' People who have been to Peponi all come back saying the same thing: that it is simply dreamy, unlike anywhere else in the world they've seen, which seems to be exactly what Hemingway was getting at.

There are 24 rooms, ten of which are superior. All of them face the sea and have private verandas (no back room views here!), plus private shower and toilet. The superior rooms are larger and either newer or newly renovated, featuring traditional decor of simple wooden furniture made locally. There are no in-room facilities like wall safes or hair-dryers but the use of both can be arranged.

The hotel is found at the beginning of a beautiful 12km beach backed by sand dunes, from where windsurfing, water-skiing and dhow trips take place. Snorkelling, diving and deep-sea fishing can all be arranged, between September and March.

The ways of Lamu are infectious and dinner at Peponi epitomises the laid-back atmosphere of this island: most guests dine shoeless and dressed in nothing more formal than a shirt and a kikoi (an African sarong) while sitting around crisp linen tablecloths and eating delicious seafood prepared in Swahili style.

PEPONI
(☎ 121-33421/3, fax 121-33029), PO Box 24, Lamu, Kenya
Closed: May and June
Reservations: Most leading specialist African tour operators and travel agents worldwide (see p11)
Getting there: The Peponi will arrange complimentary transfers by boat
Accommodation: 24 guest rooms: 10 superior, 14 standard
Amenities: 12km beach, windsurfing, water-skiing, local sailing dhow trips, plus snorkelling, diving and deep-sea fishing between September and March, small bar, two restaurants
Dress code: In the evening men are required to wear long trousers or kikois and no swim suits are allowed in the dining-room
Weddings: The hotel can help you arrange a wedding through the local ministers and can cater for a small reception
Minimum stay: None
Rates: Double rooms from US$220 to US$270, full board
Credit cards: Most major
Taxes and service charge: Included

Nomads

Perched right on **Diani** beach, Nomads is a good place to stay if you don't need luxury accommodation, but are looking for a really friendly relaxed place to flop on the beach for a few days.

With just 16 rustic bandas (cottages) actually on the beach, a dining-room and a beach bar, don't go expecting luxury hotel facilities at Nomads: this is a very low-key beach resort away from the mass market crowd, where the accommodation is basic, but clean and the food is really good.

Seven of the bandas just have a double room with en suite bathroom with a shower, if you need more space go for one of the five 'family' bandas which have a large twin-bedded room as well as a smaller twin-bedded room and a bathroom. There are three stone cottages and a 'honeymoon suite' which are a bit smarter but if you are looking for something smart this is probably not the ideal place anyway.

Days at Nomads revolve around the beach with its watersports, dive centre and beach bar, which also doubles up as the day-time dining-room and a place to relax

NOMADS
(☎ 127-2155/2533, fax 127-2391), PO Box 1, Ukunda, Kenya
Reservations: UK tour operator World Archipelago (UK ☎ 0181-780 5838)
Getting there: Transfers from Mombasa Airport can be arranged, costing US$55 each way
Accommodation: Seven bandas, five family bandas, three stone cottages, one honeymoon suite
Amenities: Main dining-room, beach bar/dining-room, dive centre, windsurfing school, deep-sea fishing centre, excursions and safaris
Dress code: Casual
Weddings: Can be organised on request
Minimum stay: None
Rates: Bed and breakfast costs between US$25 and US$70 per person depending on accommodation and the time of year
Credit cards: Most major
Taxes and service charge: Included

out of the sun. The hotel's main restaurant where guests eat in the evening serves fantastic seafood – probably the best crab you'll ever eat – and on Sundays really comes alive when the curry lunch is accompanied by a local live band, making it particularly popular with the local Kenyans.

If you tire of the beach, the hotel can easily organise excursions and safaris to **Shimba Hills, Wasini Island** or even into Mombasa. Alternatively, wander down to nearby **Ali Barbar's** for a beer and make sure you find out which nights the **Forty Thieves** hold their beach-side jump-ups: these usually happen twice a week and are popular with tourists and locals alike.

Other recommended hotels

Kiwayu Safari Village (☎ c/o 2-571661, fax 2-571665), PO Box 56923, Nairobi, Kenya, an island retreat 16km north of Lamu off the Kenyan coast, is a great honeymoon getaway. A true Robinson Crusoe-style island combined with perfectly understated luxury, faultless service and excellent dining.

The beach is idyllic white sand, the central mess tent really wonderful with lots of comfortable cushions for lounging around on and doing nothing, and the seafood is delicious. I've never heard a bad word spoken about Kiwayu, and as long as you're not the sort of person who can't live without a hair-dryer you'll fall in love with the place. If you do need a hair-dryer go to Hemingways (see above)! There are 18 rooms in individual 'bandas', reed matting and thatched cottages. They are well spread out among the sand dunes and each one has a private shower and a wonderful large veranda with colourful scatter cushions and a hammock. Rates are approximately US$200 per person per night.

Indian Ocean Beach Club (☎ 0127-3730, fax 0127-3557), Diani Beach, Mombasa, is a new hotel which is a popular honeymoon destination because it offers very economically priced packages through UK tour operators such as Tropical Places (see p11). A 14-day holiday in early July, before the school holidays start, can cost as little as US$1036/£669 for bed and breakfast, flights and transfers as well as free watersports at the hotel.

Diani House (☎ 127-2412, fax 127-2391) on Diani Beach, is an elegant homestead south of Mombasa. Diani is a private house offering wonderfully exclusive accommodation for just four couples. It is run by a lovely young couple, the Clarks, and is a very individual place to stay. Make sure you get down to the Forty Thieves, a great bar which is close by. Diani House costs around US$160 to US$180 per person per night.

Takaungu House (☎ c/o 2-571661, fax 2-571665), near Kilifi, is also really fabulous. This small private house, 48km north of Mombasa, offers three double rooms on a self-catering or full board basis. There is a swimming pool, and snorkelling, scuba diving, deep-sea fishing and local excursions can all be arranged. US$160 per person per night, full board.

Tanzania
(BEST TIME: JUNE TO MARCH)

If you are looking for the authentic safari experience and want to make it the focus of your honeymoon look no further than Tanzania. In this land of magnificent and diverse beauty you will find unparalleled game viewing, in much less touristy surroundings than in neighbouring Kenya.

From the vast, and seemingly never ending, **Serengeti Plains**, to the rugged mountains and stunning soda lakes of the **Rift Valley**, and the awesome **Ngorongor Crater** – a giant Noah's Ark crowded with black rhino, buffalo, elephant and lion – Tanzania offers an experience for real safari enthusiasts. Between November and April the plains are home to droves of wildebeest, stalking lions, hyenas, jackals and eagles. All of this with the added attraction of the idyllic Indian Ocean beaches to look forward to after a week in the bush.

Only 20 minutes off the coast of Tanzania, by plane from the capital **Dar Es Salaam**, is the famous spice island of **Zanzibar**. This intriguing Muslim island had until recently waned in popularity as news of its growing commercialisation spread, but I have found some new properties which are truly excellent and some exclusive private island resorts off the coast, which are far from being over-commercialised or scruffy.

TANZANIA
Incredible wildlife in the Serengeti, and a stunning tropical coastline
When to go: Avoid April to the end of May when the rains are bad, expect intermittent rain around November and December
Average maximum temperatures °C

JAN	FEB	MAR	APR	MAY	JUN	JUL	AUG	SEP	OCT	NOV	DEC
30	31	31	30	30	29	28	29	29	29	30	30

Capital: Dar Es Salaam
Flight times: to Dar es Salaam from:
New York (via Europe) $16^1/_2$ hours
LA: (via New York and Europe) 22 hours
London: $12^3/_4$ hours
Sydney: (via Johannesburg) 22 hours
Approximate exchange rates: Tanzanian shilling (S) – £1 = S886, US$1 = S571.24, A$1 = S451.42
Time difference: GMT plus three hours
Voltage: 240v AC, 50 Hz, although some hotels are equipped with 110v wall sockets for American plugs
Combine with: Kenya, Zanzibar and its islands
Country dialling code: ☎ 255

Safaris in Tanzania

The Serengeti is the most famous game reserve in Africa and no trip to Tanzania would be complete without a visit. In just a couple of days in the Serengeti you'll see an awesome variety of game; nowhere else is there such an abundance of lion, leopard and cheetah – you may even see a kill or two.

The best places to stay are **Migration Camp** (☎ 51-36134, fax 51-115885), c/o Kavimjee Court, 19 Sokoine Court, PO Box 409, Dar es Salaam, in the northern Serengeti or **Klein's Camp** (Kenya ☎ 2-223131, fax 2-212656), c/o Archer's Tours and Travels, Lonhro House, Standard Street, Nairobi, just outside the park in the north-eastern Serengeti. Migration costs around US$200 per person a night full board, while Klein's is marginally more expensive at around US$250. Both are really fantastic camps in beautiful settings.

Make sure you do one of the early morning hot-air balloon safaris: you take off before sunrise, drift gracefully above the majestic plains for an hour or so and then land for champagne and a full English breakfast cooked on the balloon's burner. You could even get married in one?! Balloon safaris can be arranged through either of these camps once you are out there or by talking to Mike Toogood at **Serengeti Balloon Safaris** (UK ☎ 0181-455 0065).

Apart from visiting the **Selous** and the **Serengeti**, a day at the **Ngorongoro Crater**, a World Heritage site, really should be part of any Tanzanian itinerary. There can be few who have not heard of, or seen on TV documentaries, this staggering 20km-wide volcanic crater with its 600m walls packed with just about every type of African wildlife. Apart from the staggering views from the rim, it will also allow you to see rhino, wild dogs and flamingos, which you won't have seen in the Serengeti.

A week of unrivalled game viewing in Tanzania is likely to put you back around US$5000 per couple if you stay in the camps featured in this chapter. If you are put off by this price tag then it's probably better to forget about Tanzania as it is nigh on impossible to see game in these kinds of wilderness conditions for much less. There are much cheaper safari holidays to be had, but not in Tanzania: my advice is to look at Kenya where game viewing tends to be much more reasonable, largely due to the animals' greater accessibility and the presence of more tour companies.

SELOUS GAME RESERVE

A vast wilderness in Southern Tanzania covering 54,000 sq km, the Selous has the largest elephant population in the world and is truly one of the wildest most untouched areas left to discover. This is a safari for the enthusiast, where walking with extremely knowledgeable guides will reveal the hidden Africa, but it's definitely not for the faint-hearted.

MBUYUNI LUXURY TENTED CAMP
(☎ 51-28485, fax 51-46980), PO Box 1192, Dar es Salaam, Tanzania
Closed: Mid April to the end of May
Reservations: Either direct or with Tours and Trade International (UK ☎ 01367-253810); or alternatively through most leading African specialist tour operators and travel agents worldwide (see p11)
Getting there: Mbuyuni can arrange your transfer from Dar es Salaam Airport by light aircraft or charter flight to the camp (scheduled flights cost around US$75 per person one-way but will be included in your final bill)
Accommodation: 12 luxury tents
Amenities: Open top four-wheel drive game drives, aluminium boats, game scouts for treks, swimming pool, three meals a day and open bar, laundry service, and transfer service
Dress code: Casual, but most guests wear long trousers to avoid mosquitoes
Weddings: No
Minimum stay: None
Rates: US$150 per person per day for full board
Credit cards: American Express, Visa, MasterCard
Taxes and service charge: Included

Mbuyuni Luxury Tented Camp

Mbuyuni Luxury Tented Camp is located in the north east sector of the Selous. This sector is the most densely populated game area in the whole reserve and is one of the few places remaining in the world where game can be viewed without the disturbance of hordes of other tourists.

The camp is situated on the banks of a lagoon which is part of the **Rufiji River**: you can sit on your tent's veranda and watch the game coming down to the lagoon to drink – a mesmerising sight.

The camp's 12 green tents, five doubles and seven twins, are mounted on wooden platforms which face towards **Lake Nzerekera**, and which are carefully placed in order to provide maximum privacy. Each one is 3.4m wide and 7m long, well-ventilated and luxuriously appointed with an en suite flushing toilet, a shower and a basin, plus solar powered lighting.

The bar is exceedingly well stocked and is open for as long as you want – they just keep on serving until the last guests have gone to bed. Dining is a pretty spectacular event, especially in the evening when you are served three courses with silver service. The day gets off to a good start with a hearty breakfast comprising fruit, freshly baked breads and eggs to order. Lunch is buffet style with a selection of salads.

Between all this eating and drinking guests get on with the game drives that attracted them to Selous. There is so much to see and do that you won't know whether to go for one of the three-hour safaris in the open top four-wheel drive vehicles (each of which are fitted with VHF mobile radios to keep them in touch with the other vehicles and camp), an afternoon boat trip, or a walk into the surrounding bush accompanied by one of the experienced game scouts. And when you've had enough of all that activity, there's a swimming pool to come home to.

The best time to visit is between June and October because it is the dry season and it is not too hot. Between November and December it is pleasantly hot but you can expect some short rain showers, and from January through to April it just gets hotter and hotter before the rains come. Mbuyuni is closed during the rainy season from the middle of April to the end of May.

Mbuyuni is the perfect solution if you want to experience what it's like to sleep under canvas in the middle of the African bush but don't really want to sacrifice your comforts on your honeymoon.

Sand Rivers Selous

Sand Rivers Selous consists of just six thatched cottages set amidst over 50,000km of land that is home to impala, elephant, hippos and crocodiles. Come here if you want to see game in its natural habitat and if you don't want to be surrounded by hordes of other tourists. There's no point in going to Sand Rivers if you're scared of the bush or need to blow dry your hair every evening, but if you really want to get back to nature you'll love Sand Rivers.

Set in the shade of a baobab tree on the banks of the river Rufiji, the lodge was established by Richard Bonham, who has long been known as one of the finest guides in East Africa.

The six thatched cottages have no fronts and are on stilts overlooking the river, so you can lie in bed and look straight out over your private wooden balcony to the bush. The cottages are all built in rustic style, offering complete comfort and sophistication but using local materials. Each has an en suite bathroom with power shower and a four-poster bed with mosquito netting, a fan and a cupboard with hanging space, so you won't exactly be roughing it! The lodge also

SAND RIVERS SELOUS
(c/o Kenya ☎ 2-884475, fax 2-882728, e-mail: lizzy@srs.simba.glcom.com), Selous Game Reserve, Tanzania
Closed: April and May
Reservations: Either direct or through UK representatives Roxton Bailey Robinson (UK ☎ 01488-683222, fax 01488-682977) and Theobald Barber (UK ☎ 0171-221 0555, fax 0171-221 0444)
Getting there: Guests are met at Dar es Salaam Airport and are then flown to the lodge's airstrip (45 minutes), from where it's a 10-minute drive to the lodge; scheduled flights from Dar es Salaam to Sand Rivers cost around US$95 per person
Accommodation: Six thatched cottages (there are plans to build two more)
Amenities: Dining area, sitting area, open bar (payable on departure), swimming pool with changing room; game viewing by four-wheel drive, on foot and by boat, plus fly camping trips
Dress code: Informal
Weddings: The camp's management say that the prospect cannot be discounted!
Minimum stay: Three nights recommended
Rates: From US$280 to US$360 per person per night, including transfers, meals and game viewing, excludes drinks and fly camping (US$120 a night)
Credit cards: Are not accepted so extras will have to be paid for in cash (preferably US$); your travel agent/tour operator will accept credit cards for the actual holiday bill
Taxes and service charge: Taxes are included, but tips are appreciated

features a large open bar and dining area with an open fire, sofas and armchairs. A swimming pool has been built into the rocks by the river in the shade of the baobab tree. There is a changing room with a shower and toilet, and lots of chairs around the pool.

Activities here include boat trips on the river, and game drives in Richard Bonham's open-top Land Rover but the highlight of Sand Rivers is heading off into the bush on one of his 'fly camping' treks in search of the big five – Bonham is armed only with a mobile phone and a gun. You camp under the stars with only a mosquito net between you and the African sky.

The types of game you are likely to see at Sand Rivers include elephant, hippo, crocodile, lion, wild dog, giraffe, antelope, buffalo and the most superb birdlife.

THE TANZANIAN COAST

Ras Kutani Beach Resort

Ras Kutani Beach Resort is *the* place to relax after a southern Tanzania safari. Rustic and relaxed, the hotel is built on the side of a wooded hill, overlooking the golden beach and beside a fresh-water lagoon.

Like its sister property, Mbuyuni, the Ras Kutani was built using natural materials so, while it may be luxurious, from the air it looks just like a tribal village. You'll stay in one of the 24 large cottages which have either double or twin beds, a flush toilet, shower and basin, and cover around 70 sq metres.

The cottages were built from bamboo and thatch and inside bold, coloured fabrics are used to brighten up the natural fibres of the floor, walls and ceiling. Some of the cottages are up on the hill, others span the side of the lagoon while the best are on the sea shore.

In the middle of your room lies the bed, shrouded in white mosquito netting suspended by a canopy hanging down from the ceiling. All the furniture is locally made and beautifully carved.

In front of each cottage is a fabulous veranda with a brightly coloured hammock perfectly strung to make the best of the view, as well as a sofa, table and chairs, and a wonderful Swahili day bed.

Staying at the Ras Kutani is all about chilling out big time. Watersports are available but nothing motorised is allowed to interrupt the tranquillity of the area: most people spend their days lounging around in hammocks reading or taking the occasional dip. If you do fancy getting up and doing something the hotel will pack you off with a lunch and snorkel to explore the reefs, or you could take out one of their boogie boards and surf the breakers.

RAS KUTANI BEACH RESORT
(☎ 51-28485, fax 51-46980), PO Box 1192, Dar es Salaam, Tanzania
Reservations: Either direct or with Tours and Trade International in the UK on (UK ☎ 01367-253810); most leading African specialist tour operators and travel agents worldwide (see p11)
Getting there: The lodge can arrange your transfer from Dar es Salaam Airport, taking you by scheduled or charter flight to the resort (about 15 minutes)
Accommodation: 24 large cottages, twin, double or single
Amenities: Bar, restaurant serving European food with Africa touches and an emphasis on fresh seafood; snorkelling, windsurfing, sailing, boogie boarding, fishing on nearby reefs, island trips, nature walks, laundry
Dress code: Casual
Weddings: No
Minimum stay: None
Rates: US$135 per person per day full board
Credit cards: American Express, Visa, MasterCard
Taxes and service charge: Included in the price

ZANZIBAR AND OTHER ISLANDS
Ras Nungwe

Zanzibar's west coast, around **Stonetown**, has some lovely hotels but very little to boast about in the way of beaches. The east coast has great beaches and is lovely if you're into back-packing or from Italy – it's full of back-packers and Italians – while the north of the island has the most incredible beaches, is much less tidal and is home to Ras Nungwe, a very special hotel.

Ras Nungwe has the finest beaches in the whole of Zanzibar, and the best setting of all the island's hotels. As a new hotel it is still relatively undiscovered, which makes it an even better find.

You get a wonderfully remote feeling staying there, as there are no other hotels in the area: you can walk for ages along beautiful soft sandy beaches without seeing another soul.

The food is also surprisingly good. Although it's the usual fish suppers (I wouldn't recommend a visit to Zanzibar if you don't like fish!), the hotel has stolen the chef from the **Zanzibar Reef** – apparently he is the best on the island.

The 35 beach bandas, or chalets, all have a patio, a double four-poster bed and

> **RAS NUNGWE**
> (☎ 54-25554, fax 54-33098) A Lala Salama Resort, PO Box 1784, Zanzibar, Tanzania
> **Reservations**: Through UK tour operator World Archipelago (UK ☎ 0181-780 5838)
> **Getting there**: Taxi from Stonetown costs around US$20 per person
> **Accommodation:** 35 beach chalets
> **Amenities**: Dive centre, deep-sea fishing, watersports and dhow trips
> **Dress code**: None, but smart in the evening
> **Weddings**: Can arrange both ceremonies and receptions
> **Minimum stay**: None
> **Rates**: From around US$85 per person full board
> **Credit cards**: Visa, American Express
> **Taxes and service charge**: Included, but tips welcome

are very well furnished. They would have been even nicer had they tiled the en suite bathroom and given it a slightly more substantial door but, this gripe aside, the bedrooms are extremely comfortable.

The central sitting area is full of scattered cushions which are just perfect for lazing around on, at any time of the day. Separate to the sitting area is the restaurant and bar, both of which are open plan: in the evening the tables are smartly laid for dinner and the meal is served by professional waiting staff – somewhat unusual in this part of the world. Breakfast is much less formal comprising an assortment of pastries baked freshly at the hotel, fresh ground coffee or, better still, their home-made hot chocolate which is an absolute must. You can also have your breakfast brought to your room.

Ras Nungwe is the sort of place where there is absolutely nothing to do apart from laze around on the beach all day, and maybe nip off for a bit of snorkelling or diving. The dive school is great and all the usual watersports facilities like windsurfers and dinghies are there. They are a bit short on loungers but somehow it's not that sort of hotel, it's much more of a get the sand between your toes and lie on the beach kind of place. Very relaxed, very remote and very, very beautiful.

Other recommended hotels

Mbweni Ruins (☎ 54-31832, fax 54-30536), PO Box 2542, Zanzibar, Tanzania, is definitely one of the best places in Zanzibar, particularly if you want to be close to Stonetown but don't want to be woken by the chant of the muezzins from the mosques at 4am. The beach isn't so good, but Mbweni Ruins is great for a night or two. Doubles from US$85 bed and breakfast.

Dhow Palace (☎ 54-33012, fax 54-33008), PO Box 3794, Zanzibar, is right in the middle of town and has ten rooms, many with four-posters. The rooms, which face into a central courtyard are surrounded by open verandas. The hotel is a beautiful example of old Stonetown architecture and is filled with Zanzibar furniture and artefacts. Under the same ownership is **Tembo**, (contact the Dhow Palace) a 19th century house on the waterfront which has a lovely swimming pool and superb outside restaurant area. The Dhow Palace and Tembo will cost you between US$80 and US$100 for bed and breakfast per couple.

Zanzique Ltd (☎/fax 54-31033), run by Tariq Barwany and Asha Said, is the best ground operator in Zanzibar: they can arrange almost anything you want to do. Tariq, half-English and half-Zanzibar, is extremely helpful and he is an essential contact in Zanzibar.

Mnemba Club

Created by Italian hotelier Bruno Brighetti, owner of the Blue Safari Club in Manda, Mnemba Club is the ultimate all-inclusive island getaway, for those who can afford it. Situated between two coral reefs 2km off the north-east coast of Zanzibar, the hotel was constructed with minimal impact on the local environment, using local materials and powered by a solar-power unit.

This beautiful, uninhabited island epitomises the concept of barefoot luxury. The ten timber and thatch bamboo shacks have coconut matting floors, and are decorated in a wonderfully simplistic but relentlessly design-conscious fashion – varnished director's chairs are covered in cream canvas, brightly coloured woven rugs and hand-painted cotton curtains sit side by side with rustic furniture and island artefacts such as drift wood and shells. The only slight allowance you have to make for this wonderful hideaway is that the use of solar power means there is hot water only at dusk and since there is no electricity in the cottages the hotel provides one room that has hair-dryers for guests' use.

Otherwise, the island has all the essential creature comforts you'd expect from an Italian hotelier including Dom Perignon, and fresh pasta and olive oil which are flown in from Italy each week.

Mnemba is a place to relax. Instead of a television your cottage has a large veranda with the most awe-inspiring view over the lagoon. If you want to be active the snorkelling and diving on the island's own 16km of unspoilt coral reef is captivating, and in the evening there's first rate sea food and a cold beer or cocktail to look forward to.

If you can possibly afford it this is undoubtedly a contender for the most luxurious, upmarket and expensive destination in Africa.

> **MNEMBA CLUB**
> (c/o Kenya ☎ 2-750298, fax 2-746826), Mnemba Island, Zanzibar, Tanzania
> **Closed** April, May and June
> **Reservations:** Conservation Corporation East Africa (☎ as above); Archer's Tours and Travel (Kenya ☎ 2-224069, fax 2-212656); or through tour operators specialising in East Africa (see p11)
> **Getting there**: On request Archer's Tours and Travel will arrange transport from Nairobi or Dar es Salaam by private air-charter at extra cost; Mnemba Club provides free transfers to the island by speedboat or dhow from Zanzibar Airport
> **Accommodation**: 10 cottages
> **Amenities**: Bar/lounge cottage, open-plan dining cottage, video/library cottage, hair-drying/dressing room
> **Dress code**: Casual – 'barefoot luxury'
> **Weddings**: Can be arranged, but the whole island must be taken by the wedding group – maximum of 20
> **Minimum stay**: Three nights; seven night minimum from late December to mid January
> **Rates**: From around US$360 per person per night (fully inclusive)
> **Credit cards:** American Express, Visa, MasterCard
> **Taxes and service charge**: Included

Kinasi Camp

Kinasi Camp, on Mafia Island, is one of the most beautiful places in the world. This highly exclusive lodge is one of only two hotels on Mafia Island: the island is about the size of nearby Zanzibar where there are as many as 50 hotels.

Kinasi's main lodge is set up on a hillside looking down over the sea, with a beautiful neo-classical swimming pool and large sundeck adjacent to it. The pool is elegantly tiled and looks more like something found in Greece than a Tanzanian construction.

Spread out over the grounds are 12 luxury chalets. They are built from local materials but are much more solid than some rustic bandas. Each chalet has a lovely big four-poster bed and a separate proper tiled bathroom with shower and toilet. At the front of the chalet is a veranda which is equipped with hammocks, royal blue Director's chairs and a table. The hotel staff are quite happy to bring any meal up to your veranda so that you can enjoy it in privacy.

In the main lodge there is a huge open-plan drawing-room and bar, where you can flop into one of the all-enveloping lily pad chairs and slowly drift off with a book, or if you're feeling mentally active play chess or Trivial Pursuit. The hotel's dining-room is quite smart, even slightly austere in these surroundings, with its mock Queen Anne furniture.

Every day is different at Kinasi. In the morning, most guests head off somewhere: scuba diving, snorkelling, or for a picnic on the sand bar. The hotel's dive school, under the supervision of Greg the dive master, is really well run and the area offers some fantastic diving. If you're not into snorkelling and diving and all you want to do is slob on the beach there are better places to do it than Kinasi.

KINASI CAMP
(Kenya ☎ 2-448349, fax 2-441743), PO Box 26, Mafia Island, Tanzania
Reservations: Either direct with the Nairobi number given above, or through UK tour operator World Archipelago (UK ☎ 0181-780 5838)
Getting there: Scheduled flights from Zanzibar or Dar es Salaam to Mafia Island cost US$70, the hotel will meet you from the plane
Accommodation: 12 luxury chalets
Amenities: Swimming pool, diving, watersports, bird watching, picnic boat trips
Dress code: None, but smart in the evening
Weddings: Can arrange both ceremonies and receptions
Minimum stay: No, but three nights recommended
Rates: From US$140 per person all inclusive
Credit cards: Most major
Taxes and service charge: Included, but tips are welcome

Zimbabwe
(BEST TIME: APRIL TO OCTOBER)

If you don't mind early morning wake-up calls, communal dining, or sleeping it rough for a few nights, and if you both share a thirst for adventure and excitement Zimbabwe could be the perfect destination for you.

The great thing about a holiday in Zimbabwe is that you are virtually guaranteed good weather, there's lots to do from white-water rafting to big game trekking, and also some wonderfully luxurious hotels where you can indulge yourselves.

This captivating country is home to the magnificent **Victoria Falls**, the mighty **Zambezi River** as well as an abundance of wildlife. All sorts of waterborne activities are available on the river if you are seeking adventure. It is definitely worth noting that limited places are available on the canoeing safaris, so do make sure you book as early as possible.

Excellent light aircraft services make it very easy to travel around within Zimbabwe and also make it an easy destination to combine with other countries in **Southern Africa**. For example there are flights direct from **Kariba** to nearby **Botswana**.

ZIMBABWE
Fantastic wildlife, canoeing and white-water rafting on the Zambezi and the awesome Victoria Falls
When to go: April to October to avoid the rains, but make sure you take socks and a warm jumper for
early mornings and evenings
Average maximum temperatures °C

JAN	FEB	MAR	APR	MAY	JUN	JUL	AUG	SEP	OCT	NOV	DEC
26	26	26	25	23	21	21	23	27	29	27	26

Capital: Harare
Flight times: to Harare from:
　　　　New York: (via Europe) $17^1/_4$ hours
　　　　LA: (via New York and Europe) 23 hours
　　　　London: $9^3/_4$ hours
　　　　Sydney: (via Johannesburg)$19^3/_4$ hours
Approximate exchange rates: Zimbabwe dollar (Z$) – £1 = Z$16, US$1 = Z$10.32, A$1 = Z$8.15
Time difference: GMT plus two hours
Voltage: 220v AC, US appliances will require an adapter, plugs are usually 13 amp square pins
Combine with: Botswana, Zambia, South Africa, Mauritius
Country dialling code: ☎ 263

LAKE KARIBA

The beautiful man-made **Lake Kariba** is the starting point for many of the canoeing
trips down the Zambezi river. It is also a great place for watching wildlife or for relaxing on a houseboat.

　　If you sit quietly in your boat for long enough, your patience is likely to be
rewarded with the sight of buffalo, zebra, elephant and impalas which will all come
down to the water's edge to drink. From
Kariba you can hop in a boat and head off to
the little known **Matusadona National
Park**, where there are fewer tourists than at
most of Africa's game parks.

Sanyati Lodge

Sanyati Lodge is situated at the mouth of
Sanyati Gorge across the lake from Kariba
town. This cluster of simply furnished
chalets looks out over Lake Kariba but is
camouflaged by the surrounding wooded
hills. The hotel offers game viewing on the
lake by speedboat, as well as walking and
driving safaris in Matusadona National Park
with professional guides.

　　Although nine out of the ten thatched
chalets have twin-beds (plus an en suite toilet and shower), there is one, called the honeymoon suite, which features a double bed
and a private plunge pool.

　　All the chalets are made out of stone
and have thatched roofs with ethnic decor
and overhead fans; shampoo and condition-
er, soap, insect repellent and suntan lotion
are all provided. Laundry is included in your
accommodation charge, which is too good
an offer to miss. These hideaways are open-

SANYATI LODGE
(☎ 14-161 2608, fax 14-161 2264),
Private Bag, Kariba, Zimbabwe
Reservations: Either direct or through
leading African-specialist tour operators
and travel agents worldwide (see p11)
Getting there: Transfers from Kariba
Airport to the harbour and then from the
harbour by boat to the lodge cost US$50
per person one way; self boat hire is
available but expensive and not recommended
Accommodation: Nine twin thatched
units and one double honeymoon suite
Amenities: Two plunge pools, game
safaris (walking, by boat, by vehicle),
fishing, sunset cruises, room service,
open bar
Dress code: Very casual – no jackets or
ties required
Weddings: The lodge does not perform
wedding ceremonies unless the entire
lodge is booked by the wedding party,
costs depend on the time of year and
requirements
Minimum stay: None
Rates: US$250 per person per night
which includes all meals and safaris
Credit cards: Most major
Taxes and service charge: 2% government levy, service included, an additional 15% sales tax charge added to your bill
if you pay in Zimbabwean dollars

sided so don't be surprised if you see monkeys staring at you in the mornings.

The accommodation is comfortable and the food served in the central dining-room excellent. There is also a bar and tea and coffee are available first thing in the morning, at mid-day and in the afternoon.

The lodge has always prided itself on its personalised service. It has however recently been sold to Landela Safaris, a group which has bought a number of Zimbabwe's safari lodges, so do check before booking that this hasn't changed the atmosphere of this truly beautiful and tranquil bush haven.

Musango Safari Camp

Musango has a reputation for being the very best of the best, an absolute must for that untamed bush experience. This exclusive 12-bedded camp accommodates its guests in thatched tents overlooking the **Ume River** mouth on Lake Kariba.

The camp is a great place to see wildlife: this is largely due to the fact that its owner manager, Steve Edwards, is an experienced guide and wildlife photographer. He and his team specialise in walking and driving safaris and canoeing trips, as well as taking guests out on night drives or in the speedboat to more remote areas.

Musango is a tented camp: each chalet is covered with an A-framed thatched roof, designed to keep you cool. They are all equipped with en suite bathrooms set in natural stone and have a private terrace overlooking the lake. There is only one with a double bed, typically named 'the honeymoon suite', otherwise you get twin beds.

Meals are taken in the two-storey central thatched building, together with the camp's other guests: there is also a lounge area, bar, excellent viewing platform and a shaded swimming pool with commanding views over the lake.

> **MUSANGO SAFARI CAMP**
> (☎ c/o 113-2001, fax 113-4349), PO Box 159, Victoria Falls, Zimbabwe
> **Reservations**: Either direct or through all leading African-specialist tour operators and travel agents worldwide (see p11)
> **Getting there**: Transfers from Kariba Airport by float-plane cost US$100 per person return
> **Accommodation**: Five twin and one honeymoon suite thatched tents
> **Amenities**: Swimming pool, central dining and lounge area with bar, walks in the Matusadona National Park, boat cruises, canoeing, bird-watching, fishing, cultural visits; a visit to a crocodile ranch can be arranged on request
> **Dress code**: Casual
> **Weddings:** Musango hasn't yet done any weddings but is not adverse to the idea
> **Minimum stay**: None, but two to three days recommended
> **Rates**: US$195 per person during low season (from early January to the end of June) and US$240 in high season, including all food, drinks, accommodation, safaris and tours
> **Credit cards:** Visa
> **Taxes and service charge:** 2% government levy, service is discretionary

Other recommended hotels

Senkwe River Lodge (☎ c/o 113-2001, fax 113-4349), PO Box 159, Victoria Falls, is located right on the shores of Kariba in the remote **Chete Safari** area. Run by Chris Worden, Senkwe accommodates 12 guests in six open, airy daub and thatch huts built around A-frames, all of which have an en suite shower and toilet.

There is a small swimming pool with gazebo and a summer house but most of the day is spent out on the water exploring the inlets and creeks of this massive lake. After dinner, guests often sit in the main lodge's upstairs sitting-room where there is a viewing area.

Senkwe is reached by a short flight from Kariba, Victoria Falls (US$230 per person return) or direct from Harare (US$275 per person return). Doubles from US$190 per person per night.

CANOEING SAFARIS

If you prefer to view game without the continual hum of Land Rover engines, a canoeing safari down the Zambezi is a wonderful way of seeing hippos, giraffe, elephants, fantastic bird life, and even crocodiles. You'll spend days gliding effortlessly through the tranquil waters, viewing the game that have come down to the water to drink, and at night you camp under the stars around a fire.

The great thing about canoeing trips in Zimbabwe is that you can either go for a day, three days or even six days. You can also choose to stay on the more popular strip between **Kariba** and **Chirundu** or go into the more remote waters around **Mana Pools** and down to the **Mozambique** border, or wait until you get up to Victoria Falls and canoe the reaches of the **upper Zambezi**.

A whole host of tour companies run trips on the lower Zambezi between Kariba and Chirundu: the best known is **Shearwater** (☎ 113-4471) which has gradually taken over many of its competitors including most recently Sobek, but you might also try talking to Anthony Elton at **River Horse Safaris** (161-2422) and Garth Thompson who runs **Nature Ways** (☎ 14-758841).

For canoeing trips departing from Victoria Falls try **Kandahar Safaris** (☎ 113-4502, fax 113-2014), owned by Kerry and Clive Bradford. The Bradford's small, family-run company is well suited to honeymooners because they give much more individual attention than the bigger companies and generally they are great people to go with. Their canoeing safaris start at US$80 per person for a one-day trip and go up to US$300 for a two and a half day sortie. If you don't have time for a full-day, opt for the ultimate sundowner cruise: gin and tonic in hand and nibbles at your side as you are paddled downstream watching the sunset.

Luxury houseboats

Renting a houseboat is one of the best ways to experience Lake Kariba. The lake is usually calm as there are few strong winds, and your relative quietness on the water enables you to get much closer to the animals: you'll find you can drift right up to the shore line where the elephants are bathing. Apart from observing the wildlife, being on the water also gives you the freedom to explore the various islands.

Zimbabwean-based **Run Wild** (☎ 14-792333, fax 14-792342) offers houseboats and yacht charters on Lake Kariba, while UK tour operator **Carrier** (UK ☎ 01625-582006), has a range of boats to suit all budgets costing from US$200 to US$600 per day. For US$200 you get a skipper but no guide and although the skipper may sound as if he knows about the local wildlife, it's worth paying the extra for a professional guide if you can. You also have to do your own catering.

The other option is to stay at **Water Wilderness**, a small custom-made colony of houseboats in a really quiet part of the lake, which can be booked through most leading African-specialist tour operators (see p11). The four houseboats at Water Wilderness don't actually move, but you can spend your time paddling around on your own Canadian canoe that comes with the houseboat or tracking on foot with one of the camp's experienced trackers. Water Wilderness can also be booked through Maureen Vincent at local agents **Wilderness Safaris** (☎ 113-4527). At US$250 per person each day the houseboats tend to be more expensive than the charter boats, but the price does include meals.

HWANGE NATIONAL PARK

Covering 23,000 sq km, roughly the size of Switzerland, Hwange is the largest National Park in Zimbabwe and is home to over 100 different varieties of animals and 400 species of birds. Herds of over 100 elephants have often been seen drinking at the watering holes in the park. Hwange is an hour's drive from Kariba by four-wheel drive.

Jijima

Jijima is an absolutely brilliant place to stay and is definitely one of the best lodges in Hwange. Owned and run by the White family, this beautiful camp overlooks the **Jijima Vlei** (bush) and a watering hole.

The camp is about an hour's drive through indigenous hardwood forests from Hwange Airport. It is on the park's south-eastern boundary and consists of a large central boma (thatched hut) offering open-air seating, a bar and a dining area all under thatch, and a swimming pool. During winter Jean's legendary cooking is served around a roaring fire in the boma and in summer guests eat out under the stars.

The eight chalets, seven with twin beds and one with a double, are tents under thatch: they all have en suite showers with hot and cold water and flush toilets. Do remember to bring warm clothes if your holiday falls between May and September as the early mornings and nights can be really cold.

Guests can chose between game viewing by vehicle or on foot, as well as overnight camping in the Hwange National Park at **Ngweshla Pan**. You should see many of the larger mammals including lions, elephants, sable, zebra, eland and maybe even rhinoceros and leopard if you're lucky.

JIJIMA
(☎ c/o 113-2001, fax 113-4349), PO Box 159, Victoria Falls, Zimbabwe
Reservations: Either direct with local agent Wild Horizons on the above number or through leading tour operators specialising in Africa (see p11)
Getting there: Transfers cost US$65 per person return from Hwange Airport
Accommodation: Seven twins and one honeymoon suite in thatched tents
Amenities: Swimming pool, central dining and lounge area with bar, game drives in four-wheel drive into Hwange National Park and walking safaris within the estate
Dress code: Casual
Weddings: Have been arranged in the past, costs depend on what you want
Minimum stay: None, but two to three nights recommended
Rates: US$200 per person during the low season (early January to the end of June) and US$240 in the high season, which includes all food, drink, accommodation and game drives
Credit cards: Most major
Taxes and service charge: 2% government levy, service is discretionary

---

VICTORIA FALLS

No visit to Zimbabwe would ever be complete without a visit to the mighty Victoria Falls, the world's largest waterfall and definitely deserving of its place among the Seven Wonders of the World. The volume of water cascading over this huge 90m precipice is so huge that the spray can be seen from 30km away. On my first visit to the Falls I noticed that people returning from them were soaked to the skin: I assumed this meant it was raining ahead. However, it wasn't long before I started to get wet and then I realised that the 'rain' was coming from the Falls rather than the sky. Nothing can prepare you for the immensity of the sight, or the clouds of water rising high above your head and soaking you through – earning the Falls the local name of 'the smoke that thunders'.

The Victoria Falls Hotel

For true romantics the only place to stay in Victoria Falls is, of course, The Victoria Falls Hotel. This famous five-star colonial hotel is perched close to the edge of the vast gorge and is a wonderful place to relax, especially after its recent extensive refurbishment. The Edwardian architecture and old world charm cannot fail to woo you. Set in lovely well kept gardens The Vic Falls (as it is known locally) has the most splendid views of the bridge spanning the **Batoka Gorge**, while the thundering noise of cascading water acts as a constant reminder of your prime location.

All the bedrooms are en suite and air-conditioned and feature colonial architecture and traditional furnishings. They are well fitted-out with modern amenities including

THE VICTORIA FALLS HOTEL
(☎ 113-4751/61, fax 113-4586), PO Box 10, Victoria Falls, Zimbabwe
Reservations: Either direct or through most leading specialist-African tour operators and travel agents worldwide (see p11)
Getting there: The hotel does not offer transfers, but you can jump on the Air Zimbabwe bus which offers transfers from the airport for Z$35 one way, or take a taxi which is more expensive at Z$120 to Z$140 one way
Accommodation: Capacity 300 guests in a range of accommodation including six executive suites and one Royal Presidential Suite
Amenities: Swimming pool, room service gift shop, hair salon, Livingstone Restaurant, Stanleys, Jungle Junction and the swimming pool bar
Dress code: Smart casual
Weddings: Wedding ceremonies can be arranged at the hotel either in the grounds or in the chapel and will be performed by the local magistrate
Minimum stay: None, unless you are getting married in which case you must stay for two nights
Rates: Doubles from US$290; suites from US$507
Credit cards: Most major
Taxes and service charge: Taxes are included, there is no service charge

in-room safe, hair-dryer, bathrobes, toiletries, radio, phone: the suites also have a minibar.

Facilities include two tennis courts, a swimming pool with pool-side bars as well as several other restaurants and bars. Don't miss the wonderful pool-side buffets and braes (barbecues) which are legendary.

Victoria Falls Safari Lodge
The Victoria Falls Safari Lodge may be a new hotel but it is currently giving the older contender a real run for its money. Just four kilometres away from the Falls, the lodge benefits from a relatively peaceful location and has built up quite a following in the short time since it opened.

The lodge is perfectly located to make the most of its uninterrupted views of the surrounding **Zambezi National Park** and the spectacular African sunsets, with lots of game to be seen on the property throughout the year. There is a courtesy minibus to the Falls and a tour desk at the Lodge which will help you organise anything you want to do.

What sets the Victoria Falls Safari Lodge apart from the rest of the accommodation in the area is its stunning architecture and attention to detail. The thatched rustic finish combined with vibrant patterned and checked fabrics and the omnipresent warm glow of the local hardwoods gives the lodge a distinctly African feel which at the same time is extremely homely and informal.

The lodge has 66 bedrooms and six luxury suites: all are furnished to the highest standards and have superb views over the Zambezi National Park. The rooms are decorated ethnically with bright, coloured bedspreads and African floor rugs. Each room

VICTORIA FALLS SAFARI LODGE
(☎ 113-3202/3/4, fax 113-3205/7, PO Box 29, Squire Cummins Road, Victoria Falls, Zimbabwe
Reservations: Either direct or from the UK through Three Cities Hotels (UK ☎ 0171-225 0164, fax 0171-823 7701, e-mail Anne@tch.ftech.co.uk); or by calling US toll free (☎ 800-44-UTELL)
Getting there: 4km west of the falls, 20km from Victoria Falls Airport, transfers arranged from US$12.50 per person
Accommodation: 72 rooms, including six suites, 10 doubles and 56 twins
Amenities: Two restaurants, bar, swimming pool, bungy jumping, white-water rafting/kayaking, game drives/walks, horse-riding, sunset river cruises, flights over the falls
Dress code: None – very casual
Weddings: Can be arranged anywhere within the hotel or at a watering hole in the surrounding bush for up to 150 guests, the hotel will try to cater for virtually anything you want, the service costs US$35, plus US$100 administrative costs
Minimum stay: None
Rates: Doubles from US$300; suites from US$400 including full breakfast
Credit cards: Diners Club, Visa, Access
Taxes and service charge: 2% government levy not included

also features luxury extras such as air-conditioning with a ceiling fan, mosquito net, hair-dryer, phone and smoke detector. The pristine white and blue tiled bathroom has a huge corner bath and a pressure shower. There are also binoculars and nature books on your private balcony so that you know what you are looking at.

At sundown you'll find most guests congregate for cocktails in the **Buffalo** bar, where huge thick wooden pillars support an intricately thatched roof and carved wooden buffalo heads adorn the bar. When it's time for dinner you'll move into the wonderful **Makuwa-Kuwa** dining-room softly lit with candles. The tables are covered in brilliant coloured cloths and there are co-ordinating director's chairs. After dinner, head for the **Nature Library** high up in the apex of the thatched roof: it's the perfect place to round off the day with a night-cap as you overlook the watering hole for one last sighting of the surrounding wildlife.

Tongabezi

Tongabezi, named after the local Tonga tribe and *bezi* meaning river, is on the other side of the Falls and thus is actually in **Zambia**. It has recently gained the recognition it deserves as one of Africa's most exciting hotels, and is currently very much in vogue as *the* place to go in southern Africa. There is no doubt that Tongabezi is the perfect honeymooner retreat, and it is now becoming so popular for weddings that one British party recently set their wedding date around availability at the lodge.

If you are flying into Victoria Falls Airport on your way to Tongabezi, do take advantage of the lodge's rather unusual transfer arrangements. Instead of being picked up by road they can arrange a Flight of the Angels for you, before landing at the hotel: swooping down over the Victoria Falls in a light aircraft is really the only way to get an idea of the scale and immense grandeur of this rushing torrent of water.

Accommodation at Tongabezi is spread across **Tongabezi Lodge**, **Sindabezi Island** and **Livingstone Island**. Tongabezi Lodge is found on the banks of the Zambezi, facing west into the setting sun, 20km upstream from the Victoria Falls. Guests stay either in luxury tents which have twin beds or in one of the four 'houses', which are open to the wild and couldn't be more perfect. Both the tents and houses are built using natural materials and all have their own private river frontage.

The four houses (bird, tree, dog and honeymoon) each have a four-poster bed with a large, airy mosquito canopy, private bathroom with a bath big enough for two,

TONGABEZI
(Zambia ☎ (260) 3-323235/96, fax 3-323224, e-mail: tonga@zamnet.zm)
Private Bag 31, Livingstone, Zambia
Reservations: Specialist African tour operators (see p11)
Getting there: Road transfers from Livingstone Airport (20 minutes), the Zambian border (25 minutes) are arranged on a complimentary basis by the lodge; road transfers from Victoria Falls Airport (75 minutes) and Victoria Falls Hotel (one hour) cost US$30 and US$23 respectively, alternatively air transfer on the Flight of the Angels cost US$90 from Victoria Falls Airport (20 minutes) and US$125 from Kasane Airport (40 minutes)
Accommodation: Four twin tents, four double houses in Tongabezi Lodge; three twin and one double chalet on Sindabezi Island; plus Livingstone Fly camp and Upper Zambezi Canoeing
Amenities: Swimming pool, grass tennis courts, croquet, bird-watching, fishing, boating, canoeing, walks, dining, staff soccer games, room service, private dinners, laundry
Dress code: Casual
Weddings: Tongabezi is incredibly popular for weddings and really helpful, but do book early, ask them about their four-day wedding package which costs around US$3100 per couple including your accommodation in a house and all arrangements
Minimum stay: None
Rates: Doubles from US$310 in Tongabezi houses, from US$255 on Sindabezi Island, which includes accommodation, meals, bar, house wines, picnic lunches, sunset and sunrise boat trips and several other tours
Credit cards: Most major
Taxes and service charge: Included

flush toilets with the most incredible views, and hot and cold running water.

One of the best aspects of staying in Tongabezi, and something that everyone comments on, is the privacy. While guides and management are on hand at all times, they do their best to be unobtrusive, and because of the careful positioning of the houses and tents you won't find anyone wandering around in front of your patch. The fact that there are no walls can at times be almost comical when room service arrives and instead of knocking the waiter is obliged to say

We loved Tongabezi – with its fantastic views it was the perfect place for a honeymoon – Honeymoon House and Tree House were the best.
Peter and Madeleine Harding

out loud: 'knock, knock, Missy, room service is here', but don't worry the tents are totally insect-proof.

Just 3km downstream by private motorised banana boat takes you to Sindabezi where eight guests at a time are treated to a safari experience unlike any other. Sindabezi is the only island lodge in the Falls area. As such it is unique: you may get elephants in your room, hippos on your doorstep and you will undoubtedly be woken by a vociferous dawn chorus. Try to work a couple of nights on the island into your itinerary if you can.

Although the prices are steep, you can at least rest assured that unless you are going to drink nothing but champagne, for which there is an extra charge, you will spend very little money as all meals, drinks at the bar, house wines, picnic lunches and excursions are included in the price.

A FEW THINGS TO SEE AND DO AROUND VICTORIA FALLS

There's lots to do from Victoria Falls. Many people find the river cruises and the curio (craft) villages disappointingly touristy, but there's lots of less tame entertainment to be had if that's your want. Go for the Flight of the Angels, a 15-minute trip in a twin-engined light aircraft flying low over the Falls: it's particularly thrilling at sunset. Better still, grab a paddle and head down one of the world's most exciting white-water rapids on a raft. The 5m inflatable rafts buck and leap down the wild rapids, guided by experienced oarsmen.

There are hordes of companies offering white-water rafting from Victoria Falls and whoever you go with it will cost US$95 per person: this rate is the result of an agreement between the companies. Don't pay cash as you'll be charged an additional 15% sales tax. Whichever company you pick, make sure your day starts at Rapid No 1, the so called **Boiling**

Pot at the base of the Falls: you get spectacular views and four extra rapids before you even get to the point where most companies start their day! **Kandahar Safaris** (☎ 113-4502) start from the Boiling Pot and offer a full day's rafting from 7.30am to 6pm including lunch.

From Tongabezi it is also possible to go rafting on the Zambian side with **Safari Par Excellence** (☎ (260) 14-720527). If you fancy going further afield go for one of Tongabezi's canoeing trips. These can last between one and three nights and enable you to explore upstream sections of the Victoria Falls along with a dedicated chef, waiter and service staff. Each night you camp in comfortable fly tents with twin beds (mattresses and linen), while days are spent paddling in two-seater canoes. You won't need any previous experience, just be mad enough to think this is what you want to be doing on your honeymoon!

Botswana
(BEST TIME: OCTOBER TO MAY)

Because of their close proximity, Botswana and Zimbabwe can easily be combined on a two-week holiday, giving you the best of both worlds, especially if it's game you're after. There are regular flights from Kariba to Botswana.

The **Okavango's** 15,000 sq km delta, produced every spring as the Okavango river floods into the **Kalahari** sands, is home to countless numbers of hippo, crocodiles, elephant and buffalo as well as a diverse birdlife. In the 10,000 sq km **Chobe National Park**, giraffe, lion, leopard and the endangered white rhinoceros roam the plains, while open-top game drives through the grasslands of the **Moremi Wildlife Reserve** will reveal impala, kudu, buffalo and elephants.

The following camps are the best places to stay in Botswana, and can all be booked through tour operators specialising in southern Africa (see p11): Jedibe Island Camp, Mombo Camp, Chobe Chilwero Lodge, Jack's Camp and Delta Camp.

BOTSWANA
Average maximum temperatures °C

JAN	FEB	MAR	APR	MAY	JUN	JUL	AUG	SEP	OCT	NOV	DEC
31	30	29	27	25	22	22	25	28	30	31	31

Approximate exchange rates: Pula (P) – £1 =P5.43, US$1 = P3.50, A$1 = P2.77
Time difference: GMT plus two hours
Voltage: 220v AC
Combine with: Zimbabwe, South Africa
Country dialling code: ☎ 267

South Africa
(BEST TIME: OCTOBER TO MAY)

South Africa is such a perfect holiday destination it's worth setting your wedding date between October and May just so that you can have your honeymoon there. However, like New Zealand, Australia and South America, South Africa is not the sort of destination where you are likely to fly to one resort and stay there for two weeks.

So much of the country is worth seeing, it makes the selection process painful: as the national tourist board is known to boast 'it's a world in one country'. With its spectacular landscapes of deserts, mountains, beaches and cliffs, fertile farmlands and modern cities, South Africa has all the ingredients for a wonderful honeymoon and the holiday of a lifetime.

The main elements of any holiday in South Africa should be a trip to **Cape Province**, where the Atlantic and Indian Ocean's meet, **Cape Town** and the vineyards of **Stellenbosch**; a drive up the spectacular coastline between Cape Town and **Port Elizabeth**, known as the **Garden Route**; a few days safari in the **Kruger National Park**; and perhaps an overnight journey on the **Blue Train** or **Rovos Rail** – South Africa's sumptuous answers to the Orient-Express. I would avoid Johannesburg, as it is little more than a large, essentially grey, modern, inland city.

Although South Africa's tourist industry is only just emerging from the ravages inflicted by apartheid, the country is full of first-class hotels and restaurants, originally created to satisfy the demands of an incredibly discerning local population.

I first went to South Africa ten years ago, and however backward it was politically then, it was an unforgettable culinary experience. From the brais (barbecues) on the beach to the freshest crayfish brought in by local fishermen, and some seriously elaborate six-course marathons; this is definitely a destination for gastronomes, with hotels to match.

If you like the idea of combining walks along empty beaches pounded by deafening surf, sundowners on top of the magnificent **Table Mountain**, wine tasting and dining in some of the world's greatest wineries, and donning your khakis for a few days of 'real' Africa, then this is the honeymoon for you. All the above can easily be achieved in a fortnight, with plenty of time to relax and really enjoy the surrounding countryside.

SOUTH AFRICA
Mountains, coasts, wine lands and safari all interspersed with truly luxurious hotels for gastronomes
When to go: October to May; mid-December to mid-January is holiday time in South Africa and as such the country's key destinations are a great deal busier and more expensive; the east coast is always warm(ish), and Durban really humid and unless you're up in the mountains, the winters are rarely very cold
Average maximum temperatures °C(Cape Town)

JAN	FEB	MAR	APR	MAY	JUN	JUL	AUG	SEP	OCT	NOV	DEC
26	26	25	22	19	18	17	18	19	21	23	25

Capital: Johannesburg
Flight times: to Johannesburg from:
New York: 14$\frac{1}{4}$ hours
LA: (via New York and Europe) 21 hours
London: 10$\frac{3}{4}$ hours
Sydney: 18 hours
Approximate exchange rates: Rand (R) – £1 = R7, US$1 = R4.51, A$1 = R3.57
Time difference: GMT plus two hours
Voltage: 220v/230v, AC 50 Hz, plugs have three round pins
Combine with: Zimbabwe, Botswana, Mauritius but there's plenty to keep you occupied in South Africa alone
Country dialling code: ☎ 27

THE MOUNT NELSON
(☎ 21-231000, fax 21-247472), 76 Orange Street, Cape Town 8001, South Africa
Reservations: Through Orient-Express Hotels' reservation numbers worldwide (see p12) or through The Leading Hotels of the World reservation numbers worldwide (see p12)
Getting there: The hotel can arrange transfers from the airport
Accommodation: 219 air-conditioned rooms and suites
Amenities: 24-hour room service, curio and gift shop, hairdresser and beauty salon, free parking, courtesy shuttle bus to the Blue Train at Cape Town station, the Grill Room, the Oasis Restaurant overlooking the pool, the Lounge and Veranda for coffee and afternoon tea, the Lord Nelson bar, several function rooms, two heated swimming pools, two all-weather tennis courts (floodlit), one squash court, full range of watersports available at nearby beaches including surfing, windsurfing and scuba diving; hill walking, climbing and a wide choice of golf courses nearby
Dress code: Elegant casual, jackets are requested for gentlemen diners
Weddings: Both ceremonies and receptions can be arranged
Minimum stay: None
Rates: Double room from US$240; suites from US$310, but ask about honeymoon packages
Credit cards: Most major
Taxes and service charge: Included

CAPE TOWN
Built on a peninsula where the Indian and Atlantic Ocean meet, Cape Town is, without doubt, one of the most naturally blessed cities in this world. With the most dramatic of back-drops supplied by the omnipresent Table Mountain and the craggy Apostles, plus a beautiful harbour, numerous surf strewn beaches, and the wonderfully cool south-westerly breezes, it is difficult to imagine a more perfect summer city.

The Mount Nelson
The most gracious and the most famous hotel in Cape Town is The Mount Nelson, known to its friends as The Nellie. This elegant pink hotel has been restored to its former colonial splendour since the fire in 1993 and has recently become part of the revered Orient-Express Hotels group.

The Nellie's dreamy setting at the foot of Table Mountain helps make it a wonderfully romantic hotel. It is within an easy stroll of the city centre, although you'd never know it because you're surrounded by three hectares of beautifully tended gardens.

This hotel has everything you could possibly want, from the swimming pool to the beauty centre, as well as casual and formal dining. But one of the highlights about staying in The Nellie is undoubtedly its teas, which are served either in the conservatory or on the lawn: you may well spot President Mandela and other visiting dignitaries. Sipping tea in such elegant surroundings with the chink of bone-china, it is difficult to imagine that you are in Africa and you'll immediately feel as if you've been transported back to the 1920s. The Nellie can also claim to be the only hotel to offer steak tartare on the breakfast menu, apparently a relic from Lord Kitchener's days.

The 159 bedrooms also personify the hotel's old world grandeur and have lovely views over the gardens, the city or towards Table Mountain, **Lion's Head** and **Devil's Peak**. Many of the rooms have been redecorated in the last few years by renowned South African interior designer, Graham Viney. He has worked hard to restore the feel of the colonial days and has produced bedrooms with a very light and airy feel, full of English chintz and luxurious bathrooms. The best room is No 218 with its astonishing 180° view over the gardens and nearby mountains, but you might also try one of the eight Garden Cottage suites, which are surrounded by their own individual garden and have wrought-iron furnishings and a private swimming pool.

The Cellars-Hohenort Country House

The Cellars-Hohenort Country House enjoys a prime location, only fifteen minutes from Cape Town but right in the heart of one of the Cape's best wine growing regions, Constantia. The lush valley of Constantia running between Cape Town and the **Cape of Good Hope** has been famous for its superb wines for centuries, while back in the 18th century Cellars was the Cape governor's wine cellar.

This beautiful country house, set in exquisitely landscaped gardens with orchards and vineyards all around, offers wonderful accommodation and exceptional food, making it the perfect place to wind down after a long flight and the emotional highs of a wedding. It's really easy to get into town and to the many great beaches around Cape Town but even nicer to return to serene Constantia at the end of the day.

The 38 rooms and 15 suites are individually decorated to reflect the gracious elegance of a historic Cape country house. They are decorated in chintz fabrics, period furniture and local artwork. All have stunning views over the mountains. Rooms No 2 and No 41 are particularly beautiful: room No 2 is one of the oldest rooms in the house and the most romantic with its wooden ceilings, large brass bed and its cream and blue furnishings; room No 41, a junior suite, has spectacular views of the Constantia Valley and **False Bay** in the distance, it is decorated in pale yellow and light green giving it a really fresh appearance.

As a member of Relais & Châteaux you'd expect the food at Cellars to be good. And it is. There are two restaurants to choose from, the famous **Cellars Restaurant** where you can expect dishes such as Cape Rock lobster and Karoo lamb, washed down with fine Cape wines, and the **Malay Kitchen**. Jacket and tie are expected in both – this is Cape Town and people like to take their food seriously!

THE CELLARS-HOHENORT COUNTRY HOUSE
(☎ 21-794 2137, fax 21-794 2149), 15 Hohenort Avenue, Constantia 7800, Cape Town, South Africa
Reservations: Relais & Châteaux worldwide reservation numbers (see p12)
Getting there: The hotel can help with transfers on request, Cape Town airport is 20km away
Accommodation: 38 rooms and 15 suites
Amenities: Two restaurants, private dining-room, swimming pool, tennis, golf, 24-hour room service
Dress code: Jacket and tie is required in the restaurants
Weddings: During May, June and July wedding receptions are catered for in the Cellars Restaurant (maximum 60) and in the private dining-room, the Jade and Gold Room (maximum 40), although the hotel is not licensed to perform wedding ceremonies there are some beautiful old stone churches nearby, ask the hotel for advice
Minimum stay: None
Rates: Double rooms from US$192 R880; suites from US$216/R990 to US$331/R1520
Credit cards: Most major
Taxes and service charge: Included

Guests can play tennis or golf or just relax by the lovely pool, set amidst landscaped gardens, soaking up the sunshine and the total tranquillity of Constantia. But you should also make a point of exploring the wonderful residences in the area and the beautiful **Kirstenbosch** botanical gardens.

Ellerman House

Also just outside Cape Town, and equally welcoming and tranquil, is Ellerman House, named after Sir John Ellerman, a wealthy ship owner who bought it at the turn of the century.

Today Ellerman House is a beautiful haven, situated in **Bantry Bay**, a charming part of Cape Town, with terraced gardens and palm trees facing the Atlantic. This wonderful hotel, extremely highly rated within South Africa, is run very much like a private house; helped by the fact that with only seven rooms there are never more than 14 guests.

The restaurant is for residents only and, instead of having a set menu to choose from, you are asked after breakfast each day if you'll be in for lunch and dinner and, if so, what you might fancy eating. With such a generous policy the chef has been known to prepare totally different meals for every guest. To make matters even better this small hotel operates 24-hour room service so it's no problem if you fancy eating on your balcony, or if you like they will recommend a local restaurant and book it for you.

Tucked away on the slopes of Cape Town's famous Lion's Head, there can be few better views in the city. All seven rooms are en suite and are decorated in Edwardian style, with English period furniture and lovely antiques. The Ellerman Suite, on the top floor, is the house's grandest room: it has a totally separate, fully furnished lounge and incredible views over the ocean. Alternatively, go for mini suites Nos 1, 2 and 4, which have great views and balconies.

The reception rooms offer intimate relaxation surrounded by typically Cape furnishings, such as plush leather armchairs, fine wood panelling and warm colours. A very relaxed atmosphere pervades the lounges and bar: it wouldn't be unusual for one guest decked out in black tie to be having a drink with another guest still in shorts. Ellerman House has its own gym and sauna on the premises and will also arrange any health or beauty treatments you should want.

ELLERMAN HOUSE
(☎ (021-439 9182, fax 021-434 7257), 180 Kloof Road, Bantry Bay, 8001 Cape Town, South Africa
Reservations: Relais & Châteaux reservation numbers worldwide (see p12)
Getting there: The hotel will arrange airport transfers, the price of which is included in your room bill
Accommodation: Six rooms and one Ellerman suite
Amenities: Outdoor swimming pool; tennis and golf within 5km; sauna and private fitness centre; private dining-room
Dress code: Smart/casual in the restaurant
Weddings: The hotel can do weddings as long as the entire house is taken over in which case you'll pay the usual prices for accommodation, plus whatever food you want for the reception
Minimum stay: None
Rates: Doubles from US$458/R2100 between October and May, and from US$393/R1800 between June and September; the Ellerman suite costs US$698/R3200 during peak season and US$611/R2800 out of season; rates include all meals and drinks except wine and champagne
Credit cards: Most major
Taxes and service charge: Included

THREE DAYS IN CAPE TOWN

At the end of the 17th century, the largely Mediterranean climate lured the French Huguenot refugees to the Cape where they planted the original seeds of what are now world class **wineries**. These glorious wine estates with their Cape Dutch colonial-style architecture are still well preserved today. Paarl, Stellenbosch and Franschhoek have all developed their own **wine routes** for tourists. Hire a car and spend a few days touring the wine lands: you won't need to do much driving as they are all within easy reach of Cape Town, and many offer wonderful accommodation and restaurants so you can relax in style and don't need to worry about driving home.

One of my favourites is the recently-refurbished *Lanzerac* (☎ 21-887 1132, fax 21-887 2310), PO Box 4, Stellenbosch 7599, Western Cape, a 300-year old manor house on the outskirts of Stellen-bosch where 40 individually furnished rooms all have access to the hotel's beautiful gardens. There are few better ways to spend an afternoon than lying on the beautifully mown lawns of a winery, with a bottle of Cape Blush (rosé) to share, and only the prospect of a sumptuous dinner and bed ahead of you. Double rooms at the Lanzerac start at US$68/R310 per person for bed and breakfast in a Classic room and go up to US$89/R410 per person for a Luxury Room, but there is also the most fabulous Swimming Pool Suite which has a double bedroom, a separate living-room and a beautiful small rectangular swimming pool set in a pretty courtyard, costing US$166/R760 per person, bed and breakfast. Take a wander around the winery, choose yourselves a few bottles and retire to the pool for an afternoon of decadent heaven.

Hiring a car will also enable you to drive down to the tip of the Cape peninsula, Cape Point, taking you through the **Cape of Good Hope Nature Reserve**. The road along Chapman's Peak Drive is one of the most beautiful stretches of **coastal highway** you are ever likely to see. The best way to drive it is to do a clockwise loop around the peninsula, starting at Kirstenbosch Botanical Gardens, and then going through Muizenberg. If you leave in the morning you'll have plenty of time to find your own perfect beach en route to the Cape, see the magnificent views where the two oceans meet, and get back to Chapman's Peak in time to enjoy the most wonderful moules and other seafood at **Hout Bay**. This really is paradise for seafood and wine lovers, and all with a backdrop of relentlessly crashing surf. Try *Chapman's Peak Restaurant* in the hotel (☎ 21-790 1036) and the *Mariner's Wharf Grill* (☎ 21-790 1100), which although a bit touristy is a good open-air bistro serving fantastic fish.

A trip to the top of **Table Mountain** is a must for visitors. Pick a day when there is no cloud (affectionately referred to by the locals as its table cloth because of the way it hugs the mountain top and drapes down the side), and either take the **cable car** (☎ 21-24 5148) or, if you're feeling very energetic, walk. If you do go by cable car, make sure you avoid the long queues by getting there first thing or towards late afternoon, giving you time to get up there for a sundowner – traditionally you take up your own 'cold tinnies'. It is possible to book the cable car at the Waterfront Information Centre in town. You can drive up far enough to get a pretty good view but it is worth getting to the top if you can.

You haven't really been to Cape Town until you've sampled its **beaches** – as the locals are fond of saying, 'life's a beach', and nowhere is that quite so true as in Cape Town. The city's most popular beaches are at **Clifton**: they are numbered 'First', 'Second', 'Third' and 'Fourth', and the little one at the end is called Moses (it disappears with the tide). This is where the beautiful people flock at the weekends and on holiday: to surf, to pose, to gossip and to bronze themselves. Other fantastic beaches are at **Camps Bay**, although it is normally pretty windy, **Llandudno** where the surf is great and the clientele a bit less posey (watch out for the undertow), and across the other side north of the city at **Bloubergstrand** where you get that distant picture-postcard view of Table Mountain that we always see in photographs and paintings.

THE GARDEN ROUTE

This stretch of land, along the coastal highway between Cape Town and Port Elizabeth, is renowned for its spectacular scenery and equally good hotels. Kilometre after kilometre of glorious coastline is met by mountains covered in indigenous forest, with only the occasional dolphin or whale to break up the monotony of the view. Allow four or five days to do the journey at an easy pace, and give yourselves plenty of time to get off the road and explore. The best section of the coast is between **Mossel Bay** and **Storms River**. The area is famous for its lakes and forests as well as its two National Parks (**Tsitsikamma Forest** and **Tsitsikamma Coastal Park**), both of which are worth visiting. This is also where the most famous coastal resorts of the Garden Route are found, where South Africa's affluent families come for their own summer holidays. **Plettenberg Bay**, known simply as Plett, **Wilderness** and **Knysna** all offer excellent accommodation at very affordable prices, and some really élite hideaways at greater expense. Outside December and January, the peak summer months, accommodation prices drop and the whole place becomes a great deal quieter, but in the peak season, the beachside bars hum constantly.

When you get to **George**, one of the route's major ports, take the road off the main highway which loops north over the mountains of the **Great Karoo**: the views on top of the mountains are incredible and are forever changing colour depending on the movement of the sun. The road takes you on to **Oudtshoorn**, famous for its ostriches and home to the **Kango Caves**.

Hunter's Country House

Nestling in the heart of the Garden Route between the **Tsitsikamma Mountains** and the Indian Ocean, overlooking magnificent rain forests, is Hunter's Country House: an exclusive retreat where 30 guests are accommodated in pretty thatched cottages. Beautiful gardens and almond orchards enable you to really relax into the incredibly mellow atmosphere.

The cottages with their white walls, thatched roofs and white chimney stacks epitomise the idyllic country cottage. All the cottages are individually furnished in beautiful old country house style – the chintz cushions and curtains break up the mellow colours of the walls. There is also a typical wooden beamed and thatched roof ceiling. Each suite has a fireplace and private patio as well as a phone, radio and television.

There are also three Premier Suites which are even more spacious and luxurious, the ultimate of which is the newly refurbished Forest Suite: it is really secluded, looks on to the forest and has a private pool, an enormous master bedroom with a four-poster and a separate lounge and dining-room.

The house's public rooms are all beautifully elegant and are filled with antiques and ethnic carpets: roaring fires are lit when there's a chill in the air. Hearty breakfasts

---

HUNTER'S COUNTRY HOUSE
(☎ 4457-7818, fax 4457-7878, e-mail: hunters@pixie.co.za,), PO Box 454, Plettenberg Bay 6600, South Africa
Reservations: Either direct or through most African-specialist tour operators (see p11)
Getting there: An hour from George by car and ten minutes from Plett Airport; the hotel can arrange any transfers that are necessary, but most guests hire cars
Accommodation: 21 Garden Suites: 15 standard suites, five premier suites and one presidential suite
Amenities: Wine cellar and pub, swimming pool, bar, lounges, two dining-rooms, antique shop, forest trail, tour desk, 18-hour room service and laundry service; plus fishing, hiking, climbing, golf, tennis, bowls, squash and horse-riding nearby
Dress code: Jacket and tie are not necessary, though most guests dress for dinner
Weddings: Hunter's does cater for weddings, prices are available upon request
Minimum stay: None
Rates: Bed and breakfast from US$87 R397 per person
Credit cards: Most major
Taxes and service charge: R4.56 bed levy per room is charged

are served in the cosy breakfast room, while superb five-course dinners are eaten by candlelight in the baronial dining-room of the main house.

Only a short drive from Plettenberg Bay and in the middle of the Garden Route, Hunter's is the perfect place to stop off for a few days. You can ask for a picnic hamper and head off into the forest along one of the estate's trails, laze around the pool or pop down to the beach and play in the surf.

The hotel can arrange a whole host of other activities in the area including fishing, hiking, climbing, golf, tennis, bowls, squash and horse-riding. If you do go riding or cycling ask them to prepare a sundowner basket for you and stop at **Kransheok** where the views are just magical.

Plettenberg Park

Plettenberg Park is a very special place. It is also very expensive. Situated on 200 hectares of land with approximately 3km of rocky shoreline, the setting of this exclusive hotel is quite magnificent.

From the inside, almost every window seems to look down over the dramatic cliff edge to the surf pounding below. **The Lake House**, where the rooms are, overlooks an inland wild duck sanctuary and offers privacy beyond your dreams, while the **Cliff House**, only half a kilometre away and originally an old stone castle, blends in perfectly with the craggy coastline.

The location may be good but the interiors are a designer's dream, with white plastered walls and tiled floors broken up by sea grass rugs, fine oak antique furniture, verdigris tables and huge comfy sofas and armchairs in tranquil shades of cream, taupe, white and buttermilk. Nothing is overdone. They call it 'Afro-Colonial', using only natural materials and no colour at all. The five bedrooms follow the same theme: guests sleep on extra long 'sleigh beds' covered in white linen. Each room features an open fireplace, a ceiling fan, a TV and VCR and a minibar.

A continuous strip of brilliant blue sky floods into the Lake House through a sky light which runs along the apex of the extended entrance hall. This is complemented by wall to wall windows and terraces which show off the view. And there's lots to do when you've had enough of lazing by the swimming pool or on the private beach: water-skiing, hobie cat sailing, diving, walking in Tsitsikamma Forest or shopping in Plettenberg Bay.

> **PLETTENBERG PARK**
> (☎ 4457-33067, fax 4457-33192), Robberg Road, Plettenberg Bay 6600, South Africa
> **Reservations**: Either direct or through Three Cities Hotels (UK ☎ 0171-225 0164, fax 0171-823 7701, e-mail: Anne@tch./ftech.co.uk)
> **Getting there**: 600km from Cape Town, 33km from Knysna, 3km from Plettenberg Bay Airport – transfers are available, Avis car rental in Plettenberg Bay
> **Accommodation**: The Lake House has five bedrooms (three twin and two doubles)
> **Amenities**: Scenic walks, deep-sea fishing, scuba diving, snorkelling, water-skiing, hobie cat sailing, bird, whale and dolphin-watching, excursions, river boat, golf, swimming pool
> **Dress code**: Casual
> **Weddings**: Can be arranged but all the accommodation must be reserved
> **Minimum stay**: None
> **Rates**: Small luxury room from US$164 R750, large luxury room from US$207 R950, whole house from US$1439 R6600
> **Credit cards**: Most major
> **Taxes and service charge**: Inclusive of 14% tax

Meals are discussed with the chef and created around your specific tastes, but they usually have a distinctly Mediterranean feel and are made from whatever is freshest at the time.

THE BLUE TRAIN AND ROVOS RAIL

South Africa is blessed with two sumptuous trains offering the kind of luxury epitomised by the famous Orient-Express. The **Rovos Rail**, a beautifully restored train pulled by four **vintage locomotives**, makes several wonderful trips any of which is just perfect for honeymooners who can afford it.

There is the four-day **Steam Safari**, a bi-monthly journey leaving Johannesburg on a Saturday and making its way through some of South Africa's most stunning scenery stopping for a night at one of the top private game reserves. You could otherwise opt for the monthly three-day journey from Pretoria to Cape Town.

You can now also board the Rovos Rail for a one-night trip up the **Garden Route** from Cape Town to Knysna, or even take the train right up to **Victoria Falls** in Zimbabwe. All these trips, as you can imagine, are very popular so check availability before you set your heart on one. If they are in your budget any of them would certainly be the experience of a life-time, as the train has been fastidiously restored and is truly luxurious with thick carpets, a huge double bed, en suite bathroom with black and white chequerboard floor tiles, and varnished mahogany and chrome furnishings. The train can accommodate a maximum of 40 people in either an A or a B suite. Prices are available on request. For reservations talk to leading tour operators specialising in Africa (see p11).

The **Blue Train** is a similar operation. The train's proud and noble history is said to have begun at the turn of the century when a Train de Luxe first travelled between Cape Town and Bulawayo. The service was upgraded just before the outbreak of WWII when South African Railways took delivery of the Blue Train – the most luxurious rail carriage the continent had ever seen. This year the Blue Train enters another era following its US$10 million refit.

The two **refurbished trains** – making the journey from Cape Town to Pretoria and back – will be in service again this year. Everything about the trains is luxurious so that you can guarantee you'll have a comfortable and entertaining journey. Prices per person for a luxury compartment in the newly refurbished Blue Train with a private bathroom and toilet are US$998 R4500, while a deluxe compartment with a private shower and toilet costs US$931/R4200 per person.

The Blue Train departs from Pretoria for Cape Town on Monday, Wednesday and Fridays, leaving in the morning and arriving the following lunch-time, and makes the return journey to Pretoria on the same days. Once a month the Blue Train travels from Pretoria to Victoria Falls.

For more details call **The Blue Train reservations** (South Africa ☎ 11-773 7631, fax 11-773 7643).

GAME RESERVES

South Africa has more than 700 reserves, parks and game farms so, wherever your itinerary takes you, it should be possible to see some game. For many people the game parks of Transvaal to the east of Johannesburg epitomise the 'real' Africa. This was once frontier country where the pioneering Voortrekkers fought against the British and the countryside to forge a life for themselves. This is where **Kruger National Park** is found: it's an institution unto itself, with more animal species than any other wildlife park on the whole of the African continent.

Londolozi Game Reserve

Londolozi, so famous for its leopards, has consistently been recognised as the best of all the game camps in South Africa. This world-famous game reserve has set the standards that all its competitors strive for: the camps are small, intimate and incredibly luxurious. Main Camp has been run by the same family for over 60 years and is now the flagship of the celebrated Conservation Corporation, which owns several other fabulous safari camps including **Ngala**, **Phinda**, **Singita**, **Twalu** and **Makalali**, all of which are highly recommended.

There are eight double chalets and four rondavels (thatched cottages) in Londolozi's Main Camp: each has an elevated private balcony and a pristine en suite bathroom. Main Camp also has its own swimming pool, boma (thatched central 'mess' hut) and curio shop, while the impressive lounge and bar area has a suspended balcony overlooking the Sand River. Alternatively you can stay in the luxury Bush Camp which offers eight secluded rock chalets: these have outdoor showers as well as en suite bathrooms and elevated balconies with views over the river. Lastly there is Tree Camp, the very best that Londolozi has to offer, where guests dine on a balcony 20m up in an ancient Ebony tree with, of course, breathtaking views. Each tree camp is

> **LONDOLOZI GAME RESERVE**
> (☎ 11-803 8421, fax 11-803 1810), PO Box 1211, Sunninghill Park 2157, South Africa
> **Reservations**: Either direct or from the UK through Century House (UK ☎ 01604 882565) or Relais & Châteaux and Small Luxury Hotels of the World's toll free numbers (see p12)
> **Getting there**: The camps can provide transfers, the nearest airport is Skukuza to where there are daily scheduled flights from Jo'burg with Comair, private air charters are also available on request
> **Accommodation**: Tree Camp has four luxurious suites; Bush Camp has eight suites; Main Camp has eight chalets and four rondavels
> **Amenities**: Each camp has a swimming pool, lounge, balcony, bar, plus game drives in Land-Rovers and nature walks with trackers
> **Dress code**: Casual
> **Weddings**: Can be arranged
> **Minimum stay**: None
> **Rates**: Doubles from US$382/R1750 full board including game drives
> **Credit cards**: Most major
> **Taxes and service charge**: Included

beautifully decorated and the en suite bathrooms, full of white tiles, white ceramic and white towels remind you that you may be in the bush but you're far from roughing it.

On your doorstep are 14,000 hectares of prime game land literally teeming with wildlife. You'll see the Big Five here along with a dazzling array of other wildlife amongst the beautiful and diverse bushveld of the Kruger National Park.

Londolozi being a member of Relais & Châteaux, you can expect the food to be excellent. Each camp has its own bar and superb catering facilities: the staff greet you with lavish breakfasts as you return from early morning game drives and prepare picnics for you to eat in the bush. Their delicious dinners under the stars in the 'boma' are the perfect way to round off the day.

BENGUELA ISLAND

Although it's not actually in South Africa, most visitors to **Benguela Lodge** (☎ 11-483 2734, fax 11-728 3767), PO Box 87416, Houghton, 2041 South Africa, use it as a coda to a South African holiday. Situated off the coast of **Mozambique**, Benguela is set on a secluded island surrounded by the warm waters of the Indian Ocean so it is the perfect place if you fancy a beach holiday at the end of a tour of South Africa. It offers barefoot luxury and fantastic diving and watersports among totally unspoilt and uncluttered surroundings. Nestled in the indigenous forest, the lodge's accommodation is in thatched bungalows on stilts. There are en suite bathrooms and private balconies from which you can watch the magnificent sunsets and diverse birdlife: the island is home to over 115 varieties of bird including the rare Olive Bee-Eater and the Crab Plover. However, only two of the 13 chalets have a double bed (No 1 and No 13) so book early and make sure you emphasise this request. Transfers to the island are on Tuesdays and Fridays only from Jo'burg International Airport. A three-night Tuesday to Friday package, including flights, all meals, use of windsurfers and hobie cats, and taxes costs around US$843/R3801 per person.

India
(BEST TIME: OCTOBER TO MAY)

There is nowhere quite like India; that heady concoction of all that is beautiful in the world and the harsh reality of a continent that is home to around 900 million people.

To paint India only as a romantic destination would be painfully superficial. There are such extremes of poverty and wealth in this vast, vast sub-continent, that it would be callous just to talk of the incredible sunrises and sunsets over the Taj Mahal. A honeymoon in India would undoubtedly take in fabulously romantic sights but no visit to India can gloss over the shocking filth, poverty, continual hassle and throngs of people, that is part of life. Despite all this, perhaps even because of all the difficulties, people still fall deeply in love with this fascinating country and long to return again and again.

The subcontinent has a life of its own – from the haggling buyers and sellers to the passionately revered cows in the streets, along with the vibrant colours and fragrant aroma of the flower garlands and the mounds of exotic spices piled up in the markets. It is also steeped in a complex history stretching back over 4000 years, during which the philosophies, religions and languages of its people have expanded to produce the immense wealth of culture, heritage and tradition that exists here today.

There is no doubt that India's landscapes are overwhelmingly beautiful in their variety. They range from the harsh barren deserts of Rajasthan to the rolling green hills of Darjeeling; from the snow-capped eastern Himalayas to the tranquil palm groves and lush paddy fields of the south, to say nothing of the long unspoilt beaches beside the Indian Ocean. You can stay in former palaces, explore hilltop forts in Rajasthan, haggle for an auto-rickshaw in Delhi, escape the heat amongst the tea plantations of Darjeeling or just relax for a few days on a palm-fringed beach in Goa.

INDIA
A startling kaleidoscope of religions, culture, heritage and people, amongst incredibly diverse landscapes – not for the faint-hearted
When to go: India's climate varies from region to region, the coolest weather on the plains is between November and March; head to the hills between April and June when it is hot and dusty on the plains, avoid July to September when the rains come
Average maximum temperatures °C

	JAN	FEB	MAR	APR	MAY	JUN	JUL	AUG	SEP	OCT	NOV	DEC
Goa	29	30	30	30	30	29	27	27	27	29	31	31
Udaipur	23	26	30	34	36	34	29	27	29	30	27	25
Darjeeling	9	9	13	16	16	18	18	18	18	16	13	11

Capital: Delhi
Flight times: to Delhi from:
New York: 18 hours
LA: $25^{1}/_{2}$ hours
London: 9 hours
Sydney: 10 hours
Approximate exchange rates: Rupees (Rs) – £1 = Rs55.51, US$1 = Rs35.79, A$1 = Rs28.28
Time difference: GMT plus $5^{1}/_{2}$ hours
Voltage: 220v AC, 50 Hz; two and three round-pin plugs
Combine with: Maldives, Nepal, Sri Lanka, Singapore
Country dialling code: ☎ 91

And then there is religion. Apart from the continually contrasting landscapes and the colourful pageant of its people, at the very heart of India is a religious spirit which more than anything else is responsible for making the continent so magical, so captivating. The very essence and indeed, the poignant romance, of India is religion and the strength of Hinduism and Buddhism, both of which originated there.

GOA

Goa is a wonderful place to go for an exotic sun-drenched beach honeymoon that won't cost you the earth. The palm-fringed coastline with its magnificent sandy beaches has drawn travellers for years but it has only been in the last decade that the world's travel industry has really started to realise the potential that lies in Goa. There are hundreds of decent hotels along the coast offering comprehensive facilities and comfortable accommodation. You'll also find a lively night-life as the recent wave of 'rave' dance culture moves into this long-established hippie enclave.

Because of its Portuguese roots – Goa was a Portuguese colony until 1961 – the architecture has unmistakably Mediterranean tones in the white-washed churches and colonial facades, while the influence of Catholicism also ensures that the state differs markedly from the rest of India.

Fort Aguada Beach Resort

Generally regarded as the best of the numerous hotels in Goa, Fort Aguada Beach Resort has sea-facing rooms in the three-storey main part of the hotel and 42 cottages in the grounds. The hotel is located in north Goa beside **Sinquerim** beach, with its main wing occupying the ramparts of a 17th century Portuguese fort.

Fort Aguada is managed by the well-respected Taj group. As a result it offers very good standards of accommodation and service. The Taj group also owns two other hotels, the **Aguada Hermitage** and the **Taj Holiday Village** – both of which are next to the fort. All three hotels are suitable for honeymooners, the plushest being Aguada Hermitage with its pretty, colonial-style villas, red-tiled roofs and white-washed walls, though the honeymoon cottages, which are scattered throughout the grounds in the Holiday Village, are also very pleasant. The three hotels are operated as a group so you can use any of the hotels' facilities.

The 130 rooms at Fort Aguada all have air-conditioning with either a twin or double bed (so make sure you stipulate which you want), TV, phone, fridge and bath or shower. Most have good views of the sea but again make sure you request one that does. The 42 cottages have their own private gardens and inside there are tiled floors and traditional cane furniture, while

---

FORT AGUADA BEACH RESORT
(☎ 0832-276201, fax 0832-276044), Sinquerim, Bardez, Goa 403519, India
Reservations: Through the Taj Group's reservation numbers: UK (☎ 0800 282699); US (☎ 1-800-1-LUV-TAJ); Germany (☎ 0130-852428); Australia (☎ 008-221176); New Zealand (☎ 0800-656666); Hong Kong (☎ 2866 0882); Japan (☎ 03-5561 9353)
Getting there: 45 minutes from the airport, the hotel will arrange transfer
Accommodation: 130 rooms including 24 Terrace Suites
Amenities: The Anchor Bar, Seashell Restaurant, the Trattoria, Rampon restaurant for Goan specialities, and a poolside grill, fresh-water swimming pool, sports complex offering water sports (para-sailing, windsurfing, water-skiing, water scooters, jet skis, boating), tennis, squash, badminton, table tennis, billiards and five-hole golf course, plus fitness centre with sauna, steam, jacuzzi and gym, beauty parlour, barber shop, travel desk, car rental, shopping arcade, in-room safes, bank, currency exchange
Dress code: Elegant casual
Weddings: Receptions for up to 225 people can be catered for
Minimum stay: None
Rates: Doubles US$75 to US$200 at the Beach Resort; from US$60 to US$115 in the Taj Holiday Village; and from US$135 to US$215 at the Hermitage
Credit cards: Most major
Taxes and service charge: Taxes are not included and they vary – 25% at the Beach Resort and Hermitage, 15% at the Taj Holiday Village

the 24 Terrace Suites have their own private terrace. The hotel's facilities are impressive including an air-conditioned billiard room, health club, sauna, three tennis courts, badminton, squash, volley-ball and a wide range of watersports between November and April.

There is a good selection of food including Goan, continental, Indian, Chinese, Italian and Thai. The hotel's main restaurant usually has music in the evening, but it's easy to avoid this by choosing one of the other restaurants or by opting for one of the many restaurants on the beach.

A FEW THINGS TO SEE AND DO AROUND GOA

Rent a car, around Rs4000 for a week for a small vehicle, or alternatively hire a motorbike: much more fun and just as easy in Goa. For around Rs2500 you'll get an old Enfield for a week including insurance: try **Classic Bike Adventure** (☎/fax 0832-276124) in Candolim, always carry all your documentation with you and remember that in India a highway code is virtually non-existent.

One of Goa's major attractions is **Anjuna flea market** on Wednesdays between October and March: tourists flock to see the Tibetan and Kashmiri traders, the Indian women in traditional tribal dress and, of course, the resident hippies. Anjuna is one of Goa's truly cult places where 'serious travellers' ensconce themselves for months on end just soaking up the scene.

Even if you're not staying in the hotel, it's worth visiting the moated ruins of **Fort Aguada**. The fort was built by the Portuguese in 1612 and its hilltop location means the views are great.

All the hotels mentioned above and many other good hotels have their own private beaches, the best of which are **Aguada, Bogmalo, Varca** and **Cavelossim**. If you want to get away from the tourist beaches head to **Arambol, Betui** or **Palolem**. Although you'll find these beaches colonised by a handful of hardy, seasoned travellers the coast is stunning and the local fishermen are friendly.

Another great place is **Terekhol Fort**, way up in the north of Goa on the border with Maharashtra. This small Portuguese fort used to incorporate a state-run hotel, but this was recently privatised and *Hotel Tirakhol Fort Heritage* (☎ 0832-220705, fax 0832-283326) now makes the perfect overnight stop for little more than Rs 1650 a night. Go for the honeymoon suite, where the magical views of the coast and the wonderful sunken bath adequately compensate for the fact that it has two single beds. Stop for a swim on the unspoilt and deserted **Querim** beach.

Other recommended hotels

Majorda Beach Resort (☎ 0832-220128), situated on lovely Majorda Beach, has cottages set amongst the bougainvillaea and palm trees of the hotel's landscaped gardens. With all mod cons such as air-conditioning, TV, phone, bath or shower, these are more spacious than the rooms in the main body of the hotel and afford much more privacy. If you book this through a UK tour operator such as Kuoni you can get a package, with flights, transfers and seven-nights' accommodation in a cottage for around £750, while UK tour operator Hayes and Jarvis has standard rooms in the main hotel for around £550 for seven nights, flights and transfers.

The Marbella Guest House (☎ 0832-276308), close to Fort Aguada, would be a wonderful place to rent for a week. This lovely old Portuguese villa has been carefully restored and now offers six bedrooms, all of which are individually decorated. The bedrooms are clean, comfortable and really airy with their own attached bathroom, while one even has a wonderful sunken marble tub. At around US$34/Rs1200 to US$62/Rs2200 per night this makes it a perfect place to stay especially if you want to avoid the large resort hotels like the three Taj Group five-star hotels just down the road.

The Panjim Inn (☎ 0832-226523) in Goa's capital, Panaji, is a popular place to stay. This 300-year old town house is run by a Tibetan family. It has a pretty garden as well as a huge veranda sweeping around the first floor. Do make sure you ask to see a few of the rooms when you arrive as some are much nicer than others. For around US$9/Rs315 or US$11/Rs410 you get a room with en suite bathroom. The food is also pretty good here.

Hotel Mandovi (☎ 0832-224405), the best of the colonial hotels overlooking the river in Panaji, has recently had a thorough revamp and is now much more luxurious. You can enjoy pre-dinner drinks on the balcony, before dinner in the first floor restaurant which is really good. Doubles from US$27/Rs950 to US$42/Rs1500 for rooms overlooking the river.

RAJASTHAN

Rajasthan's traditions and heritage make it one of those places that is romantic to the core. The state is known as the Land of the Kings, and the story of the Rajputs, its native warriors, is the stuff of legends. While chivalry and honour formed a quintessential part of the Rajputs' thousand-year rule, the individual clans' pride and zeal for independence also caused them to come into conflict with each other just as much as with their alien aggressors. As a result Rajasthan is littered with forts, palaces and temples and today, due to the pecuniary constraints on the 20th century maharajas, many of them have been converted into spectacular hotels.

Because of the Rajputs' glorious heritage, Rajasthan is very much India at its best for visitors: the extraordinarily colourful clothes; the almost comic moustaches of the men and their continued romantic sense of chivalry; and the crumbling palaces all make this a truly magical place, quite unlike anywhere else in the sub-continent. The best time to visit Rajasthan is between mid-October and mid-March.

Rambagh Palace Hotel

Rambagh Palace Hotel is one of the most famous and romantic palaces in all Rajasthan. Staying there will take you back to the land of the Maharaja when the building was used for royal house parties. Everything about the palace is old world ostentation; with its over the top palatial grandeur you'll never forget the experience.

Built in 1835 as a hunting lodge, in the 1920s it was transformed into a palace at the cost of Rs4 million for the use of Prince Man Singh, the Maharajah of Jaipur. In 1957, he decided to turn this glorious residence into a hotel: the first public guest was Count Artaza, the Spanish Ambassador to India.

Entering the Rambagh Palace takes you into another world. Archways and cool corridors connect rooms filled with the most incredible Rajasthani ornaments and furniture. The four Royal Suites are absolutely incredible and many of the luxury rooms are

---

THE RAMBAGH PALACE
(☎ 0141-381919, fax 0141-381098), Bhawani Sing Road, Jaipur 302 005, Rajasthan, India
Reservations: Through the Taj Group's reservation numbers: UK toll free (☎ 0800 282699); US toll free (☎ 1-800-1-LUV-TAJ); Germany toll free (☎ 0130-852428); Australia toll free (☎ 008-221176); New Zealand toll free (☎ 0800-656666); Hong Kong (☎ 2866 0882); Japan (☎ 03-5561 9353); or through specialist tour operators such as Cox & Kings, Abercrombie & Kent, Worldwide Journeys (see p9)
Getting there: 11km from the airport, the hotel can arrange transfers
Accommodation: 106 rooms including four special suites
Amenities: Suvarna Mahal restaurant, Neel Mahal coffee shop, Polo Bar, indoor swimming pool, fitness centre, beauty parlour, travel desk, car rental, shopping arcade, currency exchange, in-room safes, tennis, squash courts, cultural theatre (October to April)
Dress code: Elegant casual
Weddings: Receptions can be arranged in the hotel's two banquet halls which can cater for between 30 and 100 people, the lawns can also be used
Minimum stay: None
Rates: Standard doubles cost around US$175, but go for one of the superior rooms which start at US$200, luxury rooms from US$275, the Maharaja from US$525 and the Royal suite from US$675
Credit cards: Most major
Taxes and service charge: 10% tax

definitely worth paying the extra for as the standard rooms are a bit characterless and they often have twin-beds, though they are spacious: ask if you can have a look at a few before deciding. With their abundance of precious art, silk embroideries, golden dragons, elaborately framed European canvasses, exquisite blue pottery and beautifully laid-out rooms the Royal Suites are literally fit for a king. The Princess Suite even has a mosaic fountain in the middle of the drawing-room, with huge glass doors leading onto a private terrace, while the Maharani suite has the most exquisite mirrored bathroom.

Once the only private residence in the world with its own polo field, the Rambagh Palace maintains its grand colonial feel with the help of the **Polo Bar** which is furnished with the late Maharaja's polo trophies. The Palace has a lovely indoor swimming pool in the ground, outside which there are loungers to relax on.

The Lake Palace Hotel

The legendary Lake Palace Hotel will always be at the forefront of people's minds when they think of India. This incredible white palace, famous also as the location for James Bond's *Octopussy*, seems to float in the middle of the still blue waters of Lake Pichola.

Once the summer retreat of the rulers of Mewar, the Palace was built two and a half centuries ago by Maharana Jagat Singh II and covers the whole 1.5 hectare island. The Palace is so astonishingly beautiful that you couldn't possibly visit Udaipur without crossing the lake to visit it for lunch or dinner (all that non-residents are allowed to do), but to actually stay here is a total privilege.

What really makes the Palace is its gardens, around which the hotel is built so that what you see from the water is in fact largely a shell, enclosing the most magnificent array of lily ponds, marble terraces, formal garden beds and fountains. As you sit on one of the terraces taking afternoon tea you get this incredible feeling of being cocooned by a huge expanse of pure white marble. Whichever direction you look, there is wonderfully ornate masonry with slender carved columns, filigreed screens, domed chattris and ornamental fountains.

Inside is just as grand. The walls are frescoed with ancient water colours inlaid with miniature paintings and painfully intricate mirror mosaic. Black and white floor tiles contrast with brightly coloured stained-glass windows through which the shimmering waters of the lake are reflected, and the balconies are larger than many of the hotel's bedrooms. All the suites are decorated in different styles, but all are unquestionably ornate. When you book, do make a point of emphasising that it is your honeymoon and stress that you want a reasonably-sized room or a suite because some of the rooms are very compact and ordinary.

THE LAKE PALACE
(☎ 0294-527961, fax 0294-527974), PO Box 5, Pichola Lake, Udaipur 313 001, Rajasthan, India
Reservations: Through the Taj Group's reservation numbers: UK toll free (☎ 0800 282699); US toll free (☎ 1-800-1-LUV-TAJ); Germany toll free (☎ 0130-852428); Australia toll free (☎ 008-221176); New Zealand toll free (☎ 0800-656666); Hong Kong (☎ 2866 0882); Japan (☎ 03-5561 9353); or through specialist tour operators in the UK, such as Cox & Kings, Abercrombie & Kent, Worldwide Journeys (☎ see p9)
Getting there: 26km from the airport, the hotel can arrange transfers
Accommodation: 81 rooms including 13 suites
Amenities: Jharokha 24-hour coffee shop, Amrit Sagar bar, Neel Kamal restaurant, swimming pool, mini-gym, travel desk, car rental, shopping arcade, currency exchange, in-room safes
Dress code: Elegant casual
Weddings: The hotel can arrange outdoor receptions by the lily pond, or on the lake in its barge *Gangaur*
Minimum stay: None
Rates: Doubles from US$180, suite from US$280 to US$600 for a Historical Suite
Credit cards: Most major
Taxes and service charge: 10% tax

Shiv Niwas Palace

There is an on-going battle between Shiv Niwas Palace and the Lake Palace Hotel as to which is the better. I believe it all comes down to the matter of the view. While some argue that *the* view to have is from the lakeside Shiv Niwas Palace looking down over Lake Pichola and the Lake Palace Hotel, there are those for whom nothing other than actually staying in the Lake Palace, and gazing back at the shoreline, will do.

The residence of the Maharana of Udaipur, part of this incredible 400-year old city complex has now been converted into a heritage hotel. Shiv Niwas is undoubtedly more exclusive, attracting less attention from tour operators, and a wonderful place to experience the splendour of the maharajas in less claustrophobic surroundings.

The whole hotel is charming, from the staff who couldn't be more friendly, to the old world decor all around you. The 31 rooms, including 16 suites, are spacious with bits and pieces from the Royal collection of the house of Mewar scattered around as a reminder of where you are. They are all air-conditioned and have an in-room safe and a minibar. If you're looking for extravagance on a grand scale opt for the King or Queen suite, but most of the rooms are very comfortable.

Spend lazy afternoons around the swimming pool or take a wander down to the City Palace which is just a few minutes away and has now been converted into a museum, before returning to have drinks on the balcony and admire the marvellous views of Lake Pichola and the Lake Palace. Some suites have two balconies, one of which has a table and chairs and is where breakfast is served, while the one on the other side is tailor-made for very private sun-bathing.

> **SHIV NIWAS PALACE**
> (☎ 0294-528016/19, fax 0294-528006/12), City Palace, Lake Palace Drive, Udaipur 313001, Rajasthan, India
> **Reservations**: Direct
> **Getting there**: Local taxi from the airport costs Rs175
> **Accommodation**: Nine suites, eight de luxe suite, 18 standard rooms
> **Amenities**: Live band, swimming pool, travel desk, squash, table tennis, billiards, room service, restaurant and bar
> **Dress code**: Informal
> **Weddings**: The Palace can perform weddings for up to a maximum of 50 people, costs depend on location (whether you chose the hotel or island) and whether you want a Royal procession, fireworks, cocktail menu etc.
> **Minimum stay**: None
> **Rates**: Standard rooms cost US$70, super de luxe are US$200, historic suites US$250, Royal Suite US$350, Imperial Suite US$425
> **Credit cards**: Most major
> **Taxes and service charge:** 12% food and beverage tax, 10% expenditure tax on final bill

If you don't want anywhere too grand or too stuffy the honeymoon cottages at **Fort Aguada Holiday Village** *in Goa are very relaxed, with lots of young people around.* **Shiv Niwas** *in Udaipur, on the other hand, is the best hotel in the world, it's just so romantic, and much nicer than being at the Lake Palace.*
Rodney and Vicky Theobald

Neemrana Fort Palace

Built originally as a fort, Neemrana Fort Palace seems to rise out of the vast expanse of the Rajasthan desert from nowhere, and even when you are close enough to detect the mighty fort from the outside, it would be hard to guess the elegance and luxury that lies within.

Hidden among the folds of the ancient **Aravalli** desert mountains, this historic fort, built in 1464, is India's oldest heritage hotel. The property sprawls over 10 hectares, while the stepped palaces cover as much as a hectare: so while I feel that the word spacious is linked too readily with hotel rooms, these rooms definitely deserve the epithet. The transformation of this incredible fort began just over a decade ago, effectively turning the former ruins into 16 different suites and 21 rooms. What makes Neemrana so special is the unique way in which each suite is decorated: each has been given a different name evocative of the room's style, hence there is the Palace of

NEEMRANA FORT PALACE
(☎ 01494-6007, fax 01494-6005), Port Neemrana, District Alwar, Rajasthan 301 705, India
Reservations: Small Luxury Hotels of the World toll free numbers worldwide (see p12)
Getting there: 100km from New Delhi Domestic and International Airports, the hotel will arrange transfer on prior notice at a cost of around Rs2500
Accommodation: 21 rooms and 16 suites
Amenities: Bar, restaurant serving French and Indian dishes, morning tea served in your room, buffet breakfast in the restaurant; camel and camel cart rides; treks in the nearby hills; cultural evenings at weekends
Dress code: Informal
Weddings: The Palace can conduct Indian weddings and cater for receptions up to 250 people at a cost of US$15 per head
Minimum stay: None
Rates: Doubles from US$85; suites from US$115
Credit cards: American Express, Visa, MasterCard
Taxes and service charge: There is no tax on rooms, but there is a 12% tax on food and beverages

Mirrors, the Moon Palace, the Palace of Breezes and the French colonial suite. Most rooms have balconies, terraces, courtyards or at least an area where guests can sit out and admire the incredible views. Even the bathrooms have been designed to afford the best views of the surrounding countryside. All the rooms are furnished with Indian fabrics and an eclectic mix of colonial and Indian furniture, and the sort of Rajasthani artefacts that Western city dwellers pay fortunes for today. Lots of the rooms have wide pillars, impressive arches, and stained glass windows – the effect is simply stunning.

Other recommended hotels
Samode Haveli (☎/fax 0141-42407) was used as a set for *The Far Pavilions*, which is a fitting testament to its splendour. Located in the north-east corner of Jaipur, this wonderful old building has masses of character, a lovely terrace, a pretty painted dining-room and two incredible suites. The original town house of the nobleman of Samode, who was also once the prime minister of Jaipur, a night costs from US$28/Rs1000 for an ordinary room, and from US$31/Rs1100 to US$50/Rs1800 for a suite.

The **Narain Niwas Palace Hotel** (☎ 0141-563448), a former palace with a large garden, has four spacious suites equipped with antique furniture and some even have four-poster beds, costing almost US$32/Rs1150 for the best for a night.

A FEW THINGS TO SEE AND DO IN RAJASTHAN

No visit to Rajasthan would be complete without a trip to **Jaipur**, known as the 'Pink City' because of the pale pink hue of the old walled city. Built in 1727 by the great warrior and zealous astronomer Maharaja Jai Singh II, all seven of the city's gates remain and the old part of the town with its jewellery market and camel drawn carts is fascinating. Take a deep breath and jostle your way through the incessant wave of hurrying bicycles, rickshaws, Ambassador taxis and people to the various bazaars and the **Palace of the Winds**. Not far outside Jaipur is **Amber Fort**, which was built in the late 16th century and epitomises Rajput architecture. Ride up together on the back of an **elephant**: about Rs300 each way.

Udaipur is without doubt one of the most romantic cities in India, and not just because of the famous Lake Palace. There are scores of wonderful palaces and temples in Udaipur, both great and small but all with that noble character that imbues the whole of this incredible city. Make sure you visit the huge and exquisitely

beautiful **City Palace**. For sunset pictures of the Lake Palace go to **Sajjan Niwas Gardens**, and then follow it up with a drink in one of the bars in the old town which screen *Octopussy* nightly.

One of the greatest experiences in India is the **Palace on Wheels**' train tour around Rajasthan. This luxury train leaves Delhi every Wednesday from September to April and takes you on a tour of Jaipur, Chittorgarh, Udaipur, Ranthambhore National Park, Jaisalmer, Jodhpur, Bharatpur and Agra. The train, which originally used carriages formerly owned by various maharajahs, has recently had a US$6 million refit adding in-room minibars, bathroom toiletries and a beauty parlour, making it more luxurious than ever. The week-long tour costs US$300 per couple per day, but does include everything – tours en route, entry fees and all meals. Book well in advance through RTDC Central Reservation Office (☎ 011-381884, fax 011-382823) in Delhi, or through tour operators specialising in India (see p9).

DARJEELING

When you've had enough of the heat it is time to retire, just as the British used to, to the hills and tea plantations of Darjeeling to get some fresh, mountain air. Darjeeling straddles a 2000m ridge in the north-eastern corner of India, set between Nepal and Bhutan. Here the land is full of Tibetans and Himalayan folk, Buddhist monasteries, spectacular tea plantations and wonderful markets and incredible trekking in the near-by mountains. The most interesting way to get to Darjeeling is aboard the famous toy train, which winds slowly up from New Jalpaiguri or Siliguri to Darjeeling.

Windamere Hotel

The Windamere Hotel is quite legendary as a surviving bastion of the days of the Empire. The most refined and popular place to stay in Darjeeling, the Windamere is the perfect spot if you are looking for a little old world style and relaxation.

This wonderful colonial mansion, set on the banks of Observatory Hill, is just like stepping back in time to the days of the Raj. You'll find no frivolous modern amenities here such as televisions, central heating or minibars, and the owner of the hotel, Mrs Tenduf-La, a Tibetan octogenarian, is proud of it. Instead the Windamere has other delights in store for its guests such as open fires lit each night in the bedrooms, hot water bottles, tea served with heart-shaped biscuits on the lawn, a string quartet playing in the drawing-room, a library, and a pianist who plays during dinner – a taste of Old India at its best. For around US$130 you can get a good double room and US$150 will secure you a suite, both come with all meals included. The food at the Windamere is fabulous, not to mention hearty: they usually serve continental and Indian meals in rotation.

THE WINDAMERE HOTEL
(☎ 0354-54041, fax 0354-54043), Observatory Hill, Darjeeling, West Bengal, India
Reservations: Either direct or through Cox & Kings (see p9)
Getting there: The nearest Airport is Bagdogra (90km and three hours drive), the nearest station is New Jalpaiguri (80km) which is connected to Delhi and Calcutta by express trains
Accommodation: 35 guest rooms: 26 doubles, four suites and five singles
Amenities: Central dining-room, parlour where tea and biscuits are served in the afternoon, bar where Indian and foreign wines are served, local entertainment in the evenings
Dress code: Quite smart in the evenings
Weddings: Wedding ceremonies and receptions can be hosted as long as the hotel is given plenty of warning, maximum 100 guests
Minimum stay: None
Rates: Doubles from US$127, suites from US$153, which includes breakfast, lunch, tea, dinner
Credit cards: Most major
Taxes and service charge: Included

A FEW THINGS TO SEE AND DO IN DARJEELING

Whatever you do in Darjeeling try to either arrive or depart on the famous **toy train**, one of the last few remaining steam trains in India and a truly wonderful experience. The train runs daily leaving Siliguri at 9am which gets you into Darjeeling at around 5.30pm and costs around Rs165 in first class. If you get bored of the belching smoke and somewhat cramped conditions jump off at Kurseong and take a bus to Darjeeling.

I've heard conflicting reports about the **Tiger Hill** sunrise trip which involves hordes of Land Rovers charging up the hill at 4am. Some say it's an absolute must and that the views of the sunrise on **Kanchenjunga** are breathtaking, others say it was a total waste of time, energy and money, especially as the mountain is often obscured by cloud. The **Tibetan Refugee village** is definitely worth a visit. Their yak sweaters and rugs, which are handmade in the workshops, make perfect souvenirs.

Darjeeling is of course famous principally for its tea plantations. **Happy Valley Tea Estate**, only 2km from the centre of town, is the easiest to visit, but it's only worth going when processing is taking place (between April and November). If you have time visit **Kalimpong**, a two and a half hour journey by jeep through stunning countryside. Kalimpong is a very remote hill station and still retains its original charm. It is known for its orchid nurseries, beautiful mountain scenery and oak forests.

AGRA AND THE TAJ MAHAL

Agra was a former capital of India, and as such has a whole host of magnificent monuments and buildings dating back to the 16th and 17th century when the Mughals ruled the country. However the town is hard work to look round owing to the persistence of the salesmen, touts and beggars. Nevertheless, people flock to Agra for its most famous monument, the Taj Mahal, and are not disappointed.

The Taj is quite incredible: built by Emperor Shah Jahan in memory of his wife, Mumtaz Mahal, when she died in childbirth in 1631; it is the world's most extravagant monument to love and took 23 years to complete. The most poignant aspect of the story is that the Emperor was later deposed by his son, who then sentenced his father to life long imprisonment in the Agra Fort, where it is said he spent his remaining days looking out over the river at the tomb he'd built for his wife.

It's easy to get from Delhi to Agra and visit the Taj in just one day, if that's all you've got time for. But you can only fully appreciate the beauty of this vast white palace when you've seen it at varying times of the day, largely because of the effect the light has on the monument but also because it is majestically peaceful and uncrowded at dawn and sunset, so it's well worth staying the night.

I would recommend staying only one night as the whole city is run by people on commission trying to rip off tourists in various different guises. The best place to stay is at the **Mughal Sheraton** (☎ 0562-33 1701, fax 0562-33 1730), the ultimate 'room with a view' hotel and quite definitely Agra's top hotel. All the rooms at the Mughal Sheraton are good, but make sure you get one with a view of the Taj, and if you really feel like splashing out go for the famous Mughal Chamber Exclusive (MCE), where a picture window frames the Palace in a view that will stay with you forever. The hotel's facilities are just what you'd expect from a truly first-class residence, but with the addition of some rather unusual extras such as camel and elephant rides, as well as its own in-house astrologer. Their MCE rooms boast superb views of the Taj and cost US$275 per night including breakfast.

A cheaper option which also has good views is the **Taj View Hotel** (☎ 0562-36 1171, fax 0562-36 1179), another five-star hotel with views of the palace from most of its rooms. For around US$145 you'll get a room with a view of the Taj from the luxury of your bed.

Thailand
(BEST TIME: ALL YEAR ROUND)

There are few countries that offer Thailand's beauty and diversity and make such an ideal honeymoon for couples wanting to combine a beach holiday with some oriental culture and maybe a little adventure.

What makes Thailand so exotic is its wonderful concoction of islands, vibrant night-life, mountainous jungles offering all sorts of adventures, delicious cuisine, incredibly fascinating culture and glittering temples – and above all the charming Thai people.

Thailand has some of the finest beaches in the Orient, and with 2500km of coastline there's no shortage of romantic hideaways to discover. Although some of the major beaches on the islands of **Phuket** and **Ko Samui** have become overdeveloped and are best avoided, there are still plenty of beautiful beaches to be found there, and more at **Krabi.**

These coastal resorts are home to Thailand's most romantic hotels, offering the kind of first-class accommodation and service that has helped the area develop its reputation for superb luxury resorts. While many hoteliers tend to think a four-poster bed defines romance, the Thais have taken it one step further and given the world jacuzzi baths on outdoor decks, open-air showers, and chilled face-towels brought to your lounger on the beach. They really have got service down to a fine art, and even at the cheaper places in these beach areas you'll be looked after very well.

Just north of Bangkok is **Chiang Mai**, Thailand's second largest city. While Chiang Mai itself is a bit of a dump, it's the place to go if you're looking for easily accessible culture and adventure. This highland city is the gateway to the north: if you hire a four-wheel drive you can discover ancient hill tribe villages with their intricate costumes and age-old customs, or do an exhilarating trek through the jungle on an elephant, and white-water raft along the river.

The absolute ultimate in luxury and old world charm, the famous and fabulously elegant **Eastern & Oriental Express** makes the 1932km rail journey between Bangkok and Singapore about three times a month (see p286).

THAILAND
An exotic combination of islands, culture, night life, shopping, wonderful food and really first-class hotels
When to go: February to September (Ko Samui); November to April (Krabi and Phuket), November to March (Chiang Mai)
Average maximum temperatures °C

	JAN	FEB	MAR	APR	MAY	JUN	JUL	AUG	SEP	OCT	NOV	DEC
Bangkok	32	33	34	35	34	33	33	33	32	32	32	31
Chiang Mai	29	32	35	36	34	32	32	31	31	31	30	28
Ko Samui	29	30	31	32	33	32	32	32	32	31	30	29
Phuket/Krabi	33	34	34	34	32	32	31	31	30	31	31	31

Capital: Bangkok
Flight times: to Bangkok from:
New York: 18 hours
LA: 15 hours
London 13 hours
Sydney: 9 hours
Approximate exchange rates: Baht (B) – £1 = B39.42, US$1 = B25.42, A$1 = B20.08
Time difference: GMT plus seven hours
Voltage: 220v AC, 50 Hz, US and European-style two flat-pin plugs
Combine with: The Eastern & Oriental Express from Bangkok to Singapore, Malaysia; but there is plenty to occupy you in Thailand alone for two or three weeks
Country dialling code: ☎ 66

BANGKOK

Entering this world famous river city has to be one of the most exciting experiences imaginable. Bustling, throbbing, dirty, smelly, chaotic but at the same time quite magical, Bangkok epitomises Thailand's blend of old and new and is the most exhilarating city to visit. With several truly first-class hotels it is also a great place to unwind from your flight, shop for tailored suits and silks, and explore some of numerous fascinating temples and palaces.

The Oriental

Located right on the edge of the city's **Chao Phya River**, the Oriental has long been Bangkok's most legendary hotel and for years has fully merited its position as one of the world's greatest hotels.

All the 362 rooms and 34 suites are beautifully furnished with the kind of luxuries as standard that you'd expect in a hotel of this calibre. They are all there: air-conditioning, hair-dryer, phone, radio, television with in-house video films, in-room safe,

THE ORIENTAL

(☎ 2-236 0400, fax 2-236 1937), 48 Oriental Avenue, Bangkok 10500, Thailand

Reservations: The Leading Hotels of the World toll free reservations numbers worldwide (see p12)

Getting there: The hotel can arrange to collect you from the airport in one of their white Mercedes

Accommodation: 362 rooms and 34 suites

Amenities: Seven restaurants and one bar: the Normandie, the China House, Lord Jim's, Sala Rim Naam, Riverside Terrace, Veranda, and Ciao; two outdoor pools, tennis, squash, saunas, gym, jogging; the Oriental Spa; river cruises, 24-hour room service, fully air-conditioned

Dress code: Jacket and tie are required for dining in the Normandy Restaurant only; no shorts or slippers are allowed in the hotel

Weddings: Can be arranged

Minimum stay: None

Rates: Double rooms from US$263 B6700; junior suites from US$413 B10,500, author's wing US$865/B22,000 but ask about promotional packages which offer discounts on these rates

Credit cards: Most major

Taxes and service charge: 7.7% tax and 10% service charge

and even umbrellas to weather the usual Bangkok thunderstorms.

A particular favourite is the Noel Coward Suite: sumptuously decorated it is situated in the original wing of the hotel and is stashed full of photographs of the man and his books. The bedroom has two four-poster single beds upholstered in turquoise blue raw silk. The bathroom is huge and divided into two parts, with wardrobes and a large basin in one part and a lovely large bath in the other. There are all the usual bathroom goodies, plus two very thick bathrobes and slippers.

The service at the Oriental is legendary and deservedly so. Each suite has a dedicated butler: he arrives at your door every evening at 6pm armed with tiny tempting canapés and sandwiches which you can indulge in as you get ready for your evening out. He also appears at random times to ask if you have any laundry, or need your shoes shined, while at the same time managing to remain very discreet. He explains on arrival that you should put the huge brass Do Not Disturb sign on the door and he'll leave you alone for as long as you want. Apart from the immaculate and unobtrusive service, it's the little details that really make the Oriental so special. You'll find a bottle of champagne and red roses in your room on arrival, wonderfully posh writing paper and postcards contained in a very smart wallet and a continual stream of fresh flowers in the rooms.

The hotel's food is also good. Either dine at the famous **Normandy Grill**, which serves French cuisine, or out in the hotel's garden at the Italian restaurant. Alternatively, take the boat across the river to the other side of the hotel where the fabulous health spa is found, and the equally wonderful Thai restaurant adjacent to it. The boat ride is great – instead of normal seats it has large wooden dining-room chairs down each side, to make you feel that little bit extra special.

A recent £3 million refurbishment has made the Oriental's spa, with its 50 different Thai treatments, one of the most heavenly places on earth – there can be no better way of reviving your bodies after a long flight than this. As well as the sports complex and stunning spa facilities, the Oriental has two pools.

All the rooms were overflowing with beautiful flowers which were changed daily, and a very fragrant white flower was put on our pillows each night. There was an incredible thunderstorm the first night, and it was bliss to be able to open the windows and watch. It was also very funny to see two of the hotel staff punting their way past our window on a makeshift raft as the gardens had completely flooded.
Katie and Philip Stockton

Other recommended hotels

The Delta Grand Pacific (☎ 2-255 2440, fax 2-255 2441), 259 Sukhumvit Road, Bangkok 10110, is a perfect, cheaper alternative. The new hotel is modern in style and has almost 400 rooms, great facilities and a really good restaurant, and at US$170/B4320 per room per night it's really good value.

(Opposite): The Taj Mahal, Agra, India (see p270).

A FEW THINGS TO SEE AND DO IN BANGKOK

It is now possible to enter Bangkok via the river on a **water taxi** straight from the airport, which takes about an hour: this is definitely the best way to enter this incredible city because the river is the centre for all the activity and at the same time you avoid the appalling traffic jams on the city's crowded streets.

The best way to see Bangkok and the surrounding region is by river so, even if you don't get a boat from the airport, try to leave time for a cruise up the famous **Chao Phya River**, which for 700 years was Thailand's main communication artery. A two-day, one-night cruise aboard the *Mekhala*, a traditional teak, rice barge which has recently been converted into a comfortable hotel, costs around US$200 per person. Each of the six air-conditioned state rooms has a king-size bed, dressing table and wardrobe as well as a private bathroom with a shower. As you slip out of Bangkok in the early afternoon you'll pass the Grand Palace and the Temple of Dawn, before the *Mekhala* docks at **Wat Kai Tia**, a Thai temple set in a tranquil rural village, for a candlelit dinner on the main deck. The next day

you visit the ancient capital of **Ayuthaya**, and lunch in a riverside restaurant, before returning to Bangkok in a private air-conditioned minibus. The cruises can either be booked once you're in Bangkok through **East West Siam** (☎ 2-256 6153, fax 2-256 6665) or before you leave through UK tour operator Asia World (UK ☎ 01932-820050).

The basic 'must see' sights in Bangkok are the **Grand Palace, Wat Phra Kaew, Wat Po, Wat Arun, Chatuchak Park's Weekend Market** open on Saturday and Sunday, and the **Floating Market**.

If you can cope with getting up early there are great photo opportunities to be had watching the Buddhist monks delivering alms outside **Wat Benjamabophit** at around 6.30am, before going onto Phak Klong Talad, Bangkok's largest floating market, near the foot of the Memorial Bridge and the flower market at nearby Chakkapet Road.

From the Oriental you can also rent a boat and cruise through Klong Bangkok Noi and along the smaller canals to **Klong Bangkok Yai** for a better insight into everyday life for the residents of this mind-blowing city.

NORTHERN THAILAND

The cool mountainous landscapes of northern Thailand make a welcome change from steamy Bangkok and are well worth visiting for the hill tribes and their exquisite handicrafts. Situated in a broad river valley 305m above sea level Chiang Mai is now a modern city but there is still plenty of evidence of its former days of glory when it reigned for seven centuries as the capital of the Lanna ('million rice fields') kingdom. Chiang Mai can be reached by a one hour internal flight from Bangkok.

Regent Resort Chiang Mai

The Regent Chiang Mai is just 20 minutes outside the city centre, and definitely the most lavish and beautiful place to stay in northern Thailand. Located in the beautiful **Mae Rim Valley** amongst eight hectares of gardens filled with lily ponds, two small lakes and terraced paddy fields, the recently opened Regent epitomises everything that is luxurious and sensuous about this chain.

Wherever you walk or look there are tiny details of perfection, from the decorative paper lanterns hanging from the lobby ceiling and the local elephant carvings in the pavilion's secluded gardens, to the stencilled cabinets and string harps sitting on lacquered tables.

The designers have managed to combine the beauty of the traditional style of Thai architecture with just about every luxury that you could possibly imagine, striving to remain true to the local culture in every aspect of the hotel's design – even the horticulture is indigenous. Instead of creating a tropical atmosphere with sprawling bougainvillaea, they planted plumeria.

The 64 Pavilion Suites reflect the style of the Lanna Kingdom, when back in 1296 King Mengrai established his kingdom in northern Thailand. The houses were a blend

(**Opposite**): Getting married abroad. **Top**: Vatulele, Fiji (see p53). **Bottom**: Beach wedding, Philippines.

THE REGENT RESORT

(☎ 53-298181, fax 53-298189), Mae Rim-Samoeng Old Road, Mae Rim, Chiang Mai 50180, Thailand

Reservations: The Regent Resorts' toll free reservation numbers worldwide (see p12); and most major tour operators and travel agents offering holidays in Thailand (see p10)

Getting there: Thai Airways operates seven flights a day to Chiang Mai Airport from where transfers can be arranged, a private limo round trip costs B1500

Accommodation: 64 Pavilion suites and six Residences at the Regent

Amenities: 24-hour room service, daily and overnight laundry, VCRs for in-room use available on request, the Regent Boutique, three restaurants/bars, tennis club, spa and fully equipped fitness studio, plus there are four international golf courses close to the resort, tour desk, outdoor 20m swimming pool and covered heated jacuzzi, satellite TV, library, mountain bikes, shuttle service to Chiang Mai

Dress code: Smart casual

Weddings: Weddings and receptions can be arranged at the Regent

Minimum stay: None

Rates: Garden view pavilion suites from US$273/B6900; rice terrace view pavilion suites from US$352/B8900; one bedroom Residences from US$593/B15,000

Credit cards: Most major

Taxes and service charge: 7% tax and 10% service charge will be added to your bill

of several influences in style: Indian, Chinese and the groups which were powerful in the region at that time. The Lanna theme is even incorporated in the staff uniforms, right down to their silver accessories and the buttons on their sleeves.

The vaulted ceilings tower loftily above polished teak floors, while rich Thai cottons, cream rugs and walls, and beautiful Siamese art produce an air of tranquillity. The pavilions are extremely spacious, covering 70 sq metres in all, and comprising a separate dressing room, a sitting-room, a bedroom with an attached bathroom with deep soaking tub and glass panels looking on to the lush foliage outside. Each Pavilion also features a Thai 'sala', a private outdoor living space, which adds to the resort's village style. The in-pavilion facilities are impressive: there's absolutely everything here, from CD players to Thai cotton robes and slippers.

The most luxurious suites of all at the Regent Chiang Mai are the Residences, six units with either one, two or three bedrooms. The one-bedroom suites, covering a magnificent 350 sq metres, feature individual plunge pools on the terrace, gabled buttresses styled to imitate ancient temples, fireplaces and polished wood floors. We're talking seriously pukka stuff.

The hotel will arrange a great variety of activities for you, tailor-made to your individual requirements: exhilarating treks into the jungle on horse-back, mountain bike or foot; visits to elephant training camps or orchid and butterfly farms; trips around the city's many treasure troves, or you can merely relax in its own extensive Health Club or play a game of tennis.

Guests can enjoy cocktails in the **Terrace Lounge**, before having traditional Thai cuisine in the **Sala Mae Rim**, the resort's fantastic Thai Restaurant. The restaurant serves mouth-watering dishes like fresh sea bass with tamarind juice and coriander root and favourites like Thom Yum soup. Alternatively, breakfast, lunch and dinner can be taken at the pool-side restaurant, or even in the privacy of your own terrace for those times when you don't feel like dressing for dinner.

Other recommended hotels

Lisu Lodge (c/o East West Siam (☎ 2-256 6153, fax 2-256 6665) in the typical hilltribe village of **Dton Loong** is a small lodge, which is just perfect for honeymooners. Built out of wood and bamboo, with only four bedrooms, a restaurant and bar, Lisu Lodge offers the essential comforts in a unique setting. If you know you're not the kind of people who enjoy resort-like hotels this would be a truly magical experience. Lisu Lodge is found just 100m from a hill-tribe village: it was built and is now staffed by villagers, so it really will give you a unique insight into their lives and customs. Check with your travel agent or tour operator whether the lodge has been finished, as it was undergoing extensive refurbishment at the time of writing. Twin rooms at Lisu Lodge cost almost US$300 per night and can be booked either through East West Siam (☎ 2-256 6153, fax 2-256 6665) or from the UK through Asia World (UK ☎ 01932-820050).

A FEW THINGS TO SEE AND DO AROUND CHIANG MAI

Chiang Mai although not the unspoilt hilltop town it was once, does have many glittering gold Buddhist temples, a good covered market and is a definite must if you are keen to explore a little of this country's fascinating culture and history. Its surrounding countryside has a totally distinct flavour compared to the rest of the country, owing to its relative isolation until the 1920s when the railway linking it with Bangkok was completed.

Chiang Mai is certainly rich in history, with relics of the ancient kingdoms and their artistic achievements that preceded the founding of the first Thai capital at **Sukhothai** in the 13th century. Even in the city itself there are scores of temples, known as 'wats', with wonderful teak carvings and intricate decorations inspired by the area's Burmese neighbours. Make sure you visit **Wat Doi Suthep**, the massive temple sitting on a hill looking down over the city, at sunset when the panoramic views of the Chiang Mai valley are breathtaking. Other temples worth looking at are **Wat Chiang Man**, **Wat Phra Singh** (particularly the small **Phra Viharn Laikam** which is probably the best example of Lanna architecture) and **Wat Suan Dok** where the ashes of the royal family of Chiang Mai are found.

In the streets of Chiang Mai you'll see people from the **northern hill tribes**, driven to the city in the hope of selling their crafts. These fabulously dressed people with their clanking jewellery, heavily embroidered dresses and silver turbans are such a cultural curiosity because their relative isolation – some villages in the north are five or six days' walk away from the nearest town – means that they live today in pretty much the same way as they have for centuries. The best place to find their handiwork is on **Borsang Road**, where all the handicraft shops have now congregated. Here you can buy a large range of crafts which are still

original and not machine made, including delicate silver bowls, hand-woven cottons, gold leaf on black lacquerware, expertly carved teak, Thai celadon ceramics, embroidered handbags and paper umbrellas with their ornate hand painted designs.

Most tourists spend a few days here visiting the temples before heading further north to explore the hill tribes, trek in the mountains, white-water raft or visit elephant camps. **Mae Hong Son**, one of the prettiest hill towns in Thailand, can be reached either by a 40-minute domestic flight from Chiang Mai, directly from Bangkok, or by renting a car or a four-wheel drive jeep in Chiang Mai, driving to Hot, spending time in Mae Hong Son and then returning via the northern route through Pai, which is still incredibly remote, and back to Chiang Mai along the picturesque winding road. In Mae Hong Son drive along the mountain roads to the villages of the Hmong and Lisu hill tribes to see the beautiful women in their traditional costumes.

There are hordes of adventure expeditions leaving from Chiang Mai daily, most of which can be organised on arrival in the city: you might try a three-day **Golden Triangle Tour** which departs from **Chiang Rai** (you can fly to Chiang Rai from Bangkok or Chiang Mai) and includes trips in long-tail boats, elephant rides as well as visits to some of the ancient and more remote hilltop towns such as Chiang Saen, one of the oldest towns in Thailand.

A good day trip from Chiang Mai takes you out to **Lamphun**, just 26km south of the city, along one of the most beautiful tree lined roads in the north. Lamphun, the former seat of the Haripunchai Kingdom, is home to the 9th century **Wat Prathat Haripunchia**, one of the oldest and most magnificent wats in northern Thailand.

PHUKET

Phuket is Thailand's largest island and of course its most famous since it was used as a location in the James Bond film *The Man with the Golden Gun*. Linked to the mainland via the **Sarasin Bridge**, Phuket has become very commercialised over the last ten years and is now served by direct flights from destinations as diverse as Vienna, Sydney, Hong Kong and Singapore. However, if you stay in any of the hotels listed below all you'll see are deserted private beaches fringed by lush tropical scenery and the emerald waters of the Andaman Sea.

The Banyan Tree Phuket

The Banyan Tree in Phuket has received high critical acclaim from the world's glossy travel magazines, largely because of its incredibly lavish spa facilities. So if you fancy really winding down after your wedding in a pampered paradise, this is the place for you.

Opened at the end of 1994, the Banyan Tree is set on a private beach in **Bang Tao Bay**, and has every kind of facility you could possibly need from the first-class spa to the championship golf course, tennis courts, squash, sailing and windsurfing. There are also two swimming pools, one aimed at encouraging lap-swimming to keep you active and the other, a freeform pool with its own bubble mats, rapid water canal and jacuzzi, to relax in.

The hotel's luxury accommodation is in two different kinds of traditional Thai-style villas surrounded by lush tropical gardens and Asian water courts. Each villa has its own private garden and Thai sala (terrace). The Garden Villas come complete with their own open-air sunken baths, while the 46 Pool Villas, which cover 270 sq metres including dining area, open-air sunken bath, patio, and the most wonderful nine by three metre swimming pool, are quite simply the ultimate experience. The villas have everything from tea and coffee-making facilities to stereos and air-conditioning.

Dining can either be on your own terrace or at one of the Banyan Tree's four restaurants: the intimate **Watercourt** offers innovative Asian seafood dishes, **Saffron** has a selection of delicious curries, **The Banyan Café**, overlooking the golf course, is informal and open and features international cuisine, while the **Spa Lounge** offers meals for the health-conscious.

> **THE BANYAN TREE**
> (☎ 76-324374, fax 76-324375), 33 Moo 4, Srisoonthorn Road, Cherngtalay, Amphur Talang, Phuket, 83110, Thailand
> **Reservations:** Small Luxury Hotels of the World toll free reservations numbers worldwide (see p12)
> **Getting there:** 25 minutes from Phuket International Airport, the hotel can arrange transfers costing B1000 return
> **Accommodation:** 98 villas, including 52 Garden Villas and 34 Pool Villas.
> **Amenities:** Four Spa Pavilions offering saunas, steam rooms, loofah areas, jacuzzis, beauty treatments and massage, five rejuvenation rooms offering body and beauty treatments such as facials, and the Beauty Garden for make-overs; Fitness Pavilion, championship golf course, tennis courts, two swimming pools, Watercourt Café, Saffron Restaurant, Banyan Café, Spa Lounge, Thai Sala Restaurant, Terrace Bar, Pool Bar, Banyan Tree Gallery and bicycles for guest use
> **Dress code:** Casual smart in the restaurants
> **Weddings:** The hotel hosts receptions for up to 150 people from B750 per person
> **Rates:** Garden villas from US$260 B6609 to US$360/B9151; pool villas from US$440/B11,184 to US$640 B16,269
> **Credit cards:** Most major
> **Taxes and service charge:** Not included

Amanpuri

Amanpuri, situated on Pansea beach on the island's west coast, is a very exclusive hotel, and definitely one of the best in Phuket.

When it opened in 1988 Amanpuri was the first of the Amanresorts, a small hotel chain now widely regarded as having the world's most exclusive and luxurious properties. The word Amanpuri means 'region of tranquillity' in Sanskrit, and with just 40 rooms this small hotel is a total haven for escapists.

The bedrooms, or pavilions as they are known, are arranged across eight hectares of coconut studded hillside, with the most wonderful views of the bay and beach below. They are connected by elevated walkways with colonnades.

Each pavilion covers 115 sq metres, including the outdoor terrace, and offers unrivalled luxury with a large separate bedroom, dressing room and bathing area. The beds are king-sized, and there is also air-conditioning, a stocked minibar, electronic in-room safe, stereo system, a luxurious bathroom with a sumptuous sunken bath and separate shower, and a wonderful outdoor terrace or 'sala' ideal for sunbathing or dining alone together. All the rooms have sleek teak wood furnishings, and cream walls and bed linen: extremely simple but wonderfully elegant. Pavilions No 103 and No 105 are the best located because of their ocean views, though the three de luxe pavilions have partial ocean views.

Amanpuri has two restaurants, both of which are open air. **The Terrace** offers casual Thai and European meals, while the **Italian Restaurant** specialises in Mediterranean dishes, and the Bar which overlooks the sea offers poolside drinks and snacks. There is, of course, also 24-hour room service available, and between November and April barbecues are held on the beach.

Facilities include an amazing black-tiled fresh-water pool, two floodlit tennis courts, windsurfing, water-skiing, diving, a gym on the beach, a sauna and a teak-panelled library with an impressive array of books and music. Golf can easily be

---

AMANPURI
(☎ 76-324333, fax 76-324100/200), Pansea Beach, Phuket Island, Thailand
Reservations: Most major tour operators/travel agents worldwide (see p9)
Getting there: Frequent hour long flights from Bangkok land at Phuket airport each day, Amanpuri is 20 minutes from the airport via private limousine transfer
Accommodation: 40 suites: four pavilion suites; 27 superior garden pavilions; five superior ocean pavilions; two de luxe ocean pavilions; plus pavilions No 103 and No 105
Amenities: Fresh-water pool; two flood-lit tennis courts; watersports facilities include windsurfing, sailing, snorkelling, water-skiing, diving, as well as cruises on any of its many charter boats; health and beauty salon; golf nearby; the Gallery shop; two restaurants, a pool-side bar; 24-hour room service; beach-front gym; library; complimentary newspapers
Dress code: Smart casual
Weddings: No
Minimum stay: None
Rates: Pavilions from US$415/B10,500; superior ocean pavilion from US$576/B14,575
Credit cards: Most major
Taxes and service charge: All rates are subject to 17.7% government tax and service charge

---

arranged at any of the five golf courses nearby while, for the less active, massage and beauty treatments will be conducted in the privacy of your own Pavilion or at the salon. Golf carts are provided for moving around the hotel.

Amanpuri also has a terrific scheduled cruise programme offering guests a variety of boats and excursions from *Aman 1*, an 18m Bluewater yacht which does day and night-time cruises to **Phang-Na Bay** where the limestone cliffs and islands provide truly dramatic scenery, to the *Sealion*, a traditional Chinese sailing junk, which takes guests to **Ko Wah** for a day's swimming, snorkelling and lunch on the deserted beaches north of **Bangtao**.

Other recommended hotels
The Chedi (☎ 76-324107, fax 76-324252) 118 Moo 3, Choeng Talay, Talang, Phuket, Thailand, is a pretty cottage-style hotel overlooking the most beautiful beach in Phuket. It is the perfect place for honeymooners looking for peace and quiet. All the Thai-style cottages have separate dressing area and bathroom, as well as a minibar, electronic in-room safe, hair-dryer, air-conditioning, tea and coffee-making facilities and phone. There are two restaurants at the Chedi, the main dining-room which serves a good selection of both local and international dishes, and Rim Lay, an alfresco restaurant on the beach, which specialises in freshly caught fish. Snacks are also served by the hotel's large hexagonal swimming pool. As well as the pool, which has its own wading pond, there is a wide variety of watersports available free of charge, only scuba diving and water-skiing cost extra. Doubles from US$60/B1525 to US$143/B3635 per person per night.

KO SAMUI

Ko Samui is one of Thailand's most beautiful resorts – a small island totally covered by coconut plantations which still provide the mainstay of the island's economy. If you don't want to spend a fortune on a hotel Ko Samui's roots as a backpacker's paradise mean that you can find a rustic beach hut for around US$10 a night on any of the island's dozen beaches. However, if you fancy a little luxury Ko Samui is also home to some of the most beautiful and romantic hotels ever built.

Baan Taling Ngam

Baan Taling Ngam has the kind of fantastic rooms and really first-class service, that inspires everyone who's been to come home raving about it.

Located on Ko Samui's secluded and tranquil western coast, this wonderful hotel's name means 'your home on a beautiful cliff', which just about summarises the ethos of this wildly romantic place.

This is one of those hotels that makes you feel excited as soon as you set your eyes on it. The view from the stunning open-plan reception area out to sea with the little green dots of islands below you, is mesmerising.

There are 59 Thai-style rooms with teak wood interiors. You will be accommodated in either a de luxe room, a beach suite or a cliff villa, all of which overlook the neighbouring islands of **Ang Thong Marine National Park**. The rooms are a clever mix between traditional wooden materials and essentially very modern Thai designs. All the rooms have satellite TV, CD and stereo system, air-conditioning, in-room safes, minibar and phones, as well as luxury bathrooms and spacious balconies.

The cliff-side villas are the best of all. Set on two storeys the bedroom and bathroom are downstairs, while a centrally placed staircase takes you upstairs into a stunning open-plan lounge with the most incredible views and furnished with Thai silks, rugs and chunky wooden furniture. The cliff villas have a kitchen and dining table, a balcony running right along the length of the front of the villa and the added luxury of a beautiful horizon-style swimming pool shared between six villas, with its own jacuzzi, a continual stream of fresh towels and a swim-up bar. Alternatively go for one of the suites which have huge balconies off both the lounge and the bedroom, an extremely funky black slate toilet, a four-poster bed made out of chunky wooden posts, and the most wonderful black slate bathroom where a round window allows you to lie back in the sunken bath and gaze out to sea.

As a Mandarin Oriental resort, you'll find the service and facilities at the Baan Taling Ngam very definitely up to scratch. Choose from the two main restaurants – the **Lom Talay** serving Thai cuisine and Western grill, or **The Promenade** by the beach,

---

BAAN TALING NGAM
(☎ 77-423019, fax 77-220), 295 Moo 3, Taling Ngam Beach, Ko Samui, Suratthani 84140, Thailand
Reservations: Mandarin Oriental reservation offices: UK (☎ 0800-962667); USA, Canada, Mexico toll free (☎ 800-526-6566); Australia (☎ 1-800-653328); Japan (☎ 03-3433 3388); The Leading Hotels of the World toll free numbers worldwide (see p12)
Getting there: There are regular flights from Bangkok and Phuket to Samui, arrange your 40 minute transfer from airport to hotel at the time of booking
Accommodation: 40 de luxe rooms, 10 cliff villas, seven beach suites, two Royal suites
Amenities: Two restaurants, the Veranda bar, pool deck bar, PADI licensed diving school, two main swimming pools, plus shared pools for the cliff villas, cruises to nearby islands and beaches, general watersports, gym, two tennis courts, mountain bikes, beauty salon and Thai-massage, boutique, 24-hour room service, jeep rental, and shuttle bus to town
Dress code: Elegant casual
Weddings: Can be arranged
Minimum stay: None
Rates: Doubles from US$158/B4000 to US$435/B11,000
Credit cards: Most major
Taxes and service charge: 7% tax and 10% service charge

serving Eastern and Western seafood. **The Veranda Bar** in the lobby with its wonderful view also makes the perfect spot for a cocktail as the sun drops on the Gulf of Thailand. Bar snacks and drinks can also be enjoyed all day long on the Pool Deck.

The suite was so spacious and beautifully decorated it was the sort of place you dream about living in, if only we could have brought it back to Britain.
Martin and Meea

There are two outdoor swimming pools, a whirlpool, lots of watersports including PADI instruction, ocean kayaks, sailing and windsurfing, as well as cruises to nearby islands on the hotel's own speedboats or longtailboat for picnics à deux, or snorkelling. Other facilities include a beauty salon, Thai massage, 24-hour room service, boutique, jeep rental, gym, two tennis courts and mountain bike, so there's plenty to do.

Tongsai Bay Hotel

Tongsai Bay Hotel, perched high above its own private beach, is undoubtedly one of the best in Samui. Located a good drive away from any local bars, shops or restaurants, Tongsai Bay best suits those who really do want to relax and do nothing.

Guests are offered a choice of accommodation from the rooms within the main hotel building to secluded cottages set in the grounds. Remember to ask for one of their honeymoon rooms, which are just superb. These are laid out on two floors and, although quite basic, are really very beautiful with an abundance of bamboo and wicker. On entering the room you are shown the bedroom area with its four-poster bed shrouded in mosquito netting, off which there is a small shower room with a basic shower. You then follow a bamboo and wicker staircase down to a sitting-room where champagne and flowers await you. Everything up until now is very attractive but quite basic, but when you go through the French windows and see the dark wooden deck with its jacuzzi, outdoor shower, vanity unit, two sun loungers and table, you know you've stumbled upon a little slice of paradise!

A visit to Tongsai Bay is full of welcoming touches like the freshly sliced papaya waiting for you in your room each afternoon, and the way the pink and blue cotton robes are changed daily: fresh white towels are also left by the jacuzzi. The rooms have a full selection of luxury amenities from air-conditioning and minibar, to a TV with in-house videos and a phone.

One of the nicest things about staying at Tongsai Bay is the incredibly relaxed atmosphere. There only ever seem to be about ten couples staying in the hotel and no one's bothered what you wear for dinner – if you want to eat in shorts and T-shirts that's fine, but if you feel like dressing up you won't feel out of place. The restaurant beside the pool serves great stir-fries during the day and lots of good European dishes in the evening. Upstairs the Thai food is terrific and it's a

TONGSAI BAY HOTEL
(☎ 77-425015 fax 77-425462), 84 Moo 5, Bo Phut, Ko Samui, Surat Thani 84320, Thailand
Reservations: Either direct with the hotel's Bangkok office (Thailand ☎ 2-254 0056) or through UK tour operator Asia World (UK ☎ 01932-820050) and Kuoni (see p9)
Getting there: The hotel will collect you from Ko Samui Airport
Accommodation: 76 guest rooms, 48 cottages and 13 honeymoon rooms
Amenities: Large free form swimming pool, small beach for swimming and windsurfing, piano bar, Thai restaurant, pool-side bar, 24-hour room service
Dress code: Very relaxed
Weddings: Can be arranged
Minimum stay: None
Rates: Cottages from US$279/B7062, honeymoon rooms from US$302/B7651
Credit cards: Most major
Taxes and service charge: Included

The deck is surrounded by lush green plants and foliage so that while you lie in the bath starring out at the turquoise sea, no one can see in. We were exhausted from the wedding and found it a great place to vegetate, eat, swim and relax, it was absolutely fabulous.
Anthony and Deborah Clifden

lovely place to eat outside by lamp light with the staff fussing around you.

There isn't much of a beach at Tongsai Bay, so don't think that this is going to be a major water sporting hotel. The nearest watersport facilities, like the bars, are a 15-minute bus ride away. But don't let this put you off as Tongsai Bay is a wonderfully relaxing hotel with a lovely free form swimming pool and that tremendous deck to get back to.

Other recommended hotels

If all of the above sound too extortionate, don't worry because there's lots of more moderately priced accommodation in Ko Samui. Talk to the major UK tour operators such as Tropical Places, Kuoni Travel, BA Holidays, Silk Cut Travel and Hayes and Jarvis (see p9 for details): they get amazingly good deals on lovely hotels because of the sheer bulk they book in. For example, Tropical Places was recently offering two weeks at **Amari Palm Reef**, a really friendly hotel at the northern end of **Chaweng Beach** with Thai-style buildings set in tropical gardens for US$1935/£1249 per person which includes flights, transfers, bed and breakfast. Another good deal was two weeks at **Paradise Beach Resort,** a great Thai-style resort hotel overlooking **Maenam Beach** which was going for under £1000 including flights, bed and breakfast and transfers.

Wherever you're booking from, it's worth giving these companies a call as you might find the price of an international call from the US or Australia could save you a small fortune.

KRABI

This stunning peninsula, close to the Malaysian border, has so far escaped the commercialisation of its sister Thai beach resorts, a situation perhaps largely due to its remote location. This spectacularly beautiful province with its sweeping palm-fringed beaches overlooks countless offshore islands and dramatic limestone rock protrusions.

Dusit Rayavadee Resort

Dusit Rayavadee Resort is located two hours away from Phuket by speedboat, and is only accessible by sea. Situated on a peninsula 19km south west of Krabi town, the Dusit Rayavadee has access to three different white sandy beaches.

Several of the 98 delightful two-storey circular pavilions scattered around the grounds have their own private whirlpool, all of them have a good sized living area downstairs connected via a spiral staircase to the bedroom and bathroom above. All the pavilions are equipped with air-conditioning, minibar, tea and coffee-making facilities, satellite TV, hi-fi system with CD, cloakroom and small patio downstairs. Up the spiral staircase the second floor has a king-size bed, double bath, separate shower, hair-dryer, bathrobes and slippers, in-room

---

DUSIT RAYAVADEE RESORT
(☎ 75-620 7403, fax 75-620630), 67 Moo 5, Sai Thai, Susan Hoy Road, Tambon Sai Thai, Amphur Muang, Krabi 81000, Thailand
Reservations: Most major tour operators/travel agents worldwide; The Leading Hotels of the World reservations numbers worldwide (see p12)
Getting there: The hotel will arrange complimentary transfers from Phuket Airport which take about two hours by bus and speedboat, or you can request a limo which costs B3000 one way for two people
Accommodation: 98 pavilions, 2 villas
Amenities: Krua Phranang restaurant for traditional Thai dishes and fresh seafood, Raya Dining-room for Asian and continental fare, Phranang Music lounge, Rayavadee lounge, poolside snack bar and beach bar, swimming pool, two floodlit tennis courts, air-conditioned squash court, whirlpool, fitness centre, sauna, massage, watersports, snooker, video and CD library, book and magazine library
Dress code: Elegant casual
Weddings: Can be arranged
Minimum stay: None
Rates: Pavilions from US$231/B5850 to US$612/B15,500; villas from US$848/B21,450
Credit cards: Most major
Taxes and service charge: 7% tax and 10% service charge added to your bill

safe, a second TV with satellite and video player. The Dusit Rayavadee has had so much publicity since it opened, you'll probably get there and realise you recognise the famous pool from fashion shoots and travel articles in glossy magazines – the way the fresh-water pool floats seamlessly in to the sea is now one of the world's classic honeymoon images.

Watersports are rather limited largely because all motorised watersports are banned in order to maintain Krabi's atmosphere of tranquillity. However, both snorkelling and scuba diving are readily available and the beauty of staying there is not really to dash around doing lots of activities, but just to relax in the heavenly surroundings.

Other recommended hotels

Sea View Resort (c/o ☎ 2-411 3605, fax 2-411 4662), 98/1 Moo, 1 Laemngop, Ko Chang, Trat 23120, is the place to go in Thailand if you fancy yourselves as latter-day Robinson Crusoes. Don't go to the Sea View if either of you need constant pampering or an abundance of luxury, but do go if you don't want to spend loads on your room and are quite happy as long as the accommodation is comfortable.

All the rooms are air-conditioned with TV, fridge, and a bathroom with a shower, so all the essential items are there. In the restaurant Thai food is served, and there is also a good library, a snooker room, and small watersports centre for water-skiing and snorkelling. Other than that Sea View is all about the two of you, alone with your sea view and that glorious long white beach. Sea View is quite a trek to get to, though. You'll have to go to **Pattaya** by road until you get to **Leam Ngop** pier from where a boat will take you to Ko Chang. But for some honeymooners this overland journey through Thailand will be an adventure, and will no doubt be especially worthwhile knowing you won't have to share the beach with hordes of others once you get there. In fact you are very unlikely to see many people at this lovely little hotel set amidst coconut trees overlooking the private white-sand beach. Doubles from US$20/B500.

Malaysia
(BEST TIME: ALL YEAR ROUND)

If you are looking for something off the beaten track with unspoilt national parks, very accessible wildlife and an element of adventure then Malaysia is the perfect destination. Malaysia has borders with Thailand in the north, with Singapore and Indonesia to the south and the Philippines to the east. It comprises Peninsular Malaysia and the states of Sabah and Sarawak.

Once a British Protectorate, the states of Sarawak and Sabah on the island of Borneo form Eastern Malaysia. Here is South-East Asia at its most untouched, where vast areas of virgin rainforest are sanctuary to some of the world's rarest flora and fauna. Although Malaysia is blessed with some fabulously luxurious hotels, you have to expect quite basic accommodation in the jungle. The advantage of going to some of the more basic hotels is that you stay in traditional style buildings, right in the heart of rain forest with wildlife all around and while the accommodation might be simple, you can expect to find truly delicious local dishes.

The local guides are usually great – really informative about the flora and fauna of the region – and take tremendous pride in their country. Most visitors to Malaysia try to take in the mysterious **Mt Kinabalu,** a visit to the **Sepilok Orang-utan Rehabilitation Centre,** a few nights in the jungle and some well earned rest on one of Malaysia's islands.

MALAYSIA
An area of outstanding natural beauty, exhilarating adventure and luxury hotels – the perfect honeymoon combination
When to go: Malaysia is pretty much a year round destination: it is almost always warm and humid and has sporadic rainfall
Average maximum temperatures °C

JAN	FEB	MAR	APR	MAY	JUN	JUL	AUG	SEP	OCT	NOV	DEC
32	33	33	33	33	33	32	32	32	32	32	32

Capital: Kuala Lumpur
Flight times: to Kuala Lumpur from:
New York: $19^1/_2$ hours
LA (via Sydney): 23 hours
London: 12 hours
Sydney: $8^1/_2$ hours
Approximate exchange rates: Ringgit (MYR) (the Ringgit is often referred to as the Malaysian dollar) – £1 = MYR3.88, US$1 = MYR2.50, A$1 = MYR1.98
Time difference: GMT plus eight hours
Voltage: 220v AC, 50 Hz, square three-pin plugs
Combine with: Singapore
Country dialling code: ☎ 60

SABAH

Shangri La's Tangung Aru

Tangung Aru is a really fabulous hotel and very much the best place to stay in Kota Kinabalu. Within easy access of five idyllic tropical islands and set amidst 10 hectares of landscaped gardens, the hotel overlooks a panoramic sweeping bay.

The traditional Malay-style reception area with its lofty, raised beam ceiling and views out to sea is absolutely breathtaking; wide open space and exotic furnishings give the whole hotel a very serene and tranquil atmosphere. Honeymooners receive special check-in treatment at a separate desk in the hotel's reception area.

The whole hotel was carefully constructed to maximise the sea view from every room. The bedrooms are truly luxurious and have enormous bamboo beds, huge marble bathrooms and spacious balconies behind wooden shuttered doors. All Honeymoon, Premier and De Luxe suites have a private jacuzzi. The rooms are

SHANGRI LA'S TANGUNG ARU
(☎ 088-225800, fax 088-217155), 88744 Kota Kinabalu, Sabah, Malaysia
Reservations: Shangri La numbers worldwide: Australia toll free (☎ 1-800 222448); Canada toll free (☎ 1-800-942-5050); Germany toll free (☎ 0130-856649; Hong Kong (☎ 2331 6688); Japan (☎ 03-3667 7744); New Zealand toll free (☎ 0800-442179; UK (☎ 0181-747 8485); US toll free (1-800-942-5050)
Getting there: The resort can arrange a limo service from KK International Airport (10 minutes) costing MYR60, while a local taxi costs MYR10
Accommodation: 500 guest rooms and suites with balconies
Amenities: Six restaurants, health club, leisure centre, two free-flow swimming pools, four tennis courts, nine-hole pitch and putt, laundry and valet service, tour and travel desk, car hire, night-club
Dress code: Smart casual
Weddings: Ask about the Graceful Wedding Package, which for around MYR480 includes five-tier cake, 10 corsages, scroll, flowers and other decorations, music, one night stay in the honeymoon suite with breakfast, flowers and champagne and first anniversary stay in de luxe room and dinner
Minimum stay: None
Rates: Superior rooms US$161/MYR400, de luxe rooms US$185/MYR460, honeymoon suite US$293/MYR730, de luxe suite US$482/MYR1200
Credit cards: Most major
Taxes and service charge: 5% Government tax and 10% service charge

equipped with a large range of de luxe amenities which include cable TV, phone with bathroom extension, radio with speakers in the bathroom, hair-dryer, bathrobes and slippers, tea and coffee-making facilities and an in-room safe.

Guests tend to spend their days by the lovely swimming pool area where a continual supply of ice cold flannels is distributed by a man on a bicycle, the aim being to keep you cool as you sunbathe. He also has a selection of ice cold drinks and when you've really had enough of sunbathing there is a pool side bar serving Malay snacks. Each night at about 6pm a band plays in the pool bar, so you can sip a Long Island Ice Tea and watch the sun set over the water.

There are six restaurants at the Tangung Aru serving everything from Asian seafood to Italian. The fish restaurant on the jetty set out over the water is particularly wonderful, as are both the Chinese and Indian restaurants. The hotel has its own tour desk which will organise local excursions into **Kinabalu National Park**, and many of its guests use the hotel as a springboard from which to start their adventures.

Other recommended hotels Borneo Rain Forest Lodge (☎ 088-243245, fax 088-254227), 3rd Floor, Block D, Lot 10, Sadong Jaya Complex, PO Box 11622, 88817 Kota Kinabalu, Sabah, Malaysia, is the best jungle lodge in Malaysia. Newly built, this wonderful lodge is situated beside **Danum River** in Sabah's largest protected lowland forest, **Danum Valley Conservation Area**. It was designed by naturalists and built with local materials. There is a large, airy central lodge with imposing belianwood columns and a sweeping veranda. The river stone and core log chalets are linked to the lodge by wooden bridges. All the rooms are simply furnished with twin-beds, an en suite bathroom and a private veranda overlooking the river. You'll see incredible wildlife from the lodge including huge butterflies and moths, bearded pigs, and the biggest attraction of all, the wild orang-utans which live in the valley and form one of the largest remaining populations of these primates left in the world. Doubles from US$562/MYR1400 to US$602/MYR1500 per couple for two nights' stay including full board, all tours and transfers to/from Lahad Datu Airport.

A FEW THINGS TO SEE AND DO IN SABAH

The **Kinabalu National Park** spans 750 sq km around Mt Kinabalu, which, at 4094m, is the highest point between the Himalayas and the peaks of New Guinea. Climbing the mountain is no mean feat, although it is entirely possible for amateur climbers to get to the top – you've just got to be determined and a little bit mad on your honeymoon. The 8¹/₂km walk to the top involves a steep climb and takes you from jungle to cloud forest and eventually on to sheer rock. As one newly wed described it: 'it was without doubt the most exhausting, strenuous and challenging thing I'd undertaken and was fairly horrible all the way. The second phase was another dimension... involving rising at 2am after little sleep and climbing to the summit in the dark under the pretence of seeing the sunrise but actually preventing us from seeing how horrific the climb in front of us was. But we got there and it was awesome from the top, just like standing on top of the world, a great achievement and we've now got the certificate to prove it!'

A slightly softer adventure experience but just as interesting is the famous Canopy Walk in **Taman Negara**, the national park stretching 4400 sq km across eastern Malaysia. The 200m walk is only open between 9am and 12 noon, but from 23m above the forest floor you can see every level of vegetation. The walk can be terrifying at times as the wire bounces up and down, but it is definitely worth it for the views.

The **Gomatong Caves** are staggering in dimension and reek of bat droppings, because of the vast amount that have accumulated over the thousands of years the bats have been here. The caves are also home to millions of swallows whose nests are collected for that famous Cantonese delicacy, bird nest soup. There's even one poor chap who has to live in the caves among the roaches and bats to guard the nests!

And finally, you mustn't miss the wonderful inhabitants at the **Sepilok Orang-utan Rehabilitation Centre**, where baby orang-utans that have been orphaned as a result of deforestation and poaching are nurtured until they are strong enough to go back to the wild. In the nursery a dozen or so babies swing along a series of ropes erected between the trees and vegetation, and often just drop to the ground hugging each other and looking ridiculously cute!

PANGKOR ISLAND

Pangkor Laut

A couple of honeymooners I spoke to recently described Pangkor Laut as 'heaven on earth, the ultimate in luxury'. This wonderful island hideaway has certainly built up quite a following over the last few years.

Undoubtedly one of the world's most luxurious and spectacular hotels, Pangkor Laut is set on a private 120 hectare island, where guests are accommodated either in beautifully crafted over-the-water villas or hillside villas with glorious views. Built like a village, the hotel's architecture is Malaysian in style and exquisitely designed.

Throughout the suites there is superb detailing, but nothing is over the top or over-done: instead the simplistic beauty of wooden floors and locally made furniture creates a wonderfully tranquil atmosphere making your room the perfect place to retreat to at the end of a day on the beach. The bathrooms in the hill villas are quite incredible, there is a reconstituted stone bath which is big enough for two where you can lie back and look out to sea: if you shut your eyes all you can hear are the sounds of the jungle, and beside the bath is a stone slab just big enough for two gin and tonics.

Whether you stay in an over-water villa or up on the hillside, the suites all have a good sized area for sitting out on, wooden loungers with really comfortable mattresses and a panoramic view of the bay. For those staying in the hill villas there's a timber tower with a lift that takes you up to your level: the lift stops at the jungle walkway for the semi-detached apartments.

All the restaurants overlook the sea and there's a wide variety to choose from. There is no fixed menu in the Chinese restaurant, just a board with various meats and fish listed: it's up to you to tell the waiter how you'd like it cooked. Breakfasts are absolutely huge and are buffet-style.

Most guests spend their days either lying by one of the island's three swimming pools or down at the beach ensconced on a lounger, but there's plenty to do if you feel like being active. Get a map from Reception and head off on one of the many walks on the island, or have a game of tennis. Whatever you choose to do the staff are ready to help you: if you want to go to the beach they immediately radio for a driver who will take you to the other side of the island where the beach is. Once there you are met by one of the beach boys who will take your towels to whichever pair of loungers you choose and will keep your glasses replenished all day long.

At the back of the beach, in amongst the palm trees, there's an octagonal beach bar which does amazing satay and other traditional Malay snacks. Everything about the resort is carefully conceived and perfectly executed, so much so that you'll never want to leave.

PANGKOR LAUT
(☎ 05-699 1100, fax 05-699 1200), c/o Lamut Post Office, 32200 Lumut, Perak, Malaysia
Reservations: Small Luxury Hotels of the World toll free reservation numbers worldwide (see p12) and most leading tour operators and travel agents
Getting there: The hotel can arrange transfers from Kuala Lumpur Airport (MYR325 per car and three hours), or from Ipoh Airport (MYR125 and one hour) and Penang Airport (MYR325 and three hours); guests are then taken to the island from Lumut by ferry, there are several ferries a day
Accommodation: 177 guest rooms and three suites
Amenities: Fitness centre, hot spa and cold plunge bath, massage, sauna, three swimming pools, two squash courts, three tennis courts, resort boutiques, golf nearby, indoor board games, jungle treks, fishing trips, kayaks, sailing, windsurfing, watersports centre, boating, charter cruises, sunset cruises, TV lounge
Dress code: Smart casual
Weddings: The hotel can host wedding receptions
Minimum stay: None
Rates: Doubles from US$230 to US$322; suites from US$552
Credit cards: Most major
Taxes and service charge: Included

LANGKAWI

The Datai

Tucked away on the north-western tip of Langkawi, between the majestic Macincang mountains and the Andaman Sea, is a sumptuous and beautifully designed hotel, The Datai.

Adrian Zecha, the man behind the fantastic Amanresorts chain, is partly responsible for making this such an amazing resort through his investment and the fact that it is currently run by General Hotel Management, his own management company. The resort certainly has all the Aman hallmarks of perfect design, simple but elegant furnishings made from expensive solid materials – minimal interior decoration and stunning exterior layout.

The hotel's interiors are dominated by the deeply polished red hew of local balau timber, set off by subtle, low voltage spotlighting and beautiful rustic ornaments. Each room is equipped with luxury mod cons such as air-conditioning, king-size bed, humidity controls, satellite TV, private bar and separate shower and bath.

The hotel's cheapest accommodation is in the main building itself, close to the beach, while the 40 villas are scattered up the hillside throughout the tropical rain forest and connected to the public facilities via a series of pathways. Each villa has its own elevated veranda and sun terrace, but some do have better sea views than others, so ask when you are booking.

Like any truly first-class resort, the Datai's dining and leisure facilities are extremely impressive. During the day you can work up an appetite by swimming in one of the two beautiful pools, sailing, windsurfing or snorkelling from the resort's perfect white sandy beach, or playing tennis or golf. The Datai is a very quiet hotel, with little in the way of evening entertainment apart from the top quality cuisine. **The Pavilion** offers authentic Thai cuisine, while the **Dining-room** serves delicious Malaysian and Western dishes.

THE DATAI
(☎ 04-959 2500, fax 04-959 2600), Jalan Teluk Datai, 07000 Langkawi, Kedah, Malaysia
Reservations: Prima Hotels toll free reservation numbers worldwide (see p12)
Getting there: The hotel does arrange transfers from Langkawi Airport, costing MYR100 one way for a limousine
Accommodation: 108 guest rooms: 54 de luxe rooms, 40 villas and 14 suites
Amenities: The Pavilion Thai restaurant, the Beach Club, the Dining-room, lobby lounge, duty free boutiques, beauty salon, car rental, library, white sand beach, two swimming pools, health club, two tennis courts, bicycles, jungle treks, windsurfing, sailing, snorkelling, golf; boat charters and scuba diving can be arranged
Dress code: Elegant casual
Weddings: Can be arranged
Minimum stay: None
Rates: Double rooms from US$245 MYR610; villas from US$281/MYR700; suites from US$402/MYR1000
Credit cards: Most major
Taxes and service charge: 10% service charge will be added to your bill

We were looking for a mixture of adventure, wildlife and luxury and we got an abundance of all three! Malaysia is still relatively unspoilt which enabled us to feel like true explorers as we were whizzed up tiny rivers in boats, surrounded by thick rain forest, and watched monkeys playing in the trees . The food is delicious, a mixture of Chinese, Indian and Malay – the only negative point is that the alcohol is heavily taxed. Rice wine is lethal but a cheaper option! Accommodation can be basic but this is in true jungle style and if you have a week at Pangkor Laut planned at the end you can put up with anything! One word of advice, don't climb Mt Kinabalu immediately you get there, getting married tends to zap your energy reserves and getting to the peak of Mt Kinabalu requires all the energy you could possible muster! **Charlotte and Ian Cross**

Other recommended hotels

Carcosa Seri Negara (☎ 03-282 1888, fax 03-282 7888), Taman Tasik Perdana, 50480 Kuala Lumpur, is a wonderful hideaway just five minutes from the centre of Kuala Lumpur. It boasts one of the city's most romantic restaurants, **The Mahsuri**, which serves continental and Malaysian specialities. Most people passing through Kuala Lumpur for just one night stay at one of the large international chains, either the Shangri La or the Hyatt Regency, but if you are planning to stay on for a few days, or even want to make that one night special this is *the* place to stay. Carcosa Seri Negara, the Malaysian Government's official state residence for visiting heads of state, is owned by Amanresorts, which accounts for the incredibly elegant interior of this fantastic colonial mansion set in 16 hectares of private parkland. The 13 suites start at US$382/MYR950 for a Standard Suite and go up to US41044/MYR2600 for a Grand Suite.

THE EASTERN & ORIENTAL EXPRESS

One of the world's most incredible train trips, a journey on the Eastern & Oriental Express, will transport you back in time. Created by the same company that restored the legendary Venice Simplon-Orient-Express in Europe, this is the most magical way to travel between **Singapore** and **Bangkok**.

Within the train's distinctive shining green carriages, you will spend two nights passing houses raised on stilts among paddy fields, Buddhist temples with elaborately designed spires, children chasing water buffalo, rugged mountains, rubber plantations and deserted palm-fringed beaches. There's lots to do on the train, from palm-readers to a library, and with an Observation Car, two Dining Cars, a Saloon Car, and a Bar Car, you shouldn't suffer from claustrophobia. And in every compartment the sumptuous upholstery and intricate detailing is unbelievable – the train's sheer opulence is quite breathtaking.

The Eastern & Oriental Express, although of course expensive, really is the journey of a lifetime and the most superb way to link Thailand and Malaysia. Prices range from around US$1255/MYR2825 per person in a Sleeper Compartment and US$1130 MYR3140 for a State Compartment to a monumental US$3254/MYR5275 for the Presidential Suite. But do bear in mind you can hop on at **Butterworth** or Kuala Lumpur which reduces the prices, for example Kuala Lumpur to Bangkok is US$990/MYR2480 in a Sleeper Compartment, while Butterworth to Bangkok is US$790/MYR1975.

If you are considering making the journey do call about vacancies and train times as soon as possible, as the train gets very booked up and only runs two or three times a month. Bookings can be made through the following numbers: UK (☎ 0171-928 6000); USA (☎ 800-524-2420); Germany (☎ 0211-162106).

Hong Kong
(BEST TIME: ALL YEAR ROUND)

However much Hong Kong changes in 1997, as Britain hands the former colony back to the Chinese, it's unlikely that any of these hotels will alter. Hong Kong is hardly a haven for cheap accommodation so it's rather a case of five-star or bust. However if you are booking your holiday through a tour operator they can often wangle you a spectacular deal for a couple of days' stopover.

Taxis are numerous and readily available, and fares are much lower than in most cities. Red taxis serve Hong Kong Island and Kowloon; the green taxis in the New Territories and the blue ones on Lantau Island are even cheaper. Drivers speak limited English, but the best way to get around the language barrier is have your destination written in Chinese characters.

It is worth noting that any trip through cross-harbour tunnel costs an additional HK$20 surcharge, which includes the driver's HK$10 return toll. Taxis drivers do expect to be tipped, but just round up the fare to the nearest dollar. Note that they cannot pick you up if you're standing on a restricted street (marked by yellow lines).

The **Star Ferry**, which has connected Hong Kong and Kowloon since 1898, runs regularly between 6:30am and 11:30pm. Costing HK$1.70 on the upper deck and HK$1.40 on the lower, it must be one of the cheapest and most scenic ferry rides in the world so it's almost a disappointment that it takes only eight minutes!

HONG KONG

A heady mixture of Chinese culture with its temples, markets and tea shops as well as crowded streets, gleaming skyscrapers and luxurious hotels

When to go: All year round, but May to September are hot and humid

Average maximum temperatures °C

JAN	FEB	MAR	APR	MAY	JUN	JUL	AUG	SEP	OCT	NOV	DEC
19	19	21	25	29	30	31	31	30	28	24	21

Airport: Kai Tak International Airport

Flight times: to Hong Kong from:
 New York: $18^3/_4$ hours
 LA: $16^1/_2$ hours
 London 12 hours
 Sydney: $7^3/_4$ hours

Approximate exchange rates: Hong Kong dollar (HK$) – £1 = HK$12.02, US$1 = HK$7.75, A$1 = HK$6.12

Time difference: GMT plus eight hours

Voltage: 200v/220v AC, 50 Hz

Combine with: Australia, New Zealand, Malaysia, Thailand, Philippines, India, Singapore

Country dialling code: ☎ 852

The Peninsula

There are scores of top quality hotels in Hong Kong, all with really first-class accommodation and service, but somehow the legendary Peninsula, first opened in 1928, still manages to stand head and shoulders above them all in the romance stakes. For around US$45 the Peninsula will meet you at the airport in one of their fleet of nine green Rolls-Royce Silver Spurs, which somehow symbolises everything that is elegant, and outrageously decadent about this hotel.

Following its complete renovation in 1994, the Peninsula is now immaculate and seriously lavish, boasting some of the most incredible skyline views anywhere in the world and a sense of design and opulence that will continually make your mouth drop open. Despite its recent refurbishment, which brought many technological innovations to the hotel, it still retains the colonial elegance and character that its competitors somehow lack.

The only disadvantage is its location on the **Kowloon** side, making it not quite so accessible to the night-life of **Central** and **Wan Chai**, but the **Star Ferry** runs until about midnight between HK Island and Kowloon, the MTR underground a bit later and after that you'll have to resort to a taxi: they are pretty cheap, but the language can sometimes be tricky!

Because the hotel gets so many honeymooners and couples celebrating anniversaries it has now put together what it calls its 'Romance Packages'. These vary in content and price throughout the year, but usually comprise a de luxe room at a special rate of around US$600/HK$4650 including all sorts of glamorous extras such as champagne, breakfast in bed, round trip from the airport in one of the hotel's green Rollers, and even a dozen red roses delivered to your room by one of the Peninsula's bell boys.

The Peninsula has 246 guest rooms and 54 suites, all of which are equipped with so many mod cons and luxury gadgets there's no point in listing them all. Go for one of the De luxe Harbour View Suites which are located in both corners of the hotel's new tower: you get ceiling to floor glass walls on two sides of the bedroom providing

THE PENINSULA

(☎ 2366 6521, fax 2722 4170), Salisbury Road, Kowloon, Hong Kong

Reservations: The Leading Hotels of the World toll free reservation numbers worldwide (see p12)

Getting there: Kai Tak Airport is just 20 minutes by car, the hotel can arrange transfers in one of its green Rolls-Royce Silver Spurs for around US$45

Accommodation: 246 guest rooms and 54 suites

Amenities: 24-hour currency exchange, florist, hairdresser and beauty salon, health club and spa, helicopter sightseeing tours, fleet of Rolls-Royce Silver Spurs, shopping arcade with 132 shops, sightseeing tours, swimming pool, valet parking service, Gaddi's restaurant, Felix rooftop restaurant on 28th floor, the Veranda restaurant

Dress code: Guests are requested not to wear shorts or flip flops in public places

Weddings: The Peninsula caters for both weddings and receptions for a minimum of 80 and a maximum of 120 people

Minimum stay: None

Rates: Doubles from around US$372/HK$2883; suites from around US$697/HK$5402

Credit cards: Most major

Taxes and service charge: Tax 5%, service charge 10%

panoramic views over Victoria Harbour, and the bathroom's jacuzzi is strategically placed to make the most of the magnificent harbour and Kowloon city vistas. The views are totally captivating by day and even more so at night as thousands of lights glitter on the island.

All the suites in the newly refurbished and expanded Peninsula were designed by Richmond International, the company also responsible for the recent renovation of the Dorchester, in London. The Peninsula's suites range in size from the spacious 85 sq metre junior suites to the awesome 370 sq metre Peninsula Suite.

One of the best things about the Peninsula is the fantastically designed **Felix** rooftop restaurant, located right up on the 28th floor. Designed by Philippe Starck, the decor is about as incredible as the views making it one of the most superbly romantic places to enjoy cocktails and dinner. And if you find yourself slightly overdoing it, don't worry you can always recuperate in the distinctly Venetian-looking health spa and swimming pool or on the sundeck.

Other recommended hotels

The bathrooms in the de luxe suites of **The Regent Hong Kong** (☎ 2721 1211, fax 2739 4546), 18 Salisbury Road, Kowloon, have the ultimate view from their jacuzzi baths: you can lie back sipping champagne as the sun sets behind the myriad of skyscrapers. It's the bell boys in spotless white uniforms, the vast fleet of gleaming Daimlers, the knowledge that your every wish is being taken care of by the hotel's 1300 staff, that makes the Regent such a slick hotel. Almost two thirds of its 602 bedrooms overlook the harbour, while ultimate hedonists gravitate towards the De Luxe Terrace suites featuring outdoor jacuzzis which look straight on to the harbour. Otherwise there's Hong Kong's largest private outdoor swimming pool to relax in, three outdoor spa pools which are set in granite with glass walls to maximise the views, and the most fantastic indoor spa. Doubles from US$284/HK$2200, De Luxe Terrace suites US$1537/HK$11,900.

The Mandarin Oriental (☎ 2522 0111, fax 2810 6190), 5 Connaught Road Central, Hong Kong has the sort of solid reputation that the colonial Far East was built upon. For over 30 years this hotel has been among the best of the luxury hotels in Hong Kong. It is without doubt the most wonderful refuge from the madness that is Hong Kong, a place of utter indulgence and sophistication. Set in the middle of the business centre it also boasts wonderful harbour views. With a ratio of two staff to each guest you'll be looked after admirably. Double rooms from US$256/HK$1980 for a de luxe city view and from US$372/HK$2880 for a de luxe harbour view.

(**Opposite**) **Top:** De luxe Harbour View suite, Peninsula Hotel, Hong Kong. **Bottom left:** Alpine view from bathroom, Le Melezin, France (see p134). **Bottom right:** Bathroom, Château de Bagnols, France (p126).

THREE DAYS IN HONG KONG

If you're not staying on Hong Kong Island, take the Star Ferry from Kowloon across to the island and the Peak Tram from Central up to **Victoria Peak**. One of the most advanced tram systems in the world, the climb takes only eight minutes and costs HK$12, or HK$19 for a return. The walk around the top is really worth doing for the views, then stop off for lunch or dinner at the **Peak Café** which has excellent food, reasonable prices (for Hong Kong!) and a really good atmosphere – sit in the garden if possible.

A trip to **Stanley,** on the south side of Hong Kong Island, to visit the market is also well worth while. There's also a good selection of places to stop for lunch, particularly recommended are **Stanley's Oriental, Stanley's French** and **Lucy's.**

There are lots of organised harbour cruises but just as good, a lot more authentic, and significantly cheaper is the ferry journey to **Lantau**, which departs from one of the piers by Central.

All the major designer shops are crammed into **Central's shopping centres** – The Landmark, Prince's Building, Pacific Place and The Galleria. Look out for the World of Joyce in the Galleria, which is Hong Kong's Conran shop and is great for homeware and designer clothes; Shanghai Tang in the Pedder Building is a beautifully laid out shop and is well worth a visit for its traditional Chinese clothes which have been reworked in amazing fabrics; BeBe on Lan Street is a great place to pick up some designer bargains; and Lane Crawford in both Pacific Place and Ocean Terminal is the Harrods of Hong Kong!

If you need to refuel, **Post 97** and **La Dolce Vita 97**, Lan Kwai Fong, are the happening bars in Central – not bad value but both tend to get overrun with fashion victims, still they're good for people-watching. In the evening, the best value French cuisine on the island can be found at **Club Camargue** in the Regent Centre: the food and atmosphere are great and the views over Kowloon wonderful. Still in Central, there are some good bars on D'Aguilar Street; try **Shermans**, or if you fancy a bit of live music head for the **Jazz Club** which is open until late.

For antiques and a slightly more Oriental experience Hollywood Road, Cat Street, Western Market and the 'Lanes' in and around Central are all really worth a look.

In terms of markets, **Temple Street Market**, in Tsim Sha Tsui (TST) District, is *the* place to pick up that fake Rolex or Chanel handbag, while **Stanley Market** is good for just about everything from tourist junk to good value

clothing. While you're in TST you could eat at **Tutto Bene** on Knutsford Terrace which, although fairly pricey, is a good trendy Italian. Again, make sure you sit outside.

If you're not staying at the Peninsula you must go up to **Felix**, the rooftop restaurant designed by Philippe Starck; it is worth visiting even if it's just for a drink.

If you're on the look out for authentic Chinese food, the **American Peking Restaurant** on Lockhart Road, Wan Chai, is very reasonable and popular with gweilos (Westerners working in Hong Kong) and, better still, the waiters actually speak and understand English! Try the **Chinese Thai Restaurant** in Shek O for a really authentic south-east Asian eating experience. If you want upmarket Cantonese head for **Number 1 Harbour Road** at the Grand Hyatt Hotel: it's probably the best in town though it's painfully expensive.

Macau

Macau, situated on a tiny peninsula at the mouth of the Pearl River, is linked to mainland China by a narrow isthmus, and is only 55 minutes away from Hong Kong by jet foil. This Portuguese colony has some fantastic hotels and a totally different atmosphere from Hong Kong.

Bela Vista (☎ (853) 965333, fax 965588), 8 Rua do Commendador Kou Ho Neng, Macau is very much the outstanding hotel experience of the region. A classic boutique hotel with only eight suites in grand colonial style, Bela Vista is too good to miss. All the rooms offer panoramic views of the city and Praia Grande Bay. Set among landscaped gardens on the slopes of Colina da Penha, The Bela Vista has been part of Macau for over a hundred years and was splendidly restored in 1992. Food and service are truly excellent (the hotel is part of the Mandarin Hotel Group), and guests can choose between dining on the veranda with stunning views over the bay or in the antique-filled restaurant. Doubles from around US$282 HK$2185, suites from US$312/HK$2415.

Pousada de Sao Tiago (☎ 378111, fax 552170), Avenida da Republica, Foraleza de Sao, Tiago da Barra, Macau, a 17th century fort converted into a five-star hotel, is another contender. This pleasing building now houses 24 rooms in total, making it the ideal destination for those who like their hotels small and traditional not sparkling new. The restaurant serves great Cantonese, Macanese and Portuguese cuisine. Doubles cost US$144/HK$1118, the four suites cost US$207/HK$1600 to US$388 HK$3000. Highly recommended.

(Opposite) The Great Barrier Reef, Australia. **Top:** Hayman Island Resort, Whitsunday Islands (see p297). **Bottom:** Green Island (see p298).

Australia
(BEST TIME: ALL YEAR ROUND)

Australia, the world's largest island and its smallest continent, is an increasingly popular honeymoon destination. It is a land of dramatic contrasts which has, quite simply, got the lot. A honeymoon in Australia will allow you to: experience the outback, listen to the thrilling sounds of tropical rain forests, sail among offshore islands or in coastal waterways, dive on the world's largest coral reef, or just lie on deserted beaches in some of the most luxurious resorts imaginable. Australia also has one of the world's most vibrant, beautiful and cosmopolitan cities. When you land in **Sydney** and see the sun shining on the distinctive white sails of the **Opera House** with the harbour glistening before you, you'll know you've picked the right place for your honeymoon.

Two weeks is plenty of time to see lots of Australia but, because the country is so huge, I suggest you break down your trip to three or four 'must see' areas. Most travellers to Australia have three principal sights in mind: the **Great Barrier Reef** and **Queensland's Gold Coast**, Sydney, and **Ayers Rock**. But you could quite easily forget all about Ayers Rock: it's a long way out of the way and do you really want to be shepherded around somewhere sandy and rocky with the blistering heat burning down on you, as part of a group of tourists, on your honeymoon?

It's far better to concentrate your time experiencing the beautiful islands off the Great Barrier Reef or on the **Sunshine Coast** in the popular resort of **Noosa**, and combine your beach holiday with a few days in Sydney, perhaps also fitting in a brief stay in the nearby mountains to give you some experience of the Australian bush.

AUSTRALIA
Big sunshine, crashing surf, sandy beaches, diving and snorkelling on the Great Barrier Reef, stunning Sydney, and vast tracts of untouched tropical rain forest and rugged outback
When to go: The climate ranges from temperate in the south to tropical in the north, so there is year round sunshine in Queensland (although May and September are the driest months), while November to March is the best time to visit Sydney

Average maximum temperatures °C

	JAN	FEB	MAR	APR	MAY	JUN	JUL	AUG	SEP	OCT	NOV	DEC
Sydney	26	26	25	22	19	17	16	18	20	22	24	25
Cairns	31	31	30	29	28	26	26	27	28	29	31	31

Capital: Canberra
Flight times:
    to Sydney from:
        New York: (via LA) $17^1/_2$ hours
        LA: 12 hours
        London: (via LA) 24 hours
    to Cairns from:
        New York: (via LA) $23^1/_2$ hours
        LA: 18 hours
        London: 19 hours
Approximate exchange rates: Australian dollar (A\$) – £1 = A\$1.96, US\$1 = A\$1.27
Time difference: Queensland: GMT plus nine hours
Voltage: 240v/250v AC, 50 Hz, three-pin plugs
Combine with: Los Angeles, Malaysia, Singapore, Hong Kong, Bangkok, New Zealand, Fiji
Country dialling code: ☎ 61

SYDNEY

Situated on a magnificent natural harbour, a few days in Sydney is a great way to start your holiday. In just three days you can see a lot of Sydney, and if you're feeling too tired to do much sightseeing, hop on a ferry and cross the harbour to one of the city's beaches.

The Park Hyatt

Since it opened in 1990, the Park Hyatt Sydney has become established as the hotel with the best views in town. Whether you are in the **Rooftop** restaurant enjoying an informal grilled lunch or sitting gazing at the Harbour lights from your balcony at night, the view is just staggering.

The hotel is situated in the fashionable **Rocks District** and looks straight out over the Harbour to the **Opera House**; the hotel is so close to the water you can virtually reach out and touch it.

A classic boutique hotel with 158 rooms, the Park Hyatt is a great deal more intimate than most of the neighbouring international hotels and it was cleverly designed to maximise its greatest asset – the view of the Harbour and the Opera House. The four-storey hotel follows the contours of the harbour wall nestled beneath the Harbour Bridge, so from the moment you walk into the 'lobby' – where instead of a traditional reception you check in at an antique desk – you'll be utterly mesmerised by the view. The vast expanse of polished granite, marble and sandstone run up to sheet glass windows and doors beyond which everything is blue – it's almost like being on a ship.

Most of the rooms have balconies, all have air-conditioning, separate dressing rooms, TVs and VCRs, and personal butler service as well as hordes of other impressive features. The furnishings are a mixture of old and new and in very good taste, although the decor is very 'hotel-neutral' in style.

As a result of the numerous requests received from guests insisting on having a room with a Harbour view, the Park Hyatt's hotels are now ranked in four different categories, so you know in advance what you are getting. De luxe Harbour rooms have floor to ceiling windows leading to a private balcony, with views of **Campbells** and **Sydney Cove** – without an opera house in sight! De luxe Opera Rooms, as you'd expect, have perfect

THE PARK HYATT
(☎ 2-241 1234, fax 2-256 1555), 7 Hickson Road, The Rocks, NSW 2000, Australia
Reservations: From the UK (☎ 0171-580 8197) for Hyatt Reservations, or talk to tour operator Elegant Resorts (see p9); from the US and Canada toll free (☎ 800-233-1234); from Japan (☎ 03-3288-1234); from Hong Kong (☎ 2311-1234); and from New Zealand toll free (☎ 0-800 441234)
Getting there: 25 minutes by taxi from Sydney International Airport, the hotel can arrange private transfers for you by limousine or taxi
Accommodation: 158 guest rooms, most with balconies: 31 Executive Studios, three Premier Suites, Diplomatic Suite and Governor Suite
Amenities: 24-hour butler service, wardrobe storage service for travelling guests, daily laundry and dry cleaning service, No 7 at The Park, Veranda at The Park, the Bar, fitness centre with exercise equipment, steam room and sauna, massage and beauty services, roof terrace with sundeck, swimming pool and jacuzzi
Dress code: Smart casual
Weddings: The Park Hyatt caters for weddings big and small and has all sorts of packages on offer, such as a reception for 60-80 guests in No 7 at The Park costing A\$115 per person including welcome canapés, three-course meal and drinks, wedding night in a De luxe Harbour King room with champagne and breakfast for the bride and groom
Minimum stay: None
Rates: Superior rooms from US\$374/A\$480; de luxe harbour rooms from US\$459/A\$590
Credit cards: Most major
Taxes and service charge: Included

picture postcard views of Sydney's most famous building, while the Executive Harbour Studios are junior suites with an open-plan living area and bedroom, plus two private balconies looking out over the Harbour. There can be few more invigorating ways to start your day than swimming in the hotel's roof-top pool or just lounging in the outdoor jacuzzi, before enjoying breakfast on the sun drenched terrace looking out over the Harbour. The famous yellow ferries shuttle commuters in from the north side, and the incessantly tacking sail boats remind you that this is a city where leisure is taken seriously. The Park Hyatt may be the most expensive five-star hotel in Sydney but, if you can afford it, it's worth the extra for the views and service, especially if you are not going to be in the city for long.

The Observatory

The Observatory is just around the corner, slightly set back from the Harbour. Though it doesn't have the views of the Opera House, it is a splendidly luxurious town house hotel with a warm atmosphere. The hotel is in the fashionable Rocks District, and within easy walking distance of Sydney Harbour Bridge, the Opera House, and Circular Quay. It is widely regarded as the most comfortable hotel in Sydney.

Only recently taken over by Orient-Express Hotels, the Observatory is the group's first and only hotel in the Pacific Rim. Each room lives up to the fastidious standards set by this hotel group – all are spacious, elegant and beautifully decorated with fine antiques, paintings and tapestries, and feature first-class facilities including television, two phones, in-room safe, hair-dryer, fully-stocked minibar, CD and video player with remote control. The Observatory is one of those hotels where everything looks new and extremely plush, from the heavy curtains in the bedroom to the thick carpeting underfoot and the properly fluffy towels. It all feels marvellously expensive!

The fabulous marble bathrooms have the kind of baths with lashings of bath salts and other goodies that ensure you look forward to getting ready to go out each evening. They also have huge walk-in showers where the jets spray you from every angle, and lovely Molton Brown toiletries.

But the biggest luxury of all at the Observatory is the swimming pool and spa facilities. Above the 20m pool is a ceiling of fibre-optic lights, designed to recreate the constellations of the Southern Hemisphere.

> **THE OBSERVATORY HOTEL**
> (☎ 2-256 2222, fax 2-256 2233), 89-113 Kent Street, Sydney, NSW 2000, Australia
> **Reservations:** The Leading Hotels of the World toll free reservation numbers worldwide (see p12); toll free within Australia (☎ 008-806245)
> **Getting there:** Approximately 25 minutes from the airport by local taxi, or the hotel can arrange collection in a limousine at a cost of A$65
> **Accommodation:** 100 rooms: 77 de luxe rooms, 10 junior suites, 12 executive suites, and the Observatory Suite
> **Amenities:** Drawing-room, Globe bar, the Galileo Restaurant offering modern Australian cuisine with an Italian influence, the Orient for more informal dining on Australasian specialities, 20m star-lit pool, gymnasium, massage, sauna, steam room, floatation tank, tennis court, valet parking, 24-hour room service
> **Dress code:** Smart casual
> **Weddings:** The hotel does cater for weddings with a marriage celebrant present and can host pretty much any kind of reception you want
> **Minimum stay:** None
> **Rates:** De luxe doubles from US$261/A$335; weekend packages start at US$226/A$290 per couple
> **Credit cards:** Most major
> **Taxes and service charge:** Included

Adjacent to the pool is a jacuzzi, sauna and steam room, as well as massage rooms and float-tank facilities – guaranteed to ease jet lag or the after effects of a night on the town.

Although you probably won't be staying in to make the most of them, the Observatory's dining facilities are very good: the informal, light and airy **Orient Restaurant** serves café-style dishes, and the more formal **Galileo Restaurant** which was designed to resemble London's famous Venetian restaurant, Harry's Bar. If you are just after a drink then the club-like atmosphere of the **Globe Bar** with its cedar panelled walls is a good place to sit for a pre-dinner gin and tonic. There is also a drawing-room with an open fireplace.

THREE DAYS IN SYDNEY

For the best views of the **Opera House** stop for lunch, or just a drink at the Park Hyatt – even if you can't afford to stay there it's worth popping in because the views are just awesome and a constant reminder of where you are! Whether you stay there or not, go to the **Rocks**: it's a great place to cruise around, shop and sit in pavement cafés, especially at weekends when you'll often find live bands playing in the streets. It is the oldest part of Sydney, but the whole area has undergone substantial gentrification over the last decade and, as well as being a cool place to wander about, it also has the best city views. Either climb the 200 steps up to the top of **Sydney Harbour Bridge Pylon**, entering via the bridge walkway off Cumberland Street in the Rocks District, or alternatively take the lift up to **Sydney Tower Centrepoint's** observation level. Located right in the middle of the city centre at 100 Market Street, the Tower has 360° views and a revolving restaurant and offers a comprehensive visitor information service from 9.30am to 9.30pm Sunday to Friday and 9.30am to 11.30pm Saturday.

If you are even half-way interested in opera, then attending a performance at the Opera House is a must. Walking up the steps, all dressed up, with those famous white peaks towering above you and a faint breeze lifting off the Harbour, has to be one of the most magical experiences in the world. Contact **Sydney Opera House Tourism Services** (☎ 2-9250 7870, fax 2-9252 2085) about a dinner and performance package, or stop for some bubbly and seafood at the nearby *Sydney Cove Oyster Bar* first. UK-based **Showbiz Bookings** (UK ☎ 0171-497 9977) also offers dinner and opera packages allowing advance bookings.

If you just want to look around this magnificent building but aren't so keen on opera, do one of the **guided tours** which leaves the lower forecourt level between 9am and 4pm daily, costing A$9 each.

Without doubt the best way to get a sense of the real Sydney is to hop on a yellow **ferry**, or an organised cruise, from Circular Quay – you get the best views of the Opera House and

Harbour Bridge from the water. Head for one of the harbour beaches, **Balmoral** or **Camp Cove**, or **Palm Beach** which is further north but is easy to get to via sea-plane from Rose Bay, on the south side of Sydney Harbour.

One of the best things to do on a sunny day in Sydney is to take a ferry trip out to **Watson's Bay**, over the other side of the Harbour, for lunch on the beach at *Doyle's*, the famous seafood restaurant. Get the concierge at your hotel to book you a table on the beach front.

On Saturdays the market at **Paddington** is definitely worth a look: spend the morning there looking around the many different stalls which have everything from candles to clothes made by young local designers, and remember to take cash with you as very few stalls take credit cards. Once you're done in the market pop into *La Mensa* (☎ 2-9332 2963), 257 Oxford Street, a brand new deli-type place where you can either just stop for coffee or a glass of wine, or have a full blown meal. Sit at one of the bar stools and watch your meal being cooked, or take a window seat and watch the world go by.

Bibliophiles should go to **Berkellouws** (☎ 2-9630 3200), also on Oxford Street, where there is a great coffee shop upstairs amongst the second hand books. The food is scrummy and there are all sorts of interesting looking people and books there – get a window seat on one of the bar stools and watch the rest of Paddington do their Saturday thing.

No visit to Sydney would be complete without an afternoon on **Bondi Beach**, or its smaller neighbour, **Tamarama**. Bondi has been cleaned up in the last year or so, after the city council suddenly realised that one of their hottest tourist attractions was actually turning into a bit of a dump. There are still more beautiful beaches in the world, but it is a fun place to stroll around and of course, great for a bit of body surfing. If you're feeling peckish on the way back from the beach in the early evening, stop for a beer and some delicious snacks at the **Bondi Tratt**, 34 Campbell Parade.

THE SOUTHERN HIGHLANDS

No trip to Australia would be complete without getting a taste of the outback with its rugged but serenely tranquil countryside. The Southern Highlands are only an hour and a half's drive from Sydney and are the closest thing to bush that you are going to get without flying for hours into the interior. If you are planning to spend some time in Sydney and some on the beach, you could consider this as an interesting coda to your holiday. For shopping and a glimpse of old Australia visit the nearby towns of

Berrima, Bowral and Moss Vale, all quiet havens for antiques, books and arts and crafts. If you have time, a more scenic journey back to Sydney is to take the F3 Freeway via Kangaroo Mountain, which adds only 20 minutes to your journey and is well worth it for the views.

Milton Park

Milton Park is one of Australia's most beautiful and comfortable hotels. Under the ownership of Amanresorts, which has only a handful of exclusive properties worldwide all of them featured in this book, the rooms in this former country house are some of the most beautiful in any hotel I have ever come across.

The decor is not ostentatious but refined colonial elegance, where contemporary Mulberry fabrics sit alongside Georgian mahogany easy chairs and antique French tapestries. The stone-washed walls produce an air of European old world charm, enhanced by the fine design details that are the hallmark of Amanresorts. It is impossible not to relax here: curl up together with a book or a board game in front of the fire in the antique-filled library or, if it's warm outside, order the picnic of your choice and head off into the parklands with a rug to lie on and a chilled bottle of wine to share.

The staff are so friendly and relaxed in their chinos and open-neck shirts, that you'll probably end up knowing all their names. They will be quite happy to arrange anything for you, whether it be a guided tour of the gardens, horse-riding through the bush, or sightseeing in the nearby towns.

In the bedrooms, the four-poster beds are made from washed pine, the fireplace laid in case the mountain mist swirls in, fresh coffee and a cafetière are provided, and the twin seating jacuzzis in the six suites are large enough to swim in. The robes provided look so good that you'll consider stealing them, and the bath oils so luxurious that you will. All of this and a spacious private balcony, with rattan chairs and the most glorious views of the surrounding woodlands.

There's not much to do at Milton Park,

> **MILTON PARK**
> (☎ 48-611522, fax 48-614716), Hordens Road, Bowral, NSW 2576, Australia
> **Reservations:** The Leading Hotels of the World toll free reservation numbers worldwide (see p12)
> **Getting there:** An hour and a half's drive from Sydney airport, rent a car from any of the main car rental companies at the airport, or take the train to Bowral from where the hotel will collect you
> **Accommodation:** 40 suites and de luxe rooms, each with a view of the gardens and courtyard lawn, or the surrounding forest and bush
> **Amenities:** The Garden Court Dining-room, the Horden Dining-room, a lounge bar, library and extra lounges, Homestead Veranda with panoramic views of the grounds where light meals are served outside in the summer, day-time room service, gourmet picnic hampers prepared for guests, Heli-pad, mountain bikes, horse-riding, bush walks and local sightseeing tours, four championship golf courses within 15 minutes drive, three all-weather tennis courts, softball and volley-ball, a heated outdoor swimming pool, croquet, bocce, massage
> **Dress code:** Informal, no jacket or tie are required in the lounges or dining-rooms
> **Weddings:** Receptions can be arranged for residents
> **Minimum stay:** None
> **Rates:** Doubles from US$550/A$706, suites from US$630/A$809, including à la carte breakfast and dinner
> **Credit cards:** Most major
> **Taxes and service charge:** Included

except stroll around the grounds which in all span 280 hectares, ride across the local bush and parkland, or play croquet on the lawn, but I wouldn't worry as you'll probably find it difficult to leave your room anyway, which is why a night or two at Milton Park would make the perfect end to an Australian honeymoon. I really couldn't recommend it highly enough.

THE BLUE MOUNTAINS

Just over an hour directly west of Sydney are the Blue Mountains, named after the blue haze which perpetually hangs over these vast craggy mountains, allegedly produced by the combination of oil from the thousands of eucalyptus trees and the sunlight. The principal recreation in the Blue Mountains is bush walking: 100 km of walks are available. For the less energetic, the mountains can be seen to equal effect on horseback or with any of the many tour companies operating four-wheel drive, cycling and train tours in the area.

Lilianfels Blue Mountains

Lilianfels in the Blue Mountains, west of Sydney, has a less personal atmosphere than Milton Park but the view from the front-facing windows over the famous **Seven Sisters** is quite spectacular. Since it opened four years ago, the hotel has won several awards for its service and food, and it is now rated as one of Australia's foremost hotels.

The hotel is a lovely place to spend a few days of your honeymoon taking in the invigorating mountain air. It is equally popular for weddings which are held in the immaculately kept gardens with the most magical of backdrops provided by the blue haze clinging to the mountains.

Although the main building of the hotel is modern, there is old world charm to be found in **Darley's**, one of Lilianfels' two restaurants located in the former home of the original owner, Sir Frederick Darley. Darley named the house after his daughter, Lilian, who was reputedly sent to the mountains to recover from tuberculosis in the late 19th century.

What the bedrooms at Lilianfels lack in old world charm, they make up for in furnishings and amenities. All the rooms are large and comfortable and they have spacious marble en suite bathrooms with a separate bath and shower, TV and VCR, phone, large and extremely comfortable beds with European feather down comforters, and views over the mountains or the hotel's award winning gardens.

The suites have a great deal more character than the bedrooms, and are really prettily furnished in strong colours, with the added bonuses of jacuzzi baths, beautiful antique furniture and more staggering views over the mountains.

> **LILIANFELS BLUE MOUNTAINS**
> (☎ 47-801200, fax 47-801300), Lilianfels Avenue, Echo Point, Katoomba, NSW 2780, Australia
> **Reservations:** Small Luxury Hotels of the World toll free reservation numbers worldwide (see p12)
> **Getting there:** One and a half hour drive from Sydney, or two hours by train, the hotel will pick you up from Katoomba station only 3km away
> **Accommodation:** 81 rooms and five suites
> **Amenities:** Room service, indoor swimming pool, health club and spa with sauna, float tank, steam bath, herbal bath, gym, tennis courts, croquet, two restaurants, billiard room, library; plus four golf courses and great bush walking and mountain tours nearby
> **Dress code:** Smart casual, jackets and ties are not compulsory
> **Weddings:** The hotel is extremely popular for weddings and receptions for up to 80 people, costing around A$89 per person for a three-course dinner and drinks for $3^1/_2$ hours with table arrangements
> **Minimum stay:** Two nights over a weekend
> **Rates:** Doubles from US$220/A$283; suites from US$336/A$431; ask for packages
> **Credit cards:** Most major
> **Taxes and service charge:** Included

With its fantastic health facilities, including an indoor swimming pool, massage, saunas, steam rooms, and jacuzzis, not to mention the walks through the surrounding bush and four-wheel drive picnic excursions, Lilianfels has lots to offer those looking to escape the hustle and bustle of nearby Sydney. Whether you choose to take tea on the lawn with a game of croquet to follow, or abseil off one of the many nearby cliffs, Lilianfels won't let you down.

Withycombe

Withycombe is a much smaller, but in my mind, much more romantic, hideaway in the Blue Mountains. Near **Mt Wilson**, this elegantly furnished cedar homestead has just four rooms, all with wide verandas, and offers absolute tranquillity.

Days at Withycombe are spent planning activities over breakfast in the farmhouse kitchen with your hosts, Gary and Helen Ghent, and end with fine dining in the splendid dining-room. The Ghents have lived at Withycombe since 1980 and decided to share their home with a few privileged guests who are encouraged to treat the pretty house as their own; whether it be curling up in front of the fire in the library or finding total privacy somewhere in the three hectares of gardens, it's the sort of place where you just get on with it.

When weather permits Helen serves lunch in the garden, or she'll happily pack you a picnic if you want to explore the immense beauty of the Mt Wilson area, where nearby walks will take you to waterfalls and breathtaking views across an ocean of acacia and eucalyptus trees.

If you don't like the idea of eating meals around a communal dining-room table then you are probably better off at Lilianfels. But for just a few nights this makes the most wonderful taster of the 'real' Australia – you cannot help but feel that you've stumbled upon a real gem of a private home here. Helen is lovely, and is just as happy to cook you breakfast at 8am as at 4pm in her homely kitchen where an old Rayburn sits beside a huge pine-dresser adorned with blue and white china. With its gabled roof and wide veranda, Withycombe really is the epitome of the idyllic Australian homestead.

> **WITHYCOMBE**
> (☎ 47-562106, fax 47-562177), Mt Wilson, NSW 2786, Australia
> **Reservations:** Small Luxury Hotels of the World toll free reservation numbers worldwide (see p12)
> **Getting there:** Two hours drive from Sydney; Gary or Helen will collect you from Mt Victoria or Katoomba railway stations
> **Accommodation:** There are currently four guest rooms, but separate garden cottages are planned
> **Amenities:** All bedrooms are en suite; the house and gardens are free for guests to use as their own, and there is golf, horse-riding, abseiling and a heli-pad nearby
> **Dress code:** Informal
> **Weddings:** Withycombe is very popular for wedding receptions of up to 40 guests
> **Minimum stay:** None
> **Rates:** Doubles from US$331/A$425 including dinner, bed and breakfast
> **Credit cards:** American Express
> **Taxes and service charge:** Included

QUEENSLAND

A honeymoon in Queensland can be as lazy, exhilarating, tranquil, glitzy, laid-back or sophisticated as you want. You can choose between spending long days lounging around on the beach, scuba diving amongst the coral and tropical fish of the Great Barrier Reef, walking through the noisy jungle, living it up at the casinos or even exploring the beautiful Whitsunday Islands with the privacy afforded by your own chartered yacht. Queensland, the state where kangaroos outnumber people, is absolutely huge. But despite its size it is relatively easy to explore thanks to the great network of internal flights from Sydney, as well as a number of direct international flights flying straight into Queensland's 'gateway' towns of Cairns, **Townsville** and **Brisbane** from Singapore.

THE SUNSHINE COAST

Outside Australia, people only think of the islands of the Great Barrier Reef when they think of Australia's coast, but native Australians are just as fond of the Sunshine Coast below **Fraser Island** and, in particular, **Noosa**. A cosmopolitan village of restaurants, boutiques and sidewalk cafés, the real beauty about Noosa is that it is also just minutes away from beaches, rain forest, bushland, everglades and lakes. The best time to visit this vibrant coastal town is between October and April and make sure you stay on the river or on the bay. Noosa is brimming over with great restaurants but do go to **The Salt Water**, which is famous for its amazing seafood. If you want to really pamper yourselves there are two wonderful hotels in the area to choose from.

The **Sheraton Noosa** (☎ 74-494888, fax 74-492230), Hastings Street, Noosa Heads, is most luxurious. This lovely caramel coloured hotel, with its blue balconies overlooking the swimming pool, provides a stylish base on Noosa's famous Hastings Street. All the rooms are spacious and well equipped with microwave ovens and spa baths in addition to all the usual luxuries. Apart from Noosa's many restaurants on the doorstep, the Sheraton also has its own speciality grill and seafood restaurant, a beach-front restaurant, coffee shop and cocktail bar. Doubles from US$218/A$280 for a Noosa view room to US$239/A$307 for a river view.

The **Hyatt Regency Coolum** (☎ 74-461234, fax 74-462957), PO Box 78, Coolum Beach, at the base of **Mount Coolum** is only half an hour south of Noosa and well worth a visit for a few days. The hotel is designed as a low-rise village square which ensures that it doesn't detract from its scenic surroundings. Its facilities are endless and include shops, boutiques, bars, four speciality restaurants, an 18-hole championship golf course, eight swimming pools, beach club and spa and health centre. The hotel has its own complimentary shuttle into Noosa, allowing you to get the best of both worlds. Doubles from US$270/A$345 to US$320/A$411 including taxes.

ISLANDS OF THE GREAT BARRIER REEF

The **Whitsunday Islands**, once the tips of ancient mountains scattered either side of **Whitsunday Passage**, are among the safest and most scenic sailing waters in the world. This group of 74 hilly and wooded islands, many of them fringed with reefs, were originally named by Captain Cook in 1770. Today only nine of the 74 have been developed for tourism. Further up the coast, are the **Family Group** of islands of which **Bedarra** and **Dunk** are particularly famous resorts, and much further still is **Lizard**, Australia's northernmost island.

Hayman Island

Hayman Island is without doubt the most famous of the Whitsunday Islands, and arguably the most celebrated, exclusive and luxurious hotel in Australia. A totally self-contained resort, Hayman has been owned and operated by Ansett Australia since the late 1980s when the company totally redeveloped the island with the aim of creating a resort that would rank among the finest in the world. They have succeeded in creating an extremely swanky resort. A holiday at Hayman is all about indulgence, pleasure, elegance and the most attentive service imaginable, on an island no bigger than 8km in circumference.

The most northerly of the Whitsunday Islands, Hayman is also one of the closest to the Great Barrier Reef, so the opportunities for diving are really first rate.

The hotel is a 50-minutes boat trip away from Hamilton Island. From the moment you are handed a glass of chilled champagne aboard the hotel's private luxury launch, *Sun Goddess*, for the trip to Hayman itself, you'll know you are in for a treat. The resort's unique architectural style comprises three-storey modern buildings with tiered white terraces, so that from the side they resemble a cruise ship. Each tier has a suc-cession of balconies overlooking the most fantastic array of swimming pools, joined by jetty-like walkways and interspersed with lofty palms and lush tropical foliage. The overall effect is just like something out of a James Bond movie.

To complement the island's extraordinary natural beauty – two white coral beach-es and glistening clear blue waters as far as the eye can see – the hotel has six restau-rants serving exquisite food from casual Italian to formal French, and Oriental

HAYMAN ISLAND

(☎ 79-401234, fax 79-401567), Great Barrier Reef, North Queensland 4801, Australia

Reservations: The Leading Hotels of the World toll free reservation numbers worldwide (see p12)

Getting there: 50 minutes by luxury boat from Hamilton Island, which is reached by flights from Cairns, Brisbane, Sydney and all major Australian cities on a daily basis

Accommodation: 203 rooms and suites overlooking the pools, grounds, and beaches; 108 double rooms, 62 twin rooms, 33 suites and 11 ocean view penthouses

Amenities: 24-hour room service, six restaurants and three bars, boutiques, information centre and activities desk, weekly activities programme, a huge selection of watersports including parasailing, water-skiing, fishing, diving, sailing aboard the resort's yachts, tennis, squash, putting green, volley-ball, Hayman Health Club, the Entertainment Centre, Hernandos night-club, piano Club lounge

Dress code: Casual attire for all restaurants except La Fontaine where a jacket is required for men

Weddings: Weddings are becoming increasingly popular on Hayman, so much so that they are now building a Wedding Chapel, which will be used in addition to the Swan Pond, the formal garden and the beach which are currently popular wedding venues; ask about the Hayman Wedding Package which costs around A$1260 for cake, fees, location decoration, champagne, bride's wired bouquet and groom's buttonhole

Minimum stay: None

Rates: Palm garden view from US$327 A$420; beach-front room from US$483 A$620; West Wing suite from US$934 A$1200

Credit cards: Most major

Taxes and service charge: Included

seafood. The range of sporting facilities is equally impressive, including a large salt-water swimming pool, two fresh-water pools, a golf target range, a state of the art health club, tennis and squash courts as well as a huge range of watersports. Nothing is done on a small scale at Hayman; the West Wing Pool is seven times the size of an Olympic pool!

Inside, soft neutral colours and the cooling honey-coloured marble produce a restful air, while the bedroom furnishings are extremely plush incorporating floral designs and pastel plaids. The 203 rooms and suites are all luxuriously appointed with air-conditioning, ceiling fans, phones, television and videos, radio, tea and coffee-making facilities, in-room safe, hair-dryers, minibars, plus beautiful marble bathrooms with toiletries and bathrobes. Each room also has a private balcony or terrace overlooking either the swimming pools, the tropical gardens, or southwards over the beach across the Whitsunday Passage.

The staff will arrange day trips taking the two of you out to nearby **Bail Hai** and **Langford Reef**, two popular picnic and snorkelling spots, leaving you all alone to wallow in your private island paradise. Or else charter one of the island's fully crewed yachts and explore these stunning blue seas and islands under your own steam for a few days.

Green Island Resort

Green Island Resort looks like one of those idyllic islands straight out of the Maldives. From the air, it is just one small green oval dot with a white sandy brim hovering in a vast expanse of varying shades of turquoise, cobalt and marine blue. The only sign that it is indeed inhabited is the fragile-looking jetty strung out to one side with an assortment of boats clustered around it. Situated on Australia's beautiful Great Barrier Reef, Green Island is a small coral cay covering just 15 hectares. Home to 126 native plants, stunning birdlife and a magnificent coral reef, Green Island is one of Australia's premier heritage sites. The hotel was built with extreme care for the natural habitat, allowing the management to claim that it is one of the most environmentally friendly tourist developments in the world.

Days are spent lazing by the pool with the occasional refreshing dip, strolling along the beach, on more adventurous walks through the rain forest, or participating in any of the resort's numerous watersports. Diving, sail-boarding, game fishing and reef snorkelling are just some of the sports available. The swimming pool is a really serene place, surrounded by wonderful comfortable wooden loungers with cream cushions and cream canvas traditional sun umbrellas. All around you, the lush foliage provides a welcoming change from the blistering heat.

Ninety guests are accommodated in 46 rooms, all of which feature separate shower and bath, bathrobes, toiletries, TV and radio, minibar, air-conditioning and ceiling fan, as well as a private balcony with outdoor furniture. Natural fabrics predominate in the rooms, with highly polished wooden floorboards and furniture producing a very elegant and warming ambience.

Although all the added extras that you'd expect from a member of the Small Luxury Hotels of the World chain are there, the rooms are not fussily or over elaborately furnished. You can expect clean cream or white walls, wooden slat blinds, sleek wooden table tops and lamps, and colourful bedspreads.

Lizard Island

Lizard Island is Australia's most northern island resort located 240km north-east of Cairns and, as such, continues to be one of the most unspoilt and naturally beautiful of the islands on the Great Barrier Reef.

Lizard is so far north that even after landing at Cairns you'll have a further one-hour flight to the island. Once you get there you'll know it was worth it. If you are seeking a tropical island and underwater paradise, but don't want to share it with hordes of other tourists, it's worth making the effort to get up to Lizard.

The island, named after its first inhabitants, the monitor lizards, is blessed with 24 pristine white sandy beaches, 1000 hectares of environmentally protected woodland, and some of the most incredible diving available anywhere along this coast: the diverse underwater attractions include 150-year old clams and the ridiculous looking potato cod fish.

The 40 guest rooms, set among coconut palms on the wonderfully sheltered **Anchor Bay**, come in three different styles. The 30 Anchor Bay suites have superb views, while the two de luxe suites have separate living areas and are superbly comfortable. All the

---

GREEN ISLAND RESORT
(☎ 70-313300, fax 70-521511), Green Island, PO Box 898, Cairns, Queensland 4870, Australia
Reservations: Small Luxury Hotels of the World toll free reservation numbers worldwide (see p12)
Getting there: 10 minutes from Cairns Airport to the wharf (A$10 taxi), then 45 minutes by high speed catamaran (A$20)
Accommodation: 46 rooms and 10 suites
Amenities: 24-hour reception, two bars, restaurant, small meeting room, laundry/valet service, business facilities, two shops, 25m fresh-water heated swimming pool, Canopy grill snack bar, bird-watching, star-gazing, snorkelling, fish feeding, private guest lounge, Cairns transit lounge
Dress code: None
Weddings: Green Island hosts wedding ceremonies and receptions for a minimum of 20 people, starting at A$80 per person
Minimum stay: None
Rates: Doubles from US$390/A$501 to US$640/A$822, suites from US$440 A$565 to US$690/A$886
Credit cards: Most major
Taxes and service charge: Included

LIZARD ISLAND
(☎ 70-603999, fax 70-603991), Lizard Island, Great Barrier Reef Resort, North Queensland 4870, Australia
Reservations: Direct or toll free within Australia (☎ 1-800 812525)
Getting there: One hour from Cairns in a private plane or with Qantas, the planes land on the island
Accommodation: 40 guest rooms: eight Sunset Point villas, two Suites, 30 Anchor Bay rooms
Amenities: Fresh-water swimming pool, full range of watersports including sailing, fishing and scuba diving, glass-bottom boat cruises, dining-room, lounge, bar, tennis, room service
Dress code: Casual
Weddings: Both ceremonies and receptions are occasionally catered for
Minimum stay: None
Rates: From US$374/A$480 to US$442 A$567 per person per night including all meals
Credit cards: Most major
Taxes and service charge: Included

suites have a balcony with views of the bay, private facilities, air-conditioning, ceiling fans, one king or twin double beds (so make sure that you state that you want a king-sized bed), minibar, writing desk, phone, iron/ironing board, hair-dryer and bathrobes.

Lizard is an all-inclusive resort where all meals, bush walks and many watersports are included in the basic tariff. You won't have to pay for dinghies, paddle-skis, water-skiing, fishing gear and bait, catamarans, sailboards or snorkelling equipment, but you do have to pay for scuba diving lessons and equipment hire, game-fishing charters, Great Barrier Reef trips, as well as all refreshments and alcohol.

The hotel's bar and restaurant have a very relaxed club-like atmosphere, where guests often join each other for drinks, though you don't have to worry about your privacy being invaded too much – there is plenty of space on this lovely remote island.

THE GREAT BARRIER REEF

The Great Barrier Reef, one of Queensland's three **World Heritage** sites, is the largest marine park in the world and a scuba diver's paradise. Extending along Queensland's coastline from Cape York at the tip of mainland Australia to Gladstone in the south, the reef is more than 2000km long and comprises 2900 individual reefs and 74 coral islands. It was formed 10,000 years ago and today supports an incredibly diverse and dense population of 10,000 species of sponge, 350 different species of coral, 4000 species of molluscs, and 1500 species of fish from swarming pelagics to massive humpback whales.

The reef also has some of the **best wall diving in the world**, especially in the outer sections of the Barrier Reef, the Coral Sea or Oceanic Reefs, where sheer walls of coral disappear into the sea floor hundreds of metres below. It is not uncommon to find yourself swimming alongside sea snakes measuring about two metres long, reef sharks, giant Potato Cod, Manta Rays and turtles.

You can dive in Queensland all year round, but the most consistently good weather is between August and January. The variety of diving on offer is quite astounding. While many of the best reef dives are reached by charter boat, on some coral cays and islands you can literally walk off the beach and dive into a coral world. There are also many excellent locations for beach and river diving.

Yacht charter operator, **The Moorings** runs sailing charters on a wide range of boats around Hamilton Island and through the Whitsundays. Charters can be booked either through The Moorings' office in Sydney (☎ 2-693 5401, fax 2-317 2258), with the UK office (☎ 01843-227140, fax 01843-228 784), or with the US-based Head Office (☎ 813-535-1446, fax 813-530-9747).

Other recommended hotels

Dunk Island (☎ 70-688199), Brammo Bay, Dunk Island 4810, North Queensland, is a truly beautiful hideaway with tracts of virgin rain forest, sweeping arcs of golden sand and lush green gardens full of soaring palm trees. One of only three true rain forest islands on the coast, Dunk is a lush home to native fauna and flora, cool walking trails, a real Australian farm, and some fantastic big-game fishing. Just 4km off the mainland's Mission Beach, midway between Cairns and Townsville, Dunk is reached by either a 30-minute flight from Cairns or a 45-minute flight from Townsville. With four grades of accommodation from Banfield Units set in the gardens to the superb Bayview villas, the island offers a wide range of prices from US$265/A$340 per night which includes full breakfast, nightly entertainment and free use of non-motorised watersports and most island facilities, to US$385/A$495.

Bedarra Island (☎ 70-688233), Bedarra Island 4854, Great Barrier Reef, North Queensland, is a very luxurious and equally expensive all-inclusive private island retreat. Twenty minutes in a private launch from Dunk Island, Bedarra is unashamedly elitist; no children under 15 years of age are allowed, nor are day-visitors, so the entire island is reserved for the privileged 31 guests housed in the luxuriously appointed 16 beachside villas. The rooms, either split-level or two-storey, have beautifully polished wood floors and walls, elegant pine and rattan furniture, a queen-size bed covered in warm tones of salmon pink, and all mod cons such as TV/VCR, minibars and air-conditioning. A week of this kind of luxury, with the champagne and vintage wines flowing from the 24-hour bar, will set you back a pretty substantial US$927/A$1191 per couple per night including all meals, accommodation, all island activities and the 24-hour bar.

The Point, Mission Beach (☎ 70-688154, fax 70-688596), Explorer Drive, South Mission Beach, North Queensland, is a much more moderately priced alternative to the expensive luxury resorts featured above, with really easy access to the Great Barrier Reef. This rain forest retreat has superb views over to Dunk Island and the Coral Sea, with a beach just 500m away and shops two kilometres. Doubles from US$125/A$160.

Silky Oaks (☎ 70-981666), Daintree Rain Forest, Mossman River Gorge, North Queensland, owned by P&O, is located 80km north of Cairns which makes it a great base from which to explore **Cape Tribulation National Park**. Perched high up in the mountains above the Mossman River Gorge, Silky Oaks' guests stay in tree houses, which are en suite and have some luxuries including a fan, tea and coffee-making facilities and a hair-dryer. The hotel offers four-wheel drive wilderness safaris to **Daintree River** and **Cape Trib**, as well as day trips to the Great Barrier Reef. Doubles from US$292/A$375.

New Zealand
(BEST TIME: NOVEMBER TO MARCH)

New Zealand is the place if you are looking for a little more from your honeymoon than spending two weeks on a lounger – adventure in a truly unspoilt wilderness. Few visitors to New Zealand stay in one place because there's so much to see and do: build your itinerary around the key sights and hotels I've covered in this chapter.

You'll find such a staggering mix of scenery in New Zealand that you won't believe you have only visited one country: ancient glaciers; smouldering volcanoes; azure lakes fringed with lush green pines and surrounded by a backdrop of craggy snow-capped mountains; fertile grasslands stretching out as far as the eye can see, and everywhere the unrelenting surf crashes down on vast empty beaches.

This country is also heaven for animal lovers. You can swim with huge packs of Dusky dolphins, watch awesome 12m sperm whales surfacing and diving, visit the Fjordland crested penguin, one of the rarest varieties of penguin in the world, and sea-kayak past fur seal colonies.

But New Zealand is perhaps most famous for its adventure activity, from bungey jumping, white-water rafting and jet boat racing through narrow gorges, to heli-skiing, parapenting, and trail biking along challenging mountain paths. You can experience more exhilarating adventure in one day in **Queenstown** than a normally sporty person will see in a lifetime.

New Zealand is a land of rugged beauty, of hugely diversified landscapes, and of activities. Most of the main sights are located near enough to each other so that once there, you won't have to do much travelling around. But perhaps the country's best attribute is its space and remoteness. If you are looking for peace and tranquillity – somewhere to rediscover each other away from hordes of other honeymooners, then this is the place for you.

In honeymoon terms, New Zealand's South Island has more to offer than the North Island. It really depends on how much time you have: if you are going for two weeks or less, I would concentrate all your time on seeing the South Island because the best sights and places are in a compact area: the ever-changing landscapes of the South Island offer some of the most spectacular and unspoilt scenery the world has to offer. However, there are some good hotels and places to visit in the North Island, so if you have three weeks spend the first one in the North Island and then move to the South Island for the remaining two weeks.

NEW ZEALAND

A truly unspoilt wilderness of ancient glaciers, smouldering volcanoes, azure lakes fringed with lush green pines, crystal clear mountain streams and craggy snow-capped mountains, with lots of opportunity for adventurous pursuits from bungey jumping to swimming with dolphins

When to go: November to March are the summer months, but skiing is best in August

Average maximum temperatures °C

	JAN	FEB	MAR	APR	MAY	JUN	JUL	AUG	SEP	OCT	NOV	DEC
Auckland	23	23	22	19	17	14	13	14	16	17	19	21

Capital: Auckland

Flight times: to Auckland from:
New York: (via LA) 17³/₄ hours
LA: 12 hours
London: 28 hours (via LA/Far East)
Sydney: 3 hours

Approximate exchange rates: New Zealand dollar (NZ$) £1 = NZ$2.22, US$1 = NZ$1.43, A$1 = NZ$1.13

Time difference: GMT plus 12 hours

Voltage: 230v, slanted three-pronged plugs

Combine with: Australia, Bali, Fiji and anywhere else in the South Pacific, Hawaii, Los Angeles, Hong Kong, Tokyo, Bangkok, Singapore and Kuala Lumpur

Country dialling code: ☎ 64

CHRISTCHURCH

The best way to see the South Island is to fly into Christchurch, the island's main city, and hire a car. Driving in New Zealand is an absolute pleasure, the roads are in good condition, the sign posts are clear, efficient and easy to map-read by, and the highways are so empty that you'll very rarely have a car both in front and behind you! Besides, the surrounding countryside is invariably so beautiful, and constantly changing, that even a four-hour drive will be positively enjoyable.

While you are in **Christchurch**, stay at **The George** (☎ 3-379 4560, fax 3-366 6747), 50 Park Terrace, Christchurch 8001: it is a member of the Small Luxury Hotels of the World and is situated in the centre of town overlooking the **River Avon**. The George isn't particularly romantic, but it will provide you with an excellent place to recover from the journey and, with only 54 rooms, it offers the kind of friendly and personalised service you'd expect on your honeymoon. Doubles from US$198/NZ$287, suites from US$383/NZ$557.

Or, if you are looking for something a little more individual and don't mind being just outside town, try **Cashmere House Lodge** (☎/fax 3-332 7864), which boasts magnificent views over Christchurch, the Pacific Ocean and across to the Southern Alps. The Lodge has five bedrooms some of which have massive Irish four-poster beds. Honeymooners are given a warm welcome with nice touches such as a half bottle of champenoise and chocolates on the bed. Don't go to Cashmere House expecting everything to be luxuriously perfect – the showers are a bit small and plastic, the carpet a bit over paisley – but Birgit and Monty Claxton will look after you well. Doubles from US$165/NZ$240 per night including breakfast. From the UK Cashmere House Lodge can be booked through Silk Cut Travel (UK ☎ 01730-265211).

A FEW THINGS TO SEE AND DO IN AND AROUND CHRISTCHURCH

While you're in Christchurch, apart from all the touristy things to do such as visiting the **Botanical Gardens** and the magnificent Cathedral and punting down the River Avon, make sure you do leave time for dinner at *Espresso 123* (☎ 3-365 0547), 124 Oxford Terrace, drink margaritas at *Kyotes*, and take a look at the best outdoor clothes I've ever seen in Action Down Under on **Cashel Street**. All of these activities come highly recommended! The other great restaurants in Christchurch for dinner are *Saggio di Vino* (☎ 3-379 4006) on the corner of Bealey Avenue and Papanui, and *Scarborough Fare* (☎ 3-326 6987) on the sea front in Sumner which serves truly fantastic gourmet food.

One of the main attractions on the South Island is **Kaikoura**, a small coastal town only two hours' drive north from Christchurch, where you can watch sperm whales lolling around on the ocean's surface from a boat and afterwards actually go swimming with the local Dusky dolphins and seals. There are lots of

companies specialising in both activities in Kaikoura, but **Whale Watch Kaikoura** (☎ 3-319 5045, fax 3-319 6545) and **New Zealand Sea Adventures** (3-319 6622, fax 03-319 6868) are both run from an office at the town's railway station which makes combining both activities much more convenient. It also means that you are ideally placed to make the most of *Station Café's* fantastic all-day Kiwi fried breakfast between the two tours.

The whale watching starts at 8am, which means starting start just after 6am if you're driving up from Christchurch. But if you've recently flown in from Europe or America you'll probably be waking up early automatically because of the jet lag, so it's not as bad as it sounds, and it's certainly well worth the effort. If you share the driving it's easy, besides the scenery en route is fantastic. We did both the whale watching and dolphin swim on the same day and got back to Christchurch in time for dinner that night. Exhausted yes, but full of the day's experiences.

BLENHEIM

Blenheim, and the surrounding Marlborough region, earned its place on the international wine map back in the 1980s when Western Australian wine maker David Hohnen named his wine after nearby **Cloudy Bay**. The romantic image and the distinctly lush tropical flavours of this now famous wine caught on, earning Marlborough Sauvignon Blanc widespread international acclaim.

Timara Lodge

Timara Lodge, part of the Small Luxury Hotels of the World chain, is known for its fine food and impressive wine cellars and would be the perfect place to relax and look back on your day's adventures.

Set in beautifully kept formal gardens where swans swim in the mill pond, the Lodge was built in 1923 as a private country manor and is now run along the lines of a country house hotel, accommodating just eight guests.

Only two the lodge's four rooms are doubles so prior booking is essential, and it is expensive at NZ$700 per couple, though this does include pre-dinner drinks, a delicious dinner with the best local wines, bed and breakfast. The bedrooms are really lovely and are very well-equipped with clock radio, hair-dryer, heated towel rails, complimentary toiletries, bathrobes, ironing board

TIMARA LODGE
(☎ 3-527 8276, fax 3-572 9191), Dog Point Road, RD2, Blenheim, Marlborough, New Zealand
Reservations: Small Luxury Hotels of the World toll free reservation numbers worldwide (see p12)
Getting there: The lodge can arrange transfers from Blenheim (5km)
Accommodation: Four guest rooms
Amenities: 22m outdoor swimming pool, grass tennis court, mountain bikes, dining-room, lake and rowing boat, 72 hectares of walks, plus whale watching, winery tours, golf, sailing and fishing can all be arranged locally
Dress code: Smart casual
Weddings: The lodge does host receptions for a maximum of 160 people, starting at NZ$150 per head
Minimum stay: None
Rates: Doubles from US$482/NZ$700
Credit cards: Most major
Taxes and service charge: Not included

and a phone. There are pleasing personal touches too, from the freebie chocolates and bottle of mineral water left out for you, to the fresh flowers in every room.

Days at Timara are spent touring the surrounding countryside on the lodge's mountain bikes, or on foot. There are 72 hectares of walks to be discovered and a rowing boat on the lake making it the perfect spot for a picnic. It's also a good place to tour the local wineries from, or if all you want to do is relax for a day there's a lovely outdoor swimming pool and a grass tennis court.

A FEW THINGS TO SEE AND DO AROUND BLENHEIM

Blenheim, about two hours from Kaikoura up the one road north is the South Island's **wine capital**, made famous by the prolific Montana winery which is accountable for one in every two bottles of New Zealand wine produced.

Many of the wineries in the Marlborough region are open to visitors. The best way to see them is to drive north, from Nelson through Richmond to Motueka (on the SH60 Coast Road) and do the loop back round on the Moutere River road, stopping off for the odd tasting en route.

The best place to stop for lunch, or better still dinner, is the world famous *Hunter's Winery* (☎ 3-572 8803). Make sure you have time to sample the winery's famous Sauvignon and Chardonnay on the terrace before having dinner: looking out through the vines to the sun setting over the surrounding mountains is wonderful.

In many ways it makes sense to head straight on up to Blenheim after Kaikoura as you won't want to spend more than a couple of days in Christchurch and there's lots more to see and do around the very top of the South Island.

From Blenheim you'll be ideally placed to visit both the convoluted waterways of the **Marlborough Sounds** and **Nelson**, a small sea-side town right on the top of the island, which boasts some of the best beaches and more sunshine than any other part of the South Island.

After a few days in either place you should be ready to hit the adventure trail again. A couple of hour's drive further up the coast will take you to the **Abel Tasman National Park**, where the coastline of unspoilt and protected native forest makes for a spectacular five-day walk or, arguably better still, great sea

kayaking trips. **Abel Tasman Kayaks** (☎ 3-527 8022, fax 3-527 8032) offer all sorts of packages from one-day guided trips to five-day remote coastal trips, and even allow you to head off on your own if you've got some experience.

You don't need any experience of canoes if you're going on one of the guided trips however, just a love of water and thirst for adventure. We did the three-day trip which I think was just about the right length of time to really get into it, but not too long to miss our bed.

The kayaks are very easy to handle and definitely afford the best views of this breathtakingly unspoilt coastline, not to mention the chance to get to beaches only accessible from the sea. You'll also have plenty of chance to see lots of local wildlife from colonies of frolicking fur seals to plummeting gannets dive bombing for their supper in the clear waters around you.

Although you'll be in a group of six, plus a guide, you'll find you can get all the privacy you want, paddling along at your leisure and pitching your tent in your own private, secluded spot at night. Sitting on those beautiful, remote sandy beaches, the colour of golden honeycomb, watching the sun go down over the water at night is a must. Life simply can't get much more romantic, or heavenly, than that. The *Kahurangi Lodge* in Golden Bay (☎ 3-524 8312, fax 3-524 8316) is a good place to stay after the kayaking, as you probably won't want to drive too far on the day you finish, and you'll be ready for a good bath and a bit of luxury. The Lodge is furnished with lovely handcrafted furniture and has spacious rooms, each with its own luxury bathroom. Rates are available on request.

QUEENSTOWN

The one place that you won't want to miss out on in New Zealand's South Island is Queenstown. Now becoming famous throughout the world for its bungey jumpers and numerous other dare-devil activities, Queenstown is indisputably the adventure capital of the southern hemisphere. Because Queenstown is right down the bottom of the South Island, it might pay to fly there direct from Christchurch. The only problem with flying is the huge expense: return tickets from Christchurch will set you back around NZ$500 each – New Zealand is one of the most expensive places for domestic flights in the world. But flying does avoid a six hour drive from Christchurch, allowing you to conserve your energy for the numerous activities that await you, not to mention the extra time in this wicked resort. If you're not flying in to Queenstown, then the drive along the rugged west coast, taking in the **Fox** and **Franz Josef** glaciers and on through the **Haarst Pass** via **Lakes Hawea** and **Wanaka** is the best way to get there. On the return journey make sure you take a different route, driving via **McKenzie Country** to see the magnificent snow covered **Mt Cook**, the country's highest mountain.

The Waterfront Apartments

The Waterfront Apartments are situated right in the middle of town, overlooking the vast **Lake Wakatipu**, with the most incredible views over the **Remarkables Mountains**.

There are loads of hotels in Queenstown but we decided that staying at The Waterfront was much nicer than being in a hotel. For one thing the apartments' location is hard to beat, just metres away from the shore, and with that staggering view. It is also an advantage that it is on one of the town's quieter streets so that you're not kept up by the bars and their music. Besides, in my mind, it's lovely to have the facility to make yourselves breakfast in bed and after several nights of eating out you might fancy just the one night in – and if you don't it also gives you the freedom to check out all the fabulous bars, bistros, diners and even the curry house in Queenstown.

These fully serviced apartments are all immaculately furnished and clean, with lavish marble bathrooms that have a deep bathtub and a wonderfully strong power shower; television, video, CD player, and nice thoughtful touches like cafetières in the well-equipped kitchens. There is a huge pile of white bath towels and, as the apartment is serviced every day, you don't have to worry about keeping the bathroom clean. Judy and Jim Farquharson will even arrange to bring you continental or cooked breakfast in bed.

There are essentially two different types of apartment which are best for honeymoon-

> **THE WATERFRONT APARTMENTS**
> (☎ 3-442 5123, fax 3-442 7743), 109 Beach Street, Queenstown, New Zealand
> **Reservations**: Either direct with the numbers above or toll free within New Zealand (☎ 0800-889889)
> **Getting there**: Jim and Judy will arrange complimentary transfers from Queenstown Airport
> **Accommodation**: 19 units: 11 with two bedrooms and two bathrooms; four with two bedrooms and one bathroom; four penthouse studios with decks and spa
> **Amenities**: Tour desk, laundry, ski drying room, ski lockers, cooked or continental breakfast room service, maid service and off-street parking
> **Dress code:** Casual
> **Weddings**: The Waterfront has had couples get married in their rooms or on the decks of the penthouses and are happy to help you arrange anything you require
> **Minimum stay**: None
> **Rates**: Penthouse doubles cost US$170/NZ$247.50, two-bedroom apartments cost US$232/NZ$337.50
> **Credit cards**: Most major
> **Taxes and service charge**: Included

ers. Either opt for one of their two bedroom apartments, where one of the bedrooms is really large with a superb en suite bathroom and glass windows looking into the good sized lounge and kitchen. These also have a small balcony, with French windows looking out over the lake, but it's not big enough to sit out on. Or go for the top floor suites which have one large double room with a queen-size bed, a small adjoining sitting area, a small kitchen, and the most wonderful decked terrace featuring a jacuzzi bath. You can both sit in the spa bath watching the sun go down enjoying a glass of wine, looking out over the lake at the craggy profile of the mountains the other side. Amazing!

Other recommended hotels

Nugget Point (☎ 3-442 7273, fax 3-442 7308), Arthur's Point Road, Box 677, Queenstown, is a pretty impressive resort about 20 minutes outside Queenstown at Arthur's Point. It doesn't really matter that the hotel is outside Queenstown as lots of the activities, such as jet boating and bungey jumping, take place close to the hotel, so all you'll miss is being able to pop into one of Queenstown's bars on your way home at the end of the day. But Nugget Point is a pretty self-contained resort with impressive facilities, wonderful views over the Shotover River and 35 comfortably furnished rooms, making it particularly popular with British and American tour operators. Its modern architecture is New Zealand's answer to a European alpine lodge, which personally I wasn't mad about, but none of the hotels are much to look at and the natural surroundings more than make up for this. Doubles from US$182/NZ$265.

The Millbrook Resort (☎ 3-441 7000, fax 3-442 1145), Private Bag Queenstown, is very popular with New Zealanders', and also, because of its amazing golf course and Japanese owners, with the Japanese. I had heard a great deal about the Millbrook before we visited and have to admit to being a little disappointed at the hotel's architectural style of grey stone cottages. But the facilities, service, bedroom interiors, beautiful golf course and public rooms are just wonderful and it is a lovely place to relax. The villas each have two bedrooms with huge beds swamped in white linen and sumptuous en suite bathrooms, as well as a spacious living and dining-room area, fully equipped kitchen and two outdoor patios. Doubles from US$256/NZ$372 plus Government Service Tax.

A FEW THINGS TO SEE AND DO IN QUEENSTOWN

Queenstown feels just like an Alpine ski-resort with traditional wooden chalets overhanging bustling streets filled with four-wheel drive wagons, and numerous cafés and bars with pavement tables, all surrounded by a backdrop of vast rocky mountains. Uniquely, Queenstown is a year round resort, where skiing in the winter is just as popular as all the waterborne activities of the summer.

Here you can attempt the ultimate challenge, the **Awesome Foursome**. For around US$194/NZ$277 you can: hurl yourself off a pipeline into Skipper's Canyon – the **world's** largest **bungey jump**; catch a **helicopter** swooping 225kph down the Canyon; **white-water raft** the furious rapids through a 170m disused mining tunnel, and finish off rocketing through the Canyon's thin gorge, hurtling past rocks just millimetres away from you in the 340hp boats run by **Shotover Jet**. You'll need a drink after all that.

Queenstown is also a great base from which to see the **Milford Sound** and walk the stunning **Milford Track**, though be warned that it is very popular with tourists which does rather detract from the area's outstanding natural beauty.

THE NORTH ISLAND

Even if you only have a few days to spare for the North Island, try to make it to **Auckland**. Commonly known as the City of Sails, the picturesque harbour provides great entertainment both on the water and around it. Explore the underworld at **Kelly Taltons**, or stand on top of one of the 48 extinct volcanoes to get a 360° panoramic view of the city. Take the bus downtown to **Parnell Village**, a cluster of colonial shops all painted in bright colours with an endless choice of food. To enjoy something a little quieter take a boat ride out to **Waihete Island**.

Beyond Auckland is the breathtaking **Bay of Islands'** district extending for more than 805km of indented coastline with over 150 small islands. An idyllic setting, relaxed and wonderfully peaceful, you can hire a Laser if you're into sailing which will get you out to some of the islands on your own, or for some real action do one of the deep-sea fishing trips, or try some surfing. If you go beyond **Paihia** to **Waihangi** you can visit the village where the Treaty was signed between the colonials and the Maoris in 1840. A good round trip starts at **Russell** up the eastern coast and through **Opononi** and down the west side through the tropical nature reserve, or the bush as it's known locally. Here you'll see the huge Kauri trees – one tree trunk takes at least six men's arms linked together to circle it.

South of Auckland is **Hôtel du Vin** (☎ 9-233 6314), a lovely small hotel situated in its own vineyard which is an idyllic spot to stop for a night en route to **Cambridge** and **Rotorua**, famous for its hot mud pools and geysers which spray water as high as 18m in places.

Then head down to **Huka Lodge** (☎ 7-378 5791, fax 7-378 0427), PO Box 95, Taupo, situated besides **Huka Falls** which feeds down to **Lake Taupo**, a huge lake created by volcanic eruption and home to some of the world's best fresh-water trout fish. It's very expensive to stay at the lodge, over NZ$1000 per couple a night, but do pop in for lunch or tea. Then move on to **Hawkes Bay** to sample some of the world famous wine and munch your way through endless orchards of apples, nectarines and peaches. Finally, drive on down through the many dairy and sheep farms to windy **Wellington**, which does have some great sights and places to visit before heading back to Auckland or across to the South Island.

WORRIED ABOUT JET LAG?

Don't be put off by the prospect of the long flight or the jet-lag if you're coming from Europe or the US. With the right sleeping pills (on prescription from your doctor) you can happily miss most of the journey, as they send you to sleep for between six to eight hours, and you don't even feel lousy when you wake up – just excited that you've got to the other end so quickly. If you know anyone in New Zealand it's also worth asking them to send you a packet of No Jet Lag pills, these are NZ-made homeopathic pills to be taken every four hours throughout the flight. We found they really helped as we had no problems with jet lag on the way out and only a little on the return trip – certainly not enough to put you off going.

When to go where

JANUARY
Argentina, Australia, Belize, Brazil, Canada, Caribbean, Chile, Costa Rica, Ecuador, Guatemala, Hawaii, Hong Kong, India, Kenya, Malaysia, Maldives, Mexico, Morocco, New Zealand, Philippines, South Africa, Sri Lanka, Tanzania, Thailand, USA, Venezuela

FEBRUARY
Argentina, Australia, Belize, Brazil, Canada, Caribbean, Chile, Costa Rica, Ecuador, Guatemala, Hawaii, Hong Kong, India, Kenya, Malaysia, Maldives, Mexico, Morocco, New Zealand, Philippines, South Africa, Sri Lanka, Tanzania, Thailand, USA, Venezuela

MARCH
Argentina, Australia, Belize, Brazil, Canada, Caribbean, Chile, Costa Rica, Ecuador, Egypt, French Polynesia, Guatemala, Hawaii, Hong Kong, India, Kenya, Malaysia, Maldives, Mexico, Morocco, Philippines, South Africa, Sri Lanka, Tanzania, Thailand, USA, Venezuela

APRIL
Argentina, Belize, Brazil, Canada, Caribbean, Chile, Costa Rica, Ecuador, Egypt, French Polynesia, Guatemala, Hawaii, Hong Kong, Indonesia, Italy, Malaysia, Maldives, Mauritius, Mexico, Morocco, Spain, South Africa, Thailand, USA, Venezuela, Zimbabwe

MAY
Belize, Brazil, Britain, Canada, Caribbean, Comores, Fiji, France, French Polynesia, Greece, Hawaii, Hong Kong, Indonesia, Ireland, Italy, Malaysia, Maldives, Mauritius, Morocco, Seychelles, Spain, South Africa, Thailand, USA, Venezuela, Zimbabwe

JUNE
Brazil, Britain, Canada, Caribbean, Comores, Fiji, France, French Polynesia, Greece, Hawaii, Hong Kong, Indonesia, Ireland, Italy, Malaysia, Maldives, Mauritius, Seychelles, Spain, Tanzania, Thailand, USA, Venezuela, Zimbabwe

JULY
Brazil, Britain, Canada, Comores, Fiji, France, French Polynesia, Hawaii, Hong Kong, Indonesia, Ireland, Italy, Kenya, Malaysia, Seychelles, Spain, Tanzania, Thailand, USA, Venezuela, Zimbabwe

AUGUST
Brazil, Britain, Canada, Comores, Fiji, France, French Polynesia, Hawaii, Hong Kong, Indonesia, Ireland, Italy, Kenya, Malaysia, Seychelles, Spain, Tanzania, Thailand, USA, Venezuela, Zimbabwe

SEPTEMBER

Australia, Brazil, Britain, Canada, Comores, Fiji, France, French Polynesia, Greece, Hawaii, Hong Kong, Indonesia, Ireland, Italy, Kenya, Malaysia, Maldives, Mauritius, Seychelles, Spain, Tanzania, Thailand, USA, Venezuela, Zimbabwe

OCTOBER

Australia, Belize, Brazil, Canada, Comores, Egypt, Fiji, French Polynesia, Hawaii, Hong Kong, India, Indonesia, Italy, Kenya, Malaysia, Maldives, Mauritius, Morocco, Seychelles, South Africa, Spain, Tanzania, Thailand, USA, Venezuela, Zimbabwe

NOVEMBER

Australia, Belize, Brazil, Canada, Caribbean, Egypt, French Polynesia, Guatemala, Hawaii, Hong Kong, India, Kenya, Malaysia, Mauritius, Mexico, Morocco, New Zealand, Philippines, Seychelles, South Africa, Tanzania, Thailand, USA, Venezuela

DECEMBER

Argentina, Australia, Belize, Brazil, Canada, Caribbean, Chile, Costa Rica, Ecuador, Guatemala, Hawaii, Hong Kong, India, Kenya, Malaysia, Mexico, Morocco, New Zealand, Philippines, South Africa, Tanzania, Thailand, USA, Venezuela

6/98 Adamson House, Malibu
    Rancho de Malibu
23200 Pacific Coast Hwy. 310) 456-
                                    8432
early 1900's. adobe, Moorish hacienda
tile work, coast view.

INDEX